Laws of All the Greeks

THE HISTORY AND THEORY OF INTERNATIONAL LAW

In the past few decades the understanding of the relationship between nations has undergone a radical transformation. The role of the traditional nation-state is diminishing, along with many of the traditional vocabularies which were once used to describe what has been called, ever since Jeremy Bentham coined the phrase in 1780, "international law." The older boundaries between states are growing ever more fluid, new conceptions and new languages have emerged which are slowly coming to replace the image of a world of sovereign independent nation states which has dominated the study of international relations since the early nineteenth century. This redefinition of the international arena demands a new understanding of classical and contemporary questions in international and legal theory. It is the editors' conviction that the best way to achieve this is by bridging the traditional divide between international legal theory, intellectual history, and legal and political history. The aim of the series, therefore, is to provide a forum for historical studies, from classical antiquity to the twenty-first century, that are theoretically informed and for philosophical work that is historically conscious, in the hope that a new vision of the rapidly evolving international world, its past and its possible future, may emerge.

PREVIOUSLY PUBLISHED IN THIS SERIES

The Unseen History of International Law
A Census Bibliography of Hugo Grotius' De iure belli ac pacis (1625–1650 Editions)
Mark Somos, Matthew Cleary, Pablo Dufour, Edward Jones Corredera, Emanuele Salerno

The New Haven School
American International Law
Rían Derrig

Socialism and International Law
The Cold War and Its Legacies
Raluca Grosescu, Ned Richardson-Little

Odious Debt
Bankruptcy, International Law, and the Making of Latin America
Edward Jones Corredera

A Century of Anarchy?
War, Normativity, and the Birth of Modern International Order
Hendrik Simon

Laws of All the Greeks

International Law as Social Reality in Ancient Greece

JESSE JAMES

OXFORD
UNIVERSITY PRESS

OXFORD
UNIVERSITY PRESS

Oxford University Press is a department of the University of Oxford. It furthers the University's objective of excellence in research, scholarship, and education by publishing worldwide. Oxford is a registered trade mark of Oxford University Press in the UK and in certain other countries.

Published in the United States of America by Oxford University Press
198 Madison Avenue, New York, NY 10016, United States of America.

Library of Congress Cataloging-in-Publication Data
Names: James, Jesse author
Title: Laws of all the Greeks : international law as social reality in ancient Greece / Jesse James.
Description: New York : Oxford University Press, 2026. |
Series: History and theory of intl. law series |
Includes bibliographical references and index. | Text in English and some Greek.
Identifiers: LCCN 2025049000 (print) | LCCN 2025049001 (ebook) |
ISBN 9780197838525 hardback | ISBN 9780197838549 updf |
ISBN 9780197838532 epub | ISBN 9780197838556 online
Subjects: LCSH: International law—Greece—History | Law—Social aspects—Greece—History |
Law, Greek—History | Greece—International relations—History | Greece—Politics
and government—To 146 B.C.
Classification: LCC KL4121 .J36 2026 (print) | LCC KL4121 (ebook) |
DDC 340.5/38—dc23/eng/20251229
LC record available at https://lccn.loc.gov/2025049000
LC ebook record available at https://lccn.loc.gov/2025049001

DOI: 10.1093/9780197838556.001.0001

Printed by Integrated Books International, United States of America

MIX
Paper
FSC FSC® C183721

The manufacturer's authorized representative in the EU for product safety is Oxford University Press España S.A. of Parque Empresarial San Fernando de Henares, Avenida de Castilla, 2 – 28830 Madrid (www.oup.es/en or product.safety@oup.com). OUP España S.A. also acts as importer into Spain of products made by the manufacturer.

To the memory of my mother, and of her mother

Contents

Contents

Acknowledgments

I owe gratitude to many people and institutions for help in the conceiving, researching, writing, and revising of this book.

It was a great bit of serendipity that John Ma joined the faculty of Columbia University at the same time I began my Ph.D. studies there. His seminar in Greek epigraphy was epochal in my conception of the sources and possibilities for thinking about and writing Greek history. He turned out to be the ideal advisor for the dissertation out of which this book grew, a mentor, and a friend. The other four members of my dissertation committee were influential on my thinking and approach, offered important help at critical times, and have encouraged my efforts with this second project: Marcus Folch, Adriaan Lanni, Roger Bagnall, and Alain Bresson.

Further good luck came in the form of an email introduction to Benjamin Straumann, who expressed interest, when the dissertation was still incomplete, in including my (then only contemplated) book in Oxford's series in the History and Theory of International Law. My thanks to him for his interest, his helpful suggestions, and his support. Thanks to Robert Cavooris for guiding me through the proposal and submission process with Oxford University Press, to Rizwaan Ahmad for shepherding the manuscript into production, and to the anonymous reviewers for their many helpful suggestions. The Berger-Howe Legal History Fellowship at Harvard Law School offered the ideal conditions for beginning work on the book proper. Special thanks to Adriaan Lanni, Bruce Mann, Idriss Fofana, and Elizabeth Papp Kamali for welcoming me and for their intellectual guidance as I worked to write a book of legal history and not just Greek history. Many others have aided the writing of this book in various ways, materially and immaterially, including with comments on part or all of the manuscript or on live presentations of research that ended up in the book. They include Kerri Arsenault, Emma Aston, Charles Bartlett, Éric Baudelaire, Sophia Bönisch-Meyer, Sari Castro, Kathy Eden, Michele Faraguna, Fabiola Ferrero, Sara Forsdyke, Rudolf Haensch, Edward Harris, Meredith Hunter-Mason, Yannis Kalliontzis, Paul Kosmin, Andrew Lanham, Michael Leese, David Lewis, Rosanagh Mack, Luke Madson, Alberto Maffi, Mark Mazower, Dorothea von Mücke, Kyriaco Nikias, Marie d'Origny, Johannes Platschek, Flavio Santini, Christof Schuler, Brent Shaw, Henry Smith, Matthias Stern, and Victor Walser, as well as audiences in Cambridge (Massachusetts), Chicago, Edinburgh, Helsinki, Munich, and Zurich. I could not have completed this book without the generous material support of the Columbia University Graduate School of Arts and Sciences and Department of Classics; Harvard Law School; the Columbia University Institute for Ideas and Imagination in Paris; the American School for Classical Studies at Athens; the Kommission für Alte Geschichte und Epigraphik of the Deutsches Archäologisches Institut; and the Stanwood Cockey Lodge Fund at Columbia University. Among the many friends not already named who offered welcome camaraderie and intellectual stimulation during the writing of the book, I single out Will Austin, Amanda Ball, Francesco Cassini, Sophie Cushman, Elizabeth Heintges, Paul Johnston, Joe Miller, Sarah Norvell, Gautam Parthasarathy, Ramon Portas, Jeremy Simmons, Lien Van Geel, and all my SF Bay homies.

Rebecca has been the mainstay and companion of my life since shortly before I began work on the book proper. Her affection, humor, wisdom, taste, intellect, knowledge of art, archaeology, and Greece, and love of travel have sustained me. I cannot express what I owe her.

My family has always offered steadfast and unconditional love and support. That became especially important during the final year of writing this book, when we lost my mother not long after her own mother had passed away. I dedicate this book to their memory.

Series Editor's Preface: Jesse James, *Laws of All the Greeks*

What are the sources of the law that applies in the international realm? We tend to believe that something is law if it has been made by our legislature, but there is no legislature above or beyond the state. When it comes to public international law, the reigning doctrine as contained in the Statute of the International Court of Justice is that treaties, state practice, and the "general principles of law recognized by civilized nations" are the sources that determine the validity of international law. The extent to which there is an inbuilt hierarchy of these sources of law is a matter of contention, but treaties tend to have a higher status than does customary law at least for the contracting parties, and both treaties and custom prevail whenever they conflict with general principles of law, because these general principles, although originally tightly connected to the natural- and Roman-law matrix from which the early modern law of nations arose, are nowadays merely perceived as a plug to fill in gaps in treaty and customary law. Needless to say, this is a highly positivist way of looking at things, and it is only via the idea of *ius cogens*, or so-called peremptory norms, that the voluntarist framework of treaty and custom receives any kind of constraint.

This sketch of the sources of current international law cannot do justice to the sophisticated ways in which international lawyers have argued about the character of the individual source categories and their respective weight, but it can serve as a segue into the question asked by Jesse James in the present book: what, if any, were the laws that held, not just for the Athenians, or Spartans, or Thebans, but for all the ancient Greeks? And what, James asks, were the sources from which such a body of law for all the Greeks could possibly have emanated? James answers that there were indeed such laws that held for all the Greeks. He points to the prevalent expression, which we find in the evidence from the fifth century BCE onward, of a "law common to all the Greeks" and invites the reader to think of the Greek world as both "profoundly international" and "awash in international laws connecting people across cities and seascapes, *koina* [federations] and kingdoms." James substantiates this by adducing novel examples from the domain of both private and public international law, as we today would call it, and he insists that we are perfectly justified to view this body of "law of all the Greeks" as recognizably international and recognizably legal.

That the ancient Greek world from the eighth century BCE to the eastward expansion of the Roman empire in the second century BCE can be called "international" is certainly plausible given the more than one thousand often fiercely independent city-states (*poleis*) that dotted the Mediterranean, Asia Minor, and the Black Sea, in addition to the large kingdoms of the Hellenistic era and the important phenomenon of federal states. But was there anything resembling public international law governing the relationships between these states, or anything resembling private international law governing the commercial dealings between citizens of those states? James answers emphatically in the affirmative and presents us with sophisticated arguments as to why the Greeks must be seen to have had international law, discussing the most important philosophical conceptions of law in the process: those of Hans Kelsen, H. L. A. Hart, Joseph Raz, Scott Shapiro and, most importantly for James, Ronald Dworkin. James argues that the Greek conception of law corresponds most closely to a Dworkinian outlook where what the law is can be discovered only by reference to the moral principles that justify and underlie the legal system. This close relationship between moral principles and the law, James writes, can also be found in the Greek evidence.

It is not just legal philosophy which suggests that the Greek conception of international law is closely related to ours: James's book urges that even according to the most narrowly positivist doctrine of sources of international law—treaties and custom determine what the law is—the ancient Greek world had international law. Indeed, the most important examples discussed by James, namely the private international legal institution of self-help (*syla*); or bilateral treaties (*symbola*) between *poleis* which provided for judicial resolution of disputes between citizens of different city-states; or the league (*koinon*) of Thessalian cities between the sixth and the fourth centuries BCE; all these legal institutions, James shows, were based on either customary law or treaty.

Yet James seeks to go beyond this already impressive demonstration. He would like to answer an even more ambitious question, namely *why* "international law was a constant and often compelling presence in ancient Greek life," why it was so ubiquitous. Here James resorts to concepts drawn from social psychology and legal sociology, especially that of group identity, which he believes was key in making international law effective. Notwithstanding some evidence that the Greeks believed that the most basic rules of international law were shared by everybody, not just the Greeks—Herodotus (7.136.2) has the Persian king claim that there are common laws of all human beings—James thinks that it is via the idea of a shared Greek identity, or shared Thessalian, or shared Ionian, or shared *polis* identity, that the laws were made effective. This social psychological approach, it should be noted, also chimes very well with our current positivist doctrine of sources: custom—state practice—is only a source of law insofar as it is accompanied by a mental state, the conviction (*opinio iuris*) that the practice is owed to a legal obligation.

But James goes so far as to claim that his book need not be read as a book about international law—he writes that it might just as well be read as a book about the "rules of behavior between politically organized territorial communities and their respective citizens in ancient Greece." I for one very much doubt whether "law" in the present book can be exchanged so effortlessly with "behavior"; James's account suggests that the Greeks sometimes follow the law because it is seen as obligatory in its own right. Moreover, the present book gives us reason to believe—and James himself is sometimes drawn towards this view—that some of the Greek actors he discusses have a Dworkinian view of the law as not just depending on social facts—not reducible, that is, to behavior, mere psychology, or group identity—but as a normative concept with an important moral component. James's book, therefore, will be read with great profit by those who believe the sources of international law are treaties and custom shaped by social psychology. It will also be read, however, with as much profit by those who think that the law has a normative core not reducible to social psychology, for all readers of this remarkable, fresh book will realize that at least some Greeks at least some of the time were also convinced of this core.

Benjamin Straumann
New York City, October 22, 2025

PART I

BACKGROUND AND FRAMEWORK

1
Introducing Greek International Law

International law as social reality

Law, a largely intangible human artifact, resembles architecture, one of the most concrete. Both can be strong, effective, and durable when used as designed. They aim at timelessness but conceal fragility, since each is subject to shocks that can quickly turn it to rubble. What longevity they achieve demands changes over time, repairs and modifications to keep them serviceable for present needs, yet some features remain as traces of earlier society. Disembodied law has physical effects, not only ownership of real property and material goods but bodily punishment, enslavement, even death. And the physical architecture of buildings and their spaces holds intangible meanings for those who work and live in them. Like architecture, law was ubiquitous in the ancient Greek world, affecting practically all aspects of human life. Like architecture, law had general, recognizably Greek forms but sometimes notable local variations. Hence, like architecture, law expressed, spread, and was interpreted through profusions of "Greekness." And like the rules of architecture, some rules of law propagated across the Greek world (and beyond), were seen to hold an almost universal validity, and exerted on Greeks great normative force. This book explores that international dimension of Greek law, asking why international law was a constant and often compelling presence in ancient Greek life.

The comparison of law to architecture is not just a glib simile. It brings into view the important point that law was not a pure sui generis element of Greek civilization but was, like architecture, one of many intertwined social realities created by and guiding human activity. Yet, as with architecture, specialized techniques have been developed to study and talk about law, treating it as sui generis. These differences in how we study the two domains sharpen my analogy between them. But noting their similarities suggests fruitful ways to study both, and in this book I address questions about Greek international law that one could also ask about Greek architecture: Why did Greeks use it? What made it effective? How did it spread across the Greek world? When and why did it change? How did it express (and, in turn, affect) layers of identity—local, regional, panhellenic? While many have studied the social nature of Greek *domestic* law, similar sustained attention has not been directed to international law. As I will show, however, Greek law was just as socially immersed on an international scale

Laws of All the Greeks. Jesse James, Oxford University Press. © Jesse James 2026.
DOI: 10.1093/9780197838556.003.0002

as it was locally. This is why we can study Greek international law not only as a specialized artifact of jurisprudence but, like Greek architecture, as a social phenomenon.[1]

International law in action

To glimpse the ubiquity of international law in the ancient Greek world, the force it could exert, and how it was one of many mutually entwined social realities, one need not look further than the outbreak of the Peloponnesian War, one of the most familiar episodes of Greek history.

The war was triggered partly by a conflict between allies. Potidaia was a Greek city clenching the narrow isthmus of a peninsula in the northwest corner of the Aegean Sea (see Map 1 on the facing page). Founded in the late seventh century BCE as a colony of Corinth when that city was ruled by the tyrant Periander, Potidaia became a tribute-paying ally of democratic imperial Athens in the fifth century. The Potidaians' mother city Corinth, on the other hand, was a member of the Peloponnesian League, the military alliance led by the Spartans that had clashed occasionally with the Athenian alliance in the decades after the Greek coalition victory in 479 against a massive Persian invasion. In 446/45 the Athenians and Spartans had committed themselves and their respective allies to peace with each other, by a treaty intended to last for thirty years.[2] Halfway through that term, in 432, spurred by their mother city's encouragement and seeking to preempt perceived Athenian threats, the Potidaians revolted from the Athenian-led alliance. The immediate military response resulted in an Athenian victory over a force of Potidaians, Corinthians, and mercenaries, and a subsequent Athenian siege of Potidaia (Thuc. 1.57–65). Shortly afterwards the Spartans hosted an emergency summit of the Peloponnesian League at which representatives from Corinth and other cities accused the Athenians of breaking the thirty years' peace treaty. The representatives in Sparta did not restrict their complaints to the Potidaia debacle but deluged the Spartans with accusations against the Athenians.

In his history of the Peloponnesian War, Thucydides highlights three complaints made against the Athenians at this meeting, in addition to Corinthian complaints about the siege of Potidaia. First, representatives from the island city of Aigina, forced into the Athenian alliance in the early 450s, asserted they were not actually "autonomous" from the Athenians as they should have been in accordance with the peace treaty (Thuc. 1.67). Second, Megarians, neighbors to Athens but members of the Peloponnesian League, alleged another violation of the treaty: their traders and merchants were being excluded unfairly from the harbors of the Athenian empire and from the Athenian (or "Attic") marketplace.[3]

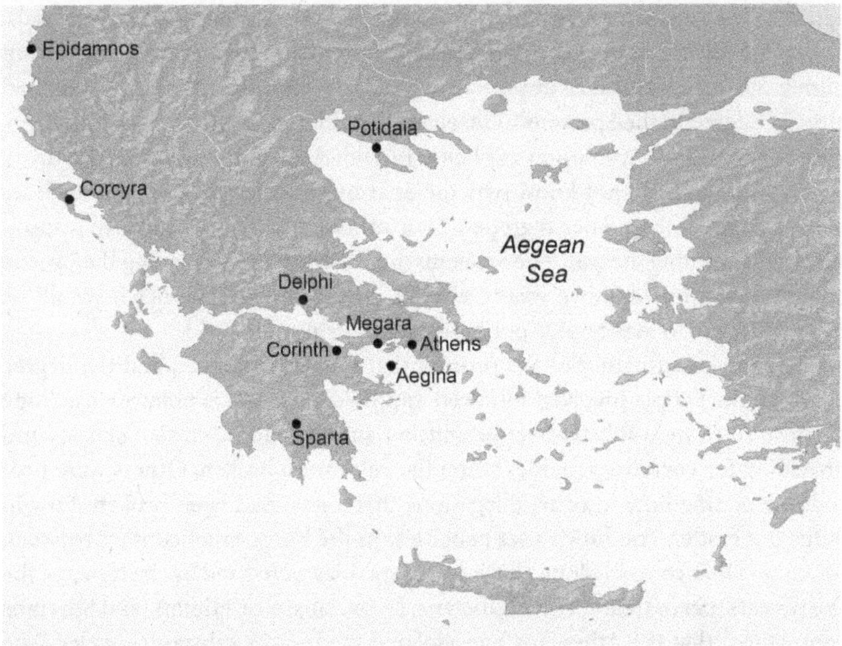

Map 1 Key locations involved in the outbreak of the Peloponnesian War. Map by R. Salem.

Third, a Corinthian envoy criticized the Athenians for using force to assist the Corcyreans (an island community off the northwest coast of Greece) in a naval engagement against Corinthians and Epidamnians, an action the Corinthians had already condemned as a violation of the treaty.[4] The summit culminated with the Spartan hosts voting that the Athenians had violated the treaty and the Spartans should declare war. At a later congress of the full Peloponnesian League a majority of representatives from member states voted for war (Thuc. 1.125).

Even after this vote for war, the Spartans and their allies did not immediately launch military action. Instead they sent multiple embassies to the Athenians to communicate officially the Peloponnesian complaints and stipulations. First, they insisted the Athenians must "drive out" a curse connected to the family of Pericles, the leading Athenian politician of the day, who seemed unintimidated by the prospect of war, even eager for it.[5] A later embassy made more substantive demands directly related to the treaty terms: that the Athenians end the siege of Potidaia; let the Aiginetans be autonomous; and revoke the decree excluding Megarians from the empire's harbors and from the Attic marketplace. The members of the final Spartan embassy simply stated there would be peace if the Athenians would let "the Greeks" be autonomous (Thuc. 1.139). Pericles at last called an assembly of Athenian citizens to discuss the Spartan proposals, urging flat rejection; the Athenians approved his recommendation. This was not purely obstinate refusal of any peaceful solution, however: the Athenians had already offered to the Spartans to resolve their differences through adjudication, a means of dispute resolution explicitly provided for in the terms of the thirty years' peace.[6] We do not know why the Spartans rejected this, but Thucydides tells us some of them later regretted their refusal and held themselves responsible for beginning the war. The Spartans' final step before convening the League congress mentioned above was to ask the god at Delphi whether it would be better for them to make war. Apollo gave his blessing.[7]

The rule-based nature of the process that finally led to war, and the degree to which the people involved followed and invoked rules, is noteworthy. Some of those rules were substantive: permitting and forbidding certain actions and providing for coercive penalties when the rules were broken. Others were procedural: stating how to bring allegations that a rule had been broken, how to judge the matter, and how to set penalties. In the burgeoning conflict between Athenian alliance and Peloponnesians, many rules were fixed by the terms of the thirty years' peace treaty. The Aiginetans, Megarians, Corinthians, and Spartans complained that the Athenians had violated the treaty's substantive rules. The Athenians in turn followed a procedural rule by offering adjudication, a rule then arguably broken by the Spartans, who apparently disregarded the offer.

The thirty years' peace was not the only set of rules governing behavior in what turned out to be the run-up to war. There were also the internal rules of the Spartan and Athenian alliances. As full defensive and offensive *symmachiai*, or military alliances, both the Peloponnesian League dominated by Sparta and the Athenian alliance were governed by agreements under which the members were "to have the same enemies and friends."[8] The Peloponnesian League had further rules, for example, those establishing the two-stage process under which the Spartans and then the other members of the League debated and voted on the alleged Athenian violations, and declaring that a "yes" vote by a majority of League members was binding on all.[9] The Athenian alliance also had rules, the best known being that each ally had to provide a specified number of ships or amount of money ("tribute") to the alliance.[10] In the organization's earlier form as the Delian League, the allies deliberated together at common meetings, albeit with Athenians as leaders. But by the time of the Peloponnesian War it seems that a foreign policy decision of the Athenian assembly could by itself bind all cities of the alliance: it had effectively become, as admitted by Athenians themselves, an "empire" (ἀρχή).[11] In this regard, prominent among the rules imposed on the allies by the Athenians was the decree the Megarians had complained about, which forbade the allied cities from admitting Megarians to their harbors.

Also shaping the series of decisions prodding the Greeks into war were the partly customary rules governing relations between colonies and mother cities. The conflict between the Epidamnians, Corcyreans, and Corinthians revolved around the duties and privileges of colonies and mother cities, and George Sheets has argued persuasively that Thucydides's narrative of the Corcyra affair provides strong evidence of applicable customary rules.[12] These rules formed the background against which cities established specific arrangements such as we see in a number of decrees relating to colonies. In general, the government of a *metropolis* was expected to exercise some hegemony over its colonies, hegemony that could include a right to send later settlers, to suppress uprisings, to regulate some economic affairs, and to have a say in the making of the colonies' treaties.[13]

The diplomatic activities that ultimately failed to prevent the Peloponnesian War were facilitated by customary rules protecting heralds and ambassadors.[14] The universally understood inviolability of these vital organs of communication made the Spartans confident they could send multiple embassies to negotiate in Athens even after the Spartans had declared that the Athenians were in violation of the treaty and that the Spartans were prepared for war. This same period provides a demonstration of the influence of that customary rule on state action. In his *Life of Pericles*, Plutarch (writing centuries later) tells us the Athenians sent a herald named Anthemokritos to the Megarians and Spartans in order to publicly denounce the Megarians for cultivating sacred land. When Anthemokritos turned up dead, apparently killed by Megarians, the Athenians retaliated. Approving a proposal by a certain Charinos, they decreed, first, that there be an official state of hostility between Athenians and Megarians, with no truce and not even communication by herald permitted; second, that the Athenians invade Megarian territory twice each year; and third, that Anthemokritos receive an official state burial.[15] The date of the decree of Charinos and its relation to the decree excluding the Megarians from the Attic marketplace and from the imperial harbors (mentioned above) are impossible to determine from our surviving sources. But the Athenians' vehement reaction to what they perceived as a violation of a core rule of interstate relations should not be doubted.[16]

One respect in which law and architecture resemble each other is in having both foundation and superstructure. A foundational rule governing Greek international affairs, of critical importance because it created the normative framework supporting the other rules, was that international agreements bound by oaths must not be broken. This Greek form of the principle *pacta servanda sunt* was a central factor in the outbreak of the Peloponnesian War.[17] The Athenians who addressed the Spartan assembly in 432, responding to the numerous complaints against their city, solemnly invoked the oaths that sealed the thirty years' peace: "We tell you, while each of us still has the ability to choose the correct path freely, don't violate the peace or transgress your oaths, but resolve our differences through adjudication in accordance with the agreement. Otherwise, with the gods of oaths as our witnesses, when you begin the war we will strive to defend ourselves just as vigorously as you attack."[18]

Breaking an oath incurred divine disapproval, which in itself was bad enough but could also attract both human and divine punishment upon perjurers. In fact, the Athenian emphasis here on the power of oaths responds to an attempt by the Corinthians, in another speech reported by Thucydides, to soothe the Spartans' worry about violating oaths. Encouraging the Spartans to approve a Peloponnesian invasion of Attica, the Corinthians insisted they would *not* thereby be guilty of breaking the oaths with which they sealed the thirty years' peace: "And we would not be doing anything wrong (ἄδικον οὐδέν), neither in the eyes of the gods of oaths nor in the eyes of men who learn of our action. For the people violating truces are not those who seek the help of others when they've been abandoned but those who don't help the people they've sworn to help."[19] The Corinthians, aware of Spartan reluctance to violate oaths, argued that the Spartans were no longer bound by their oaths to the Athenians because the latter had already violated the treaty. Corinthians made this argument again, according to Thucydides, at the League meeting that ended with a decision for war.[20]

Belief in divine support of agreements sealed by oath and in divine disapproval and punishment of oath breakers was a key element of the ideological foundation underpinning the great number of Greek interstate agreements. When Greeks inscribed on stone or bronze the texts memorializing treaties, they often included the exact wording of the oaths; named the gods by whom the oaths were to be sworn; and specified which officials were to swear them as representatives of their states.[21] But the danger to oath breakers was not of divine origin alone. The Athenian threat quoted above reveals that *human* willingness to take action against oath breakers also fortified oaths' effectiveness. Nor did compliance with oaths stem wholly from fear. The formal solemnity of swearing oaths in public communal ceremonies impressed on people the seriousness of the commitment they were entering upon and tied them, by the joint ritual, to everyone who swore the same vow. In these many ways oaths made international agreements more binding and enforcement more likely.

All these rules structured and guided the actions and responses that led to the Peloponnesian War. What is more, war itself was among the actions and responses envisioned and even demanded by those rules. And other rules shaped how Greeks waged that war. Therefore, it is easy to see that these were not ordinary everyday rules, like the rules of chess, or of etiquette, or of language, spheres of action in which it matters relatively little (in most people's eyes) if the rules are broken. And although deeply imbued with ethics, a serious and important domain of human society, these also were not simply rules of ethics. Unlike most ethical rules, the rules governing Greek international conduct permitted parties to impose serious sanctions on transgressors, including war.[22] For these reasons and more, I will argue, it is accurate and useful to understand the rules governing the behavior of the Athenians, Spartans, Corinthians, and the other Greeks involved in the outbreak of the Peloponnesian War as *legal* rules (the sense of which I clarify in the next chapter) and specifically as rules of international law.

The plan of the book

The claim that the Greeks recognized and maintained international law is not new or radical, but the case for it is worth making explicitly. The institutions of international law in the twenty-first century are much more complex and developed than those of the ancient Greek world (or even of the modern world until 1950 or so), and it is reasonable to wonder whether and how the expression "international law" can be used for a phenomenon of the fifth century BCE just as for one twenty-five centuries later. And while (as I will argue) we may appropriately speak of international law in the ancient Greek world, I am far from claiming it is identical to international law now. In much of this book, I describe details of Greek international law; and while this is mostly not a comparative work, some of the differences from contemporary international law will be apparent even to non-lawyers. Perhaps most importantly, Greeks had no equivalent to the United Nations and its International Court of Justice. Yet the number of similarities between contemporary and ancient Greek international law, some of which I describe in this book, may be surprising.

Although scholars have talked about and studied ancient Greek international law for over a century, a few have practically denied that it even existed. Arthur Eckstein may be the most vocal recent proponent of this view, having claimed that "ancient Greek city-states existed in a world that was essentially bereft of international law."[23] In the next chapter, I will discuss three main reasons it is fair to speak of an ancient Greek international law: first, Greeks used and observed treaties and customary laws, the key elements of what is called international law in the modern world; second, it makes sense to talk about the Greek world as "international"; and third, there are grounds for using the word "law" in referring to the system of rules governing Greek international behavior, as we are justified in using it with comparable rules in the modern world.

My arguments for the existence and effectiveness of Greek international law should not be taken as praise of it. Many now agree with a founding premise of certain "critical" schools of legal scholarship: law can be used to reify inequalities and promote injustices just as easily as it can be a tool to nurture fairness and punish wrongdoing. The oppressive possibilities of law have often been emphasized by scholars of ancient Greece, a society in which the low status and degraded condition of women, slaves, and others was always *legally* codified and enforced. Similarly, much scholarship has described how international law in recent centuries has often been a tool of rich, European, "Western" nations to exploit the rest of the world economically, politically, and socially.[24] Ancient Greeks as well often used international law, especially in the form of unequal treaties, to institutionalize and legitimize hegemony and introduce arguably *less* just legal procedures, as Greeks themselves sometimes complained. We have already encountered this legitimized hegemony in the form of Spartan and Athenian domination of their respective alliances in the fifth century. In arguing that international law existed in the ancient Greek world and affected how Greeks acted, I am not claiming we should applaud those effects.[25]

In any case, demonstrating the existence of Greek international law is a preliminary and subsidiary matter here. I will argue it in the next chapter and fill that argument out over the course of the book. Many examples will make apparent international law's significance to ancient Greeks. And while this historical point is worth making in its own right, I have a more ambitious goal than describing what Greek international law consisted in. As I stated in the opening paragraph, my larger question is *why* international law was a constant and often compelling presence in ancient Greek life. Therefore in much of the book, interwoven with the historical discussions, I also explore why Greeks used international law and how it influenced their behavior; what made specific elements of that law effective (or not); and why Greeks seem, usually, to have obeyed international law and to have enforced it when broken by others.

It is well understood that the question "why" any phenomenon or event happens usually can be answered in many ways. This is not only because most events have multiple causes but also because those causes can be of quite different sorts. For example, a particular person's commission of a crime might have psychological, economic, political, and social causes. A certain mental phenomenon might have personal-historical, biological, chemical, and physical causes. The start of the Peloponnesian War might more or less plausibly be attributed to the personal psychology of Pericles, perceived violations of international law, Spartan fear of growing Athenian power, or an "anarchic" international system.

Let me pause and expand on this last point, because it bears directly on my earlier discussion of the outbreak of the war. There I deliberately focused on events and decisions leading to war that directly implicated Greek international law. I made no effort to canvass the current state of scholarship on the origins or causes of the war, an old cottage industry of Greek history. This is not only because I was not trying to find the "deepest" or "truest" cause of the war but because I believe there is no such thing. Rather, there are levels of cause, and one's answer to "What caused the Peloponnesian War?" will depend on one's level of analysis. It is Thucydides's immense authority and his magisterial assertion that there was a "truest cause" that has largely spurred historians' search for one. But it is not to be found. In any case, because human life is finite, all who search for causes or reasons, including historians, must choose which kinds of reasons they are most interested in exploring and discussing.[26]

As I said above, my primary interests in this book are why Greeks used international law and how it influenced their behavior. In a sense, then, this book is about international relations between Greek states. But only certain aspects of those relations: aspects explicitly involving law or more or less directly affecting the international use of law. There were many of these. Greeks *might* have interacted with each other in a world where there truly was no international law; a world in which it was understood that no rules governed the behavior of people from different city-states in their interactions with each other; a world with no treaties; no laws of war; no "heralds" or "ambassadors" strictly speaking, because no laws offered them special protection; no borders between states, aside from rivers and seashores, because a border is a legally recognized figment of the human mind. Far from being a lawless anarchy, though, the Greek international world was permeated with law; and that law seems to have guided Greek behavior much of the time.

To the extent that one of my main goals is to offer some explanations for why Greek international law was as effective as it was, this book can be seen partly as a contribution to what Benjamin van Rooij calls "behavioral jurisprudence," the study of how law influences behavior. Van Rooij distinguishes this from traditional jurisprudence concerned with interpreting the law (saying what the law is) and applying it to particular legal disputes or questions. His distinction goes back at least to the legal sociology of Eugen Ehrlich, who over a century ago delineated the "practical legal science" of judges, lawyers, and most law professors from the "pure legal science" of legal sociology.[27] As Ehrlich noted, traditional legal history has been more closely aligned with practical than "pure" legal science, largely concerned with stating what the law was in a particular time and place, in a manner that fits the kinds of legal analyses typically used by judges and lawyers. Stating the law in such a way is an essential part of legal history, and important to get right; I unapologetically tackle substantive doctrinal legal history in places. But my larger goal is to interpret the operation of law within its social-historical context. My approach therefore fits into a robust tradition of social histories of ancient Greek and Roman law, among which this book finds much congenial company. It also fits the often-noted fact that Greeks themselves never developed the sort of "practical legal science" practiced by the Roman jurists and by legions of lawyers since.[28] Yet my approach differs from most other socially inflected histories of Greek and Roman law by being focused on international rather than domestic law and by my interest in applying studies by contemporary social psychologists and sociologists to understand Greek legal behavior.

Modern research in legal sociology confirms that moral and ethical motives, and those deriving from peer pressure and group identity, as well as the pull of habituation, explain much of our compliance with domestic law in the contemporary world. I describe this research and some theories arising from it in Chapter 3. People enact laws not only for their material benefits ("This law will make us richer, or safer.") but also to express and promote ethical values ("This is more fair, or more just."). And people comply with laws not only because they fear the material consequences of punishment but also because they believe the underlying act is the right thing to do; they think it will keep them safer; they expect disapproval from others if they break the law; they (consciously and unconsciously) favor following the rules of the groups with which they identify; they respect legal authorities; or they have developed a strong habit of following laws. Similarly, people sue in court not only for financial compensation but from a belief of having suffered an injustice and driven by the emotions that accompany such belief. I argue that Greeks often used and complied with international law for all these sorts of reasons and violated or ignored international law when such reasons were absent.

Socialization is the process by which social forces—exerted by the people of a society in their various social relations—shape beliefs and behavior not based strictly on a cost-benefit analysis of material effects. Researchers in social psychology and related fields have revealed many ways the local environment socializes people. Socialization also occurs across national borders, through the rich networks of international contacts carpeting the world. In fact, people now speak of "states" being "socialized" by other states. Although that terminology is misleading (as I will explain), I will present a view of state behavior within which the socialization of people in international society affects how "states" act. The decision makers of states are subject to the same psychological phenomena and the same socializing pressures that affect all people; therefore we need to understand those phenomena and pressures in order to understand state action. State action is, at bottom, human action.

In sketching a picture of international law partly rooted in studies of domestic legal socialization, I reject an old-fashioned dichotomy between domestic and international law. That dichotomy (perhaps never strictly insisted on by anyone) goes back at least to the English positivist legal scholar John Austin, who defined (domestic) law as rules made by a sovereign and backed by sanctions. He also drew a fundamental distinction between law in the strict sense and morality. On his view, what was called "international law" was nothing more than international morality, in part because there was no international sovereign.[29] Setting aside weaknesses in Austin's definition of law, we can note that, even if it were correct, his theory provides only a limited explanation of why people use and comply with domestic *or* international law, one apparently based solely on the power of material sanctions. Emphasis on the power of sanctions still dominates much scholarship regarding the operation of legal systems. But, as "legal realist" scholars pointed out almost a century ago, philosophy of jurisprudence cannot fully explain legal behavior without taking into account the findings of social psychology and sociology.[30]

Because of the similarities between domestic and international social structures and legal rule systems, persuasive explanations of domestic and international legal compliance largely overlap. Domestic law compliance is not due solely to the deterrence threat of sanctions, and international law compliance is not due solely to the pull of morality (as Austin suggested) or the coincidence of international law rules with national interests (as argued by Jack Goldsmith and Eric Posner). Instead, in both realms, varying mixes of material and nonmaterial motives, psychological drives, social pressures, and habits determine when people comply with or violate laws, invoke or enforce them. This complexity means I hesitate to ever speak of the "causal efficacy" of law itself. No one obeys a law just because it is the law, and there is no such thing as a "self-enforcing" law or institution. International law's efficacy is derivative, relying on the sorts of social and psychological factors I listed above.[31]

The effectiveness of international law among Greeks therefore arises from their socialization to it, a phenomenon I describe in Chapter 4. It has long been recognized that the ancient Greek world was radically international and that many Greeks maintained numerous and varied contacts with people from sometimes distant communities. These human contacts constituted a web of international networks across and beyond Greek society, richly documented and theorized in recent scholarship. They included diplomatic networks, commercial trade networks, connections made by people who traveled to international religious festivals, "proxeny" networks connecting cities to individuals, and more. These networks socialized Greeks, encouraging the use and observance of international law by shaping the moral and ethical motives, the peer pressures, and the habits that modern research tells us are key elements in legal behavior.

One effect of international networks I focus on most is group identity. This is a person's sense of belonging to various social groups (everyone has many group identities), which vary in size from tiny (a few friends or colleagues) to enormous ("all Chinese people"). International networks shaped and strengthened group identities by bringing Greeks together in contexts that made salient common membership in certain groups. For example, panhellenic religious festivals emphasized the common Greekness of participants, while more local festivals reinforced senses of belonging to smaller clubs ("Ionians," "Thessalians," "Thebans"). People cooperate more with and have stronger senses of trust, fairness, and justice toward those with whom they consider themselves to share some group identity. I will argue that group identities on various levels often encouraged Greeks to guide their international behavior in accordance with legal rules. In turn, the process of agreeing to mutually binding legal rules, in the form of treaties, could reinforce group identities.

My approach should be distinguished from recent studies, strongly rooted in economics, of the relative success of some ethnically homogeneous business or trade networks in creating private legal systems that substitute for state-established laws, police, and courts. The studies I am familiar with attribute almost all the economic and (quasi-)legal effects of these groups to their ability to enforce contracts and business rules by transmitting reputation information and applying punishments. Their conclusions are important as far as they go. But I go beyond them to explore ways other than punishment and sanctions in which group identity made law and commerce effective.[32]

Hence, Part I of the book, through Chapter 4, provides essential background and a theoretical framework. In Chapter 2, I defend "Greek international law" as legitimate subject matter to discuss in the first place. In Chapter 3, I lay out the theories of human social psychology, socialization, and legal sociology I use in interpreting the ancient Greek world later in the book, argue for their applicability in an international context, and contrast them with certain other approaches. And in Chapter 4, I describe the Greek international world as heavily networked, with many opportunities for legal socialization and the formation and strengthening of international group identities.

The second, longest section of the book describes specific aspects of Greek international law and interprets them partly from the point of view of social psychology and legal sociology. Greek international law is an immense field, and I do not re-map its whole territory. Emphasizing depth over breadth in Part II, I explore two components of Greek international law: in Chapters 5 and 6, the customary law of *syla*, or legal seizure, which permitted people to take self-help measures to retrieve anything (or its equivalent in value) that had been wrongly taken from them; and in Chapters 7 and 8, *symbola* agreements, bilateral judicial treaties by which cities agreed to permit each other's citizens to bring claims in their domestic courts.

One reason for focusing on *syla* and *symbola* is precisely that they are not the first things that come to mind when one thinks of Greek international law. Those would probably be the common use of treaties of military alliance or peace or the customary laws of war. Going beyond these relatively familiar fields, my discussions of *syla* and *symbola* reveal the extent of Greek international law. In addition, *syla* and *symbola* seem to have been largely economic measures, expected to be used mostly by businessmen and aimed at lubricating international commerce. If I can show that even these kinds of international law are susceptible to a sociological analysis rather than pure economic rationalist explanations, it will be good evidence that such an analysis could be applicable to the whole variety of Greek international law. Finally, neither *syla* nor *symbola* have recently received thorough scholarly treatments, particularly in English. My discussions are the most comprehensive histories of these topics that I know of from the past several decades, incorporating a few new inscriptional finds and addressing recent scholarly contributions on particular inscriptions and issues.[33]

In these chapters, I argue that a sociological approach can complement much important work done on the Greek economy, including with the tools of new institutional economics and law and economics.[34] This book contributes to that work by emphasizing two points that are underemphasized in recent scholarship. First, I look beyond domestic *polis* law to international law as also contributing a fundamental institutional framework to the operation of the Greek economy. Josiah Ober has turned on its head Eckstein's lament of the Greek international world as a "grim," "ruthless," and "violent" anarchy leading to constant wars, not by rejecting his description of an anarchic system but by arguing that the fear the system generated inspired rational cooperation among Greek cities that encouraged economic growth.[35] Yet, with his extensive development of Plato's analogy of Greeks around the Mediterranean to ants around a pond, Ober still perhaps underemphasizes the degree to which Greek international life was structured and institutionalized by international law, especially where it related to economic activity. The Greek world may have been "anarchic" by the definitions of international relations theorists, but it was no anarchy.

The second way this book complements recent work on the Greek economy is in my insistence that because institutions, including law, exist only in the human mind, they require human agency to have effect. Therefore, as I noted above, human nature and the social environment make an enormous difference in how (well or badly) institutions work. We cannot explain economic activity simply by pointing to laws on the books; we have to consider how they may have been used in real life. More generally, to understand the effectiveness of law, domestic or international, we must study it with an accurate view of human nature, as I try to offer in Chapter 3, and in its particular social and human contexts, as I try to do throughout the book. Christopher Casey has noted recently that "encounters between international law and economic history have been rare until the past two decades, and remain only slightly less rare" (2024, 163). In Part II, I help fill that gap.

In Part III, I move beyond *syla* and *symbola* to suggest how my broad approach to international law can be applied to other aspects of that law. I offer three shorter case studies: the practice of and enforcement against piracy (Chapter 9); the use of oaths (Chapter 10); and the Thessalian *koinon* as evidence that Greek federalism was sometimes a creature of international law

(Chapter 11). Because these phenomena—piracy, oaths, and federalism—have received recent significant treatment in the scholarship, I focus on aspects that have been underinvestigated.

The book's chronological scope is, roughly, the sixth through second centuries BCE. Before the sixth century we have too few reliable sources to write a history of Greek international law (although I use the evidence of the Homeric poems in several places); and by the end of the second century the Greek world had become so thoroughly dominated by and absorbed into the Roman empire that the purpose and meaning of international law between Greeks changed forever. I return to this point in the final chapter. Although in the "historical" chapters of this book I offer only a partial history of Greek international law, in the theoretical chapters I have my eye on the entire broad scope of that law during the time period I just described. There I give more attention to some topics than may seem merited in light of the historical chapters. One example is my relatively detailed discussion, in Chapter 2, of the major Greek kingdoms, which feature slightly in the rest of the book. My purpose is to offer a theoretical framework broad enough to be relevant to a complete history of Greek international law although I do not offer that complete history here.

This book's place in international law scholarship

Polly Low observed a decade and a half ago that "the study of international law in ancient Greece has never been a particularly vibrant field" (2007, 80). The same year saw the publication both of her book, focused on international relations but with a chapter on law, and of a detailed book-length survey of Greek international relations and law by Adalberto Giovannini. Nevertheless, the general neglect continues, and Low's observation is still accurate: while never ceasing entirely, publications about Greek international law also never seem to exceed a trickle. This lack of attention may be a symptom of what was for a long time a wider disregard of the history of international law, whose "scandalous neglect" was bemoaned by Stephen Neff as recently as 2010 (2010, 3). The past couple of decades have seen a blossoming of scholarship into the history of international law, as seen in the work of Neff himself but also, for example, of Martti Koskenniemi, Lauren Benton, and Antony Anghie, to name a few well-known authors.[36] Recent scholarly work on the history of international law has, however, focused largely on the "post-Westphalian" world of the past four centuries and its more or less immediate intellectual and philosophical background, perhaps partly in the belief that the seventeenth century saw such a clean break in the meaning of statehood and sovereignty that "international law" became something ineluctably distinct from *ius gentium*, the law of nations, or whatever it had been before.[37]

That Westphalian barrier has never been absolute (it was artificial to begin with), and legal historians have occasionally included antiquity in their histories of international law. But much work on ancient Greek international law is either old; treats Greek matters briefly; engages with the materials only in translation; or limits itself to individual aspects of the topic.[38] Giovannini's (2007) work, which I mentioned above, offers a survey of the whole field of Greek international relations and law and was written by a specialist in Greek political history. Moreover, it provides extensive bibliographies covering over a century of scholarship in multiple languages and is sensitive to the social and ethical aspects of Greek international law I emphasize. It is therefore an excellent first stop for anyone researching the subject. But Giovannini's book is more handbook than monograph, lacking in depth what it achieves in breadth, and largely avoids making overarching arguments about the nature of Greek international law. Finally, his work coyly avoids calling itself a history of international law, instead describing its subject more generically as "relations between states"; and the U.S. Library of Congress does not even classify his book under the subject category "history of international law."

In light of the state of scholarship, one of my goals with this book is to contribute to a new history of Greek international law in terms permitting integration of that history into the ever-expanding global history of international law, a task whose importance was recently proclaimed by Emiliano Buis (2021). But I must emphasize my self-imposed limitations. As already noted, I myself do not offer here a complete history of Greek international law. And my restriction of the subject matter to international law *between Greeks* is artificial and potentially misleading, since I almost entirely ignore how law helped guide relations between Greeks and the many non-Greek people in the ancient Mediterranean basin and beyond.[39] The fullest possible understanding of Greek international law can be achieved only by taking an even broader view, one that accounts for a two-thousand-year history of ancient Mediterranean and Near Eastern international relations and the attitudes, behaviors, rules, and organizations that structured them. In other words, I myself do not here integrate Greek international law into a larger global history. I will consider this book to have been a success if it helps inspire others to do so and to conduct similar research with broader temporal and geographic scopes.

Another goal of this book is to demonstrate the usefulness of a social-psychological and sociological approach to the history of international law. Although law was a subject of sociological study from the early days of that discipline, in the work of such founding practitioners as Émile Durkheim and Max

Weber, only in recent decades have social psychology and legal sociology started to enter the main stream of legal scholarship, part of a wider trend toward empirical and "behavioral" approaches to understanding law. Their application to the study of international law is even more recent, beginning to multiply in the last decade or so. I am aware of no other current scholar interpreting the *history* of international law in the light of recent studies in social psychology and legal sociology. I hope this book shows some benefits of doing so.[40] Although it is, at heart, a work on Greek history, I have tried to write it in terms that make apparent at least some of the connections, correspondences, and relevancies between that story and the long history of international law.

2
The Reality of Greek International Law

Justifying the project

"How can you write a history of ancient Greek international law, since Greek states were perhaps not states at all, since international law did not even exist until the seventeenth [or "nineteenth" or "twentieth"] century, and since international law is not real law anyway?" In this chapter, I justify in more detail my use of "international law" to describe the institutions, activities, documents, and rules of ancient Greece that I discuss in this book.

My justification in a nutshell is that the ancient Greek world was international in the sense of containing political entities we can reasonably call "nations" or "states," and that institutions and rules governing relations between these entities are reasonably called "law." In developing the argument in this chapter, I will briefly touch on some philosophical and theoretical discussions and definitions of "state" and "law." But this is a work of legal history and sociology; not a legal brief, not a judicial decision, and not a work of legal philosophy. A sociologically inflected history of international law concerned mostly with its effects and operations in human society should take a flexible and open-minded view of what counts as "international law" in the first place, treating it as what Ronald Dworkin calls an imprecise "criterial concept" (2013, 11). It should not start from narrow and sharp definitions of "state" and "law." Over the roughly four centuries of Greek history I consider in this book, many kinds of political entities interacted in the Greek world, and no single, unchanging set of rules guided all those interactions. My use of "international law" is intended to embrace as many of those entities, institutions, and rules as it can without becoming meaningless, as well as to imply the continuity of a generally coherent normative system over time.

Therefore, although I argue here that there really was an ancient Greek international law, apart from this chapter the book would remain largely unchanged if I labeled my topic not "international law" but instead (for example) "the acknowledged, often followed, and sometimes enforced rules of behavior between politically organized territorial communities and their respective citizens" in ancient Greece. This is because much of the research in social psychology and legal sociology I present in Chapter 3, and from which I derive some of my arguments

Laws of All the Greeks. Jesse James, Oxford University Press. © Jesse James 2026.
DOI: 10.1093/9780197838556.003.0003

(especially those involving group identity), are not focused on the international world as such and are not based on law defined so narrowly as to exclude international law (modern *or* ancient Greek). Therefore, any reader who reads to the end of this chapter and still thinks that either part of the term "international law" is a misnomer for what I discuss in this book should feel free to replace "international law" with that longer phrase throughout.

Yet the reality of international law in the ancient Greek world, that is to say, its legality and its international nature, may have significance for questions other than those I focus on in most of this book and therefore be important for some readers. Because I am not aware of a recent scholarly discussion of the matter that I find satisfactory in both historical and theoretical terms, that seems reason enough to consider the question at some length here. Alternatively, it may be that the "legality" of Greek international law is more relevant to my own arguments than I yet understand. If so, better to bolster the case now so that my larger claims are less vulnerable on that ground. In addition, readers who are not specialists in the ancient Greek world may find useful my descriptive survey of the Greek world as international.

I insist on using the term "international law" not just because it is accurate but also to highlight two important connections. One is between Greek international and domestic law: by using the term "law" for each, we will be inclined to see the real similarities between them, similarities I point out at times and that help us understand both phenomena.[1] The second connection is between ancient Greek and modern international law. If we are willing to see the two "systems" (a word that may be controversial to apply in either case) as sharing important similarities, then the study of ancient Greek international law may help move us past either a presentist bias (believing that the way things are is the only way they can be, or all that matters) or a teleological developmental assumption (believing that we are always and inevitably moving toward a future that is different from and better than the past, sometimes called "Whig history"). Greek international law may turn out not to have important lessons for those of us concerned with modern and contemporary international law, but better that this be a conclusion arrived at after studying the question than an assumption preventing inquiry in the first place. I briefly revisit this point at the end of the book.[2]

The ancient Greek world as international

What makes law international? A simple answer is, when it applies not within a state but rather among and between states. On this view, then, you first need states. This is clear in the definition of international law offered by the twentieth-century judge and scholar Hersch Lauterpacht: "the body of rules of conduct, enforceable by external sanction, which confer rights and impose obligations primarily, though not exclusively, upon sovereign States and which owe their validity both to the consent of States as expressed in custom and treaties and to the fact of the existence of an international community of States and individuals" (1970, i.9). A community of states makes possible a space for international law on the conventional view that each state is defined by a boundary, both physical and legal, demarcating an inside domestic space and an outside international space.[3] The international space is inhabited by all other states, which typically means that a political entity within any state's domestic realm (a province, county, or city, for example) is not itself a state with respect to the international space. Therefore, one route to defining Greek international law begins from defining what counted as a state in the Greek world.[4]

"International" is used generally, and I use it here, as synonymous with "interstate." But the slightly more old-fashioned word suits the Greek context well because "nation" applies not only to states but to various kinds of human communities, including political and ethnic unities, and it is not always clear which ancient Greek political entities should count as states in a narrow modern sense.[5] This observation supports abandoning a strict dichotomy between the domestic and the international in favor of acknowledging that there was a political and legal continuity between them. This continuity in turn suggests one should not insist that the "legal" somehow stops at the physical or conceptual borders of the state, in part because those borders often cannot be discerned clearly.

Before heading to ancient Greece, we should consider briefly how the state is defined in the modern world. Having seen the difficulties and ambiguities besetting the question even now, we will be less distressed to encounter them in the Greek case. The concept of the state is controversial and has never been satisfactorily theorized, especially in the field of international relations and international law.[6] There is no universally accepted definition of the state, although Max Weber's formulation has been claimed to have "best stood the tests of fashion and time": a territorially-based compulsory administrative and legal order that claims binding authority both over its citizens and over all action within its territory and monopolizes the legitimate use of physical force in enforcing its order.[7] But Weber's definition is not inclusive enough. It does not accommodate the federal state, not allowing for the sharing of authority and of legitimate use of force between federal and sub-federal governments. The member units of a federal state are, like the "parent" state, territorially defined and they retain authority over certain defined spheres of the administrative and legal order within their territories, while the central government exercises authority over and makes laws pertaining to all citizens in certain other defined spheres.[8]

Another problem with Weber's definition as worded, as he realized, is its failure to explain how an "administrative and legal order" can *do* anything. Weber elsewhere expresses the view that *people* do things, "administrative and legal orders" do not.[9] In this respect, Peter Steinberger improves on Weber's wording by describing the state as a "structure of intelligibility . . . reducible, at one level, to a series of propositions . . . that collectively embody the various judgments that the citizens of the state have made about how things really are" (2004, 13). By inserting people ("citizens") into his definition, Steinberger indicates their central importance and hints that states only ever act through people, a point to which I will return.

The attempt to define international law by first defining the state is therefore problematic.[10] Furthermore, no matter one's definition, there have always been state-like entities whose status within the international realm was not clear. Contemporary examples include Somaliland, Kosovo, Northern Cyprus, Palestine, the Autonomous Republic of Crimea, Nagorno-Karabakh, Artsakh, Transnistria, Taiwan, Greenland, and the Faroe Islands.[11] As we go back in time, the variety of state-like entities seems only to grow. Robert Phillimore, writing in the latter half of the nineteenth century, identified thirteen different categories of state, several of the categories being individual "peculiar cases" where the matter of sovereignty was unclear.[12] It was only in the first half of the twentieth century that international law became the exclusive domain of "sovereign states" at all, at least as that term is generally used by Western political and legal theorists.[13] India and four dominions of the British Empire (Canada, Australia, South Africa, and New Zealand) were founding members of the League of Nations in 1919, although they had no acknowledged right to pursue their own foreign policies. And Ukraine and Belarus were founding members of the United Nations, although they were, at the time, constituent republics of the Soviet Union, and their policies and voting records quite closely tracked those of Moscow.[14] A popular question in contemporary European political theorizing is whether the European Union has become a state. The ever-present existence of such definitional border cases means that, at least in the real world, the concept of the state, and with it the concept of international law, has wide border zones rather than distinct edges.[15]

Partly because a precise definition of the state may be elusive, I propose that, for the purpose of delineating "international law," an important element of being a state is engaging in relations with other states.[16] As Jens Bartelson puts it, "the state and the international context in which it finds itself [are] mutually constitutive yet opposed spheres of politics" (2001, 12). To avoid circularity, we might define the "international context" of interstate relations as the highest, outermost context existing in the world political order (relations that, from within the state, can be called "foreign affairs"). And we can then define states as territorial political entities with enough sovereignty to interact with each other in this outermost world, even if they often participate in such interaction as part of a larger collectivity such as an alliance. In a federal state, on the other hand, the constitutive units (confusingly often also called "states," but sometimes, e.g., "provinces" or *Bundesstaaten*) interact with other units of their "sovereign state" or "nation-state" (*Bundesrepublik*) but do not, normally, have significant independent interactions with political units outside of that larger state. British Columbia does not send diplomats to Malaysia but rather representatives to Ottawa.[17] Of course, in discussions of foreign affairs, alliances are often spoken of as the most relevant actors: it is easy to find references to decisions and actions by, for example, "NATO," "the Allies," "the Peloponnesians." But the role of such organizations in foreign affairs has not, in itself, made them states, not only because they lacked most internal markers of statehood but also because their members always maintained at least a high latent potential for individual action in foreign affairs. Yet a primary role in foreign affairs is, in general, a key marker of the state with respect to international law.

I am speaking loosely and abstractly in saying a state engages in relations with other states. As I insisted above and discuss further in the next chapter, *people* carry out these relations. This means that, for practical purposes, for states to be cognizable under international law there must be ways to determine whose acts and words represent the state as a collective of people. At a minimum, at least in a world with anything more than customary international law, someone has to be able to negotiate and sign (or swear to) treaties on behalf of the state, even if there are ambiguities or uncertainties concerning who is authorized to do so. Therefore, we should complicate our rough-and-ready definition of a state by adding that there are normally particular people—individuals or groups—recognized as having authority to interact, on behalf of a state, with equivalently authorized people in other states. This "functional" understanding of the state seems generally valid for describing international relations in ancient Greece, where there was *usually* little difficulty in determining who was authorized to speak and act on behalf of a particular state.[18]

Greek states: Their variety and relations

The *polis* (plural *poleis*), the city or city-state, has always been considered the Greek state par excellence and was for almost a millennium of Greek history the most common and important organizing unit of many aspects of Greek communal life, including in politics, law, economics, religion, and art. The nature of the *polis* changed over those many centuries, to be sure. But the transformation was surprisingly slow and limited, given the large number of *poleis* that existed, over how broad a geography, and for how many centuries.[19] And the *polis* was never the universal principle of Greek communal organization. There were always Greeks who were members of no *polis* but lived in rural villages or were organized as non-urban "peoples," *ethne*. And entities other than the *polis* could claim the label "state." The most important examples of non-*polis* state-like entities are federations of *poleis* (often called leagues or *koina*, singular *koinon*) and kingdoms or empires, especially the Macedonian kingdom and those arising from it. I will consider these three categories in turn: *polis*, federal league, and kingdom. I hope that, by showing the variety of relationships existing over the centuries between these three basic types, I will begin to demonstrate the usefulness of keeping a flexible idea of what qualifies as "state" and therefore as "international" law in the Greek world.[20]

Partly because the *polis* has always been viewed as the central case of Greek political organization, it is only mildly controversial to classify as states the *poleis* that were not members of closely bound federal systems or under the tight control of kings. The common (if now somewhat outmoded) translation of *polis* as "city-state" betrays an assumption that a *polis* was typically *some* kind of state. In this book, I often use the (Latin-derived) English word "city" in place of "*polis*." Cities were territorial. The people who ruled them made their own laws and enforced them within those territories (possessing the political and judicial apparatuses to perform both kinds of activities), fielded soldiers when necessary, often minted money, and granted citizenship and created other rules to determine who could be full political participants.[21] Cities were also (to briefly coin an ugly term) "identitorial," fundamental *loci* of identity for their citizens. But never exclusively so: both sub- and super-*polis* identities also mattered to Greeks in ways that varied with time and place. This multiplicity of group identity, along with its ability and tendency to shift and alter, plays a central role in my interpretation of Greek international law, as I will explain in detail in later chapters.[22] As with "state," I do not find it useful here to define *polis* carefully; not all cities exhibited all potential markers of *polis*-hood; and sometimes by the term *polis* I may include communities to which some Greeks might not have applied the word.

I similarly find it unhelpful to distinguish sharply between "autonomous" and "dependent" cities, as Mogens Hansen and Thomas Nielsen do.[23] On the contrary, one result of the presence of international law in the Greek world, in particular customary law, is that no city was truly *autonomos*, literally "ruled (only) by its own law": certain laws applied to all Greek or even all human communities and could be enforced by other communities. Autonomy arose as a Greek political norm probably in the fifth century and operated, like "freedom" and "democracy" (both in ancient Greece and today), more as a vague theoretical ideal than as true actuality for any particular community.[24] Yet some communities that were called *poleis* lacked significant elements of independence, particularly in foreign affairs. Well-known examples are the perioikic ("surrounding") Lacedaimonian towns subordinate to Sparta, as well as similar communities in Thessaly and Crete.[25] Unsurprisingly, the cities of most relevance for the history of international law are those whose citizens or rulers made historically significant foreign affairs decisions. But because "significant" is a vague term and not always discernible in our limited evidence, we should hesitate to omit any *polis* from that history at its outset.[26]

In some parts of the Greek world, groups of neighboring cities were joined at times by their citizens into federal leagues. These confederacies were often referred to in Greek as *koina* but also sometimes as *ethne* because of their usually explicit identification with a particular *ethnos* (or "ethnic" group), an identification that posited actual kinship relations between members.[27] Federalization was especially common in the fourth through second centuries. References to around two dozen federal *koina* survive in our sources. Some are fairly well known, including the Achaians, Boiotians, Aitolians, Thessalians, and Lokrians. The scholarship on Greek federalism has blossomed in recent decades, documenting and theorizing these *koina* in ever more detail and conceptual sophistication.[28] But that scholarship, in which *koina* of all sorts are commonly called "states," has not explained in a satisfactory way when a *koinon* was a state. Or, to phrase it differently, it has not established satisfying criteria to determine when the constituent cities ceased being states (in a sense that matters most under international law) and ceded that statehood to the *koinon*.[29] This is not for lack of trying. For example, Georg Busolt defined the most centralized form of Greek confederacies, which he called federal states (*Bundesstaaten*), as characterized by dual federal and *polis* citizenship and by direct jurisdiction over individual citizens exercised by both federal and *polis* governments. Jakob Larsen used the same criterion in defining his "true federal state." Yet both criteria are problematic, and neither is concerned with the state's role in foreign relations or international law.[30] Part of the problem is that Greek federalism varied widely. It was bookended on one side by actual synoikism (i.e., full unification into a single city, such as the unification of the villages of Attica into the single large *polis* "Athens") and by bare military alliance, *symmachia*, on the other, and filling many shades between those extremes.[31] As I will discuss further in Chapter 11, in the world of Greek *koina*, statehood had nebulous borders, and distinguishing between "domestic" and "international," even if desirable, can be difficult.

A similar ambiguous variety affects characterization of the Macedonian, Seleukid, and Ptolemaic kingdoms, the "big three" successor kingdoms to the Macedonian realm made enormous by Alexander the Great's conquests in the late fourth century. Here the resistance to a neat dichotomy lay in the fact that certain areas and political units within those kingdoms should not be considered actual parts of a particular kingdom's "state" for purposes of international law, although they were to varying degrees under the coercive military and fiscal-extractive power of that kingdom.[32] First, there was a range of statuses held by the cities within the spheres of influence of the kings.[33] Second, the landscape of those spheres of influence sometimes shifted rapidly. It might even be excessive to describe the kingdoms as having borders when they changed so easily (but see Map 2 in this section for one attempt at portraying them).[34] And third, there always existed cities affiliated with the three largest kingdoms, as with the Persians before them and the Romans after, that were not annexed territories fully incorporated into the royal state but were more like allies, even if the alliances binding them to the kings were always lopsided and frequently coercive. Therefore, while it is common and reasonable to call these kingdoms "states" (because of the authority they claimed and the power they exerted, at all times, over *some* territory and people, and because of their "international" interactions with similar entities), they always to some extent ruled over and hence "contained" other entities also reasonably called states.[35]

Each of the three kingdoms that arose out of Alexander's defeat of the Persian empire was unique and must be considered on its own terms. But each resulted from imposing Macedonian and "Alexandrian" practices on populations and governing institutions in place before the Macedonian army conquered them. This process of imposition began under Alexander and continued during, and

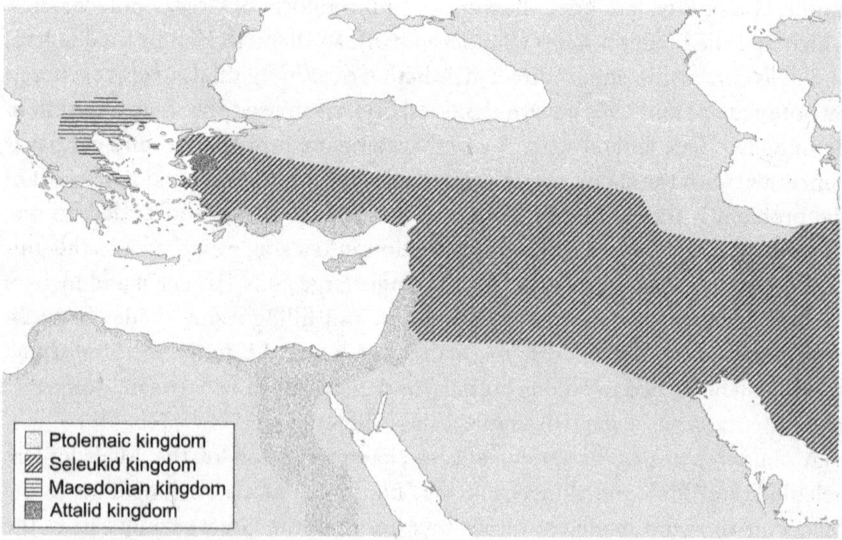

Map 2 Approximate extent of the Seleukid, Ptolemaic, and Macedonian kingdoms circa 250 BCE. Map by R. Salem.

in the aftermath of, the wars of his successors in the decades after his death.[36] Alexander "freed" many of the Greek cities of mainland Asia Minor by replacing oligarchies with democracies, letting them have "their own laws," and ending the tribute payments they had made to the Persians.[37] Alexander's successors, led by Antigonos Monophthalmos at Tyre in 315, invoked, enshrined, and defended the notion that the Greek *poleis* should be free and autonomous.[38] But many, if not all, of the successors also violated this principle, although *polis* autonomy was guaranteed by the peace treaty of 311.[39] A further sign that *polis* autonomy was recognized under international law is that enforcement of alleged violations of a city's freedom could also be a pretext for attacks between the successors, as it already was for Ptolemy against Antigonos in 310. Warring powers often used the language of "freeing" the cities affiliated with their opponents.[40] In the third century, the quasi-official status of "free and autonomous" was held by only some cities and did not always mean the same thing for those that had it. But it is reasonable to consider nominally free cities to have been states, even if the realities of power normally induced them to follow the lead of a particular monarch in most foreign affairs. I discuss the three major kingdoms individually here to give an idea of the rich complexity of parts of the Greek international world for the centuries between Alexander's conquests and those of the Romans.

In the Ptolemaic kingdom we can distinguish between Egypt (always the center of Ptolemaic political gravity) and the overseas territories, in many of which there was frequently greater local control than anywhere in Egypt and little or no territory directly owned by the king.[41] Roger Bagnall describes the varieties of relationships between the Ptolemies and their overseas possessions. These varied from, on one hand, "friendly relations" such as with the Byzantines, and treaty-sealed alliances such as with the Iasians and many cities of Crete, to, on the other hand, closer control over places like Samos, site of an important Ptolemaic naval base where "[t]he king interfered freely in the internal affairs of the island through his admiral"; Cyprus, the longest-lasting Ptolemaic overseas possession, heavily garrisoned and overseen by the highest Ptolemaic officials; or Cyrene, where—early in the reign of Ptolemy I and then again after Cyrene's reannexation into the Ptolemaic kingdom around 250—the king exerted authority over certain key security and judicial functions of that city's government.[42] The Cyreneans, then, came to be almost fully integrated into the administration of Egypt proper. But their ability to undergo various changes of status suggests that, at least before this integration, "the Cyreneans" were a state or state-like entity to which those changes could take place.[43]

Unlike the Egypt of the Ptolemies, the Asia Minor that the Seleukids took over (from Alexander, via Antigonos and Lysimachos) already contained in its west and southwest many Greek cities, which made up only a portion of the enormous variety of peoples, languages, religions, and political organizations within the vast Seleukid territory.[44] These cities, long accustomed to Persian garrisons and tribute payments (to say nothing of previous Athenian and Lydian hegemony), had been "freed" from Darius by Alexander.[45] John Ma characterizes the variety of relationships between the Seleukid kingdom and the Greek cities within its influence. He distinguishes four categories of *polis* in the Seleukid world. There were the "genuinely independent cities like Smyrna or Lampsakos" in the years around 200 BCE, which were at most allied to the king; superficially similar to these were the "autonomous" cities granted freedom by the king. The explicitly subordinate cities fell into two groups: those fully "integrated in the royal dominion" and those "formally subordinate to the king, but not integrated within the royal land."[46] Hence, in the Seleukid realm as with the Ptolemaic dominions, a primary feature was the variety of relations between *polis* and king. I propose that most if not all of the cities in Ma's first two categories, both of which were described as "free and autonomous," may be considered as states even when under some form of Seleukid hegemony, and therefore their relations with the Seleukids can be described as governed by international law.[47]

Macedonia presents, again, a different situation, and not only because it was centered on the core region inhabited and ruled by ethnic Macedonians for centuries before Alexander the Great's massive expansion of the kingdom. That region included much of the territory bordering the northwest end of the Aegean, roughly between Thessaly and Thrace. Here, one feature for potentially distinguishing a domestic from an international realm is the existence of what Miltiades Hatzopoulos calls the federal territory of the Macedonians, consisting of a more or less contiguous domain that was, as Hatzopoulos has done much to show, heavily settled with Macedonian cities that had their own vibrant civic lives while still projecting little or no independent existence onto the international stage.[48] Control over this territory shifted frequently and violently in the years between Alexander's death in 323 and the late 270s, when Antigonos Gonatas established control there. "Macedonia proper" in this sense (as opposed to the vast domains conquered by Alexander) experienced an overall expansion over the course of the fourth and third centuries. Hatzopoulos has argued that two cities founded within this Macedonian territory, Cassandreia and Philippi, were established at least in principle as independent cities allied to the Macedonian king.[49]

There were also usually cities outside of this Macedonian geography and its national structure that were more or less closely allied with or subject to the king of "the Macedonians." And there were always such cities attached to the Antigonid dynasts, both before and during their rule of the Macedonian homeland. The spectrum of these relations between Antigonid king and Greek cities outside of Macedonia proper seems to have run a gamut similar to *polis* relations with the Ptolemies and Seleukids. On the one hand, the Antigonids held the three cities later called the "fetters of Greece" under close control and heavily garrisoned. On the other hand, already in 302 Antigonos Monophthalmos and his son Demetrios announced the Hellenic League, whose (now uncertain) members were not outright subjects of the kings but rather subsidiary allies. Hence they were, there seems little doubt, states in their own right.[50]

Yet the freedom proclaimed for those cities was incomplete and, like the composition of the Hellenic League itself, varied over time. But this fluctuating subjection to Macedonian domination did not, or not necessarily, terminate their status as states. The Athenians are only the most well-known example of a city that, after centuries of (mostly) autonomy, vacillated between independence and Antigonid subjection. A brief pause, here, to focus on the case of Athens will give an idea how far the status of individual cities could swing with respect to royal hegemony. Although freed in 307 by Demetrios Poliorketes from the one-man rule of Demetrios of Phaleron, within a few years many Athenians began to feel less than free under the influence of this new Demetrios (Polybius says relations with kings always came to feel oppressive, 15.24.4). They refused Demetrios Poliorketes reentry to the city after the Antigonid forces were defeated at the Battle of Ipsos in 301, only to welcome him again after suffering for five years under the tyranny of Lachares (Plut. *Demetr.* 34). This new welcome, in turn, lasted only until 287, when Athenians rejected Demetrios's rule once again and drove him out, now remaining independent until their next loss to the Macedonians, in 262, in the Chremonidean War. The Athenians not only oscillated between independence and subjection. Even their experience of Macedonian dominance varied between what seemed like freedom and something that felt more like oppressive tyranny. Hence it seems more useful to speak of Athenian sovereignty under the Macedonians as growing and shrinking by turns than to describe the Athenians as successively "losing" and "gaining" statehood.[51]

The Athenian experience thus exemplifies the range and fluidity of relations between *polis* and kingdom that began in the fourth century and carried on, with important similarities and continuities, even to the Romans' dominance in the second century BCE and beyond. As my sketch of the complex and variable Greek international scene has shown, it is often difficult or impossible to determine whether a particular political-legal organization at a particular time is a state, or to draw firm boundaries between "domestic" and "international." All the more reason to adopt a generous understanding of which rule-bound relations in the Greek world fell within the ambit of international law.[52]

With this flexible understanding, I do not restrict discussion of international law to situations involving uncontroversially independent, sovereign, and "juridically equal" entities. Instead I deliberately include situations in which sovereignty may be incomplete but significant independence is still in evidence. We should not think of a city such as Athens after Alexander's death as alternately "not a state" and then "a state," subject to and then not subject to "domestic" Antigonid law. The Athenians were continuously part of a system of international law under which Antigonid hegemony over them was alternately more and less close, and local Athenian legal independence was correspondingly less or greater. The same general approach would apply to other cities, including their relations with the Ptolemaic and Seleukid kingdoms and, later, the Romans. In this way we can understand at least some aspects of kingdom–city relations from a legal point of view without insisting on a firm definition of the state and also without treating those relations entirely legalistically.

I should clarify what I mean here by "from a legal point of view." For my purposes, taking a legal point of view means seeing relations as involving a subjective understanding, by the parties involved, of the existence of rules and of mutual rights and obligations, rather than seeing them as involving, for example, only considerations of power, wealth, and safety. That subjective understanding is what some legal philosophers talk about as the "internal aspect" or "internal point of view" of law. In taking a legal point of view, I consider that kind of subjective understanding of legal rules as affecting behavior in international contexts.[53]

We saw in the first chapter that the Aiginetans believed (or at least claimed) that the terms of the thirty years' peace treaty granted them a certain autonomy within the Athenian empire. When they perceived violation of that autonomy, Aiginetan complaints to the Spartans contributed to the outbreak of war. Seeing the Aiginetan dispute with the Athenians in this way, with a focus on perceptions of what the law required and permitted, is taking a legal point of view of that historical event. A similar view of city–king relationships could be fruitful: it may be that cities under the subjection of the great kings, as well as the kings themselves, had a sense of certain mutual obligations *and* rights even within their hegemonic power structures; obligations and rights whose violation could lead to attempts at "enforcement" by either side. As I insisted in the first chapter, arguing that certain relations were governed by international law should not be seen as defending or justifying those relations.[54]

Even if we deny sharp and firm conceptual boundaries to statehood, we can say Greek states took three main basic forms: *polis*, kingdom, and federal *koinon*. In a simplified model, "international" could refer to any interactions between cities, kingdoms, and *koina*, and between people who identified with or claimed to represent those entities. But I have argued such a simplified model does not fully portray Greek historical reality. The degree of sovereignty of cities in particular could vary widely, so that a city's interactions with a kingdom, *koinon*, or another city could be understood as falling anywhere on a spectrum from essentially domestic to fully international. Among the three, the *polis* was always most important with regard to most aspects of Greek life, including international law. This holds even from the late fourth to second centuries, when kingdoms and *koina* waxed widest. Those larger political entities were constituted largely or entirely *by* cities, which often retained significant sovereignty within them. This is the main reason cities figure much larger in this book than do kingdoms or *koina*. And city autonomy was always prized by Greeks. Even when their world was dominated by kings and confederacies who fought wars against and made treaties with each other, cities also made treaties with kings and *koina*, city loyalties shifted, and their citizens rebelled or changed sides and often otherwise acted "autonomously" on a recognizably international stage.

Greek international law as "law"

Having shown there was a Greek international world constituted by state-like entities, I will argue we can reasonably call a group of rules within that world "law." It may help to begin, again, with international law in the modern world. I quoted above Lauterpacht's definition of international law, which includes "the consent of States as expressed in custom and treaties." Customary law and treaties are the main sources of modern international law. One authoritative statement of those sources is Article 38 of the Statute of the International Court of Justice, which declares that, in deciding disputes, the Court relies on four kinds of legal sources: "a. international conventions [i.e. treaties], whether general or particular, establishing rules expressly recognized by the contesting states; b. international custom, as evidence of a general practice accepted as law; c. the general principles of law recognized by civilized nations; [and] d. . . . judicial decisions and the teachings of the most highly qualified publicists of the various nations, as subsidiary means for the determination of rules of law." As we have already seen illustrated by our opening discussion of the outbreak of the Peloponnesian War, examples of customary law and treaties in the Greek world are easy to find. I will first discuss each again in a wider Greek context and then consider why it makes sense to call them sources of Greek "international law."

Like English "law," the Greek word *nomos* (νόμος, as well as its cognate *nomima*, νόμιμα) had a wide semantic range. It encompassed both legislated and customary law, written and unwritten, and included customary rules of international behavior.[55] Expressions such as "the laws of the Greeks," "the laws of men," and even "the laws of the gods" referred to those rules. Herodotus reports that, after the Spartans had killed the Persian heralds sent to them in 491 to demand the Spartans give them earth and water (which would have indicated Spartan subservience to Persia), the Persian king Xerxes declared the Spartans had "destroyed the common laws (*nomima*) of all people by killing the heralds."[56] We saw in Chapter 1 how an alleged Megarian murder of a herald spurred Athenian retaliation in the form of the decree of Charinos. Despite Herodotus's quotation of the Persian king, in our sources such rules of international behavior are often described as being peculiarly Greek.[57] A key fact driving the plot of Euripides's play *Suppliant Women* is that the Thebans have refused to turn over for burial the bodies of the seven chief soldiers killed while attacking Thebes. The requirement to permit burial of enemy dead is referred to there both as "laws of the gods" and as "laws of all Greece."[58] Isocrates, referring to the same legendary event Euripides dramatized, describes the requirement to permit burial of enemy dead fallen in war as "the common law of all the Greeks."[59] The centrality to Euripides's play of the theme of this law concerning enemy dead has long been connected by scholars to a contemporary historical event: the dispute between Athenians and Thebans over the inviolability of sanctuaries and the burial of dead soldiers during the Delion campaign of the Peloponnesian War in the winter of 424/23. This is around when the play was likely written, as judged by independent criteria. In his description of that dispute, Thucydides reports that the Thebans accused the Athenians of first violating "the laws of the Greeks" by occupying the sanctuary at Delion and used that as a pretext for their refusal to turn over the Athenian battle dead. Similar statements of the "laws of the Greeks" are made by the historian Diodorus Siculus, writing a few centuries later about events long before his own time.[60]

Customary law applied not only in warfare and the treatment of heralds and ambassadors. I noted in the first chapter that there seem to have been customary laws of colony–metropolis relations, partially modifiable on a case-by-case basis. In Chapters 5 and 6, I will delve into the customary rules of *syla*, seizure as a form of international legal self-help. Greek customary international laws were rooted not in any acts of human legislation, not even semi-legendary acts such as those that instituted the Spartans' "laws of Lycurgus" or Athenians' "laws of Solon." Instead, they were recognized by the fact of their near universal observance and by common agreement regarding their authority. The description of them, sometimes, as "laws of the gods" underscores the deep respect in which Greeks held these rules. In Aeschylus's *Suppliants* (ll. 381–86), the chorus describes granting asylum to suppliants as being a form of "justice required by law" (δίκη ἔννομος) enforced by the anger of Zeus. In the *Politics*, Aristotle calls customary laws more valid, or more authoritative (κυριώτερος) than written laws (*Pol.* 3, 1287b). As Adriaan Lanni explains, "To say that the law of war was customary is not to imply that it occupied a lesser status in the eyes of the Greeks than written laws and treaties. . . . If anything, customary law may have enjoyed more respect than positive law in ancient Greece."[61]

As in the modern world, the other main source of Greek rules of international behavior was treaties. Treaty law consisted of rules agreed to by individual *poleis* or supra-*polis* structures (*koina*, kings) by means of explicit bilateral or multilateral agreements, which were often written down, even inscribed on stone or bronze. The essential role that Greeks reserved for treaties in their international relations is reflected in the cultural significance of the legendary "Oath of Tyndareus" that bound Helen's suitors to join Agamemnon's and Menelaus's expedition to Troy (Hes. fr. 204 M–W, ll. 78–84). We have direct evidence of hundreds of treaties between Greek states.[62] What appears to be the earliest surviving copy of a written Greek treaty is that between the Sybarites of southern Italy and the otherwise unknown Serdaioi, recorded on a bronze tablet discovered at Olympia that has been dated to between 530 and 510 BCE.[63] In the category "treaty," we could include not only such long-term treaties, often called *symmachiai*, but also truces, *spondai*, that were usually shorter-term. *Spondai*, however, could also be long-term: Thucydides's description of the thirty years' peace as *spondai* indicates Greeks did not always recognize a firm distinction between *spondai* and *symmachiai*.[64]

The most familiar kind of Greek treaty is the military pact, an agreement to come to each other's aid in cases of armed attack; and peace treaties were used to forswear military aggression. But Greeks entered into treaties in nonmilitary contexts as well. *Symbola* agreements were judicial conventions under which cities agreed that each other's citizens would have particular legal rights.[65] I discuss these in detail in Chapters 7 and 8. And treaties sometimes included trade or economic terms. For example, the "agreement" (συνθῆκαι) between the Macedonian king Amyntas III and the Chalkidians, from the early fourth century, states first that Amyntas and the Chalkidians shall be *symmachoi* and defend each other against attack. But it also provides for export by the Chalkidians of shipbuilding materials from Macedon and for export by both parties of various goods from the territory of the other.[66] *Sympoliteia* agreements provided for shared citizenship and often for synoikism, political merger into a single city, which typically terminated the separate existence of at least one of the signatory *poleis*.[67] And *isopoliteia* agreements were usually bilateral (but sometimes unilateral) mass grants of the right of citizenship, but in which both *poleis* retained a separate, sovereign existence.[68]

Other written agreements were also likely sources of international law in Greek eyes, even if not traditionally categorized as treaties, *symmachiai*. Here I classify in particular the constitutions (written or not) of any *koina* that are better understood as alliances of independent *poleis* than as federal states in their own right. In Chapter 11, I argue this is the case with the Thessalians from the sixth through the early fourth centuries. As suggested by my arguments in the previous section, also treaty-like are any agreements between kings and significantly sovereign *poleis* (whether within or outside their realms). Like treaties between cities, such agreements between two or more parties provided for standards of mutually obligatory behavior, often memorialized in written form.[69]

In ancient Greece, as in the modern world, the terms of treaties were not themselves typically referred to as "laws."[70] As I explained in the first chapter, they acquired binding power through the oaths sworn by the parties when entering into them. In this way, they resemble contracts in private law, which have to meet certain conditions to acquire legal effect. This feature also made Greek treaty law subordinate to the customary law stating that treaties sealed by oaths must be adhered to.[71] And although in English we do not normally say that someone violating a contract has "broken the law," breaches of contract are just as legally cognizable as breaches of the peace are: they can result in litigation and enforcement. By the same token, violating the terms of a treaty in Greece could justify a breach of the peace to enforce it. This combination of binding power and enforceability indicates the legality of Greek treaties.

The lawfulness of international "law"

One might concede that Greek international law had important similarities to modern international law, that Greeks called some customary rules "laws," and that treaties were similar to contracts. But the question may linger: did this really add up to law? A traditional critique, made for over two centuries by a varied group of people whom I call the "international law skeptics," argues international law should not be called law at all because it differs so greatly from the "real" domestic law internal to states. The skeptics often point out that international law lacks a written code of law, an international court system, and an international police force. Furthermore, largely as a result of these absences, they sometimes assert, there is little compliance with or enforcement of international law. Such claims have been made about international law in the ancient Greek world just as in the modern global system. Although it has been called a "tired old question" (Franck 2009, 161), some readers are surely unfamiliar with the debate, are themselves skeptics, or have not considered the question in the ancient Greek context. Therefore it is useful for me to discuss the lawfulness of Greek international "law."[72]

Four (somewhat overlapping) kinds of response are normally made to the international law skeptics. The first is to point out that, in determining what law is, we should not start from domestic law, granting it definitional primacy; doing so simply reflects a "statist" bias. One can just as reasonably take international law as the core case of law and then decide whether domestic law matches it.[73] Second, one might concede or ignore the claim that international "law" is not law in exactly the same way (modern) domestic law is, but insist it is still an institution, closely entwined with the state, consisting of authoritative and binding rules, often enforceable by sanctions, with effects in the real world, and that many people call it "law" and react to its rules similarly to how they react to domestic legal rules.[74] Third, one might largely accept the critics' definition of law based on the domestic case and argue that international law resembles domestic law more closely than these critics admit. Finally, one might reject the critics' definition of law and offer a new definition that better encompasses both domestic and international law.[75]

I offer bits and versions of all these approaches. First, why start from domestic law? The mere cognitive availability of domestic law as the most ready source of examples from which to draw in conceptualizing law does not justify granting domestic law definitional primacy. Hans Kelsen has offered theoretical grounds for taking international law as the most basic valid form of law in the world and then defining legitimate states, and their national domestic legal systems, from *its* standards: that is, only if they meet the norms of international law.[76] Second, we have already seen some cases of Greeks calling international law "law" and treating its rules as authoritative and enforceable. Maybe this is enough for us also to call it law.[77]

Regarding the third approach: can one reasonably claim that Greek international law actually resembled domestic law more than is often acknowledged? Before offering such an argument, we should distinguish between two sorts of international law skepticism: formalism and functionalism. Formalists focus on the formal institutional features of a legal system. Skeptics of a formalist bent would point out that the Greek world had no permanently sitting international courts, no international police force, and no international legislature.

To these formalist objections we might counter that Greeks did have established sources of international law, in particular, customary law and treaties, as we have seen. In addition, court-like adjudication was often available, in the form of international arbitration under which a neutral tribunal settled disputes. And, in the absence of international police, states relied on themselves and their allies to enforce international law.[78] In the first chapter, we saw all of these elements in play at the outbreak of the Peloponnesian War. Despite the similarities to domestic law systems, though, it is unlikely that strict formalist skeptics will be persuaded: they can argue that self-help military action is importantly different from police officials; that the availability of mutually agreed arbitration is no substitute for standing courts with statutory jurisdiction over disputes; and that a web of treaties and customary law bears insufficient resemblance to a code of laws enacted by a legislature. Hence, formalist skeptics might insist, Greek international law is an entirely different creature from domestic law.

Yet formalist critique of international law has its own weakness: by tying the definition of law too closely to institutions considered constitutive of the state, this critique easily turns the claim that "there is no international law" into a logically irrefutable tautology. Let us accept, for the sake of argument, that you can have law only if you have a legislature, courts, and police. If international law were eventually to earn the status of "law" by acquiring those institutions, it would simultaneously cease to be "international," because everyone subject to that law would now, presumably, belong to a single state. In short, to the extent that formalist skeptics insist in effect that, by definition, law exists only within states, they simply define away international law. For these reasons, I will go no further in trying to persuade strict formalist skeptics.[79]

The other class of international law skepticism is functionalism. Functionalist criticisms of international law as being "less" than domestic law are, at bottom, complaints not that it lacks certain formal institutions but that the absence of these institutions renders it functionally ineffective. The accusation of ineffectiveness can mean either that actual rates of compliance with and enforcement of international law are low, or that something other than the institutions of international law bring about the complying behavior.[80]

The claim that international law is not really law because it is ineffective assumes the premise, or criterion, that law must be usually effective in order to be "real law." This criterion in turn implies that any legal system that is properly called "law" is in fact effective.[81] The implied standard seems to be the domestic law of modern, western, "global north" states such as the United States.[82] But I am unaware of any functionalist critic of international law offering data to show that the domestic law of the United States (or any other country) is more effective than international law.[83] This gap in argument is understandable, considering the lack of reliable data indicating rates of legal compliance with and enforcement of domestic law and the even greater lack of such information for international law. But it leaves completely unsupported by data the assumptions apparently underlying the functionalist critique: that rates of law compliance and enforcement in domestic systems are typically high, that they are low in the international realm, and that there is a meaningful way to compare the two.

The limited data that are available do not support the functionalist critique. Beginning at the top, it has been argued that modern constitutional law does little to restrain the activities of state executives.[84] And the trend continues in the more routine lives of private citizens. For example, it appears that a great mass of domestic law is violated constantly and enforced rarely. For most crimes and non-criminal violations alike, accurate statistics are difficult or impossible to compile. The US Department of Justice does conduct a widely cited annual review of "crime victimization" based on surveys asking people to state whether and how often they have been the victim of a property crime or a violent crime in the previous year. These reviews indicate that in recent years about 15 million American households (out of 130 million total) have been the victim of a property crime each year, and about 3 million Americans (out of 325 million total) have been the victim of a violent crime.[85] Are these annual rates high or low? In any case, these statistics do not include "victimless" crimes such as illegal drug use, underage alcohol consumption, traffic violations, tax violations, illegal firearm possession, and much much more.[86] Regardless whether one considers the rate of law violation in the United States to be high or low, a good case can be made that there *is* a low rate of sanctioning, or punishing, domestic criminal law violations. In the United States, even murder, which one expects to be one of the most frequently punished crimes, results in an arrest about half the time and in a conviction even less often.[87] The rates are lower for other crimes: federal estimates indicate that fewer than 20 percent of violent crimes and fewer than 7 percent of property crimes in the United States result in an arrest.[88] The situation is similar with civil law. For example, as few as 2–3 percent of Americans injured by medical negligence ever file malpractice claims.[89] Any skepticism about international law based on the assumption that compliance and enforcement rates in domestic law systems are high must explain how the available data tell that story.

On the other hand, the functionalist skeptics' assumption of international law's *in*effectiveness—that it is violated often and enforced rarely—is difficult or impossible to back up, and in fact the contrary claim is also often made. For example, Hans Morgenthau and Kenneth Thomson (1984, 295) state that since the era of Hugo Grotius and the Peace of Westphalia "international law has in most instances been scrupulously observed," and Louis Henkin has famously claimed that "it is probably the case that almost all nations observe almost all principles of international law and almost all of their obligations almost all of the time."[90] The truth, though, is that we have less data for international law than for domestic law and simply do not know. Our ignorance about compliance and enforcement rates is, of course, even deeper in the case of ancient Greek law, domestic *or* international. All of this makes it unreasonable to assert, from what data do exist, that international law is too ineffective to be considered law.

Some functionalist skeptics will still not be satisfied: they will accept Henkin's and Morgenthau and Thomson's claims about high rates of international law compliance but still argue that the best explanation of this situation is not that states are intentionally complying with international law, but that they are independently doing what they see as most in their national material interests, and that it just happens that actions demanded by those interests often comply with the rules of international law.[91] Yet, as Robert Howse and Ruti Teitel point out, it is not evidence of a legal system's ineffectiveness if compliance with its rules coincides with the self-interest of its subjects: in fact, that should perhaps be one goal of law. And the evidence of history shows the "behavior" of states is affected by much more than narrow "rational" considerations of self-interest. I argue throughout this book that this was true in the ancient Greek world.[92]

The fourth kind of response to claims that international law is not really law is to offer a definition of law not closely tied to the (arguably incidental) features of most modern domestic legal systems. Hans Kelsen maintains that the rules of international law count as law because they are obligations backed by sanctions, those sanctions traditionally being reprisals and war.[93] Christoph Kletzer, clarifying a Kelsenist approach, claims that law by definition permits the use of force under certain circumstances.[94] Oona Hathaway and Scott Shapiro (2011) argue that international law enforcement is mostly not effected by force, but that this does not lessen its status as law. H.L.A. Hart, in elaborating his view that advanced legal systems consist of a set of both primary and secondary rules, argues that it is not the secondary rules that make the primary rules obligatory as laws, nor the availability of sanctions, but rather the acceptance of the primary rules as guiding standards for behavior: "The rules of the simple structure are . . . binding if they are accepted and function as such."[95] Joseph Raz describes a legal system as consisting, in part, of norms that provide what he calls "exclusionary reasons," that is, second-order reasons to refrain from acting for some first-order reason and that always prevail over the first-order reason.[96] Raz suggests that international law counts as a legal system under his definition, but calls it a "border case" because of his doubts whether it is an "institutionalized system."[97] And according to Scott Shapiro's "planning" theory of law, legal activity is a special form of shared social planning. It is "not simply the creation and application of rules. It is an incremental process whose function is to guide, organize, and monitor behavior through the settling of normative questions and which disposes its addressees to comply under normal conditions."[98]

The previous paragraph severely simplifies complex and subtle theories of law. But I suggest it permits us to see that a case can at least be made for the "legality" of Greek international law under a number of theories of what law is. There seems little doubt that Greek international law would count as law under Kelsen's definition, since it imposed obligations backed by sanctions, which included reprisals and war, as we see in the case of the Peloponnesian War. Kletzer points directly to the permissibility of forceful self-help under international law as proof of its status as law.[99] I suggest that Greek international law counts as law also under Hart's definition, since Greeks appear overwhelmingly to have accepted its rules as binding. Greek international law also seems to fulfill Raz's conditions at least as well as modern international law does. For example, the Spartans cited the terms of the thirty years' peace as a reason for the Athenians not to do certain things they had decided to do. The rules of the peace thus appear to have functioned as potential exclusionary reasons under Raz's definition. Greek international law would seem to have a claim to be at least a Razian "border case" of a legal system.[100] And someone adopting Shapiro's theory might accept the "legality" of Greek international law partly on the basis that Greek practices of treaty formation and Greek norms relating to treaty compliance and enforcement count as the kind of "group planning" Shapiro posits at the heart of legality, with customary law as an entirely acceptable backdrop to and supplement of the rules created by treaties.[101]

If I were, however, to propose a theory of law that seems most compatible with Greek notions and practice of international law as well as most philosophically defensible as a theory, it would be something close to Ronald Dworkin's conceptualization. Unlike legal positivists, who argue that law is distinct from morality and who ground international law in the consent of nations, Dworkin grounds law, including international law, in moral principles.[102] As a general matter, Greek international law was rooted in a ground of shared morality, as has been shown by a number of scholars.[103] One of Dworkin's foundational principles in this regard is "associative obligation," the intensifying effects that certain social and political structures have on the ethical duties people owe to each other.[104] I will describe in Chapter 4 how the Greek international world was constituted by a great web of social networks that, among other things, heightened ethical obligations among Greeks. That there was a "Greek world" with a core of shared ethical values and legal principles also helped create a community of international practice that gave Greek international law what Dworkin calls "salience." This is the power of a set of rules that has been adopted by a significant percentage of a community (even a global community of states) to become obligatory upon and accepted by the entire group.[105] This "salience" seems especially relevant to the formation of customary law, but also probably contributed to Greeks' willingness to make treaties with each other. While no surviving Greek work theorizes international law (although we will see a couple of gestures in that direction in Chapter 4), if there ever was one, it might very well have taken a strong Dworkinian direction. This book, however, as a sociologically tinged work of history, is not the place to pursue such theoretical possibilities further.

Conclusion

There may be no authoritative answer to the question "Was Greek international law really international law?" and any attempt at such an answer would have to be built in part on the evidence I will present and discuss in later chapters. But I hope to have shed light on what the question even asks, and I have suggested several ways of responding to it. What I consider most important to understanding the use and effectiveness of international law is its nature as a system of rules treated as authoritative and binding upon, and subject to enforcement by, people acting somehow beyond the borders of an individual state. As will become more clear in my discussion of legal socialization in Chapter 3, similarities between human responses to different rule systems (such as those found in the legal system, within the household, at school, and in most workplaces) means that studying how people act in one law-like, rule-bound environment can illuminate how they act in others. Furthermore, social and socializing forces cross state boundaries. Hence, rule-affected behavior at an international level likely resembles, in important ways, such behavior on smaller scales. My goal in this book is to explore and explain the history of Greek international law as a social phenomenon rather than to offer a precise philosophical analysis of law or the state. I do not insist that Greek international law was "international" in a sense based on a narrow definition of the state, nor that it was "legal" under any particular definition of law. But in this chapter I have explained why I call it "international law" throughout.

3

Psychology, States, and International Legal Socialization

> "In one aspect law is as broad as life, and for some purposes one will have to follow life pretty far to get the bearings of the legal matters one is examining."
>
> — Karl Llewellyn (1930, 432)

Law as social reality

I opened this book by describing it as a study of Greek international law as a social reality rather than a sui generis phenomenon. This means, among other things, explaining why law is effective. The mere existence of legal rules and institutions does not ensure they will be used, or used justly. And explaining legal behavior means explaining not only law's rules but how law exists within society, how it interacts with human psychology, and how that psychology translates into law-related action. In this chapter, I describe the framework of theory and research, especially in social psychology and legal socialization, that informs much of my interpretation of Greek international law as a social reality. And I begin to argue in earnest that psychological and social factors, including group identity, were central to that law's effectiveness. Readers who find these matters obvious, uninteresting, or unimportant to their purposes may want to skip ahead. But, because my interpretation of Greek international law relies on positing certain psychological and social premises and rejecting others, I want to make as clear as possible just what my premises are and explain why I favor certain forms of explanation over others.

To help motivate the rest of the chapter, I open with a concrete example of what I mean by seeing Greek international law as a social rather than a strictly legal reality. Let us return to the beginnings of the Peloponnesian War. In Chapter 1, I started from the Athenian siege of Potidaia in 432 BCE. But Thucydides begins his narrative of the war with earlier events, domestic conflicts in 435 between factions in Epidamnos (modern Durrës, Albania). Epidamnos was a port city far up the Illyrian coast, where broad beaches silt slowly westward

Laws of All the Greeks. Jesse James, Oxford University Press. © Jesse James 2026.
DOI: 10.1093/9780197838556.003.0004

into the Ionian Sea toward the heel of Italy (see the map in Chapter 1). Although Epidamnos was understood to be a colony of the slightly less remote island *polis* of Corcyra (Corfu), it lacked a precise colonial status. Corcyreans "founded" (ἀπῴκισαν) Epidamnos, but its chief founder (οἰκιστής) was a Corinthian, and some Corinthians had been cofounders (συνῴκισαν, Thuc. 1.24.2). To complicate matters further, Corcyra itself was a colony of Corinth, which was therefore simultaneously a mother city and a "grandmother" city of Epidamnos.

In 435, the Epidamnians in political power sought help from the Corcyreans, in both protecting them from and reconciling them with a group of Epidamnian exiles. Their appeal had both political and geographic logic: Corcyra was not only their mother city, it was also one of the closest Greek neighbors at this verge of the hellenic world. The Corcyreans, however, refused to intervene. The desperate Epidamnians resorted to their other founders, the Corinthians, whose city guarded the crossroads and geographic heart of mainland Greece. The Corinthians granted their assistance. According to the Corinthians, this was the lawful or just thing to do (κατά τε τὸ δίκαιον), since Epidamnos was as much a Corinthian as a Corcyrean colony; and in Corinth there festered a hatred (μίσει) for the Corcyreans, who did not grant to Corinthians the "customary honors" at public festivals and appeared to hold the Corinthians in contempt (Thuc. 1.25). Corinthian involvement, in turn, spurred the Corcyreans to side with the Epidamnian exiles. They promptly besieged Epidamnos, a domestic dispute mushrooming thus into an international incident. Both the Corcyreans and Corinthians soon appealed to the Athenian assembly. Their competing speeches in Athens invoked pragmatic and legal considerations: on one hand, the practical consequences of Athenian aid to Corcyra; on the other, customary rules of colony–*metropolis* relations and the Athenians' rights and obligations under the terms of the thirty years' peace. The Athenians sided with the Corcyreans (Thuc. 1.31–44).

George Sheets has argued persuasively that the Corcyreans and Corinthians approached this crisis legalistically: that is, seeing the conflict as implicating international legal duties and rights, rules and enforcement. In other words, their actions came down to considerations not just of power but also of international law. In this sense, Sheets takes a "legal" view of the conflict.[1] This is a valid and important approach, implied by my argument in Chapter 2 that Greek international law does count as "law" on many views of the concept. But I want to focus not on the legality per se but on factors that interacted with legal rules and relationships to result in the Peloponnesian War.

Although there were customary rules governing colonies and *metropoleis*, why did the Corinthians not simply ignore those rules, or decide not to apply them in this situation, and reject the Epidamnian appeal? What gave the legal rules special "bite" in this case? At least three factors are apparent, all of them social: the perceived genetic and political connections between Epidamnians and Corinthians, and the sympathy deriving from them (Corinthians had helped found the city); the uniquely eminent moral and religious authority throughout the Greek world of the Delphic oracle, which had advised the Epidamnians to appeal to the Corinthians; and, as Thucydides claims, a Corinthian antipathy toward Corcyreans for their defiant insubordination, their refusal to honor the Corinthians in the manner prescribed for a colony (Thuc. 1.25.2–4). Although, in this case, the Corinthians were ultimately willing to help the citizens of one colony by taking steps against another, disobedient one, they explained to the Athenians that such enforcement was normally unnecessary because most colonies followed the rules voluntarily (1.38.2–3). This sort of colonial obedience likely resulted less from a fear of sanctions than from the social, affective ties binding together the citizens of mother cities and colonies, decades and even centuries after their founding.[2]

We must be careful, also, not to think of social and psychological factors as acting simply at a *polis*-wide level, by saying for example that "Corinth" had a sympathy for "Epidamnos" and disliked "Corcyra." General sympathies and antipathies may have existed, but they were created and nourished by actual relations between real people and felt by individuals. The Epidamnians probably selected ambassadors to Corinth who had particular connections to that city, connections of trade, family, proxeny, or some other sort, although Thucydides does not tell us as much. And specific Corinthians must have been insulted by not receiving special honors at Corcyra over the years. Individual Corinthians, in turn (and not a corporate "person" called "Corinth") had to be persuaded to help the Epidamnians. Thucydides offers no details of the Corinthian decision-making process, but a fairly small governing body would have had the relevant authority in Corinth's government, which was oligarchic in the fifth century.[3] And Thucydides does portray the Athenian democratic assembly, presented with the appeal from Corcyra, as leaning to the Corinthians one day but voting to support the Corcyreans at their next meeting (1.44). This detail invites the reader to imagine the assembly not as a solid political whole but as a collection of people, of whom likely only a few changed their minds. In other words, it was not just the rules of colonial relationships that determined the Corinthians' (and later the Athenians') intervention, but human psychology and human relationships interacting with those rules.

Considering the effects of Greek international law at the human level helps us make the theoretical connection I argue for in this chapter: that recent research in social psychology and legal sociology can help illuminate the operation of international law. This is because international law, like domestic law (and in fact all social phenomena), ultimately comes down to the perceptions, beliefs, emotions, words, activities, and interactions of individual people. And in this chapter, I offer a model of human (and, derivatively, state) behavior that helps explain how and why Greeks used, complied with, and enforced international law. I describe empirically founded theories of legal socialization that make intelligible some portion of law-related behavior at the domestic level within states. This kind of domestic legal socialization certainly took place in the Greek world as well, as Greeks themselves explained.[4] And I argue that many of the same social-psychological and socialization phenomena operate at an international level, helping to explain international legal behavior—both now and in ancient Greece.

My main focus in this regard, in this chapter and the rest of the book, is on group identity and its effects: I argue that international group identities were fostered by the many interwoven social networks connecting the Greek world. These networks and their associated group identities encouraged the use of and compliance with international legal rules, by spreading knowledge of those rules but also by fostering goodwill that made people tend to follow the rules in their interactions with each other.

In the fifth book of Plato's *Republic*, Socrates describes a Greek international society united by similarities. He claims, "the Greek race is related to itself, and is one race" (συγγενές, 470c2), in contrast to non-Greeks who are foreign and different from them. Greeks are "naturally friends" to each other (φύσει μὲν φίλους, 470c8); war between Greeks should therefore be called civil war and is a form of sickness. Consequently, citizens of the ideal city he describes will be "Greek-lovers," *philhellenes*; they will consider Greece to be something their own (οἰκείαν) and will maintain the same religion as other Greeks (470e9–10). Socrates paints this image of panhellenic community within a larger discussion of how the citizens of his theoretical city will conduct warfare: by adhering to rules even more stringent than the customary Greek laws of war. Soldiers will strip nothing more than armor from the enemy dead, whose burial they will always permit; they will not dedicate enemy arms in temples; they will not enslave Greeks defeated in war; they will not burn enemy houses; and they will destroy no more than one year's crop when ravaging the countryside (469b–471c). Socrates posits a direct connection between a common Greek identity and the establishment and observance of rules of international law.

In this and the following chapters, I argue that the relationship sketched by Socrates in the *Republic* is basically correct: common group identities make international law more effective. As we will see, however, the historical reality was more complex than Socrates suggests. The group identities relevant to international legal behavior were often other than simple "Greekness," and the range of international laws whose observance was affected by those identities was wider than the laws of war. The case of Epidamnos, Corcyra, and Corinth demonstrates both points, since it concerns the rules of colony-*metropolis* relations and involves a "greater Corinthian" rather than a panhellenic identity. I describe forces and historical examples of Greek group identity formation in Chapter 4.

In this chapter and the next, then, I lay out the theoretical and social science background and tools I use in interpreting the historical Greek behavior I describe in detail in Chapters 5 through 10. Because my interpretations of that behavior incorporate premises and conclusions argued for in these two chapters, I set them forth in full before considering specific legal institutions in depth. My focus is on theoretical approaches that not only are fruitful for understanding Greek international law but have been relatively neglected both in Greek historical scholarship and in international law scholarship generally. This emphasis on a few approaches, however, should not be taken as a claim that they have a special or comprehensive explanatory power. While I often ignore, and sometimes criticize as inadequate, other approaches (for example, some international relations theorizing, law and economics, new institutionalism, game theory), that should not be taken as a dismissal of their potential value for understanding Greek international behavior. My hope is to introduce international legal socialization into the conversation as a useful supplement to other forms of explanation.

Going below the state level

The role of the state has been over-inflated in the study of international law. States are not always the actors in international activities, and to understand why international law works, we must look below the state to the level of the human. Tamar Megiddo has argued that scholars of international law have overwhelmingly suffered from a "statist" bias that has prevented sustained attention to the role of individual people in international law.[5] Much behavior governed by international law, including by Greek international law, simply was not the direct product of state decision-making. For example, certain entirely private acts fell at least partly under international law's jurisdiction. Piracy, which I discuss in Chapter 9, is a vivid example (although enforcement *against* pirates was often a public act). International trade, aspects of which I discuss at length in Chapters 5 through 8, is a more banal but arguably more important example. In addition, many actions by state magistrates acting in their official capacities were the result of individual rather than collective decision-making; one thinks especially of generals in the field following (and sometimes breaking) the laws of war, or judicial officials dealing with foreign litigants. In a very straightforward way in these cases, in order to fully understand legal behavior in an international context, we have to take directly into account the complexity of individual human psychology and behavior.

But my point is more radical than the claim that states are not always the actors in international activities. It is that states are *never* the actors. Yes, it is common to speak of states as actors and decision makers. We debate whether "Sparta" or "Athens" was more responsible for the Peloponnesian War, shudder at how close "the United States" and "the Soviet Union" came to nuclear war during the Cuban missile crisis, and wonder why "Britain" chose to leave the European Union. But these are merely convenient ways to say that some individual or group, typically empowered through constitutional and legal features of a state, made a decision or took an action on behalf of all the people of that state. States themselves do not act. My claim, of course, is not uncontroversial, and in fact contradicts a long tradition in political and international relations theory. Therefore, it may be worthwhile to lay out both views in a bit more depth.[6]

The tradition I am arguing against sometimes literally anthropomorphizes the state. In claiming that "states are people too," Alexander Wendt argues that "states are real actors to which we can legitimately attribute anthropomorphic qualities like desires, beliefs, and intentionality." Political and international law theorists have anthropomorphized the state for centuries (it was common already in antiquity), and the strategy is adopted across the ideological spectrum of international relations thinkers, by "constructivists" like Wendt as well as by so-called realists and neorealists.[7]

According to realists, state psychologies are fairly simple, with two overriding concerns: survival (in the state's current form) and power. Realists do not ground these concerns in actual human psychology, attributing little importance to the mechanisms for converting the psychology of people into the "psychology" of a state. Realists take the nature of the international system itself as almost completely determinative: an anarchic "state of nature" in which war may break out at any time, and frequently does. States do not have the "mental bandwidth" to be concerned with anything beyond survival, which comes down to maximizing power.[8]

Constructivism offers a more complex but still state-centered view. Constructivists consider a state's interests to be not mere exogenously given facts determined solely by the interstate system but partly determined, or "constructed," by factors of "intersubjective beliefs" (beliefs affected by what others believe), language ("discourse"), and identity. This central argument of constructivism—that social construction plays an important role in interest formation—is persuasive yet marred by frequent reliance on a unitary anthropomorphic "psychology" of states and state action.[9]

Anthropomorphizing the state and thereby ignoring the individual psychology of actual people is sometimes defended as applying a set of simplifying assumptions that are useful for developing basic theories of state behavior. But these assumptions flatten out just the sort of psychological complexity I seek to understand.[10] And states simply do not have minds, or emotions, senses, predilections, and prejudices, so that ascriptions to states of mental phenomena such as desires and fears, intentions and interests, are at best convenient fictions. At worst they badly distort our understanding of how states work.[11] More realistic are models like that advocated by Ryan Goodman and Derek Jinks, in which the psychological characteristics of individual "relevant actors" in states are proposed as determining policy decisions, those actors themselves having been influenced by various internal and external factors. Their work is part of a relatively recent surge of interest among international relations scholars in the role that psychology and related factors play in international affairs, interest that is already paying off with richer understandings of international relations.[12]

We can compare the explanatory effectiveness of a simplifying state-level approach to history versus that of a complicating bottom-up social psychological approach by considering alternative interpretations of the beginning of the Peloponnesian War. Here we are fortunate to have Thucydides's double explanation of the war's causes. On one hand, he famously attributes the "most important cause" of the war (ἀληθεστάτην πρόφασιν, 1.23.6) to Spartan fear of the growth in Athenian power, claiming that it "compelled" the cities to war.[13] On the other hand, as we have already seen from my discussions above and in Chapter 1, his actual narrative shows that the war broke out as a result of many events and historically contingent circumstances. Thucydides does not explicitly anthropomorphize the Spartan and Athenian states, not even when offering his "deepest" cause. But the starkly simple psychologizing he displays in that passage is consistent with such anthropomorphizing and is one reason he is seen by many as an iconic forerunner of the "realist" approach to international relations. Yet we have seen that Thucydides's narrative makes readily available "bottom-up" interpretations that take into account human psychology and complex social and political interactions.[14] And, as I argued in Chapter 1, he indicates the central role played by the rules and obligations of international law in triggering armed conflict. My claim is that we can determine *how* international law played that role only by understanding the social-psychological processes of legal socialization. Because socialization affects individual people, to understand it we need a realistic model of human psychology. I turn to this now.

A basic psychological model

People have physical and psychological needs, personality dispositions or traits, emotions, motives, values, beliefs, memories, and perceptions. These elements, several with a significant genetic basis, are connected by cognition. Cognitive processes can be highly conscious, entirely unconscious, or anywhere on the spectrum between. One factor that is often conscious is *motives*, understood as "preferences directing choices."[15] Most psychologists believe we act from a variety of motives. Those frequently proposed include a "survival motive" (the wish to live rather than die), "hedonic motives" (desires to experience pleasure and avoid pain), "material motives" (desires to possess material wealth), normative motives (desires to do what is right according to some rule), and peer pressure motives (desires to please others or fit in).[16] In Tory Higgins's model of human motivation, the central motive is people's desire "to be effective in their life pursuits" (2012, 14, 47). Roy Baumeister and Mark Leary (1995) argue for a fundamental human motivation to "belong," which people do by forming and maintaining connections to others (we will see this basic human impulse in action when we consider group identities). Pleasure, wealth, and power are sometimes grouped together as "material" motives. But desires for pleasure, wealth, and power are not the only, nor necessarily the most important, motives of human action, and any model that ignores nonmaterial motives is incomplete.

The situation is complicated immensely when people translate their variety of motives into action. In deciding to act, someone must have a conception of what is possible. After a field of possibilities is established, different motives can simultaneously push a person toward incompatible paths. Conflicting motives can be difficult to compare and judge between, since they may not be commensurate (we cannot simply assign everything a "utility" value, for example) or may have differing timescales. How do I decide how to spend my afternoon if my self-determined options are working several hours at the office, watching sports and drinking beer with friends, mowing the overgrown lawn, visiting with my grandfather who may die soon, or writing an editorial about the long-term environmental benefits of nuclear energy?

One important demonstration of psychological research is that decisions are affected by internal processes and factors not consciously available to us: we do not have access through introspection to all the causes of our own decisions and actions.[17] We often do not even perceive our own lack of access and sometimes provide explanations for our actions that can be shown by experimental methods to be most likely false. For example, we often incorporate unconscious stereotypes and biases, as well as emotional factors, into conscious reasoning. And innumerable cognitive "shortcuts," or heuristics, make it possible for us to get through an ordinary day without endlessly analyzing every situation and decision.[18]

A factor frequently escaping awareness in decision-making is how the situation is being "framed" or conceptualized: for example, as an increase in loss or a reduction in gain; or as primarily an ethical rather than an economic question. Framing is one example of a set of phenomena described by Kahneman and Tversky's "prospect theory," which explains how people do not follow pure mathematical probabilities in evaluating future losses and gains. It is also a familiar rhetorical strategy, understood and used in ancient Greece.[19] Another example of cognitive bias is revealed by studies showing that voters are more likely to select candidates similar to themselves in perceived physical or personality traits. And *transference* is the tendency, when we meet a new person who resembles (even in subtle ways) someone we know well, to respond to the new person similarly to how we respond to the known person. The transference response can make us, for example, more or less open to arguments that the new person might put forward about a decision to be made. These are just a few examples of typically unconscious factors in human decision-making identified by experimental psychologists.[20]

This thumbnail sketch of human psychology may be fairly uncontroversial but cannot easily be expressed in a mathematical formula and used in simple models predicting behavior. Social scientists' desire to model human behavior with algebra and game theory has for decades lured many of them into the welcoming arms of rational choice theory. This psychological model assumes an idealized, deliberately simplified, and essentially normative scheme of how people make—and should make—decisions. Because of its popularity, and because I do not adopt rational choice theory, I describe it here briefly, pointing out a few central elements that occur in most versions. It assumes that humans exhibit "rationality" by making decisions not based on a variety of motives such as those I described above but from a single core motive of maximizing "utility," which is defined as whatever a person wishes—consciously—to have or achieve. Rational choice theory also assumes that people's desires are stable and can be compared to each other and ranked transitively as preferences (so that if I prefer A to B, and B to C, I also prefer A to C). Rational choice theorists often insist that "utility" does not have to be some form of selfish gain, such as wealth, and that the concept can include other-regarding and altruistic desires, such as for a healthy environment or the elimination of disease. Yet still it is assumed by rational choice theory that all desires can be converted into the subjectively universal currency of utility.[21]

It should be clear from the psychological model I proposed above that I find the rational choice model overly simplistic, and it has been criticized in part for its failure to account for well-attested "irrational" phenomena such as I have mentioned. Like anthropomorphism of the state, rational choice theory is sometimes defended as useful for further theory-building even if it is not an accurate description of human psychology. But like anthropomorphism, rational choice theory assumes away psychological phenomena important in explaining actual human behavior: it achieves simplicity at the price of accuracy.[22]

State and psychology

How does human psychology translate into state action, in the ancient Greek world in particular? Both individual psychology and group dynamics are complex and variable, they interact in multiple ways, and this interaction is highly determinative of historic events. The process may vary widely depending on the political structures. Even limiting ourselves to the primary political forms offered by the Greek world, we can say that a democratic *polis*, an oligarchic *polis*, a close federation, a monarchy, and a tyranny will all follow different procedures, first in political deliberation and then in mobilization into action. The internal political dynamics of each historic Greek political system are themselves fields of study. Each system followed its own peculiar means of reaching political decisions, and any two systems would often have reacted differently under similar circumstances. In other words, human psychology worked through political institutions, in interactions that shaped decisions and deeds at the state level.[23]

Political psychology studies humans within political institutions, and one subfield focuses on the psychology of international relations.[24] While I do not focus on political psychology factors in this book, the questions that political psychologists ask, and their attempts at answering them, are allied and complementary to my social psychological consideration of international law. It is also important to note that there has been, over the decades, some scholarship in international relations that looks carefully below the state level.[25] For the sake of example, I describe here one set of approaches I find particularly promising for explaining how psychology can affect international actions. Schafer and Crichlow (2010) and Mintz and DeRouen (2010) attempt realistic accounts of how individual psychology and the dynamics of small-group decision-making have large effects on the international activities of modern states. They present a rich set of explanatory frameworks for understanding the many psychological factors affecting how state decision makers actually make foreign policy choices within particular institutional and social environments. These frameworks can be sorted along various lines, including by distinguishing between (1) the pre-existing psychological characteristics of the people involved in the decision process, (2) dynamics within the decision-making group, and (3) external domestic and international conditions.[26]

Both works follow in the steps of Irving Janis, who made famous the notion of "groupthink." This was Janis's name for a phenomenon that he argued can afflict fairly small, homogeneous groups and is characterized by placing a high value on group cohesion, discouraging dissenting or skeptical opinions, curtailing analysis, failing to question assumptions, and not seeking to understand the group's biases. Janis's approach, while focusing on intragroup dynamics, acknowledges that external conditions and individual psychologies also play a role in group decision-making. Personalities demonstrating a need for power, low self-esteem, a low appetite for complexity, distrust, and high nationalism appear to have a propensity toward conflict. Those with a high need for affiliation, optimism, a high appetite for complexity, and a low need for power tend to be more cooperative. All personality types seek "cognitive consistency" by processing new information in accordance with expectations rather than on its own terms, and can be affected in their information processing by strong emotions, which limit the options considered and the information deemed relevant.[27]

Groupthink, in its permutations, is just one example of the psychological group dynamics directly affecting state decisions regarding international relations and international law in the modern world.[28] In the same way the decisions of Greek states, whether *polis*, *koinon*, or kingdom (a difference that could matter very much), were made and carried out by people with their own psychological traits assembled in institutional groupings with their own structural features. Greeks understood that psychological factors mattered, and our sources offer abundant Greek examples of human psychology affecting considerations of international affairs and international law.

Psychology, politics, and international law in the Greek world

Thucydides suggests the importance of individual psychology, group dynamics, and emotional factors in foreign policy decisions in a number of passages, but I single out two.[29] We can start with our now-familiar international crisis: the outbreak of the Peloponnesian War. In this context, Thucydides provides insight into the psychology and group dynamics of decision-making at Sparta. As he reports it, when the Spartans debated among themselves whether to go to war against the Athenians over violations of the thirty years' peace, the Spartan official in charge of the proceedings, the ephor Sthenelaidas, determined that the assembly's first vote, by voice (βοῇ), was too close to call. Because he supported the proposal to go to war, Sthenelaidas developed an ad hoc voting procedure he believed would encourage members of the assembly to support the war: voting "by foot." He made the supporters of war all stand in one area and the opponents in another, on the pretext of making a precise count. According to Thucydides, Sthenelaidas's reasoning was that, without the relative anonymity of a voice vote, more Spartans would vote for war, out of fear of appearing cowardly to their peers. Here we see the power of peer pressure in international law. Even as Thucydides tells it, Spartans were perhaps more afraid of the opinions of their fellow citizens than of the growing strength of the Athenians.[30]

A few years later, in 427, the Athenians enforced international law—the rules of their treaty-bound alliance—by quelling a revolt from that alliance by the

Mytileneans. Thucydides reports that the Athenians in assembly, under the influence of anger (ὀργή) and impulsive eagerness (ὁρμή), resolved on a fierce punishment for the Mytileneans: to execute all the adult men and enslave the women and children (3.36.2). The next day, however, many Athenians, regretting the "savagery" (ὠμόν) of their decree, were relieved to reconvene and reconsider it. First to speak at this second assembly, in favor of maintaining the harsh penalty, was Cleon, the man Thucydides describes as the most violent Athenian as well as the most persuasive (3.36.6). Nevertheless, the Athenians narrowly voted to ease the penalty, sentencing to death only those Mytileneans involved in the revolt. By Thucydides's account, the psychologies and emotions of Cleon and other Athenian citizens, along with the procedural rules permitting reconsideration of a motion, were part of the mix contributing to the final Athenian decision in this violent yet rule-guided international conflict. And that is not all. The Mytileneans were ultimately spared the harsher punishment in fact only because the sailors of the ship sent to announce the first sentence traveled slowly, deterred by the awfulness of the message they were bearing (3.49.4). Personality and psychology, emotion and political structures, determined an important question of international law and foreign affairs.[31]

Individual psychology and group dynamics played roles in foreign relations decisions beyond the fifth century *polis*, such as in the great monarchies that grew out of Alexander's conquest of the Persian empire. Here, the king was the central decision maker but always socially embedded in a family and court. Hence the psychologies of the people within these networks, and their interactions, would have affected multiple dimensions of foreign policy. Most significant in this respect were the *philoi*, the official "Friends" of the king, "to be found in all Hellenistic courts, where they form[ed] a council of state in daily session, advising the king on matters of policy."[32]

Historians in antiquity pointed out some of the decision-making traps facing a king and his *philoi*, traps familiar to those aware of Janis's groupthink model. For example, we see a concern with the vice of flattering speech tempting a king's advisors away from the virtue of frank talk, *parrhesia*.[33] Plutarch relates the famous story of Alexander the Great's companion Kleitos: Kleitos's complaint that Alexander no longer valued "men who are free and free-spoken" incited a drunken Alexander to run him through with a javelin, a deed Alexander immediately regretted (*Alex.* 51.3). In a letter to Antipater attributed to Isocrates, the writer, in recommending a certain Diodotos to Antipater, praises Diodotos's *parrhesia*. Both monarchies and constitutional governments (πολιτείας), he explains, are harmed by advisors who speak only to please, but are preserved even in the direst circumstances by those who speak freely with an eye to what is best (Isoc. *Ep.* 4.4, 7). These passages recognize in a nutshell the very dangers in group decision-making accounted for in Janis's groupthink model.[34]

Polybius portrays a king's advisors significantly affecting foreign relations, and not always through the calm presentation of reasoned argument. For example, Aratos of Sikyon, a general of the Achaian League and, in that capacity, officially an ally of the Macedonians starting about 240, became an advisor to the young Macedonian king Philip V after the latter's accession in 221. Although an ally and therefore perhaps not technically one of Philip's *philoi*, Aratos was an important advisor whose normative influence on Philip can be seen in an incident at Messene described by both Polybius and Plutarch (who follows Polybius closely).[35] In 215 or 214, Philip entered Messene under arms while the city was gripped by civil tension. Detecting an opportunity to capture the easily defended Messenian citadel and gain a strategic advantage in the Peloponnese, Philip sought advice from both Aratos and Demetrios of Pharos. Demetrios encouraged Philip to seize the acropolis and thereby cow the Peloponnesians into fearful submission; Aratos encouraged him to leave the Messenians independent and make the Peloponnesians cooperative out of gratitude. Philip followed Aratos's advice. According to Plutarch it was because Philip had been "compelled" by Aratos (ἐκβεβιασμένος, Plut. *Arat.* 50.6); according to Polybius he "yielded out of shame" (ἐνετράπη, 7.12.9). In either case Philip's decision is attributed by our sources not to the perceived *strategic* superiority of Aratos's advice but rather to the esteem in which the young monarch held the much older advisor and, it is implied, the ethical superiority of leaving Messene free. We cannot know how accurate this story is but there is no obvious reason to disbelieve it.[36]

Greeks, we see, attributed great weight to psychological and social factors in the determination of policies and actions in foreign affairs and international law. The point hardly needs arguing and is demonstrated as early as the first book of the *Iliad*, where Agamemnon's psychology and the dynamics among the leading officers of the Achaian army are crucial to the progress of the war. Greek historians were concerned with the practical effects of the psychology both of leaders and of rank-and-file members of political bodies, as evidenced above; so were the Greek political thinkers. We see this in the rich considerations of such matters in Plato's *Gorgias*, *Republic*, and *Laws*, and in Aristotle's *Nicomachean Ethics*, *Politics*, and *Rhetoric*. Their concern was warranted.

For the reasons presented so far in this chapter, I insist on the explanatory force of the reality that state actions are in fact human actions, based on decisions made by people in specific social and political settings. This point is crucial for understanding the role of international legal socialization in "public" international law, where states themselves are considered the primary actors. But "state" use of and adherence to international law cannot be fully explained by the state-level psychology posited by some international relations theorists. One must also take into account the psychology of those involved in state decision-making within the social matrices of groups large and small.

When the Corinthians, Aiginetans, Megarians, and others encouraged the Spartans to declare war against the Athenians, a key argument was that the Athenians had violated the thirty years' peace, and therefore international law, in several ways. This argument was premised on a belief that most of the Spartans hearing it cared about the obligations created by that law. In the next section, I will argue that legal socialization helps explain human attitudes toward law of all kinds, including international law. One implication will be that, although the theorist Thucydides was correct that Spartan fear of Athenian power helped drive the groups to war, the historian Thucydides helps us see another important reason for the Spartan declaration of war: the socialization of individual Spartans to a Greek international legal system.

Legal socialization, networks, and identity

Seeing state action as rooted in human psychology is the first step in understanding what makes international law effective. And it points to a second step: exploring why law, and rules more generally, are effective. Awareness of how law works at local levels offers insights to its operation in international realms.

The question "What makes law effective?" is sometimes asked differently: "Why do people obey the law?" When framed this way, the most common answer is, "To avoid punishment." Since at least the time of Cesare Beccaria and Jeremy Bentham in the late eighteenth century, efforts to explain compliance with the law have been dominated by such deterrence theory.[37] It assumes many people are generally motivated to do things forbidden by law and claims that the most effective way to prevent this is deterring them with fear of detection and punishment. Deterrence theory aligns easily with rational choice theory when one views the benefits or fruits of rule-breaking as an increase in utility and detection and punishment as its decrease.[38] Yet much evidence suggests that deterrence efforts have real but limited effect on crime rates and little or no effect on tort rates.[39] These small effects are disproportionate to the prominence of deterrence in much criminological and tort theory. Contemporary research suggests that often more important than such "external" deterrence efforts are peoples' internalized norms of behavior, their identification with the community, and their views of the legal or rule system's legitimacy. These conflicting views reflect a debate already held among Greeks themselves.[40]

I focus here on socialization: how the social environment, especially through the influence of overlapping social groups, shapes the psychological factors of action. Our propensities to abide by legal and law-like rule systems derive largely from socialized and group attitudes. And socialization is an international phenomenon: we are all influenced by people in other countries; hence international socialization affects the administrative and legal structures of states as well as a state's adoption of, compliance with, and enforcement of international law. These discussions lay the groundwork for my argument in Chapter 4 that social networks in the ancient Greek international world socialized people to compliance with international law.

Socialization

Socialization is learning how to act in human society. It has long been understood—since antiquity—that socialization affects our acquisition of language, values, norms, habits, social roles, and processes of thinking, judging, and decision-making.[41] It is formative of individual psychologies. People are socialized by each other through relationships partly determined by social and institutional structures. We are affected and shaped by our families, friends, those who share in our religious life, schoolmates and teachers, coworkers, media personalities, authors of books we read, professional colleagues, business competitors, police, government officials, and strangers with whom we interact, both in everyday life and occasionally. The influence is reciprocal, as we all, even as children, affect the world around ourselves.[42] And people help choose which socializing environments they are exposed to. Mechanisms of socialization vary from active intentional and motivational instruction to passive teaching by example. And influence can travel through in-person contact or through media such as books, television, radio, and the internet. It is now common to conceptualize the set of contacts leading to such influences as a *network*, a concept I return to below. Core elements of socialization take place during childhood and adolescence, and much research has focused on those ages. Yet it continues through life into old age.[43]

The complexity multiplies: every society contains countless overlapping social subgroupings, each with its own accepted ways of acting. Everyone belongs to many groups, for varying periods of time, and may participate in socialization processes in all of them.[44] Socialization does not only train people to fit in to one dominant majority society: most of us adjust our behavior according to the group and situation at hand. Two kinds of subgroups are "subcultures" and "communities of practice." Subcultures are social groups whose habits, viewpoints, and norms differ from, and may conflict in marked ways with, those of society at large. Subcultures can counteract mainstream socialization forces, as a source of "deviance." Some theories explain deviance partly as a person's response to an inability to conform to the norms of society: people become "deviant" by first internalizing the values of society, ultimately rejecting them only after failing to embody them.[45] Subcultures can encourage this rejection of mainstream norms. Communities of practice, discussed already by Durkheim, are groups united by common activities rather than close and frequent contact. Much research has focused on professions as socializing groups. "Reference group" theory points out that people are also shaped by the norms of groups to which they do not belong but aspire to. Because of the multiplicity of social groupings in any society, I mean by "socialization" the processes by which any social group affects a person's language, values, norms, habits, perceived roles, judgment, and decision-making.[46]

Recognizing what is socially appropriate is not the same as doing it. Acquiring a tendency or preference to act according to social norms is sometimes called "internalizing" them. Actions performed in accord with internalized tendencies or motives to follow social norms can be contrasted with "rational choice" decisions based on calculations of the rewards and punishments for following or disobeying the same norms. Internalization and rational choice are not mutually exclusive if one posits that the desires and preferences engaged during rational choice are those previously internalized through socialization (i.e., as exogenous to the processes that rational choice theorists are concerned with). Yet much social theory focuses on the dominance of habit in human life, and, as I pointed out in the previous section, psychological research confirms the importance of unconscious factors, including habit, biases, and automatic processes, in human decision-making. The processes of socialization can therefore be seen as affecting both the conscious and the unconscious aspects of human action.[47]

The most relevant aspect of socialization for this book is "legal socialization," which refers specifically to attitudes toward and relations with law and law-like systems of formal rules with formal sanctions. Unlike lawyers and some philosophers of law, sociologists and psychologists usually do not single out the domestic legal system as a unique rule system but consider it similar enough to other normative social compliance systems to be studied together with them. Studies of legal socialization look at how and why people comply not only with domestic law but also with, for example, the rules of households, schools, and workplaces. Because international law is also a normative social system of rules, it is reasonable to assume that much research into legal socialization is also applicable to understanding socialization to international law.[48]

We should not elide potentially important differences between domestic and international law. For example, much legal socialization scholarship has studied the role of attitudes toward legal authorities.[49] But international law, traditionally enforced mostly through self-help by interested parties, largely lacks figures, such as police and judges, seen specifically as enforcement authorities. This lack, apparent in much (but not all) of Greek international law, is one reason that some discount international law as *law*, as I discussed in Chapter 2. Yet the lack of legislators, police officers, and judges did not deprive Greeks of sources of international legal authority with potentially socializing effects. For instance, the "establishment" authority of Greek international law may not have been any less than that of domestic law. By establishment authority I mean the perceived authority of the institutions that established various rules of international law. Customary laws ("the laws of all the Greeks") were established by common consent over a long period of time and may even have been seen, at times, as more legitimate than domestic laws.[50] Treaty laws were established by acknowledged political authorities of the state parties (even if, sometimes, by different particular bodies and processes than for domestic law). Their perceived legitimacy was probably at least similar to that of domestic laws. Still, we should not simply assume that studies of legal socialization focused on attitudes toward "legal" authorities (parents, teachers, police, judges) apply to Greek international law.[51]

Socialization is at least as important as deterrence in explaining legal behavior. Compliance with law is moderately correlated to sanction-based deterrence methods; but is more strongly correlated to the existence of a rule system, to identification with the social groups associated with the norms, and to "morality"—that is, positive attitudes toward the specific norms embodied by the rules and the rule system in question.[52] Often we obey the law mostly because we agree with it: we have internalized the rules and accepted them as authoritative norms of behavior applicable to ourselves.[53] We also accept law's authority over us: law-favoring values, largely internalized during childhood and adolescence, "establish a two-way relationship through which people learn that they should respect the law and defer to legal authority when that authority is being exercised in a way that is appropriate" (Trinkner and Tyler 2016, 422). The normative environment in which one lives and operates as an adult is also important: people are more rule-abiding when surrounded by rule followers and less so where, although rules may be "on the books," the local culture adheres to them less closely.[54]

Legal socialization also involves thoughtfully judging and participating in rule-bound systems. A person will not simply follow any set of rules just because he or she was socialized during childhood as a "rule follower." Instead, some of the values internalized include ideas about how rule systems should be structured and operate. The development of the cognitive ability to make such judgments is part of legal socialization. These judgments are, in turn, directly correlated to perceptions of the procedural justice or fairness of the system and its authorities. In short, personal morality, the system's perceived legitimacy, and one's position and relationships within society all affect a person's willingness and tendency not only to comply with law but to cooperate with the operation of a legal system.[55]

Group identity and the effectiveness of law: Helping friends

One social factor that makes law effective and plays a large role in this book is group identity. Also called social identity, this is a person's sense of belonging to a certain social group "together with some emotional and value significance . . . of this group membership" (Abrams and Hogg 2010, 180). Group identity has concrete effects beyond a person's internal thoughts and feelings. People cooperate more with and have stronger senses of trust, fairness, and justice toward those with whom they share a group identity.[56] I noted above that some psychologists have posited a basic human desire to belong to social groups. Cooperation with and generosity toward fellow group members has been explained as resulting from consciousness of a connection between one's own well-being and that of the group; this consciousness may in turn derive from the basic need to belong to a group in the first place: the group's well-being *becomes* the individual's well-being.[57]

Group identity likely contributes to law's effectiveness in two main ways: substantive and procedural. The substantive effect comes about because we are simply less likely to harm and more likely to help people we see as fellow group members. To the extent that legal rules track what people see as right and wrong, positive group attitudes encourage law-abidingness within the group. If I perceive you as being in my social group, I will be more likely to care for you and less likely, for example, to steal from you or cheat you in business.

Group identity also has procedural effects. People often uphold rules less because of inherent agreement with those rules than just because they are the rules of a group with which they identify. Human social groups are inherently rule-governed, regulated by more or less formal rules and procedures.[58] There are rules about internal group hierarchy and relations of authority, how people are expected and allowed to participate in the group, and how infractions of both substantive and procedural rules are to be negotiated, adjudicated, and settled. "When people identify more strongly with a group, they are motivated to support and legitimize its authorities, and to cooperate within it and on its behalf" (Bradford et al. 2015, 177). To the extent that a legal system is connected to a particular social group, identifying with that group can reinforce one's opinion of the legal system's legitimacy, making one, in turn, more law-abiding and more cooperative with perceived legal authorities. William Miller has argued that medieval Icelanders' noteworthy respect for Icelandic law was partly a product of their sense of a shared Icelandic identity. The same phenomenon has been documented in studies on contemporary societies.[59] This means that, even in cases where other social values encourage conflicts within the group, such as in rivalries for honor, group identities can make the legal system an effective venue for resolving such conflicts. Miller has described how this happened in Iceland.

More directly relevant to the present book, David Cohen has described how ancient Athenians used their court system partly as a field for the contestation of honor. In both cases, the legal system worked for these purposes because it was operated by members of a relevant social group.[60]

In short, by belonging to a group and interacting with other members, people tend to become socialized to its values, to trust and cooperate with other group members, and to uphold and comply with its rules. Group rule compliance is also correlated to belief that the group's rules are moral and that its procedures for ensuring compliance are fair. Tom Tyler uses the term "social motivations" to describe motives driven by socialized and internalized traits, values, and attitudes that encourage people to cooperate within a group. Buttressing arguments made by authors such as Montesquieu, Durkheim, Freud, and Weber, Tyler presents evidence that much of the reason people cooperate within groups is that the creation and maintenance of social links develops social motivations to cooperate in the pursuit of group goals and the maintenance of group values. The scale of the groups seems to have little effect on these phenomena: similar results are found at small scales (for example, in workplaces and college dorms) and at large scales (in the context of city, state, and federal legal systems).[61]

The other side of identity: Harming enemies

Group identity, however, is not all about generosity and cooperation. This is because defining a social group of which you are a member—your in-group—simultaneously and necessarily defines an out-group: everyone not in your in-group. The very sense of group identity that encourages norm-alignment and cooperation within the group also produces competition with out-groups, a sense of the superiority of one's in-group, and bias against members of the out-group. That this tendency is universal has been confirmed by hundreds or thousands of studies over the past decades, since the first important experiments by Henri Tajfel and his associates. It is sometimes called the "minimal group" effect, since it occurs even with groups that meet only the minimal definition of a group.[62] Generally speaking, no matter the kind of group, "in intergroup contexts people generally behave so as to gain or maintain an advantage for their own group over other groups in terms of resources, status, prestige, and so forth" (Hogg 2006, 480). According to social identity theory this differentiation arises in part because, as I noted above, people connect their personal identities and their self-esteem to the groups to which they perceive themselves as belonging, and therefore seek to strengthen their self-esteem by maintaining a sense of their groups' distinctiveness and superiority over other groups.[63] The phenomenon has both cognitive and social elements by which divergent thoughts, feelings, and evaluations lead to divergent treatment. The effect is seen even in minimal groups but tends to increase as a group becomes more coherent through similarity, proximity, and interdependence of its members.[64]

The Athenian political reformer Cleisthenes may have understood the power of the minimal group effect when he radically transformed the tribal and deme organization of Athenian citizens: one of his goals appears to have been not only to break down old tribal ties but to foster new group allegiances. To the extent to which the reforms he spearheaded were achieved, such group identity realignment through "mere" political reorganization suggests the power of the minimal group effect. The large number of groups in most societies produces a high potential for intergroup conflict, but this potential is tempered by most people identifying with multiple groups.[65]

Intergroup conflict is ameliorated, for example, simply through increased contact with members of the out-group. Contact can "blur" intergroup boundaries, reducing the salience of group identities; or may "decategorize" people in out-groups, that is, cause one to see them as individuals rather than to categorize them as members of an out-group. Simply being exposed to people increases the chances of liking them, and this effect can be reflected in attitudes toward others deemed similar to those one knows. Intergroup contact can increase empathy between groups, making members of an advantaged group more likely to act in ways that benefit a disadvantaged group.[66]

Intergroup conflict can also be decreased, and cooperation increased, by heightening identification with a larger, inclusive superordinate group. Perception of a common threat is one factor that can drive such superordinate group identity. Group identities often form at multiple levels. A modern example is the United Arab Emirates ("UAE"), which over the past several decades formed a strong superordinate "Emirate" identity among a group of disparate subordinate sheikhdoms. The UAE is also part of the six states of the Gulf Cooperation Council, which itself has formed a fairly strong "Khaliji" identity. On the other hand, there is support for the theory (the "ingroup projection model") that if a subgroup believes it is most prototypical of the superordinate group and that other subgroups are less prototypical, this belief can increase out-group bias against the other subgroups.[67]

International identity and socialization

Socialization and group identity formation are not stopped by national borders, as we see from the UAE example. Of course, nationality has long been a dominant form of identity, while the relevant "nation" in a particular case may be more a political or social grouping. Whichever way you define nation, transnational group identities exist and have socializing effects. For my purposes, it is useful to distinguish three overlapping forms of international legal socialization. I will call them "international weak ties," "state level socialization," and "affective international identity."

Socializing influence spreads internationally even without, or in spite of, the obvious mechanism of salient group identities. People travel abroad for education, business, religion, tourism, and other purposes, often for long periods of time. We also meet foreigners at home. These international connections expose us to new ideas, institutions, and ways of life. Although their novelty and foreign origin cause many such ideas to be quickly forgotten, sometimes they have a lasting effect. Most of us are in regular contact with small circles of people resembling each other along multiple socioeconomic and ideological axes; so our daily circles tend to be intellectually and normatively "calm." Contact with one person from outside these close circles can therefore impress us with strikingly new information, ideas, and points of view that find some purchase and then "diffuse" into our close contact groups. Mark Granovetter, who first studied this phenomenon in an influential article, calls it "the strength of weak ties," since such "weakly tied" people appear to be responsible for much of the spread of new ideas and cultural patterns in societies: the ties are weak but their effects, cumulatively, can be strong.[68] If this theory is correct, it might mean there is a certain unavoidable level of instability and unpredictability to socializing influences: most contacts with people outside of one's main social groups will have negligible influence, but a small number will reverberate resoundingly; yet it may be impossible to predict which those will be. When such contacts occur across state borders, I call them "international weak ties."

International weak ties may play a role in a second form of international legal socialization, the well-documented phenomenon I call "state level socialization." The modern world has seen a remarkable convergence in how states of all kinds, all over the globe, not only structure their governments but also address various social and political matters. Researchers have mapped significant global convergence in, for example, constitutional structures, educational practices, and environmental, economic, and human rights activities and policies.[69] Goodman and Jinks distinguish two mechanisms of such convergence in addition to "material inducements": what they call "persuasion" and "acculturation." Their "persuasion" resembles Granovetter's "weak ties" in relying on social contact but not group identity. International persuasion involves argument and deliberation, and "the practices of actors are influenced through processes of social 'learning' and other forms of information conveyance that occur in exchanges within international organizations and transnational networks" (Goodman and Jinks 2013, 24). "Acculturation," though, generally depends on the existence of group identities: "varying degrees of identification with a reference group generate varying degrees of cognitive and social pressures to conform" (2013, 26). As in the domestic sphere, both persuasion and acculturation are aspects of international socialization.

But the socialization Goodman and Jinks focus on is "international" more in its causes than its effects. Their book is mostly concerned with how international forces can influence states to adopt particular *domestic* legal institutions, practices, and organizational forms. As they argue, international socialization has tended to encourage states to converge on roughly similar responses to roughly similar problems: for example, how to structure a modern democratic constitution; how to educate an entire population; how to preserve the local environment; how to defend human rights within state borders. These are largely domestic problems whose solutions have often been sought abroad.

There have been few empirical studies of the third kind of international legal socialization, the form that interests me most and which I label "affective international identity." The basic idea is that, just as group identity plays a role in domestic legal socialization, international group identities likely affect the use of, compliance with, and enforcement of law in international contexts. We saw above that group identity encourages, among other things, social motivations to cooperate more with and be more generous and fair toward in-group members. Part of legal socialization therefore is a tendency to be law-abiding and law-enforcing with people you perceive to be in your social group. Social groups can be small or very large, and I am aware of no evidence that this affective element occurs only in groups of a certain size. My suggestion, therefore, is that the positive affective consequences of group identity also form at an international scale.

While little research has been done into the ways that international group identities affect law-relevant behavior, a few recent studies offer evidence of group identity's quasi-legal purchase at an international level. For example, one study looked at varying degrees of cross-border solidarity among Europeans in the form of support for economic assistance for people in other countries both within and outside of Europe. It identified three factors that increased the probability of feelings of solidarity: sharing a language, being geographically close, and sharing membership in the European Union.[70] Another study suggests that success in naturalizing as a citizen in Switzerland is strongly tied to in-group and out-group identities: western Europeans have had significantly higher success rates than applicants from Yugoslavia and Turkey, and statistical analysis shows that country of origin was "by far the most important determinant of naturalization success."[71] While neither of these studies concerns international legal rules per se, both indicate affective results of international group identity that could easily ramify in effects on international law compliance and enforcement. And one recent study *does* explicitly connect international group identity with the effectiveness of international law. A study of German politicians found that those with a high "European" self-identity were more willing to support and uphold EU law than were German politicians with a low European self-identity.[72] In other words, a sense of belonging to the international social group "Europeans" seems likely to make EU law more effective.

These affective consequences in the minds and feelings of individual people should also scale up to a state level of socialization and decision-making. On the model of state action and state "psychology" I proposed earlier in this chapter, state-level socialization is basically an aggregation, within certain political structures, of individual socialization. If this is correct, we should expect group identities to have similar effects on state attitudes and action to those they have on individual attitudes and action. For example, we should expect countries to act with more cooperation, restraint, and generosity toward other members of their perceived groups than toward out-group countries. We should also expect them to follow the norms of their perceived "groups" partly from having internalized those norms and from a desire to fit in with the group, rather than solely out of a fear of material punishment. Drawing on legal socialization research, we should also expect states' compliance with international law to correlate with their opinions of the procedural justice of the international system. The more fair that decision makers perceive the international legal system to be, the more likely they will be to comply with international law.

Thucydides appears to have recognized just this sort of identity-fueled attitude toward compliance with international law in the speech he attributes to the Mytileneans when they justify their revolt from the Athenian alliance in 428, early in the Peloponnesian War. Envoys from Mytilene addressed the Spartans and other members of the Peloponnesian League at Olympia after the festival had concluded (Thuc. 3.8). Justifying their revolt, the Mytileneans suggested that their enlistment into the Delian League was driven by common Greek identity made especially salient by its contrast with the Persians: "We became allies, not to the Athenians for the enslavement of the Greeks, but to the Greeks for freedom from the Persians."[73] And they gladly followed the rules of the alliance so long as the Athenians led it in a fair and just manner on the basis of its members' equality (ἀπὸ τοῦ ἴσου, 3.10.4). But their devotion to the alliance and its rules faltered as they saw the Athenians turning the international legal system to unjust uses, treating some members more like subjects than allies (3.10.4–6). Nevertheless, the Mytileneans make an elaborate defense of their behavior to the Spartans because of a firm belief across the Greek world that the terms of alliances must be followed except in extraordinary circumstances (3.10–14). Closing with a rousing invocation of the panhellenic god Olympian Zeus, within whose temple the envoys are speaking "as though suppliants," the Mytilenean speech demonstrates the sometimes dramatic dynamic of identity and notions of justice in Greek international law.

Networks and socialization in the Greek world

There is one final theoretical matter to put on the table before I turn in the next chapter to considering how international legal socialization built on group identities in concrete ways in the ancient Greek world. This matter is networks. Networks have become a primary way for scholars to visualize and theorize many social processes. I noted above that sets of contacts between people are often described as networks, and social network analysis has developed as a discipline studying how networks connect and affect people.[74] Social networks are a sort of "dark matter" of social life, largely invisible but essential to the "social gravity" binding human communities. Your social network is a group of people who might exert a socializing influence on you through direct or indirect contact. In the simplest sort of social network model, people are represented as nodes and the personal relationships connecting them are lines between the nodes.[75] These lines represent a collation of actual instances of personal contact that permit information to travel. Such information can be transmitted in any of the ways people communicate with each other, verbally and nonverbally, intentionally and unintentionally.

Complications arise quickly. Not all connections are equal. We have daily contact with some people in our networks, infrequent exposure to others. Some connections are intimate, others impersonal. The feelings that accompany connections affect how information from them is processed: information from someone in an out-group might be rejected as false or unreliable simply because of the messenger.[76] So we see that, while networks are essential to creating group identities, a social network is not the same as an "in-group" of group identity theory. A further complication is that socialization, as I noted, can occur through exposure to media (books, television, internet). When I watch Stephen Colbert's television show, in a sense he becomes a member of my network (although I do not become a member of his in the same sense). Something similar happens if I read a book, or watch a film, by someone now dead. Consider biographies. To readers of Ron Chernow's biography (or Lin-Manuel Miranda's musical), Alexander Hamilton has probably been more personally influential than have been many people they have known. Information and socialization spread between people in many ways, which a network analysis of socialization should account for. And more than information travels through networks. For example, network analysis is used to study the spread of disease.[77]

Social networks develop through and along nonsocial networks. We travel on sidewalks, bicycle paths, highways, trains, and through airport networks; we communicate through telephone, internet, and satellite networks passing electromagnetic signals between machines. I send text messages to my sister, email my editor, telephone my grandmother, walk to class, take a train to the annual academic conference (or attend by videoconference). Infrastructure networks can therefore offer good indications of the strength of social networks: wider highways, more flights, and thicker internet cables between two towns suggest thicker social networks between their inhabitants. We mostly lack direct evidence of who knew whom in ancient social networks, and therefore the "network" studies of Greece and the Mediterranean world often exploit proxy data such as pottery, coins, amphora stamps, colony and alliance relationships, and religious and athletic festivals to reconstruct social networks in the ancient Mediterranean.[78]

Even when particular names survive in the evidence, as they often do in honorary decrees, artists' signatures, and various kinds of inscribed lists of names, we seldom know more about the person than what is reported in that single source; sometimes we have a mere name, perhaps with a patronymic and the name of the person's city or deme, and the fact that someone had a reason to inscribe it. This lack of detailed evidence means we normally cannot use it to test theories of network effects or even to offer detailed models of specific networks. Instead we are limited to using theories already tested on modern data to understand the likely *general* implications of the ancient data that do survive. Irad Malkin does this in applying the notions of "phase transition" and "information cascade" to Greek colonization of the Mediterranean, which, he suggests, at some point reached a critical number that led to a network-wide notion of "Greekness" in a form that had not previously existed.[79]

Some of the scholarship on ancient Greek networks is less concerned with using network theory to understand historical phenomena than with mapping historical networks to the extent possible from our surviving evidence.[80] My interest is not in mapping networks but in understanding their effects. The existing research suggests Greek networks fed international socialization by connecting many Greeks across *polis* and *ethnos* boundaries. My argument regarding Greek networks therefore largely comes down to: networks are a vehicle for socialization; the Greek world had many international networks; those networks therefore likely had an international socializing force.

But we can at times attempt more detailed hypotheses. Our social networks connect us to the social groups with which we identify and to society as a whole. Because everyone in a society is always embedded within a social network, it is misleading to conceive of people simply as atomized, independent individuals, on one hand, or as merely a part of undifferentiated "society," on the other. As Granovetter puts it, networks form a "meso" level that connects the individual to a society-wide level (2017, 15). He emphasizes several other features of networks that may be relevant for understanding their effects in the Greek world. First, he notes that norms spread faster and are complied with more reliably in dense sections of networks than where connections are sparser. Second, as mentioned above, Granovetter emphasizes the importance of "weak ties": how a network section whose members are densely connected to each other spreads new information from someone connected to the dense section only loosely, perhaps by a single tie. These weak ties might help explain, for example, the apparently large role that traveling intellectuals such as sophists, poets, and doctors played in the Greek world. Third, he describes the "strategic advantage" possessed by people who are the only, or among the few, connections between otherwise separate networks. This position can give them "social capital" as brokers between networks. *Xenia* and proxeny in the Greek world may be examples of practices promoting such brokerage.[81]

This strategic position of the broker is one form of what Matthew Jackson describes as network centrality, an umbrella term for describing how well connected someone is compared to everyone else in a network.[82] People with the most centrality in the network are likely to have the most influence, all else being equal. This is true even when the people with the most connections are just as liable to be influenced by others as everyone else in the network. That is, they are not more influential because people care more about their opinions. They are more influential just by virtue of having higher centrality in the network.[83] As Jackson expresses it, "more central opinions have more of an impact. . . . Being friends with other people who are well connected means that my opinion will spread to them, and then outward from them, and so having well-connected friends is as important as having many friends" (2019, 168). One effect of network centrality is that most societies have fields in which there are "opinion leaders" and "opinion followers." This is perhaps more obvious now than ever, with the rise of "influencers" with millions of followers on ubiquitous social media such as Instagram, TikTok, X, and Facebook. Although perceived authority may play a crucial role in expanding influencers' networks in the first place, with their resulting immense network centrality they forge public opinion and shape commercial markets.[84]

Network centrality also offers social capital. Pierre Bourdieu has defined social capital as "the aggregate of the actual or potential resources which are linked to possession of a durable network of more or less institutionalized relationships of mutual acquaintance and recognition—or in other words, to membership in a group—which provides each of its members with the backing of the collectivity-owned capital, a 'credential' which entitles them to credit, in the various senses of the word." Definitions of social capital vary (and Bourdieu developed the concept in elaborate ways I do not explore here), but this central concept of *resources available through a social network* is common to many of them.[85] It supports my claim of a close relationship between network centrality, social influence, and social capital. Network connections help people become wealthier and more influential and there is, therefore, a general positive correlation between wealth, social position, and social influence. In short, elites tend to have larger networks and more influence than non-elites. This fact is important in understanding how ancient Greek international networks helped bring about international socialization, since many of those networks, as we will see, were made up largely of elites, who in turn likely had disproportionately large influence in their hometowns. Elites in Greek states were more likely to come into contact with people from other cities and therefore to socialize them and be socialized internationally. Back home, they would spread the information, norms, and values they acquired abroad.[86]

In short, socialization was a central aspect of Greek international law's social reality, helping not only to transmit legal rules and norms but to give them effect in people's minds and social relationships. Greek networks that crossed the boundaries of *polis*, *ethnos*, *koinon*, or kingdom participated in this social reality. Those networks transmitted information about norms and rules: information such as the terms of the thirty years' peace; the unwritten rules of trade among merchants in the Black Sea; the rules governing retrieval of the dead after a battle. People from different states but networked together would have encouraged each other, both deliberately and subconsciously, to adopt specific norms. This encouragement would have operated through all three of the mechanisms identified by Goodman and Jinks: material inducement, persuasion, and acculturation. Finally, networks make possible group identity and bias, which can strengthen *or* weaken tendencies to follow, apply, and enforce the norms that have been transmitted and encouraged by networks. One of my central arguments in this book is that group identity formation through international networks was a key element inducing Greeks to follow and enforce the norms of international law. I describe that group identity formation in the next chapter.

4
International Identity and Socialization in Ancient Greece

A networked world

The Greek world was knitted together by a mesh of social networks reflecting the Greek penchant for forming relationships across physical distance. These networks took shape through diplomacy, religion, commercial trade, traveling professionals and craftsmen, law, war, athletics and equestrianism, intellectual activity, and the performing arts of music, dancing, and poetry (and drama, which combined all three). By nurturing the solidification of international Greek identities, these networks fostered the spread of and compliance with international law.

I focus in this chapter on a central example: international networks of Greek religion. A certain shared body of religious beliefs and practices was a sure indicator of Greekness.[1] Herodotus reports an Athenian opining to a group of Spartans, while the Persian army ground toward them in 479 BCE, that Greeks are united by blood, language, religion, and customs (8.144.2; cf. 5.92.η.5). His point is that the Athenians will remain loyal to the Greek alliance. No need to express *why* those factors induced fidelity to the group: their effect is taken for granted. I take up the task of supplying the Athenian's omitted logic, considering just how shared religion, among other things, bound Greeks together. And despite the Athenian's implication, Greek religion was not always a panhellenic force uniting all Greeks: it could be regionally specific and intensely local; religion often divided Greeks at levels of *ethnos*, *polis*, or below; and it acted as a site (literally and figuratively) of competition and contention. I will touch on these more complex interactions of religion and identity.[2]

Because religious networks were just one of many kinds of network connecting Greeks and shaping identities, I will more briefly consider other ways that Greeks interacted across borders, making international identities salient. One of my claims is that the Greek international world was a community less of states than of people, all belonging to many social groups, only one of which was each person's set of fellow citizens. As Greeks themselves existed in more than just the realm of "state" identity, their networks and group identities socialized them to laws beyond the domestic laws of their home cities.[3]

Laws of All the Greeks. Jesse James, Oxford University Press. © Jesse James 2026.
DOI: 10.1093/9780197838556.003.0005

International religious festivals

The lived experience of Greek religion offers an example of how the thick web of Greek international networks was woven by bringing people together under the umbrella of multiple social practices. Consider religious festivals. Religious practice was always the central pretext for festivals, and the core cultic activities of procession, prayer, and sacrifice were any festival's heart and climax. But celebration of large festivals also included formally organized competitive events: not only the familiar contests between human athletes, but also horseback and chariot races, as well as contests in *mousike*, which included instrumental music, dancing, and singing of poetry. All this transpired over a festival's several days. And much other activity was pursued before, during, and after the officially sanctioned proceedings: eating and drinking, buying and selling, diplomatic maneuvering, political and philosophical conversations.[4]

Although almost every cult and sanctuary was run by citizens of a single city, many had international visibility and at times were overrun with visitors from abroad, especially during formal and periodic celebrations highlighted on religious calendars. Most prominent was the circuit of quadrennial or biennial "crown" festivals: Olympic, Pythian (at Delphi, home of Pythian Apollo), Isthmian, Nemean; less prominent were regional but still well-known ceremonies such as those at Dodona, Epidauros, Delos, Samothrace, and the sanctuary of Zeus Ammon at Siwa in north Africa, as well as the Athenian Eleusinia, Greater Panathenaia, and City Dionysia (see Map 3); and Greeks everywhere celebrated many smaller and now mostly little-known events.[5] The number of festivals with an international profile, or at least aspiring to one, grew until the first century BCE or later, in what Angelos Chaniotis has called "the explosion of a festival culture."[6] Celebration of them by Greeks from many cities acted as a continuous wellspring of supra-*polis* identities, including panhellenic identity. Ian Rutherford, who has described the international networks forged from Greek religious practices, notes that "one of the main ways religion works in ancient Greece is by facilitating connections with the broader world through networks that connected individuals and cults in different locations, and through a framework of common sanctuaries, where polis-identity comes up against the larger identity of being Greek."[7]

The Athenian orator and political theorist Isocrates portrays international festivals—often called *panegyreis*—as opportunities for Greeks from everywhere not only to congregate but to interact meaningfully. He insists those interactions had affective, identity-building power. In his speech titled *Panegyricus*, written in the 380s BCE for the occasion of an unspecified international festival, Isocrates commends such festivals for nourishing warm panhellenic sentiments:

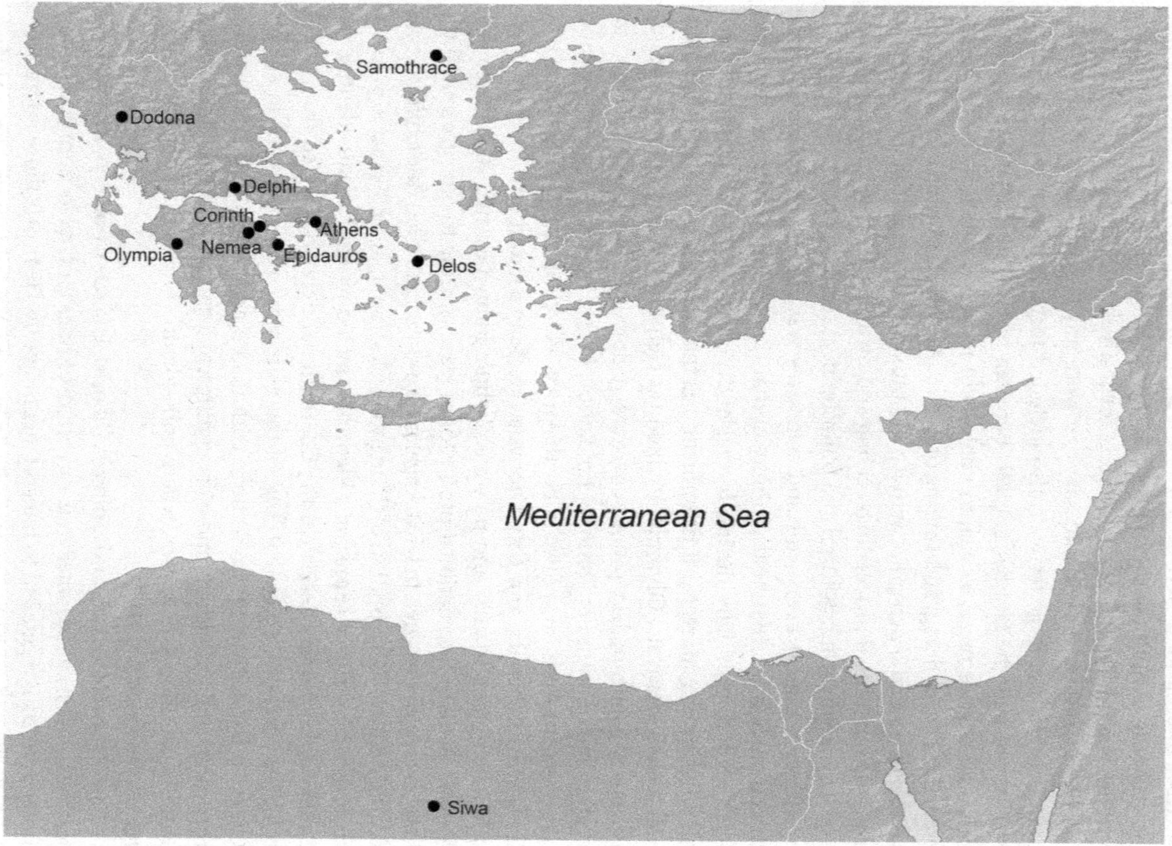

Map 3 Locations of major Greek sanctuaries. Map by R. Salem.

> Those who established panegyric festivals are justly praised for having handed down to us a tradition like this in which we make truces, cease current hostilities, and come together to the same place. Then, after making prayers and sacrifices in common, we remember our ancient kinship (συγγενείας ὑπαρχούσης) with each other, we become very well-disposed (εὐμενεστέρως) toward each other for the future, we renew old ties of guest friendship and make other, new ones. . . . And in addition, at our festival most of all one can discover faithful friendships (φιλίας πιστοτάτας) and participate in all sorts of conversations (συνουσίαις).[8]

Isocrates's explicit goal in the full speech is to encourage the Greeks to coalesce in a war against Persia. His characterization of putting aside differences, strengthening old friendships, and creating new relationships is intended to have rhetorical impact—to induce the very effects he describes. This does not render his description inaccurate, since the speech assumes a festival audience in a position to judge; an audience that might have been experiencing exactly the friendships and conversations he describes.

Other contemporary speeches emphasized the power of religious festivals to nurture international affection among attendees and the propriety of doing so. At the Olympic festival of (probably) 388 BCE, the orator Lysias described the occasion as an opportunity for Greeks to form and cement mutual friendships. In fact, he claims that Heracles founded the Olympics for just this purpose.[9] Like Isocrates, Lysias was rallying the Greeks to unite in opposition not only to the Persians but also to the Syracusan tyrant Dionysius, whom he accused of teaming up with the Persians (33.4–7). Since Lysias's father had migrated from Syracuse to Athens, where his family lived as resident aliens, Lysias knew about building relationships with Greeks of different citizenship. Another intellectual of wide experience, the famous itinerant orator and rhetorical teacher Gorgias of Leontini (also in Sicily), had delivered a previous Olympic oration, probably in 408 BCE, already then exhorting the Greeks to unite against the Persians as a common enemy.[10] In contrast, Diogenes Laertius relates that, at the Isthmian festival one year, the Athenian Antisthenes, a follower of Socrates, "had planned to deliver a speech in which he both criticized and praised the Athenians, Thebans, and Spartans; but he begged out of his commitment when he saw how many visitors had arrived from those cities."[11]

These anecdotes show that international religious festivals were venues for positive messages unifying Greeks more than for critical, divisive rhetoric. The speeches I mentioned were delivered within decades of each other, and we do not know if they represent long-lived festival practices.[12] But a large festival drawing participants from across the Greek world was an obviously attractive venue for performers seeking an audience, including rhetorical performers. Formally scheduled speeches seem to have been a regular feature of some festivals, for centuries. Although Greeks sometimes recognized in these speeches the power of the festivals to build community among Greeks, they took this for granted rather than analyze the specific mechanisms. These deserve consideration.[13]

Large religious festivals fostered creation of international networks, identities, and communities in both their preparation and their realization. First, the city hosting the festival sent delegates called *theoroi* to often widespread parts of Greece to announce the festival, its dates, and any associated truce for the protection of attendees. In each community they visited, these *theoroi* were hosted by so-called *theorodokoi*, who could be appointed either by the *polis* organizing the festival or by their home city. This act of hosting created or strengthened personal relationships between host and guest. And the visitors must typically have interacted, during their stay, with many locals. The arrival of a delegation of *theoroi* would have been a noteworthy event, especially in small and remote towns.[14]

When the time for the festival arrived, each *polis* accepting an invitation sent its own official delegation of festival attendees, also called *theoroi*, typically two to five people. They might be accompanied by athletes, musicians, or private citizens visiting the festival as participants or unofficial observers. Anyone with the time and money to go might yield to the temptation of the promised spectacles, and performers of all sorts would be lured by anticipation of audiences larger and more diverse than those they ever saw at home. Over 100 people from a single city might travel to attend a given festival. Probably hundreds of cities sent theoric delegations to the larger celebrations.[15]

The visitors would be crowded together with strangers all day and night, not only while watching the contests, performances, and religious rites, but while eating and even sleeping.[16] Of course, festivals could bring people close together but still not force them to socialize. The amount of actual interaction among Greeks from different places must have varied widely, some mingling mostly with fellow travelers from their hometowns. But several factors suggest there usually was real inter-*polis* mixing. First, almost all visitors would have been at any festival for multiple days. Some festivals are known to have taken place over a week or longer. Even if the officially organized events themselves lasted only three to five days, as the Pythian and Olympic crown celebrations typically did, uncertainties of transportation times would have led to many people arriving several days before official proceedings began: more time to meet strangers, if only out of boredom.[17]

Both participants and spectators needed lodging. Some boarded with local citizens of the host city, often with locals connected somehow to their hometown, for example as *proxenoi* or *theorodokoi*. Others stayed at purpose-built inns; this was a more viable option when the festival took place in or next to an established city. Not only a major urban center such as Athens, but even modest Delphi, would have such public accommodations.[18] At many festivals, most attendees would have set up camp, pitching tents or even sleeping in the open air. This is best attested at Olympia, which was not itself a *polis* and was situated a fair distance (thirty-five kilometers) from Elis, the city whose citizens managed the Olympia sanctuary for centuries (although other towns were closer). Plutarch tells us about the lavish temporary quarters erected at Olympia for the Athenian aristocrat Alcibiades in 416, when he was victorious in a horse race there: the Ephesians supplied his magnificent tent; the Chians provided him with sacrificial animals and feed for his horses; and the Lesbians gave him wine and food to feast a multitude.[19] It is especially significant that at this festival Alcibiades, although an Athenian, was explicitly "sponsored" at Olympia by non-Athenian Greeks from far away. Surely the Ephesians, Chians, and Lesbians also socialized intensively both with Alcibiades's delegation and with each other at this encampment to which they all contributed. Alcibiades himself was extraordinary, but such international mingling at Olympia was not.

On the contrary, festivals were times of communal celebration, of group sacrifice, and feasting and wine-drinking. Most sanctuaries regulated who could participate in the actual sacrifices and who would get the meat from them. But a sacrifice proper is not the same as even a ritual meal or feast, and we must imagine that the meat distributed from sacrifices was taken away from the altar area by whoever was entitled to it, brought to locations around the festival site, and prepared with other ingredients into meals served at multiple venues.[20] Mixed crowds often enjoyed those meals. This is Plutarch's implication about the meals served at Olympia by Alcibiades. Athenaeus makes it explicit, describing not only Alcibiades but also a certain Leophron as wealthy Olympic victors who celebrated by inviting everyone (πᾶσαν) to a massive feast.[21] We also have some evidence for large joint sacrifices that must formally have brought together visitors from various cities, and of delegates sharing sacrificial meat with strangers. There was surely a hierarchy of meals: the powerful, wealthy, and famous would often have eaten together, and pre-existing group identities would have influenced who ate with whom.[22] But as attendees at weddings and academic conferences know, common meals and drinking parties encourage strangers to interact with each other, more than formal ceremonies do. Shared meals help to create and define social groups, and at large festivals they allowed extended interactions between people from different parts of Greece.[23] People engaged in other affairs, including the obscure and puzzling: beauty contests (male and female); cross-dressing; bathing the statues of the gods in the sea; stealing food; feigned slaughter of an infant. Markets set up for the purpose of supplying so many people with food and other products brought visitors in contact with merchants, many no doubt local. Finally, the contests and other spectacles, athletic and artistic, would, after crowding people close together, give them much to talk about at their meals and parties.[24]

The identities nourished by any religious event would depend very much on the social groups permitted and welcomed to participate.[25] Panhellenic festivals, open to all Greeks, were obvious and explicit forums for nurturing panhellenic identity. Shared religious rituals would frequently have had a community-strengthening effect. Although every cult and sanctuary had its own local, idiosyncratic practices, the passage from Herodotus discussed above (8.144.2) states a reality we know of from abundant evidence: Greeks generally recognized a certain group of gods and certain forms of religious ritual as being characteristically Greek. The latter included animal sacrifice, prayer, feasting, and processions. These rites were almost always communal. Robert Parker describes sacrifice in particular as "a preeminently communal activity, one that is performed by groups and also helps form them."[26] Spectators observing the rites, although they did not personally walk in procession, restrain the sacrificial animal, plunge in the knife, or cook the meat, would still have felt like members of the full religious community simultaneously created and reinforced by the ceremonies. And this community was often international. Barbara Kowalzig, echoing Isocrates, argues that "theoric ritual"—all the practices associated with participating in and especially attending international festivals—"was perceived as crucial for the social and political order between cities, and for the creation of a sense of communality among them" (2005, 43). Regular participation in panegyric festivals by people from many cities, according to Kowalzig, was seen as "a way to prevent stasis, and to grant 'harmony and peace' among perennial competitors" (56). The mere close contacts fostered by so many people from different cities and regions being so close together would often have had a harmonizing effect, even in the absence of a religious context, through the ability of contact itself to reduce prejudice and encourage positive feelings. Religious rituals, in which participation was generally limited to a particular group, certainly fostered group identity even more.[27]

The centrality of the common gods of the Greeks to both international festivals and international law meant that participation in the former likely reinforced participation in the latter. Cities sent representatives to international festivals in order to strengthen relationships with other Greeks, but especially in order to honor, and strengthen relationships with, the god or gods being celebrated. One small example of the gods' centrality to all aspects of Greek participation in such festivals is that, when cities appointed *theorodokoi* as hosts of the *theoroi* sent out to announce festivals, the decrees sometimes described them as *theorodokoi* of the gods to be honored.[28] The gods were also central to several aspects of international law, from the laws of war forbidding harm to sanctuaries, to the religious rite of pouring libations (*spondai*) to mark a truce, to the swearing of sometimes elaborate oaths while concluding treaties. We saw in Chapter 1 how much focus was placed on the religious aspect of oath violations in the prelude to the Peloponnesian War. Socialization at festivals centered on religious practices and beliefs would have encouraged further behavior in line with legal rules implicating those very practices and beliefs.[29]

The religious significance of treaties often induced Greeks to post inscribed copies of them in sanctuaries, usually sanctuaries under the control of one of the parties involved. We know of dozens of specific treaties the Athenians were party to, inscribed copies of which were exposed to public view while protected by the goddess on the Athenian acropolis. Olympia stands out as a sanctuary where many cities displayed treaties and other documents relating to international law (such as judgments in international arbitrations). This "panhellenic" display of treaties was practiced at Olympia from the sixth through the second centuries. In included major multiparty treaties such as the thirty years' peace between the Athenian and Spartan alliances, which I have discussed in earlier chapters, as well as agreements between otherwise unknown communities. Delphi was used similarly.[30] After oaths were sworn and libations poured to seal a treaty, posting it in a sanctuary tinted it even further with holy dye by placing it almost literally under the watchful eyes of the gods. Visitors' exposure to physical copies of treaties within sanctuaries must have reinforced respect for interstate agreements. This respect would have extended beyond the treaties themselves to the very principle underlying them, the customary rule that treaties must be adhered to: *pacta servanda sunt.*

Another rule of customary law would inevitably have been at the forefront of people's consciousness at major religious events: the rule providing for a truce during certain festivals, requiring safe passage for *theoroi* and other participants, and protecting the territory of the festival itself from attack. These truces, usually called *ekecheiriai* (ἐκεχειρίαι) or *spondai* (σπονδαί), are attested in the fifth and fourth centuries for festivities at Olympia, Delphi, Nemea, and Eleusis, and for other festivals in the third and second centuries. They were probably openly declared by the festival announcers themselves, first at their departure from the host city and then at each subsequent stop.[31]

Like much Greek religious practice, international festivals were strictly regulated. There were, of course, rules for how the local officials should manage events, but I am concerned here with rules of "international" reach: those explicitly applying to people from abroad.[32] We have surviving texts of festival regulations concerned in part specifically with the conduct or treatment of foreigners, for example from the Athenian Eleusinia in the fifth century, and from the similar festival at Andania, in the southwest Peloponnese, in the first. Athletic contests had their own particular rules. The common experience of international festivals as highly regulated affairs would have enforced a notion that all Greeks were equally subject to certain rules, which were necessary to organize and run a complicated event while maintaining general order.[33]

Considering just the athletic regulations at Olympia, there was a basic rule forbidding cheating by athletes, in addition to specific rules defining cheating for different events.[34] Pausanias describes the system by which the Elean officials of the Olympic contests fined cheaters and used the proceeds to set up statues of Zeus called *Zanes*. The bases of these statues were inscribed with messages to the effect that Olympic victories must be earned fairly. Flogging was another prescribed penalty, as was expulsion from the contests. Cheating violated not only the rules, but the athletes' oath to abide by them, an oath they swore while standing in front of a statue of Zeus *Horkios* ("the 'oathy' one," Paus. 5.24.9). This oath-swearing ritual would have reinforced the belief that the gods cared about the rules and compliance with them.[35] As I discussed in Chapter 3, group identity formation typically reinforces norms operative within the group. The centrality of rules to the contests of international Greek festivals would have reinforced the connection between being Greek and abiding by certain rules of behavior. It is especially significant that the rules of festivals concerned matters of war, contests, and oaths. The panegyric festivals therefore strengthened a notion of Greek identity specifically tied to the principle, "Greeks must follow rules when contesting with each other."

Polis, competition, and conflict

International festivals were not always and only about panhellenic unity. *Polis* identities, and divisions arising from them, persisted and could be highlighted. As already noted, even the most panhellenic sanctuaries were (mostly) managed by the citizens of particular cities, such as the Eleans in Olympia and the Delphians in Delphi.[36] The festivals too, especially the strictly religious aspects but also the athletic and other contests, were typically controlled by officials from the local city. This point is emphasized by advocates of the "*polis* religion" model articulated most forcefully by Christiane Sourvinou-Inwood. On this model, "the *polis* provided the fundamental framework in which Greek religion operated."[37] Josine Blok has emphasized the centrality of *polis* cult participation in revealing and determining who counted as a citizen of the city. For Sourvinou-Inwood, the *polis* religion framework meant, in the context of international festivals, that "the *polis* was the basic unit": it was a *polis* that hosted the festival, and all attendees were present in the name of and as representatives of their respective *poleis*.[38]

The special status of the host city at any international festival could reify distinctions of identity between the hosts as in-group and everyone else as out-group.[39] Julia Shear argues that identity formation along these lines took place at the Great Panathenaia in Athens. This festival, which was international but not panhellenic in the same sense as those at Olympia and Delphi were, emphasized an Athenian's "identity as an Athenian in contrast to the inhabitants of other cities" and "also allowed the Athenians to impose identities on their visitors." Shear's model of identity formation at the Panathenaia is more complex than this quotation indicates, and she is surely correct that the festival highlighted the various roles that different groups played in Athenian society.[40] But she gives little consideration to the possibility that the festival fostered international identity that did not count either as "all the Athenians" or as a subgroup within Athenian society. We know that non-Athenians attended the Greater Panathenaia, probably since the sixth century, as Shear notes.[41] Such visitors must have been drawn by the prospect, not of feeling *excluded* from the core ceremonies reserved to Athenians, but of feeling *included* in common, recognizably Greek worship of a major panhellenic god. International festivals were international only to the extent they were welcoming of an international audience; festival organizers could not have done this by reifying attendees' differences and highlighting their exclusion from the central elements of celebration. And Blok's more general point, beyond her claims about citizenship, is that sharing in cult fosters community. In the Greek world this community-fostering aspect of cult took place at scales from the single family to the panhellenic community.[42]

None of my emphasis on international identity-building is meant to deny that large festivals were key sites of competition between communities and identities. On the contrary, they were pregnant with its possibility. Rivalry was both explicit—in the athletic contests above all—and implied, especially in the form of conspicuous displays of wealth or military success.[43] Theoric delegations seeking to outdo those from other cities could bring impressive flocks of animals to sacrifice. Sanctuaries and temples were decorated with spoils of war, including from battles against other Greeks.[44] And Greeks could be competitive even in their panhellenism: much of Isocrates's *Panegyricus*, which I quoted above, is devoted to arguing why the Athenians were the best choice as leaders of a joint Greek expedition against Persia. The order of appearance of *theoroi* from different cities in any festival's sacred procession (*propompeia*) would have been a matter of honor and hence competition, as were the seating positions (*proedria*) for spectators at the many public events. Plutarch describes the lavish and impressive procession the Athenian general Nicias staged when he led the Athenian delegation to Delos in 421 or 417. Nicias, having arranged the Greek ships as a bridge to Delos from the nearby island of Rheneia, at dawn led a choral procession of Athenians across the ships to the sanctuary. At the Olympia of 416, mentioned above, Alcibiades performed a separate grand parade on the night before the official event.[45]

Thucydides describes high international tensions at the Olympia of 420, which almost led to outright violence. The Eleans, who ran the festival, had recently entered into a treaty with the Athenians, inscribing the text on a bronze *stele* erected at that year's festival. They also fined the Spartans for having violated the Olympic truce with two minor military engagements. The Spartans denied that these engagements were, legally speaking, violations of the truce, and refused to pay the penalties imposed by the Eleans, who then excluded them from the festival. They were afraid the Spartans would come nevertheless, under arms, and force their way to the altar. Therefore they posted soldiers to protect against a Spartan incursion, which never occurred. In the actual sporting events, a Spartan named Lichas, having been disqualified because of his Spartan citizenship, apparently lent his four-horse chariot team to some Boiotians to enter in the race. After his horses won, however, Lichas proudly strode onto the racecourse and indicated that the team was his, an act of bravado that the Elean officials punished with a beating. Simon Hornblower calls this sequence of events "one of the most tense and dramatic moments in the history of the ancient Greek Olympic Games."[46] But it also shows a remarkable commitment by most parties to the rule-bound nature of the event. Both rule violations (first of the truce, by the Spartan army, then of the ban, by Lichas) were punished, and the Spartans (aside from Lichas) ultimately respected the Olympic ban. Despite the tensions, the incident confirms the power that international rules wielded among the Greeks. It must have made a similar impression at the time.[47]

In any case, athletic and musical competitions were themselves vehicles of Greek identity. Greeks seem to have (inaccurately) perceived athletic competitions in particular as something that only Greeks engaged in. In fact, people judged to be non-Greek were not allowed to compete at Olympia.[48] By participating in such competitions, Greeks would have reaffirmed their Greekness, to themselves and each other. At festivals that were largely premised on valuing competition, where contests played an identity-affirming role, it is not clear that the mere existence of competition would have weakened rather than re-knitted ties of identity.

Sanctuaries, memorials, and identity

So far in this chapter, I have focused on the effects of person-to-person contact at major religious festivals. International networks of such contacts encouraged group identities socializing Greeks to be law-abiding and law-enforcing toward each other. But we should also take into account the effects of the architectural environments where those festivals took place. Like the festivals, the built environments were sites of competition. That competition was always played out in a space defined by Greekness and governed by rules, in a landscape that forged a normative sense of what it meant to be a member of an international Greek society.

I noted in the previous chapter that we can be socialized by the dead. They can also shape our identity, through the words, images, and artifacts they leave behind. In Greece, religious sites were magnets of deliberate visual commemoration, the most important sites exerting the strongest attraction. The weight of commemoration left by prior generations was especially heavy at major sanctuaries such as Delphi and Olympia, which teemed with monuments and messages, many explicitly religious in nature. One effect of the many altars, temples, statues, and other dedications to gods, many of them crowded together, must have been simple religious awe. But sometimes more specific messages were conveyed.[49]

Some meanings were obvious, with a lesson. The *Zanes* statues at Olympia, which I mentioned above, warned against cheating. At Delphi, the most famous deliberate messages were the maxims inscribed on the temple of Apollo, such as "know yourself" and "nothing too much."[50] The massive altar of Apollo, built and dedicated by the Chians in the sixth or early fifth century and located directly in front of the temple, was inscribed with a record of the Delphian grant to the Chians of *promanteia*, the right to consult the oracle before people from other cities. This inscription informed everyone of the Chian privilege and implied that the Chians had performed an excellent deed worthy of it—likely the building of the altar itself.[51]

Also close to Apollo's temple at Delphi stood a coiled pillar of bronze six meters tall, three entwined snakes supporting a golden tripod, commemorating the allied Greek victory over Persia in 479. Cast from the metal of Persian spoils, the serpent column stood near the temple of Apollo and the Chian altar as a conspicuous emblem of Greek unity in their desperate resistance against the overwhelming Persian invasion.[52] At first, Pausanias, Spartan commander of Greek forces and hero of the battle of Plataia, engraved the tripod with an epigram implying that he had defeated the Persians himself. Embarrassed and angry at Pausanias's arrogance, the Spartans had the epigram erased, replacing it with an inscription on the snakes' coils, naming all the cities that participated in the Greek victory. The Spartans said that Pausanias had committed an injustice (ἀδίκημα) with his inscription, one of a series of offenses that led to his arrest and eventual death by starvation.[53] In this way, the serpent column communicated to its viewers not only an identity unified by opposition to Persia but also a lesson that what mattered was this alliance of Greeks, more than any individual. Monuments of the allied victory were set up also at Olympia and at the "Isthmian" sanctuary of Poseidon near Corinth.[54]

Some "monumental" messages were more ambiguous and subject to contesting interpretations. The pediments of the temple of Zeus at Olympia each featured a sculpted depiction of a mythological event. At the west end, Lapith men fought Centaurs, the latter having turned violently drunk at the wedding of the Lapith king Perithoos. In the east pediment, Pelops (the beloved of Poseidon) and Oinomaos (king of Pisa, the nearby city that originally controlled Olympia) prepared for their chariot race, Pelops seeking as the trophy of victory Oinomaos's daughter Hippodameia.[55] In Greek myth, the Lapiths and Pelops would win their respective contests, both with divine aid (the Lapiths helped by Apollo and the hero Theseus, Pelops by Poseidon). But recognizing the stories depicted is only a first step. Why depict them on this temple? After Zeus, the hero Pelops was the most prominent recipient of cult at Olympia, with his own sanctuary in the *altis*, the central sacred area. His chariot race against Oinomaos was sometimes taken as the founding event of the Olympic athletic contests, which offers an obvious explanation for carving that event into the temple's pediment. The lesson of the portrayed event, though, is not obvious. Even more so for the east sculptures, whose mere presence on the temple Pausanias felt the need to explain. Did these stories have a message for visitors to Olympia?[56]

Judith Barringer interprets both depictions in the context of nearby sculptures in the sanctuary, including the statue of Zeus before which athletes swore to compete fairly and the *Zanes* that memorialized punishment of past cheaters. She sees references to Olympic events in the chariot race at the east end and in the wrestler-like holds of the struggling Centaurs and Lapiths at the west, and finds a reference to marriage in the presence of Hippodameia. Hence, Barringer argues, the pedimental sculptures delivered a unified message to viewers, "an inspiring exhortation to the Olympic athletes: 'Successful athletes, who behave like heroes such as Pelops, Theseus, and Perithoos, will win honor, glory, and wives not by violence like the Centaurs but by athletic prowess and martial honor in both types of *agones*. Win, and win honorably, and all will be yours.'" On Barringer's view, rather than honoring "the reestablishment of order in the face of *hubris*" or denouncing discord among Greek states, as others have interpreted them, the sculptures commend honesty, fairness, and physical excellence.[57]

At Olympia, people seeing these sculptures came from all over Greece and knew that other viewers did so as well. The message, therefore, would have been understood as panhellenic, urging all Greeks to excellence, *arete*, in all its forms.[58] It would have urged a healthy ecology of panhellenic competition at Olympia, one that existed also at Delphi. That competition was enacted by the monumental dedications themselves, which competed for space, for viewers' attention, and to tell their own versions of historical episodes and of what it meant to be a "good" Greek. Monumental competition could play out in many ways.

One highly visible example took place at the southeast entrance to the main, upper sanctuary at Delphi. Over the course of a century or so, the Athenians, Spartans, Argives, and Arkadians built monuments here in succession, each new structure or statue group to some extent blocking the view of or access to another. What is more, the Spartan dedication commemorated their victory over the Athenians to end the Peloponnesian War in 404, and the Arkadian dedication celebrated their participation in weakening the Spartans after their defeat at Leuctra in 371.[59]

Victories of Greeks over Greeks were also celebrated at Olympia. The enormous temple of Zeus itself, built in the first half of the fifth century and so luxurious that it was roofed with slabs of glowing Pentelic marble rather than terracotta tiles, celebrated an Elean victory over the Pisans, their sometime rivals for control of the sanctuary (Paus. 5.10.2–3). Not long after the temple was built, the Spartans used it for a cheeky memorial of their victory over the Athenians, Argives, and allies at the battle of Tanagra in 457. The Spartans affixed a golden shield at the very peak of the temple roof's gable end, an epigram on it declaring sardonically that they brought the shield from Tanagra and dedicated it as "a gift from the Argives and Athenians and Ionians, a tithe of their victory as a consequence of war." The Spartan memorial emphasized victory and specified the defeated opponents by name. Both celebratory and agonistic, it fit well at Olympia.[60]

This competitive quality of many dedications, especially at Delphi and Olympia, has often been noted.[61] For Michael Scott, it is evidence that Greeks contested over what "panhellenic" meant, over "the extent to which they were part of a wider community, and these sanctuaries reflected that conflict and acted as a resource for its articulation" (2010, 267). Perhaps. But this contestation was also a way to constitute the community of Greeks: being Greek meant, among other things, coming together with other Greeks and arguing what it meant to be Greek. It meant fighting against Greeks in war, competing against them in athletics and *mousike*, contesting with them to honor the gods most magnificently. Tonio Hölscher (2018, 134–42) is right that Greek communities sought to assert unique identities, to stand out and impress. But they wanted to stand out among Greeks and to impress, above all, other Greeks. Gabriel Zuchtriegel has argued that this competitive effort to be "most Greek" was a central cause of the speed and uniformity of the development of early Greek sculptural styles and the Doric architectural order, a development most visible at major religious sites like Delphi and Olympia. On his view, panhellenic festivals, highly uniform sculptural dedications, and a standardized "Doric" style of architecture all "enhanced both the sense of identity and the spirit of competition among urban elites in Archaic Greece" (2023, 205). The international sanctuaries socialized Greeks and shaped a "Greek" identity by offering a venue for Greeks to interact both in person and, monumentally, across generations.

The socializing effects of international festivals would not end when the final sacrifice had been burnt, the last brow crowned with victory. The competitors, spectators, and other participants would return home, bringing with them new information and changed or strengthened attitudes. Influential people attended these festivals. Competitors and *theoroi* were almost always male citizens, usually from an upper social stratum, publicly visible. *Theoroi* would be familiar to the appointing body of their home city, "known quantities" trusted to represent the city in a particular way.[62] They would need to have the time and money to take a possibly long voyage that would not in itself be materially profitable. Surviving evidence shows, unsurprisingly, that *theoroi* were typically from the elite. Athenians who served as *theoroi* include well-known figures such as Themistocles, Cimon, Nicias, and Alcibiades. Aristotle even reports complaints that Themistocles's family was of too *low* status for him to be an appropriate *theoros* to Olympia.[63] In Plato's *Laws*, the Athenian declares that the leaders of *theoriai* sent by his hypothetical city of Magnesia are to be drawn from the *euthunoi*, the auditors among the city's most honored officials (12.946e–47a). Although the names on surviving inscribed lists of *theoroi* to various festivals are often otherwise unknown to us (due to our ignorance about the local history of most cities), Ian Rutherford describes several *theoroi* whom we know from other sources to have been politically important. And Paula Perlman provides a prosopographic catalog of Peloponnesian *theorodokoi*, noting those *known* to have been from prominent families. *Theoroi* and *theorodokoi* were usually the well known, well connected, and wealthy; in other words, the elite.[64]

The network centrality and social capital of these internationally mobile elites gave them outsize influence in their own cities, for reasons I discussed in Chapter 3. The socializing effects of international festivals upon such elites would be more likely to seep into their home communities than if the same number of ordinary people attended the festivals instead.[65] One straightforward example of how these socializing effects would travel is people reporting back what they saw and heard at a festival. Sometimes, undoubtedly, these reports would mention rule violations and their punishments: "The Spartans violated the truce, and the Eleans barred them from the entire festival!" or "One of the runners cheated, he was beaten by the officials, expelled from the event, and forced to pay a fine." Other socializing effects back in the home *poleis* might be more subtle. Elites who had traveled internationally and encountered many other Greeks would be more likely viewed as authorities about other communities and their views more influential in deliberations. To the extent that their personal contact with foreigners made them less biased against other Greeks, that lower bias would affect the attitudes of others and permeate group deliberations.[66]

Networks beyond festivals

Festivals at the major panhellenic sanctuaries were just one reason Greeks crossed *polis* borders. They came together and had contact "internationally" under many circumstances and for different reasons.[67] As already mentioned, many sanctuaries drew a smaller but still international clientele of worshippers. A few sanctuaries were even *managed* internationally by the religious cartels known as amphictyonies. Best known is the one we have already encountered at Delphi, but amphictyonies also managed the sanctuary of Poseidon on the island of Kalauria (Calaurea, modern Poros) just off the mainland in the southern Saronic Gulf, and of Poseidon in Onchestos, west of Thebes. These amphictyonies consisted of nearby member communities, whether *polis* or *ethnos*, who sent delegates to attend periodic "board meetings." As with a board of directors, their role seems to have been mostly supervisory, making important decisions but leaving daily year-round management of a sanctuary to local officials. Common membership in the amphictyonies and participation at regular meetings would have built networks between communities, as would a feeling of a special connection to the same sanctuary.[68]

The rules of amphictyonies are rightly seen as a form of international law. Pylaio-Delphic amphictyonic identity blazed in the explicit context of international law enforcement in various so-called sacred wars fought by members of that religious body from the sixth through the third centuries. To generalize, these wars were seen as defending the interests of the god, Apollo, against a member of the amphictyony who had violated rules governing the use of sanctuary resources in the form of land or precious metals. Aeschines describes the members of the Pylai-Delphi amphictyony as swearing an oath not to till the sacred land and to defend it, and the god, against anyone who did so.[69]

In a less formal religious mode of network building, seers (*manteis*), along with other religious or quasi-religious figures such as oracle collectors (*chresmologoi*), seem often to have traveled widely. In Isocrates's *Aegineticus*, the speaker describes the traveling seer Thrasyllos of Siphnos as "becoming itinerant and living in many cities."[70] Esther Eidinow argues that "Thrasyllos was not remarkable . . . in the combination of his profession and his wanderlust. From a variety of ancient sources we glimpse a world of traveling ritual specialists." At least some traveling religious professionals such as seers would have mingled in both the high and low social echelons of the communities they visited, simultaneously gaining and disseminating not only religious and quasi-religious expertise, not only international news and gossip, but attitudes and norms.[71]

Greeks engaged in economic, political, legal, and military activities across political borders. International trade was necessary and common, and in Chapters 5 through 8 I discuss international laws concerned especially with trade. Although trade is largely motivated by material concerns, the relationships formed through it easily take on personal and ethical dimensions. These in turn will have affected compliance with the formal and informal rules of international business.[72] Greeks traveled "both for commerce and to see the world," as Isocrates puts it.[73] Some private associations had significant international dimensions, either because their members actively traveled or because some of their members were foreigners, or both.[74] Establishing a colony was not only a founding act, but usually also created lasting ties between "mother" and "daughter" city, as well as among "sister" cities.[75] Proxeny, a special relationship between one *polis* and a particular citizen of another, has been called by Josine Blok "the most conspicuous and ubiquitous institution of (non-military) inter-polis relationships in ancient Greece," and William Mack has made a "very conservative" estimate that 1.2 million proxeny grants were made by Greek communities from roughly the sixth through the first centuries.[76]

Metics, the non- (or no-longer-) enslaved immigrants of the Greek world, must have richly fertilized international networks, overlapping identities, and international norms.[77] Earlier I mentioned Lysias, whose family migrated from Syracuse to Athens. Xenophon distinguishes between Greek and non-Greek metics in Athens: the former can be expected to be loyal and to assimilate, unlike the latter (*Vect.* 2). Although some metics settled permanently, like Lysias's family, others were more itinerant professionals and artisans. Architects, craftsmen, performing and visual artists, as well as doctors and philosophers, and even mercenaries, were highly mobile professionals and intellectuals who crisscrossed the Greek world to fulfill the immense appetite for their expertise and skills.[78] Metics, especially the highly paid professionals among them, were often a privileged class of foreigners; but they were still foreigners, not local citizens. They would have taken part in much of the communal life of their current city of residence, including business, religion, and even war, but their metic identity kept even lifelong metics permanently distinct from those holding full political rights. At times, this status difference surely alienated metics from local citizens. Considering the social and legal status of slaves in Greek communities drives this point home, since their low position must often have alienated enslaved people from much of the community. The topic is too big to discuss here beyond emphasizing that the details of particular situations matter; but since those details are usually inaccessible to us, group identity in the Greek world (and the socialization that may follow from it) must often be approached with generalities and probabilities.[79]

Greeks appreciated the social and ethical consequences of international relationships. Andocides, in his defense speech *On the Mysteries*, delivered in 399, argues that one reason for the Athenians to acquit him of the charge of illegally participating in the Eleusinian Mysteries is the large international network he has formed and can use to help the Athenians: "I have come to know many people and have experience of an enormous number, as a result of which I have gained *xeniai* and friendships with many kings and *poleis* and with other foreigners who are private citizens, friendships that you will share in if you acquit me, and you can take advantage of them whenever it is convenient for you to do so."[80] Andocides does not here suggest that legal socialization in particular has taken place, but he emphasizes his positive, friendly relationships with non-Athenians. Networks of positive relations encourage trust, agreement on norms and rules, and legal socialization generally. They bound the Greek world with rules, obligations, and affection.

Complications of Greek identity: Delos, Ionians, and Islanders

Greeks, of course, could identify with many social groups at the same time. It has long been argued that a broad "hellenic" identity (often called "panhellenic") took shape by the sixth century or earlier, partly as a result of commonalities of language, literature, and religion, partly as a result of Greek colonization around the Mediterranean basin and a resulting increase in contact with non-Greeks. The Persian invasion's effect in uniting Greeks in opposition to the "Great King" is familiar. It is in this context that Herodotus emphasizes the notion of a hellenic identity, united by kinship, language, cult, and customs, in the passage I quoted early in this chapter.[81] Below the level of hellenic identity, Greeks recognized several more, sometimes intersecting, layers of identity, and hence of potential conflict and unity. These layers included the Greek "tribes," Ionian, Dorian, Aiolian; the layer of *ethnos* or *koinon*, such as Boiotians, Thessalians, Arkadians, Achaians; a colonial layer, binding some cities to their mother or "grandmother" city; the *polis* identity layer, such as Corinthians, Pharsalians, Milesians, Syracusans; the layer of intra-*polis* identities such as demes and tribes; identities that cut across *polis* boundaries, such as democrats and oligarchs, "mass" and "elite"; and more.[82]

One reason identities below the panhellenic level are important to international law is that treaties created the great bulk of that law, and even multilateral treaties likely implicated group identities that were not panhellenic. Local or regional factors, ethnicity, colonial status, and kinship, as well as historical or legendary friendship (or enmity) between communities, could reinforce or counter the effects of a baseline of common Greekness. Below the panhellenic level, Greeks came together in smaller international organizations, which varied in their rules and the effects of those rules, but in which group identity mattered for cohesion. Consider, for example, two organizations, separated by a century,

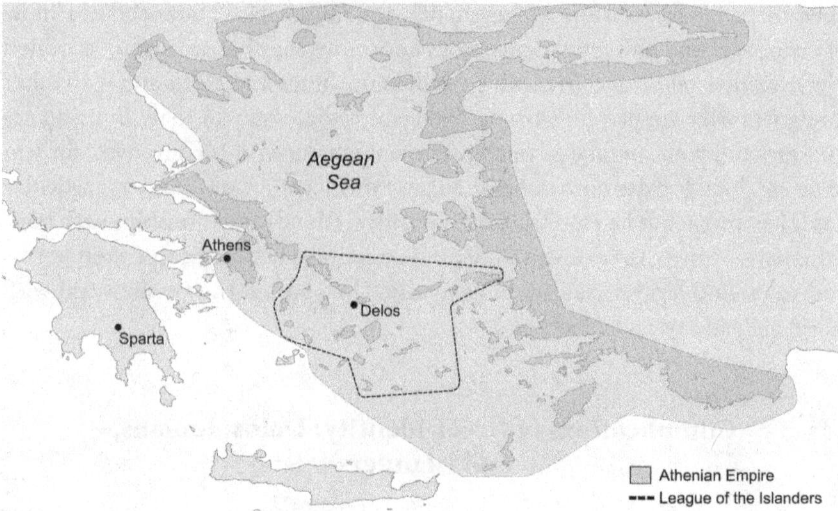

Map 4 Approximate extents of the Athenian Empire and League of the Islanders. Map by R. Salem.

both centered on the small but significant island of Delos: the Delian League and the so-called League of the Islanders (see Map 4).

Delos, a scrawny, unpromising island even by Greek standards, nevertheless had greatness thrust upon it: by its location at the center of the Cycladic islands, which Greeks already in antiquity considered as a geographic unit (Hdt. 5.30; Thuc. 1.4); by its status as the mythical birthplace of Apollo; and relatedly, by the presence there, at least since the end of the second millennium BCE, of cult for Apollo, his sister Artemis, and their mother Leto. By the fifth century at the latest, this cult was associated with the Athenians and especially with the Ionians, which helps explain its selection as the first headquarters of the eponymous Delian League.

The Delian League was founded in the aftermath of the Persian Wars, probably in 478, as a successor to the Greek wartime alliance against the Persians. According to Thucydides, the cities that came together into this alliance adopted the Athenians as leaders out of disgust at the increasing aggression of the Spartan general Pausanias: "Because he was already being aggressive, the rest of the Greeks grew angry with him, especially the Ionians and those recently free of the Persian King. So they approached the Athenians, thinking that the Athenians should become their leaders because of kinship (κατὰ τὸ ξυγγενές), and so as not to rely on Pausanias if he should become aggressive."[83] Hence the Delian League was founded on trust in the binding power of a perceived common Ionian identity rooted in kinship (ξυγγενές) and also, perhaps, on a current of

Ionian-Dorian *hostility* that may have fed fear of the Dorian Spartans.[84] Although probably not *all* the League's founding members were Ionian, the choice of Delos as the home base and treasury likely strengthened the League's Ionian identity and its cohesion: Thucydides later explains that Delos had long been a center of Ionian *and* Athenian worship of Apollo.[85] After the Athenians moved the treasury to Athens, probably in 454, they began dedicating one-sixtieth of each ally's annual tribute to Athena; even later the Athenians decreed that all allies were to contribute a cow and a panoply at the Great Panathenaia festival. These explicitly religious contributions may have been intended partly to create a sense of allied identity around the cult of Athena, as a sort of replacement of Delian Apollo, although Athenians continued to lead cult activities on Delos through the end of the Peloponnesian War and beyond.[86]

But common Ionianism and cult were not the only group identities buttressing first the Delian League and then the Athenian empire. The empire came to be defined by a "democratic" identity. In the Athenian assembly debate over how to deal with the Mytileneans after their revolt from the alliance, Thucydides reports Diodotos as stating that the *demos* in all the cities is friendly to Athens.[87] Geoffrey de Ste. Croix perhaps overgeneralizes in claiming that "the general mass of the population of the allied (or subject) states, far from being hostile to Athens, actually welcomed her dominance and wished to remain within the empire." But there was "class" or "factional" identity of this sort in fifth-century Greece and it played a role in keeping the Athenian empire together: the democratic Athenians tended to support democrats more than oligarchs in the allied cities; democrats in the allied cities reciprocated more than oligarchs did.[88]

Identity also appears to have played a role in a later interstate organization based on Delos. From the late fourth century the island probably acted as headquarters of the League of the Islanders. This organization is more obscure than the Delian League: it is unclear, for example, when it was formed and under which monarch's influence. Some evidence points to a founding of the League in the late fourth century, perhaps 313, at least partly for the purpose of celebrating festivals in honor of Antigonos Monophthalmos and his son Demetrios Poliorketes (who may themselves have encouraged formation of the League). But arguments have been made for foundation in the late 280s by Ptolemy II Philadelphus. In either case, the League came under Ptolemaic influence by about 280. This is the likely approximate date of the well-known Nikouria decree regarding the League's participation in contests and sacrifices in honor of Ptolemy I Soter.[89] The League participated in the Ptolemaia festival held in the royal capital Alexandria and held local festivals on Delos in honor of various kings. Member cities sent delegates to (presumably) regular meetings where League decisions were made, and group activities included organizing festivals and getting members to pay for them. The League also granted honors such as proxeny. Yet, there was an element of indirect royal influence on League decisions. The League's highest official, the *nesiarch*, was probably appointed by the Ptolemaic monarch, at least during the years of Ptolemaic dominance; and the three *nesiarchs* we know of were not natives of any League member.[90]

Despite the royal hand in League operations, Christy Constantakopoulou argues that the existence of a League of the Islanders is evidence of an "islander" identity among inhabitants of southern Aegean islands, an identity connected especially with Delos and its religious significance.[91] She shows that "the kind of political unity that the islands experienced in the years of the League's activity . . . depended on the solid background of interaction these islands had experienced for centuries before the Hellenistic kings and their games for world domination came to the fore," and that this unity "was the result of an active regional identity" (2017, 53–54). Andrew Meadows posits that the League had an "internal religious cohesion . . . apparently with old Ionic resonance" (2013, 35–36). Furthermore, the "minimal group" effect documented by group identity theory suggests that the mere operation of the League would in itself have spurred identity formation, even more so since it was building on pre-existing salient group characteristics (Ionianism, islander identity, religious connections to Delos).

Constantakopoulou may therefore be correct that, even if the League was goaded into existence by Antigonos (or Ptolemy, as Meadows prefers) and was considered a useful subsidiary ally both by the Antigonids and by the Ptolemies, it may still have been "an expression of a strong regional island identity, which can be interpreted as a resistance to power . . . [that] provided a suitable venue for the Aegean islanders to negotiate their position within the changing world of power of the Hellenistic kings."[92] If Constantakopoulou is correct, and the citizens and political decision-makers of the member states of the League of the Islanders had a subjective sense of a League identity, that identity likely not only was a venue to resist royal power but also fostered feelings of trust, ethical duty, and loyalty that encouraged the members to abide by League rules and to follow international law in interactions with each other.

Conclusion

The mesh of international networks I have described in this chapter and the attendant variety of group identities available to any Greek at any particular historical time contributed to the tenaciousness of those identities. They could also be unpredictable, even fickle. The comparative strengths of different identities vacillated, although *polis* identity often trumped the others.[93] Greeks frequently saw various groups with which they identified as having competing interests. The apparent size, proximity, and particular nature of outside threats could make different interests salient to different identity groups. Consider the Persian War of 480–79. Athenians, Spartans, and others allied themselves as "Greeks" when faced with an imminent Persian invasion, but common Greek identity did not keep the two strongest Greek powers united after the Persian threat was beaten back.[94] And certain Greeks allied themselves with the Persians before and during their invasion of the Greek mainland. Some of those alliances can be attributed to compulsion, from a desire simply to survive, but Herodotus (7.6.2) tells us that the Peisistratids of Athens and the Aleuads of Thessaly, both well-known oligarchic families, encouraged Xerxes to invade Greece. This internal split among Greeks shows that outside forces could aggravate intergroup conflict.[95] Thucydides claims the Peloponnesian War widened schisms between democrats and oligarchs within cities.[96] Some research suggests that when a superordinate identity is seen as threatening the identity of a subgroup, the superordinate identity may, in the long run, fail to prevent intergroup conflict. But recognizing and publicly acknowledging the distinct contributions each subgroup brings to the whole sometimes overcomes this problem.[97] One might speculate that the anti-Persian alliance held together so long as the Spartans' strength at land warfare was needed to repel the Persian army, but that Spartan distinctiveness was underappreciated when the Greek alliance's activities became predominantly naval and thus fell within an area of particular Athenian strength.

Hence there was the potential for "collateral damage" from group identity, in its ability to create conflict *between* groups. Yet various forms of overarching identities among Greeks seem often to have contributed to channeling those conflicts through institutions of international law. Even when superordinate identity does not eliminate conflict within the group, it can still encourage group members to resolve conflicts according to procedures perceived as just. Greek international law did not always accomplish this, but its rules arguably pushed conflicts toward more just resolution. At the panhellenic level it reinforced shared norms that were explicitly connected to Greek identity. These norms included customary law, as it was "laws of the Greeks" that provided for the protection of shrines and temples; truces to gather the dead; encouragement of communication, including the airing of grievances, through the protection of heralds and ambassadors; and the possibility of international arbitration as a form of nonviolent dispute resolution. More "local" group identities, below the panhellenic level, would have further encouraged people to actually follow international law when dealing with fellow group members, treating them not just "legally" but fairly and in good faith.

The power of written treaties between states was protected by a common understanding that *pacta servanda sunt* and by the binding force of the oaths sealing them, sworn in the names of (mostly) common Greek gods. Individual treaties were often similarly bolstered by identities between the party states. I have discussed here the Delian League and the League of the Islanders, but the list quickly expands. To cite just three, the Peloponnesian League, the Second Athenian Naval Confederacy, and the early Thessalian League (on which, see Chapter 11) are all candidates for treaty "organizations" held together not only by material, strategic interests but by the affective power of identity. In this chapter, I have suggested some ways that such identities took root and grew among Greeks.

The vigor of identities waxed and waned over time and varied from person to person. But it may be the case that a sense of hellenic identity generally strengthened over the four centuries considered in this book, roughly 500 to 100 BCE. At least, there was a broad homogenization of Greek culture over those centuries that could indicate a solidifying Greek identity. This homogenization can be seen, for example, in language, with the development and spread of the Attic *koine* dialect, which dominated the Greek world by the third century; in the growing ubiquity of democratic *polis* institutions; in the rise of the gymnasium as a marker of the "Greek" city; and in the canonization of a small set of standard authors and texts.[98]

Such cultural "homogenization" can also be described as, or be a result of, socialization; the process of Greeks, ever more tightly connected by social networks, slowly teaching each other and learning from each other how to speak, what to read, how to build a city, how to run a city. Also teaching each other rules for interacting across *polis* borders, while reinforcing social motivations to follow those rules, motivations deriving in part from identities: as speakers of the same language, as worshippers of the same gods, as emulators of the same heroes, as competitors in the same games, as readers of the same books, as descendants from common ancestors, as allies in war, as united by cooperation—and competition—across generations.

I should not be understood as painting here a triumphal picture of Greek civilizational harmony. For one thing, as I claimed in Chapter 1, there never was such a thing as a Greek world, strictly speaking. Greeks were always mixed with non-Greeks, living, working, trading, and fighting with people of different languages, gods, and customs from around the greater Mediterranean basin. What precisely it even meant to be Greek was perennially contestable. Greeks were constantly exposed to influences from non-Greeks. Hence social networks in the Greek world, along with the forms of socialization they facilitated, also always included non-Greeks.[99] Furthermore, conflict, violence, and war were always present in that world, within and between cities, leagues, and kingdoms, with Greeks often fighting against Greeks and allied with non-Greeks.[100] But Greeks still saw their international interactions—violent and conflicted as they might be—as guided by laws subject to enforcement. Although those laws were often ignored and violated, sometimes with impunity, they were frequently followed and sometimes enforced. That these laws existed at all, that they were known throughout the Greek world, and that they affected the behavior of Greeks as much as they did, was partly thanks to the varieties of identities tying Greeks together across political borders and geographic barriers.

PART II

SYLA AND SYMBOLA

International Law and Commerce

5
Syla
Approaching Legal Self-Help in the Greek World

Socioeconomics of private law

That the Greek world was heavily networked across long distances would have been obvious to the merchants, traders, and sailors who made possible the vast trans-Mediterranean economy within which Greeks existed. That this international world was governed by law was also obvious to them. It was probably a precondition for many of them to operate in an international realm at all. In fact, the international laws governing commerce probably arose largely *because* traders insisted on them and enforced them among themselves.

Private international law is likely the form in which Greeks encountered international law most often. Therefore, although military treaties and the laws of war, with their glamour of high politics and violent conflict, have a stronger grip on scholarly and popular imaginations, Greek international law played its most important role in the humdrum daily interactions of private commerce. This is one reason I devote so much attention to the topic in this book.[1]

These next few chapters are also a response to the recent flourishing of scholarly investigation into ancient economies and the application of modern economic understandings to the limited information we have about them. One of my hopes is to show how a sociologically flavored approach can supplement recent studies by providing new insights into the intersections of Greek economic and legal activity, emphasizing that people are more than just rational actors whose behavior in economic and legal realms results simply from calculations of material rewards and penalties, gains and losses. To better understand the causes of, reasons for, and benefits of international commercial law, we must examine it not only from economic and legal but also from psychological and social viewpoints. In these chapters, I provide a history of Greek private international law. And I argue that the formation of social identities in an international sphere across the Greek world both encouraged certain developments in private international law and helped make that law effective.

Laws of All the Greeks. Jesse James, Oxford University Press. © Jesse James 2026.
DOI: 10.1093/9780197838556.003.0007

Trade beyond the *polis*

International trade was structurally fundamental to ancient Greek economic life, the arteries that fed the capillaries of local markets.[2] Such trade occurred from at least the Bronze Age and appears to have continued in Greek-speaking lands, if only at a trickle, even during the most isolated periods of the eleventh and tenth centuries BCE, between the late Bronze and early Iron Ages. By the eighth century, a denser network of international exchange had regrown, a network that thickened and expanded over the coming centuries.[3] Greeks recognized the prevalence and importance of such trade. In the late fifth century, the anonymous author known by scholars as the "Old Oligarch" claimed that "there is no city that does not have to import or export something," and later observers such as Isocrates, Aristotle, and others believed that international trade was a necessity.[4]

Greeks distinguished between domestic retail trade, often confined by law to a city's *agora*, and international wholesale trade, which took place in the dockside *emporion*.[5] The *agora* served as the political and commercial heart of the *polis*, home both to civic buildings and to the shops and stalls of dedicated retailers as well as of producers (farmers or manufacturers) selling directly to consumers. In contrast, the *emporion* was a zone of traders, merchants, and wholesalers, and was always by a city's harbor, that perennially seedy district haunted by the rootless and the grasping. It could also be several kilometers from the main *polis* center, as at Athens.[6] Yet some differences between domestic and international trade were more of degree than of kind, and commercial actors likely had the same basic goals whether they operated on a local or an international stage. These would have included profit, physical security, financial security, predicting outcomes, and resolving disputes. In addition, there were ordinary human desires to interact with people they knew and liked, to make new acquaintances, and to have a good (and wide) reputation. International trade offered opportunities for enormous profit, but those opportunities offered less physical and financial security, decreased predictability, more occasions for dispute, and higher risk overall than encountered in domestic trade. Greeks did not simply accept this compromise but found ways to lower the risks accompanying what they recognized as the necessity of international trade. One way they did this was by developing and enforcing rules and procedures of international commerce and dispute resolution.[7]

Disputes are a perfectly ordinary byproduct of economic exchange. They can arise from criminal or tortious intent of one party (such as in theft or fraud) or from sincere disagreements over the parties' actions or the terms of contracts.[8]

Purely domestic disputes between fellow residents, when not ignored, forgiven, or resolved informally, as they usually are, could be handled with domestic legal procedures and courts. But international trade and travel created jurisdictional ambiguities: cargo moved from one legal jurisdiction to another, and transactions typically involved citizens of different communities. As is still the case today, in the ancient Greek world there was no universally accepted set of rules to determine in which community's courts or under whose laws a particular dispute would be decided. Shared borders also inevitably led to private disputes between citizens of neighboring cities, sometimes over access to and use of resources such as pasture or woodland, at other times over accusations of theft, especially livestock rustling. Travel beyond the local community similarly exposed international traders to greater risk of attack by highway robbers and pirates.

Greeks lowered such risks with customary laws forbidding piracy and highway robbery; with bilateral judicial treaties called *symbola* agreements, providing for judicial resolution of disputes between citizens of different *poleis*; and, in the absence of such bilateral agreements, with customary laws of seizure, *syla*, under which a wronged party was permitted to seize people or property in compensation for the injury claimed. In the next several chapters, I discuss private legal seizures and *symbola* agreements. I describe the main features of these institutions and the most important surviving evidence of them. And I compare them to similar provisions of domestic law in Greek lands, especially Athens, for which we have the most evidence.

Greek private international law seems to have been effective, judging by the apparent vigor of international trade. Therefore, beyond describing the international laws of commerce and tracing their history, I offer explanations for why they were effective, following the theoretical path sketched in Chapters 3 and 4. In this regard, my focus is mostly on the effects of group identity. Panhellenic Greek identity fostered a baseline level of trust and encouraged Greeks to treat each other in law-abiding ways, including after one party had broken the rules and violated that trust. In these chapters, I point out situations in which more local or more narrow identities might have strengthened those effects. As I explained in Chapter 3, legal rules have always been followed mostly not from a fear of formal punishment but from a complex of psychological and social factors, one of which is group identity. We saw in Chapter 4 that trade networks were just one of many international networks that fed group identities across the Greek world. I argue in these chapters that those group identities in turn strengthened the networks by encouraging trading practices in accordance with established and agreed rules.

Law, economics, and institutions. Or, How I learned to stop worrying and love Moses Finley

My sociologically tinged approach to understanding the operation of law is in contrast, but not opposed, to an economic approach. Economics and law are studied together in two similar and largely overlapping fields: "law and economics" (also known as "economic analysis of law") and the "new institutional economics." Although the modes are similar, they may be distinguished by their dominant tendencies. Law and economics is usually concerned with contemporary problems, while new institutional economics often attempts to explain economic history. Law and economics frequently focuses on economic price theory, treating legal penalties as "costs" of breaking legal rules (this focus brings the field into continuity with the traditional deterrence theory of law I discussed in Chapter 3). Both disciplines emphasize transaction costs and how they are affected by legal and informal institutions. Law and economics typically adopts mainstream economic theory uncritically, applying it to the analysis of legal problems or the formation of legal rules. New institutional economics, in contrast, finds fault with "neoclassical" economics and claims to offer an improvement, partly by taking greater account of law's role in economic activity. It has sought to go beyond a focus on consumer choice, production, and consumption, beyond assumptions of perfectly "rational" and fully knowledgeable economic actors in frictionless efficient markets.[9] Economists always knew, but were too little bothered by the fact, that these assumptions do not describe the real world.[10]

One claim of the new institutional economists is that ignorance drives institutionalization. Economic actors' ignorance of others' intentions as well as of the future leads people to create institutions—basically, rules—designed to decrease uncertainty by restricting the activities of others to a limited set of possibilities. Those institutions, in turn, both guide action and affect transaction costs, with effects on economic activity and performance that are large, yet underappreciated by mainstream economic theory.[11] Under the umbrella concept of "institution," Douglass North and others distinguish between "formal rules" (especially laws) and "informal norms" and emphasize the importance of both. Formal rules typically emphasized by new institutionalists include those establishing private property rights and providing for the enforcement of contracts and the "rule of law" more generally. Informal norms include those encouraging compliance with the law and government officials, encouraging fairness, honesty, integrity, reliability, and openness, and discouraging their opposites.[12] Because both new institutional economics and law and economics provide important and influential modes of studying how legal rules affect economic behavior, in these chapters concerned with Greek international commercial law I engage with and use some of their modes of analysis.[13]

In seeking to improve the assumptions of neoclassical economists, new institutional economists have been part of a wider movement, which has waned and waxed in the discipline, to adopt more realistic models of human actors than economists have typically employed. The more realistic models incorporate the findings of fields such as cognitive psychology, social psychology, rhetorical practice, and sociology into understanding economic behavior. I mentioned some of that work in Chapter 3.[14] At times, these efforts, at least among the new institutional economic historians, have been less fire than smoke: after declaring the important roles of complex human psychology and informal social phenomena, in their historical analyses they at times have fallen back on the assumption of the wealth- and power-maximizing rational actor and focused largely on formal institutions.[15] This focus is reinforced by an assumption that formal institutions work only when and because they are backed by a credible threat of punishment by a third party, an assumption made explicit even in studies of privately ordered legal systems.[16] At other times, new institutionalists have gone too far in attributing almost all large-scale economic change to institutions. These problems appear to be receding as economics again becomes more welcoming of and familiar with the findings of other social sciences.[17]

Somewhat parallel to the traditional but narrowing distinction between a wealth-maximizing versus a sociological view of human economic activity has been the century-long debate concerning the economies of ancient Greece and Rome. The two basic alternatives dominating the debate are that (i) the ancient Greek and Roman economies were similar to modern economies, with profit-maximizing economic actors operating within recognizable markets that set prices through supply and demand (a view advocated by Eduard Meyer); or (ii) ancient Greeks and Romans were not profit maximizers like us moderns but differed from us in guiding their economic activity by social considerations such as status and honor; impersonal markets and mercantile exchange played only a small role; and states had no meaningful economic policy (the Karl Bücher/Moses Finley view).[18] The debate has largely gone stale, with the Meyer position currently ascendant, although mostly in a form that adopts the teachings of new institutional economics and therefore at least formally acknowledges the importance of social and nonmaterial factors in economic activity.[19] I would emphasize what I see as an important truth on each side. Meyer was right in arguing that the ancient Greeks and Romans largely resembled modern people in important respects relating to economic activity, but part of that resemblance was in the very qualities that Bücher and Finley ascribed (accurately) to the ancients but (inaccurately) not to modern industrialized people: namely, in the psychological and social motivations, beyond pure wealth maximization, that guide our economic activity. In these next few chapters, I consider some ways that economically inflected approaches help us understand Greek usage of international law that related to trade. But my emphasis is on factors often overlooked by self-consciously economic approaches.

International commercial legal disputes in the Greek world

The simplest forms of international trade might rarely result in legal disputes. Consider the case of a merchant with goods in hand that he owns outright, traveling in his own boat, arriving at a foreign land and selling his goods on the spot for cash or in barter. He takes out no loans, receives no financing, has no business partners whom he might cheat. He advances no credit to customers and has no insurance.[20] If such simple trade was ever common among Greeks, by the fifth century it seems not to have been the dominant mode. Greek international commerce was sophisticated, often involving multiple parties and the advancement of credit, loans, or other forms of agreement, the terms of which were memorialized in oral or written contracts; it was also highly regulated by states.[21] One of the best-known examples of credit-based commerce is the fourth-century loan contract reported in the speech *Against Lakritos*, transmitted among Demosthenes's speeches but maybe not written by him ([Dem.] 35.10–14, ca. 350 BCE). The complete set of transactions envisioned here was not only financially, legally, and logistically complicated; it also spanned a wide geography. In this business deal, two men from Phaselis on the south coast of Asia Minor borrowed 3,000 drachmas from an Athenian and a Euboian (from Karystos) (the locations are marked on Map 5 in this section). The purpose was to buy wine in the Chalkidike, sell it in the Bosporos in exchange for other cargo (probably grain), and return to Athens with the Bosporan cargo. The entire voyage was to take place in a boat operated by another man, a certain Hyblesios (35.20). The Phaselite traders never owned their merchandise outright, since one condition of the loan was that the changing cargo (first the wine, then whatever replaced it) was the security for the loan, and the lenders had rights over that cargo until the loan was repaid.[22]

The dispute was heard in a formal court in Athens. It was probably the monthly court dedicated to hearing so-called *dikai emporikai*, legal disputes concerning maritime trade. This court, at least after a fourth-century reform, was apparently open to litigants of any origin or citizenship but heard only cases concerning alleged harms to commercial ship captains and merchants that occurred in relation to trading into or out of Athens and for which there was a written contract.[23] Even before the formation of this specialized court, international commercial

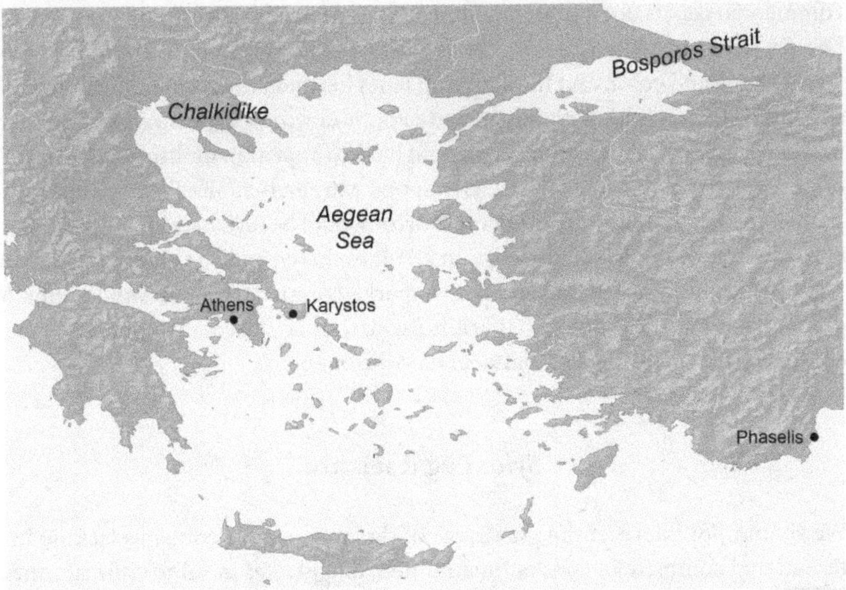

Map 5 Map showing Athens, Phaselis, and key locations mentioned in *Against Lakritos*. Map by R. Salem.

actors often had access to formal legal process in Athens and elsewhere under the terms of bilateral judicial treaties usually called *symbola*, which I discuss in detail in Chapters 7 and 8.

But courts were not always accessible to those ensnared in international commercial disputes. A certain amount of commercial business fell outside the jurisdiction of *symbola* agreements or special maritime courts. It appears that the courts of most cities were fully accessible only to their own citizens and resident metics. One reason for cities to make *symbola* agreements was precisely to expand their citizens' access to justice in each other's courts. We do have some evidence that even without *symbola* agreements, cities sometimes allowed foreigners to litigate in their courts, but this may have been at the discretion of officials on a case-by-case basis.[24] Yet even in the absence of formal legal process for resolving disputes, Greeks eagerly pursued international trade, and some trade occurred with no automatic right to judicial recourse and perhaps no practical judicial recourse at all.

Consider a hypothetical map of access to judicial process for international commercial disputes in the Greek world, perhaps a kind of cross between a demographic map and a map of shipping routes. On this map, cities would be coded graphically by their volume of trade, by their trading connections, and by the availability to foreign merchants of formal law and procedure. Those with commercial courts open to all merchants, such as Athens at certain times, would be a particular shape and color. Those with *symbola* agreements would be a different shape and color, and the shipping lanes between them would be drawn in a colored stripe. Cities with larger trade volumes would appear larger. In order to show historical change, the map would have to appear in multiple "snapshots" of perhaps twenty-year intervals. Given our extremely limited knowledge, any such map we could draw from extant sources would be seriously incomplete. But even if we had complete knowledge, at all times there would be cities that had no colors, shipping lanes that would not be marked. Parts of the map would remain gray, indicating cities without a maritime court, and in places there would be few colored stripes denoting judicial *symbola* agreements.

Syla: Legal seizure

We should not interpret the gray areas of the map just described as lacking international commercial law. As I mentioned, magistrates in some cities at times unofficially offered domestic judicial recourse to foreigners. But Greeks also developed and recognized a customary international law of self-help seizure called *syla*. This allowed people who had been legally wronged and suffered a financial loss to compensate themselves by making seizures of goods or people—so long as those goods or people were foreign, from *poleis* or *ethne* not their own. In other words, the law of *syla* permitted a citizen of city A who claimed to have been legally wronged by a citizen of city B to seize the goods or person of a citizen of city B in order to be compensated for his loss or injury.[25]

Beyond this simple description, however, the international rules of *syla* are uncertain and may have changed over time. Questions for which our evidence does not provide definitive answers include: What injuries granted the victim a right of seizure? Was there, in effect, a substantive customary international law, maybe based on significant similarities in law between domestic jurisdictions? Who was permitted to perform the seizure—only a victim, or someone acting on his or her behalf? Could reprisal be taken only against the wrongdoer and his property, or against any of his fellow citizens? Were the things or people seized always taken as security or hostages and held until the wrongdoer paid compensation, or were they sometimes taken as compensation themselves? When, if ever, did a person need the explicit approval of his community before making a seizure? What relation did a community-wide "declaration" of a right of seizure have to a declaration of war? These questions have been debated by scholars, but none can be answered definitively. I will discuss our main evidence for legal seizure to show what we can say with some confidence, proceeding chronologically to try to discern whether and how the rules and practices changed over time.

Despite our great ignorance about the details of *syla*, the centrally important fact is that Greeks did recognize a customary right to self-help seizure. This norm—or the entire set of norms around *syla*—must have spread through the international networks I describe in Chapter 4. And *syla* must have been permitted, and effective, because Greeks normally did not take their self-help too far, into violent vigilantism or lawlessness. There was always an international law against actual piracy, as we will see in Chapter 9. And part of the reason *syla* was effective was, likely, group identities and the attendant norms encouraging people to treat each other reasonably and humanely, even in the midst of a legal dispute.

One question about *syla* has stood out in scholarly debate: whether reprisal could legally be taken only against the wrongdoer and his property, or against any of his fellow citizens as well. In 1889, Rodolphe Dareste suggested that the wronged person could legally perform seizure against the wrongdoer *or* any of his fellow citizens. This interpretation was largely accepted for almost a century, until Benedetto Bravo disagreed, arguing at length that private disputes permitted seizures only against the wrongdoer himself and his property, unless the wronged person's city "declared" a state of seizure against the wrongdoer's city.[26] Bravo's disagreement with what he took to be Dareste's position was motivated partly by his worry about what he saw as the likely consequences if Dareste's rule had actually been in force: any Greek merchant traveling abroad would understand he was everywhere at risk of being seized by a foreigner because of some wrong committed by a fellow citizen, a wrong that he himself need not even be aware of, much less responsible for. This fear, Bravo believed, would have had a strong chilling effect on international commerce. But in fact, according to Bravo, we see little or no evidence of such a chilling effect; therefore, the rule must not have been so broad as Dareste believed.[27] Bravo argues that *only* a declaration of seizures by the city of the wronged person permitted seizures against any fellow citizen of the wrongdoer. These declarations were relatively uncommon and therefore had little chilling effect on trade.

As we will see, the evidence is too ambiguous to resolve the question. But Bravo may not correctly interpret the implications of the apparent general briskness of Greek international trade. As he admits, because of the common use of *symbola* agreements, the occasional availability of informal judicial procedures, and the existence of maritime courts at some times and places, *syla* would not in fact have been legally available for many legal disputes, or at least not a first resort. To express it in terms of the hypothetical map I described above, much of the map would have been colored much of the time, and many of those colored zones would have been between cities with some the highest volumes of trade.[28]

Even in situations where *syla* was the only legal option, social and psychological factors often would have prevented Greeks from pursuing remedies when they had been harmed by a foreigner. As I noted in Chapter 2, litigation rates in the modern world are much lower than the rates of legally actionable harms. For example, in the allegedly hyper-litigious United States, physically injured people rarely make *any* effort—even informal—to recover from the person who may have caused their injuries: perhaps around 10 percent of the time. Rates of pursuing legal claims vary widely according to the kind of claim, but people rarely go so far as even hiring a lawyer.[29] Of course, this is not direct evidence concerning ancient Greek international commercial grievances. But it shows that in many contexts, people do not pursue disputes to the stage of a high-stakes confrontation. Instead, if they make any attempt at compensation, it usually goes no further than a direct communication with the person they hold responsible. Why is this?[30]

One explanation of human reluctance to bring legal claims is that, often, it literally is not worth it. Pursuing the claim beyond informal communication with the other party may cost more, in money or time, than the value of the claim. In law and economics terms, its likely "administrative costs" may be deemed too high.[31] But noneconomic social and psychological considerations also often discourage people from bringing legal action. Many societies have a community norm against pursuing certain kinds of legal claims.[32] For some people, a tendency to blame oneself for harms one suffers, or feelings of shame, can have a similar effect. On the other hand, a strong feeling that the other party is to blame can lead to lawsuits that seem "irrational" from an economic point of view. David Cohen has argued influentially that some litigation in Athens was a form of elite feuding, valued for its own sake in an agonistic society. Edward Harris, on the other hand, has emphasized the importance of feelings of "civic duty." People often view legal disputes as "conflicts of principles and values" rather than simple financial matters.[33] In the *syla* context, even if Dareste is correct that customary law permitted seizure against an innocent fellow citizen of the wrongdoer, some people may have been deterred from performing such seizures because the absence of the wrongdoer would deprive them of the feeling of really vindicating the wrong they had suffered; or they might have been deterred by a personal belief that seizing compensation from an "innocent" third party, even if doing so was strictly legal, would be unjust.[34] Hence even if Dareste's interpretation of the law of seizure is correct, we see a number of factors that would likely prevent those wronged in international commerce from vindicating their rights against "innocent" fellow citizens of the original wrongdoer. In short, we have reasons to question Bravo's belief that a rule permitting such seizures would create a heavy drag on international commerce, and this undermines one of his key arguments against Dareste's interpretation. As we will see, though, we still cannot state definitively what the law of *syla* was.[35]

This discussion raises the question how effective the international law of seizure might have been if it was in fact rarely enforced. We have no way of knowing. But its very existence, as revealed in the surviving sources surveyed below, shows that there were norms of international trade so well known that parties acting in self-help were permitted to apply them. That the institution of legal seizure existed for centuries—as we will see—is evidence that it was an important way to enforce those norms, even without neutral third parties to act as judges. Profit motives and concern for reputation no doubt played an enormous role in this success. But it is also evidence of a process of the socialization and internalization of norms of honesty and fair dealing among Greeks on an international scale.

Seizure in domestic law

Before plunging into the detailed evidence for seizure in international commercial law (in Chapter 6), it will be helpful to consider the role seizure played in the domestic law of Greek communities. Similarities reveal conceptual and practical continuity between international and domestic private law. In both realms, there was a shift, over time, toward decreasing self-help and increasing judicialization of disputes through adjudication by third parties. But, even in matters that would be classified under the label of criminal law in modern legal systems, private initiative was usually the most important element in pursuit of a legal remedy within a city. The acceptability and even necessity of seizure as self-help in early Greek domestic law is suggested in a story about the gods sung by the musician Demodocus in the *Odyssey* (8.266–369). Hephaestus ensnares in chains his wife Aphrodite with her lover Ares, while they are in bed together. Hephaestus will let Ares free only after he promises to pay a fine for adultery (μοιχάγρια, 332) and Poseidon swears to act as Ares's guarantor (347–58). The formal legality of this fictional episode must be based on the social reality of the poet's world, where physical seizure of a wrongdoer in certain matters was probably both lawful and common.[36] Seizure retained its importance in some aspects of Greek commercial law while communities came to limit the role of legal self-help generally. In fact, the important role that seizure had once played in at least some domestic jurisdictions is suggested by the explicit restrictions placed upon it by the fifth and fourth centuries.[37]

The question of seizure is placed front and center in the great law code of the Cretan city Gortyn.[38] Its very first rule states that if someone believes a person claiming to be free is in fact a slave, it is forbidden to seize that person (μὲ ἄγεν) before the question has been litigated in court: "Whoever is going to dispute concerning a free person or a slave is not to seize him before trial. If he does seize him, let (the judge) rule that he pay ten staters for a free person and five for a slave because he seized him, and let him rule that he release him within three days."[39]

Michael Gagarin and Paula Perlman make much of this provision, taking it as representative of what may have been one of the motivations that drove the Gortynians to publish the city's laws so prominently: namely, a desire to use judicial procedure in place of self-help wherever it was feasible to do so.[40] The provision's prominence also suggests a recognized temptation to practice seizure as a form of self-help in Gortyn, and perhaps a customary law permitting it.

The Gortynians' code did not entirely eliminate seizure. In fact, it granted immunity to someone who seized (ἄγοντι) a person who had either lost a legal dispute or indentured himself to a creditor, and perhaps to a guarantor of the self-indentured.[41] The former case would not be "pure" self-help, occurring as it would only after a court judgment. But, by listing the exceptions disjunctively, the code indicates that in Gortyn, seizure of an indentured debtor did *not* require a preliminary court decision. Another provision inscribed at Gortyn, separate from but not contradicted by the great code itself, established limited conditions under which it was forbidden to seize goods securing a loan.[42] The limitation tells us that such seizure of security *was* permitted under most conditions. In the fifth-century Gortynian procedural landscape that emerges, judicial procedure was a central feature, but self-help seizure continued to play a role in some cases where the seized person indisputably owed money or property.[43]

A similar but more detailed picture emerges in our evidence from fourth-century Athens: private initiative was essential for enforcement of many aspects of law, but physical self-help in the form of seizure of people or property was carefully restricted.[44] We see this in the restrictions on the most violent form of self-help: killing. Deadly force in defense of a legal right was permitted in just a few situations. They included: in hot pursuit of a thief caught red-handed; in self-defense when attacked by ambush on a highway; and when a man caught another man having sexual intercourse with his wife, daughter, sister, mother, or unmarried partner with whom he had children.[45] In all these situations, there was always the option to arrest rather than kill the offender and to either bring him to the authorities or privately negotiate a form of compensation. In other "criminal" situations, one had to summon the proper officials, empowered by law to make an arrest when appropriate.[46]

Athenian law also permitted self-help seizure in certain cases of unpaid debts, an important aspect of commercial law. The two main categories of debts in which private seizure was allowed in Athens appear to have been unpaid court judgments and unpaid secured debts. As in Gortyn, seizures in cases of unpaid court judgments were not pure self-help because a court had already found that one party owed a specific amount of money or piece of property to the other.[47] In *Against Meidias*, Demosthenes describes a law forbidding the seizure, during the City Dionysia festival, either of property won in a lawsuit or of an amount due from a defaulting debtor; the implication is that both sorts of seizures were allowed at other times.[48] And Demosthenes's speech *Against Euergos and Mnesiboulos* describes, as an entirely legitimate act, the speaker's attempt to seize property (ἐνέχυρα λαμβάνεσθαι), including a slave woman, from the house of the man who owed him certain trireme equipment. He did this only after having received a decree from the *boule* permitting the seizure.[49] In contrast, it appears that no court judgment or *boule* decree was needed for a creditor to seize—without using force—the security for an overdue loan.[50] The right to such seizure is implied by the law described in the passage mentioned above from *Against Meidias* (Dem. 21.11–12) and is an explicit provision of the contract quoted in *Against Lakritos* ([Dem.] 35.12). This right is also implied by an Athenian law forbidding litigation against someone who possessed land that had been mortgaged to him. In this case the current possessor, protected against litigation, was presumably the creditor who had seized it legally from the debtor in default. Even in this situation, however, the rightful owner could not use force to eject someone.[51] If the wrongful possessor refused to abandon a piece of real property, the rightful owner had to prove his ownership in a suit for ejectment. This is the type of suit that Demosthenes brought when, as a young man, he made the speech *Against Onetor I* (Dem. 30).[52]

Like the Gortynians, the Athenians even after Solon's reforms of the early sixth century seem to have permitted a third type of private seizure, one that bordered on enslavement: seizure of a debtor to place him into debt bondage, making him work for the creditor until the debt was paid off. This could happen if the debtor was so impoverished that seizure even of all his money or goods would not cover the amount due.[53] In Aristophanes's comic play *Clouds* (first performed in 424/23), Strepsiades explains to Socrates that his debts have motivated his desire to learn how to speak well. When he says, "I'm being led off, and plundered, and having my property seized by debts and harassing creditors," he may be expressing a fear that he will be seized into debt bondage.[54] The small amount of evidence for the practice of debt bondage in Athens does not reveal whether a creditor was permitted to seize a debtor into bondage without a court judgment, but the provision from Gortyn discussed above shows that such "unlitigated" seizure of a person was not unthinkable in the fifth century. In any case, as with goods and property, the "seizure" of a debtor likely was often a mostly nonviolent matter.[55]

To round out the domestic law picture I briefly mention later evidence from two other jurisdictions. Some papyri from Greek communities in third- and second-century Ptolemaic Egypt indicate that private seizure was allowed as a form of self-help after a court judgment, although in most cases there would have been official involvement at various stages of the dispute.[56] And Polybius reports an incident from Epizephyrian Lokroi in southern Italy apparently showing that self-help seizure of property (in this case human property, a slave) was permitted, although the ownership question was subject to subsequent litigation.[57]

Conclusion

Overall it appears that self-help, including by seizure, was a familiar and important aspect of domestic law in the Greek world. It was restricted in important ways, however, sometimes by a requirement for judicial recourse and sometimes by the involvement of public magistrates. These elements were often lacking in cases of international seizure. Yet, as I will describe in the next chapter, Greek international law not only recognized a similar right to self-help seizure under certain circumstances; judicialization and restriction of that international right also developed. These resemblances across Greek jurisdictions thus seem to reflect the existence, in the law of seizure, of what Hans Julius Wolff would call a Greek legal *Denkform*, a characteristically Greek way of thinking about certain legal questions. It is perhaps one place we can find some degree of an elusive and contested "unity of Greek law."[58]

6
Syla as Self-Help in Greek International Law

Legal seizure in international law

The earliest clear example of an international legal seizure in the surviving written Greek sources is fictional, in book 11 of the *Iliad*: old Nestor's tale of a seizure he participated in as a young man. It illuminates Greek international law not by relating an historical event but by reflecting, and in turn having helped shape, Greek views on the appropriate circumstances and forms of legal seizure. In the poem, Achilles's close friend Patroclus comes to Nestor's tent to learn the news of battle. Nestor, criticizing Achilles's withdrawal from fighting, makes a pointed rhetorical contrast with a story showing off his own eagerness for battle as a young man. It happened decades earlier, in the western reaches of the Peloponnese, border lands between Pylos and Elis, far from the battlefields of Troy (see Map 6).[1]

Nestor narrates a tale of "when conflict arose between Eleans and us [i.e., the Pylians] over the driving of cattle" and Nestor killed a man "while driving off what I had seized" (ῥύσι' ἐλαυνόμενος, *Iliad* 11.671–74). He and his fellow Pylians defeated a small group of Elean herdsmen and took from them many flocks. Nestor, introduced as a "sweet-tongued orator of the Pylians" in the poem's opening book (1.248), takes pains to justify this seizure with a rhetoric of morality and law: he claims the cattle were seized as repayment of debts that some Eleans owed to a number of Pylians. The source of these debts was prior violent attacks by the Eleans (whom Nestor also calls Epeians) upon Pylians. For instance, Augeias of Elis had seized the four prize racehorses and chariot of Nestor's father Neleus; now in recompense Neleus took for himself a herd of cattle and a flock of sheep with their shepherds; "and the rest he gave to the people to divide up, so that no man go away deprived of a fair amount" (11.704–05).[2]

Nestor hammers home the legal justification of the Pylian seizure, three times repeating a version of the phrase "they owed a debt" (χρεῖος ὄφειλον, 688; also 686, 698); he describes a specific theft against his father; and he explains that the property seized was divided up only among those men to whom a debt was owed. Nestor's account could almost be a courtroom speech defending the

Laws of All the Greeks. Jesse James, Oxford University Press. © Jesse James 2026.
DOI: 10.1093/9780197838556.003.0008

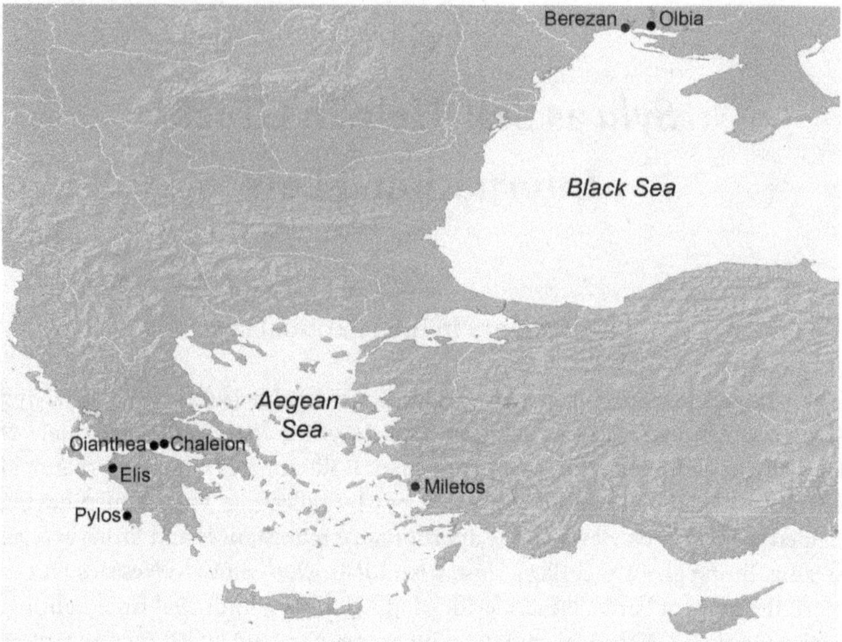

Map 6 Map showing key locations discussed in this chapter. Map by R. Salem.

Pylians. He insists that Eleans violated law by unjustly depriving certain Pylians of property, and some Pylians made a seizure in return, which they used specifically to compensate those harmed by the Eleans. The Pylian seizure seems to have been sanctioned by the community and performed not only by those directly harmed by the Eleans. This resembles the "declarations of *syla*" we will see later, although the word for seized goods here is *rhusia* (ῥύσια, 674). From the Pylian point of view, this should be the end of the matter: a specific wrong has been righted through a legal act by the community.[3]

The limited, legalistic nature of this attack contrasts with the more war-like character of what follows: the Eleans soon launch a new attack on Pylos, making the Pylians eager "to wage war" (πολεμίζειν, 717). The ensuing conflict, which the Pylians win and in which Nestor himself (by his own account) fights heroically, unfolds like a battle of war, preceded by sacrifices to the gods. Although in this later altercation the Eleans are again in the wrong according to Nestor, he no longer mentions any "debt" for which individual Pylians are to be compensated. It has turned into a more existential crisis of war-like attack and defense, community against community. In this fictional account, as in actual Greek history, legal seizures, although not themselves acts of war, could be part of an escalating sequence of violent events leading to war.

Nestor's story presents a world of international law. Pylos and Elis are recognizable as independent political and territorial communities in an international space where raiding and seizures are illegal unless performed to collect a debt, a debt that could have been incurred by a previous illegal raid. And the law we see portrayed here is recognizable as effectively the same law of self-help seizure revealed by our more straightforwardly historical sources. In this chapter, I survey the history of international seizure through those sources. And, through consideration of individual historical incidents, I propose ways that group identity, especially but not only a common sense of "Greekness," encouraged recognition and enforcement of a simple but sturdy set of rules for resolving international legal conflicts without courts. Despite the lack of courts, rhetoric still played a role in the use, recognition, and dissemination of those rules. And although we will not resolve here all the scholarly debates over *syla* introduced in the previous chapter, we will come to see it as an institution that remained remarkably consistent and robust for centuries.[4]

Olbia and the northern Black Sea

Our earliest nonfictional evidence for international legal seizure comes from the uppermost edge of the Greek world, on the north shore of the Black Sea, and probably dates to between 550 and 500 BCE. Greeks had begun establishing cities on the Black Sea by the mid-to-late seventh century, and by the late sixth century dozens of settlements had been established. Most of these were organized by settlers from Ionian cities on the west coast of Asia Minor, Miletos chief among them.[5] Complex layers of international identity that could exist between Black Sea *poleis* thus already become visible, as various combinations of "Milesian," "Ionian," and "Greek." And many Greek cities on the Black Sea either themselves included significant populations of (more) local non-Greeks, in particular Scythians from the north, or at least were sites of contact between Greeks and non-Greeks.[6]

Irad Malkin has argued that the very process of Greek colonization activated the coalescence of a panhellenic Greek identity in the first place: seeing how different they were from people who did not share their language, gods, and customs made Greeks of different cities realize just how much they had in common with each other. Ionian identity, in turn, seems to have distinguished Ionians mostly from other Greeks, and was coherent by the seventh century.[7]

This is one context within which we should interpret two letters inscribed on lead that were found relatively close to each other, both likely dating between 550 and 500. One was found on what is now a small island named Berezan, a low, flat plateau, about a third of a square kilometer, almost teardrop-shaped, rising out of the Black Sea at the mouths of the Dnieper Gulf and the Berezan River where they both drain to the Black Sea. The other is from the site of the city of Olbia, about forty kilometers to the east, where the Bug River empties into the Dnieper estuary. On Berezan, there was a settlement perhaps called Borysthenes, the first Milesian colony on the Black Sea, founded in the late seventh century on what was at the time a peninsula. Olbia was also "Milesian," founded by people either from Berezan or directly from Miletos, perhaps in the middle of the sixth century.[8] Like most *poleis*, Olbia consisted not only of an urban center but also a large countryside or *chora*. By the fifth century, the Olbians' *chora* likely reached east as far as Berezan, whose citizens seem to have lost their political independence: Berezan may be what Herodotus, who visited in the late fifth century, calls the *emporion* of Olbia. The Olbian *chora* was bordered by navigable waters on three sides, with the Bug River in particular permitting deep northward penetration by boat. It was within easy coasting distance of many other Greek communities. It seems, accordingly, that Berezan and Olbia formed perhaps the major trade hub of the north shore of the Black Sea.[9]

The first letter was discovered on Berezan in 1970; hence it is often called the "Letter of Berezan." The text is scratched into the surface of a small sheet of lead, a rectangle about 7 by 15 centimeters. The letter itself was written on one side (Side B), then rolled up, and the "address" written on the outside (Side A). It says:[10]

[SIDE A:] The lead of Achillodoros to his son and to Anaxagoras.

[SIDE B:] Protagoras, your father sends a message. He is being wronged by Matasys, for he [Matasys] enslaved (or "defrauded") him and took away his cargo (or "cargo ship"). Go to Anaxagoras [and] explain, for he [Matasys] says that he [Achillodoros] is [5] a slave of Anaxagoras, saying, "Anaxagoras has my things, slave men and slave women and houses (κοικίας: perhaps "household effects" or "female household slaves"?)." But he [Achillodoros] protests and said that there is no business between himself and Matasys; he is a free man and there is nothing between himself and Matasys. What there is between Matasys himself and Anaxagoras, [10] they know on their own. Say this to Anaxagoras and to his [Achillodoros's] wife. And he sends you a further message. Your mother and your brothers who are in Arbinateis: take them into the *polis*; and the captain himself will go and come down to him.

The situation appears to be as follows: Matasys and Anaxagoras had some sort of relationship, perhaps business, putting Anaxagoras in a position to possess property Matasys claimed as *his*. Hoping to get this property back from Anaxagoras and realizing that Achillodoros knew Anaxagoras, Matasys seized Achillodoros and his cargo (and perhaps boat). Matasys claimed Achillodoros was enslaved by Anaxagoras; Achillodoros insisted he was free.

Scholarly speculation has filled out the picture in various ways, but I will focus on a few points that seem fairly clear. Achillodoros believes he is being treated improperly by Matasys (ἀδικε̃ται, B1). Matasys feels justified in having seized Achillodoros, since "Anaxagoras has my things" (B5). Matasys wants to resolve his dispute with Anaxagoras. There is no indication the letter was sent without Matasys's permission or that Achillodoros was in actual physical danger. The third person narrative may indicate that Matasys even provided someone to do the writing for Achillodoros.[11] In short, this appears to be a case of legal seizure, Matasys using self-help to seize what he claims is property of someone who has wronged him. Achillodoros believes his status, as a free man against whom Matasys has no legitimate complaint, makes Matasys's seizure of him unjustified. Awareness of the importance of Achillodoros's status may explain Matasys's perhaps insincere claim that Achillodoros is a slave of Anaxagoras.

Compare this to another private letter from approximately the same time and place. The "Letter of Apatorios" was discovered in the excavation of Olbia's *agora* in 1971 and has been dated to the late sixth century.[12]

[SIDE A:] Apatorios to Leanax.

[SIDE B:] Apatorios to Leanax. My goods have been seized by Herakleides son of Eotheris. It is in your power that I not lose the goods, for I said that the goods are yours. And Menon said that you put them into his care; and whatever other things [5] you put into his care.[13] And in addition he said it is your goods that are in my possession. If you present the documents to Herakleides and Thathaies, your goods [. . . he will return?]. For they say they will return what they have of yours. Twenty-seven staters in all [were] seized. [What will you wish?] to do? Concerning the house slaves of Thymoleos [10] [. . . . . to ——]thumios. For myself, I don't know if things will turn out well.

Here the underlying dispute is apparently between Herakleides and Apatorios: Herakleides seized goods in Apatorios's possession thinking they belonged to Apatorios, in compensation for some unnamed harm that Apatorios committed against him (probably an unpaid debt). This could explain the final sentence: perhaps Apatorios was afraid Herakleides might keep him under arrest even after letting the goods return to Leanax. Despite Apatorios's fear, it seems to have been a generally calm and legalistic affair, with Herakleides willing to accept the authority of documentary evidence of ownership. Leanax seems to have known Herakleides, who wished to stay on good terms with him. It is noteworthy that Apatorios twice uses the verb *sylan* to describe the seizure (σισύλημαι, 1; συλη[θὲν?], 8): this is the ordinary term for legal seizure in an international setting.[14]

This letter and that of Achillodoros, we see, offer good evidence for a law permitting self-help seizure in recompense for a legal wrong, a law applying to Greeks living and trading in and around Olbia and Berezan in the late sixth century. There is general scholarly consensus on this point. It might be objected, however, that the law of seizure these letters reflect is not obviously a matter of Greek international law: neither situation is undoubtedly international. So do they really belong in this book?[15]

The uncertainty on this point is real, but the weight of evidence tilts international. It is true that neither letter mentions the name of any city, much less two different cities, to clearly signal an international context.[16] The personal names lack city-ethnics indicating where people are from; city-ethnics are a good indicator, when they are used, that someone is a foreigner. In the Berezan letter, Matasys appears to have houses in the country where Anaxagoras is located: maybe they are residents, even citizens, of the same city.[17] Some features, however, do point to an international context. If either dispute was purely a matter of domestic law, there would probably be a domestic judicial procedure for the parties to follow, both the person resorting to self-help and the person seized. We have seen that the first provision of the code of Gortyn prohibits seizure in exactly this sort of status dispute. Yet neither letter hints at the possibility of recourse to any magistrate or civic body.[18]

In addition, "Matasys" is apparently not a Greek name, making it less likely that he and Anaxagoras share citizenship.[19] Achillodoros has apparently been seized while on a shipping expedition and sent the letter from outside the town where Protagoras and Anaxagoras live. I noted above that the Olbia/Berezan region appears to have been a hub of international trade. Both letters explicitly involve transport of goods. And there were many politically independent Greek communities around the shores of the Black Sea. All things considered, then, both letters likely come from an international context.[20]

These letters are also evidence of a moderately sophisticated sixth century commercial-legal culture in the northern Black Sea. International disputes arose for which the best option was self-help, but self-help that followed rules, in which both oral and documentary evidence were important for reaching solutions. The effectiveness of those rules is evident from these letters, key links in the process of resolving the underlying legal disputes. And it likely resulted in part, at least some of the time, from a recognition among the people involved that they belonged to common social groups: Greeks, Ionians, "people of Milesian descent" being just a few obvious candidates. Jessica Lamont argues that letters such as these "served as assertions of Hellenic identity in this frontier region," and she notes the likely existence of a regional Pontic "cultural *koine*" encouraged by local networks.

She also suggests that the name Apatorios may reflect the popularity of the pan-Ionian Apatouria religious festival in this region settled by Ionian Greeks.[21] The latter point evokes my discussion in Chapter 4 of how religious festivals in particular were events for forming and consolidating identities among Greeks. Such group identities often would have triggered social obligations to abide by group rules. Especially when there were apparently no obvious magistrates or courts to appeal to, identity-based obligations to follow the group's rules could have been critical to managing social and business relationships.

Other factors could also weigh heavily. The people in these letters knew each other. It appears that part of what made them abide by the rules were their personal relations, not simple group membership. Business considerations could have been paramount: if Herakleides had ignored Apatorios's assertion about ownership of the goods, he would have alienated not only Apatorios but also Menon and Leanax. Those men might have been important business connections for Herakleides, whom he did not want to antagonize. Both letters transmit a rhetoric of justification that presupposes a common social context and shared ethical and legal rules, the very principles upon which rhetorical argument must be based. Matasys has felt the need to justify his seizure of Achillodoros, and Herakleides similarly disclaims any effort to seize the property of Leanax. No single factor can explain *syla*'s effectiveness. But these letters are good evidence that it was acknowledged as customary international law already in the sixth century, here at the frosty northern rim of the Greek world.

The fifth century: Why not ban seizure on the open sea?

Our fifth-century evidence for the international customary law of *syla* mostly comes down to one famous inscribed treaty, which I discuss at length below. But first we should consider briefly an early fifth-century reference to *syla*. This is an agreement between an otherwise unknown group of people called "the Chaladriens" and a man named Deukalion. It was inscribed on a small sheet of bronze (10 x 26 cm.) found near the temple of Zeus at Olympia. The brief document (ϝράτρα, 1) grants Deukalion citizenship among the Chaladriens and gives him a piece of property. A final clause forbids seizure against him: "And if anyone commits *syla* against him, let that man be exiled/perish in the eyes of Zeus, unless it seems right to the people."[22] Seizure here, as indicated by the verb *sylan*, refers to an act against someone who has been a foreigner up to the moment of this agreement. The text makes clear that, now that this man's status has changed from foreigner to citizen, the mode of proceeding against him legally has also changed. You may no longer simply perform self-help *syla* but, it is implied, must proceed through judicial avenues.[23] It demonstrates a recognition at this time, among communities around Olympia, far from the north shores of the Black Sea, of a law of *syla* operative between citizens of different cities. The bronze plaque's storage or display near the temple of Zeus at a major panhellenic sanctuary illustrates, again, the mutually reinforcing entanglements of religion, international identity, and law that created and animated Greek international law in ways I described in Chapter 4.

The law of *syla* was made more effective by group identities but never by the closest such identities. As far back as our earliest sources, we cannot discern a time when judicial processes were not available for at least some legal disputes within Greek political communities.[24] Just as common Greek identity acted as a kind of baseline level of group identity for Greeks, on top of which other "thicker" identities could build, customary international law such as *syla* acted as a baseline set of legal rules for interaction among Greeks. But communities could always agree to rules above that baseline. Therefore, one way to understand the nature of legal seizures is by studying decisions by two cities to ban them. This was often done through *symbola* treaties. I study them at length in the next two chapters, but here I discuss one of the best-known examples because it mentions seizure practices permitted in the absence of a special treaty. This *symbola* treaty also offers an opportunity to consider different explanations for why cities might have decided to permit or forbid *syla*.

About 450 BCE a small plaque, or tag, of bronze was inscribed with an agreement between Oianthea and Chaleion.[25] These two neighboring *poleis* in western Lokris, southwest of Delphi, were perched on a rugged coastline where the foothills of Mount Giona finally slide into the Gulf of Corinth. That body of water plays a central role in the agreement between these close communities. The agreement opens with a prohibition of seizures:

> Do not forcibly carry off a foreigner, neither the Oianthean from Chaleion nor the Chaleian from Oianthea, and not his property. [But] if someone makes a seizure (συλο̃ι), one may without penalty seize the man making the seizure. One may forcibly carry off foreign property at sea, without being seized oneself, except from the harbor by the city.[26]

The agreement, phrased in desperately unclear language (and translated by scholars in correspondingly varied ways over the years), seems to prohibit a practice previously permitted: citizens of one *polis* seizing people or property from the other in their mutual territories. This now forbidden form of seizure is contrasted with two things that are permitted: seizure on the open sea, as we see here; and the use of judicial procedure, which is laid out later in the document and which I will discuss in the next chapter.[27]

One implication of establishing a judicial procedure, though, is especially relevant in this chapter: how it illuminates what kind of seizure is being regulated. Since seizure here is, as we will see, replaced by a requirement that people go to court, the goal of that seizure must be the same as the goal of going to court: namely, to resolve a legal dispute. This means the seizures envisioned in the above lines must be the same kind of self-help legal seizures we have already encountered. They are founded on a belief (or at least a claim) that the person performing the seizure has previously been harmed by the person subjected to seizure.[28]

This agreement, then, is not about piracy. Yet a few scholars have suggested it is, based on Thucydides's claim that the western Lokrians were among a few groups of Greeks who openly committed raiding in his day (the late fifth and early fourth centuries): there are "some people even now for whom performing such acts well brings prestige." On the basis of Thucydides's assertion, Simon Hornblower believes this inscription's regulation of seizure "implies piratical activity."[29] This is not persuasive. As I discuss in Chapter 9, piracy is seizure performed simply for gain, with no legal pretext. With a legal pretext it is not piracy but *syla*. And, as I have noted, judicial process is not a reasonable replacement for piracy but *is* for an act of seizure premised on an underlying legal dispute. Second, even if we posit that the Oiantheans and Chaleians considered piratic seizures and forceful enslavement of other Greeks to be legal in some places, it is still difficult to believe that these acts had been, until the time of this agreement, permitted even within their *polis* territories, which is emphatically specified as the geography of regulation here. Furthermore, if Oiantheans and Chaleians were regulating piracy in this document, why would they leave the very large loophole for seizures on the open sea, where piracy is so often practiced in the first place? It would be puzzling for two communities to agree that violent piratical seizures against each other's citizens were forbidden on land and in the city harbor but permitted on the open sea. As we will see though, the "open sea" exception does make sense in the context of a regulation of *legal* seizure.[30]

This partial ban on seizures has not previously been satisfactorily explained by scholars. Andrew Lintott suggests there were "practical difficulties in regulating maritime seizures by law; it would have also been difficult for a wronged party to gain redress from those responsible" (2004, 344). Philippe Gauthier offers two explanations. First, *polis* authorities could not judge the legitimacy or illegitimacy of a seizure unless it took place in the *polis*, because they would need the adversary parties, the goods, and any eyewitnesses of the seizure all to be present. Second, he claims seizures on the sea were more like acts of piracy than like the exercise of a right of retaliation. According to Gauthier, pirates could be punished only by generals, not by ordinary magistrates.[31]

Lintott is right that seizure on the open sea might have offered certain advantages; I will discuss them below. But these explanations are otherwise unsatisfying. Practical enforcement difficulties might prevent the creation of a law in the first place, but they would not motivate carving out a special exemption. Just imagine how elaborate laws and treaties would be if they were drafted to include exceptions for all the situations in which their rules might be difficult to enforce.[32] If ease or frequency of enforcement were a precondition for laws, the world would have very little legislation indeed. Gauthier's arguments about seizures being "too similar" to piracy makes little sense. And the passage he cites as supporting his claim that only generals were legally empowered to bring pirates to justice does no such thing.[33] Alberto Maffi's solution is to interpret the agreement differently from most scholars: as simply containing no open sea exception. But his interpretation—that seizure is permitted *only* in the port and *not* on the open sea—introduces problems that, to my view, are intractable. We should look further for possible rationales for an open sea exception.[34]

How might a law and economics approach interpret the exception? It might seek evidence for an economic advantage in continuing to permit seizures at sea. Under the law and economics theory of legal procedure presented by Robert Cooter and Thomas Ulen, the "economic objective of procedural law is to minimize the sum of administrative costs and error costs." Administrative costs are the time, money, and energy needed to work through the stages of a legal dispute. Error costs arise if the legal process comes to the wrong result.[35] From the law and economics viewpoint, errors in the legal process are bad because they "distort incentives." Applying this theory to the treaty between Oianthea and Chaleion, self-help justice in the form of seizure has a clear advantage in its low administrative cost: it can be done quickly and probably involves few people. But the error costs are potentially high, since plaintiffs might perform seizures based on one-sided and incorrect views of both the facts and the law. It may be that decision makers from Oianthea and Chaleion decided the error costs of permitting self-help seizures had become too high and were not offset by their low administrative costs. This agreement was perhaps designed to minimize the total procedural costs.

This conceptualization could also help explain permitting seizures on the open sea to continue. Oiantheans and Chaleians might have perceived a difference in procedural costs between seizures on the open seas and those in a city's territory. Seizures at sea might prevent someone seen as a high flight risk (by virtue of already being at sea) from escaping justice entirely. Or, to phrase it differently, seizure might grant to the wronged party a last resort. The danger of a complete failure of justice is not clearly an administrative cost or an error cost but could perhaps be accounted for with an additional term in the formula. Let us call it a "futility cost."

A new institutional economic analysis might be similar. New institutionalists could note the flexibility of the Oiantheans and Chaleians in implementing a "mixed" regime and suggest it represents an intermediate stage in institutional evolution.[36] But their focus is often drawn to large-scale trends, and if they saw one here they might argue it was caused by an efficiency gain—path-dependent, to be sure.[37] Such a gain could reflect either decreased transaction costs, which could just be the sum of administrative and error costs; or a change in the balance of political power within the cities, such that the revised judicial arrangement was believed to favor some newly powerful political classes.[38] In my discussion of *symbola* agreements in the next two chapters, I will consider the possibility of a long, slow, efficiency-driven shift in the Greek world toward the formation of judicial treaties.

Law and economics, with its focus on costs, is at risk of omitting from its accounting the *benefits* of litigation. Especially prone to omission are benefits not fitting easily in the economist's notion of "utility."[39] This is one advantage of a sociological approach. The sociologist tries to understand people as social creatures and law as a web of phenomena embedded within social contexts. Some aspects of public litigation can be seen as potential advantages when we view litigation as a social event at which both sides tell their stories, make ethical appeals, and argue for particular interpretations of the law. One way to judge the fairness of a litigation process is participants' belief that their voices have been heard and their stories made known. Besides making dispute resolution seem more fair, the social process of litigation can lead to healing for the plaintiff, shame for the defendant, and bringing to community consciousness what may be a little-known social problem. As Aristotle points out, "the trial and punishment are (also) forms of healing."[40] Self-help seizure does not present the same opportunities. Litigation also offers an opportunity for participants to shape their public personas. David Cohen interprets the speeches made in Athenian courts as "quintessentially public acts by which individuals invite judgment through their attempts to establish a particular social biography" (1995, 85). As Socrates and Plato both understood (if we are to trust Plato's *Apology of Socrates*), persuading the jury is not the only goal of courtroom rhetoric, which could be used to win a larger war while losing a battle. On the other hand, as I will discuss in the next chapter, serving as a juror was understood as one of the most important ways in which citizens of Greek cities exercised their political existence *as* citizens. Less litigation would mean fewer opportunities to create political community. Finally, public legal procedure advertises the state's laws and norms of justice as a reminder and reinforcement to the community. This is the expressive, or communicative, function of law.[41]

There are, to be sure, negative social effects of litigation, as I mentioned in Chapter 5. Some communities have a norm against formalizing disputes.

Making a dispute public can exacerbate it, in part because merely publicizing an accusation damages the accused's reputation. Once a dispute is public, the positions of the opposed parties may harden, neither side wanting to be seen as giving in or admitting fault. For commercial actors in particular, such public airing of grievances might harm a business relationship more than a privately resolved dispute. In many societies, the victims of certain wrongs are especially hesitant to bring public legal complaints; sexual violence is a common example. Litigation therefore has real social costs. But such drawbacks do not seem to apply especially to disputes that might lead to seizures on the open sea. So it is hard to see how consideration of such litigation costs would have led to a carve-out permitting such seizures.[42]

Larger forces might have been at play. By advertising a *state*'s laws and norms, public litigation does not just resolve disputes but also contributes to what Mauricio García-Villegas describes as the symbolic force of law that, under classical liberal theory, gives legitimacy to the state's exercise of power: "Under this view, power and legal rhetoric exist in a kind of symbiosis: state actions are justified through juridical norms, and juridical norms are upheld when they enjoy the support of the state" (2018, 23). Legal rhetoric helps constitute statehood. By adjudicating some international commercial disputes in the same or similar public forums as domestic lawsuits, the Oiantheans and Chaleians may have been bolstering their cities' claims to authority as states. This "liberal" interpretation, however, still seems unable to explain the exception permitting seizures at sea.

The "open sea" exception may become more clear by combining the liberal view with a sociological interpretation of the very act of citizens of two neighboring cities entering into a judicial treaty. I suggested earlier that identity formation and rule formation can be mutually reinforcing. In the next chapters, I argue that *symbola* agreements were often entered into by communities that already had a special relationship of some sort. That is likely the case here. The treaty between the Oiantheans and Chaleians might reflect a sense of a preexisting shared identity. Both cities were in western Lokris, they were physically close to each other, and they had sufficient interactions to want this treaty in the first place.[43] Although there may have been no formally organized confederacy of west Lokrian *poleis* until the fourth century, the cities of west Lokris were connected to each other and to the cities of east Lokris through notions of common Lokrian ethnicity and religious cult, while distinctions between east and west were salient early on.[44] We should view the agreement between Oianthea and Chaleion as building on this background of common ethnicity and cult, a conscious thickening of already dense interactions. The new, mutually applicable judicial rules would only have strengthened the notion that citizens of the two cities formed some sort of larger community, at least in a judicial sense, but perhaps also in a physical and economic sense: communities bound by both the sea and the mountains that formed the major elements of a shared landscape. There must have been discussions in both communities when they were contemplating this treaty. We can only guess what considerations were aired, since the surviving text does not rhetorically justify the treaty. But there can be little doubt that Lokrian connections and positive relations between the two cities were at least a subtext of the arguments that clearly won the day.[45]

It would have been reasonable to wish to regulate legal acts within the controlled physical space of that combined community, that is, within its land territory and main harbors. Here is where the liberal view comes in: these newly applicable judicial rules would in turn have helped justify an overall expansion of state authority by the Oiantheans and Chaleians. Previously, state authority extended primarily over only acts between fellow citizens or those that occurred entirely on one state's territory; now the authority of both cities extended explicitly over transactions between citizens of either or in the territory of either.[46]

Acts of seizure on the open sea, however, might have been seen as outside of even this larger combined community—the open sea was always open to all—and therefore inappropriate objects of regulation by it. Prior to the treaty, seizure was appropriate for resolving all disputes between Oiantheans and Chaleians, all relations between the cities seen as simply international rather than as "Oianthean-Chaleian." After the treaty, the only relations that were still international in the strongest sense and therefore still subject to customary international law were those on the open sea, the most international of all places. The treaty was shaped by a culturally influenced sense of *where* customary international law was most appropriate. In short, the exception permitting seizures on the open sea was likely inspired by the practical advantages such seizures offered plaintiffs and by the social appropriateness the practice continued to present, even in the face of the group identity reflected in the existence of this treaty between two closely situated Lokrian cities.[47]

Syla in the fourth century

Our picture of the customary rules of seizure slowly fills in as we move into the fourth century. We learn that seizure could be used even when the debtor was a foreign government, and we confirm that it was seen as a legitimate means of pursuing payment of an overdue debt. We also find cases in which the seized property or person was taken not as compensation in itself but as security to be returned when the debt was paid.

Athenians

At the end of the fifth century, Athenians suffered *syla* over unpaid loans taken out after their final defeat in the Peloponnesian War. A prosecutor's speech written by the orator and speech writer Lysias blames these seizures on an Athenian named Nikomachos.[48] Nikomachos had been twice appointed in Athens as a "transcriber of the laws," an official charged with consolidating and organizing official versions of the laws of Athens. In this speech the anonymous prosecutor accuses Nikomachos, among other things, of adding unauthorized festival days to the sacred calendar (Lys. 30.19). The great public expense of these additional festival days overtaxed Athenian revenues, creating debts whose impending effects the prosecutor warns of: "And he did all this although he sees that the city is hurting for funds and that the Lacedaimonians are making threats if we don't send back their money, and Boiotians are making seizures (σύλας) since we aren't able to repay two talents."[49] It is well documented that in 403, in the immediate wake of the Peloponnesian War, the board of thirty men installed by the Spartans to govern the Athenians had borrowed from the Spartans one hundred talents, which is presumably the sum not yet paid back to them.[50] While the Spartans were merely threatening Athenians over these debts, Boiotians were making seizures, *sylai*, to recover a comparatively paltry two talents. This was a public debt owed by the Athenian people, as we see from the first-person plural expression, "we aren't able to repay." Hence this is our earliest good evidence that people or their goods could be seized because of public debts owed by their city.

Although the Spartan loan is confirmed by other sources, we know nothing beyond what this sentence tells us about the Boiotian loan and seizures: who performed them, where, upon whom, or what they seized. Léopold Migeotte suggests that small loans were made by individual Boiotians only to certain Athenians, probably the democrat Thrasyboulos and his partisans when he was a refugee in Thebes during the regime of the Thirty.[51] The speech makes no suggestion that the Boiotian seizures were improper or illegal. Rather the blame, the speaker implies, belonged with Nikomachos, for hindering the Athenians' ability to climb out of debt.

Salaminians

A work by Isocrates, probably written in the 360s, takes us to the eastern end of the Greek world, to Salamis, a city-state kingdom on the island of Cyprus.[52] Written in the voice of Salamis's king Nikokles, the work describes seizures that, like the Athenian seizures just discussed, were likely in response to public government debts. Isocrates (as Nikokles) argues that the king has been a responsible ruler who dealt effectively with a depleted treasury. He offers as evidence his management of a rash of seizures: "Although Greece was off limits to us because of the war that broke out, and we were suffering seizures (συλωμένων ἡμῶν) on every side, I paid off most of them; some people I paid back entirely, others in part, and from others I requested postponement, coming to agreements with them over their claims as much as I could."[53] The context of an empty treasury tells us the debts here were public. And, even more than Lysias's speaker, Nikokles acknowledges the propriety of the seizures: he either paid the claims immediately, negotiated a payment schedule, or negotiated a settlement. A good king would not have boasted of paying off unjust seizures such as pirate attacks. The most respectable way to meet those would have been open force. Paying off the seizures, in contrast, validates both the underlying claims and their enforcement mechanism.[54]

This work must be considered in the distinct context of Cyprus and Salamis, which merits a brief discursion since it will be unfamiliar to many readers.[55] Greek speakers had arrived on Cyprus in some numbers by 1000 BCE. They partly displaced and partly absorbed a non-Greek population that retained its own language, at least in pockets, until around 300 BCE. By the eighth century there had arrived a significant Phoenician presence, which is unsurprising given how near Cyprus was to Phoenician cities of the Levant. From the eighth until the end of the fourth century, Salamis was only one of the independent cities inhabiting Cyprus's landscape. Two of them maintained a distinct non-Greek identity: Phoenician Kition and "autochthonous" Amathus. But most were ruled by kings with Greek names who identified as Greek. These included Salamis, which has been described by Maria Iacovou as having a "staunch Hellenic identity" that "was continuously reaffirmed throughout antiquity."[56]

Cypriots were always Greek in their own way. This was perhaps most noticeable in their language, which was not only old-fashioned but also written in a syllabic script rather than the alphabetic script adapted from Phoenicians and used in the rest of the Greek world.[57] Yet both literary and archaeological evidence shows, from the sixth through the fourth centuries, a strong Cypriot alignment with the rest of the Greek world and away from Persian, Phoenician, and other "eastern" influences. Evagoras, who preceded Nikokles as king of Salamis, was the first Cypriot monarch to write official documents in the alphabetic script used by the rest of the Greek world; this in itself was a rhetorical performance of "Greekness." In other words, when Isocrates wrote the *Nikokles*, Cypriots (and the Salaminians foremost among them) operated quite deliberately within a largely "Greek" space, although one with Phoenician elements.[58]

It is in the context of Cyprus at the edge of the Greek world, with Phoenician contacts and presence but turning strongly to Aegean Greece, that we must ask certain questions about this passage. How reliable is Isocrates's report about seizures of Salaminians and their goods? And were these seizures all conducted by Greeks? In other words, is this passage evidence that the customary law of *syla* was accepted as applicable by non-Greeks? Answering that question goes beyond the scope I have defined for this book, but an affirmative answer is entirely compatible with my picture of Greek international law. As I noted in Chapter 1, the expression "Greek international law" is a sort of legal fiction, since there was always a degree to which Greeks followed international legal rules with non-Greeks.[59] My claim is not that international law was purely Greek but that group identities, including a panhellenic Greek identity, helped make that law effective among Greeks. In any case, given the Salaminians' long-standing Hellenic identity and Cyprus's "Aegean" orientation since the second half of the fifth century, it is reasonable to conclude that Salaminians followed Greek customary international law, at least with regard to much of their trade. Furthermore, it was most likely Greek sources that informed Isocrates's portrait of Nikokles; and if he invented details, to be persuasive to a Greek audience his inventions would be based on his understanding of Greek practice. Therefore it seems reasonable, overall, to take this passage as evidence for the Greek law of *syla*.

Neither the Isocrates nor the Lysias passage describes who or what was seized, or where. But in both cases the seizures were probably performed on private people and their goods; an attack on public goods, ships, or buildings (including treasuries), or on public officials, might have been seen as an act of outright war. If this is right, both passages are evidence of an international law under which, when a city defaulted on loan payments, the creditors could make seizures upon its citizens, presumably detaining their goods and possibly their bodies. In addition, the *Nikokles* shows that the seized object might be taken not as compensation in itself but as a leverage or hostage for payment: when Nikokles says, "I paid off (διέλυσα) most of" the seizures, it must mean that he paid to have the seized items or people returned.

Cyreneans

Proceeding chronologically, as well as clockwise around the Mediterranean, we arrive at Cyrene in North Africa. Established in the foothills of the "Green Mountain" that bulges into the Mediterranean, west of Egypt and due south of the Peloponnese, Cyrene was favorably located in the wettest part of Libya, which contributed to the region's eminence in grain production.[60] An inscription from Cyrene, dated to the 330s, offers further evidence that private creditors could make seizures against many citizens of a single city; in this case against Cyreneans.[61] The fragmentary inscription was found in the sanctuary of Apollo at Cyrene, near the small treasury known as the "Strategeion." The inscribed text begins with six verses honoring a certain Timagoras, then memorializes payments made by ambassadors from Cyrene (presumably led by the honoree Timagoras) to specific people in various parts of mostly mainland Greece. The inscription states that "seizures were paid off" and "we paid off a seizure for eight talents."[62]

These seizures were probably made *against* Cyrenean citizens rather than *by* them. This would explain why Cyrenean ambassadors traveled around Greece giving people money: to pay off whatever debts had instigated the seizures in the first place, just as Isocrates tells us Nikokles had done. Fragmentary lines near the beginning of the inscription seem to indicate that copies were placed at the temple of Zeus at Olympia; in Delphi; at the temple of Zeus *Lykaios* in southern Arcadia; and in Athens with the officials called *thesmothetai*. By depositing these copies at important religious locations, the Cyreneans left highly visible evidence of their payments. This not only helped prevent any double claims but also advertised the Cyreneans' payments—made in accordance with "laws of all the Greeks"—precisely at sites of significant Greek group identity formation. The amounts memorialized in the surviving fragments vary from roughly two to fifteen talents, and the inscription names the recipients, including "Apollodoros the singer to the *aulos*" and "Nikias the pharmacist" in Megalopolis, "Charon the disabled man" in Arcadia, "Thoropidas the general" in Argos, "Demetrios the orator" in Athens, and in Melos to an Olympic wrestling champion whose name is lost.

Unlike the description of Nikokles's payments, the Cyrene inscription does not tell us the seizures being paid off were responses to unpaid debts. But, by memorializing and advertising the amounts paid to "settle" the seizures, the Cyreneans acknowledged the legitimacy of the seizures themselves. It is hard to imagine what would legitimize peacetime seizures in Greek eyes aside from debts of some sort. Furthermore, the presence of Charon "the disabled man" (τὸγ χωλὸν, 24) is evidence that creditors could authorize agents to make seizures on their behalf (as Charon presumably did) rather than perform them personally. But we cannot tell if the Cyrenean debts were public or private. This inscription therefore leaves unanswered the disputed question: in the case of debts owed by private citizens, did the customary law allow creditors to make seizures against any fellow citizen of the debtor or only against the debtor himself? Seizures had become a problem for the Cyreneans, as their concerted public response shows. Perhaps Cyreneans had been getting harassed for the private debts of their countrymen or for debts incurred by the city itself.[63]

Like the seizures against Athenians mentioned by Lysias, but unlike the seizures against Salaminians, in the Cyrenean case the evidence explicitly points to seizures made by Greeks against Greeks. Although located in north Africa, Cyrene was a thoroughly Greek city, founded in the late seventh century by settlers from Thera (modern Santorini), which itself had been colonized by Spartans.[64] The Cyreneans were ruled for two centuries by a monarchy begun by Battos, who led the founding expedition from Thera. But in the middle of the fifth century they overthrew their last king and established what was probably a democracy. The history of Cyrene from this political revolution until the time of the *syla* inscription is obscure. But Cyreneans kept in contact with the rest of Greece throughout their history, as is revealed by scattered but telling evidence relating to architecture, sculpture, theater, trade, legend, religion and festivals, and quasi-military relations.[65] This inscription, at least as it survives today, situates itself in an entirely Greek world. All the payments were made to people with Greek names living in Greek cities. And copies were displayed at some of the most religiously and culturally significant places in Greece. It should be understood, accordingly, as reflecting *Greek* customary law. The Cyreneans here are acknowledging and promoting the force of that law.

This inscription also hints at the workings of international Greek networks and identity. It tells us that, at major nodes of the Greek world, and religious nodes in particular, the Cyreneans advertised their adherence to Greek international law. Their adherence was not mere abstract dedication to the "rule of law": specific people in particular cities had now been treated justly by Cyrene, and all their neighbors who came to these major sites could read about it. Although there was an underlying wrong committed by some Cyreneans (the unpaid debts), the collective Cyrenean action to correct those wrongs portrayed Cyreneans as a whole as rule-abiding, trustworthy Greeks embedded in the larger Greek social world despite living at its southern edge.

This "hellenic" rhetoric of Cyreneans embedded in a Greek social and legal sphere is filled out by two other well-known inscriptions from Cyrene. One, dated to about the same time as the *syla* stele, memorializes enormous amounts of grain that Cyrene "gave" (ἔδοκε) to forty-one cities around Greece in response to grain shortages. These shipments were not motivated by power politics alone. As Alain Bresson interprets their act, the Cyreneans "played the role of 'saviours of the Greeks', at least of many of them, probably accepting a loss of their financial income in exchange for a reputation as universal benefactors."[66] Read next to the *syla* stele, the record of grain shipments is part of a pattern of Cyrenean advertisement of their ethically motivated behavior reflecting and strengthening the Cyreneans' place in a Greek network of political and social connections bound by normative commitments.

A third important Cyrenean inscription from the fourth century reaffirms the Cyreneans' commitment to a provision of their founding constitution, which guaranteed land and citizenship to later settlers from the mother city Thera. Those later settlers likely would have found urban Cyrene uncannily familiar. Richard Neer and Leslie Kurke have noted how the layout of Cyrene's city center, linearly oriented along "a single ridgetop thoroughfare," is unusual for a Greek city and seems deliberately modeled on Thera's, which it matches closely.[67] This inscription shows that early Cyrenean attempts to create and maintain a Theran "feel" in the city may have also contributed to maintaining substantial ties with the mother city. Unlike with the acts recorded in the two inscriptions discussed above, the international social effects of the citizenship grants that presumably resulted from this confirmation of a long-standing right were not "panhellenic," but they would have strengthened social ties and group identities between Cyreneans and Therans.[68]

In these three inscriptions, we see Cyreneans in the fourth century strengthening connections to other Greeks and publicly upholding norms both of law compliance and of generosity towards fellow Greeks. These were not abstract commitments simply recorded for posterity. They were real acts performed by and benefitting real people, people who would have established or renewed personal ties to Greeks from other cities. This *human* network was key to the operation of Greek international law.

Granting seizures

Several times in this book I call *syla* a form of private law. By this I mean law primarily governing relations simply between people, rather than between people and their own state or between two or more states. We saw in the previous section that *syla* was not always strictly private, since seizures were sometimes performed to recover debts owned by a state. At least by the middle of the fourth century we see a related but apparently distinct *syla* practice that also involved the state: cities sometimes granted their citizens a general right of performing seizures against the citizens of another city.

In the speech *Against Lakritos* delivered probably around 350, the Athenian litigant Androkles, criticizing the refusal of two men from Phaselis to repay a loan to Athenians, compares their refusal to an act of seizure: "In our own city, even though we haven't done anything wrong and haven't lost a lawsuit to them, we've had our goods seized by these men, these Phaselites, as though Phaselites had been granted *syla* (δεδομένων συλῶν) against Athenians. After all, since they aren't willing to give back what they've taken, how should one describe these men other than by saying that they are taking other people's property by force?"[69] This passage tells us that seizures, *syla*, could be "given" or "granted" to the citizens of a *polis*, presumably by its own governing authority.[70] An earlier passage indicates that blanket declarations, allowing citizens of one city to make seizures against citizens of another, were common. The contract quoted by Androkles (which must be used cautiously since it may not be original to the speech) includes the following provision: "and if they do not enter [the Black Sea] after waiting ten days past [the rising of] the dog-star, let them unload [the cargo] wherever *sylai* have not been granted against Athenians." There is dispute over the interpretation of this passage.[71] But on my translation the contract forbids the merchants from unloading the cargo—cargo in which an Athenian has an ownership interest—in the harbor of a city that has granted seizures against Athenians. Unfortunately, neither passage suggests what circumstances might compel a city to grant *syla*.

The declaration of a state of seizure became common enough that cities took it into account in awarding honors: we have a number of decrees from the late fourth and third centuries granting honorees, among other things, "freedom from seizure during times of seizure."[72] These "times of seizure" appear to refer to situations in which cities granted *syla* in response to specific wrongs, often financial wrongs, that their own citizens had suffered. It is Bravo's position that it was always a Greek customary international law that such a declaration of *syla* was required before seizure could be performed on anyone other than the original wrongdoer himself or his goods. But *Against Lakritos* is our first clear evidence for such seizures, and there is no strong evidence that a public declaration of *syla* was ever required for these "indirect" seizures rather than being simply official encouragement of them.[73]

Demosthenes suggests in several speeches that Athenians in positions of military authority serving abroad sometimes exploited their power to seize goods in legally questionable ways. Other cities often responded, it seems, by "granting" or "declaring" legal *syla* against Athenians. For example, in *Against Timokrates*, delivered about 353, Demosthenes describes an Athenian trireme carrying ambassadors that came upon a merchant ship from Naukratis, a Greek city in Egypt. The Athenians seized nine talents and thirty *minai* worth of property. The Athenian perpetrators justified the seizure on the ground that the Egyptians were at the time enemies of the Athenians.[74] Unlike the Boiotian seizures against Athenians in the late fourth century, there was no claim here that the seizure was in response to a public debt owed by the Naukratians collectively to Athenians. The cargo owners came to Athens and supplicated the assembly for return of their money. The assembly voted, though, that the property had indeed belonged to enemies of Athens and therefore now belonged to the Athenians (Dem. 24.11–12). One can imagine that these events might have pushed the Naukratians to declare *syla* against Athenians.

These arguably illegal Athenian activities may have stemmed from a deeper corruption that had taken root in the Athenian naval system. In that system, the expense of outfitting a trireme warship was assigned to a rich man as a form of taxation called a *leitourgia*, or liturgy, under which he became a "trierarch." In the speech *On the Trierarchic Crown*, delivered in 359 and attributed (probably wrongly) to Demosthenes, the speaker decries the practice of trierarchs not only paying the traditional costs of the trireme's gear and the sailors' pay but also hiring another man to serve as captain of the ship.[75] This position was usually filled by the trierarch himself; paying another to do it led to abuses. "Someone *hired* to captain a trireme," the speaker protests,

> attacks all people, seizing them and pillaging their property, and enjoys the profits himself while random individuals among you pay the penalty for his acts, and you alone can't go anywhere without a herald's staff because of the seizures of people and property that they've committed. . . . If you're going to receive the services you deserve, the man serving as trierarch for the *polis* should not expect to get rich from public matters but rather to improve the city's affairs with his personal wealth. But each of these men sails off with the exact opposite in mind, since all the harms they cause with their practices are set straight by the penalties for them that fall upon you. — [Dem.] 51.13–14[76]

In other words, ersatz trierarchs tried to get rich by making illegitimate seizures, and innocent Athenian travelers paid the penalty by becoming the victims of retaliatory or compensatory seizures.

In *Against Aristokrates*, delivered about 352, Demosthenes complains about a wider problem: "All those with soldiers under them, whenever they encounter people they think are weaker, plunder and pillage them in their search for money." He makes clear that, unless performed against an actual state enemy, such seizures, which did not even claim to be justified by an outstanding debt, were illegal.[77] Both written law and "the common law of all people" permitted the victim of such unjust seizures to defend themselves, up to the point of killing the perpetrator.[78] Demosthenes is probably exaggerating for rhetorical effect how often Athenians in positions of military authority were abusing their power. But these speeches are good evidence it did occur, at least during wartime, and that it was a rule of Greek international law that both immediate defense and compensatory seizures were permitted in response. It is also clear that the international law against such unjustified seizures was enforced by the retaliatory acts of the victims' states against Athenians. This enforcement was effective, as we can tell from this speech proposing measures to reduce Athenian violations of the law.

We see more evidence for declarations of *syla* in the second book of the *Oeconomica*, a work misattributed in manuscripts to Aristotle. This book (which, although not by Aristotle, may still have been written in the late fourth century) describes the practice of *syla* declarations by the Chalkedonians. Their city, Chalkedon (also spelled "Kalchedon"), sat at the site of modern Istanbul on the Asian side of the Bosporos straits, the busy shipping route into and out of the Black Sea.[79] This was a convenient place for their strategic seizures:

> The Chalkedonians had among themselves many mercenaries to whom they owed wages they could not pay. And so they declared that if any citizen or resident alien had a claim of *syla* against a city or private person and wanted to make a seizure, he should sign up. After many people had signed up, they made seizures of ships sailing into the Black Sea, on justifiable grounds. And they set a time within which they said that people [i.e., the victims of the seizures] could make claims concerning the seizures. After collecting a lot of money, they paid off the soldiers and judged the claims concerning the seizures. And anyone who had suffered a seizure unjustly was compensated by the city from the money collected. — [Arist.] *Oec.* 1347b20–31[80]

This passage states unequivocally that rights of *syla* could be held by people against other people and against an entire city. Distinguishing those two situations implies the difference mattered. It may be that claims against a person could be exercised by *syla* only against that person, while a claim against a city could be exercised against any of its citizens.[81] The passage also shows a city assuming individual peoples' rights of *syla*, probably by "purchasing" the legal claims of its residents. It seems that Chalkedon here acted like a collection agency and paid the claim holders some percentage of whatever was collected.[82] The author does not tell us if he views the practice of the Chalkedonians as exceptional or exemplary. But it is a remarkably sophisticated legal device to be found operating among the rules of customary international law, highlighting just how "lawful" Greeks could consider those rules to be. Overall, the Chalkedonians were careful to adhere to a reasonable interpretation of the law of *syla*.[83]

Declarations, or grants, of *syla* seem to have been a way of mixing politics with law, and their use is compatible with a Darestian view that the declarations were never legally necessary. Their use may have been less about authorizing seizures than about advertising the need for them; and sometimes, as with the Chalkedonians, about creating a state mechanism for dealing with some of their effects. State intervention of this sort might be authorized after a citizen had suffered a particularly egregious wrong; when a prominent citizen had been harmed; or when many crimes or torts had been committed by citizens of the same foreign state. Or, as the anonymous author claims for Chalkedon, when the city's treasury was in crisis.

Other reasons could spur states into becoming officially involved in *syla*. Staying in the late fourth century and on the southern edge of the Black Sea, let us move one long day's sailing voyage from Chalkedon, through the Bosporos and east to the next city on that coast, Herakleia Pontica. In the early 320s, citizens of Herakleia seized the sails of a grain merchant named, ironically, Herakleides of Salamis (on Cyprus), apparently while he was shipping grain to Athens. Herakleides got word of the seizure to Athens, where he was popular as a benefactor to the Athenians. We know of his popularity from the series of inscribed Athenian honorary decrees that mention his misfortune in Herakleia.[84] What we do not know is why the Herakleians, governed at the time by a tyrant named Dionysius, seized Herakleides's sails. As Andrew Lintott points out, they do not appear to have taken the grain that Herakleides must have been carrying (2004, 346). So this may have been a limited legal seizure in response to a specific harm. On the other hand, one of the decrees suggests the Athenians believed the Herakleians had acted unjustly in taking Herakleides's sails (ἀδικεῖν, 40–41), so it may be that no legal pretext for the seizure was even offered. It is also not clear if Herakleides was harassed because of something he himself had done, because of an act by a fellow Salaminian, or because he was heading to Athens.[85]

It seems the conflict was resolved by a minor diplomatic intervention. This resolution was made easier by Herakleides's status in Athens and by what seem to have been good relations between Athenians and Herakleians in the fourth century. The Herakleians and Athenians had *proxenoi* in each other's cities. We know at least one Herakleian merchant, in the 370s, who had Athenian guest-friends (*xenoi*) and did banking business in Athens. And in the 330s, not long before this incident, the Athenians decreed honors to two Herakleian grain traders for selling grain in Athens at reduced prices. The ties between Athenians and Herakleians—partly economic, to be sure, but also social—must have assisted in the peaceful resolution of this legal dispute.[86]

Despite how legalistic the practice of *syla* seems often to have been, and the apparent fact that *syla* could sometimes be resolved by minor diplomacy, reciprocal seizures could also slide toward war. We saw this depicted fictionally in Nestor's account from the *Iliad*. To jump forward in time, Polybius also narrates a declaration of seizures serving as a preliminary to war. In about 220, he reports, the people of Eleutherna in Crete, believing that a Rhodian force had deliberately killed one of their citizens, "first declared seizures (ῥύσια) against the Rhodians, and after this waged war against them."[87] This declaration of seizures, though, was in response to a public crime by a Rhodian military commander, not for collection of a delinquent private debt. The difference between the two seems significant, both legally and socially, as may be indicated by the use here of the term *rhysia* rather than *syla*. Seizures in response to debts seem to have been usually quite limited in scope, even when they included in their purview fellow citizens of the original wrongdoer. War, on the other hand, was a more encompassing circumstance; and a state of war could in turn justify seizures on a larger scale than could private debts alone.[88]

Limited restrictions on seizures

The incidents described in the previous section show that, while the law of *syla* addressed a need, it created problems of its own. So it is unsurprising that Greeks often sought to avoid its use. We have already seen, briefly, one way this was done: with *symbola* agreements, which typically included a ban on seizures between the citizens of two cities.[89] But Greek states sometimes granted specific people legal protection against seizures. I noted above several blanket grants of "freedom from seizure in times of seizure." The ordinary term for this protection was *asylia*. "*Asylia*" could refer to several forms of inviolability, but I use it here with only one of its meanings: personal protection from the form of legal *syla* that is the subject of this chapter. Personal *asylia* was not born in the fourth century but may have become more common then.[90]

These grants of *asylia* could be limited to particular conditions. In the late fourth century, the Eretrians (in Euboia) contracted with an apparent foreigner named Chairephanes to drain a marsh and farm the drained land for ten years.[91] The Eretrians granted *asylia* to Chairephanes and his associates, on land and sea, during peace and war, while they performed the contracted work.[92] Around the same time, Ilion (the Greek city at the site of ancient Troy) decreed extensive honors to four brothers from the nearby island of Tenedos, granting them (among other things) protection from seizure, *asylia* during peace and war, and the right to perform seizures upon foreigners within the territory of Ilion.[93] By providing special exemptions, the grants memorialized in these inscriptions offer further evidence that customary international law normally permitted *syla* against foreigners.

It must still have been possible to seek justice against people who were specially protected from seizure. The substitute for *syla* in such cases would have been ordinary domestic judicial procedures. On this assumption we can explain grants of *asylia* both sociologically and from a more calculative law and economics point of view. From the law and economics perspective, consider the formula I described earlier: administrative costs plus error costs plus risk of futility costs. Grants of *asylia* were made to foreigners with special ties to the granting city, people who had demonstrated loyalty and reliability. They were likely to fulfill their obligations to the city (or had committed contractually to doing so), including the obligation to respond to a legal complaint rather than flee the territory. In other words, they presented a relatively low risk of futility costs. I already proposed that ordinary judicial procedure probably had higher administrative costs but lower error costs than reliance on private *syla*. That some cities granted *asylia* only to select foreigners, leaving the rest exposed to *syla*, suggests from a law and economics perspective that the lower risk of futility costs they presented were a decisive factor. And the typical foreigner probably saw protection from *syla* as a material benefit, since it would often have made it more difficult for a claimant to recover from him.[94]

Social factors also likely made grants of *asylia* attractive to both city decisionmakers and individual foreigners. To grant *asylia* was to remove one of the identity barriers separating a foreigner from a local, a way of saying, "In this respect, you are one of us." To people who had already performed deeds making them worthy of *asylia*, this form of social acceptance was probably valuable in itself. To the extent the foreigner was now more like a member of the citizen group, that identity would in turn make him likelier, on average, to adopt and internalize the city's norms. This adaptation to group standards is of obvious value to members of a community.

Continuities and novelties in the third century and beyond

After the fourth century, our evidence for *syla* comes almost entirely from inscriptions. The practice seems to have been notably stable, although with a few apparently new variations. An example of continuity is found in several surviving inscriptions indicating that debts of a city could still be grounds for seizure of a person or his cargo. Probably sometime between 275 and 250, the Delphians granted privileges to a certain Philistion in exchange for payments he made when he had been seized by a creditor to the Delphians. We know it was a creditor to the Delphians because the inscription describes the payment made by Philistion as being "on behalf of the *polis*" and because one of the privileges granted him was tax relief, which has been interpreted (rightly) by commentators as a way of compensating Philistion for his payment of a *polis* debt.[95] Around the same time, a citizen of the island city of Delos was honored by an unknown city for twice having paid off seizures of wheat shipments; these shipments had been seized by other Delians as repayment of debts owed them by the unknown city.[96] A similar situation probably provoked the honors granted by the citizens of Eresos on Lesbos to Damon son of Polyarchos. A fragmentary inscription of the late third century claims that Damon earned his honors by having "lifted the state of seizure against the *polis*."[97]

An international right of legal seizure was recognized at least into the second century BCE. This is implied in a few surviving agreements among cities prohibiting seizures between their respective citizens. A treaty between the Cretan cities Lyttos and Malla, perhaps from the mid-third century, prohibits *syla* by the citizens of each *polis* in the territory of the other.[98] An early second-century treaty between the Milesians and Magnesians on the Maiander, neighbors on the west coast of Asia Minor, forbids the citizens of either city from giving a base of operation to anyone performing *syla* against a citizen of the other.[99] The reference to *syla* here is probably to legal seizure and amounts to an acknowledgment of its legality as well as an attempt to curtail it (presumably with a preference for judicial resolution of disputes). A very fragmentary inscription from Priene, believed to date to the second century, may honor a man who paid off a seizure made in response to debts owed by the city.[100]

Cities continued to grant personal *asylia*, protection against seizure, in the third century. An example among several from Tenos is an inscribed decree honoring Melesias of Mytilene with a crown, proxeny, and *asylia*.[101] The Andrians awarded Dromon of Babylon proxeny, *asylia*, and the right to have his legal cases heard first, among other things. The last privilege reveals a *polis* explicitly connecting the grant of *asylia* to a foreigner's use of local courts.[102] At least two third-century decrees guaranteeing personal *asylia* survive from Siphnos. One, perhaps from the late 270s, is for Perigenes of Alexandria, an *aulos* player apparently connected with the Ptolemaic court. His many honors from the Siphnians included a gold crown, proxeny, front seats at festivals, and *asylia*.[103] The Naxians similarly honored judges from Kos in the early third century.[104]

In these examples a city forbids only its own citizens and residents from performing seizure on one or a few specially protected people. But we also see broader declarations of personal *asylia* beginning in the third century. For example, around 220 the entire Aitolian League granted protection from seizure to all citizens of Keos, decreeing that "no one of the Aitolians, or those living as citizens in Aitolia, is to perform a seizure upon (ἄγειν) the Keans, operating from anywhere, neither on land or sea, not on account of an amphictyonic complaint nor any other."[105] An enforcement provision allows Kean victims of Aitolian seizures to seek justice with Aitolian officials. The Aitolians made a number of similar decrees in the second half of the third century, sometimes using the word *asylia* and sometimes not (as here), and typically including enforcement provisions. This testifies to an Aitolian concern with the substance of the privileges: they were not empty, formulaic honors.

At the very end of the third century, *asylia* was granted to the people of Teos in western Asia Minor by a number of international powers, among them Antiochos III, the Aitolians, the Delphians, and a number of Cretan cities.[106] The Aitolian decree and some of the Cretan decrees make clear that the protection forbade their own citizens from carrying out seizures against any Teans. The little-known Cretan city Sybrita provided specific penalties for violation: "If anyone setting out from Sybrita should wrong any Tean or anyone residing in Teos, publicly or privately, contrary to the rule concerning *asylia* adopted by the city of the Sybritans, it shall be permitted to one who is one of the Teans or one of the residents of Teos to take possession of the persons or goods, if someone takes them away. The *kosmoi* in office are to compel those in possession to give back (the seized items)."[107] These cases make clear there was some overlap between personal *asylia* and the mostly distinct phenomenon of territorial *asylia*, in which a particular territory was declared off limits to violent seizures. Indeed, blanket grants of personal *asylia* might be made in response to requests seeking the territorial variety.[108]

One special case of mass grants of international personal *asylia* was for the performing artists known as *technitai* of Dionysus. They were specialists in music and theater who performed at religious and dramatic festivals throughout Greece. By the third century, they began to organize into associations called *synodoi* or *koina*, the four most important of which were based in Athens, Isthmia-Nemea, Teos, and Egypt.[109] In 278/77 the Pylai–Delphi Amphictyony declared that the Athenian *technitai* were protected from seizure by any Greek and claimed that this protection was "a firm declaration by all the Greeks."[110] At some point in the third century, the Aitolians recognized *asylia* for at least some associations of *technitai*. Another inscription found in Delphi records the decision of the Aitolian League "to grant [securit]y and asylia to the *technitai* inscribed among those of I[onia and the Hellesp]ont, just [like for those] who assemble in Isthmia and Nemea."[111]

The *asylia* granted to the *technitai* was not absolute. The amphictyonic declaration clarified that the *asylia* did not protect a *technites* with regard to his personal debts to a city or for other personal liabilities.[112] This limited *asylia* therefore did not conflict with a joint decree of the four cities on the island of Euboia explicitly *permitting* seizure of a *technites*. The Euboian decree applied only to situations in which the artist had been fined for not completing the performance he contracted for: in that case, the artist and whatever property he had with him could be seized anywhere within Euboia.[113] These artists were being protected from seizures based on liabilities owed by their fellow citizens, a legitimate concern to those whose profession involved constant travel abroad. Unfortunately, the amphictyonic and Aitolian declarations of *asylia* do not help us decide between the theories of Dareste and Bravo I presented in the previous chapter. Neither indicates if the kinds of seizures they mention—permitted in most cases but forbidden against *technitai*—were seizures declared by a city or undertaken by a private victim of wrongdoing on his own initiative.

It is noteworthy that many of the restrictions of *syla*, an element of customary international law, were themselves forms of international law. This is most obvious in the case of treaties between two cities, such as Lyttos and Malla, or Oianthea and Chaleion. But *syla* restrictions for *technitai* agreed by the Pylai–Delphi Amphictyony and by the cities of Euboia were also international legal agreements. The Amphictyony was always an international body, and in 278/77 not yet dominated by the Aitolian League as it came to be later in the third century.[114] And the Euboians' decree, clarifying their continuing right to seize *technitai* for personal debts, explicitly calls itself a "law," *nomos* (*IG* XII 9 207, l. 61). Although this inscription is evidence of the four cities of Euboia regulating certain affairs jointly, no evidence indicates that they acted at this time, in any sense, as a federal *state.*[115] That they nevertheless called the enactment a law is an indicator of Greeks viewing international law as "law."

Conclusion: The social aspects of syla

The *technitai* are an example of one kind of Greek international network. At least by the third century BCE, organized groups of artists were traveling around the Greek world, to festivals large and small, making contacts, bringing news, and literally representing "Greekness" in two of its central forms: religion and *mousike*, especially drama. Brigitte Le Guen argues that hiring and honoring the *technitai* was a rhetorical gesture by monarchs after Alexander the Great portraying themselves as publicly and emphatically adopting explicitly Greek cultic and cultural practices to secure legitimacy and acceptance in the Greek world. By working through and building on networks founded on core elements of Greekness, the *technitai* would also have shaped and solidified a notion of a common Greek identity. This group identity, in turn, was part of the ethical basis for the observation of international law among Greeks.[116]

The *technitai*'s effect on international law was probably even more direct, precisely through the international legal protection they enjoyed. Official recognition of *asylia* for *technitai* likely made the idea of *asylia* recognition generally more familiar, encouraging cities to grant it in other situations as well. We saw the Aitolians, when offering *asylia* to the Teans, referring to the *asylia* they had previously granted the *technitai*. We do not know if Perigenes of Alexandria, the musician honored by the Siphnians, was a *technites*; if not, the fact that he was a musician may nevertheless have made it seem obvious to the Siphnians that they should grant him *asylia*. Treatment of *technitai* indicates how Greek international legal practice was grounded on international networks that shaped changes in that practice over time.

The law of *syla* exhibits a fundamental continuity over the period surveyed here. At least as early as the sixth century and as late as the second, Greeks recognized an international legal rule allowing self-help recourse to people who believed they had suffered torts or contractual violations at the hands of a foreigner. The permissible recourse included seizing the wrongdoer or his property. The seized property might itself be taken as compensation, but more often it seems it was held as hostage or collateral until the underlying obligation was paid off. A city would sometimes "declare" *syla* against all citizens of another city, for the declaring city or its citizens to get lawful compensation. These elements endured.

What seem to have developed over time are efforts to create alternatives to this form of self-help. That was done, it appears, mostly through *symbola* treaties, which permitted and required some private international legal disputes to be settled judicially. I discuss these in the next two chapters. Another development was granting *asylia*, freedom from legal seizure, to individual foreigners and more rarely to groups. Although such grants appear to have become more common over time, the need for grants of *asylia* shows the basic law of *syla* remained in force and legal seizure continued to be used by Greeks at least through the second century.

Syla's long life tells us that Greeks saw this form of legal self-help not only as necessary in an international world but as a socially and ethically appropriate form of dispute resolution. The use of self-help in domestic law, more limited though it was, drives this point home. And the perceived appropriateness of *syla* suggests it was not often abused in practice. If this is right, it is probably largely due to international social ties connecting those whom the law affected. In Olbia, we saw, Herakleides apparently would have accepted written evidence of ownership of the goods he seized. The Cyreneans were eager not only to pay off seizures their citizens had suffered but to advertise their settling of debts to the Greek world at large. And when the speaker of *On the Trierarchic Crown* connects illegitimate seizures by Athenians to a corruption of the naval system, it is partly a social diagnosis: his implication is that the wealthy, politically prominent, socially connected Athenians who should be commanding their own triremes would not blemish the Athenians' international reputation with such disgraceful acts.

I will not dwell on *syla*'s disadvantages, but only point out the two most obvious. One is the potential for violence. This should not be exaggerated but is real enough. Several people may have died from Teisilaos's use of *syla* to get compensation for some wrong done to him by a Cyrenean, an incident mentioned in the Cyrene inscription discussed above. And the need for physical coercion likely deterred many people from seeking justice through *syla*. The other obvious disadvantage is the lack of a neutral judge to weigh both sides of a dispute. Aristotle claims that "most people are, I dare say, poor judges concerning their own affairs," and therefore err in disputes they are personally involved in. This must have meant that *syla* came down, sometimes, to the law of the stronger. These disadvantages are surely two of the main reasons cities often agreed to forbid *syla* among their citizens.[117]

I would like to close this chapter, however, by noting briefly a few advantages offered by *syla*, which may help explain why the institution survived so long.

One I have already mentioned: it could be a quick and efficient way to end a dispute. As anyone knows who has ever been in litigation, speed of resolution is certainly a value to be weighed against the justice of the result. "Justice delayed is justice denied," as the saying goes.[118] Second: it is true that self-help suffers from its lack of a neutral judge to decide between competing claims of biased parties. But adjudicatory legal process always operates through humans, and no one is without bias or prejudice. In Chapter 3, I pointed to studies about human bias that suggest what reasonable people have always known: judges and jurors bring their prejudices and biases into court. Legal rhetoric, theorized and refined by the Greeks and well suited in many ways to seeking truth and justice, was also regularly used to make factually or legally weak cases seem persuasive. This is the source of so much Greek anxiety about rhetoric: that it could "make the weaker argument the stronger," in the words of the famous sophist Protagoras. Bypassing judicial process entirely, *syla* avoided these rhetorical pitfalls.[119]

One aspect of human bias and susceptibility to rhetoric deserves special notice in the context of international law. This is the role that group identity plays in those biases, and the effects it could have on judges and jurors. Often in this book, I note the positive affective elements of group identity *within* the group. But there is also, always, the dark side of group identity, the balancing of in-group favoritism by a countervailing prejudice against outsiders. Greeks were well aware of such group biases against foreigners, as Paul Vădan has recently discussed (2022). I will argue in Chapter 8 that *symbola* agreements, which replaced *syla* with judicial procedures, were usually concluded between especially friendly cities. One reason for this selective use of *symbola* may have been a well-founded fear that jurors or judges in any city would tend to be biased against "random" foreigners. An advantage of *syla* becomes obvious in this light: why prefer judicial process over self-help if you think a jury will be stacked against you?

7
Symbola
Social Origins of a Legal Institution

Introducing symbola

Symbola agreements were bilateral interstate treaties that guaranteed certain legal rights, especially procedural rights, to the citizens of each state in the territory of the other. This is what Aristotle tells us: that *symbola* gave people in different cities "the right of being sued and suing." And Harpocration, a lexicographer writing in the second century CE, defines *symbola* as "treaties that *poleis* make with each other granting their citizens the right to defend and prosecute lawsuits."[1]

I closed the previous chapter by emphasizing that *symbola* were often explicitly designed to replace *syla*, self-help seizure in international legal disputes. Hence a good starting point for understanding *symbola*'s advantages is considering *syla*'s disadvantages. I have mentioned the two most obvious: the potential for violence and the lack of a neutral, third-party judge. Cities made *symbola* with each other to lower these risks by the use of judicial process.[2]

But we should not be under the illusion that *symbola* eliminated violence or bias from the resolution of international legal disputes. As I explained in Chapter 5, Greek domestic legal systems—which *symbola* themselves implicated—always retained elements of self-help, making physical encounters between parties common and inevitable. This is exactly what the speaker describes in Demosthenes's speech *Against Euergos and Mnesiboulos* (Dem. 47.37–38, 47–61). Judicial process does not take place through words alone. And judicial process, despite eternal claims about efforts to make it neutral and disinterested, always reflects the biases of those who carry it out.

One of my arguments in this and the next chapter is that use of *symbola* agreements was partly shaped by Greek awareness of judicial biases against foreigners. Judges or jurors of a legal dispute between a fellow citizen and a foreigner will tend to be biased toward their fellow citizen. Awareness of this bias could sometimes have made *syla* preferred to *symbola*. It helps explain why cities entered into *symbola* selectively. This usually happened, I argue, when there was already a special or close relationship between the cities; barring that, when they hoped to create such a relationship. Awareness of judge and juror bias also

Laws of All the Greeks. Jesse James, Oxford University Press. © Jesse James 2026.
DOI: 10.1093/9780197838556.003.0009

motivated a shift in *symbola* practice in the third and second centuries. In this period, *symbola* sometimes provided for certain disputes to be resolved not by jurors from the two cities that were parties to the agreement but by jurors or judges from a third city, deemed less likely to be partial to the litigants on either side of an international dispute. This process indicates an expanding, not contracting, circle of *symbola*-related group identity.

Aristotle conveys a view of *symbola* reflecting especially close ties between cities, in a well-known passage of the *Politics* where he discusses what it means to be a citizen. He begins by explaining that certain groups of people resemble citizens in important ways, although they are not actually citizens:

> And the citizen is not a citizen by virtue of dwelling somewhere, for both metics and slaves partake in dwelling in a city; nor are citizens those who have a share in legal matters to the extent of being sued and suing, for this right also belongs to those who share as a result of *symbola*. In many places, not even metics have these judicial rights fully but have to provide a *prostates* when they go to court, so that they share in this sort of community incompletely. But it is just like with the boys who are not yet enrolled in the citizen lists because of their youth, and the old men who have been removed: one must say that they are citizens in a way; not in the most basic sense, but adding the qualification that the former are "incomplete" and the latter are "past their prime," or some other expression of this sort. It makes no difference, since it's clear what it means. . . . A citizen in the basic sense is distinguished from the others by nothing more than participation in legal judging (κρίσεως) and ruling (ἀρχῆς). — Arist. *Pol.* 3, 1275a7–19[3]

This passage and the larger discussion in which it occurs has been a recent object of scholarly debate, with much emphasis on how far Aristotle's narrow definition of the citizen in his "basic sense" (ἁπλῶς) diverges from the actual practice of cities.[4] The key observation is that Aristotle omits from his basic definition of citizenship aspects such as owning property, serving in the military, participating in *polis* religious rites, and creating new citizens through reproduction, all of which are prominent elements of citizenship in the literary, epigraphic, and archaeological evidence. And a central complaint is that Aristotle's narrow view of citizenship is blind to the central role that citizen women played in *polis* life. The critiques make clear that this passage should not be granted special authority but rather should be treated as one among very many sources for understanding the meaning of citizenship to Greeks.[5]

Despite its limitations, Aristotle's discussion is useful as one of the few surviving literary passages to mention *symbola* agreements. That Aristotle describes *symbola* generically is a sign they had, in his day, broad similarities across the many cities that used them. This passage also reveals his understanding that two populations connected by *symbola* had a notably close relationship, one that overlapped with the relationship among fellow citizens. Note Aristotle's four-part comparison between (i) citizens, (ii) metics, (iii) slaves, and (iv) foreigners covered by *symbola* agreements, and his distinction between citizens in a "basic sense" and those too young or too old to be full political participants in the city. Both reveal his view that legal status within a city was varied and hierarchical. While interested, for philosophical reasons, in finding a strict definition of the citizen, Aristotle openly acknowledges a fuzzier social and philosophical reality.[6] Cities connected by *symbola* were deep within that fuzzy zone. With respect to judicial access, Aristotle sees *symbola* agreements as bringing a foreigner closer to citizen status than did enrollment as a metic. Metics had to bring along a local citizen representative, a *prostates*, when going to court; those connected by *symbola* lacked this form of dependency.[7]

Even more telling is that those bound by *symbola* agreements also shared one of Aristotle's two core elements of citizenship: namely, participation in making legal judgments, *kriseis*, by serving as a juror.[8] Aristotle does not make the point explicit in this passage, but "being sued and suing" in each other's courts also meant sharing in legal judgment. This is because, in most cases, a suit between citizens of two different cities would have to be judged by citizens of one of those cities, or by a mixed jury with citizens from both.[9] Insofar as Aristotle is correct that jury service, *krisis*, was a constitutive element of citizenship, those connected by *symbola* were very close indeed to being fellow citizens.

But there is more. By actively subjecting themselves to each other's substantive laws, the citizens of two cities connected by *symbola* also shared to a certain extent in the other half of Aristotle's core of citizenship, *arche*, which I translated above as "ruling." Certainly they could not be magistrates in the other city. But a major part of *arche*, for Aristotle, was serving as a member of the assembly. To the extent that *symbola* made citizens of two cities subject to laws enacted by each other's assemblies, they all shared in a common *arche*.[10]

In general, although Aristotle's point is that *symbola* agreements did *not* turn foreigners into citizens, that he found the distinction useful indicates that the rights granted by *symbola* agreements overlapped with citizen rights.[11] And they did so on the basis of greater equality than that enjoyed by people mentioned earlier in the passage, enslaved people and metics. Those legally connected by *symbola* were all free adult men, presumably resident in their own home cities. In a *symbola* relationship there is, legally speaking, no imbalance in the relationship, such as the imbalance that exists most obviously between free and enslaved but also between citizen and metic. Of course, there often were real power imbalances between two cities connected by a *symbola*, just as there often were between fellow citizens despite any laws declaring them equal. But enactment of a *symbola* agreement was an effort to put aside such differences and deal together on some grounds of equality. Given how carefully Greek cities controlled access to the levers of legal decision-making, how sparingly they gave outsiders access to those levers in the form of citizenship grants, it is unlikely two cities would enter into *symbola* except when their citizens already had close relations and good reason to trust each other.[12]

Unless imposed from the outside, a domestic legal system applicable to a community requires a self-identified community to bring that system into existence. To some minimal extent, people have to agree that a certain set of legal rules applies to "us."[13] I argued in Chapter 3 that social identities within communities, with their affective and normative consequences, make legal systems more effective. In this and the next chapter, I argue that *symbola* agreements also implied and built on a sense of "us." There was often a preexisting group identity among the members of the two communities participating in the agreement. And the agreement itself would have nourished that identity, or planted the seeds for it if it did not already exist. Furthermore, just as within a domestic community, a common identity between citizens of two states would have tended to encourage compliance with the underlying laws whose enforcement was contemplated by the *symbola* agreements.

Aristotle was writing in the second half of the fourth century and, moreover, generalizing across all Greek *poleis*. The similarity he posits between fellow citizens and those connected by *symbola* may not have applied in every case over the centuries. But in these two chapters I offer more evidence that Greeks saw a connection between *symbola* and fellow citizenship; that *symbola* had affective impacts on Greeks; and that they implicated group identity. I try not to downplay the importance of the specific legal provisions of *symbola* nor of their significance to international trade. But the legal and economic effects of *symbola* were buttressed and nourished by the social factors including group identity that made a *symbola* agreement palatable and viable to the people in two communities who entered into it.

An inscription roughly contemporary to Aristotle seems to confirm his implication that the mutual rights created by a *symbola* relationship were in a continuum with citizenship rights. In the previous chapter, we became familiar with Olbia, founded as a Milesian colony in the mid-sixth century. At least two centuries later, probably sometime between 330 and 250, the Milesians and Olbians affirmed special prerogatives between themselves. These included the opportunity for actual citizenship in the other city (*isopoliteia*) as well as rights probably first laid out in a *symbola* agreement.[14] The inscription specifies three categories of Milesians in Olbia: (1) those who registered with the Olbian *boule* and henceforth could (and presumably must) take part in full Olbian citizen life including by holding local magistracies (this indicates the availability of *isopoliteia*); (2) those who continued to hold only Milesian citizenship but had special privileges in Olbia, including exemption from taxes and access to something called the *demotikon dikasterion*, or "people's court"; and (3) those who held (or "exercised") citizenship in a different, third city and were apparently therefore excluded from any special status in Olbia.[15] The *demotikon dikasterion* probably was the ordinary court used by Olbian citizens and hence likely also composed of Olbian citizen jurors or judges, presumably in contrast to a court especially for or consisting of foreigners.[16] On this interpretation, the judicial aspect of the agreement between Miletos and Olbia aligns with Aristotle's description of *symbola*: Milesians who were not full citizens of Olbia nevertheless had a special relationship to the Olbians and special privileges in their city, similar to but not quite as integrated as the Milesians who accepted full *isopoliteia*.

This text likely records certain terms of a reciprocal agreement between Olbians and Milesians, terms recorded on this *stele* in Miletos for the information of Milesians about to travel to Olbia. Christel Müller proposes that a similar *stele* had been set up in Olbia informing Olbians of their rights in Miletos.[17] Like the Aristotle passage, it reveals a conception of a continuum of citizen-like relations between members of two communities. Reciprocal access to local courts is not the same as joint citizenship, but it approaches it. That access is one of many elements (several of which are mentioned in this inscription) of an "Olbian-Milesian" identity, an identity likely existing since the founding of Olbia by Milesians two centuries earlier.[18]

Access and economics

Let me immediately complicate the picture of identity-fueled *symbola* I sketched above. A passage from a fourth-century speech simultaneously questions *symbola*'s judicial usefulness and highlights their explicit economic purpose. Called by scholars *On Halonnesus*, the speech was transmitted among Demosthenes's works ([Dem.] 7) but probably written and delivered in the Athenian assembly in about 342 by Hegesippus, a political ally of Demosthenes. It concerns a dispute between the Athenians and Philip II of Macedon over possession of the small island Halonnesus in the north Aegean. The pirate Sostratos had captured the island from the Athenians, and Philip in turn had captured it from Sostratos.[19]

In negotiations with the Athenians over rightful possession of the island, Philip apparently offered to have the question arbitrated while also proposing that he and the Athenians enter into a *symbola* agreement.[20] Hegesippus, urging the Athenians to reject Philip's entire offer, focuses briefly on the *symbola*. He protests that a *symbola* agreement would offer no advantage to Athenians and Macedonians:

> Your past experience is evidence that Macedonians don't need a *symbola* agreement with Athenians. Neither Philip's father Amyntas nor the other kings ever made *symbola* with our city. Yet the intercourse with each other then was greater than now: Macedonia was dependent on us and paid us tribute, and we used the trading centers there, and they used ours, more than now. And unlike now, there were no strict monthly mercantile courts, which eliminate the need for *symbola* agreements between people so distant from each other. But even though we had no such agreement then, there was no advantage in making *symbola*, neither for Macedonians sailing to Athens to litigate nor for Athenians going to Macedonia: we simply litigated cases there under Macedonian laws and they litigated here under ours. — [Dem.] 7.11–13[21]

The precise meaning of the end of this passage has been debated, but I follow Harrison and others in taking Hegesippus not to be contrasting the requirements for suing with and without *symbola* but rather to be saying there *is* no relevant difference.[22] The claim is polemical but was probably not without basis in the eyes of Hegesippus's audience. And it is evidence that, even without *symbola,* some foreigners in some Greek cities had at least limited access to local courts. If this is correct, Greeks would not have felt the need to enter into *symbola* simply to share a minimal level of judicial access; they would have wanted better reasons. An especially close relationship with another city was such a reason.

This speech is also noteworthy in presenting a law and economics view of *symbola*, judging a legal institution by its expected effects on commerce. Hegesippus assumes that *symbola* were widely understood as encouraging "intercourse," *epimeixia*, between states, specifically by stimulating the use of international trading centers, *emporia*. Of course he argues that, in fact, this would not happen between the Athenians and Macedonians; but he does not contradict the premise that *symbola* generally encouraged trade. Aristotle reveals a similar view in his *Rhetoric*, in the section describing some of the central issues that should be of concern to the orator who speaks about political issues in the assembly: "When it comes to food, the deliberative orator should understand how much the city needs, what kind is grown locally and what is imported, what needs to be exported and imported, so there can be contracts and *symbola* with the right people. You have to keep the citizens blameless in the eyes of two groups: those who are more powerful, and those who are useful in these matters."[23] In other words, politicians have to understand a city's trade patterns and encourage *symbola* agreements with communities who are "useful" for trade. The assumption, again, is that *symbola* encouraged that trade.

Neither Hegesippus nor Aristotle explains how *symbola* stimulated interstate commerce. But law and economics thinkers and new institutionalist economists would likely agree with them, on the theory that, by making it easier (or even possible) to sue in court, *symbola* helped define and ensure enforcement of property laws and international contracts. This is because a reliable ability to sue under clearly defined law and procedure is seen as increasing certainty for commercial parties. Say that two Greek merchants, A and B, from different cities, have a business contract. If B knows that A has the right to sue him in his home city, where B lives and has his assets, B's commitment in the contract becomes more credible: A can harness the legal coercive power of B's city to recoup any damages B may inflict on A by breaching.[24]

Symbola may also have lowered some transaction costs. I might forgo paying for armed guards to escort each shipment of goods (guards who could prevent a shipper from cheating me) when I know I can sue the shipper, even in his home state, with a reasonable likelihood of success. And economies of scale can make it more efficient for a government, rather than private individuals alone, to play a role in protecting people, property, and contract terms and to provide for adjudication of disputes.[25] Such potential cost savings can be seen as advantages over the self-help procedures of *syla* in particular. Of course, as I pointed out in the previous chapter, *syla* offered its own efficiencies. But the considerations laid out here suggest some of *symbola*'s potential attraction.

There is little doubt, then, that in the fourth century Greeks saw *symbola* as having economic importance. They were not simply legal treaties existing in a pure juristic realm but had a place and a role in the great economic web of the Greek world. Yet, further consideration of these passages shows that economics, too, fails to tell a complete story about *symbola*.

Just below the surface of Hegesippus's speech, which admits assumptions of human action as profit-maximizing, there lurks a fear not of the rational economic actor but of the social actor and of the potential psycho-social effects of *symbola*. By criticizing the Macedonia sympathizers in Athens throughout his speech, Hegesippus expresses his antipathy toward the pro-Macedonian sentiment that had become common among Athenians.[26] He seems also to fear that a *symbola* agreement with Philip will only improve relations between Athenians and Macedonians. Hegesippus claims a *symbola* agreement will have no effect on Athenian-Macedonian relations, but behind his blustery façade he fears that in fact it will: that guarantees of judicial process will increase both commerce *and* goodwill between the communities and make it even more difficult for the Athenians to avoid subordination to growing Macedonian power. On this reading, Hegesippus, while focused on the economic effects of *symbola* agreements, betrays a (perhaps hazy) understanding of their potential social effects.[27]

Aristotle similarly believed that *symbola*'s effects were not just economic. Yes, his emphasis on citizens in one city being "useful" to those in another looks like pure economic rationality. According to Aristotle, though, usefulness is not the only consideration in play. He thinks citizens of cities that trade with each other should be not only useful but also "blameless" (ἀνέγκλητος) in each other's eyes. Implied in his reasoning is that a potentially useful trading partner will take that blamelessness into account. Aristotle sees an ethical, emotional foundation to trade relations. And he hints that *symbola* contributed to this foundation. I argue in these chapters that Aristotle was right.

In this chapter and the next, I trace the history of *symbola* agreements, with an emphasis on how they likely affected and were affected by social relations, social identities, and processes of socialization. Building on my discussion of *syla*, I show that *symbola* agreements were about more than bare access to the law, about more than simple economic interests. They were also about acknowledging and cementing relations between communities. Because entering into a *symbola* meant both recognizing and nourishing a larger group identity, forming this pact not only created legal institutions between two cities but also increased the odds those institutions would be effective.

Symbola were proposed, discussed, and approved by a *polis*'s assembly or other decision-making body.[28] When successful, the very negotiation of a *symbola* agreement and subsequent deliberative processes of approving it in each *polis* probably contributed to the goodwill the citizens of each *polis* had for each other, by encouraging the expression of reasons they had for making relations even closer. This is one aspect of what I called, in the previous chapter, the expressive function of law, the ability of legal enactments to affect other social norms. Formally agreeing and establishing, as a community, that the citizens of another city were juridically almost equal to local citizens would have fostered social norms to treat the former group in ways encouraged by law.[29]

Furthermore, by putting each city's citizens into the class of "most favored foreigners" in the other city, *symbola* may have induced positive feedback loops. As claimed in the passages discussed above, granting judicial privileges likely tended to encourage trade, which would have increased contact and expanded social networks between citizens of the two cities. This increased network contact in turn would have tended to decrease out-group biases, making business transactions more trusting and cooperative. The increase in trust and cooperation within this expanded social network would increase the odds that, when disputes did arise, they would be more often resolved informally. When informal procedures failed, in the local court the *symbola*-connected foreigner would be more likely to be treated justly, as a member of an especially friendly city. And if, after a formal trial, he concluded he had been treated justly by the legal system, he would be more likely to support it in the future: obeying its rules himself, helping others enforce them, and spreading his positive views among his network contacts.[30]

Adriaan Lanni has argued that, in Athens, argumentation in public trials served both to shape and to enforce community norms. She suggests that "courts facilitated the operation of informal sanctions" by the community "by encouraging litigants to publicize their opponent's norm violations" in the public forum of the court—another way that law can have an expressive function.[31] To the extent that trials involving foreigners protected by *symbola* agreements resembled ordinary trials between two citizens, the participation of such foreigners in trials where community norms were expressed and debated might have led to a similar effect among *symbola*-protected foreigners in Athens and other communities. For example, if a Chian defendant were colorfully accused of some commercial misbehavior in open court in front of two hundred Athenian jurors, word would probably spread among the Chians who visited Athens frequently, and it might tend to make them less likely to act as their countryman was accused of acting. This could be so even if the commercial misbehavior was not the basis for the underlying charge but simply held up as evidence that the defendant was a "bad character": hearing a particular behavior frequently condemned often leads people to internalize that condemnatory attitude.

My proposal, in short, is that the formation and use of *symbola* agreements had social and ethical effects on the people who fell within the ambit of those agreements and tended to strengthen compliance with the legal rules encompassed by them. As I have repeatedly emphasized, my social and ethical understanding of *symbola* agreements supplements rather than replaces other accounts of their use. Economic factors especially would always have been important considerations in both the conclusion and operation of *symbola* agreements. But they do not explain everything. In my historical survey, in addition to tracing the development of *symbola* agreements and describing their varieties, and without ignoring economic and political factors, I emphasize features most implicated with social and ethical considerations.

Symbola "Origins": Social and literary context

We can better understand the social import of *symbola* by considering their social and philological origins and context: the social practices, both predating and contemporary with *symbola*, that filled some of the same social roles and functions as *symbola*; why the latter were called *symbola* in the first place; and use of the terms *symbolon* and *symbola* in literature. This "archaeology" of *symbola* will highlight social aspects not always obvious in our epigraphical evidence, offering suggestive possibilities of *symbola*'s psychological effects.

Historical social background: xenia and proxenia

Judicial treaties may have roots in the Greek cultural practice of *xenia*, or at least in the social and political feature that gave *xenia* its importance: a desire to provide protections to some foreigners. There is no satisfying single translation of *xenia*, variously rendered in English by "hospitality," by the old-fashioned term "guest friendship," or by the more technical "ritualized friendship." It derives from *xenos*, "stranger" or "foreigner." Two forms of *xenia* are recognized in our earliest literary sources: a universal respect for all foreigners or strangers, who were under the protection of Zeus *Xenios*; and a special relationship between two elite families from different communities. The latter form was more formalized and ritualized, primarily in the exchange of gifts, and of hospitality when either *xenos* visited the other's community.[32] In both cases the *xenia* relationship was predicated on a distinction between locals and outsiders that created ethical problems alleviated by *xenia*. As Gabriel Herman explains in his fundamental study, a *xenos* differed from, for example, a "friend" (φίλος) or "companion" (ἑταῖρος) on one hand, and "kin" or a "relative" (συγγενής) on the other, by invariably being from a different community.[33] Like international law, the social institution of ritualized friendship was not invented by or restricted to Greeks. There is evidence of ritualized friendship among Near Eastern societies, Etruscans, Romans (as *hospitium*), Germans, Gauls, Carthaginians, and Celtiberians.[34]

The protections offered and obligations imposed by *xenia* were independent of local community obligations, with which they could even conflict. In the *Iliad*, Diomedes and Glaukos, although meeting as enemies on the battlefield, recognize their family bond of *xenia* and agree not to fight each other, while acknowledging this may conflict with their duties as soldiers (*Il.* 6.226–29). And both Thucydides and Plutarch report that, in 431, the opening year of the Peloponnesian War, Pericles feared that *xenia* between himself and the Spartan king Archidamos might cause Archidamos to spare Pericles's property—and no one else's—from destruction by the Peloponnesian army when it invaded Attica, potentially stoking Athenian enmity against Pericles.[35]

Herman describes *xenia* as a form of "ritualised friendship," "a bond of solidarity manifesting itself in an exchange of goods and services between individuals originating from separate social units."[36] The bond could also be manifested in naming practices, in particular naming one's son after a *xenos* or his city. *Xenia* was practiced almost exclusively among socially elite men, leaders of their communities with influence over foreign relations. As mentioned above, their *xenia* was formalized through ritual. More than a simple exchange of gifts, the ritual typically included a pledging of faith by means of a handshake (*dexiosis*), a concrete demonstration of nonaggression, and often by sharing a meal and exchanging oaths.[37]

The coalescence of Greek communities into forms recognizable as *poleis* created an urgent problem in the potential for conflict between private and public interests. One apparent reaction to this potential was the development, by the sixth century, of proxeny as a public variant on private *xenia*.[38] A *proxenos* was a citizen of one *polis* appointed by the governing body of another *polis* to be its unofficial assistant and representative in his own home *polis*. To describe it differently, a *proxenos* acted toward an entire community as a *xenos* acted toward an individual or family. William Mack describes the *proxenos* as "an intermediary figure who could be expected to help visitors from the granting city negotiate any difficulties or barriers in his own political community which their status there as strangers and non-citizens might cause them."[39]

Xenia and proxeny also shared a strong affective element. Although relations of *xenia* were established and reinforced partly through reciprocal exchange of material goods or benefits, *xenia* was about more than material benefits. The exchange acted as evidence of real affection, and that affection could arise instantly upon learning of a particular relationship. The battlefield embrace of Diomedes and Glaukos, when they learn each other's lineages, vividly demonstrates this: "After the two said these words, they leaped from their chariots, / grasped each other's hands, and swore to be true to each other."[40] Affection was also a fundamental basis for grants of proxeny. Most proxeny decrees explicitly premise the grant on the honoree's demonstrated goodwill (εὔνοια), affection (φιλία), or zeal (προθυμία; σπουδή) for the granting city. The feelings were manifested, of course, in concrete acts.[41]

Those concrete acts were usually favors done for citizens of the granting city. They ranged from the very practical (finding local lodging when they came to town) to the entirely political (speaking for the interests of the granting city in one's own assembly). One important subset of those services was helping a visitor navigate the legal system of the *proxenos*'s home city. Proxeny was not a legal relationship between two cities, and it is unlikely that a *proxenos* could have had much formal sway in a lawsuit involving a foreigner. But I have repeatedly emphasized the role of the human element in law, including biases. When a foreigner had any legal affairs in a city, having a local *proxenos* to vouch for him—not just his identity but also his character—could have made a real difference.[42]

The legal assistance given by *proxenoi* was probably almost always informal, though. And granting proxeny was a unilateral act by a city, premised partly on a hope that one local citizen in another city could be of assistance. Institutionally, then, proxeny falls short of the formal, legal, bilateral nature of *symbola* treaties. We will see that our earliest evidence for *symbola* agreements is from the fifth century, later than our first evidence of proxeny. This does not necessarily mean that *symbola* developed from proxeny. But both institutions were communal responses to an awareness of the practical and legal problems created by foreigner status. I argued already that *symbola* agreements had an affective element. That is another way in which they resembled proxeny, implicating the kinds of bonds instantiated and strengthened by *xenia*. *Symbola* and proxeny seem to be related developments, outgrowths not only of high international mobility in the Greek world in the sixth and fifth centuries but also of the *politicization* (in its etymological sense) of a long tradition of familial and personal long-distance relationships.

Philological perspectives

Use of *symbola* agreements, then, should be understood as rooted in a cultural context of *xenia* and proxeny in which special treatment of foreigners had a marked affective dimension. We can also seek the origins of *symbola* agreements philologically, investigating why they were called *symbola*, the word's use in literature, and some possible implications of the nomenclature. We find in *symbola*'s philological origins strong resonances of recognition, authentication, positive emotion, and inclusion into a community. These resonances likely reached the lived experience of interstate *symbola* agreements, tinging them with a further social and affective dimension.[43]

In this book, I generally use the term *symbola* (σύμβολα), the plural form of the neuter noun *symbolon*. But in some sources a feminine form is used, *symbole* (συμβολή) or its plural *symbolai*. When referring to judicial treaties, all these variants were probably synonymous, although the question is debated by scholars, as I discuss below.[44]

The earliest surviving attestations of the word *symbolon* indicate three connected meanings: "agreement," "physical token of agreement," and "physical token of identity." The Homeric *Hymn to Hermes*, likely composed in the sixth or fifth century, describes how a mischievous young Hermes steals the cattle of Apollo, as a prank, before managing to reconcile with his older divine half-sibling. At the poem's climactic resolution, the two affirm their undying friendship with mutual oaths. Apollo states, "And I will complete an authoritative *symbolon*, immortal, and also trusted and honored in my heart. So then I will give you a very beautiful wand of prosperity and wealth, golden and three-leafed."[45] Lines in the Theognidean corpus, not securely datable but perhaps from as early as the sixth century, decry men who plot together to steal from others, "having made shameful *symbola* for [or "with"] their wicked deeds."[46]

Most interpreters take the *Hymn to Hermes* and Theognis passages to mean by *symbolon* and *symbola* "agreement" or "pact."[47] This is reasonable in both contexts. But in the *Hymn* the use of *symbolon* may also refer to the wand as Apollo's "token" of the agreement, reciprocating the lyre that Hermes gave to him, here where it is first indicated they have become friends. Each item would now be a proof of the respective god's presence and a continuing sign of their firm friendship.[48]

Herodotus relates a story from the early fifth century in which *symbola* are physical tokens used to confirm identity. The Spartan kings Kleomenes and Leutychides, having taken hostage some people from the island of Aigina, brought them to Attica for safekeeping. After Kleomenes died, Leutychides alone went to Attica to retrieve the hostages. The Athenians refused to release them because both kings had deposited the hostages but now one alone requested them back (6.86.1). Leutychides's response took the form of a story. A Milesian had once come to Sparta and deposited a quantity of silver with a certain Glaukos, with the following instructions: "And you, accept this money and these *symbola*, take them and keep them safe; and whoever has these and makes a claim, give them back to him."[49] In this story the *symbola* are physical tokens serving as proof of the bearer's identity. The *symbola* provided by the Milesian must somehow match other *symbola* that someone will later present to Glaukos, whereupon Glaukos is to hand the money over to that person.[50]

A similar use of *symbola* as "identifying tokens" occurs in Euripides's *Medea*, produced in 431. Jason, attempting to ease the harshness of Medea's impending exile from Corinth, offers her assistance abroad: "But if you want to receive more help for the boys and yourself in your exile, from my resources, tell me. Because I'm ready to give with a generous hand, and to send *symbola* to my *xenoi*, who will treat you well."[51] The scholion to this passage explains, for readers many centuries later, the concrete meaning and use of *symbola* at the time: "Those entering into *xenia* relations with people would cut a vertebra, keep one part themselves and leave the other with those receiving them in their home, so that, if it should be necessary again for themselves or their relations to practice *xenia* toward each other, by bringing together the half-vertebrae they would renew the *xenia*." It then quotes a passage from another Athenian playwright, a comic poet of the fourth century: "Euboulos in his *Xouthos*: 'Why is everything sawn through carefully in half, just like *symbola*?' "[52]

Like guest friendship itself, *symbola* as tokens of guest friendship were a trans-Mediterranean phenomenon. Actual examples have been found from Sicily to southern France to Spain, evidence of the use of such tokens not only by Greeks but also by Etruscans, Romans, Carthaginians, and Celtiberians. They are typically small bronze, bone, or ivory pieces, often in the shape of animals. A few particularly striking examples are ivory models of two human hands in a handshake gesture of *dexiosis*. These pieces are carved in relief on one face but flat on the other; the flat face is typically inscribed with a text, usually at least a name, sometimes also with further text leaving no doubt the item served as a *symbolon*.[53]

The Latin word for such an item was *tessera hospitalis*. One example actually refers to itself as a *tessera hospitalis* in its inscription.[54] We know this term also from Plautus's play *Poenulus*, produced probably in the early 180s. In a scene late in the play, a Carthaginian visitor to the Greek city of Calydon in Aitolia learns he has met the son of one of his father's guest friends. To confirm this, he offers to match up his *tessera hospitalis* from when the relationship was formed; he has brought it with him from home: "If you want to match up your *tessera hospitalis*, look, I brought mine."[55] Plautus's play is based on a Greek original, probably *Karkhedonios* by Alexis, a fourth-century Athenian comic playwright. Plautus's *tessera hospitalis* must be a direct translation of *symbolon* in the original Greek version, although in another play, *Bacchides*, Plautus uses the word *symbolum*, the Latinized form of *symbolon*.[56] It is no surprise that *symbola* appear in plays by Alexis and Euboulos, a fragment from whom I quoted above. Both wrote "Middle" or "New" comedy, dramas rife with kidnappings, family separation, and mistaken identities and, ultimately, their resolution through forms of recognition and identity confirmation.

Walter Müri argues the term *symbola* derives from an intransitive or middle meaning of the verb *symballein* (συμβάλλειν), "come together, make an agreement." On his view, *symbole* originally referred to the abstract agreement created by the action of *symballein*, while *symbolon* was a physical token of the agreement. The plural of *symbolon* then came also to refer to the abstract agreement. Gauthier suggests, in contrast, that the primitive meaning comes from the active sense of *symballein*, "to put together," and refers to a partial object completed by something else; *symbolon* and *symbole* came to mean "agreement" because such objects were used to commemorate agreements.[57] It may be a mistake to think that one of these etymologies is true (*etymos*) and the other false, as it could have been that their very compatibility contributed to the term's use in referring both to agreements and to physical tokens used to commemorate and confirm them.

Much evidence survives for the use of *symbolon* and *symbola* understood in these ways. *Symbola* as tokens were used as markers of agreements under which each party's identity might need to be confirmed through physical evidence; for example, with pacts of *xenia*, commercial agreements, or personal agreements of a quasi-commercial or quasi-political cast. This is their use in the Herodotus and *Medea* passages quoted above.[58] *Symbola* tokens were also used publicly as authentication, including for entry into a city. An agreement between the Athenians and Strato, king of Sidon in Phoenicia, probably dating to the early 380s, provides: "The *boule* shall make *symbola* for the king of the Sidonians, so that the Athenian people will know if the king of the Sidonians sends anything making a request of the *polis*, and the king of the Sidonians will know when the Athenian people send someone to him."[59] In Aristophanes's *Birds* (produced 414), when the goddess Iris attempts to enter Cloudcukooland, Peisetairos demands a form of identification: has any bird-magistrate matched up her *symbolon*?[60] Aeneas Tacticus, writing in the mid-fourth century, implies a similar use when he recommends that a city under invasion forbid residents to depart the city "without a *symbolon*" (ἄνευ συμβόλου, 10.8). A military "passport," a token identifying its bearer as official and authorized, was also called a *symbolon*. The presentation of the proper *symbolon* at the gates of a city or military fortification would have reassured the guards that the stranger presenting it was friendly and trustworthy.[61]

Aristophanes's speech in Plato's *Symposium* brings out the physical nature of the *symbolon* as half of a whole and its potentially strong emotional effect as an authenticator and a sign of belonging.[62] Offering an origin for affections such as love and friendship, Aristophanes claims that ordinary two-legged humans are just one half of what were originally four-legged creatures. "Therefore each of us is a *symbolon* of a person, since he's been cut like flat fish, two coming from one. And each of us is always looking for his own *symbolon*."[63] Whenever someone finds that other half, according to Aristophanes, both are overcome by friendship, a sense of belonging, and love (192b7–8). The striking point is that the person *is* the *symbolon*, recognizing his or her other half by literally fitting together perfectly, both physically and psychically. The *symbolon*'s goal is reunification with its other half.[64]

Symbolon also referred to any physical item distinct enough to authenticate a person or message. Fifth-century literary instances of this usage show the recognition of such *symbola* having strong emotional effects. It could create instant warmth among apparent strangers and lead to a person's integration or reintegration into a family or civic community. One well-known example is the scar next to Orestes's eye in the recognition scene between him and Electra in Euripides's *Electra*: the scar is the unfalsifiable mark by which Electra recognizes her brother, a mark she calls in turn *charakter*, *tekmerion*, and *symbola*.[65] Even more literal is the use in the recognition scene in the same poet's *Ion*, where the *symbola* are actual physical items Creusa placed in the newborn Ion's cradle that prove, at the play's climax, that she is his mother.[66] In the *Electra*, the *symbola* serve to turn a man who has been repeatedly described as a *xenos* (e.g., at lines 548, 552, 555, 562) not only into a "beloved" (τοῖς φιλτάτοις, 576), but also into a true citizen of Argos. Similarly in the *Ion* the *symbola* prove that the young man who believed he was not Athenian is in fact half Athenian by blood. They ease his transition from Delphi back to Athens to reside as one who belongs there.

In Sophocles's *Oedipus Tyrannus*, a *symbolon*, while not a sign of authentication, still aids in integrating a person into a community.[67] Early in the play Oedipus explains why he has not solved the mystery of Laius's death: Oedipus was a foreigner when the murder happened but is now a Theban citizen. The distance between the two statuses is metaphorically bridged by a *symbolon*: "I will tell them as a stranger to this tale, and a stranger to what happened; for I would not myself follow such a long trail unless I had some connection (σύμβολον). And now, since I recently am enrolled as a citizen among citizens, I will announce these things to all you children of Cadmus."[68] I follow Patrick Finglass in translating *symbolon* here as "connection." No precise meaning is clear, but Oedipus's point seems to be that acquiring this *symbolon* has brought him far enough into the Theban community that it is his responsibility to solve Theban civic problems.[69] The *symbolon* here is explicitly *not* a sign of recognition of Oedipus's true identity; but that the word could refer to such a sign adds to the already thick irony of this passage, which plays on Oedipus's ignorant claim to be a foreigner. In Oedipus's eyes the *symbolon* makes possible his inclusion in the community, but true recognition will come only late in the play.

Finglass has recently reinterpreted a similar Sophoclean usage of *symbolon*. In the *Philoctetes*, Odysseus and Achilles's son Neoptolemos have come to the island on which their estranged comrade Philoctetes has been languishing with an incurable injury. The Achaians besieging Troy have come to believe they need Philoctetes and his bow in order to conquer Troy. But Philoctetes now hates the Achaians, believing they have wronged him. In order to gain Philoctetes's trust, Neoptolemos invents a story of also having been wronged by the Achaians. Having heard the story, Philoctetes replies that Neoptolemos and his close companions bear "a clear *symbolon* of grief"; hence "you sing in harmony with me."[70] As Finglass points out, "Philoctetes' point is that Neoptolemus' tale of woe matches his; like Philoctetes, Neoptolemus too has been betrayed by the Greeks" (2023, 35). Neoptolemos's presentation of this metaphorical *symbolon* induces Philoctetes to trust him, to take this stranger into his confidence. As in the *Oedipus*, though, the *symbolon* of the *Philoctetes* is dyed in darkest irony, here fabricated to induce a misplaced trust.

In the fifth and fourth centuries the word *symbolon* was associated with agreements, recognition, authentication, and belonging. It often had strong, positive emotional resonances connected with the role of bringing people together and marking agreement. By authenticating an identity, a *symbolon* announced or confirmed a preexisting relation, and this confirmation could instantly turn an interaction marked by suspicion or even hostility into one of sincere affection and trust. Whatever the historical reasons *symbola* agreements came to have that name, the close connection of their name to the *symbola* that authenticated agreements and asserted belonging can only have reinforced the affective aspect of *symbola* agreements for their Greek users.[71]

symbola vs. symbolai

I noted above that we find slight variation in the terminology for judicial treaties. In particular, in surviving fifth- and early fourth-century inscriptions they are mostly referred to by the feminine plural *symbolai*, while by the mid-fourth century the neuter plural *symbola* is most common in our sources. Probably because much of our evidence during these two centuries is Athenian, the apparent shift from *symbolai* to *symbola* has sometimes been taken to be connected to the shift from harsh fifth-century Athenian imperialism to the "kinder, gentler" Athens of the fourth century.

Müri argues that in the fourth century there was a conscious abandonment of a term connected with previous Athenian dominance, and in particular with Athenian interference in the judicial affairs of allies. Gauthier developed a more complex thesis. On his view, in the fifth century, Athenians entered into treaties they called *symbolai*, which were concerned mostly with merchants and traders, and concluded them only with distant cities of the Delian League and Athenian empire. According to Gauthier, there may have been one or a few large multilateral treaties of this sort. These fairly simple treaties only guaranteed particular legal procedures: foreigners protected by *symbolai* were assimilated to the status of metics and *proxenoi*, but like them were judged according to ordinary Athenian laws. Similarly, Athenians abroad, if involved in a lawsuit in a *polis* under a *symbole* agreement with Athens, were judged by the laws of the local *polis*, with protections similar to those offered in Athens. In the early fourth century, perhaps around the time of the Second Athenian Naval Confederacy, the Athenians began entering instead into strictly bilateral *symbola* agreements that had more specific juridical rules. These pacts were concluded with a variety of communities, including some geographically close to Athens, and carefully enumerated the torts, penalties, and rules of procedure that applied between citizens of the two cities. Cataldi offers a more complicated picture yet, in which the nature of Athenian *symbolai* changed during the course of the fifth century, so that it would be a mistake to say that *symbolai* meant one thing and *symbola* one other thing.[72]

These hypotheses have the ring of plausibility but are founded on meager evidence. We have the remains of six fifth-century inscriptions referring to *symbola* agreements between Athens and other *poleis*, only three of which provide definite examples of the feminine form of the noun.[73] The scanty fifth-century literary references are similarly indeterminate, although in fourth-century literary sources the neuter plural dominates.[74] Second, the thin testimonies of the agreements' substance do not confirm Gauthier's conjecture of a shift from solely procedural treaties to those with a mix of procedural and substantive provisions, or Cataldi's of a shift, within fifth-century Athenian practice, from fairly equal treaties with willing partners to highly unequal forced agreements.[75] Another source of unclarity is that the surviving fifth-century sources refer to *symbolai* (or *symbola*) agreements but are not themselves, and do not quote, the texts of those agreements; hence we cannot be sure whether or how the fifth-century Athenian agreements differed from those of the fourth.[76] The sole exception (*IG* IX 1^2 717, discussed below) is not Athenian and therefore casts no more than indirect light on the agreements between the Athenians and their allies.

From the fifth through the second centuries there was a slight shift in terminology from the feminine (*symbolai*) to the neuter (*symbola*), and from the plural (*symbola*) to the singular (*symbolon*). But this change was not uniform, and it is difficult to connect to particular observable changes in the nature of *symbola* agreements. Those changes must be sought in the surviving evidence of their substance rather than in minor shifts of terminology.

The first-known symbola agreements

Ionia

Greeks were probably using *symbola* agreements—whether calling them *symbola* or *symbolai*—by the first quarter of the fifth century. The absence of evidence for earlier usage does not mean *symbola* were not used sooner, the literary and epigraphic record for that period being so sparse. But no history of *symbola* agreements before the fifth century can be written.[77]

Herodotus tells us about what may be the earliest known *symbola* agreements. In the 490s, citizens of the Ionian Greek cities of Asia Minor failed in their revolt against Persian imperial rule (see Map 7 (Ionia) on the facing page). Herodotus reports that the Persian commander Artaphernes, having punished the Ionians severely, also provided them great benefits (χρήσιμα κάρτα) by compelling the Ionian cities to make what appear to be *symbola* agreements: "Artaphernes the governor of Sardeis sent for representatives from the *poleis* and forced the Ionians to make agreements with each other so that they would settle their disputes by litigation and not make seizures against each other (μὴ ἀλλήλους φέροιέν τε καὶ ἄγοιεν)."[78] According to Herodotus, this measure, and Artaphernes's simultaneous decision to survey the Ionian lands for purposes of accurate tax assessments, brought peace to Ionia (6.43.1).

Herodotus calls these pacts "agreements," *synthekai*, rather than *symbola* or *symbolai*. But the single provision he mentions is typically a core provision of what are elsewhere called *symbolai* and *symbola*: prohibition of seizures. The expression I translated as "make seizures" is a *hendiadys* of two common verbs, *agein* and *pherein*, which together are frequently translated as "plunder." But it is a broad expression covering many kinds of acts: it could refer variously to seizures

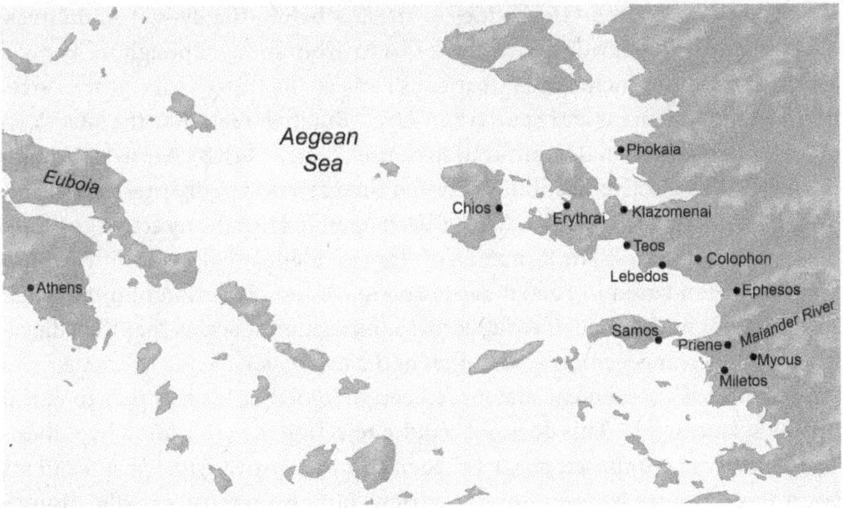

Map 7 Map of Ionian cities. Map by R. Salem.

performed during war, by pirates or troops outside of war, or by individuals, within a city or against foreigners, illegally or as *syla*, the form of legal self-help discussed in the previous chapters.[79] Herodotus himself elsewhere uses the expression to refer to ransacking by troops in war or pirate-like raiding with no legal pretext (e.g., 1.88; 1.166; 3.39; 6.90; 9.31). Here, however, Herodotus contrasts this form of seizure with litigation (ἵνα δωσίδικοι εἶεν); in other words, Artaphernes is replacing the practice of seizures with judicial dispute resolution. The implication is that the seizures were also a form of dispute resolution but taking the form of self-help rather than judicial litigation. Artaphernes forced the Ionians to start resolving their international disputes through judicial means rather than by self-help seizure.[80]

But were they public law disputes between entire communities, private legal spats, or both? Many scholars have thought Artaphernes here forced the Ionian cities to submit their public disputes to international arbitration.[81] Support for this view has been seen in an inscription from a century later commemorating an arbitral decision in favor of the Milesians over the Myusians; that case was decided by judges from Ionian cities and ratified by the Persian satrap Struses.[82] Oswyn Murray goes so far as to claim that the international arbitration provisions he believes Artaphernes instituted in the 490s existed continuously for at least a century until the time of this inscription, through the entire existence of the Delian League and the Athenian empire. This is unlikely, and belied by the evidence of a conflict over Priene that the Samians and Milesians fought in 441.[83]

Arbitration between Greek cities is attested before the 490s.[84] And Greeks never needed a preexisting treaty to resort to arbitration, although we know of arbitration clauses included in treaties as early as the thirty years' peace agreed between the Athenians and Spartans in 446.[85] But that treaty, like the later Peace of Nicias, which also had an arbitration clause (Thuc. 4.118.8), had as its primary purpose ending active hostilities between the parties. Artaphernes's provisions in 493, however, do not appear to have been intended to halt any active hostilities between Ionian cities. The formation of "Ionian" identity before the fifth century may have been based in part, it has been argued, on resolution of intra-Ionian conflicts, but at the time of Artaphernes's imposition it seems that the cities of Ionia had been at peace with each other in the recent past.[86]

Artaphernes's settlement may have been designed at least in part to curtail private seizures, *syla*. This does not require rejecting the arbitration hypothesis. The *synthekai* he imposed may have been comprehensive *symbola* agreements, governing disputes between private citizens but also referring public disputes between Ionian cities to international arbitration. A measure applying to private disputes makes sense in the context of Artaphernes's other action mentioned by Herodotus: assessing tribute on the basis of accurate land surveys. This assessment betrays a concern with income for the Persian empire, which could also be addressed by encouraging judicial resolution instead of self-help in private commercial disputes. As we saw in the discussion of *syla*, the boundary between private and public disputes could be both fuzzy and easily crossed (consider the Pylian self-help raids described by Nestor in *Iliad* 11). Artaphernes could well have had both in mind.[87]

If the *synthekai* imposed by Artaphernes were *symbola* agreements, this has implications for a sociological understanding of *symbola*. It means our first known example of them arose among communities already closely connected to each other by a common Ionian identity. Herodotus (1.141–48) makes much of treating "Ionian" as an ethnic and religious identity and describes the Ionians as organizing themselves around the "Panionion," the shrine of Poseidon *Helikonios* on the Mykale peninsula. I discussed in Chapter 4 how international use of sanctuaries likely built networks and common identities among their users. Naoíse Mac Sweeney, Jan Crielaard, and Barbara Kowalzig, in separate works, have recently explored Ionian identity; one focus has been on the roles that the Panionion and its festival may have played in forming, and transforming, what it meant to be "Ionian." This identity was likely a unifying element in the two joint Ionian attempts to throw off Persian dominance in the sixth and early fifth centuries.[88]

The Ionian cities flourished commercially in the sixth century and there must have been lively trade relations between them, leading to frequent private legal disputes.[89] Their proximity to each other, especially by sea, would have made it relatively convenient for people from different Ionian cities to participate in lawsuits in each other's courts. In fact Mac Sweeney argues that "fighting themselves was a crucial part of what it meant to be Ionian," because conflict between Ionian cities in the Melian War led both to agreement on terms of peace and to the founding of the Panionion. Michael Loy argues that the Ionians in the sixth century displayed strong economic collaboration but political distinctness and competition.[90] Commercial disputes and their resolution by peaceful adjudication could easily have been seen by Ionians themselves to fit that conflict-founded yet strongly connected identity. All these factors make Ionia a reasonable candidate as the birthplace of *symbola* agreements in the Greek world. It is possible that Artaphernes heard of such agreements existing and functioning between some Ionian cities before he ordered all the cities to adopt them. This would fit well with Briant's view of the Persian empire as frequently adopting and adapting the local institutions of subject communities for the benefit of the ruling power.[91]

Oianthea and Chaleion redux

In the previous chapter, I discussed aspects of our earliest surviving *symbola* agreement, the inscribed text of a pact between Oiantheans and Chaleians of west Lokris, dated to the mid-fifth century. This agreement has two parts: the first, which I focused on earlier, deals with limitations on self-help seizure; the second specifies judicial procedures for dispute resolution. The key judicial provisions appear on side B, but for context I provide here a translation of the entire text, divided into what I call Part 1 and Part 2.[92]

> *Part 1*
> [*Side A, line 1*:] Do not forcibly carry off a foreigner: neither the Oianthean from Chaleion nor the Chaleian from Oianthea, and not his property. [But] if someone makes a seizure, one may without penalty seize the man making the seizure. One may forcibly carry off foreign property at sea, without being seized oneself, except from the harbor by the city. If someone seizes illegally, [the fine is] four drachmas. [5] But if he holds the seized goods longer than ten days, he is liable for one and a half times what he seized.
>
> *Part 2*
> [*Side A, continuing line 6*:] If he is resident more than a month, either the Chaleian in Oianthea or the Oianthean in Chaleion, he is to enjoy the legal rights of foreign residents (ἐπιδαμίαι δίκαι). With regard to a *proxenos*: if he acts falsely as *proxenos* he shall pay double.

> [*Side B, line 10*:] If the *xenodikai* set aside a case for trial, let the foreigner bringing the suit choose sworn (judges), other than a *proxenos* and a personal host, from among the best men. For cases concerning a *mina* or more, fifteen men; for smaller sums, nine men. If a citizen [15] brings suit against a citizen in accordance with the *symbolai* (συνβολᾶς), the *damiorgoi* are to choose the oath-sworn (judges) from among the best, who have sworn the five-fold oath. The oath-sworn (judges) are to swear the same oath. The majority wins.

I mentioned already the scholarly controversy this difficult document has elicited. Every interpretation is subject to many objections; none is satisfying. But a history of *symbola* must grapple with it. I focus here on a few main points and offer my interpretation without defending it in detail.[93]

One question is whether the entire text belongs together, and if so whether that text is complete. Although the letter forms change slightly in line 8 of the first side, and the topic changes from prohibition of *syla* to judicial procedures, many commentators take the two parts as belonging together.[94] On some interpretations, Part 1 (lines 1 to 8) is the text of a *symbola* agreement between Oianthea and Chaleion, while Part 2 (lines 8 to 18) contains a local law of Chaleion (where the bronze inscription was found) governing procedures to be followed when suits under the agreement were brought in Chaleion.[95] I take Part 2, however, as itself part of the agreement between, and applying to procedures in, both cities. Moreover, the reference to *symbolai* in line 15 and to the "five-fold oath" in 16 to 17 suggests this text may be incomplete; perhaps a missing earlier and/or later section contained the more general terms of the *symbola* and the text of the oath.[96]

If the surviving inscription is (part of) a single agreement, that agreement does two main things: it forbids most *syla* between Oiantheans and Chaleians (as discussed earlier) and it provides for judicial procedures under certain circumstances. Unfortunately, those circumstances, and the procedures themselves, are not clear in the inscription's ambiguous language. One unclarity is whether the judicial procedures specified here are to apply in all legal disputes between citizens of Oianthea and Chaleion or only to claims that someone has performed an unjust seizure. The former option seems much more likely; it would be strange to forbid self-help resolution of disputes without providing for the judicial resolution of the underlying disputes.[97]

There is further unclarity whether two or three procedures are prescribed for dealing with legal disputes. One interpretation sees three scenarios here: (1) lines 6 to 9 concern procedure involving at least one metic, specified here as a foreigner resident for over a month in the other city; (2) lines 10 to 14 concern procedure involving one nonresident foreigner and one local citizen; and (3) lines 15 to 18 concern procedure involving only fellow citizens.[98] A second interpretation, which I prefer, sees two scenarios: (1) lines 6 to 14 concern procedure involving a metic, and (2) lines 15 to 18 concern procedure involving citizens of two different cities, each resident in his own city.

On my view, under the first scenario (lines 6–14) the agreement states that a Chaleian residing in Oianthea for at least a month (or vice-versa) will be subject to a form of local legal process (under the ἐπιδαμίαι δίκαι). But the process is customized in two ways: a *proxenos* is to play some role in the procedure (perhaps to confirm the foreigner's identity or his minimum month of residency), and the foreigner may choose his own judges.[99]

This provision reveals sensitivity to the role that bias plays in judging legal cases. On one hand, the resident foreigner is not permitted to include among the judges a *proxenos* of his city or any personal *idioxenos*, presumably because they are likely to be biased in his favor. On the other hand, he is permitted to choose judges from among the local citizens. The reasoning here may be that, since locals would tend to be biased in favor of their fellow citizen, the foreigner should at least be permitted to select from among them.[100] And as Zunino (2017, 137) has suggested, the "best men" (ἀριστίνδαν, 12) from whom the judges are to be selected—the elites—would have been likely to have the richest contacts with outsiders; these external contacts may also, in turn, have lessened their local biases. The mere fact that the drafters felt the need to exclude *idioxenoi* from the jury pool suggests that ties of *xenia* between Oiantheans and Chaleians were widespread and such *idioxenoi* common.[101]

The second scenario (lines 14–18) appears to concern what I would call *symbola* procedure "proper" (κὰ(τ) τᾶς συνβολᾶς, 15), namely when each party to a dispute is resident in his own city. The contrast is with the previous case where one party is a local citizen and the other is a metic in that citizen's home city: in such cases, the metic is the "foreigner" and the other party is the "citizen." In this latter case, although the parties are from different *poleis*, each litigant is equally a citizen, and neither is a foreigner—not in the way that a metic is, who will be judged under a form of local legal process.[102] In this case the *damiourgoi*—as opposed to the foreigner in the previous scenario—are to choose the judges. *Damiourgos* is a magistrate, and the plural here could mean that *damiourgoi* from each city would take part in the selection of judges from both cities.[103] The number of judges is probably to be inferred as being the same as in the previous scenario, and the oath to be sworn specified only in this latter scenario because, for cases under the previous scenario in which only one of the litigants was a foreigner, local rules would have governed the applicable oath.

If my interpretation is correct, one noteworthy feature of this *symbola* agreement is that, aside from cases involving metics, it seems to have provided for a tribunal separate from the local courts of either city. This contrasts with at least some *symbola* to which the Athenians were a party, which seem to have provided for protected foreigners to sue and be sued in the local courts. Our evidence is admittedly thin, but this is the implication of the Aristotle passage quoted above (*Pol.* 3, 1275a7–14). The provision for a separate tribunal in the west Lokris case indicates that the two communities considered themselves able to cooperate repeatedly in the resolution of disputes between their respective citizens; that is, able to have a common view of justice that would benefit the joint community as a whole, no matter which *polis*'s citizen won a particular suit. Their agreement on common rules for determining metic status is another noteworthy marker of legal cooperation. This implication of mutually beneficial justice and common substantive and procedural laws likely was a result of, and in turn contributed to, an overarching group identity among Oiantheans and Chaleians, which I discussed in the previous chapter.

As with the Ionian *synthekai*, the agreement here appears to have been agreed between cities that already had a relationship based on more than commerce alone. And the forms of public litigation provided for here must have had a further socializing effect on both Oiantheans and Chaleians. If it is true, as seems likely, that the officials from the two cities would usually have chosen a jury consisting of a roughly equal number of judges from each, the courtroom speeches on either side frequently would have appealed to common identity and shared ethics and ideology, not to the biases of one city. Each side also would have argued that its legal claim accorded with the international rules agreed to by the two communities. In this way, the practice of *symbola* litigation would have reinforced the institution. Economic considerations, broadly speaking, were undoubtedly an important factor in the formation and success of this agreement, but they do not fully explain why and how the agreement could be effective in practice.

Conclusion

In everyday life and language, *symbola* were tokens of identity and signs of close relations, used to mark, affirm, and strengthen attachments. *Symbola* agreements between cities played the same roles. Attachments with foreigners from outside a community often began as primarily personal matters between individual people or families, shaped and played out largely within the forms and rules of *xenia*. As cities became more institutionalized through the sixth and fifth centuries and beyond, so did relations with foreigners, in ways that included the formalities and informalities of proxeny. As citizenship became reified as a privileged status within each *polis*, many cities included among those privileges full access to the *polis*'s legal apparatus. Close but informal relations persisted between citizens of different cities. And it must quickly have become obvious to many that the formal barriers between communities encouraged by strict rules of citizenship needed to be counteracted by new modes of formal international connection. *Symbola* were an official means of joining communities often already tied by informal bonds of identity, history, religion, and affection. And while cities entered into *symbola* in part to avoid or cure legal and economic problems that could regularly arise between communities, *symbola*'s ability to solve such problems was always connected to the social factors encouraging their use. In the next chapter, we will see how the forms and use of *symbola* developed in the Greek world from the fifth to the second centuries, maintaining their social aspect while reflecting changing attitudes toward international judicial practices.

8

Symbola from the Athenian Empire to the Hegemony of Rome

Continuing the history

Symbola were not treaties between states designed to achieve purely economic results. They were agreements between two communities of people, usually based on already close relationships with recognized histories, intended to solidify those relationships and bring the communities even closer. This is the basic view of *symbola* I laid out in the previous chapter, where I also began tracing a history of those agreements. Here I continue that history, following it to the time when the Roman empire absorbed most of the Greek world. Following *symbola* across historical contexts from the fifth to the second centuries, we will find a few developments in their use. But we will see they never ceased to be a way for Greeks in separate, juridically bounded communities to break down those boundaries in their search for legal justice.

The history of *symbola* presents us with an evidentiary problem familiar to historians of Greece: the predominance of the Athenians in the surviving evidence. Therefore much of this chapter deals with *symbola* to which the Athenians were a party, during the century or so from about 460 to 360. But, as we have already seen, *symbola* agreements were never a narrowly Athenian phenomenon, and entirely non-Athenian evidence for them begins to predominate by the end of the fourth century. Athenian and non-Athenian examples alike reveal close interactions between group identities and Greek juridical thinking.

The Delian League and Athenian Empire

Any consideration of Athenian use of *symbola* agreements in the fifth century must place them in the context of Athenian imperial hegemony in those years. And it must wade in, however hesitantly, to the long debate over the "character" of that hegemony, whether it was, in a view contested by Geoffrey de Ste. Croix, "a selfish despotism, detested by the subjects whom it oppressed and exploited."[1] Some have seen the use of *symbola* as a typical facet of Athenian imperialism, a

Laws of All the Greeks. Jesse James, Oxford University Press. © Jesse James 2026.
DOI: 10.1093/9780197838556.003.0010

tool of their "detested despotism." But I argue that the continuing use of *symbola* agreements even at the height of empire shows us an Athenian hegemony that was not simply enforced, but reinforced. Not only enforced by heavy-handed, violent terrorism on those who resisted Athenian supremacy, but more often reinforced with the virtual cooperation of, and meaningful support from, people making their way within one more layer of hierarchy in an already stratified world. The use of a *symbola* agreement by two cities is consistent with, even evidence of, positive, harmonious relations, positive enough that the decision makers of both cities wanted at least some private disputes involving their own citizens decided by judges from the other city. Athenian use of *symbola* throughout the fifth century therefore highlights the picture painted by scholars who emphasize the variability and (in some respects) even subtlety of judicial relations under Athenian imperial hegemony.[2]

Again, none of this is to deny the blatantly imperial ways in which the Athenians used law and courts to practice and enforce their international hegemony. The judicial aspect of that hegemony was emphasized by the anonymous author known among scholars as the "Old Oligarch." Writing perhaps in the 420s, he criticizes the Athenians "because they force the allies to sail to Athens for trials."[3] We know of some rules requiring transfer of certain classes of lawsuits (or appeals) from allied cities to Athenian courts. For example, Antiphon's speech "On the Murder of Herodes," dating perhaps to the 410s, states that at that time the Mytileneans were not permitted to sentence someone to death "without [the approval of] the Athenians."[4] But while the Old Oligarch's claim could be read sweepingly as describing a root-and-branch Athenian seizure of allies' entire legal systems, other evidence makes clear that Athenian imperial judicial measures could be severe but were always limited. And *symbola* should be distinguished even from these.

The specific imperial legal enactments we know of did not compel citizens of allied cities to travel to Athens to litigate most cases. Known measures include the decree imposing rules for the government of Erythrai, on the central western coast of Asia Minor; the decree setting new terms for the city of Chalkis, on Euboia, to remain in the Athenian alliance; Kleinias's decree regarding collection of imperial tribute; and the decree (or decrees) imposing the use of Athenian measuring standards for payment of tribute.[5] The Erythrai regulations, for example, established penalties for certain serious crimes such as murder, but seem to envision the trials in such cases as being held in Erythrai.[6] In Chalkis the Athenians appear to have left most cases under local jurisdiction, while permitting appeal to jury courts in Athens for cases where the penalty was exile, death, or disfranchisement.[7] Even the "standards" decree, often taken as a sign of Athenian "micro-management" of the empire, specifies merely that imperial officials known as *hellenotamiai* were to be tried in Athens if they violated the decree; local officials within allied cities were presumably to be tried locally.[8] The specificity of each measure makes clear there was no sweeping rule such as that "all cases within Athenian or allied jurisdiction are to be heard in Athens." And all of them should be distinguished from the friendly, balanced terms of *symbola* agreements.

In contrast to Athenian techniques for managing the empire on a large scale or dealing with intransigent allies as political collectives, *symbola* were understood as granting certain mutual protections to people in foreign lands. This point will be demonstrated by the specific examples examined below. But it is supported generally by a statement in a speech attributed by our manuscripts to Andocides that urges the ostracism of Alcibiades.[9] The year is 415, after the violent Athenian invasion of Melos and the Olympic festival of 416 but before the disastrous Athenian expedition to Sicily or the scandal involving the Eleusinian Mysteries and the desecration of the herms. The speaker catalogs the many ways that Alcibiades has shown disrespect for the laws. For example, he commissioned work by the famous scenery painter Agatharchos of Samos, but then held Agatharchos in confinement for three months, forcing him to keep painting.[10] The speaker laments this imprisonment of the citizen of an Athenian imperial subject as a violation of the Athenians' judicial treaties: "And with other *poleis* we agree in our *symbola* [ἐν τοῖς συμβόλοις] that it isn't permitted to lock up or tie up a free man. And if someone violates this rule we lay a heavy penalty upon them. But when this man did such a thing no one brought any private or public claim against him."[11] He claims that at least some Athenian *symbola* agreements contained a clause forbidding seizure of a person; hence this is evidence that *symbola* were seen as a replacement for the customary law of *syla*. This is also one of the few descriptions of a substantive provision of *symbola* in the fifth century. Finally, by invoking *symbola* provisions and Alcibiades's violation of them to prove the outrageousness of Alcibiades's conduct toward a citizen of an allied city, the speaker betrays a conception of *symbola* as agreements intended to prevent such "imperialistic" treatment. *Symbola* here are not judicial tools of a "detested despot" but legal protections against abuse. As we will see, the rest of our evidence is consistent with this picture.

Eleusis

Our earliest evidence for Athenian use of *symbola*, from the first few decades of the Delian League, does not reveal them as instruments of Athenian oppression. It is a marble post inscribed on all four sides with rules concerning the Eleusinian Mysteries in Attica, dating between 475 and 450.[12] The highly fragmentary upper lines of Face A appear to concern use of the sanctuary by people from outside of Attica. The final fourteen lines of the face survive more fully.

> . . . [30] And exact a penalty. [And if it does not] surrender the debtor/accused, [it may not use] the rites. If it main[tains] that he was not summoned in the *po*[*lis*] . . . going unjust[. . .] . . . [35] later the [council] . . . Of Athenians (none) is to be expelled from these *poleis* nor anywhere to be disturbed except for those convicted in a local court or discovered among [40] the enemy. Whichever of the *poleis* is not willing [to agree to these measures], let them litigate with Athenians from ["in accordance with"?] *symbola*.[13]

These rules prescribe how the home cities of non-Athenian worshippers should treat Athenians accused of illegal behavior in their territories.[14] They seem designed to replace the terms of *symbola* agreements between Athens and those cities. This is why the clause at the end allows cities to opt out of these terms and follow those of their respective *symbola* agreements instead.

In other words, if there are private disputes between Athenians and citizens of cities that have *symbola* agreements with the Athenians, the other cities can permit those disputes to be settled in one of two ways: according to the procedures outlined earlier in the inscription or according to existing *symbola* agreements. The concern is not with "public law" disputes between two governments: it is with how people will be treated in domestic legal systems. And note the apparent concern here with *syla* procedures: the Athenians do not want people in other cities to permit seizure of Athenians except under specified conditions. Because *symbola* agreements were also designed partly to prevent *syla*, the terms of such agreements were an acceptable alternative to *syla* restrictions set forth in this inscription.[15]

The Eleusis inscription does not tell us about the specific content of *symbola* agreements. But it implies that some cities whose citizens wanted to participate in the Mysteries had *symbola* with the Athenians. Gauthier is therefore probably wrong that the Athenians' fifth-century *symbola* were all with distant communities (1972, 201). Some *symbola* even at this early date were probably with nearby cities, those whose citizens were most likely to come celebrate the Mysteries. The inscription also suggests that, in the first half of the fifth century, Athenian *symbola* likely were not overtly "imperial" in tone. Not only because the early Delian League did not have a strong imperial cast, but also because some *symbola* at this time were probably with cities that did not belong to the League at all, including cities near Attica in the northern Peloponnese, the Megarid, Boiotia, Phokis, and Lokris. This is implied by the inscription's discussion, on Face B, of the international truce that is to be in place during celebration of the

Mysteries. That truce was necessary only because it was possible that Athenians would sometimes be at war with the home cities of people coming to Athens to celebrate the Mysteries.

The connection these rules imply between *symbola* and celebrating the Mysteries is meaningful. As I argued in Chapter 4, religious worship and legal dispute resolution were both effects of and, in turn, drivers of social identity formation among Athenians and other Greeks. For example, Ionians probably were inducted into the Mysteries in significant numbers, and they of course *were* distant from Athens and were members of the Delian League. Long bound to each other by religious practice centered on the Panionion, and having already perhaps made *symbola* agreements among themselves, in the 470s the Ionian cities became part of the League.[16] At the same time that the Athenians were presenting themselves as leaders of "panhellenic" military defense against Persia, this inscription from Eleusis is evidence of the degree to which the Mysteries had also moved toward becoming panhellenic.[17] And although Athenians could use religion in heavy-handed "imperial" ways, religious worship, mutual defense, and *symbola* often would have worked together in forming social identities; these in turn would have made the exercise of judicial rights guaranteed by *symbola* less biased and, on the whole, more fair.[18]

Athenians and Phaselites

Our earliest evidence for an Athenian *symbola* agreement with a specific city reinforces the picture of imperial-era Athenian *symbola* as signs of especially friendly relations rather than tools of detested despotism. It is an inscribed Athenian decree for the Phaselites, citizens of a Pamphylian *polis* near the border with Lycia on the southern coast of Asia Minor (see Map 8 on the facing page). Inhabiting a city reportedly founded by Rhodians in the seventh century perhaps because of its favorable position with regard to trade between the Aegean, Cyprus, the Levant, and Egypt, the Phaselites were heavily dependent on trade. Their coins, for example, bore the image of one end of a ship. And the Phaselites are one of the twelve cities Herodotus lists as co-founders of Naukratis, a maritime trading settlement on the Nile delta.[19] Likely from the 420s (although it has often been dated to the 450s) survives an Athenian decree modifying the terms of a *symbola* agreement between the Athenians and Phaselites, a decree much studied for the light it may cast on the nature of Athenian imperialism at whichever time it was in fact passed.[20] Phaselis, one of the last Greek cities in Asia Minor to remain allied to Persia after the Persian Wars, was besieged by an Athenian and allied force led by Cimon shortly before the battle of the Eurymedon in the early 460s. The siege ended peaceably with a Phaselite capitulation brokered

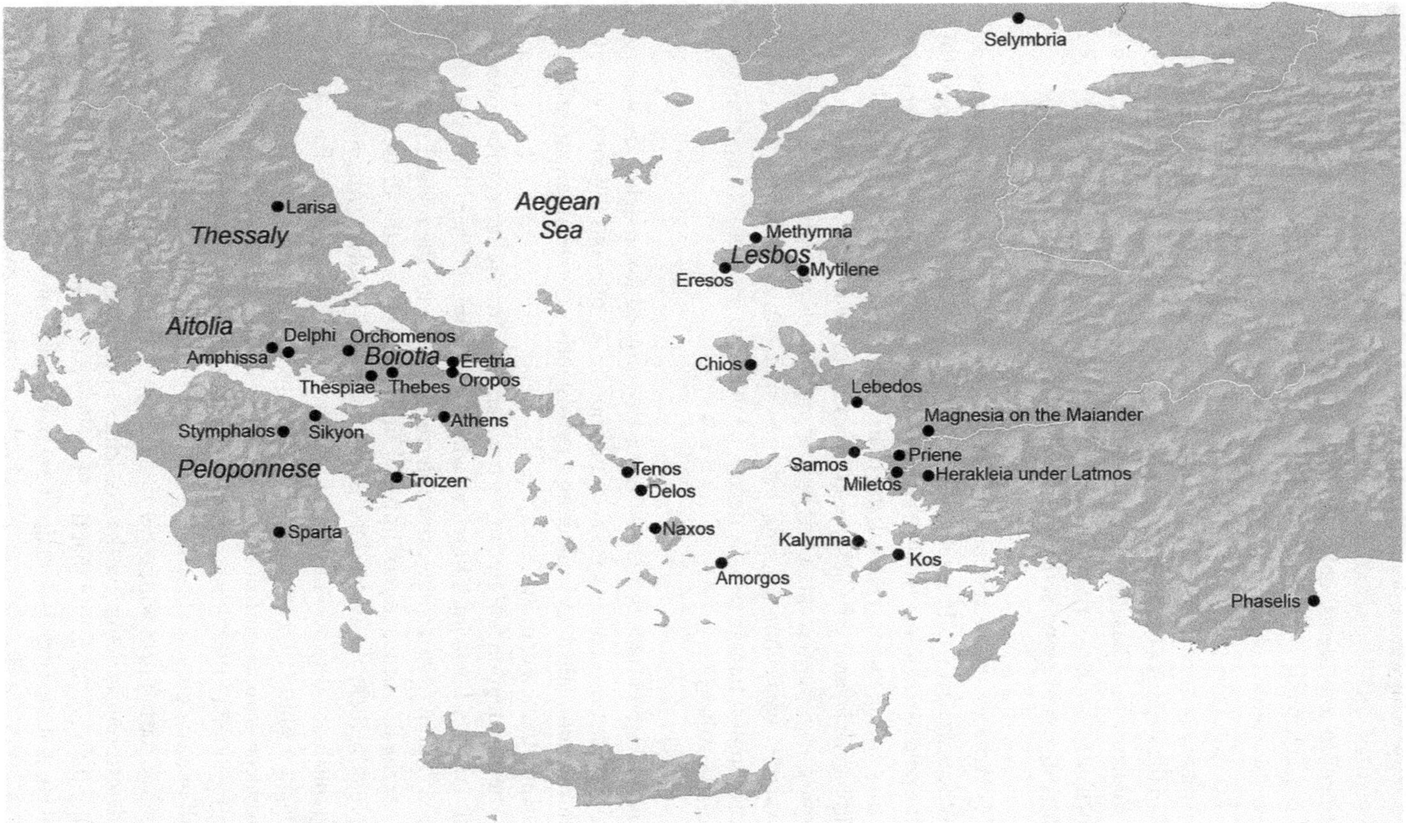

Map 8 Map showing key locations mentioned in this chapter. Map by R. Salem.

by Chians, who were allies of the Athenians and old friends of the Phaselites; a payment of ten talents from the Phaselites to the Athenians; and Phaselite commitment to join the Athenian expedition.[21] The Phaselite surrender may have been accompanied by a regime change at Phaselis from oligarchy to democracy. This would help explain how the city went from being consistently loyal to the Persians before the 460s to having apparently quite good relations with the Athenians, even after an Athenian siege of the city: local propaganda may have styled the siege as a liberation.[22]

We know the Phaselites at some point made a *symbola* agreement with the Athenians because our surviving decree modifies a previous treaty. The main substantive provisions, starting at line 5 of the inscription, are as follows:

> [5] Write up the decree for the Phaselites. Whatever legal dispute arises in Athens against any Phaselite in Athens, the trial is to take place before [10] the polemarch, just as (is done) for the Chians, and nowhere else. As for other cases arising under *symbolai*, the trials are to be in accordance with the existing *symbolai*. [. .?? . .][15] is to eliminate/prevent/remove [. .?? . .]. If any other magistrate accepts a case against any Phaselite in Athens, if he declares a verdict against him the verdict shall be void. [20] And if anyone (i.e., of the magistrates) transgresses the decree, he shall owe ten thousand drachmas sacred to Athena.[23]

This translation reflects a Greek text I have argued for in detail elsewhere. By slightly moving a comma from its position in all previous editions, we reveal a more grammatical text reflecting a consistently positive Athenian attitude toward and treatment of the Phaselites.[24]

The punctuation reflected in my translation shows the decree to be concerned with lawsuits involving Phaselites who are in Athens when the legal dispute arises.[25] Contrary to some prior interpretations, with the revised punctuation we see the decree makes no "imperial" impositions upon the Phaselites: it does not require them to travel to Athens for any lawsuits involving Athenians. Rather, it grants a privilege to Phaselites in Athens, permitting them to have any suits brought against them in Athens heard in the polemarch's court. That this was a privilege is apparent from the decree's clarification that it was the same treatment granted to the Chians, who were loyal and favored allies of the Athenians until about a decade after this decree was probably inscribed.[26] Granting this privilege harmonizes with other pro-Phaselite features of the decree, including its description as being "for the Phaselites"; being written in the Ionic alphabet, rather than the Attic; and that the Phaselites paid to inscribe it. Furthermore, it is likely that the large 10,000 drachma fine applied only to any *Athenian* official who violated the decree: such fines became relatively common in Athens in the late fifth century. This decree is not a flexing of Athenian imperial muscle but a favor done to bring a friendly city even closer.[27]

We do not know the terms of the original *symbola* agreement modified by this surviving decree. It must have permitted lawsuits between Athenians and Phaselites, in Athens and almost certainly in Phaselis as well. But we can only guess what kinds of suits were permitted and in what venues or by what procedures they were to be resolved. All we know is that it did *not* specify the polemarch's court as the sole venue for such suits in Athens, since that provision is added here. I know of no evidence to support Gauthier's proposal that the original *symbola* provided for suits between Phaselites and Athenians to be heard by a single judicial official with power to hear and decide cases on his own without referring them to a jury. On his view, the new provision that cases must be brought to the polemarch would mean that they would now, for the first time, be heard by a full citizen jury.[28] But such an important change—that charges previously heard in "bench" trials before a single judge would now be contested in front of a full democratic jury of Athenian citizens—would surely be spelled out in the decree. In fifth-century Athens some suits *could* be decided by an official acting alone, but these were almost always limited to disputes valued below relatively small amounts such as ten drachmas.[29] This decree seems worded broadly enough to include such disputes ("Whatever legal dispute arises"). One of its goals may have been to simplify and centralize litigation in Athens for Phaselites by eliminating an Athenian's right to bring a Phaselite to "small claims court" for minor legal squabbles.[30] In the fourth century, the default rule in Athens was that disputes under *symbola* were brought to the officials known as *thesmothetai*, but it would be rash to assume this was already the rule in the fifth century.[31] In any case, nothing in the decree suggests that Phaselites did not already have a right to a jury trial in Athens under their original *symbola* with the Athenians.

This decree is evidence that Athenians and Phaselites became closer through the middle decades of the fifth century: from being a subject of the Persian empire, the Phaselites had first joined the Delian League, then entered into a *symbola* with the Athenians, and now, in the 420s, began to receive even more favorable treatment. This growing attachment probably indicates formation of a group identity between citizens of the two cities, due in part simply to greater contact between Phaselites and Athenians. After the Phaselites joined the Delian League, Athens and Piraeus probably became the main focus of Phaselite trade, especially under the legal regime of the *symbola* agreement.[32] Socialization might also have occurred between Phaselite and Athenian soldiers, starting with the Eurymedon campaign. And the Chians, it seems, served as a special link between Athenians and Phaselites. They not only brokered the original peace between the cities; the Chian *symbola* agreement with the Athenians served as the model for our decree's amendment. The especially positive relations between

Athenians and Chians, demonstrated above all by the remarkable practice of Athenians wishing well for the Chians in their prayers at public events, may have further encouraged Phaselites already friendly to the Chians also to have positive feelings for Athenians.[33] Hence it may be not only that Phaselites developed some form of "Delian League" identity connecting them to Athenians; there may have arisen an even more special "Athens—Chios—Phaselis" identity of three cities bound, among other things, by their joint defense and a mutually beneficial trading relationship.[34] A Phaselite–Athenian identity could also have been facilitated by the prominence of the cult of Athena in both *poleis*. Two of the earliest known inscriptions from Phaselis are dedications to Athena *Polias* from the fifth century, and a fifth-century inscribed stone found in Piraeus marks the grave of "Athenodotos son of Iatrokles, a Phaselite": Athenodotos may have been named in honor of Athena, or even of Athens.[35]

The common identity formation I propose between Phaselites and Athenians is speculative but based partly on the studies presented in Chapter 3 suggesting that increasing contact can lead to the formation of common social identities. The contact, however, should be "positive": if our evidence indicated that Athenians from the beginning imposed restrictions on Phaselites that they strongly resented, one would not expect increased contact in the framework of such a negatively valenced relationship to build a common social identity; we would expect it to result more often in alienation.[36] Yet it seems that here the relationship was positive. To the evidence already presented, I add Thucydides's report that in the winter of 430/29 an Athenian squadron cruised the coast of Caria and Lycia, not only to collect tribute but also to put that tribute to good use by protecting merchant ships from Phaselis and Phoinike from Peloponnesian piracy. If this was anything more than a one-off stunt by an Athenian general, it is easy to see how Phaselite merchants (and their personal networks back home) could quickly become loyal to the Athenians.[37]

It might be objected, against my speculation, that not only do we lack much direct evidence of a strong social identity between Phaselites and Athenians, but we also have evidence (albeit from many decades later) of Athenian prejudice *against* Phaselites, in the opening of the speech *Against Lakritos* attributed to Demosthenes (no. 35):

> The Phaselites are achieving nothing new, gentlemen of the jury, but instead just what they normally do. For those men are the best at borrowing money in the *emporion* and then, when they take it and sign the shipping contract, they immediately forget the contracts and the laws and the fact that they have to return what they took, and they think that, if they do return it, it's as though they've lost their own personal property; and instead of returning it they come up with fancy arguments and counter-pleas and excuses; and they are the most

> useless and unjust people. And here is the proof: while many people come to your *emporion*, both Greeks and barbarians, more lawsuits each session involve Phaselites than all the others put together. This is what kind of men they are. — [Dem.] 35.1–2[38]

This passage is a direct attack on the defendant as a Phaselite. But in that respect it is merely typical of Athenian oratory, of which personal attack, *diabole*, is a common feature, whose factual accuracy should be the object of deepest skepticism.[39] Such attacks could be good for a laugh and likely induced some bias in the audience against an individual or group. But this attack, as phrased, does not even purport to reflect a preexisting Athenian bias against Phaselites. The speaker does not say, "This man is a Phaselite, and we all know how awful *they* are!" Instead he argues, "This man is a Phaselite. They are very shady businessmen. The proof of this is that they have more lawsuits in Athens than any other foreigners." If any Athenian bias is being exploited here, it is against those who "come up with fancy arguments and counter-pleas and excuses."

The speaker immediately goes on, after this passage, to further undermine any attempt to use this speech as evidence of Athenian bias against Phaselites, suggesting that Athenians were in fact generally trusting of Phaselites. We see this in his description of how he himself came to have a business relationship with a Phaselite. He had no previous familiarity with the defendant Lakritos, or with his brother Artemo (with whom he actually made the contract in question); they were introduced by a mutual friend, Thrasymedes. Yet the speaker nevertheless blithely trusted "that they were honorable men and would do what they said."[40] Understood properly, this passage is evidence not of Athenian bias against Phaselites but its contrary—high baseline trust between Athenians and Phaselites, as well as the enormous amount of business that Phaselites must have been doing in Athens in the mid-fourth century: so much that they could be accused of participating frequently in lawsuits there.

Thucydides 1.77

A much-discussed passage in Thucydides reinforces the impression that *symbola* agreements between Athenians and their allies were reciprocal and even-handed, including with tribute-paying allies who did not receive the special treatment enjoyed by Chians and Phaselites. In 432, during the assembly at Sparta at which the Peloponnesian allies were invited to voice their complaints against the Athenians (discussed in Chapter 1), Athenian ambassadors who happened to be in Sparta on other business were granted permission to address the assembly to defend Athenian behavior. As evidence that the Athenians acted more fairly and moderately than would most cities in their position, yet did not get credit for it, the ambassadors described interstate lawsuits between Athenians and citizens of their allied cities:

> And so we certainly think that whether we are acting moderately would be revealed by others getting what we have. But a bad reputation rather than praise has inequitably encircled us as a result of our equity. And although we're disadvantaged (ἐλασσούμενοι) in the lawsuits conducted against our allies in accordance with *symbola* agreements, and have rendered decisions in our own city under fair laws, we're considered to love litigating (φιλοδικεῖν). And none of them [*viz.* "our accusers"] looks at those who have an empire anywhere else and blames *them*, even though they're less moderate toward their subjects than we are. — Thuc. 1.76.4–77.2[41]

The meaning of the middle sentence of this passage ("And although we're disadvantaged . . . ") has been relentlessly debated. I take the Athenians to be pointing out an irony: those accused of loving to litigate (φιλοδικεῖν) presumably love it because they expect to win; but Athenians have no advantage in trials against citizens of allied cities, whether held abroad or at Athens; so they do not expect to win and certainly do not enjoy going to court![42] I also agree with the interpretation of Ste. Croix: the *symbola* agreements in force between the Athenians and their allies provided for certain interstate lawsuits to be brought in courts of one of the two cities and some to be brought in the other; the Athenians claim here to be abiding by those provisions, and the "lawsuits conducted against our allies in accordance with *symbola* agreements" were mostly brought in allied cities. Hence, like the Phaselis decree, this passage is not evidence of Athenian "legal imperialism" in the form of transferring all *symbola* lawsuits to Athenian courts.[43] The likely kernel of historical truth here—that Athenians were accused by allies of enjoying litigating in court, *philodikein*—suggests that lawsuits involving Athenians under *symbola* agreements were a familiar sight in allied cities of the empire. Like the similar accusation against the Phaselites discussed above, this stereotype probably resulted less from a special Athenian litigiousness than from the commercial centrality and dominance of Athens and Athenian involvement in many business dealings throughout the empire.[44]

Athenians, Mytileneans, Selymbrians

A *symbola* agreement between Athens and Mytilene, on the island of Lesbos, is referred to in an Athenian decree perhaps dating to the 410s restoring many rights the Athenians had stripped from the Mytileneans after their failed revolt from the empire in 428.[45] The highly fragmentary inscription mentions "being sued by Athenians and suing them in accordance with the *symbola* agreements that existed previously."[46] The imperfect verb "existed" (ἔσαν) indicates that the *symbola* were not in force at the time of this decree (we would then expect a present tense), but that the decree is restoring the judicial relations in force before the revolt. This clause of the decree is therefore in line with its apparent grant of autonomy to the Mytileneans (line 11) and is further evidence the Athenians did not generally force citizens of allied states to come to Athens for lawsuits between themselves and Athenians; if that were the case, it is hard to see what advantage the Mytileneans would have gained from a restoration of their *symbola* with Athens.

We see a similar situation in an agreement between the Athenians and Selymbrians from 407, restoring rights to the Selymbrians after their revolt from Athens in the wake of the Athenian oligarchic revolution of 411.[47] Lying on the northern European shore of the Propontis, Selymbria was entered in 408 by an Athenian force led by Alcibiades, who also proposed this ratification of the agreement he made with the Selymbrians. Importantly, some Selymbrians opened the city to Alcibiades and his forces, and the city surrendered with no fighting after Alcibiades announced to his men that Athenians were not to bear arms against Selymbrians. A pro-Athenian faction must have come back into influence in Selymbria in the wake of that surprisingly peaceful confrontation, and this friendly decree the following year would have further encouraged reciprocal Selymbrian goodwill toward Athenians.[48]

The *symbola* provision of this decree is noteworthy in applying explicitly both to disputes among individual people and to those between a person and the community. After limiting the ability of Athenians to be compensated for property confiscated by the Selymbrians during the years of revolt, the agreement states: "And whatever other legal claims existed previously, either belonging to private individuals against private individuals, or belonging to a private individual against the community, or belonging to the community against a private individual, or if any other one arises, they should settle those with each other. But whatever they cannot agree on, the lawsuits shall be in accordance with *symbola*."[49] That the disputes envisaged here are between Athenians and Selymbrians is indicated both by the fact that the quoted provision immediately follows an explicit mention of Athenians and by the reference to *symbola*.[50] Already by the late fifth century, then, at least some *symbola* agreements provided procedures, either explicitly or implicitly, for judicial resolution of legal disputes between foreigners and the local government.[51] The decree's main concern may be with disputes arising in Selymbria in the wake of the political changes there, but the reference to *symbola*, which so far as we know were always mutual, should be taken to indicate that Selymbrians could also sue in Athens.[52]

The *symbola* procedures might have applied to the confiscation cases mentioned earlier, and lawsuits between an Athenian individual and the community (*koinon*) of the Selymbrians may have arisen from those cases as well as, for example, from relations between the *polis* of Selymbria and individual Athenians, such as creditors and contractors of public works. Later in this chapter we will see just such a dispute (although much later and involving different cities) decided under the procedures of a *symbola* agreement.[53]

Rather than punish the Selymbrians for their prior revolt, the Athenians made an agreement that seems to limit the legal liabilities of Selymbrians. This treatment may be a symptom of a generally "softening" Athenian approach to their allies in the wake of disaster in Sicily, unrest at home, and continuing concern with securing the sailing route for grain from the Black Sea.[54] The latter consideration might have been prominent in the minds of some Athenians who voted to ratify Alcibiades's agreement with the Selymbrians, happy to have the dispute resolution procedures of a *symbola* agreement in place with this strategically located city. As I have emphasized, however, a right to legal procedure could be little comfort if that procedure was going to be managed by uncooperative officials and heard by hostile jurors. The terms of this decree and the conditions of the Selymbrian return to the Athenian alliance suggest that this *symbola* was also a token of friendship—even if a reinstated friendship—between Selymbrians and Athenians. This impression is reinforced by the decree's penultimate provisions, granting Athenian *proxenos* status to two Selymbrians, one of whom was belatedly inheriting it from his father: "[and there shall be] proxeny for Apollodoros ju[st as] for his father." In this way the inscription closes by reminding its reader of a history of close relations between Selymbrians and Athenians, engaging the affective synapses of family and tradition.[55]

Athenians and Evagoras of Salamis

Around the same time as their rapprochement with the Selymbrians, the Athenians made an alliance with Evagoras, king of Salamis in Cyprus, far off at the eastern edge of the Greek world. Three badly damaged fragments of an inscribed decree record the pact. They mention a grant of Athenian citizenship to Evagoras as well as a *symbola* agreement and the handling of lawsuits.[56] Evagoras, eulogized in detail by Isocrates in an eponymous speech (Isoc. 9), claimed descent from Telamon, legendary Argonaut, king of the island of Salamis off the Attic coast, and father to Ajax and Teucer (Paus. 1.3.2). After having seized, in about 411, the throne of Cypriot Salamis back from a short-lived Phoenician dynasty that had usurped it from his family, Evagoras sought to expand Salaminian influence and pursued hellenizing, and in particular pro-Athenian, policies, both political and cultural. Isocrates (9.51) reports that many Greeks fled to Salamis, apparently in the aftermath of the Peloponnesian War; they included at least Andocides, Nicophemus, and Conon. Evagoras was instrumental in helping the latter build part of the Persian fleet that, under the command of Conon and Pharnabazus, defeated the Peloponnesian forces off Knidos in 394.[57]

The document that survives, which is primarily an honorary decree, does not appear to have enough space for the full terms of a *symbola* agreement with Evagoras. It must have referred briefly to that agreement, simply to approve or ratify it, or perhaps to modify or clarify a term (as with the decree for the Phaselites discussed above).[58] Circumstances suggest that Evagoras and the Athenians sought a *symbola* agreement not only for its legal and economic effects but also for social and psychological reasons. Our sources emphasize the legendary connections of Evagoras's family with the island of Salamis and with Athens; Pausanias even reports that Evagoras considered himself Athenian.[59] Excavations in Salamis on Cyprus have uncovered evidence of post-Bronze Age revival as early as the eleventh century, perhaps confirming a grain of truth in the legend of Teucer's settlement. They have also found signs of continuous trade with mainland Greece from at least the seventh century, with evidence in particular of trade with and artistic influence from Athens. For example, a royal grave contained eighth-century Athenian ceramics; and Athenian "SOS" amphorae, as well as black-figure and then red-figure vases, indicate continuing Athens-Salamis trade in the late sixth and early fifth centuries.[60]

The cult of Aglauros may demonstrate a further connection between Athens and Salamis on Cyprus, a connection that could have both facilitated and strengthened relations when Evagoras led Salamis. Aglauros (also known as Agraulos) played a significant role in the legendary early history of Athens and in certain religious festivals as "one of the most important figures of Athenian mythology" (Sourvinou-Inwood 2011, 108). A complex pattern of myth and ritual developed around her. In myth, Aglauros was the daughter of Kekrops and earliest priestess of Athena who sacrificed herself by suicide to save the city. In Athenian cult, she was patroness of the young soldiers-in-training known as ephebes; she had a cave sanctuary on the east slope of the Acropolis; enjoyed a dedicated priestess; and received cult (with Athena *Polias*) in the very old Attic festivals of the Plynteria and Kallynteria. Significantly for our purposes, by the fourth century at the latest the priesthood of Aglauros was supplied by the Athenian *genos* named the Salaminioi.[61]

The only other site of Aglauros cult known to scholars is Salamis on Cyprus, although the evidence for this is late. The third century CE neoplatonist philosopher Porphyry, in his pro-vegetarian tract *De Abstinentia*, uses examples of human sacrifice to argue against claims that eating meat is defensible because of its connection to religious sacrifice. One of his examples of human sacrifice is from the cult of "Agraulos" in Salamis on Cyprus. In the early version of the rite, he explains, a human was sacrificed to Agraulos, the daughter of Kekrops. The victim was led in by the ephebes, and ran around the altar three times before a priest struck his throat with a spear and then burnt him whole.[62] Note three key similarities with the myth and cult of Aglauros in Athens: (1) she is the daughter of Kekrops; (2) the rite is closely associated with ephebes; and (3) a human is sacrificed. Scholars have debated whether and to what extent the Athenian *genos* Salaminioi was historically connected to the island of Salamis, but have given little consideration to the *genos*'s possible connection to Salamis on Cyprus. Guía (2005), however, emphasizes the likelihood of a real Aglauros connection, suggesting that the adoption of an Aglauros cult in Salamis on Cyprus was based on links of commerce and *xenia* between citizens of that *polis* and Athenians.

The religious connection of the Aglauros cult could have fed a network of social and economic connections between the distant communities. This is speculation, but such connections could help explain how Evagoras, apparently immediately after seizing power in Salamis, was able to obtain the favorable treatment at Athenian hands that the decree reflects, as well as the positive relations with Athenians that soon resulted in a "colony" of Athenian expatriates in Salamis and continued throughout his long reign.[63] In short, the Athenians and Salaminians had a special connection rooted in cult and legend, a connection that could be emphasized, nourished, and exploited when other circumstances permitted.[64] In the late fifth century, this connection may have provided the foundation upon which the institutions of a *symbola* agreement could function effectively, put into practice by communities of people connected not only by commerce but by religious and historical identity.[65]

Athenians and Samians: the "Samos stele"

The Samians, a traditionally powerful Ionian community occupying a large island just off the west coast of Asia Minor, were founding members of the Delian League. Although they had pressed against Athenian hegemonic interference in their affairs in 440, from the time of a pro-Athenian "democratic" revolution on Samos in 412 the Samians were, in Hornblower's words, "obstinately and heroically loyal to Athens right down to the end of the [Peloponnesian] war" (2002, 198). This loyalty is the context of three Athenian decrees for Samians near and shortly after the end of the Peloponnesian War.

All three decrees were inscribed on a marble *stele* placed on the Athenian Acropolis. The first dates to 405, after the final major Athenian defeat of the war, at Aigospotamoi, but before the Athenians or Samians surrendered to the

Spartans. The two later decrees affirm the first decree, have it (re)inscribed, and grant honors to a particular Samian.[66] The Athenians honor the Samians for their good services to Athens, grant them autonomy, offer Athenian citizenship to any Samian who wants it, and affirm the validity of their existing *symbola* agreement. As with other examples we have seen, the surviving decree refers to but does not contain the terms of the *symbola* agreement. Instead it simply states, "And concerning any legal disputes that arise among them [*viz.*, the Athenians and Samians], let them defend and prosecute the cases in accordance with the existing *symbolai*."[67]

Certain features of the decree of 405 and its inscription show that it was the product of remarkably warm sentiments among Athenians toward Samians. The decree was proposed not by a single person but by the entire board of *prytaneis*, our only known example of such a procedure being used.[68] It begins by explaining why the Athenians are granting these honors to the Samians: "Because they are fine men (ἄνδρες ἀγαθοί) and eager to do whatever good they can, and because they seem to have done what they have done correctly for both Athenians and Samians; and in exchange for the things they have performed well for the sake of the Athenians and [the fact that] they now value them highly and introduce good things."[69] This is the earliest surviving example of such a "motivation" clause in an Athenian decree. Its presence here could only have fostered the feelings of positive fellowship and group identity reflected in the official terms of the decree, especially the grant of Athenian citizenship. As John Ma suggests, motivating clauses in inscribed decrees create an official truth and provide the decreeing city's narrative of historical events, however generally phrased. The official truth proclaimed here is that the Samians are "fine men," and the historical narrative is that they have done things "correctly" and "well" for the Athenians and themselves.[70]

The public impact and significance of these statements in Athens is shown by several circumstances. The oligarchic junta known as the "Thirty," a group of Athenians installed by the Spartans to rule the city after the final Athenian surrender, apparently found it convenient to destroy the original monument declaring these sentiments. This is the reasonable explanation proposed by scholars for why the decree was inscribed two years later: it was actually a re-inscription to replace a destroyed *stele*.[71] The content of the decree of 405 must have struck the oligarchs as both important *and* offensive. And it was of equal importance to the Athenian democrats in the restored government, who took the trouble and expense of re-inscribing it. The decree's proposal by the full board of *prytaneis* indicates overwhelming popular support. Perhaps many Athenians stepped onto the speaker's platform to address the assembly in support of the measure; or doing so may have been unnecessary because of the raucous shouts of approval from the assembly-goers when the decree was introduced. A further sign of goodwill is how the Samian envoys were treated during their visit: having been picked out for particular praise, they were also offered traveling expenses. As warmly welcomed foreigners, during their time in Athens they must have formed or strengthened personal relationships with well-connected Athenians, thickening the network that bound Athenians and Samians together.

No amount of Athenian goodwill, however, could prevent Spartan capture of Samos and close Spartan control of affairs there, including imposition of a garrison, a board of ten overseers, and a Spartiate harmost, or governor. The democratic regime that had been so loyal to Athens was deposed by the Spartan commander Lysander in 404/03 and replaced by a government run by the anti-Athenian contingent previously expelled in the revolution of 412. It was now the pro-Athenian democrats who fled Samos, some to the mainland of Asia Minor (especially, it seems, Ephesos and Notion) and others undoubtedly to Athens, where they recently had been guaranteed citizenship.[72] The new Samian regime's stance was so pro-Spartan that it not only erected a statue in Olympia to Lysander but also, according to Plutarch (*Lys.* 18.4), changed the name of the major festival of Hera in Samos to "Lysandreia"; and a certain Ion of Samos composed the verses on the statue of Lysander at Delphi that led the enormous array of statues erected there in celebration of the Spartan victory at Aigospotamoi in 405.[73] These facts hint at how meaningful are the words preceding the decrees on the Athenian Samos *stele*: just beneath the largest letters announcing that "Cephisophon of Paiania was secretary," in letters slightly smaller but still much larger than the main text, and displayed on its own two lines, is written "For the Samians, those who were on the side of the *demos* of the Athenians." It is certain that the top two lines, mentioning Cephisophon, were not part of the original decree from 405; it is likely that these next two lines, specifying which Samians the decree is for, were also added only to this later *stele* with the reinscribed decree. The narrowing down to a group of Samians now mattered because the pro-Athenian Samians were no longer in power in Samos.[74]

To understand the potential meanings of *symbola* agreements in this complicated historical context, we must finally consider the visually most prominent element of the *stele* containing the three decrees.[75] The stone is topped by a carved relief, two adult female figures framed by columns and an epistyle. These standing figures are grasping each other's right hands in a *dexiosis* handshake gesture. The figure on the right wears a crested helmet and gorgon medallion, holding a spear with grounded butt-spike while a shield behind her leans against a tree trunk whose branches have been sawn off. The figure on the left holds a tall staff, draped in a sleeveless *peplos*. Based on the content of the decrees beneath, scholars have usually identified these figures as Athena and Hera, the patron goddesses of Athens and Samos, respectively. This is likely correct, the identification of Athena in particular appearing certain based on her trappings, but it has been noted that the other figure's lack of iconography makes identification insecure: from the image alone she could just as well be Demeter, or a human woman. Such relief carvings—Athena in *dexiosis* with another deity—are common in conjunction with Athenian inscribed interstate agreements from the mid-fifth to mid-fourth centuries.[76] Nathan Arrington has argued that representations of touch on funerary sculpture can provoke an empathetic response in the viewer. If we extend his claim to a nonfunerary context, we can surmise that viewers of this monument, especially Athenian and Samian viewers, may have felt a physical, embodied sense of the close connection between Athenians and Samians that the sculpture and the decrees represented.[77]

In his recent study of this *stele*, however, Jaś Elsner emphasizes the image's ambiguity, compounded as he notes by the ambiguity of *dexiosis*. While "everyone, without exception, assumes that *dexiosis* in document reliefs and especially when involving deities is an allegory for agreement, affection, sociability," *dexiosis* is in fact "extremely common in leave-taking scenes, especially in death—above all on relief sculpture." Hence the ambiguity: does this *dexiosis* represent a friendly greeting between the patron goddesses of Athens and Samos, or is Athena saying "farewell" to Hera, recognizing that the island's government has split from the Athenians and sided with the Spartans?[78]

Elsner's larger point in his article, which centers on a rich re-reading and complicating of the Samos *stele*, is that ancient historians have paid too little attention to *images*, and material culture more generally, in attempting to understand Greek and Roman history and culture.[79] We can take even further Elsner's complication of the meaning of the *dexiosis* on this *stele*. In Chapter 7, I discussed the likely social origins of *symbola* agreements in the practice of *xenia* and noted that *dexiosis* was one of its instantiating acts. But *symbola* themselves—and here I mean the small physical tokens—could be necessary for proving one's identity and thereby making possible the *dexiosis* as well as the welcoming attitude behind it. In 403/02, it had arguably become especially important for Athenians to be able to determine which Samians were "on the side of the Athenian *demos*" and hence the intended objects of this decree's goodwill and privileges; the question now was (as it had perhaps to some degree always been), "Are you a good Samian or a bad Samian?" The *dexiosis* depicted on the relief may be a greeting between Athena and Hera, with the latter representing a "good" Samian, one whose loyalty has been demonstrated by some sort of evidence, even if not literally by tokens, *symbola*.[80] If so, this *dexiosis*, implicitly conditioned on confirmation of identity, may hint at how we are to imagine the *symbola* agreement between Athenians and Samians operating after 404: that is, also conditionally. We may speculate that Athenian courts continued to respect the judicial rights of Samians under the *symbola*, but only of those Samians who showed they had consistently supported the Athenian democracy and were not part of the new regime in Samos. Conversely, in Samos the new, oligarchic regime may have entirely rescinded, or simply ignored, the *symbola* agreement with the Athenians.

Reading the Samos *stele* within its complex and changing context thus drives home how delicate group identities could be and the risk of assuming that *polis* identity was most important for any Greek in any situation. The internal turmoil documented for so many communities at different times, such as for Athenians in 411 and 404/03 and for Samians in 412 and 404/03, hints at how fragile and fragmented *polis* identity could be. This is why it does not always suffice to say, for instance, "Athenians identified with Samians in 403 BCE." When our information permits, we have to specify which Athenians and which Samians; or at least acknowledge that intra-*polis* divisions existed and could matter very much. When interpreted in its entirety, this *stele* suggests that Athenian and Samian democrats identified more with each other in 403 than either did with each *polis*'s own oligarchic element.

What role did the *symbola* agreement play in Samian-Athenian relations at the end of the fifth century? I offer two observations. First is that the reaffirmation of the existing *symbola* agreement in the decree of 405, which seems not to have been legally necessary, was primarily a rhetorical strategy of that decree, a means for the Athenian assembly to affirm the special relationship with the Samians. Recall Aristotle's implication that enjoying *symbola* protections was short of but similar to sharing citizenship. The Athenians here seem to agree that the two statuses are akin: even those Samians who choose not to adopt Athenian citizenship, the decree declares reassuringly, will still enjoy their honored status as *symbola* partners and still be special in Athenian eyes.

The *symbola* would also have had more practical effects, encouraging commercial activity between Athenians and Samians and perhaps making that activity more profitable. Transaction costs would be lower, with commercial relations reinforced by informal norms of cooperation and high trust. In case a dispute did arise, a public trial presumably provided for under the *symbola* agreement would have permitted these good relations to be used to rhetorical advantage. A Samian defendant before an Athenian jury, or an Athenian defendant in Samos, could have invoked the special relationship between the two cities. This strategy could have decreased out-group biases against the foreigner and increased the likelihood of a result perceived as fair. Of course the *symbola* agreement did not create most of these positive notions of community identity I am presuming between Athenians and Samians (although it may have played a role, especially in the earlier years), but its provisions would have magnified the effect of those positive feelings.

On the other hand, a pro-oligarchy Samian, one who had perhaps been in exile from 412 to 404 and returned to the island after Lysander's conquest, would have had a more difficult time in an Athenian court as the object of a democratic jury's anti-oligarchic bias. I am not aware of any surviving record of an Athenian trial under such circumstances, but perhaps instructively similar is the case from which survives Antiphon's speech number 5, "On the Murder of Herodes," which I mentioned above. In this case the speaker Euxitheos, from Mytilene on Lesbos, defends his father as a reluctant participant in the revolt of the Mytileneans from the Athenians in 428 and in fact, at bottom, a strong supporter of the Athenians (5.76–79). As Michael Gagarin notes, "the prosecution must have attacked Euxitheos's father in the course of their speech, probably in order to discredit Euxitheos by association and perhaps also to stir up hostility toward Mytilene among the jurors."[81]

Consider also the case of Andocides, an elite and wealthy Athenian who admitted to participating in the sacrilegious defacement of herms in 415, received immunity in exchange for "naming names," yet still went into exile after a new law effectively prevented him from participating in public life. As Andocides himself describes it, he sought to win back the goodwill of the Athenians by supplying oar timbers to the Athenian navy at Samos in 411 or 410. Yet when he returned to Athens to argue in person for his return, the oligarchic regime of the Four Hundred rejected his request and imprisoned him instead (Andoc. 2.11–16). Andocides had not realized the regime in Athens had turned oligarchic while the navy remained democratic, and his assistance to the navy was described by Peisander, a leader among the Four Hundred, as "providing grain and oar timbers to the enemy" (2.14). Andocides's claim to have been damned by his affiliation with the wrong faction of Athenians, in this speech addressed to the assembly, suggests not only that the biased treatment actually occurred but also that he thought his claim of bias at the hands of the Four Hundred would be credible to a democratic audience. In short, both Athenians and non-Athenians believed that aspects of group identity could have a significant effect on how jurors arrived at verdicts.[82]

Just as the Athenians oscillated, between 412 and 403, from democracy to oligarchy to democracy to oligarchy and back to democracy, the Samians oscillated in those same years from anti-Athenian to pro-Athenian to pro-Spartan. And a few years later the islanders turned back to Athens. Presumably after an Athenian, Conon, led a victory over the Spartans at Knidos in 394 and expelled the Spartan *harmosts* from the Ionian cities, the Samians erected a statue of him in the Heraion of Samos (Paus. 6.3.16). This event must have encouraged Athenians and Samians to make use of their legal rights in each other's courts under the *symbola* agreement and contributed to their success at trial. And the *symbola* agreement itself, so long as it existed (and we do not know if or when it ever was retracted or went into abeyance) would have been a stabilizing force, a reminder that Samians and Athenians had agreed to treat each other according to legal rules like those they applied to themselves.

As patchy as our evidence is for the use of *symbola* agreements in the Athenian empire, the picture that evidence adumbrates is not of a direct, harsh tool of imperialism. Most importantly, we have no good evidence that Athenian *symbola* were ever not reciprocal. On the contrary, *symbola* signal positive, friendly relations between Athenians and certain allied cities.[83] Of course the Athenians had overtly imperial legal tools at their disposal by which they imposed and enforced rules directly upon the subjects of their empire. I mentioned them at the beginning of this chapter, and it is helpful to contrast them again with *symbola* as our consideration of imperial Athens comes to a close. Ste. Croix distinguishes three kinds of measures Athenians used to regulate legal relations between Athens and Athenians, on one side, and allied cities and their citizens on the other. His categories are: (i) *symbola* agreements; (ii) rules of imperial administration whose infractions (wherever they occurred) were tried in Athens, whether in a formal court of law or through deliberation of the assembly; and (iii) provisions by which the Athenians interfered directly in the normal administration of justice *within* the allied cities.[84] Unlike *symbola*, the other two categories include the sorts of rules that existed only because there was an empire. Most obvious here are rules concerning the payment of tribute. Three surviving decrees are concerned with tribute assessment. Two of these appear to provide for trial *in Athens* of citizens of allied states who violate their terms.[85] The so-called "standards" decree has been interpreted also to provide for non-Athenian defendants to travel to Athens for trial, but I believe the surviving fragments are better interpreted as providing for such defendants to be tried in their local courts.[86] Ste. Croix includes in his second category the apparent rule that allied cities were fined five talents if an Athenian (or specially protected *proxenos* to the Athenians) was killed in that city.[87] He describes his category (iii), direct Athenian interference with the administration of justice *within* allied cities, as "by far the most important" for administering the empire (1961b, 270). It included trial or appeal to Athens in legal cases that involved either certain severe penalties (death, exile, loss of citizenship) or certain privileged individuals, in particular Athenian citizens or *proxenoi*. In short, the Athenians had means by which they imposed imperial laws and enforced imperial jurisdiction on subject cities, but *symbola* were not one of them.[88]

The fourth century

As in the fifth century, in the fourth century the Athenians were a party to many of the *symbola* agreements for which evidence survives. Our working hypothesis should be that this reflects the biased centrality of Athens in our sources rather than actual frequency of *symbola* agreements throughout the Greek world. We have no independent reason to think *symbola* were used by or associated with Athens more than other cities. But the Athenocentrism of our sources means that the variety of *symbola* practice may have been wider than our meager evidence indicates, one more reason we should not attempt definitive claims about what *symbola* agreements were and were not.

Possible source bias may affect our understanding of fourth-century *symbola* in another manner: it is now that we first see fragments of detailed provisions regarding specific offenses and their penalties. We do not know if such detail was in fact a new development of this period; if it was a largely Athenian development; if it reflects a change in the practice of recording *symbola* agreements (using stone rather than more perishable or more frequently recycled materials); or if it is just an accident of survival. We have only one agreement from the fifth century with detail remotely comparable to what we see in our fourth century evidence, that between Oianthea and Chaleion discussed in the previous chapter, a rare surviving inscription on bronze.

Troizenians, Stymphalians, and Athenians

Two highly fragmentary inscriptions from the first half of the fourth century appear to have memorialized detailed *symbola* agreements between Athenians, on one hand, and citizens of the northeast Peloponnesian cities Troizen and Stymphalos, respectively, on the other.[89] Although it seems that already in the fifth century the scope of *symbola* agreements was not restricted to commercial disputes, these inscriptions are the earliest unmistakable evidence of *symbola* agreements discussing violent tortious or criminal offenses such as wounding, blinding, crippling, and killing.[90] The surviving fragments of the Troizen agreement contain more such language, but larger similarities between the Troizen and Stymphalos agreements suggest that equivalent provisions from the latter treaty have simply been lost. In particular, both appear to lay out detailed procedural rules, specifying officials and penalties, although the content of those rules is impossible to reconstruct with any confidence.[91]

Troizenians and Athenians

The agreement between the Troizenians and Athenians has not been reliably dated more precisely than roughly between 400 and the early 360s. The letters and layout point to the 390s, but historians have pushed it later, trying to fit the agreement into their understanding of larger geopolitical movements of the first several decades of the fourth century.[92] The Troizenians were members of the Peloponnesian League led by the Spartans, and Xenophon mentions two incidents when Troizenians and Athenians clashed in war in the early decades of the fourth century. In 394, Troizenian soldiers were among the Peloponnesians who fought against Athenians at the battle of Nemea, and they again sided with the Spartans against the Athenians in the late 370s.[93] But the rapidly shifting ground of Greek international relations in the early fourth century means that, despite those two conflicts, there were periods when Athenians and Troizenians could have seen fit to enter into a *symbola*. If we exclude the entire period of the Corinthian War of 395 to 386 (when Athenians and Troizenians were on opposite sides), the agreement could date to the few years before then or the dozen or so years after. The parties certainly need not have waited for the time after the battle of Leuctra in 371 when friendly Athenian-Troizenian relations are clearly attested in other sources.[94]

The Corinthian War, whose main antagonists were the Spartans on one side against Thebans, Athenians, and Argives on the other, was concluded with the multilateral King's Peace, so-called because its main terms were set by the King of Persia, Artaxerxes. A central term was agreement that most Greek cities outside of Asia would be autonomous.[95] This term would have offered a useful justification for a member of the Peloponnesian League that wanted to make a nonmilitary pact with the Athenians any time starting in 386. A purely judicial treaty with no military terms, such as the surviving *symbola* agreement appears to be, may have been calculated by Athenians and Troizenians to be unthreatening to the Spartans: being so close to each other (just across the Saronic Gulf), Athenians and Troizenians likely had commercial reasons to have a *symbola* agreement; and, not being a military treaty, the *symbola* is unlikely to have violated the terms of either city's pacts with Sparta, either before 395 or after the King's Peace.[96]

Legend and history might have contributed to a stable stratum of Athenian-Troizenian identity that remained uncorrupted by hostilities between Athenians and Spartans and even by actual wartime fighting between Athenians and Troizenians. The Athenian hero Theseus was said by both Athenians and Troizenians to have been born in Troizen, and his maternal grandfather Pittheus to have founded that town.[97] Perhaps more importantly, Theseus's son Hippolytos was the object of cult in both Athens and Troizen—and maybe nowhere else. Troizen was certainly the major cult center for this hero. Modern excavations have confirmed Pausanias's report of an entire sacred precinct devoted to worship of Hippolytos, including a stadium for athletic competitions and a late fourth-century temple (17 x 32 meters).[98] At least three Athenian tragedies of the second half of the fifth century centered on the story of Hippolytos, doomed by the love of his stepmother Phaedra. One of Euripides's plays still exists complete; it is set in Troizen and makes much of Hippolytos's relationship with Theseus, his Athenian-Troizenian father.[99] As W.S. Barrett notes, it seems significant that in both Athens and Troizen the Hippolytos sanctuary contained a temple of Aphrodite. This cannot be coincidence and is probably due to the influence of the Troizenian cult on Athenian developments.[100] Since the Troizenian cult appears to have been large and important, it may have drawn Athenian worshippers to Troizen. And regardless of how much direct influence there was between the cults of Hippolytos in Athens and Troizen, it is very likely that the cult itself, as practiced in each city, created feelings of connection toward citizens of the other, paralleling the connection between Hippolytos and Theseus.

Those connections were strengthened by historical events. Before the battle of Salamis in 480, some of the Athenians who evacuated the city fled for safety to Troizen, where they were welcomed.[101] That this kindness was remembered by the Athenians long afterwards is attested by a legal speech composed by Hyperides, probably in the 320s, praising the Athenians for (recently) taking in refugees from Troizen and granting them Athenian citizenship, and characterizing the act as fair recompense for Troizenian kindness to Athenians during the Persian Wars.[102] The wish, perhaps a half-century before this speech, to conclude a *symbola* agreement between the two cities may have been inspired not only by strategic and economic factors but also by these legendary and historical ties.[103]

Stymphalians and Athenians

The *symbola* between Athenians and Stymphalians already mentioned above (*Agora* XVI 47) has been dated to the early 360s based on paleographic and historical grounds. The Stymphalians were members of the short-lived Arkadian confederacy that was unified from approximately 370 to 363 BCE. Xenophon reports the Athenians made an alliance with this confederacy in 366 (when the Athenians were friendly with the Spartans but the Arkadians were, in Thomas Nielsen's words, "consistently democratic and anti-Spartan"), and that the Athenians were soon "compelled, in accordance with the treaty, to send cavalry in defense of the Arkadians."[104] This alliance reflected a change in the Athenian approach to Arkadian cities, since the Athenian general Iphikrates had besieged Stymphalos perhaps as recently as 369.[105] Although the alliance was with "the Arkadians" as a whole and the *symbola* agreement apparently only with the Stymphalians, it seems unlikely that Stymphalians would have made such a friendly agreement with Athenians before the Athenians had made a firm alliance with the Arkadians and thereby tacitly disowned the recent invasion. Therefore, also taking into account the epigraphers' judgments concerning letter forms, I would date the *symbola* agreement no earlier than 366.[106]

Why did the Stymphalians and Athenians enter into a *symbola* agreement? The lack of known or presumed trade ties between Athens and Stymphalos means we have no evidence for a strong economic motive.[107] Woodhead proposes that the agreement served primarily to support Athenian hegemonic goals during the period of the Second Athenian Naval Confederacy, but does not offer an explanation for why the Athenians—much less the Stymphalians—would have been eager for this particular form of treaty rather than a *symmachia*.[108]

Religious networks may have played a role in connecting Athenians and Stymphalians. By this time the Eleusinian Mysteries had been of panhellenic significance for over a century (Clinton 2005–2008, ii.39), and Stymphalos in the northeastern Peloponnese was close enough to Eleusis that Stymphalians likely participated in the Mysteries in generous numbers. In the mid-fourth century, the Athenians erected a *stele* with an extensive set of revised regulations concerning all aspects of celebrating the Mysteries, including the participation of non-Athenians.[109] Kevin Clinton suggests these revisions were a response to an increased popularity of the cult in the decades after the Peloponnesian War, and George Mylonas describes the large amount of construction at the sanctuary in Eleusis in the first half of the fourth century, construction consistent with a desire to accommodate increasing numbers of initiates.[110] We saw above that, in the fifth-century regulations for the Mysteries, existing *symbola* agreements provided "fallback" rules for cities that chose not to adopt the specialized Eleusinian regulations. It may be that, in the fourth century as well, some cities saw an advantage in the more general legal protections of bilateral *symbola* agreements in part because many of their citizens came to Attica as celebrants of the Mysteries and other festivals. Of course this explanation applies not only to Stymphalians; Troizen, for example, was even closer to Athens and Troizenian initiates must have made the journey to Eleusis each fall. As I argued in Chapter 4, it is likely that the week of festivities helped create and strengthen the sorts of networks that would have encouraged the establishment of *symbola* agreements.

In any case, the identities nourished by the Eleusinian Mysteries that I have just speculated about are underdeterminate of a *symbola* agreement, even if such identities existed between Stymphalians and Athenians. Michael Walbank, however, has suggested a religious explanation with a relevance restricted to those two cities. Noting that an early second-century inscription found in Stymphalos mentions the placement of a bronze *stele* "in the sanctuary of Artemis *Brauronia*," Walbank proposes that use of this peculiarly Attic cult name in Stymphalos "suggests family or religious ties with Attica."[111] Pausanias (8.22.7), visiting Stymphalos in the second century CE, describes what he calls the sanctuary of Artemis *Stymphalia*. Two separate sanctuaries in Stymphalos that have been at least partially excavated have been proposed as associated with Artemis, one on the acropolis and another at its foot, next to the lake and fountain house.[112]

Sanctuaries of Artemis were frequently associated with water, and the presence of a nearby spring is a feature shared by one of the sanctuaries at Stymphalos and that at Brauron in Attica. Perhaps the lakeside sanctuary was dedicated to Artemis *Brauronia* and reflects an especially close religious connection between Stymphalians and Athenians and personal relations that could have spurred the formation of a *symbola* agreement.[113]

Naxians, Knossians, and Athenians

Sometime probably in the second quarter of the fourth century, the Athenians entered into what appears to be a *symbola* agreement with the citizens of Naxos, largest island in the Cyclades. Diodorus Siculus explains that the Naxians, although once members of the Delian League, were Spartan allies from the end of the Peloponnesian War until 376, when an Athenian force besieged Naxos and defeated the Spartans in a naval battle. It is unclear if Naxians ever joined the Second Athenian Naval Confederacy, but in any case there is no necessary connection between the Confederacy, which was a defensive alliance organized as a precaution in the event of armed conflict, and a *symbola* agreement concerned with regulating judicial relations.[114] The surviving inscription, which is quite fragmentary, commemorates a judicial agreement of some sort. Although it is impossible to reconstruct any of its provisions precisely, it mentions courts in both Naxos and Athens, *thesmothetai*, court fees, and cases in which there is a right to appeal or transfer, among other "judicial" elements.[115] There is also an apparent provision for appeal to citizens of Thera (modern Santorini), possibly the earliest such *symbola* provision in our surviving evidence, presumably to arbitrate a certain class of disputes.[116] Some scholars have taken a mention of people "reconciling" to mean reconciliation between Naxians and Athenians, but others have suggested it refers to reconciliation of internal *stasis* on Naxos. The inscription tells us little more.[117]

The Athenians also appear to have had a *symbola* agreement with the Knossians on Crete in the second quarter of the fourth century. We know this from one fragment of an inscription that recorded what was likely a *symbola* between Athenians and a third, unknown *polis* referring several times to an agreement with the Knossians.[118] As Woodhead notes in his commentary, a separate Athenian inventory inscription indicates that the Knossians, like the Naxians, gave the Athenians a crown in 345/44. The same positive relations indicated by that gift may have played a role in the decision to make a *symbola* agreement. If so, the agreements with both Knossos and Naxos may represent not an unwelcome Athenian imperialism but rather a mutual preference for closer relations.[119]

Economic and social factors

From the uncertainties of dating these four *symbola* agreements from the first half of the fourth century, we should be skeptical of Woodhead's suggestion that the Athenians concluded a cluster of such agreements in the early 360s.[120] We should also resist seeing them as part of a coherent Athenian foreign policy, one that included the aim of resisting Spartan power, as the Second Naval Confederacy was apparently designed to do.[121] Furthermore, the surviving examples forbid the conclusion that Athenians in the first half of the fourth century concentrated on concluding *symbola* agreements with geographically close neighbors, as Gauthier proposes (1972, 204). So why did the Athenians enter into these agreements, during these decades, with Troizenians, Stymphalians, Knossians, and others? And conversely, why did the other cities enter into them with the Athenians? In Chapter 7, I discussed the evidence of the speech *On Halonnesus* in the Demosthenic corpus (but likely by Hegesippus) and suggested that it assumed that *symbola* agreements served "law and economics" motivations, as reflected by their presumed goal of increasing interstate "intercourse" or commerce ([Dem.] 7.11–13). Because this speech was delivered in approximately 342 and specifically discusses interstate judicial practices of the first half of the century, it is worthwhile revisiting it here.

Recall Hegesippus's argument:[122]

> Your past experience is evidence that Macedonians don't need a *symbola* agreement with Athenians. Neither Philip's father Amyntas nor the other kings ever made *symbola* with our city. Yet the intercourse [αἱ ἐπιμειξίαι] with each other then was greater than now. . . . [W]e used the trading centers there, and they used ours, more than now. And unlike now, there were no strict monthly mercantile courts, which eliminate the need for *symbola* agreements between people so distant from each other. But even though we had no such agreement then, there was no advantage [οὐκ ἐλυσιτέλει] in making *symbola*, neither for Macedonians sailing to Athens to litigate nor for Athenians going to Macedonia: we simply litigated cases there under Macedonian laws and they litigated [τὰς δίκας ἐλάμβανον] here under ours. — [Dem.] 7.11–13

This argument assumes that the goal of entering into *symbola* agreements is some sort of advantage or profit (ἐλυσιτέλει) and believes that increased intercourse, or commerce (ἐπιμειξίαι), serves as evidence the advantage is being achieved. Hegesippus does not specify what the advantage or profit is presumed to be. It may be the ability of citizens of one state to litigate disputes in the courts of the other. Or the increased commerce resulting from assured access to a civic legal system. Or the increased profits that derive from increased commerce. Or the greater consumer access to imported goods resulting from increased commerce. Or the import and export taxes accruing to the state from increased commerce. Perhaps he has all these hypothetical results in mind.

As I noted previously, Hegesippus here *denies* that a *symbola* agreement between Athenians and Macedonians would have encouraged commerce, and this denial is important evidence that, even without *symbola*, some Greek states offered at least informal, case-by-case access to domestic courts. We should not trust Hegesippus's implication that the judicial access between Athenians and Macedonians was just as easy without a *symbola* agreement as it would have been with one, and we certainly should not trust his claim that commerce between the states had been greater before Philip's reign: since Hegesippus opposed such an agreement, he had good reason to misrepresent that situation. And how could he have had any more than a vague (and easily inaccurate) impression of the historical trend in trade volumes?[123] But his claim that Athenians and Macedonians could already sue in each other's courts was likely true, since some members of his audience would know if he was blatantly lying about that. We also should not draw strong conclusions about *symbola* from his claim that the monthly mercantile courts eliminated the need for *symbola* between distant states. The mercantile courts heard only cases concerning alleged harms to commercial ship captains and merchants that occurred in relation to trading into or out of Athens and for which there was a written contract (Dem. 32.1), whereas *symbola* agreements, as we have seen, covered a wider range of cases. Yet Hegesippus's claim may be based on the reasonable assumption that Macedonians were more likely to sue in Athenian courts over trade disputes than in other types of cases.[124]

I argued earlier that fear drove Hegesippus's opposition to a *symbola* between Athens and Macedonia, fear not of its economics but of its social and political fruits. Hegesippus may intuitively grasp that *symbola*, by granting a select group of foreigners judicial rights normally reserved for citizens, tended to increase group identity and goodwill between the two populations. Because he fears the Macedonians and is wary of Philip's attempts to win over Athenians diplomatically, he denounces *symbola* as pointless.[125] This speech is therefore evidence of a Greek understanding of *symbola* as having social in addition to economic motives and effects. As we have seen, social motives may have predominated in the conclusion of *symbola* agreements between Athenians and Stymphalians and between Athenians and Troizenians, both cases in which religious and historic social connections might have played a significant role in drawing the communities together and fueling intercourse between them. As Athenians acknowledged with their Eleusinian regulations of both the fifth and the fourth centuries, providing official legal regulations of religious celebrants, no matter their citizenship, was essential. When aspects of those regulations were specially governed by bilateral *symbola* agreements rather than applying to every religious pilgrim, a greater sense of group ownership probably encouraged higher rates of compliance among the specific groups covered.

Quite particular social, political, and economic forces might have motivated the conclusion of individual *symbola* agreements, but they were always entered into by a political process. And we must place elites at the center of any such process, while acknowledging that, in democratic cities, it could involve a complicated dynamic between elite initiative and popular decision-making. For example, to speculate boldly, the *symbola* agreement between Athenians and Troizenians may have originated in a visit by a group of Troizenians to an Attic religious festival such as the Eleusinian Mysteries or the Panathenaia. Perhaps these (likely elite) Troizenians, while being hosted by (elite) Athenian friends, encountered a legal problem that would more easily have been solved if there had been a *symbola* in place between the two cities. These Troizenians and their Athenian friends might have then agreed to begin lobbying at home for a *symbola* agreement, perhaps invoking Theseus as an ancient tie between the communities and reminding listeners of the assistance rendered by Troizenians during the Persian Wars. Once the *symbola* was in place, those same ties as well as the existence of the *symbola* itself might have contributed to strengthening the joint Athenian-Troizenian group identity that would have encouraged the internalization of the norms enforced and protected by the *symbola.* In particular, the fact that *symbola* embodied a set of legal procedures jointly agreed between two *poleis,* rather than imposed by one *polis* on the citizens of the other, would have encouraged citizens from both cities to respect those procedures as fair and just.[126] The right to invoke the *symbola* in assertion of one's legal rights in the other city would have reflected a certain social standing in that city and encouraged a sense of belonging within a larger two-city group. It is less a case of, "If you want to come to our city you have to follow our rules" than of "The representatives of our two cities have come together to create a shared set of rules governing all of us equally."

My point is not to deny, or even play down, the importance of economic considerations and "power politics" but to argue that those are not enough to understand the formation of, use of, and compliance with *symbola* agreements. Even where economics was a dominant consideration in concluding an agreement, its success would rely in part on legal socialization processes. The mere existence of a formal institution in the form of a *symbola* agreement and its underlying laws would not have been enough to ensure compliance or fair enforcement, just as the mere existence of laws and courts was not enough to ensure domestic law compliance and enforcement within a city. But, under favorable circumstances, a *symbola* agreement could have been part of a positive feedback loop in which the existence of the formal institution encouraged trade and other forms of intercourse between two cities, which in turn strengthened group identities, common normative commitments, and mutual respect; and which later, when legal disputes arose under the *symbola*, resulted in jury verdicts less biased against the foreign litigant, in turn further encouraging commerce, and on and on. This model applies not only to *symbola* of the first half of the fourth century but also to earlier agreements of the fifth century and those that came later. It is to the latter, and their historical development, that I now turn.

Symbola beyond Athenian networks: The late fourth century and after

Up to this point I have offered a history of *symbola* through close consideration of specific agreements from the fifth and fourth centuries. One goal with this form of historical account has been to demonstrate that Greek use of *symbola* agreements cannot be explained solely by reference to practical considerations of economic and political questions. We must also invoke noneconomic forces such as ethics, religion, and emotion to understand why *symbola* were used and why they were effective. In the discussions above, I have suggested ways in which socially and ethically inflected readings can nuance our understanding. In surveying the later history, my emphasis will shift to considering how *symbola*—their recording, their terms, and their use—reflect and interact with certain trends in the history of the Greek world from the fourth to the first centuries.

One trend *symbola* exemplify is that after the middle of the fourth century the Athenians are less over-represented in the surviving evidence. This is partly a result of changing epigraphic practices across the Greek world: whereas in the fifth and early fourth centuries Athenians were outliers with the great volume of their epigraphic production, inscribing public texts on stone became more widespread in the later fourth century.[127] It may be that *symbola* also became more common in the wake of Macedonian expansion, as decision makers in cities, responding to the imbalance of power between themselves and well-armed kings in grand questions of war and peace, sought to maintain what control they could over the workaday details of their own internal and "minor" international relations—minor in the sense that they did not obviously threaten royal power. In this respect, it is noteworthy that monarchs are largely absent from our evidence for *symbola*. Mostly in the background if seen at all, they rarely entered into such agreements themselves.[128]

One of the uncommon examples of a "royal background" to a *symbola* agreement is noteworthy mostly for the light it sheds on close relations between the two cities that were parties to it. In probably 307 or 306, the Athenians entered into a *symbola* agreement with the citizens of the Cycladic island of Tenos; we know of the agreement's existence from an Athenian decree honoring two Tenean ambassadors and ordering ratification of a *symbola*.[129] Beyond confirming the *symbola* (yet without describing any of its terms), the decree shows warm goodwill toward the Teneans, proposing to award them a gold crown worth 1,000 drachmas, praising and crowning their two ambassadors, and granting them and their descendants status as *proxenoi* and benefactors of the Athenians as well as the right to own property in Attica. In a fragmentary early section, the decree appears to note the allegiance of both Teneans and Athenians to Antigonos Monophthalmos and Demetrios Poliorketes, which seems to place it in the aftermath of the latter's "freeing" the Athenians from Demetrios of Phaleron in 307. The Teneans may have earned Athenian gratitude by assisting Demetrios with this military action. But that cannot be the whole story behind the extraordinary package of privileges awarded to the Teneans. They and the Athenians probably had close relations already, motivating the Teneans to assist in liberating their friends in the first place.[130]

The decree echoes the affection displayed in another Athenian decree for the Teneans that has been dated sometime in the second half of the fourth century. This decree also awards a 1,000-drachma gold crown and, to all Teneans living in Athens, the same tax rates as those paid by Athenian citizens—a mass grant of a sort rarely made by Athenians. This and other evidence testifies to affection and close connections between Athenians and Teneans in the fourth and third centuries.[131] While these would be enough to merit a *symbola*, they also would only have been encouraged by both cities becoming allied to the same would-be king. Although there is no sign that Demetrios Poliorketes played a personal role in concluding the *symbola*, the mutual alignment of Athenians and Teneans with him is surely one reason he is mentioned in the decree.

Our surviving evidence offers one case in which a *symbola* agreement was decreed by a monarch. That case also shows just how fragile *symbola* could be when imposed from above. A few years after the *symbola* between the Teneans and Athenians, around 303, Antigonos (now styling himself "King") pushed strongly for a civic merger, a synoikism, between the cities of Teos and Lebedos, neighbors on the west coast of Asia Minor. His proposal for how that synoikism was to be carried out, which he detailed in surviving letters to the Teans, included suggestions for resolving many outstanding lawsuits.[132] Antigonos said that existing lawsuits and actionable liabilities (τὰ δὲ ἐγκλήματα καὶ τὰ συμβόλαια, *RC* 3, l. 24) between fellow citizens of either city should be resolved within two years under the current laws of the respective city and under the terms of a certain declaration (διάγραμμα) by Antigonos himself. But, with regard to any currently existing cross-border disputes between Teans and Lebedeans, the two cities should make an agreement, *syntheke*, concerning how to adjudicate them.[133] With the term *syntheke*, Antigonos is pretty clearly referring to a *symbola* agreement. A *symbola* must not already have existed between the Teans and Lebedeans, or

Antigonos would at least have mentioned it, and probably also dictated its use in resolving the existing disputes, perhaps on an accelerated timeline.[134] The fact that the Teans and Lebedeans nevertheless had preexisting lawsuits with each other shows that, even without a *symbola* agreement, they had ways to litigate private disputes between their citizens. That it nevertheless took the coercion of a powerful monarch to persuade these neighbors to enter into a *symbola* is evidence that Greek communities did not do so lightly. And the Teans and Lebedeans were likely not on warm terms, since their synoikism, if it ever was completed at all, lasted no more than a few years. Their *symbola* may have been as fragile as Antigonos's and Demetrios's hold on that corner of the world, which ended with the father's death at the Battle of Ipsos in 301.[135]

We can contrast the two examples above, in which royal influence is apparent, with its conspicuous absence a century later. A *symbola* agreement between the Prieneans and Milesians dating shortly after 200 makes no mention of the great regional powers of the time, in particular Philip V of Macedonia, Antiochos III (the Seleukid king who ruled most of Asia Minor and much territory further east), or the Romans.[136] About this time, Philip probably reallocated some territory among the Milesians, the Magnesians on the Maiander, and the Herakleians under Latmos. And the Prieneans likely lost some independence to the Seleukid realm around 197, when Antiochos III campaigned in southwest Asia Minor and extended his influence there. It is uncertain, however, if the Milesians came under Seleukid control at the same time. In any case, after the Romans defeated Antiochos III's forces and imposed the peace of Apamea in 188, both the Milesians and Prieneans were nominally "free" of monarchic hegemony.[137] And their inscribed *symbola* agreement, which is admittedly fragmentary, reveals nothing about maneuvers by the great powers, which therefore do not help us date the document. This is consistent with the surprising general omission of the Seleukids from the surviving inscribed documents of Priene.[138] It reflects the fact that many cities exhibited genuinely vital civic (and inter-civic) functioning in the face of violent tectonic global power shifts taking place around them and the general readiness of powerful actors to interfere directly in *polis* matters.[139]

Although quite fragmentary, the inscription is of further interest because it contained the text of the actual *symbola* agreement between Miletos and Priene. That agreement appears to specify the venue of any lawsuit as the home city of the defendant.[140] Milesians bringing cases in Priene are to file them with the so-called *strategoi* of that city; and Prieneans are to bring cases in Miletos before the overseers of the Milesian *emporion*.[141] The surviving text does not make clear what kinds of lawsuits were covered by this agreement or the details of how cases were actually to be tried, including how juries were to be composed. There seem to have been some procedural rules in common for suits in both cities but also distinct procedures for each venue. We can say little more.

There is an intriguing possibility that this was the first *symbola* concluded between Prieneans and Milesians. If so, the case resembles that of Teos and Lebedos: a shared border caused more tension than friendliness between neighboring communities, preventing them until this date from engaging in the judicial intimacy fostered by a *symbola* agreement despite its apparent economic benefits. And, in fact, we are aware of border disputes between Milesians and Prieneans. They are first clearly attested after the time of this *symbola* but may have begun earlier.[142] The two known boundary disputes between the Prieneans and Milesians may be late symptoms of long-running tensions between neighbors, tensions that prevented them, most of the time, from trusting each other enough to enter into a judicial treaty. If so, there is no evidence of what caused this (temporary) warming of relations.

Related to the juridical independence from the major royal powers that many cities enjoyed is Roman reluctance to participate decisively in Greek interstate legal affairs, at least through the first half of the second century and despite frequent appeals to the Senate by Greeks. Such appeals were mostly made in the context of public law disputes between cities, especially over state boundaries, and were usually in turn referred by the Romans to Greek arbitrators.[143] But sometimes the disputes involved *symbola*. One example, from the 180s, is also the only case we know of a major monarch entering into *symbola*. A number of Greek communities complained to the Romans that Philip V was not complying with the terms of his *symbola* agreements with them, or was complying only with their letter but not their spirit. The Senate chose not to interfere, although the complainants were so numerous that it took three days for all of them to voice their grievances in the Senate. Instead the senators, preferring to leave this flock of Greeks dissatisfied rather than get involved in a morass of legal disputes, accepted the word of Philip and his young son Demetrios that all the cases had been handled "in accordance with justice."[144]

A couple of decades later we again see, in the *symbola* context, the Roman preference for Greek solutions to Greek problems. After the Third Macedonian War, in 167/66 the Romans "gave" Delos to the Athenians and ordered the Delians to evacuate the island. Many of them emigrated to Achaia in the northern Peloponnese, some apparently having left behind significant property. After having received Achaian citizenship, a number of former Delians brought legal claims against Athenians under the terms of a preexisting *symbola* agreement between Achaians and Athenians.[145] The Athenians, however, denied that the Delians-turned-Achaians were covered by the *symbola*, which predated their Achaian citizenship status; in response, some of these new Achaians threatened or even began performing seizures (ῥύσια) against Athenians. Ultimately, the two groups sent ambassadors to the Senate to solve their argument over how to deal with the Delian claims. The Roman response was that they should resolve the disputes themselves in accordance with the *symbola*.[146]

A third trend visible in *symbola* starting in the third century is the participation in them of *koina*, also called leagues or confederacies. Although some Greek communities had been joining into *koina* since at least the sixth century, the late fourth to early second centuries saw this phenomenon at its apogee, in terms both of the number of cities belonging to *koina* and of the strength—political, economic, and military—of those organizations.[147] *Koina* are most visible in the *symbola* record in cases where the *koinon* itself was a party. We have records of *symbola* entered into by the *koina* of the Aitolians, Boiotians, Achaians, Perrhaibians, and Thessalians.[148] The *koinon*-level participation is symptomatic of a high level of centralization of the federal organizations in question at the time the particular agreements were made, centralization in the realm not only of foreign relations but also judicial matters.[149] Unfortunately, because the evidence for these *symbola* is in no case the actual text of the agreement itself but mere references in other documents or in Polybius, we do not know their terms, including which judicial bodies were used to decide disputes arising under them.

The final trend in *symbola* I will draw attention to is provisions for having cases decided by "foreign" judges, that is, judges from a city with no direct connection to the disputes in question.[150] This practice is most familiar from Greek international arbitration and from the use of foreign judges to decide domestic disputes within a *polis*. International arbitration among Greeks is known as early as the sixth century, but its frequency seems to have reached a peak from the fourth to second centuries. Using foreign judges to resolve domestic disputes may have been even more rare before the late fourth century, although it became common about the same time as arbitration. It is unsurprising to see a similar, contemporary trend with *symbola* agreements.[151]

The earliest situation I know of in which there is no doubt that judges from a third city might be asked to decide a dispute under a *symbola* agreement is from the Cyclades, around 300. We learn of it from the inscribed text of a loan contract between Praxikles of Naxos and the *polis* Arkesine on nearby Amorgos.[152] The contract refers to a *symbola* agreement to describe Praxikles's rights of self-help seizure in case of default by Arkesine: Praxikles may make such seizures "just as from those who lost a lawsuit before the arbitrating city in accordance with the *symbolon* of the Naxians and Arkesineans." The "arbitrating city," *ekkletos polis*, must mean a group of judges from a third city.[153] Strikingly, this contract does not use the verb *sylan* to describe Praxikles's right to self-help. Instead it uses three verbs typical in the context of a domestic legal system to describe exacting payment or seizing a deposit or an amount owed. The terminology thus assimilates Praxikles's right to act unilaterally to acting with the sanction of a presumably neutral legal authority.[154] And the contract terms show just how much leverage one wealthy man had in his negotiations with the Arkesinean officials. This inscription is one of the early pieces of evidence for Greek cities financing their activities by borrowing money from private lenders rather than from temple treasuries or simply raising money through taxes that did not have to be repaid. As we see here, and will see again below, one risk of this method of public finance was default by the city and subsequent self-help seizure or litigation by the creditor. In the latter case, the litigation might be presided over by judges from a third city.[155]

Foreign judges were used by Athenians and Boiotians in a *symbola* context half a century later. Two Athenian decrees dated 251/50 honor the people of Lamia, a *polis* in Malis between Boiotia and Thessaly, along with the particular Lamians who judged a number of disputes between Athenians and Boiotians in accordance with their *symbola* agreement. One inscription describes Lamia as an *ekkletos polis* and the other says the Lamian judges decided some of the lawsuits justly.[156] We do not know what the underlying legal disputes concerned, but since the second decree mentions "disputes" in the plural (τὰς δίκας), they were probably suits between private citizens, the ordinary subject of *symbola* agreements.[157] In the early second century, two judges came from Miletos to resolve disputes between citizens of the Lesbian cities Methymna and Eresos. Three inscriptions honoring the judges refer to the governing agreement not as a *symbola* but more generally as an "agreement" or "treaty" (συνθήκη). Although the judges appear to have been resolving disputes between private citizens of the two cities, it is unclear whether this situation should properly be called "international" since the four cities of Lesbos at this time may have been members of a small federal state.[158]

In this context—using foreign judges to decide private international disputes under a *symbola* agreement—belongs the most significant new *symbola*-related inscription published in the more than fifty years since Philippe Gauthier's landmark book on the topic. Appearing on a mysterious stone whose find spot, provenance, and date of acquisition by the Archaeological Museum of Thebes are all unknown, the inscription was first published by Yannis Kalliontzis in 2020.[159] It describes just the kind of situation that Praxikles the Naxian sought to avoid: litigation over a loan to a city. In this case the litigation was between the Boiotian *polis* of Orchomenos and two men from Amphissa, a city about sixty kilometers to the west. The inscription, written in a strong Boiotian dialect, is dated by Kalliontzis very close to 228/27 on prosopographic grounds.[160] Although the find spot is unknown, the text of the inscription and those on two other faces of the same stone leaves little doubt it was set up in the *polis* of Orchomenos. Because an English translation has not yet (to my knowledge) been published,

I provide a complete translation here and reproduce the Greek text in a postscript to this chapter:[161]

> Dorkoulos was archon of the Boiotians and Timon son of Sosippos was archon of the Orchomenians. The polemarchs Kaphisodoros son of Damatrichos, Philomeilos son of Phillis, Damoteleis son of Lysidamos—the secretary to the polemarchs being Perilaos son of Anaxion—and the *syndikoi* Euareis son of Euchoros, Philomeilos son of Philon, Athanodoros son of Hippon, Karaichos son of Hermaios, Aristion son of Eurouphantidas—the secretary to the *syndikoi* being Klioxenos son of Polykritos—wrote up the decision for the *polis* against Amphisseans concerning the contract (συγγραφή) in accordance with the *symbola* agreement (καττὸ σούμβολον).
>
> [line 10] The *polis* of the Orchomenians (against) the Amphisseans Timokrates son of Damokratios and Cheirikrates son of Archoutas, who say they are the legal heirs of Xenophanes son of Timokrates, an Amphissean, (claims) that since I paid back the money in the contract deposited with Xenophanes son of Timokrates, an Amphissean, and the contract was annulled by Xenophanes, you have brought forth a counterfeit contract and have claimed, in addition to seventy minas times two, the interest on each of the seventy minas, as written in the contract; the interest comes to forty-five talents. Thus I plead in accordance with the *symbola* agreement (καττὸ σούμβολον), with regard to the forty-seven talents and twenty minas that you allege and claim for yourselves.[162]
>
> [line 22] The [jud]ges gave a decision (ἔκριναν) after (the parties) had turned the matter over by agreement and entrusted their pleading(?) to the polemarchs of the Orchomenians: Kaphisodoros son of Dama[trichos], Philomeilos son of Philleis, acting as advocates on behalf of the *polis* of the [Orchom]enians; and to the *syndikoi* Euaris son of Euchoros, Karaichos son of Herma[ios, Philo]meilos son of Philon, Athanodoros son of Hippon, Aristion son of Eurou[phantides], all Orchomenians; as well as to Timokrateis son of Damokrates and Cheirikra[teis son of Archoutas], Amphisseans—concerning the claim that the city brought against Tim[okrateis and Ch]eirikrateis, that these men presented a false contract [. . .] to/by Nion son of Askondas, a Theban, and Lioukos son of Diokleis, a Kal[ydonian, what]ever they decide unanimously, let it be authoritative. [. . .] and in the month of Dionysios [or] Prokouklios as the Aitolians cal[l them . . .], the first ones after the verdict, or, as the Boiotians [call them, in Thy]ios or Pamboiotios, in the first ones. And if Lioukos [. . .] to decide (κρινέμεν), let them provide as decider (κρίνοντα) Timokrate[is . . .] Alexamenos the former *hipparch* of the Trich[onians . . .] the current *hipparch* of the Trichonians or Timaio[s . . .].

A few points are clear. The city of Orchomenos, whose first-person speech is a remarkable feature of this text, had borrowed seventy minas from Xenophanes, a citizen of Amphissa. Xenophanes died, his heirs eventually coming forward to claim that the Orchomenians had never repaid the loan. This was years or decades later, since the sum claimed by the heirs—forty-five talents—is stupendously greater than the original loan (one talent is sixty minas).[163] At some time the dispute was formalized and began to be litigated under the terms of a *symbola* agreement (καττὸ σούμβολον), a point the Orchomenians who wrote this document were at pains to emphasize. That emphasis might imply the Amphisseans first brought a claim under another procedure, before the Orchomenians insisted on the process laid forth by the *symbola*. Also fairly clear is that a verdict has been rendered in favor of Orchomenos: the polemarchs "wrote up the decision for the *polis* against Amphisseans" (8–9).

But because the stone is damaged near the bottom, parts of it are impossible to read, and the language in places is simply ambiguous, other details are less apparent. It is not clear where precisely the legal process stood when this document was inscribed. As I just noted, it seems a verdict has been rendered. Other passages also suggest the process is complete: the officials "wrote up the decision" (ἀνέγραψαν τὰ κριθέντα, 8–9); "the judges gave a decision" (ἔκριναν τὺ [δικα]στῇ, 22–23). But it is not clear if the two men named in line 31—Nion of Thebes and Lioukos of Kalydon—were designated as trial judges or, rather, to judge any appeal that might be brought. Appeals were a common feature of Greek legal process, and we have already seen an apparent appeal clause in the *symbola* agreement between the Athenians and Naxians from the second quarter of the fourth century.[164]

As Kalliontzis notes, the situation here closely parallels a dispute from seven decades earlier pitting the island city of Kalymna, off the southwest coast of Asia Minor, against private citizens of nearby Kos.[165] The Kalymnians had borrowed money from Koans whose descendants decades later sued Kalymna, alleging the city had never repaid the loan. The case was heard by 204 Knidians, who found for the defendant Kalymnians. We should not overstate the parallels. The surviving text of the Kalymnian inscription commemorating their legal victory does not describe that case as having been heard in accordance with a *symbola* agreement, and we have no independent evidence for an agreement. In fact there is evidence the litigation was endorsed, if not instigated, by Demetrios Poliorketes.[166] So it may have been a one-off dispute not governed by a preexisting *symbola* between the Kalymnians and Koans. But a reference to a *symbola* agreement could easily be restored in the decree's fragmentary early lines. And our newly published document from Orchomenos shows that a *symbola* agreement could govern a legal dispute between one city as a corporate entity and private citizens of another city.[167]

The Orchomenians learned the lesson of their negative experience with the heirs of Xenophanes. We know this from a long inscribed dossier dated just a few years later that shows the Orchomenians taking pains to document publicly their repayment of a large loan made to them by a certain Nikareta of Thespiae, a Boiotian city.[168] There is little doubt that institutional memory played a role here: several Orchomenian officials named as responsible for writing up our inscription are also named in the later inscription as involved with the loan transactions with Nikareta.[169] Unlike our inscription, the Nikareta inscription nowhere mentions a governing *symbola* agreement. This is presumably because Orchomenos and Thespiae both belonged to the state-like federal Boiotian *koinon*, which likely had rules for resolving disputes arising from this kind of transaction. In other words, the Nikareta loan probably did not count as an international transaction.

The Orchomenian dispute with the Amphissans was undoubtedly international because the two cities belonged to different federal *koina*, Orchomenos with the Boiotians and Amphissa with the Aitolians. This prompts a currently unanswerable question: whether the *symbola* mentioned in the inscription was an agreement between those *koina* (which governed all the member cities of both) or just between the Amphissans and Orchomenians.[170] If we did know, it would tell us something about the degree of independence retained by cities within the two *koina*. We also do not know when the *symbola* dates to; specifically, whether it was already in place when the loan contract was entered into, perhaps twenty years before the dispute, or was agreed to during the intervening years.[171] Relations between the Boiotian and Aitolian *koina* vacillated sharply in the two decades preceding this litigation; unfortunately we cannot map the loan or the *symbola* onto those fluctuations.[172] But in the decades preceding this dispute the Aitolian *koinon* appointed a few Orchomenian citizens as *proxenoi* to the Aitolians.[173] Regardless of what other Boiotians thought or felt about Aitolians, these proxeny ties may indicate generally warm Orchomenian attitudes toward them. Those attitudes may have encouraged the business deal between the Orchomenians and their Amphissan creditor and later convinced the Amphissan plaintiffs that they could get a fair deal in their lawsuit against the city of Orchomenos.

Let us wrap up our historical survey of *symbola* by lingering a bit longer in roughly the same time and place. Midway between Amphissa and Orchomenos, famously perched above a dramatic valley, stood Delphi. In the late third century, Delphi's citizens honored a certain Satyros son of Polemarchos, of Agrinion (in western Aitolia). He had resolved disputes between Delphians and foreigners living in Delphi, in accordance with a *symbola* agreement.[174] Much is unclear here, but the decree states that Satyros had been appointed *epimeletas* by the Aitolians, and Agrinion at this time was a member city of the Aitolian *koinon*. It may be that the *symbola* was between the city of Delphi and the entire *koinon*, and that the foreign residents in question were citizens of member cities of the *koinon*.[175] Many decades later, in 131/30 the Delphians granted proxeny and other honors to three judges from Hermione who had decided cases between Delphians and Lokrians "in accordance with the *symbolon*."[176] In 109/08 the Athenians honored judges from Larisa in Thessaly for resolving disputes, governed by a *symbola* agreement, between Athenians and Sikyonians.[177] And at some point in the second century an uncertain *polis*, perhaps Eretria, issued a decree in honor of judges from Oropos after they decided disputes between citizens of the unknown *polis* and Thebans in accordance with a *symbola* agreement.[178]

Conclusion

Why did cities entering into *symbola* agreements begin turning to judges from third cities? In the case of both international arbitration of public law cases and foreign judges hearing private law disputes, modern scholars reasonably believe one goal of the parties was to have their cases decided by unbiased (neutral, impartial) judges.[179] For arbitrations between two cities in their corporate capacities, finding unbiased judges meant recruiting them from a third city (a so-called *ekkletos polis*), or from several different cities. But this is not obviously necessary for disputes between private citizens of the same city. On the contrary, there was among Greeks, as there is now, a general assumption that unbiased, or at least minimally biased, judges and jurors are available to solve local disputes in practically any community. This is an important basis for the notion that what is commonly called "the rule of law" is attainable in human societies, since neutral application of the law is a pillar of most conceptions of the rule of law.[180] And most cities, most of the time, used local citizens to judge local, private disputes. Yet in the late fourth century it appears to have become more common for communities to conclude that, in the case of certain disputes, there was no way to ensure a neutral jury composed of locals and that the goal of impartiality could be fulfilled only by a jury of foreigners.[181] We have seen that some *symbola* agreements contained, in addition to their provisions for private disputes between individuals, clauses pertaining to disputes involving the other community as a corporate litigant. This flexible use of *symbola* might have accelerated the willingness of cities to provide for decision by judges from a third *polis* under certain circumstances.

We should be cautious in following Gauthier in concluding from these decrees that there was a wholesale shift in the nature of *symbola* agreements in the second century, away from a model in which local domestic courts typically decided disputes to one in which decisions by judges from a third city predominated.

The examples cited two paragraphs above are known from decrees honoring the judges. Because they do not report the language of the *symbola* themselves, we do not know if any of those *symbola* provided for third-party judges as the rule, or only in special situations.[182]

Yet a shift toward the use of judges with civic identities separate from those of any of the litigants reflects a move away from the "Aristotelian" view of *symbola* I have argued for in much of these two chapters. On that view, *symbola* created a citizen-like status for the foreigners protected by them and probably succeeded in achieving just decisions (when they did achieve them) in part because of how *symbola* both built on and nourished common identities between citizens of different *poleis*. Opting for judges from a third city indicates a fear (or an awareness) either that civic identity was itself rent or that the immediate goal of impartiality was more urgent than the long-term cross-*polis* community building that could be nourished by the reciprocal use of domestic courts and jurors. Or it may reflect a "judicial habit" that developed out of using foreign judges in particular domestic disputes. Perhaps resort to foreign judges in international arbitrations and in cases of domestic crisis showed Greeks that the advantages of presumably disinterested judges more than made up for the apparent loss of local sovereignty and community reliance that resorting to such judges could represent.

We should also resist concluding that Greeks came to value an ideal of true disinterest on the part of judicial decision-makers, at least to the extent that disinterest might imply unconcern for the well-being of the communities involved. On the contrary, the decrees honoring judges from a third *polis* in *symbola* cases, like those honoring foreign judges in domestic disputes, take as a premise of those honors that the judges, or the city that sent them, showed their friendship and goodwill, or even a connection of ancestral relation, *syngeneia*, in performing a task that benefited the local community.[183] I would highlight this aspect of the use of foreign judges: it is evidence not only of concern within one city for the achievement of legal justice within another city or between two of them, but also of a trust, by citizens of those other cities, in both the goodwill and the good judgment of the judges and the people sending them. From this point of view, resort to judges from a third city can be seen as reflecting and encouraging a form of international identity-building similar to that fostered by the more traditional local judging provided for by *symbola*, but on a larger canvas, one now involving three communities instead of two. Rather than a *dégradation* of *symbola* reflecting the *décadence* of civic legal institutions (Gauthier 1972, 346), the use of judges from a third city reflects a development of the social logic of *symbola* as institutions encouraging the internationalization not only of law but also of community, identity, and socialization.

Symbola began as a way for two communities that already had close connections to strengthen them with the formalities of institutionalized forms of justice and to become, in limited respects, a single community. But *symbola* were flexible enough to be adapted to a world in which Greek communities were more and more trusting of outsiders, of Greeks from other communities: trusting them not only to be able to understand and apply local rules but to have the affection and goodwill to do so for the benefit of the local community. It may be no coincidence that the change happened as the grip of Roman power over the Greek world tightened. I noted in an earlier chapter Irad Malkin's proposal that a sense of Greekness first took shape in the eighth to sixth centuries as more and more encounters with non-Greeks highlighted all that Greeks had in common with each other. The ever-growing presence of the Romans in the Greek universe may have had a similar effect.

Postscript

I print here the Greek text of the inscription describing the legal dispute between the city of Orchomenos and two private citizens of Amphissa, which I translated into English above. *Editio princeps*: Kalliontzis 2020, no. 33. See also *SEG* 70.191; *BE* 2021, no. 237 (Rousset).

Δορκούλω ἄρχοντος Βοιωτοῖς, Ἐρχομενίοις δὲ Τίμ[ωνος]
Σωσίππω, τὺ πολέμαρχυ Καφισόδωρος Δαματρίχ[ω],
Φιλόμειλος Φίλλιος, Δαμοτέλεις Λυσιδάμω, γραμ-
ματίδδοντος τῦς πολεμάρχυς Περιλάω Ἀναξίω-
νος, τὺ σούνδικυ Εὐάρεις Εὐχώρω, Φιλόμειλος Φίλω-
νος, Ἀθανόδωρος Ἵππωνος, Καράϊχος Ἑρμαΐω, Ἀρισ-
τίων Εὐρουφαντίδαο, γραμματίδδοντος τῦς σουν-
δίκυς Κλιοξένω Πολυκρίτω, ἀνέγραψαν τὰ κριθέν-
τα τῆ πόλι ποττὼς Ἀμφισσείας, οὑπὲρ τᾶς σουνγγρά-
φω καττὸ σούμβολον· *vacat* ἁ πόλις Ἐρχομε-
νίων Τιμοκράτι Δαμοκράτιος κὴ Χειρικράτι Ἀρχού-
ταο Ἀμφισσείεσσι, ἐπινόμυς φάντεσσι εἶμεν τῶν
Ξενοφάνιος Τιμοκράτιος Ἀμφισσεῖος, ὅτι ἐμοῦς ἀπο-
δώσας τὸ ἀργούριον τὸ ἐν τῆ σουνγράφυ τῆ τεθείσῃ πο-
τὶ Ξενοφάνειν Τιμοκράτιος Ἀμφισσεῖα κὴ ἀνηρεθείσας
τᾶς σουνγράφω οὑπὰ Ξενοφάνιος, ἐπεινίξατε οὑμὲς
ψευδεῖν σούνγραφον κὴ ἅψασθε ποτὶ μνᾶς ἑβδομείκον-
τα διπλασίας κὴ τόκων τῶν ἐν τῆ σουνγράφυ γεγραμ-
μένων οὑπὰ μνᾶς αὐτοκώλως ἑβδομείκοντα, γίνυτη
[ὁ] τόκος τάλαντα πετταράκοντα πέντε· οὕπω τοὶ δικάδ-
[δω]μη, καττὸ σούμβολον, ὧν ἐπεινίξατε κὴ ἐφάψασθε ταλάν-
[τω]ν πετταράκοντα ἑπτά, μνάων ϝίκατι· *vacat* ἔκριναν τὺ
[δικα]στὴ ἐπιτρεψάντων αὐτῶν ἐσς ὁμολόγων κὴ ποτενι-
[ξάντ]ων τῦς πολεμάρχυς Ἐρχομενίων Καφισοδώρυ Δαμα[τρί]-
[χω], Φιλομείλυ Φίλλιος διαδικιόντεσσι οὑπὲρ τᾶς πόλιος [Ἐρχο]-
[μ]ενίων κὴ τῦς σουνδίκυς Εὐάρι Εὐχώρω, Καραΐχυ Ἑρμα[ΐω],
[Φιλο]μείλυ Φίλωνος, Ἀθανοδώρυ Ἵππωνος, Ἀριστίωνι Εὐρου[φα-]
[ντίδαο] Ἐρχομενίυς κὴ Τιμοκράτι Δαμοκράτιος κὴ Χειρικρά[τι Ἀρχ]-

Laws of All the Greeks. Jesse James, Oxford University Press. © Jesse James 2026.
DOI: 10.1093/9780197838556.003.0011

[ούταο] Ἀμφισσείυς ούπὲρ τᾶς δίκας ἅς ἐγράψατο ἁ πόλις Τιμ[οκρά]-
[τι κὴ Χ]ειρικράτι φάσασα ψευδεῖν σούνγραφον ἐπιφέρεμεν· [–ca. 4–]
[–ca. 5–]Ν Νίωνι ϝασκώνδαο Θειβήυ κὴ Λιούκυ Διοκλεῖος Καλ[υδωνίυ]
[–ca. 2– ὅ,τι δ]έ κα οὗτυ κρίνωνθι σουμφωνίοντες, κούριον ἔστ[ω –ca. 5–]
[–ca. 5–]ω δὲ ἐν τῦ Διωνυσίυ μεηνὶ εἰ [ἐν τ]ῦ Προκουκλίυ ὡς [Ἡτωλὺ]
[μεν ἄγ]ονθι τῦς πράτυς μετὰ τὸ κρίμα ὡς δὲ Βοιωτὺ [ἄγονθι]
[–ca. 3– Θυ]ίυ εἰ Παμβοιωτίυ τῦς πράτυς, ἡ δέ κα Λιούκυ [– – ca. 5– –]
[–ca. 5–]Ι κρινέμεν, παρέχονθω κρίνοντα Τιμοκράτε[ι– –ca. 6– –]
[–ca. 3–]Ἀλ̣εξαμενὸν τὸν ἱππαρχείσαντα Τριχ[ονεῖα – – ca. 6– –]
[– – ca. 6– –]Α τὸν ἱππαρχίοντα Τριχονεῖα εἰ Τιμῆο[–ca. 10–]
[– – – –]ΤΑΛΙΟΝΤΑΠΕ[– – – – – – – – – – – – – – – – – – –]
– –

Apparatus:
20–21: δικάδ[δω]μη καττὸ σούμβολον ὧν ἐπεινίξατε Rousset: δικάδ[δω] μὴ καττὸ σούμβολον, ὅν ἐπεινίξατε Kalliontzis

PART III
EXPANDING THE VIEW

9
Piracy

Expanding the view

So far in this book I have argued that the concept of international law is useful for understanding Greek history; offered a theory of social psychology and legal socialization that explains some of international law's effectiveness in the Greek world; and provided detailed histories of two aspects of that legal field, *syla* and *symbola*, partly through the lenses of social identity and legal socialization. My focus on *syla* and *symbola* was an act of triage. They have received less (and less recent) scholarly treatment than other elements of Greek international law, especially in English; new, thorough accounts of them are therefore particularly desirable.

But *syla* and *symbola* are not the only areas of Greek international law deserving fresh treatment, nor the only phenomena that can be better understood by being seen as aspects of international law. And so, in this section, I discuss more briefly three elements of Greek society that, unlike *syla* and *symbola*, have been robustly addressed in recent scholarship: the practice and prohibition of piracy, the use of oaths, and Greek federal leagues. Each discussion is a small exploration, nothing approaching an exhaustive treatment of any of these topics. Instead I focus on aspects that are most relevant to my larger project, suggesting ways to illuminate each topic either by a social-psychological approach, from the point of view of international law, or both. I use these final chapters not to fold the book back in upon itself into a neat, closed package but in the hope of creating an open-ended spiral that encourages further exploration. I also hope that these discussions will not only reinforce my claim that law, variously manifested, permeated Greek international life; but also further illustrate how the legal, the social, and the ethical were intertwined for Greeks both within and beyond the borders of the *polis*.

Piracy

An old story relates that Alexander the Great, in the course of his global conquests having taken custody of a pirate, asked the man what wickedness drove him to

DOI: 10.1093/9780197838556.003.0013

make the sea unsafe. His captive's retort: "The same wickedness that drives you to make the whole world that way!"[1] Brief and fanciful as it is, this anecdote hints at several aspects of Greek piracy I focus on in this chapter. Although our accounts do not use the word "law," the exchange reflects the Greek view of piracy as a violation of international law; otherwise Alexander would not rebuke the pirate in the first place. Second, in its original Greek version, it may have played on ambiguity resulting from the Greek language's failure to distinguish, as English and other languages do, between "piracy," "privateering," and wartime raiding by armies. Third, the pirate's reply underscores the role of justice, or at least justification, in determining a behavior's legitimacy. Similar tactics of violence and seizure, considered legitimate when prompted by considerations of justice or retaliation, are illegitimate when motivated solely by desire for gain. And desire for gain is the implied motive the pirate throws back in Alexander's face.[2] Finally, although we are not told his ethnicity, the pirate's sardonic tone suggests that Greeks accused of being pirates often felt unfairly singled out, condemned for acts seen as acceptable when committed by others. Among Greeks, group identities helped shape which states' imprimaturs were seen as legitimizing and who was given the benefit of the doubt when judging the legality of "raiding" behavior.

Group identity dynamics affected both the commission and the enforcement of piracy in the Greek world of roughly 500 to 100 BCE. I argue in this chapter that, to the extent certain marginal ethnic groups within the grand identity tent of "Greekness" actually engaged more than other Greeks in piratic behavior, their piracy was less a cause than a result of their ethnic marginality.[3] Already seen by others as outside the main cultural group of Greeks who viewed piracy as unjust and illegal, members of these marginal groups—Aitolians and Cretans above all—were, because of their marginality, more likely to reject the mainstream legal and ethical norms condemning piracy and not trust its mainstream "enforcers." Less accepting of anti-piracy norms, they were more willing to engage in piracy, reinforcing the prejudices against them. On the other hand, those overtly assuming the role of "police of the seas," especially the Athenians and Rhodians, held themselves out as representative members of the main stream of Greek culture. By actively opposing piracy in words as well as deeds, they were recognized by many Greeks as embodying and upholding ideals of Greek culture, reinforcing their identity with a common notion of Greekness constituting an in-group to which pirates were one of many out-groups. Piracy and its suppression were therefore two sides of a single coin of Greek identity, ramifications of in-groups and out-groups viewing themselves in the others' light.

My hope in my brief treatment here is to show how social identity complements other approaches to piracy in the Greek world. Many scholars, for example, have justly stressed economic factors as central to piracy and its suppression. Noteworthy in this regard is a recent emphasis on the likelihood that wealthy elites participated in piratic activity. Others have argued that state structures influenced piracy: either because states, as legal structures, are inherently anti-piratic or on the theory that certain kinds of Greek states embraced piracy while others actively opposed it.[4] And many have, like me, stressed pirates' marginality. But the emphasis on marginality has tended to take two forms, each dissatisfying in its own way. An earlier approach, which some might call "naive" and has been long out of fashion, adopts the viewpoint of mainstream Greek culture and blames the evil of piracy on an uncivilized "other," whether that means non-Greeks (Illyrians, Karians), "fringe" Greek populations (Aitolians, Cretans), or isolated social outcasts. More recent scholars have gone to the opposite, cynical extreme, seeing the supposed marginality of piracy, and indeed piracy itself, as almost entirely a rhetorical construct, a subjective determination, piracy "in the eye of the beholder." I take a middle path, considering Greek piracy to have been a real phenomenon whose actual practice was shaped in part by the construction of marginality in Greek international society.[5]

I *will* argue explicitly against one interpretation, traceable at least as far back as Thucydides, that posits a major change in Greek ethical views toward piracy. On this interpretation, Greeks before the fifth century considered piracy to be an entirely legitimate way to make a living, as honest and admirable as any other, perhaps reflective of a broad dominance of what Vincent Gabrielsen has called a "raid mentality." It argues that, although by the middle of the fifth century piracy had become widely discredited among Greeks, a few Greek ethnic groups maintained the hypothesized early attitudes and continued to treat piracy as completely permissible.[6] I find this interpretation incomplete and unpersuasive. There is, in fact, little evidence for a change in Greek ethical attitudes toward piracy—Greeks always generally condemned it. And, by understanding piratic activity of the fifth century and later as a behavioral fossil motivated by a combination of archaic ethics and timeless economics, this interpretation does not take into account how social relations across the Greek world, and psychological responses to them, likely affected piratic activity. The social and psychological causes of piracy were more complicated than lingering pockets of bygone lifestyles or raid mentalities. Group identity dynamics alone did not cause piracy among Greeks, but they help us understand certain aspects of that piracy and its suppression.

The vocabulary of piracy

Piracy, as well as legal forms of raiding, were common activities throughout ancient Greek history, widely practiced and just as widely condemned. The topic is a large one, has been much studied, and is beset by interpretive problems that cannot be solved here.[7] One of the major problems is lexical. The most common Greek words translated as "pirate" are *leistes* (ληστής) and, of later origin and less common, *peirates* (πειρατής). Both terms could refer to those who performed raiding, robbery, or kidnapping on sea or land. And both could refer to (i) entirely private actors; (ii) those acting independently but with the sanction of a state; or (iii) those acting in close coordination with a state military or under the direct command of a general or admiral.[8] Therefore, while in English "pirate" refers to an entirely private actor who performs robbery and kidnapping on or from the high seas, *leistes* and *peirates* can also refer to robbers or brigands on land as well as to privateers and irregular naval forces. Regardless of legality, two characteristics that make someone a *leistes* or *peirates* are the manner of operation and the immediate intent: they make swift targeted strikes, typically for the immediate purpose of food or profit rather than a larger military or political goal, even if that profit serves a larger military goal such as keeping an army in the field.[9]

Leistes, *peirates*, and their cognates, then, often referred to some sort of state-sponsored activity rather than private criminal piracy in the modern sense. And although both terms were usually derogatory (as I discuss below), the kinds of raiding practices they labeled could be legitimized under Greek international law.[10] This should not surprise us. We have already seen, in the discussion of *syla* in Chapter 5, that Greeks distinguished between just and unjust, permissible and impermissible forms of forceful seizure under both domestic and international law. *Leisteia* was (similarly) seen as capable of being legitimized by conditions of war, so long as it was performed under the authority of one of the states at war and had a war-related purpose such as seizing supplies.[11] But the lexical ambiguity means that any particular use of *leistes* or *peirates* might not refer to a pirate in the narrow sense; hence "raider" is a better default translation than the more specific "pirate." Context matters, but is often ignored. Hence it may be that the similarity in tactics between illegal pirates and legal raiders contributed to the ancient characterizations of Aitolians and Cretans as pirates, which I discuss below. Despite the lexical and tactical ambiguities, however, Greeks did distinguish between the legal and illegal forms of outwardly similar activities, which means that "piracy" and "pirate" cannot just be dismissed as purely rhetorical constructs or "entirely subjective descriptions," as "whatever the enemy does."[12]

Piracy as a violation of international law

Perhaps because of the ambiguous vocabulary that failed to distinguish illegal piracy from permissible raiding, no surviving Greek source I am aware of states bluntly that the *leistes* or *peirates* violated "the laws of the Greeks" or describes him, as Cicero would do in Latin, as "the common enemy of all."[13] But surviving sources leave little doubt that Greeks recognized an international prohibition on piracy—private raiding not authorized by any state—from at least sometime in the fifth century. Piracy's illegality is probably reflected in Herodotus's account of a certain Dionysios from Phokaia, an Ionian city on the west coast of Asia Minor. Dionysios was a naval leader in the Ionian revolt against the Persians in the 490s. When he saw the revolt fail, and knowing he would be enslaved if he stayed in Phokaia, Dionysios fled to Sicily: "operating from there, he became a pirate (ληιστής); not against any Greeks but against Carthaginians and Tyrrhenians."[14] Herodotus presents Dionysios's new way of life as an act of desperation by a man who could not be free in his own land; and he partly salvages Dionysios's reputation with the key detail that he did not attack Greeks. This detail would be unimportant if Dionysios had not turned to activity viewed by Greeks as illegal, at least as practiced against other Greeks. Herodotus was writing in the late fifth century, but this passage suggests he believed piracy was already illegal at the beginning of the century.[15]

Our earliest fifth-century documentary evidence for piracy's illegality is also from Ionian shores, an inscribed *stele* from Teos dated around the 470s.[16] This much-studied document contains a series of curses to be publicly pronounced several times a year by a Tean magistrate against those who might cause various kinds of harm. Among other things, it curses with death anyone who "commits highway robbery, or receives highway robbers, or commits piracy (ληίζοιτο) or deliberately receives pirates (ληιστάς) who are carrying things off from the Tean land or the sea, or who plots any bad thing concerning the community of the Teans knowingly, either against (πρός) Greeks or against (πρός) barbarians."[17] The mention of *leistai* so close to "highway robbers" (κιξάλλας) leaves little doubt that the proper translation here is "pirates" rather than the more generic "raiders." And the omission from these curses of "ordinary" domestic criminals such as thieves or murderers suggests that pirates, highway robbers, and those plotting "any bad thing concerning the community" had a heightened wickedness or harmfulness in common.[18]

There is an ambiguity in the final clause quoted above. What I translated as "either against Greeks or against barbarians" is translated by Mustafa Adak and Peter Thonemann as "with reference to either Greeks or barbarians." And they interpret this clause as concerned with the possibility of "harmful collaboration with external powers of any ethnicity" against the Teans, rather than piratic action against any Greeks or non-Greeks (2022, 113). But on their interpretation the phrase adds no information and makes little sense. *Any* plotting against the Teans would involve either Greeks or barbarians (the phrase itself does not specify Greeks "external" to Teos). And it is not clear why the Teans would want the curses to apply *only* if there are external co-conspirators, a condition implied by Adak and Thonemann's translation. Therefore I prefer to take the construction of the preposition *pros* with accusatives to mean "against Greeks or barbarians." On my reading, the purview of the Tean curses potentially reaches far beyond Tean territory: the harm they target must somehow concern the Tean community (ξυνός), but not necessarily be directed personally upon Tean citizens; and we at least glimpse here the Ciceronian notion of pirates as the common enemy of all.[19]

My interpretation is supported by a related text. Perhaps eighty years before this inscription was carved, settlers from Teos had founded a colony at Abdera, on the north shore of the Aegean Sea. The two cities had close relations during the following centuries. In fact, another stone found at Teos bears inscribed curses that are probably contemporary to those quoted above and indicating they were pronounced by Abderites as well as Teans. This suggests that copies of both sets of curses were publicly displayed at Teos and Abdera.[20] It also helps contextualize a statement that perhaps comes closest in that era to expressing the notion that the pirate is the common enemy of all. Democritus of Abdera, who lived in the late fifth and early fourth centuries and is now most famous for his atomic theory of physics, also wrote works with ethical and legal content. These survive only in brief passages, but two of those passages attest Democritus's strong condemnation of piracy. In one place he writes, "Anyone who kills any highway robber or pirate should (or "shall") not be guilty, whether he does it by his own hand, by a command, or by a vote."[21] In another passage perhaps closely connected to this he writes, "Just as it is written regarding foxes and snakes, since they are enemies, it seems to me we should act in the same way regarding people: it is in accordance with ancestral laws to kill an enemy in any particular social order (ἐν παντὶ κόσμῳ) in which the law does not forbid it."[22] No surviving Democritean text draws the logical connection between these passages. But the most obvious connection is that "anyone" (τις) can kill pirates with impunity (Passage 1) *because* pirates are the common enemy of everyone in the human social order (Passage 2).[23]

We also have evidence that Athenians and Spartans considered piracy a violation of international customary law by the fifth century. Aeschylus's protagonist Eteocles expresses what may have been common anti-piratic sentiment in the play *Seven against Thebes*, produced in Athens in 467. Eteocles bemoans that "if a pious man boards a ship with hotheaded sailors bent on wickedness, he perishes along with a group of god-detested men."[24] More historically, the first-century BCE Roman historian Cornelius Nepos credits Themistocles with pushing the Athenians to suppress pirates (*praedones*) in the 480s. According to Plutarch, writing even later, in the 470s the Athenian general Cimon "freed" the Aegean sea from pirates by seizing the island of Skyros from the Dolopes, people who "pirated the sea from early times."[25] Scholars have argued these were just two instantiations of a general Athenian policy of piracy suppression in the fifth century, and that the tribute paid by members of the Delian League and Athenian empire funded these efforts.[26] This view may be supported by a fragmentary inscription of a treaty between the Athenians and the citizens of Halieis, a coastal city of the Argolid in the northeast Peloponnese, dating probably to the 420s. As the inscription has been reconstructed by scholars, the Halieians promise, among other things, not to harbor raiders (*leistas*) or commit raiding themselves (*leizesthai*).[27] A recognition of a general prohibition of piracy is also reflected in the practice of the Spartans in the fifth and fourth centuries actively authorizing people to act as privateers. There would be no need to authorize privateering if actual piracy were not forbidden.[28]

Despite the ambiguity of piracy vocabulary, authors could make clear in context that they were referring to private piracy in the narrow sense, unsponsored by any state. When they do so they leave little doubt they are condemning it as harmful and forbidden. For example, in Plato's *Laws*, written in the mid-fourth century, the Athenian proposes that the citizens address to the young a prayer that includes the following wish, "May no desire come upon you for chasing down men at sea and for piracy (ληστεία), and turn you into savage and illegal (ἀνόμους) hunters. And may it absolutely not come into your mind to engage in theft (κλωπείας) in the countryside or the city."[29] Here the context indicates that the Athenian is referring to piracy as an illegal act, the equivalent of simple theft. The same equivalence is drawn in the speech *On Halonnesus* attributed to Demosthenes: "And concerning pirates (ληστῶν), [Philip] says it is right for you and him together to defend against criminals (κακουργοῦντας) on the sea." The passage's context and the word I translated as "criminals" (literally "evildoers") leave no doubt the speaker is talking about pirates, who are harming both the Athenians and Philip II.[30] Aristotle, also writing in the fourth century, seems to be referring to the illegality of piracy when he describes Greeks making seizures from Carthaginians as "acting unjustly."[31] Much later, an honorary decree from the Cycladic island Syros, dated to the second or first century, declares that the honorand, Onesandros of Siphnos, took measures on behalf of Syrians in response to "evildoing ships" (κακοῦργα πλοῖα), later calling the perpetrators *peiratai*. The context and vocabulary in all these cases shows they are referring to the illegitimate and especially "wicked" kind of raiders: pirates.[32]

Run-of-the-mill private piracy is, to my knowledge, never spoken of positively in surviving Greek sources, and a desire to suppress "genuine" piracy is one thing that most powers in the Greek world could agree on. When Philip II and the Athenians were in conflict in the mid-fourth century, both sides claimed to oppose piracy while accusing the other of an inability to suppress it. Their dispute over Halonnesus partly concerned competing Athenian and

Macedonian efforts to fight pirates.[33] And, in a letter to the Athenians, preserved among Demosthenes's works but written by Philip II, the Macedonian king accuses the Athenians of ignoring the fact that the Thasians, contrary to their agreements, had admitted to their island "whichever pirates wanted to come."[34] Demosthenes, in turn, argues that Philip was overwhelmed by pirates at various times and that he would not have prevented piracy from Euboia.[35] Both sides express opposition to piracy and insult the other by claiming they are unable or unwilling to oppose it. Through the next couple of centuries, reports survive of active opposition to piracy by Alexander the Great, the Ptolemies, the Bosporan king Eumelos, the Rhodians, and ultimately the Romans. Many inscriptions honor people who either helped repel pirate attacks or worked to recover goods or people seized. Piracy was universally denounced in the "mainstream press" of our surviving sources.[36]

Even state-sponsored raiding, while generally seen as legitimate, was often tainted in the minds of Greeks. Raiding was considered a normal and necessary part of war, and Greek writers could be bland and matter-of-fact in discussing it.[37] But wartime *leisteia* was sometimes seen as harsh and cruel. Thucydides reports that exiled Corcyrean oligarchs, by means of raiding their home island, caused "great harm," including a famine (3.85.2); and characterizes the exiled Megarians in 424 as "harsh in their raiding" (4.66.1). When Xenophon labels Alexander of Pherai "an evil pirate (ληστής) on land and sea," he may have in mind his reputation for raiding tactics.[38] And Diodorus's description of Philip V encouraging his Aitolian naval commander Dicaearchus to engage in raiding (πειρατεύειν) appears designed, by its language and in its context, to depict both men in a negative light: Diodorus calls Dicaearchus a "brazen man" (ἄνδρα τολμηρόν) and details how far into impiety Philip had fallen.[39] Such examples suggest that even raiding activities sanctioned by a recognized state power could lose legitimacy on account of their resemblance to pure piracy or their excessive brutality.

I mentioned above a line of scholarship that, while agreeing piracy was widely condemned by sometime in the fifth century, insists this was a change from an earlier Greek ethic that considered piracy, and raiding generally, to be no worse than any other profession or occupation. On this view it was only with the rise of the violence-monopolizing state, whether *polis* or kingdom, that individual piracy came to be seen as a threat to government-imposed order.[40] The view seems inspired by Thucydides's well-known description of early Greeks and non-Greeks having "turned to piracy" on land and sea. He claims that, although king Minos of Crete had long ago taken the first steps toward ridding the sea of pirates, and by the late fifth century most Greeks had laid aside arms in their daily existence, in his day there were still some Greeks, including the Ozolian Lokrians, Aitolians, and Akarnanians, who continued to follow "the old manner" by carrying weapons on their person (1.5–8). But little evidence supports the Thucydidean view of early Greeks as accepting and approving of piracy. The history of piracy before the fifth century may seem of little importance to my arguments, since my focus in this chapter, as in the rest of the book, is on the fifth through second centuries. But because my understanding of the social dynamics of piracy differs from accounts that posit a crucial historical change in Greek attitudes, I must take time to show how thin the evidence is for such a change and why we need a different explanation.

Thucydides justifies his evolutionary view with a reference to "the old poets," who he claims "are always having people ask travelers by sea the same question—whether they are raiders (λῃσταί), as though those they are questioning are not embarrassed by the deed and those wanting to know do not mean it as an insult."[41] It is widely agreed that Thucydides here is likely referring to two passages of the *Odyssey* and one from the Homeric *Hymn to Apollo*.[42] Although some scholars agree with Thucydides's reasoning, I find it to be a poor interpretation of the poems, where the question actually appears as follows: "Are you traveling on (particular) business or are you wandering thoughtlessly like raiders (ληΐστῆρες) upon the sea, who wander, staking their lives, bringing evil to strangers?"[43] Seen in its original form rather than its Thucydidean paraphrase, the question's unfavorable judgment of piracy is apparent. First there is the strong negative tenor of the expression "wandering thoughtlessly upon the sea." The word I have translated as "thoughtlessly" (μαψιδίως) is, along with its cognates, always used as a criticism in the *Odyssey* and *Iliad*. In fact, "vicious" might be a better translation in many contexts. Penelope and Telemachus use it to describe the suitors' consumption of Odysseus's food and wine, and Zeus to characterize the act of one god harming another. It is probably no accident that this strongly negative word has dropped out of Thucydides's paraphrase.[44]

The condemnatory characterization of raiders in these passages is especially clear because the question implied, "Do you bring evil to strangers?" is, in the contexts of our surviving examples, always asked by a stranger. At its core, then, the formula comes down to the following disjunctive question: "Are you traveling on legitimate business, or do you want to harm me (a stranger), as a raider would?" We must reject the interpretation of Thucydides and those who follow him that those asking this question do not mean to insult raiders. In fact, the Homeric passages leave little doubt that "pirates" is a better translation here than "raiders," since the assumption underlying the question is that these men are not motivated by an underlying military purpose.[45]

Another passage from the *Odyssey*, although not mentioned by Thucydides, has been offered as "strong" evidence of the legitimacy of piracy in the world of that poem, bolstering the Thucydidean interpretation. This is the doubly fictional life of the Cretan refugee persona Odysseus adopts on his return to

Ithaca. Odysseus fabricates for his old swineherd Eumaeus a baroque tale of war and adventure, fortunes won and lost (14.199–359). He declares he married the daughter of a wealthy Cretan family and led nine armed expeditions before joining the Greek invasion of Troy (14.211–31). Hans van Wees interprets these expeditions as piratic raids and claims they brought Odysseus's fictional character "to the very top of the social hierarchy" in Crete. Hence for van Wees this story portrays piracy as legitimate and even honorable.[46] But Odysseus's description of the nine expeditions suggests they were military campaigns presumably based, at least facially, on some sort of justification (like the Pylian retaliatory raid described by Nestor in the *Iliad*, which I discussed at the opening of Chapter 6). In describing the nine expeditions, Odysseus-as-Cretan speaks of his ability "in war" (ἐν πολέμῳ, 222) and his love of "wars" (πόλεμοι, 225). In fact, the fictional career Odysseus narrates is, if anything, a warning *against* piracy. The only expedition he marks as clearly piratic, a raid on coastal Egypt after his participation in the Trojan war, ends in disaster (*Od.* 14.243–72). What is more, three books later, Odysseus, still in the guise of the Cretan and referring again to the Egypt episode, claims that Zeus "overpowered" him by letting him join the "wandering pirates" and sail to Egypt. He offers that mistake as the original cause of his current desperate situation.[47]

Interpreted properly, then, these *Odyssey* passages reflect a negative view of piracy, the opposite of what Thucydides and some modern scholars claim.[48] This negative view is bolstered by other anti-piratic passages in the *Odyssey*, above all Penelope's brief account of the suitor Antinous's father: he incited the anger of the people of Ithaca by joining in a raid with Taphian pirates upon the Thesprotians, allies of the Ithacans. A mob of Ithacans would have murdered the man for his participation if Odysseus had not prevented them (16.424–30). The story contains several morals, but Penelope's specification that the Taphians were pirates (ληιστῆρσιν Ταφίοισιν, 16.426) lends a more negative color to the character of Antinous's father and is intended to help explain the Ithacans' anger: why mention that detail if their anger was due only to violation of a treaty and fear of reprisals?

It may be objected that Odysseus, in the narration to the Phaiacians of his ten years of travels and travails, depicts piracy in a good light by describing himself as having acted piratically. For example, his raid on the Cicones shortly after leaving Troy seems unprovoked (*Od.* 9.39–61). Must we not imagine Odysseus as presenting himself to the Phaiacians in a wholly positive light and therefore take this story as an implicit praise of piracy? No, I would say. As Richard Rutherford has argued, in his long tale to the Phaiacians Odysseus is not presenting himself as never having erred. Rather, he portrays himself as having made many mistakes but also having learned from them, and as now a wiser and a better man *because* of his errors. Notably, the "piratic" acts Odysseus describes himself as having taken part in are crowded near the beginning of his voyages, and all come to a bad end, teaching him implied lessons. On the whole, the *Odyssey* is critical of piracy.[49]

The *Odyssey* is the main evidence scholars have used to support the claim that piracy, as opposed to wartime raiding or privateering, was viewed neutrally or positively by Greeks before the fifth century. But they also cite, as a corroborating document, a text reported as part of Solon's Athenian legislation in the early sixth century. It lists several groups within the city and declares that private agreements made by those groups are to be honored unless forbidden by "public written things" (δημόσια γράμματα, presumably specific laws or decrees). Two of the groups listed are people "going off to plunder (λείαν) or to a trading port."[50] This text has been taken as straightforward evidence that piracy was seen by early sixth-century Athenians as a perfectly legitimate way to make a living.[51] But a few observations cast into question the reliability of this evidence. First, our source for this law is the sixth-century CE *Digest*, part of the compilation of Roman legal texts ordered by the Byzantine emperor Justinian. The *Digest*, in turn, is quoting the second-century CE Roman jurist Gaius, who could not have seen the original text of Solon's laws. Likely as a result of the many centuries and stages of transmission, there are multiple problems with the Greek text as we have it: the precise wording here is certainly not Solonian.[52] While there is no glaring textual problem with the specific words I translated "going off to plunder," the other linguistic difficulties the passage acquired through its transmission make the entire quotation's accuracy suspect. Second, even if the law's text were accurately reported, the word I translated "plunder" probably refers here not to private piracy but to wartime raiding or privateering against public enemies of the Athenian state. This interpretation is supported by the presence, in the same list, of groups with official recognition and important public functions including demes and phratries.[53] Third, state regulation of some aspect of an activity does not necessarily mean the state declares the activity itself legal. A well-known contemporary example is that US tax law requires illegally derived income to be declared as income and tax paid on it. This does not render the income-generating activities legal.[54] The *Digest*'s quotation is not evidence that Solonian Athenians considered private piracy to be legal.

On my interpretation and taken together, then, the Homeric and Solonian passages support a claim that Greeks as a whole never considered private piracy to be permissible or legal. There is, on the other hand, much evidence that raiding on behalf of states at war was *always* seen as permissible. Taken together, these observations suggest there was no great shift in Greek attitudes toward raiding, whether private or state-sponsored. And Thucydides's statement about piracy is evidence, not that Greek attitudes toward piracy changed, but of two related phenomena: first, of mainstream Greek biases against groups such as the

Aitolians, which I discuss below; and second, of Thucydidean recognition of the importance and effectiveness of Greek international law in his own day, a recognition I discussed in Chapter 1. Therefore, what needs to be explained about piracy is not why it came to be considered illegal under Greek international norms; its illegality reaches back as far as we can see. What needs to be explained is why Greeks of certain ethnicities were especially reputed as pirates and why other Greeks sought and developed reputations as public enforcers who took on the task of suppressing them.[55]

Piracy and enforcement as social phenomena

Two Greek populations were especially reputed as pirates: Aitolians and Cretans. And two populations were especially reputed as police of the seas: Athenians and Rhodians. All these reputations likely were grounded in reality—in fact, their reality is critical to my interpretation—but their truth probably developed partly through Greek group identity dynamics. We have seen that mainstream Greek ethics viewed piracy as illegal before the fifth century. This early "institutionalization" of anti-piracy meant that one way people could assert their identity as "good Greeks" was by condemning or fighting against piracy. On the other hand, because piracy was seen as a criminal, outsider, anti-Greek behavior, the commission of piracy could be partly a reaction against exclusion by mainstream Greek social groups, what Paul Kosmin has described as a piratic "politics of resistance" (2024, 150). This is why it is likely not a coincidence that surviving evidence for Greek biases against Aitolians and Cretans—their marginalization—predates our evidence for their participation in piracy.

Aitolians

Claudia Antonetti perceives the first clear signs of anti-Aitolian biases among Greeks in our surviving sources in Aeschylus's play *Seven against Thebes*, mentioned above. In that play, a Theban scout reports the attackers' positions to Eteocles, describing the warriors in vivid detail. He portrays Tydeus, a legendary Aitolian, in singularly animal, bestial terms, as hissing like a snake and raving like a maddened horse.[56] A similar attitude is reflected in Euripides's *Phoenician Women*, produced around 409, where Tydeus is described as "carrying an Aitolian war spirit in his chest" and as "strange, half-barbarian in his armor."[57] Thucydides, writing about the same time as Euripides, leaves no doubt that this reputation for raw fierceness was not limited to Tydeus but extended to Aitolians generally. I have already mentioned Thucydides's claim that Aitolians still showed traces of the piratic ways that had (he asserts) once been normal and acceptable across Greece: "And they also used to raid (ἐλῄζοντο) each other on the mainland. And up to the present day many parts of Greece live in the old way, around Ozolian Lokris and Aitolia and Akarnania and the mainland around there. And the habit of these mainlanders of carrying weapons has lingered from their old raiding ways (λῃστείας)."[58] Note how Thucydides insults the Aitolians without accusing them of still practicing raiding: they represent an intermediate stage between old piratic Greeks and modern civilized Greeks.

Thucydides also relates anti-Aitolian biases in the mouths of others. In 426, he reports, the Messenians of Naupaktos, close to Aitolian territory, pleaded with the Athenian commander Demosthenes to attack the Aitolians. They argued as follows: although the Aitolians were numerous, and tough fighters, the Athenians could defeat them because Aitolians lived scattered in unwalled villages and wore light armor. And the largest group of Aitolians, the Eurytai, ate raw flesh and spoke the least understandable form of Greek (3.94.4–5). It is not clear what relevance these final details might have to war-planning, but they serve to mark the Aitolians as inhabiting the fringes of the social group "Greeks." Their language is barely intelligible as Greek; eating raw flesh implies they do not burn animal meat in sacrifice to the gods of the Greeks; wearing only light armor means they do not participate in respectable, heavy-armed hoplite warfare; and living in unwalled villages means they do not live in proper *poleis* like most Greeks (the city wall being the embodied architectural metaphor for a *polis* constitution).[59] In short, not only can the Athenians defeat the Aitolians; they also should have no qualms about attacking them. Anti-Aitolian biases were well established by the fifth century, and these biases do not derive from experience of Aitolian piracy.

The earliest surviving concrete claim of Aitolians violating Greek international law also has no piratic element. It comes, again, from Athenians. In 367, the Athenians sent out the customary *spondophoroi* to announce the celebration of the Eleusinian Mysteries and the associated religious truce that all Greeks were expected to observe.[60] But this year, although the federal Aitolian league accepted the truce, people in the city of Trichonion arrested the *spondophoroi* who arrived there. We learn this from an inscribed Athenian decree sending another herald to demand their release and declaring the Trichonians' action "contrary to the common laws of the Greeks."[61] The *stele* bearing this inscription appears to have been erected near the City Eleusinion in the Athenian *agora*, where for (probably) centuries it publicly witnessed to Athenians this alleged Aitolian disregard of international law.[62]

Our earliest possible evidence of an Aitolian reputation for piracy, however, dates decades later. Aitolian piracy may have inspired an early third-century Athenian religious hymn sung during celebration of the Eleusinian Mysteries.

The song honors Demeter and Persephone, the goddesses of Eleusis, and includes a prayer to Demetrios Poliorketes as a god on earth. The Athenians ask Demetrios (who in 307 had "freed" the Athenians from the increasingly harsh rule of Demetrios of Phaleron) to protect them from the Aitolians: "And the Sphinx who now is master not just of Thebes but of all Greece, the Aitolian one, seated on the rocks, just like the old one, snatches and carries off all our bodies, and I cannot fight back. For the Aitolians snatch things from their neighbors and now also from those further away."[63] This highly metaphorical passage may not refer to piracy at all (there is, notably, no sea imagery) but rather to Aitolian military aggression.

Polyaenus explicitly describes some Aitolians around this time as pirates. Writing much later (in the second century CE), Polyaenus reports that "ten Aitolian pirates" (πειραταί) assisted Antigonos Gonatas in his attack on Cassandreia, probably in the 270s. Their assistance here was not in itself piratic, but Polyaenus or his source had some reason for calling the men pirates.[64] A more concrete but still ambiguous piece of evidence of Aitolian piracy dates perhaps to the second half of the third century. An inscription from an otherwise unknown community calling themselves the Aulonians, on the Cycladic island of Naxos, appears to honor several men for having ransomed 280 local residents seized by "the Aitolians." This may have been piracy, although the surviving portion of the inscription does not use the term. As John Grainger has observed, it could also have been a wartime raid (although there is no obvious known war to connect it to).[65] An Athenian inscription from the 220s mentions a raid on Attica, apparently from some previous year, by a certain Boukris, who seized a number of citizens and took them to Crete, from where he ransomed them.[66] He is probably the man named and described as Aitolian in a Delian inscription dating between roughly 250 and 230.[67] The Athenian inscription does not label Boukris a pirate, but he "ravaged" (καταδραμόντα, 5) the country and led many citizens away to Crete, where a Cretan named Eumaridas of Kydonia helped to ransom them back to freedom. This was probably private piracy but could have been wartime raiding.[68] I mentioned above that Diodorus Siculus claims that, at the end of the third century during the first Cretan War, Philip V encouraged his Aitolian naval commander Dicaearchus to engage in piracy. Diodorus specifically claims that Dicaearchus "made piratic attacks on merchant ships and extracted money with raids on the islands."[69]

Polybius finds much to criticize in the Aitolians, the frequent enemies of his own Achaeans. He accuses them of being violent and greedy and of violating the laws of war with their aggressive raiding tactics, although he rarely baldly accuses Aitolians of private piracy.[70] Polybius asserts that "the Aitolians were accustomed to make their livelihood off of raiding (ληστείας) and similar lawlessness" and that they "pillaged and sacked the Greeks" (φέρειν καὶ λεηλατεῖν,

30.11.1–2). Perhaps the closest he comes to a specific accusation of piracy is his claim that a group of high-ranking Aitolians effectively declared a private war on the Macedonians, Messenians, and others. They first dispatched a group of pirates (πειρατάς) who seized a Macedonian boat that they brought to Aitolia and sold off, crew and all. They also made raids on the coast of Epirus, north of Aitolia, raids Polybius characterizes as "unjust deeds" (ἀδικία, 4.6). If Polybius is correct that these attacks were undertaken without a declaration of war or official approval of Aitolian political organs, they might count as piracy. But "guerrilla warfare" may be a more accurate term, since even Polybius ascribes political rather than financial motives and says that these Aitolians "carried out war" (πόλεμον ἐξήνεγκαν, 4.5.10). This is essentially all the concrete evidence we have for Aitolian piracy.

Cretans

Cretans were, it seems, just as marginal as Aitolians to the social world of the Greeks, although anti-Cretan biases were perhaps less pronounced. Paula Perlman has observed that Greek literature "figured the island of Crete as a distant and remote place" and that "Greek thought conceived of the Cretans as inhabitants of a remote island situated at the edge of the Greek *oikoumene* whose behaviour was antithetical to the normative Greek model." Scholars have often noted the paucity of evidence for much contact between Crete and the rest of the Greek world between the sixth and fourth centuries.[71] We have seen that when Odysseus wants to create a persona whose reality no one on Ithaca can refute, someone who plausibly would have suffered many experiences before arriving at Ithaca, he claims he is from Crete.[72] Well into the fourth century Aristotle could say Cretans "live on an island far from those who might corrupt them."[73]

For Athenians, the distance and danger Crete represented were summed up in the story of King Minos's demand that the Athenians send him seven girls and seven boys every year to be sacrificed to the Minotaur, the half-man, half-bull monster whose existence resulted from Minos's irreligious behavior and his wife Pasiphae's divinely inspired passion for a bull.[74] Only the Athenian hero Theseus was able to end the annual sacrifice to the Cretan king. The grip that this story held on the Athenian imagination is indicated by its great popularity in both visual and literary art of the fifth and fourth centuries. Although we have no source stating explicitly that Athenians drew from this story the moral that all Cretans are bad, there was likely some anti-Cretan biasing effect from their constant repetition to themselves of the story of an Athenian vanquishing a dark threat from Crete.[75]

Wider anti-Cretan bias is apparent in an expression preserved most famously in the *Letter to Titus* attributed to St. Paul. It recites the sixth-century statement by Epimenides (himself a Cretan) that "Cretans are always liars, wicked animals, idle stomachs."[76] In the third century, the poet and scholar Callimachus, who was from Cyrene but lived and worked in Ptolemaic Alexandria, had already quoted the first part of Epimenides's sentiment: "Cretans are always liars" (*H. Zeus* 8). The belief clearly had currency in the Greek world. About the same time as Callimachus, Leonidas of Tarentum wrote a funerary epigram accusing Cretans of perpetual piratic tendencies:

> Always pirates and sea-destructive, and unjust
> are the Cretans. What Cretan knows justice?
> And so, while I was sailing with a splendid cargo,
> Cretans pushed me, Timolytos, into the sea,
> pitiful me. I am by the sea-dwelling birds
> bewailed, but there is no Timolytos under the tombstone.[77]

This fictional epigram is probably playing, like Callimachus, with a literary allusion to Epimenides; but also, it seems, with well-known Greek biases against Cretans. These biases have not only, perhaps, affected how scholars read the largely circumstantial evidence for Cretan piracy; they also likely fed any Cretan disposition to piracy. Again, my claim is not that Cretan piracy is a mirage. On the contrary, my group-identity-based explanation of piracy is premised on evidence that certain ethnic groups of Greeks did "turn pirate" more often than others. But questioning how we read the evidence can indicate just how sensitive its interpretation is to preconceptions.

David Lewis has argued that Greek biases against Cretans were partly based on real differences in how Cretans waged war: not with spears and shields in close-ranked hoplite formation, where leaving the battle line was a sign of cowardice, but with bows in open ranks designed for skirmishing, where tactics such as retreat and ambushes were deliberate. Furthermore, Cretans were reputed to have a great concern with the plunder of war.[78] That such qualities were also associated with pirates may have facilitated a belief that Cretans were piratic: simply because they waged legitimate war in uncommon ways.

One frequently cited piece of circumstantial evidence of Cretan piracy is an Athenian decree from 328 or 327 honoring a certain Eurylochos who ransomed some Athenians from Crete.[79] This decree does not specify the Athenians had been captured by pirates, or even by Cretans, but says that Athenian captives were brought to Crete. It is possible that non-Cretan pirates had brought their captives to Crete in the hope of selling them. Delos had a large slave market where, it seems, pirates could sell their captives (Strabo 14.5.2). This does not mean Delians engaged in piracy; so far as I know, they never had a reputation for doing so. Similarly circumstantial evidence survives in the form of three treaties inscribed on a single stone found at Miletos. The treaties, usually dated to the 250s, are between the Milesians and three Cretan cities: Knossos, Gortyn, and Phaistos. They prohibit the citizens of each city from knowingly purchasing the free citizens of the other.[80] Pierre Brulé interprets these inscriptions as proof that Cretan pirates were seizing Milesian citizens and selling them as slaves in Crete. He takes the bilateral nature of the agreements as mere façades for the one-sided reality of the underlying problem being addressed: Cretan pirates were seizing Milesians and not vice-versa.[81] This is more clearly evidence that Milesians feared their fellow citizens were being trafficked on Crete than that Cretan pirates were seizing them. Yet none of the inscriptions mentions piracy or explicitly accuses Cretans of it. Cretan cities may have been seen by the Milesians—rightly or wrongly—as places where illegally acquired captives were "laundered" into slavery and where stolen slaves were sold to new owners. While these inscriptions do not prove that Cretans were making piratic raids on the coast of Asia Minor, they are evidence of the practice.[82]

Our earliest specific claims in Greek historical sources that Cretans engaged in piracy date half a century later, to the very end of the third century. Diodorus Siculus relates in a fragmentary text that Cretan piracy provoked a response from the Rhodians: "Cretans engaged in piracy (πειρατεύειν) and plundered (ἐλῄστευον) many who voyaged by sea. Because this discouraged many merchants, the Rhodians, believing these injustices would also affect them, began a war against the Cretans."[83] This episode has often been connected to the outbreak of the so-called First Cretan War, a connection encouraged by the perceived Rhodian role as police of the seas, which I discuss below.[84] Interestingly, Polybius's earliest mention of more or less specific Cretan piratic activity is from roughly the same time, in his claim that Nabis of Sparta "partnered with the Cretans in piracies (ληστειῶν) upon the sea."[85] Polybius is characterizing generally the entire rule of Nabis, who acted as the tyrant-like leader of Sparta from 207 to 192. This means Polybius is referring to Cretan piratic activity dating to 207 or later. Later still, Strabo, describing Crete near the end of the second century, states that pirate ships filled their ranks with Cretan mercenaries (10.4.10). As with the Aitolians, Polybius is generally considered to have held anti-Cretan biases, which cast some doubt on the reliability of his characterization of any Cretan activities as piracy.[86] Diodorus, however, does not seem infected by such bias, and Strabo assures his readers (in the very passage cited) of his personal connection to Crete. The smoke of so many reports of Cretan piracy, then, probably indicates some fire.[87]

In light of all the evidence, I accept the broad scholarly consensus that Aitolians and Cretans did engage in piracy at higher-than-average rates. Even if some evidence is biased or circumstantial, there is simply too much of it to ignore.[88] Yet the late appearance of concrete evidence for Aitolian and Cretan piracy suggests it was not an archaic hangover from a primitive and lawless age, but something new; and its appearance well after evidence of Greek group biases against Cretans and Aitolians suggests a possible causal connection from the biases to the new behaviors. Before exploring further why these Greeks in particular engaged in piracy, however, we should consider how some other Greeks made vigorous efforts to suppress it.

Athenians and Rhodians

In comparison to Aitolians and Cretans, who were seen as marginal Greeks from the sixth through the second centuries, Athenians and Rhodians for long stretches represented the mainstream. For Athenians, the claim hardly needs defending: their role in the Greek world during the fifth and fourth centuries was so significant and visible that it has become commonplace for scholars to apologize for "Athenocentrism." By the fifth century, in domestic and interstate politics, international trade, drama, visual art, philosophy, mathematics, and oratory, Athens was both a center of innovation and a main hub of distribution. Greek consciousness of Athenian cultural supremacy is apparent in the epitaph reported to have adorned the cenotaph of the Athenian playwright Euripides, probably by the first half of the fourth century: it describes his hometown as "the Greece of Greece" (Ἑλλάδος Ἑλλάς).[89] From the late third century to Roman times, the rich and powerful from east and west donated buildings and monuments in Athens, apparently recognizing the city as being, like the panhellenic sanctuaries, particularly representative of a certain desirable kind of Greekness. This reputation and influence endured for many centuries and flourishes today.[90]

The long-term influence of Rhodes has not been nearly as profound, and in "power politics" it was always overshadowed, first by the Macedonian kingdoms and then by Rome, but for much of the third and second centuries Rhodes was perhaps in some ways more central to Greek life than Athens.[91] Polybius indicates how high the Rhodians stood in the estimate of contemporaries in his description of the generosity of many of them to the island nation after the late third-century earthquake that caused extensive destruction, most famously to the Colossos in the harbor. He mentions as among those donors the rulers of Syracuse; Ptolemy III; Prusias of Bithynia; Mithridates II of Pontos; other *dynastai* of Asia Minor; and an enormous number of cities. Vincent Gabrielsen argues they were all "anxious for the quick recovery of a thrifty and able maritime state that had taken upon itself the job of servicing their needs in the Mediterranean."[92] This importance to so many was partly a result of what Diodorus took to be a Rhodian position of deliberate, even assertive, neutrality amidst many of the disputes that rent Greeks in those centuries. This neutrality of Rhodians and their ability to please a variety of parties suggest the city was seen as representative of a similarly neutral mainstream Greekness.[93]

One way both Athenians and Rhodians played out their Greekness was as enforcers of international order and defenders of Greeks. In both cases it was about not merely asserting state power but also cultivating an image as *philhellenes*. For the Athenians, this role began by leading resistance to Persian power in the early fifth century, first in the Ionian revolt, then in the Persian Wars, and ultimately with leadership of the Delian League. But I focus here on Athenians and Rhodians as opponents of piracy and "police of the seas." Citizens of both cities seem to have prided themselves during their decades of ascendancy, and were credited by others, contemporaneously and later, with suppressing piracy and making the seas safe for travel and commerce by all. Earlier in this chapter I described some Athenian anti-piracy efforts of the fifth and fourth centuries. Other fourth-century evidence includes Isocrates's statement in the *Panegyricus* that the Athenian *arche* prevented pirates (καταποντισταί) from possessing the sea; and a decree proposed by a certain Moirokles to guard against and punish those who harm traders, in order to make "the sea clean."[94]

The Rhodians are generally credited with having taken over Athenian policing of the sea, or on other accounts of turning Athenian rhetoric into Rhodian reality.[95] Diodorus, as part of his praise of Rhodians cited above, claims that Rhodes "advanced to such a degree of power that it personally, on behalf of the Greeks, took on the war against the pirates (πειρατάς) and cleansed the sea of criminals."[96] Polybius supports the image of Rhodians as "police of the sea" (although not, in this case, policing against pirates) with his story of the Rhodian-Byzantine war that took place about 220. The war began because the Byzantines were levying tolls on shipments from the Black Sea through the Bosporos straits; the maritime traders, upset at this expense, complained to the Rhodians as authority figures, since they seemed to be "in charge of what happened at sea." The Rhodians began an enforcement action against the Byzantines, who soon yielded, promising to end their tolls on Black Sea commerce.[97]

Several inscriptions support the image of Rhodians as defenders against piracy. A grave inscription for three Rhodian brothers, dating sometime between 310 and 280, announces to passersby that they died fighting against "Tyrrhenians" and "pirates."[98] A Delian decree from the mid-third century honors four Rhodian naval commanders as *proxenoi* and benefactors of the Delians because they worked for "the protection of the islands and the safety of the Greeks."[99] The inscription does not specify from whom these Rhodians kept the islands and the Greeks safe; it may have been pirates or state-sanctioned raiders. But as Pierre Roussel suggests, the decree depicts the Rhodians as "police of the sea." Even if they were never more than mildly effective in curbing piracy, our evidence suggests the Rhodians succeeded in being seen as doing so.[100]

A Sociology of Greek Piracy

I have described a Greek world in which two marginal groups became particularly prone to piracy and two core groups purported to act as enforcers of piracy's prohibition. We have also seen that specific claims or evidence of Aitolian and Cretan piracy first show up in the third century, whereas there is no good evidence that piracy was ever seen by Greeks in general as legal, much less honorable. This casts doubt on efforts to explain Aitolian and Cretan piracy as simple continuations, among very conservative people, of time-honored ways to make a living.[101] Instead, I believe we can partly explain the piracy that some Aitolians and Cretans engaged in as predictable responses to their marginal identities within the Greek international community and to the fact that piracy was seen as a "policed" crime in the Greek world starting in the fifth century.

If Aitolians and Cretans engaged in piracy more often than other Greeks, it was probably in part a result of their experience of prejudice based on their ethnicity. Contemporary research in the context of domestic law has shown that a society's discrimination against ethnic minorities increases psychological depression, violence, and rule-breaking among members of those minority populations. The phenomenon has been documented, for example, among Black and Latino populations in the United States, Arabs in Israel, and Moroccans in the Netherlands. For example, gang membership by Latino adolescents in the southwestern United States is strongly and positively correlated to the number of discrete experiences of ethnic marginalization or discrimination they have experienced.[102] It has sometimes been interpreted within the framework of "strain theory," which argues that crime, along with violence and rule-breaking more generally, can be a response to negative emotions such as anger and frustration that arise from various strains or stressors upon people. Discrimination appears to be just such a strain.[103]

It may be objected that domestic crime by ethnic minorities in modern states is a far cry from piracy in the ancient Mediterranean. But there are correspondences between the two.[104] First, as I have argued throughout this book but especially in Chapter 4, while the Greek international world was not a single state, it was a social community with widely acknowledged norms: rules and laws. Second, we have seen in this chapter that Greeks considered piracy to be a violation of those laws and discussed it with language or in contexts equating it with crime. Third, Aitolians and Cretans were ethnic minorities within the Greek world, minorities against whom other Greeks expressed strong prejudices. Fourth, scholars of Atlantic piracy in the seventeenth and eighteenth centuries have argued that identity-based marginalization from mainstream culture was one driver of piratic activity at that much later date; this finding helps bridge the perceived gap between ancient Mediterranean piracy and modern domestic crime.[105]

Finally, chronology supports the causation I have proposed. In order to be exposed to prejudices, ethnic minorities must have significant contact with majority in-groups in the first place. I suggest this is one reason we see the strongest evidence for Aitolian and Cretan piracy in the third century: this is when both groups had become most fully (re)integrated in the larger Greek world. Only starting in the fourth century, but especially in the third, do we see strong signs of significant Aitolian and Cretan involvement in Greek international affairs.[106] This involvement would have meant more exposure to bias from other Greeks, especially for Cretans and Aitolians involved in international trade, working on or around ships, or serving as mercenaries: precisely those with the skill sets to engage in piracy. Perhaps surprisingly, it may not have been their isolation from other Greeks that spurred Aitolians and Cretans to piracy but their increasing contact with them. As I noted in Chapter 3, although contact generally contributes to decreasing biases and forging group identities, that result is not inevitable; the quality of the contact matters. Sometimes, increasing contact between subgroups can heighten perception of differences and sharpen biases. This may have happened often as Cretan and Aitolian contact with other Greeks grew more frequent.[107]

Resulting partly from the discrimination against them, Cretans' and Aitolians' failure to identify fully with the mainstream social group of "Greeks" may have weakened their felt obligation to abide by the rules of Greek international life. In Chapter 3, I mentioned a study showing that German politicians who feel less "European" are also less willing to support and uphold EU law.[108] Because prohibition of piracy was understood as a rule in place among Greeks, alienation from Greek identity might have lowered inhibitions about engaging in piracy, particularly against Greeks. Furthermore, in keeping with piracy's similarity to domestic crime, we have seen that among Greeks there were specialized "enforcers" of its prohibition, "police of the seas." This fact may bring into relevance modern research showing that law compliance is directly correlated with people's beliefs about the legitimacy of law enforcement authorities. I am not suggesting that Aitolian and Cretan pirates resembled Eric Hobsbawm's "social bandits," heroes to and supported by a local peasantry, much less that they represented a subaltern social resistance movement.[109] But if the Athenians and Rhodians were seen by some as illegitimate enforcers of the law against piracy, as enforcing the law unfairly, or as hypocrites with regard to piracy, these perceptions might have alienated some Aitolians and Cretans from the "Greek" norms that the Athenians and Rhodians claimed to represent. This is one way to understand the pirate's quip to Alexander with which I began this chapter: that the pirate saw Alexander as, effectively, also a pirate, and therefore an illegitimate enforcer of piracy's prohibition.

Conclusion

My hypothesis that group identities within Greek international society contributed to Aitolian and Cretan involvement in piracy cannot itself, of course, be proven by quantitative studies like those I cite in support. Given the dearth of our evidence, it will always remain a hypothesis.[110] But I have argued it is more plausible than the "Thucydidean" evolutionary hypothesis that the Aitolians and Cretans, into the second century, were simply conservative groups clinging to an old-fashioned, early Greek ethic that was permissive toward and even approving of piracy. If there is truth to the claim that Aitolians and Cretans shared a "raid mentality" in the third century and later, and if that mentality helps explain their alleged predilection for the legitimate (but not unproblematic) activities of wartime raiding and privateering, it still does not explain a willingness to engage in blatantly illegal activity such as piracy. Economic factors doubtless always weighed heavily in decisions to turn to piracy, but their importance also is easy to exaggerate, not only with respect to pirates but also for the anti-piracy "police." Most impoverished people do not turn to crime. And we have seen that Athenian and Rhodian identities within the Greek world became imbued with their role of keeping the seas safe; they were not in that business just for the money. Social factors were crucial on both sides. Vincent Gabrielsen has emphasized the close economic relationship, even mutual dependance, between Greek pirates and the police of the seas. That interdependence extended to how those groups socially identified themselves and were viewed by Greeks generally: often with reference to a specific other, and always with reference to "the Greeks" as a whole.

10
Oaths

Oaths in Greek international life

Broad swaths of Greek international law were underwritten by the power exercised on the minds of Greeks by swearing oaths. Oaths sealed international pacts such as *sympoliteia* agreements, offensive and defensive alliances, and long-term peace treaties, as well as truces to end sieges or permit gathering of the dead after battle. Within cities, oaths buttressed crucial activities such as becoming a full citizen, assuming magistracies, serving as judge or juror, and litigating in court. Hence, reliance on oaths is one of many features that Greek international and domestic law had in common. Yet we still do not have a complete understanding of how and why oaths were effective in playing their many roles, many commentators being content with the single explanation of divine deterrence. As I will argue in this chapter, however, to understand the power of oaths for Greeks we must look beyond their purely religious dimension to their social contexts and ethical features. Considering oaths in their variety of contexts and functions across Greek society will reveal more connections between Greek international and domestic law and uncover a further dimension of international law as a social reality.[1]

That oaths were effective among Greeks is rarely disputed. Andrew Bayliss not only calls oaths "the glue that held the ancient Greek city together" but claims "the same could and should be said for Greek interstate relations."[2] The widespread use of oaths by Greeks indicates they shared this view, which they sometimes openly articulated. In his speech *Against Leocrates*, delivered about 331, the Athenian politician Lycurgus endorses the value of oaths in a city. Supporting his charge that Leocrates committed treason by fleeing Athens after the Athenian loss to Philip II at Chaironeia, Lycurgus argues Leocrates violated his ephebic oath, which all Athenian male citizens had to swear upon becoming an ephebe; that is, coming of age and taking up military service for the city. The ephebic oath contained, among other clauses, a vow not to "shame the sacred weapons nor desert the man next to me, wherever I am in battle formation." Claiming tendentiously that Leocrates's hurried flight from Athens broke these clauses of the oath, Lycurgus insists on the civic value of oaths generally: "Oath is what keeps the democracy together," he claims (*Leoc.* 79).

Laws of All the Greeks. Jesse James, Oxford University Press. © Jesse James 2026.
DOI: 10.1093/9780197838556.003.0014

Lycurgus's emphasis on the ephebic oath (and, immediately following, on the oath of Plataia) reveals his belief that his audience considered that oath and others to play a special civic role.[3]

There is also wide agreement on why Greek oaths were effective: fear of divine retribution. This is surely correct, as I will discuss. But I will argue that oaths were likely effective for reasons beyond divine deterrence. Some of their effectiveness likely resulted from a wish either to establish or maintain a reputation for honesty and reliability. In addition, some people feel an ethical responsibility to abide by promises, of which an oath is a special form. I also will argue that in some circumstances oaths strengthened group identities encouraging oath takers to fulfill their obligations to members of the group. The solemnity and ritual aspect of swearing an oath also lends it greater force than ordinary expressions of intent. Finally, the high social status of people who swore the oaths undergirding international agreements would have reinforced their binding power for all concerned.

Oath structure, the divine, and deterrence

Greek oaths were usually built from three basic elements: an invocation of the gods; an agreement, action, or fact being sworn to; and a curse on those swearing falsely or violating the oath in the future.[4] We see all three elements in a fragmentary Athenian decree from the 450s approving the formation of an alliance with the members of the Pylai–Delphi Amphictyony. As reconstructed by editors, it states, "Agree on the alliance as announced by the men from the Pylaia to all the Amphictyons who have a share in the sanctuary, swearing to abide by the alliance by Apollo and Leto and Artemis, invoking ruin on ourselves if we transgress."[5] We have here (i) the agreement being sworn to ("swearing to abide by the alliance"); (ii) the gods invoked ("by Apollo and Leto and Artemis"); and (iii) a curse ("invoking ruin on ourselves if we transgress").

Uttering an oath was typically accompanied by other ritual elements. Sometimes this involved as little as standing in a certain place, as Athenian archons did when taking office; or touching a particular statue of a god.[6] When representatives of two states swore a treaty, they usually also poured libations, *spondai*. Some especially serious oaths involved animal sacrifice. At times, the ritual seems to have been customized to the occasion. For example, at the founding of the Delian League the parties sank lumps of iron into the sea.[7]

In fact, an oath's verbal aspect consisted of more than the three elements I noted above (an invocation of the gods, a statement sworn to, and a conditional curse). The oath also contained, in most contexts, communication with at least two distinct parties, the oath's human and divine audiences.[8] An audience is essential to an oath. On one hand, gods cannot enforce an oath unless they learn its content and the swearer's specified sanctions. On the other hand, need for a human audience highlights that an oath is an attempt to persuade other people *about* the swearer's commitment: "You should trust me because I am swearing, subjecting myself to divine punishment if I am lying or do not follow through." In other words, an oath is a promise. And as the philosopher John L. Austin has explained, a promise must be heard by someone who understands the utterance as an act of promising. An oath, like a promise, signals a special, heightened commitment or undertaking, communicating to a human audience that the person speaking and the statement being made are more reliable or trustworthy than ordinarily.[9]

Indeed, heightening trust appears to be the central goal of an oath. We see this if we imagine a society in which everyone always believes the truth of what everyone else says and their sincerity in any undertaking. It is hard to see a significant role for oaths in such a society because there would be no need to indicate *heightened* trustworthiness.[10] Trust involves at least two parties, a trustor and a trustee. Modern psychologists and sociologists frequently distinguish between "general" and "particular" trust. "Particular" trust pertains to a specific situation or relationship, typically between two parties, rather than to a "general" disposition to trust any random person. Oaths would mostly have affected only particular trust. Below I discuss specific ways in which they likely did so.[11]

Divine deterrence, as a deliberately built-in enforcement mechanism, is the most obvious reason oaths increased trust between parties. When Lycurgus praises the power of oaths to act as a "social cement," he attributes that power to the gods' punishment of perjurers: "Many people, by deceiving humans and escaping their notice, have not only escaped punishment at the time but even gotten away with their unjust actions for the rest of their lives. But no one who broke his oath would escape notice of the gods or get away from their punishment."[12] According to Lycurgus, this guarantee of divine retribution, if not against the oath breaker himself then against his offspring, deters people from breaking their oaths. Because oaths are sworn by (among others) those who perform vital civic functions, they "keep the democracy together" by ensuring the honesty of the people performing those functions. Greeks appear to have commonly believed that divine retribution against perjurers was inescapable.[13] Modern scholars have largely accepted the Greek explanation for their compliance with oaths. Walter Burkert asserts that, among Greeks, "the conviction exists that only fear of the gods provides a guarantee that oaths will be kept; consequently, only a man who honours the gods can be party to a contract." Sebastian Scharff emphasizes the frightening nature of the divinities who punish perjurers and argues that divine deterrence based on treaty oaths played an important role in Greek states' compliance with treaties. Greek oaths were always made in the name of one or more divinities, and the importance of this divine element is believed to be, as Lycurgus expresses it, that gods cannot be deceived or evaded. As Bayliss puts it, "Why else would the gods be invoked as witnesses in the first place?"[14]

Beyond deterrence

Emphasis on divine deterrence is merited to a degree, but the divine element of oaths had other effects. It is true that certain gods invoked in oaths were closely associated with divine vengeance. Zeus, especially under his epithet "Zeus Horkios," was the oath god par excellence precisely because he was believed to enforce oaths. Pausanias describes a statue of Zeus Horkios in the *bouleuterion* at Olympia: it held a thunderbolt in each hand and was, according to Pausanias, "of all statues of Zeus, most designed to cause terror in unjust men."[15] The Erinyes, or "Furies" from their Latin name, were closely associated with oaths, in particular with the task of punishing perjurers. In Athens, the members of the Areopagus council swore an oath of office that invoked these "revered goddesses," *semnai theai*. But the Erinyes appear to have been rarely invoked in the oath itself, so that their role as oath avengers was not dependent on their explicit invocation by a perjurer.[16]

In fact, aside from Zeus, there seems to have been some separation of functions between the gods commonly invoked in oaths and those who punished their violation. This is clearest with the "son of oath" (ὅρκου πάϊς): Herodotus reports the Spartan king Leutychides as narrating an incident to the Athenians when the Delphic oracle warned Glaucos that the son of oath destroys the families of perjurers. But one must presume that because he has no name, as the oracle itself emphasizes, he *could* not be invoked in an oath.[17]

On the other hand, certain gods commonly invoked in oaths, such as Apollo and Demeter in Athens, are not closely associated with punishing perjurers.[18] In the *Odyssey*, Helios, although himself a god, asks Zeus to punish Odysseus's men for eating his sacred cattle (12.377–84). As in other realms, the Greeks here envisaged a division of divine labor. Hence we see in some oaths an invocation of deities who represented the main aspects of the physical world—air, earth, and water—probably not as divine avengers but rather to ensure that a swearer could nowhere escape divine witnesses to perjury.[19] This is also evidence that, despite what Lycurgus thought was a "guarantee" of divine retribution, Greeks did not see oaths as somehow automatically bringing about punishment when broken. Gods had to witness the violation and impose the punishment. "Witness" gods could also be important support for human vengeance against oath breakers.[20] In many cases, the specific group of gods invoked in swearing an oath perhaps was not considered crucial to the binding nature of that oath nor determinate of which divine figures might actually punish subsequent perjury. According to Richard Janko, the key requirement was to invoke "powers greater than oneself," whose authority was recognized especially by the person swearing but also by the community. By the late fourth century, a fairly standard core list of oath gods was frequently invoked in many parts of the Greek world: Zeus, Ge, Helios, Poseidon, Ares, and Athena Areia. Among this group only Zeus is commonly treated as an oath avenger.[21]

Underemphasized both in our literary sources and in the scholarship on the role of gods in oaths is the "carrot" as opposed to the "stick." The surviving texts of many oaths specify two possible mutually exclusive outcomes: the person breaks his oath and suffers divine punishment or keeps his oath and receives divine rewards. The "consequences" section of the Athenian ephebic oath states five pairs of diametrically opposed results, both personal and communal: (1) personal health versus sickness; (2) a healthy versus sick city; (3) fertile versus barren land; and normally fertile versus monster-bearing (4) women and (5) livestock.[22] The gymnasiarchic law of Beroia states more simply, "If I abide by my oath, may many good things come to me, and if I break my oath, the opposite."[23] Here again, Greeks may have envisaged a division of labor, with some gods invoked based on their association with punishment and vengeance, others on an association with positive outcomes. Such "positive" gods are apparent in the Athenian ephebic oath's invocation of "Flourishing" (Θαλλώ) and "Growth" (Αὐξώ), and perhaps also in its invocation of "wheat, barley, vines, olives, figs" (*RO* 88, ll. 18–20). In swearing, the Greeks used gods not only to deter with fear but also to encourage with hope.

At times, a god may have been invoked, or referred to by implication, to emphasize an oath's subject matter rather than invoke divine deterrence or encouragement. An Athenian deme decree from Ikarion mentions an oath sworn by deme officials regarding production of dramatic performances featuring in the deme's celebration of the rural Dionysia festival. It implies the oath had to be sworn while touching a statue of Dionysos.[24] Because the inscription itself does not appear to name any specific gods to be sworn by, and since Dionysos was the patron god of drama, the oath was probably sworn in the name of Dionysos. But the implied invocation of Dionysos does not mean the residents of Ikarion deme envisioned Dionysos himself as inflicting punishments on perjurers of this oath. Rather, touching his statue connected those involved in his festival to a sacred object, a focus not only of that festival but also of the communal life in the deme generally. This would have driven home, to the man swearing, that his oath involved a serious ethical obligation to the community and the god. Although Greeks understood that Dionysos could be a vengeful god (as in Euripides's *Bacchae*), vengeance is not his main significance in this context.

Similarly with Athenian archons, for whom the oaths may have been less about divine deterrence than reminding people of their duties and inculcating a commitment to them. The *Athenaion Politeia*, written in Aristotle's Lyceum in the second half of the fourth century, reports that archons swore twice when taking office: once while standing on a particular stone in front of the Stoa Basileios in the agora, and again up on the acropolis (55.5; 7.1). Swearing an oath twice, in two different places, probably was not intended to increase the likelihood of divine deterrence (although different humans may have witnessed each oath). The practice more likely was intended to remind all the archons of their range of obligations to various aspects of Athenian public life: the political, legal, and economic functions, symbolically centered on the agora, and their religious functions, symbolically centered on the acropolis. It is also noteworthy that the punishment for violating the archon's oath was the requirement to dedicate a golden statue of Apollo at Delphi. That penalty was imposed by humans for the benefit of gods, rather than vice versa. To this extent, *divine* deterrence apparently was not central to the archon's oaths.[25]

Divine deterrence and reward is one aspect of the effectiveness of oaths that can be explained by "rational actor" psychological theories.[26] Another is the sort of social cohesiveness cited by Lycurgus: "oath is what keeps the democracy together" (*Leoc.* 79). One way to interpret this statement is as claiming that, to enjoy the material benefits of democracy, citizens must comply with their oaths. Oath keeps the democracy together by making it work to the material advantage of the whole community. In the context of Lycurgus's speech, it does this by compelling Athenian men to commit to participate in military defense. Similarly, Athenian jurors, by abiding by their dikastic oath, made the laws effective at guarding and regulating the community, protecting not only public safety but also the operation of the marketplace.[27]

A third "rational" explanation of oath compliance is based on reputation: that people want a good reputation because of the material benefits they think it provides and they believe oath compliance enhances their reputation (or avoids harming it).[28] People are thought more likely to enter valuable business and personal relationships with those who have good reputations. On this view, even "altruistic" oath compliance may be a rationally "selfish" strategy over the long term, so long as that compliance can be witnessed by others and might therefore enhance the reputation of the compliant person.[29]

The ethical and social elements of oaths

A fourth way to account for the effectiveness of oaths is based on their resemblance to promises: that many oath takers feel a special ethical obligation to abide by the heightened commitment indicated by the act of swearing. Contemporary empirical studies on promising show that people tend to have a stronger desire to keep promises than non-promised statements of intent. This preference likely derives partly from a wish not to disappoint a promisee's expectations after having previously encouraged those expectations (what some researchers call a form of "guilt aversion") and partly from a desire to abide by one's promises per se, independent of their effect on others' expectations.[30] Greeks, therefore, probably used some oaths not only to invoke gods who might punish a perjurer (or reward an oath keeper) but also to communicate to a human counterparty a formal and *heightened* commitment to a certain claim or course of behavior.[31] An atmosphere of formality would also tend to increase people's attention to the specific wording of an oath (the precise claim or behavior being sworn to), to ensure compliance with the "letter of the law," so to speak. Formal oath procedure might have not only helped summon potentially vengeful gods but also heightened expectations among the human participants, raising the ethical stakes.[32]

Here we must distinguish, though, between voluntary and compulsory oaths. Only voluntary oaths implicate the same ethical stakes as promises because only voluntary oaths are "up to us," to use the expression of Aristotle. He explains in his seminal discussion of the question in the *Nicomachean Ethics* that we are neither praised nor blamed for actions that are not "up to us" but due to circumstances such as compulsion or ignorance.[33] Because Athenian ephebes had no realistic option to avoid swearing the ephebic oath, that act is importantly distinct from a voluntary promise. On the other hand, because treaties were often more voluntary than coercive, treaty oaths may bear important resemblances to promises.[34]

I emphasized above the trust-instilling aspect of oaths. And in Chapter 3, I noted one of the common consequences of group identity is greater trust toward fellow group members.[35] These premises suggest a fifth possible explanation of the effectiveness of oaths: if group identity increases trust, and if oaths encourage the formation of group identities, then oaths could further enhance trust through that path. But did oaths encourage the formation of group identities among Greeks? The answer must depend both on the kind of oath and on the circumstances. Here I only suggest some possible factors in determining the group-formation potential of oaths.

Some oaths seem unlikely to have fostered group identity because they did not obviously draw on identity. This includes the oaths sworn by Athenian litigants when bringing a dispute to trial. The oaths (ἀντωμοσίαι) were made at the preliminary *anakrisis* procedure and seem to have been more or less bare statements by each litigant that his claim was true.[36]

Other oaths, however, seem largely aimed at creating or strengthening a social identity among the participants. These include citizenship oaths such as the Athenian ephebic oath. One goal of such oaths was to foster a feeling of loyalty between the swearers. For example, the Athenian ephebic oath includes a promise not to abandon comrades in arms and to act "together with everyone." I noted above Xenophon's claim that "everywhere in Greece a law is in force that the citizens must swear to agree (ὁμονοήσειν), and everywhere they swear this oath."[37] The civic oath of the Chersonesos, commonly dated to the first part of the third century, seems to confirm Xenophon: it includes promises to "be in agreement (ὁμονοήσω) concerning the security and the freedom of the city and the citizens," to protect the *demos*, and to be an enemy to anyone who plots against the city. Oaths of this sort seem designed to encourage group identity among citizens by not only fostering unity among them but also imagining a common enemy.[38]

Citizenship oaths therefore might not only memorialize membership in a group but also involve a conscious decision to defend that group and look out for its interests, an active adoption of loyalty to the group with an awareness of others making the same conscious decision.[39] It seems likely that the sense of group identity formed by such an active stance would be stronger than a more passively acquired identity, for example in modern states in which natural born citizens do not swear a citizenship oath.[40] And the invocation, in some oaths, of particular gods of local significance might have supported a feeling of connection to all the other people inhabiting the land watched over by those gods. Among the witnesses to the Athenian ephebic oath are several who were either particularly associated with Athens (Aglauros, Athena *Areia*) or who seem to be envisioned in their peculiarly Attic instantiation, that is, as representative of "the home" or "the homeland," for example Hestia, as well as the non-personified "boundaries of the homeland" and wheat, barley, vines, olives, figs. The oath invokes Hestia as goddess of *Athenian* hearths in particular, and the listing of essential crops immediately after the "boundaries of the homeland" makes clear that it is the crops occurring within those boundaries that are intended as witnesses.[41] Swearing an oath so explicitly tied to a place is likely to have strengthened the swearer's connection to all other people understood as belonging to the place. The specifically ephebic context is also important here. Service as an ephebe seems to have been designedly liminal, not only to patrol the boundaries of the state's territory but also to transform teenagers into young men (*neoi*) by means of a social and military experience calculated to bond them tightly: to each other first, but ultimately to the entire community.[42]

Treaty oaths

While citizenship oaths suggest that oaths *could* strengthen group identity, oaths made to seal international treaties are not as likely to have done so. There would typically have been less preexisting sense of group identity between citizens of different cities than between fellow citizens. Still, to the extent that agreement to an interstate treaty was, in an important sense, the formation of a single group, the attendant oaths would have fostered *some* sense of that group. There seems to have been a range of treaty-oath practice, some oaths worded to evoke a common identity but many not clearly doing so. The treaty between the Eleans and Heraeans, from around 500, states that "if anything is needed, either word or deed, they shall stand by each other in all matters and especially in war; and if they stand not by each other, those who do the wrong shall pay a talent of silver to Olympian Zeus to be used in his service."[43] The promise to "stand by each other in all matters" here is a notably broad declaration of group loyalty similar to the Chersonesean oath to "be in agreement."[44] The invocation of Olympian Zeus would also have fostered a sense of the Eleans and Heraeans as members of a common group. The sanctuary of Zeus at Olympia, where this inscription was found, was the major sanctuary lying close to and between both communities, and by this time Elis had been in control of Olympia for decades.[45] Even before this treaty was made, the worship of Olympian Zeus likely fostered a group identity among all the nearby communities whose members regularly worshipped there.[46] Hence this oath likely did both evoke and strengthen a belief in the Eleans and Heraeans as forming a group that relied on mutual trust and loyalty to prosper.[47]

A special category of international treaty is the agreement of synoikism or *sympoliteia*, under which citizens of two (or more) cities joined to become a single political community.[48] The wording of such agreements often betrays efforts to create a common group identity. A fourth-century *sympoliteia* agreement between Mantinea and Helisson asserts, "the Helisseans ["Heliswasians" in Arkadian dialect] are to be full and equal Mantineans, sharing all things that the Mantineans share, bringing their country and their *polis* to join Mantinea and the laws of the Mantineans."[49] The wording of the oath sealing this agreement does not survive, so we do not know if it reiterated this unity and equality, but the sentiment was central to becoming a single polity. An inscription from a century later, documenting the synoikism of Magnesia under Sipylos into Smyrna, does record long oaths. Each of the Magnesians was to swear not only to abide by the synoikism agreement but also that "I will act as a citizen, in agreement, causing no disruption, in accordance with the laws of the Smyrnaians and the decrees of the *demos*, and I will maintain the city's autonomy and democracy and the other things granted to the Smyrnaians by King Seleucus with all eagerness in every crisis, and I will not wrong any of them nor betray them to anyone else, as much as I am able. . . . I will help by striving with all eagerness and I will not give up (or "abandon," ἐγκαταλείψω), as much as I am able."[50] The Smyrnaians were to swear a similar complementary oath, including a promise to "be well-disposed to" (εὐνοήσω) the Magnesians, to make them and their descendants citizens on the basis of equality and commonality, to not wrong them, to prevent others from wronging them, and to aid them eagerly. The oath of a third-century *sympoliteia* agreement between Koans and Kalymnians includes promises not only to be faithful to the democracy and the common constitution but also to be friends and allies of King Ptolemy; to maintain the democracy against oligarchy, tyranny, or any other form of government; and to oppose anyone who tries to change the government. Like citizenship oaths in already-constituted communities, these oaths seem well designed to encourage solidarity among the groups involved.[51]

Aside from *sympoliteia* agreements, however, most treaty oaths may, by their language alone, have done little to evoke group identity between the allied parties. The parties often swore to vigorously defend the other when attacked or, in the case of offensive alliances, whenever they went to war. For example, in the alliance between the Athenians and Thessalians of 361/60, the Athenians swore, "I will come with all my strength as much as possible if anyone goes against the *koinon* of the Thessalians in war, or deposes the archon whom the Thessalians have chosen, or establishes a tyrant in Thessaly." The Thessalians swore with almost identical language.[52] Often the text of the oath either was not included in the inscribed version of the treaty, is not preserved in surviving pieces of the stone, or merely states something such as "I swear to abide by the agreed alliance." In a third-century treaty between the Athenians and Spartans, the oath promises simply "to remain in the established alliance." Such oaths seem unlikely to have fostered strong feelings of group identity.[53]

I have focused on the aspects of oaths directly implicated in their spoken, verbal elements. But we should briefly consider a nonverbal feature that may have strengthened international treaty oaths: who swore them. Unsurprisingly, promises made by high-status people are trusted more than those made by those of low status.[54] This points to another advantage of Greek oath practice in the concluding of international agreements, since it was usually high-status officials—generals, chief magistrates, or kings—who personally swore those oaths.[55] Their oaths gained credence from public perception of their power and political wisdom. They were well positioned to know if their state would be likely to uphold the treaty and keep their oath valid. And they could personally influence their state's compliance with a treaty. The oaths of such power brokers would carry weight with people representing the treaty's counterparty.[56]

At times a treaty, even when sworn by a small group of officials, would subsequently have to be ratified by another authority, whether an individual ruler or a more democratic body.[57] In such cases, the counterparty likely had an eye also to the predictive nature of that ratification process: if the treaty was ratified (even by people who did not personally swear to abide by it), that approval served as further indication of the community's commitment to respecting the treaty. Even then, the high status of the oath-taking officials must often have reassured the other side that the treaty partner would be reliable.[58]

A final note on high-status oath takers. Interstate oath ceremonies are one of many ways Greek elites formed and reinforced international networks that, for reasons I explained in Chapter 4, likely socialized those elites to abide by a common code of ethics and rules. A common identity among the Greek international elite would, overall, have encouraged those oath takers to have confidence in each other's commitments to what was sworn, and to believe they would do what they could to ensure that their home states abided by the agreement in question.

Conclusion

Greek use of treaty oaths, and especially the effectiveness of those oaths, was based on more than a belief in divine enforcement or a concern for reputation. Oaths likely made treaties more effective by fostering common identity, triggering the oath takers' ethical commitment to the terms agreed and, usually, engaging high-status oath takers. Even if Greeks themselves pointed only to deterrence to explain the power of oaths, it does not fully account for the centrality of oaths in Greek society. It is exaggerating to say that oaths were the glue that held the Greek interstate system together, but they did catalyze psychological and social effects that helped make it operate recognizably as a system.

11

The Thessalian *Koinon* as an International Legal Structure

Levels and spectrums of international organization

In Chapter 2, I considered the problem of applying the term "international law" in the ancient Greek context. One of my points was that, because there is not a precise line, even in the twenty-first century, between "domestic" and "international," the highly permeable and often difficult-to-discern boundary between domestic and international in the Greek world should not deter us from describing some Greek contexts and some Greek law as international. In fact, the very continuity of domestic and international realms, to the extent it derives from similarities of structures, norms, and rules at various levels of Greek society, implies related continuities between domestic and international law. Greeks found international law to be as ordinary as domestic law, requiring no special explanation or qualification. This permeability and continuity between what are now sometimes seen as separate domains supports my interpretations of Greek international law (partly) in light of modern research into domestic legal socialization: domestic and international contexts overlap and run together and human behavior in those contexts is broadly similar.[1]

The continuity and permeability of "international" and "domestic" in Greek law becomes particularly apparent in *koina*, federal leagues. I noted in Chapter 2 that Greek federalism varied on a spectrum terminating on one end at synoikism into a single city and on the other end at the ordinary military alliance between largely independent cities. In this chapter, we will see more concretely that there were *koina* very far toward the "international military alliance" end of this spectrum: international legal organizations of largely sovereign *poleis*.[2] Because such an argument is necessarily case-by-case and grounded in close consideration of historical detail, I limit myself to the example of Thessaly down to the early fourth century. In contrast to more centrally organized *koina* such as the Achaians or the Boiotians, which seem to have been largely state-like for long periods, the Thessalian cities from the sixth to early fourth century appear to have worked together mostly for military purposes. Decision-making of "the Thessalians" is visible in the historical record almost exclusively in circumstances of military urgency. Whatever "constitution" governed the Thessalians as a whole did not

Laws of All the Greeks. Jesse James, Oxford University Press. © Jesse James 2026.
DOI: 10.1093/9780197838556.003.0015

differ much from a *symmachia*, yet its rules could still be called "laws," *nomoi*. The Thessalian case therefore offers evidence of the reach of Greek international law, showing that even the law governing certain *koina* was international. More generally, the wide spectrum of Greek federalism, constituted by a variety of specific organizations whose rules can all be understood as "legal," is evidence of the even wider spectrum of Greek legalism as a whole.

By using Thessaly as an example to enrich our understanding of the range of Greek contexts in which international law was implicated, I also intervene in the long scholarly debate over how best to conceptualize the legal and political reality of the Thessalians down to the middle of the fourth century. The dominant tradition has understood Thessaly in the sixth and fifth centuries as a rural land of kings and barons rather than of cities, a largely unified feudal state that trailed most of Greece in developing a culture of self-governing *poleis*. This view has given way on multiple grounds, most importantly that Thessalians adopted a *polis* culture as early as Greeks in other regions. The challenges have recently culminated in Emma Aston's thorough demonstration of how thin the evidence is for the unified statehood view. She replaces the idea of a single Thessalian state with her picture of a group of *polis* communities led by hereditary elites who, bound by multiple aspects of "Thessalian" identity, cooperated with each other when it suited their interests.[3] Aston, however, may go too far in the antistatehood direction, giving little credence to our evidence for formal structuring agreements and cooperation among Thessalians. Maria Mili has offered a middle way, a view of a more or less socially unified Thessalian *ethnos* without the institutional rigidity of a federal state but still amounting to "a network of competing alliances" (2019, 281). I agree with her implication that we do not have to choose between a black-or-white dichotomy of a "formal state" bound by domestic law versus a "loose *ethnos*" bound by no law at all. Therefore in this chapter I outline our evidence for the public lives and activities of Thessalians from the seventh through early fourth centuries and propose that international law offers a useful concept for theorizing the Thessalians in a third way, along the lines sketched by Mili. My claim is not that Thessaly in this era was a purely international realm (such a realm has never existed anywhere) but that it is best understood as structured and connected by rules amounting to a form of international law. In other words, having international law as an available concept in the Greek world lets us see Thessaly as a law-bound institution although not an ordinary domestic state.

Theorizing Thessaly as an international legal organization, though, poses a version of one of the central questions animating this book: what made the rules of Thessalian communal action as effective as they were? In the interest of keeping this chapter focused on its central theme of the political and legal conceptualization of Thessaly, I will not answer that question in depth, but recent scholarship offers the material to do so. One of the many virtues of Aston's book (building on recent work by Mili, Bouchon, Helly, and others) is its rich account of how a Thessalian identity, shaped over the centuries, bound Thessalians to each other regardless of the extent of formal political and legal structures among them. In this way, her identity-sensitive account of Thessalian history builds on Emily Mackil's analysis of the complex ways in which identity, economics, and politics interacted in the formation and coherence of the more state-like *koina* of the Boiotians, Achaians, and Aitolians (2013). Aston's synthesis of the Thessalian historical experience therefore not only complements Mackil's history of those three better-known federal leagues but also connects to my proposals throughout this book for how group identity could reinforce the operation of international law among Greeks. I return to this point at the end of the chapter.

The shadowy unity of early Thessaly

The people called "the Thessalians" inhabited the parallelogram-shaped plains of central Greece bounded on the north by the foothills and mountains of Perrhaibia (including Olympos and the Cambunian range), on the west and south by the massifs of Pindus and Othrys, and on the east by Mt. Ossa and Pelion bordering the Aegean (see Map 9 on the facing page). This area is sometimes called "tetradic" Thessaly, from the four districts or tetrads into which it was divided for apparently military administrative purposes: Pelasgiotis, Phthiotis, Thessaliotis, and Hestiaiotis/Hestiotos (listed in clockwise order from the northeast). The Thessalian *koinon* consisted of the more than two dozen cities of this region, chief among which were Larisa, Pharsalos, and Pherai. In addition to the free population of tetradic Thessaly, there was a serf-like population of agricultural laborers called *penestai*, often compared by scholars to Spartan helots. And inhabiting the mostly upland areas around tetradic Thessaly were the so-called *perioikoi*, groups of free peoples with their own political arrangements but who were at times politically or militarily subjected to the tetradic Thessalians to various degrees. The structures of this *koinon*, relations between *koinon* and *polis*, and the free population of tetradic Thessaly that may have participated in political and legal decision-making are what concerns me here.[4]

Some sort of early Thessalian unity is indicated by "Thessalian" membership in the Pylai–Delphi Amphictyony, the international organization whose primary task was to govern aspects of the panhellenic sanctuary of Apollo at Delphi. Membership in the Amphictyony was by *ethnos*, and the Thessalians appointed two representatives. It is unclear if Thessalians were members since the Amphictyony's founding, which Pierre Sánchez cautiously dates somewhere in the long stretch between 750 and 600, but the Thessalians as a group, even if not founding members, had probably joined the Amphictyony by the

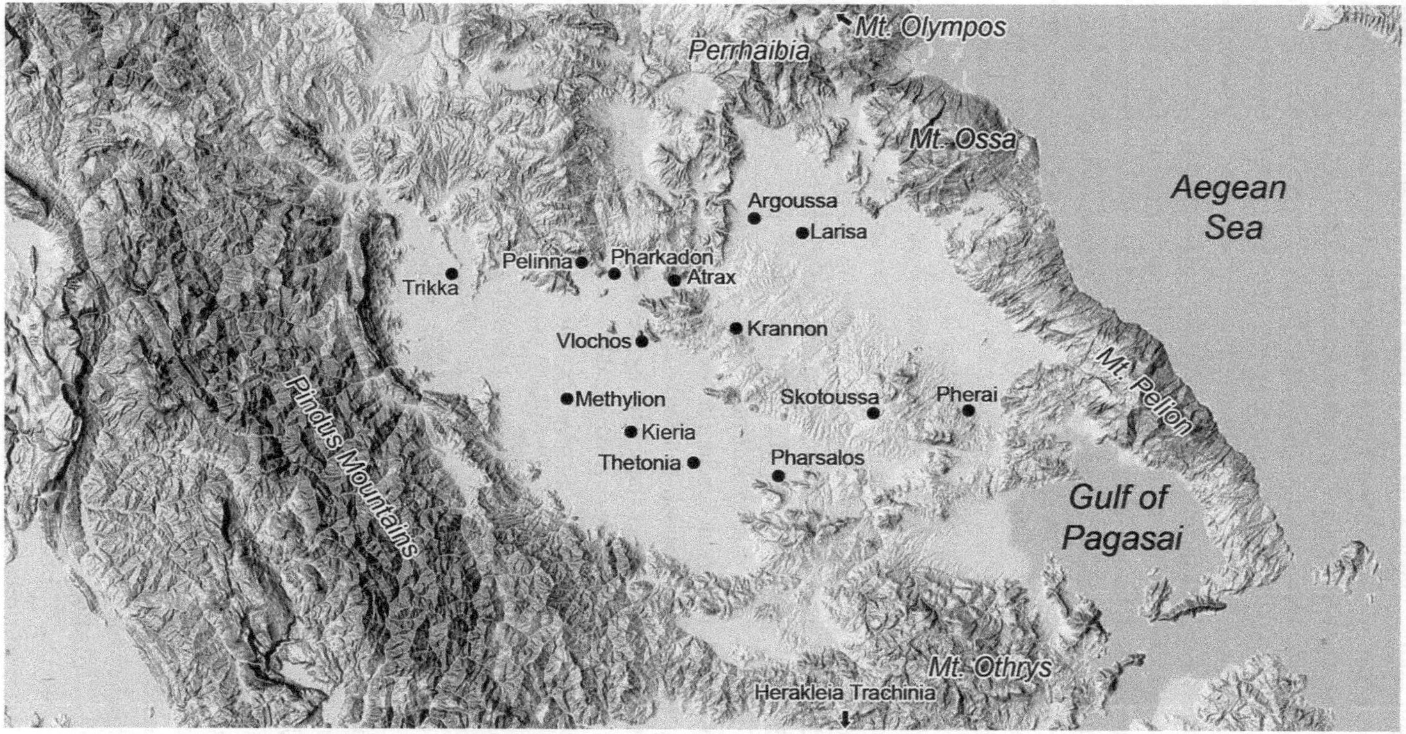

Map 9 Topography and cities of Thessaly. For Thessaly's location, see the map in Chapter 8. Map by R. Salem.

mid-sixth century.[5] By this time, then, there was presumably already some sort of "Thessalian" identity, although it is possible that the formal organization of the Amphictyony was itself a formative act of that identity, similar to how the Cleisthenic deme reorganization likely reset some forms of local identity among Athenians in the fifth century, as I suggested in Chapter 3. In either case, the Thessalians must have had rules for selecting their common representatives to the Amphictyony, in a forum that both reflected and reinforced Thessalian unity. We have no idea what those rules were, and the appointment of amphictyonic representatives is the only nonmilitary communal Thessalian decision-making for which we have good evidence in the period I am concerned with.[6]

Down to at least the middle of the fourth century we have no evidence for the existence among Thessalians of federal (as opposed to *polis*) citizenship or of a regular federal assembly or council, two features that have long been seen as most characteristic of a federal state.[7] Nevertheless, a form of early Thessalian political or military coherence may be seen in our evidence for a few rich and powerful families, and of certain men described as "kings" (*basiles*, sing. *basileus*), wielding power in Thessaly by the sixth century. For example, Aristotle reported that Thessaly was divided into the divisions called tetrads that I mentioned above in the time of a legendary "Aleuas the Red," perhaps the founder of a family based in Larisa.[8] But it is unclear how many Aleuases there were, whether he was an historical figure, when he (or they) lived, and whether his power was usually wielded over Thessaly as a whole or mostly in Larisa. A family called the Echekratidai also appears to have been based in Larisa. A third great Thessalian family was the proverbially rich Skopadai of Krannon. Skopas the son of Kreon is the most famous member, thanks to Simonides, who wrote for him the poem whose interpretation is debated in Plato's *Protagoras* (339a). Dating him from Simonides, scholars have proposed that this Skopas probably died late in the sixth century. And from Pharsalos came the rich and prominent family of Meno, also most famous now from his role in a Platonic dialogue.[9]

Yet we cannot say that members of such families held formal political positions. Herodotus calls the Aleuads at the time of the Persian Wars in the early fifth century "kings of Thessaly." In a slightly earlier context, he also uses "king" to describe Kineas, the man chosen by the Thessalians to help the Peisistratids—the family that ruled the Athenians as tyrants for a over generation—repel Spartan attempts to drive them from Athens around 511. According to Thucydides, in 454 the Athenians assisted a certain Orestes, "son of Echekratides king of Thessalians," in his unsuccessful attempt to seize Pharsalos. The "kings" mentioned are sometimes associated with a particular city although they are called kings "of Thessalians" or "of Thessaly."[10] Bruno Helly has argued persuasively that Thessalian men called *basileus* in our sources were essentially hereditary aristocrats exercising power in individual cities: several men of the same family could be called *basileus* simultaneously, as could men from different families and *poleis*. In other words, being a *basileus* should not be mistaken for being the sole executive leader of the Thessalians. Aston suggests "lords" as a more fitting translation. The rank, or status, may have indicated membership in a decision-making council or been a qualification for certain local or *koinon* offices, in particular as a military leader. But the existence of multiple politically active and powerful families based in different Thessalian cities is consistent with a view of the *koinon* as a system of allied cities protective of their independence.[11]

Although the "kings" of Thessaly were not central federal executives, there was another office that does seem to have exercised broad power across Thessaly as a whole, at least at times. Most scholars call this figure the *tagos*, following Xenophon's description of Jason of Pherai's ambition in the 370s to become *tagos* of all Thessalians. When the Thessalians had a *tagos*, according to Jason, the cavalry numbered six thousand, the hoplites ten thousand, and the *perioikoi* became Thessalian subjects. Jason eventually became *tagos* "by common agreement." He immediately accounted for all available cavalry and hoplites and ordered the perioikic communities to pay the same tribute assessed upon them in the time of Skopas. Xenophon's account portrays the *tagos* as an elected official with some sort of military authority over all Thessaly and the right to collect tribute from the perioikic communities, but in an office that was not always filled.[12]

Xenophon's account of Thessalian events in the early fourth century has been used in reconstructing sixth- and fifth-century Thessalian political structures and led some to conclude that Thessaly was continuously organized around a strong central executive called a *tagos*. A century and more ago, the historians Eduard Meyer and Julius Beloch both (separately) went so far as to draw up lists of Thessalian *tagoi* for the sixth and fifth centuries. But no source earlier than Xenophon in the mid-fourth century, and no inscriptional evidence of any period, mentions a Thessaly-wide office of *tagos*; it is always *polis*-level.[13] Bruno Helly has therefore argued against the conclusion that the leader of Thessaly was named *tagos* at any time before Jason of Pherai. He proposes instead that *tagos* was a military officer, but not commander-in-chief, and that the head of all Thessaly was called variously *archon*, *archos*, or *tetrarchos*. Yet his alternative is based on similarly scanty evidence and on his tenuous argument that a *tetrarchos* was a leader of all Thessaly rather than of a single *tetrad*.[14]

Although an intermittent military commander likely indicates less concentration of centralized power than a continuous *archon* or *tagos*, it is consistent with a rule-bound alliance of cities connected in an international legal structure. Under that alliance, it seems, already in the sixth century the cities of Thessaly agreed to appoint a leader (whether he was called *tagos*, archon, or something else) in times of military need and to endow him with authority to raise an army and the funds to operate it. Herodotus suggests this arrangement when he reports that the Thessalians, "by a common resolution," sent a thousand cavalry with the *basileus* Kineas (5.63.3). From roughly the time of division into tetrads, then, there seems to have been an agreed, established mechanism by which Thessalians from different cities could come together for joint military action. That mechanism, as well as the division into tetrads itself, could be elements of a form of international law equivalent to a military alliance. Aston has emphasized the "fundamental importance" of the division into tetrads as the "earliest known articulation of the boundaries of Thessaly as distinct from the perioikic *ethnē* around it" (2024, 227). Hence it seems that the Thessalians were reifying a "Thessalian" identity at about the same time as, and perhaps through the same means by which, they were establishing a skeletal form of Thessalian law: a law whose very effectiveness likely drew strength from that cohering sense of group identity, even if the law's purpose was to coordinate joint military efforts among a group of "Thessalian" tetradic communities that had just recently been officially delineated.

And there is, indeed, evidence for early joint Thessalian military activity. Herodotus describes a late sixth-century conflict between the Phokians and "the Thessalians" in the years before the Persian Wars. And I mentioned above his account of Thessalian assistance to the Peisistratids of Athens, around 511, because of a preexisting alliance. Here Herodotus claims the decision was made by the Thessalians in some collective sense: "having come to a common decision." His specification shows that collective action by those called (or calling themselves) Thessalians was not assumed but that there were procedures for Thessalians to act collectively.[15]

Although Thessalians regularly acted in apparent unity for military purposes, Herodotus sometimes indicates awareness of localized military decisions and actions within Thessaly. Describing Thessalians siding with the Persians in their invasion of the Greek mainland in 480, Herodotus distinguishes between the Aleuads and the rest of the Thessalians. It is the Aleuads specifically who "invited" the Persian king Xerxes to Greece, and Herodotus suggests that Xerxes *mistakenly* believed they represented all Thessalians in so doing. As Herodotus tells the story, other Thessalians (perhaps led by the Pharsalians) were displeased with the schemes of the Aleuads, first tried to resist the Persian invasion in the north of Thessaly, and went over to the Persian side only after it became clear that the Greek alliance would not try to defend Thessaly. Overall, Herodotus's references to the Thessalians are consistent with a view of them as a (mostly) united military alliance of a sort easily understood as a creature of international law.[16]

Pindar tantalizingly but vaguely refers to a "law of the Thessalians" in his tenth *Pythian* ode, composed at the beginning of the fifth century before the Persian invasion.[17] More concretely, the rules of the Thessalian alliance are explicitly referred to as "law" in two texts of the fourth century referring to an earlier era. Xenophon specifically declares the legal nature of the *tagos*'s office when he states that Jason "was appointed *tagos* in accordance with the law (*nomos*) of the Thessalians."[18] Although this happened in the 370s, Xenophon's statement comes in the context of Jason's own claims, mentioned above, that the office of *tagos* reached back to (probably) the sixth century. Xenophon's language may reflect a Thessalian understanding that the role of *tagos* was governed by Thessalian "law" from its beginnings. Fifth-century rule among the Thessalians as a whole is described with legal terminology by Daochos, a fourth-century Thessalian official who commemorated, in a statue group at Delphi, the achievements of his grandfather and other family members, including himself. The inscription under the grandfather's statue reads in part, "I am Daochos son of Agias, Pharsalos is my native city, having ruled all of Thessaly, not by force but by law [*nomos*], for twenty-seven years."[19] The contrast of "law" with "force" indicates that Daochos is claiming his grandfather ruled in accordance with regulations agreed to by the Thessalians. Here again, the wording, presumably drafted by Daochos the grandson, may record actual language used by the grandfather and reflect a fifth-century Thessalian view that Thessalian "law," *nomos*, governed the highest Thessaly-wide office.[20]

The international nature of Thessalian unity

I have just argued that the rules governing Thessalian joint action count as a form of law. They also count as a form of international law, rules agreed to by, and applying to, a group of fundamentally independent cities, each of whose citizens governed their own internal religious, civic, and financial affairs. In Aston's words, "the polis, so far from being weak and under-developed in Thessaly as used to be claimed, was actually the prime unit of religious, civic and political life" (2024, 7).

Cities took root early in Thessaly. Archaeological and inscriptional evidence before 500 BCE or so, while sparse, indicates there was active *polis*-level organization in the region by the seventh century, continuous with quite old local settlement patterns, even if not all those *poleis* were centered in dense urban settlements at this time.[21] At the sites of at least two Thessalian cities, archaeologists have found evidence of early cult activity for Athena *Polias*, a goddess whose special realm was the *polis* itself.[22] Another *polis*-oriented inscription from the sixth century, on what may be a boundary stone for a sanctuary of Hera, seems to call the goddess "Hera of the *demos*."[23] Hecataeus, writing probably in the late sixth century, named at least four Thessalian cities.[24] Pausanias (10.16.8) tells us that Echekratidas of Larisa dedicated the first statue at Delphi. If, as is almost certain, Pausanias took the dedicator's name from the statue base itself, it suggests that at an early date (probably in the sixth century) Echekratidas chose to identify himself with the city of Larisa rather than as a Thessalian.

In the fifth century, we see evidence for real political life in Thessalian *poleis*. An inscription has been found in Argoussa that calls itself "a law for the demos." Upon violation, it requires payment to the civic deity Athena *Polias*. It mentions what appear to be local officials called *tagoi* and shows the city regulating religious activity. This inscription is firmly rooted in *polis*-level civic life.[25] A mid-fifth century inscribed dedication from Vlochos describes its dedicator as *archegetes*, perhaps a civic office.[26] Another inscription, a bronze plaque from perhaps the third quarter of the fifth century, shows the Thetonians awarding a Corinthian named Sotairos with *asylia*, tax exemption, and the title of *euergetes*, "benefactor." The local *tagos* is assigned with enforcing the decree and another apparently local official is mentioned: the forest warden.[27] Around the same time, the Pheraians made two grants of proxeny whose records survive on bronze plaques.[28] Proxeny grants are especially relevant indicators of *polis* status and independence for my purposes because they show a city developing relations directly with citizens of other cities. When a city granted proxeny, instead of the *koinon* as a whole doing so, the city government asserted itself as an entity with its own presence on the international stage. As William Mack argues, proxeny "emerges as the characteristically Greek form of inter-*polis* networking and was . . . closely bound up with ideas of what it meant to be, and to be seen to be, a *polis*."[29] In this case, because the home *poleis* of both recipients were outside of Thessaly, it is especially telling that "the Pheraians" rather than "the Thessalians" made the grants.

Three fifth-century dedications to goddesses appear to have strong civic significance. One is a private dedication from Larisa, dated between 450 and 425, to Enodia *Astike*, "Enodia of the city" (*astu* meaning "city" or "town"). The other two are from Atrax: one, dated to the early fifth century, is dedicated to Athena *Agoraia*, "Athena of the *agora*," by officials called *archons*; the other, dated to the mid-fifth century, is dedicated to Themis *Agoraia* by the *tagoi*.[30] In all three cases, people are dedicating a monument to a goddess who indicates by her name her local political importance. The civic aspect is especially forceful in the Atrax dedications: apparently local officials enacting public worship of goddesses whose function was overseeing the *agora*, the space that, perhaps more than any other, served as the center of public life of a Greek city, not only as marketplace but as the *locus* of political and judicial activity.[31] And Aristotle reports in the *Politics* that Gorgias of Leontini, on a visit to Larisa, made a joke about the Larisaians granting people citizenship. The joke, based on the existence of professionals called *larisopoioi*, works best if the Larisaians did in fact grant citizenship and had a reputation for doing so.[32] Taken together, this evidence indicates that within individual cities local officials were managing their own civic affairs independently from other cities in Thessaly.

Coinage also indicates a significant degree of *polis* independence in fifth-century Thessaly, yet also cooperation among some cities.[33] A number of Thessalian cities began minting coins in the first half of the century. The Larisaians seem to be the first in Thessaly to have minted, and their earliest issues have been dated immediately after 479. The striking similarity of the earliest Larisaian coinage to that of Macedon to the north has often been noted and may indicate a specifically Larisaian friendliness to the rulers of Macedon.[34] Several other cities soon began minting coins in their own names, with coinages that fall into several groups, each identifiable by its common iconography and weight standard. One group included certain coins of Larisa, along with coins from Krannon, the Perrhaibians, Pherai, Trikka, Pharkadon, Pelinna, and Skotoussa. These coins, issued starting in the late 470s, portray on their obverse a man maneuvering a bull, which scholars have taken as representing a traditionally Thessalian rodeo sport. Another group, minted starting in the 440s, included coins from Methylion and Skotoussa, as well as coins labeled with abbreviations apparently meaning "of the Thessalians." They all portray on their obverse the front half of a jumping horse and a sprouting grain on the reverse. On some, the horse is emerging from a rock, apparent reference to the creation of the first horse by Poseidon. The Pharsalians and Kierionians minted their own coins, both bearing some similarities to but distinct from the coins of the other groups.[35]

On one hand, the cooperation of multiple cities in what may be interchangeable common coinage suggests a monetary union of sorts within each group. Furthermore, portraying on one group of coins a distinctly Thessalian rodeo activity indicates that this cooperation was connected to and fueled by Thessalian identity. And Poseidon's creation of the first horse, portrayed on another group, was placed by legend in Thessaly generally rather than at a specific city. Hence this iconography reinforces the pan-Thessalian ideology of these coins, although they may have been minted by a city whose ruling class simply had pan-Thessalian ambitions.[36] On the other hand, even the coins within a group show discernible iconographic differences and are labeled with the names of individual *poleis* indicating where they were minted, and there were at least four distinct sets of coins being minted in the second half of the fifth century. It seems that individual cities had sufficient independence for their governments to decide whether to join one of these loose monetary unions. And the Skotoussans appear to have either switched groups or belonged to two groups simultaneously. This variety suggests that in the fifth century Thessalian coinage practices reflected an underlying city independence more than federal centralization. Aston has suggested that Thessalians minted a common coinage in the mid-fifth century to facilitate the financing of joint military activities. If so, this twofold cooperation on an apparent underlying bed of city independence indicates the existence of formal inter-*polis* agreements reasonably seen as a form of international law while not approaching a federal unity that could be interpreted as Thessalian statehood.[37]

Our evidence for the internal lives of the Thessalian cities through the fifth century, relatively sparse as it is, shows local citizens controlling their own religious, civic, and fiscal affairs. They seem to have been independent polities by some significant indicators, and therefore it is reasonable to view Thessaly in the sixth and fifth centuries as an international region populated by cities whose agreements to coordinate action on amphictyonic affairs and military action was a matter of international law. As our view of Thessalian military action becomes more granular down through the fifth century, my picture of Thessaly as a military alliance rather than a unified state is supported further by the increasing visibility of internal divisions and of the possibilities for independent action within the alliance.

Distinctions in focus: the fifth century to Philip II

Immediately after the Persian Wars, we see evidence that the Thessalian *koinon* was more like a military alliance of independent cities than a unified federal state. At this time, according to Pausanias, the Spartan king Leotychidas led an expedition against the Aleuads in Thessaly, presumably as retribution for their recent support of Persia. But Leotychidas, having arrived in Thessaly, accepted bribes from the Aleuads and left the territory when he might have conquered the entire country.[38] Plutarch, however, claims that in Thessaly Leotychidas did manage to depose from power two men, Aristomedes and Agelaos, and thereby "stopped the *dynasteia* among Thessalians."[39] These men are otherwise unknown. But if Plutarch can describe Leotychidas as having ended the *dynasteia* among Thessalians while Pausanias can indicate that he did not depose the Aleuads, it suggests Thessaly at the time was composed of politically distinct entities, presumably individual cities or small groups of them.[40] Leotychidas overturned one or two cities (Aristomedes and Agelaos may have been in the same family) but left the Aleuads, based in Larisa. In this way Pausanias and Plutarch corroborate a distinction already suggested by Herodotus between Thessaly as a whole and political centers within it.[41]

Encouraging the view of Thessaly as an alliance rather than a state is that even on the international military stage the Thessalians were not always viewed monolithically. In the context of the Peloponnesian War, Thucydides in several places distinguishes Thessalians geographically and, more importantly, describes what appear to be differences in foreign policy within Thessaly. As the conflict between the Athenian and Spartan alliances escalated into war in 431, Thessalians fought alongside the Athenians, but Thucydides provides *polis*-focused details of the Thessalian forces: "This assistance from the Thessalians was in accord with their old alliance with the Athenians, and the Larisaians, Pharsalians, Krannonians, Pyrasians, Gyrtonians, and Pheraians came to help them. Their leaders were: from Larisa, Polymedes and Aristonous, one from each party; and from Pharsalos, Menon. And there were also leaders from each of the other cities."[42] Here we see a *polis*-based organization within the Thessalian army that was distinguishable even to non-Thessalians. This passage also suggests that only a subset of Thessalian cities even sent soldiers to help the Athenians. Each city contingent had a leader (or two, as with Larisa), and Thucydides names no commander-in-chief of Thessalian forces (whether such a figure would have been called *tagos* or *archon*). The admittedly sketchy picture is of a Thessalian *koinon* that, even in matters of foreign affairs, is not presenting a monolithic face to the outside world but rather behaving as a group of cities acting in concert, honoring an alliance they made as a group.[43]

Thucydides offers similar localization of Thessalian foreign policy in his description of opposition to the founding of Herakleia Trachinia at the southern edge of Thessaly by Spartans in 426, in the heat of the Peloponnesian War. He specifies the opposition came from "the Thessalians who were in power in the region."[44] Several years later, in 420/19, "some Thessalians" joined the Ainianians, Dolopes, and Malians in attacking and defeating a Herakleian force led by the Spartan Xenares (Thuc. 5.51). Despite these southern Thessalian pockets of active hostility to the Spartan colony, it seems that the small action of 431 discussed in the previous paragraph was the only time Thessalians actively took sides in the war between the Spartans and Athenians.[45] The Spartans apparently did not consider these attacks on their colony by southern Thessalians to be a general Thessalian declaration of war against Herakleia's mother city, because two years later the Spartan general Brasidas could call the Thessalians his "friends" without any apparent objection from them (as discussed below). It is also noteworthy that Thucydides does not name the Thessalians in his two separate catalogs of Athenian allies: neither at the beginning of the war nor during the great battle at Syracuse in 413. Therefore it seems that, after 431, the Thessalians as a whole were neutral in the Peloponnesian War.[46]

Thucydides further depicts a fragmented view of Thessalian foreign policy in describing how, in 424, Brasidas led Spartan forces north (4.78). At the southern border of Thessaly, Brasidas sent messengers to his "friends" (ἐπιτηδείους) in Pharsalos seeking safe passage. Thucydides names several Pharsalians who, with "other Thessalians," led Brasidas and his men into Thessaly. Still south of Pharsalos they were confronted by another group of Thessalians opposing their passage. These latter men claimed Brasidas was committing a wrong in proceeding "without the common consent of all" Thessalians. Brasidas's Thessalian friends replied they were simply taking care of their *xenos*, their guest-friend, who had arrived unexpectedly, while Brasidas claimed to be a friend (φίλος) of the Thessalians—in other words, not just of these Pharsalians. The opposing group withdrew, and Brasidas led his soldiers on a forced march northward. Thucydides attributes Brasidas's success in traversing Thessaly to a form of government that was fundamentally oligarchic rather than democratic: "If the local Thessalians didn't have *dynasteia* [as their form of government] instead of *isonomia*, he never would have proceeded."[47] Thucydides may be indicating that the local, presumably Pharsalian, oligarchic *dynasteia* had a foreign policy distinct from that of the Thessalians generally and that the local dynastic rulers realized this and hence did not seek the common consent of all Thessalians or of all Thessalian cities. The picture, again, is of a Thessaly with strong localized politics that had direct effects on a variegated foreign policy.

The internal peace between Thessalian cities that apparently accompanied Thessalian neutrality ended, with the Peloponnesian War, about 404. This is when Lykophron of Pherai, "wanting to rule all of Thessaly," fought and defeated in battle a group of Thessalians that included Larisaians. In 402 Aristippus, an Aleuad of Larisa and *xenos* of Cyrus the Persian prince (as the Aleuads had been during the Persian Wars), reportedly received from Cyrus six months' pay for four thousand mercenaries. These soldiers were intended to help Aristippus against his political opponents. It is unclear whether these opponents were within Larisa itself or from another part of Thessaly, but the most obvious candidates are either Lykophron or Larisaians who supported him.[48] In 395 Lykophron was still in power in Pherai and fighting once more against Larisa, where a man named Medios now held authority, as Diodorus reports (14.82.5–6). Hence we see a splintering of the Thessalian *koinon*. From at least 404 until 395, the Pheraians broke away to such an extent that they were fighting against several other Thessalian cities, who may in turn have considered themselves to be representing the *koinon* and seen Pherai as the rebellious member.[49]

Two speeches suggest the Larisaians at this time may have been pursuing their own foreign policy. One, called *Peri Politeias*, is attributed in the manuscripts to a certain Herodes. It is generally agreed that "Herodes" refers to the second-century CE politician and sophist Herodes Atticus, but there is an old debate whether this ascription is accurate; whether the speech is by a rough contemporary of Herodes; or whether it in fact dates to the late fifth century. Regardless of when or by whom it was written, the speech (about six pages long) may represent the late fifth-century historical situation accurately.[50] The speaker argues that the *polis*, which remains unnamed throughout, should make an alliance with the Spartans against the aggressions of its close neighbor Archelaos.

Because Archelaos inherited the Macedonian throne from Perdiccas in 413 and ruled until 399, and the speech does not discuss the Athenians as a significant force, those believing the speech to be authentically of the period typically date it to sometime between the defeat of Athens in spring 404 and Archelaos's death in 399.[51] The speech appears to show an individual unnamed city debating formation of an alliance with the Spartans and declaration of war on Archelaos.[52] If the speech is not from the fifth century, it is still evidence that an apparently well-informed later writer (Herodes or a contemporary) found it reasonable to present at least one Thessalian *polis* as debating and making its own foreign policy in the late fifth century.[53]

A fragment from another speech that dates uncontroversially to the late fifth century explicitly concerns relations between the Larisaians and Archelaos, thus indicating the Larisaians' independence in foreign affairs. The orator and sophist Thrasymachus, most famous now for his fictional role in Plato's *Republic*, is reported to have composed a speech "On Behalf of [or "Concerning"] the Larisaians," from which the following line was preserved by Clement of Alexandria: "Are we, being Greeks, to be slaves to Archelaos, a barbarian?"[54] Theodore Wade-Gery plausibly suggests this speech was written to be delivered on behalf of Larisa before a non-Larisaian audience (1945, 21). That a speech concerning relations with Archelaos is titled "On Behalf of the Larisaians" rather than "On Behalf of the Thessalians" is evidence that the Larisaians were at least partly conducting their own foreign affairs at the end of the fifth century.

Xenophon in the *Hellenica* reinforces the image of an atomized Thessaly in his description of the Spartan king Agesilaos's voyage through Thessaly from his successes in Asia Minor in 394. Agesilaos was harried by "the Larisaians, Krannonians, Skotoussans, and Pharsalians, allies of the Boiotians, and all Thessalians except those who happened to be in exile."[55] Xenophon makes no mention of Medios, the *dynastes* of Larisa who had driven the Spartan garrison out of Pharsalos the previous year. His phrasing suggests the Thessalian cities were acting individually as allies of the Boiotians and that it is almost by chance that "all Thessalians" were on the same side in this fight.[56] A similar impression is made by Plutarch's much later account of Agesilaos's passage, in which Agesilaos, plundering "the land of the Thessalians, who were allied to his enemies," sent two envoys into Larisa to make a pact.[57] He may have been trying to peel the Larisaians out of the general Thessalian alliance with the Boiotians rather than to convert all of Thessaly to the Spartan side. As Agesilaos proceeded south, according to Plutarch, it was the Pharsalians alone rather than a united force of Thessalians who harassed Agesilaos and whom Agesilaos defeated in a cavalry battle (*Ages.* 16.5). We could even reconcile the accounts of Xenophon and Plutarch if we took Xenophon's list of Thessalian cities as deliberately ordered from north to south and understood him to mean that Agesilaos was opposed, *in turn*, by "the Larisaians, Krannonians, Skotoussans, and Pharsalians." This interpretation would also explain Xenophon's highlighting of the fact that it was a Pharsalian cavalry commander, Polycharmos, who died fighting the Spartans: not because Polycharmos was leading a pan-Thessalian force but because it was the Pharsalians alone who opposed Agesilaos when he reached the southern edge of Thessaly.[58]

Events in Thessaly are almost undocumented for the nineteen years from Agesilaos's defeat of the Pharsalian cavalry in 394 until Jason of Pherai claimed to be reinstituting the office of *tagos* in 375. Xenophon describes the late stages of Jason's rise to power as a re-formation of a splintered Thessalian *koinon*. By the time Jason approached Polydamas of Pharsalos and tried to persuade him to bring the Pharsalians into alliance with the Pheraians, Jason claimed already to have the most powerful Thessalian cities as his allies, *symmachoi*. Polydamas ultimately persuaded the Pharsalians also to become Jason's *symmachoi*.[59] Xenophon's use of this word—twice—suggests that he saw Thessaly as a *symmachia*, an alliance, rather than a state. But like all alliances, this one had rules, in this case both for appointing a *tagos* and for supplying money and soldiers. As noted above, Xenophon declares that Jason was appointed *tagos* according to Thessalian law.[60] As Jason explains to Polydamas in a passage I quoted earlier, "Whenever Thessaly has a *tagos* the number of cavalry amounts to six thousand and the hoplites amount to more than ten thousand." These rules extended to exacting tribute from the *perioikoi*: Jason ordered them to pay the tribute that he claimed had been assessed in the time of Skopas (6.1.19).[61]

After Jason's assassination in 370 and a subsequent power struggle, Alexander of Pherai came to power as *tagos*, ruling harshly and unpopularly. But Thessalians outside of Pherai (Diodorus mentions Larisa by name) disputed his rule, appealing for help first to the Macedonian king, then to the Thebans, and finally to the Athenians.[62] Diodorus treats the anti-Alexander faction as representative of the *koinon*, and the *koinon* as a group to or from which cities could be added and removed: defeated by the Thebans, Alexander "was forced by agreement to give back to the Thessalians the cities he had subdued, to give back Magnesia and the Phthiotic Achaians to the Boiotians, and for the future to rule only Pherai, as an ally of the Boiotians."[63] It is not clear that outsiders ever considered Alexander to represent the *koinon*; he was instead the tyrant of Pherai who sometimes controlled other cities in Thessaly. The Athenians apparently viewed their alliance with him to be with Alexander personally rather than with the Thessalians. This is indicated in the later treaty between the Athenians and "the Thessalians" (who are referred to, in the inscribed version, as the *koinon*): the Athenian decree of that treaty required the removal of "the stele for Alexander."[64]

Another point of terminology suggests that our surviving sources for Thessaly in the early fourth century did not view the *koinon* as a unified state. None of them describes these decades of on-and-off strife among Thessalian cities as *stasis*, the ordinary Greek word for civil war. Diodorus describes the fighting between Alexander and the Thessalians as "conducting a war" (διαπολεμοῦντες, 15.80). He uses the same term to describe the conflict between Medios of Larisa and Lykophron of Pherai in 395 (14.82.5). Diodorus elsewhere follows the Greek conventional wisdom that war (*polemos*) and *stasis* are different things. *Stasis* is typically within a city, and when Diodorus applies the term also to civil strife within Rome he indicates that *stasis* is strife within a state more broadly defined, rather than just within a Greek *polis*.[65] Xenophon, in turn, does describe the situation *within* Pharsalos in 375 as *stasis* (*Hell.* 6.1.2). To Greek eyes, it seems, when the cities of Thessaly fought each other, they were conducting an ordinary interstate war rather than engaging in civil strife.[66]

Conclusion

I stop my historical survey in the 360s, before some Thessalians invited Philip II (in the 350s) to assist them against Pherai. Philip's acceptance of that invitation commenced a century and a half of Macedonian hegemony in Thessaly, a period in which the already vestigial *koinon* institutions seem to have been entirely in abeyance.[67] I have argued that Thessaly was, up to this time, less unified and more *polis*-centered than it is sometimes described and that the primary and almost sole function of *koinon* institutions was coordinating military activities of the Thessalian cities and making alliances with states outside of Thessaly. There was, at least at times, centralized responsibility for military and foreign affairs and for directly related organizational measures (raising armies and funds for them) but, so far as we can tell, for little else.

None of this is to say that the Thessalians were, or were viewed by other Greeks as, a typical alliance or a "bare" *symmachia* of cities joined solely by military considerations. On the contrary, with regard to military affairs the Thessalians normally acted together and were seen by other Greeks as a unity. Although I have noted many cracks in that unity, the default for much of the period I am considering was that Thessalians fought together.[68] And indeed, as I discuss in this chapter's epilogue, Thessalians were united by far more than war-making, while throughout this book I have argued that most Greek international relations were tied by more than pure material considerations such as security. But my argument is that their often closely unified military activities did not make the Thessalians a federal state. Aside from electing representatives to the Pylai–Delphi Amphictyony, nonmilitary functions were, it seems, exclusively under the jurisdiction of individual cities, which at times exercised independence even in military matters and foreign affairs.

The basic substance of this view is not novel. I already mentioned Aston's and Mili's recent separate disassembling of the "unitary federal state" narrative dominant in the twentieth century. Before them, Hans Beck and Peter Funke had characterized Thessaly as "effectively resembl[ing] a fighting alliance" (2015b, 11). Even Bruno Helly, who calls Thessaly at all periods a state, *état*, admits that the *koinon* down through the fourth century was "simultaneously a unitary and multipolar construction" as opposed to the more centralized Thessalian *koinon* of later times.[69] The theoretical contribution of my analysis is to insist that the rules governing relations between Thessalian cities were therefore a form of international law.

Viewing the Thessalian *koinon* as an international organization contributes to a wide vision of the varieties of Greek international law. If we admit that at least some *koina* count as international, we must take them into account in writing the history of Greek international law, a process I have begun with this chapter. It helps us see we do not have to view "Greek international law" as an all-or-nothing proposition, as a phenomenon that either always existed everywhere in Greece or never existed anywhere. Instead, international law may have sprouted, taken root, and grown into a wide variety of forms at different times and places in Greece. The Thessalian *koinon*, with its rules, was just one of those forms.

Epilogue: Thessalian identity and international law

In most of this chapter I have used "the Thessalians" in a political sense, as a way of referring to the people and cities of the Thessalian *koinon*, a group of cities that cooperated especially in military matters. But "Thessalian" also referred to a socially and historically constructed *ethnos*, a group of people who imagined they shared a common descent, either from a single mythical founder named Thessalos (a son of Heracles) or from a group of Thessalians who, sometime in the legendary past, invaded the territory that later became known as Thessaly, driving out the Boiotians who resettled further south.[70] This common descent was once accepted as a fact by historians as it was by many Greeks in antiquity; but scholars now generally speak, as I just did, about the "construction" of *ethnos* identity, a process that can often be traced in our literary and archaeological sources. Emma Aston has now performed this tracing thoroughly for the Thessalians, describing how Greeks—Thessalians and non-Thessalians alike—used mythology, cult, literature, and coinage to mold an identity of the "Thessalians" (2024). I noted a few instances of such identity construction in my main discussion above but would like to focus on it briefly here in order to tie my exploration of Thessalian history more tightly back into the question of identity with which so much of this book is concerned.

The name "Thessaloi" is known at least since the seventh century, where we find it in a fragment of the Spartan poet Alcman, who seems to group Thessalians among shepherds and other "country folk."[71] Certainly it was not just their shared name but also shared experiences that brought the Thessalians together. I mentioned briefly, in a footnote above, shadowy early military events such as the Lelantine War and First Sacred War, in which Thessalians fought together against a common enemy.[72] But our sources for those wars date much later and it is unclear to what extent the historical events themselves brought Thessalians together, compared to how the later *tradition* of their occurrence molded a common Thessalian identity. It may be that these wars helped create "the Thessalians" both when they were fought and in their successive retellings over the centuries. In any case, it seems to have been perfectly ordinary to refer to "the Thessalians" as a coherent group by the beginning of the fifth century at the latest, as is reflected in the writings of Herodotus and Hekataios, among others.

Certain religious beliefs and cultic practices had pan-Thessalian resonance. I already mentioned the two Thessalian representatives to the Pylai–Delphi Amphictyony, probably starting in the sixth century. Through this membership, worship at one of the most important religious sites in the Greek world marked "the Thessalians" as a distinct group. The cult of Athena *Itonia* has often been considered not only distinctively Thessalian but also pan-Thessalian, a reason for people from across Thessaly to come together for communal rituals, although the variety of evidence for cult activity before the third century could also reflect more localized practices.[73] The cult of Poseidon, specifically in his guise as Poseidon *Petraios*, seems even more likely to have united all Thessalians. Legends reported that Poseidon effectively fabricated Thessaly by cleaving the mountains at what became the valley of Tempe, permitting what had been a huge lake to drain into the sea and reveal the plains of Thessaly. He also created the first horse by ejaculating on a rock in Thessaly—or by striking it with his trident. Thus the plains of Thessaly, exposed for human habitation by Poseidon's action, were also the Greek region best suited to raising horses, creatures begotten by Poseidon; and Thessalians were always known for their use of horses and the quality of their cavalry. The relevance for Thessalians of this connection between Poseidon, horses, and the land of Thessaly is shown by some of their earliest common coins, the "Thessalians" coins mentioned above, from the first half of the fifth century: these depict a horse apparently springing from a rock, a gift from Poseidon to all Thessalians.[74]

In short, on a stratum above all the local variation and fragmentation of cult, politics, and coinage *within* Thessaly, there was a recognition of a common Thessalian *ethnos* identity connecting the region's inhabitants. This *ethnos* identity, formed in part by legends of united Thessalian combat against other Greeks such as Phokians and Boiotians, would have encouraged Thessalians from different cities to trust each other, to look favorably on each other, and to cooperate with the primarily military regulations, the international laws, of the *koinon*. Thessaly was not a state, but it was bound by law, and a common Thessalian identity helped socialize Thessalians to respect that law.

12
Conclusion

Reconsidering Greek international law

The Greek world was profoundly international. For centuries, around a thousand cities co-existed in varying degrees of independence and interdependence. Sometimes, cities subjugated cities, whether by brutally forcing them into unequal military alliances or milking them for people or cash. Sometimes, ambitious, charismatic, and violently successful men formed kingdoms over wide territories, using their control of armies, logistics, and rhetoric to coerce and persuade the people in cities to do their bidding, although those people rarely became "citizens" of a royal "state." In some places, cities coalesced into federal leagues, complex political and legal structures that left *polis*-based institutions largely intact. The degrees of city independence varied but the fundamentally international nature of the Greek world long subsisted, beyond the first century BCE.

Although this was a landscape of charisma and coercion, rhetoric and repression, it was also a landscape of law, of relations governed by written and unwritten rules, treaties and traditions, ethics and enforcement. Greeks traveled and traded over long distances and across political borders; made contracts—and broke them; took out loans—and defaulted on them. The victims in turn often sued for justice or grabbed someone's goods in legitimate self-help. Pirates and highway robbers often attacked, but with the knowledge they were violating a universally recognized law and of the harsh penalties awaiting them if caught. Cities made treaties, normally abided by them, sometimes argued over their interpretation, and often went to war because of them. It was an uncertain and violent world but awash in international laws connecting people across cities and seascapes, *koina* and kingdoms.[1]

This Greek international complexity yielded to the encroaching relative uniformity of the Roman empire, but only slowly, over centuries. Absorption by the Romans began concretely with the formation of the Roman province of Macedonia in 146 BCE but was complete only three and a half centuries later, in 212 CE. This is when the emperor Caracalla bestowed Roman citizenship on all free residents within the empire's borders, and with that citizenship the full jurisdiction and repertoire of Roman law. It is beyond the scope of this book

Laws of All the Greeks. Jesse James, Oxford University Press. © Jesse James 2026.
DOI: 10.1093/9780197838556.003.0016

to explore the process by which Greeks shifted from being allies, *socii*, of the Romans to being provincial subjects and, ultimately, citizens. But I suggest one fruitful way to study that process may be as a gradual "domestication" of international law. One circumstance that would have eased this process, as least conceptually, is that the Greek international world the Romans entered in the late third century BCE was not a lawless universe of atomized states but a law-suffused ecosystem of people, communities, treaties, arbitrators, and courts. So the gradual Roman absorption of an international Greek world into a single Roman state with universal citizenship is not a story of the imposition of law into "empty" spaces between Greek states. Rather it may be a story of the transformation of preexisting Greek legal matter into Roman *ius*.[2]

This book has been a start on a new history of Greek international law. The project required some ground clearing and foundation laying, including a new defense of the very act of addressing a topic under that name. Beyond that I have had two main aims. First, I have written a new history of select aspects of Greek international law. My focus has been on elements that, to my mind, have been underemphasized or misunderstood in the main stream of scholarship. My selection of topics should not be taken as a claim that what I have explored at length was historically most important. For example, although I omit detailed discussion of military alliances and peace treaties while devoting two chapters to *symbola*, this does not mean *symbola* are the more significant phenomenon. But I do believe they were more common and more important to everyday life and commerce than is widely appreciated.

My second chief aim has been to treat Greek international law neither as simple power politics on one hand nor as pure legality on the other but as an essentially social phenomenon that must be understood partly as the consequence and conjunction of the social psychologies of vast numbers of actual people. I have tried to show the fruitfulness of understanding international law with the tools of sociology, or at least in light of the results of legal sociology studies (since it is impossible to perform such studies on long-dead people). The particular "sociological" route of this book has largely followed the implications of group identities that formed across the various social networks traversing the Greek world. I have argued that social identities were critical to the effectiveness of Greek international law, nourishing psychological conditions essential not only to law-abiding and law-enforcing behavior but in some circumstances even to violation of international law, in the form of piracy. Here again, my focus on social identity is a corrective of previous neglect in studies of international law, not an assertion of its causal primacy. While I have focused on the social psychology of identity over power politics and economics, I have not claimed that the former was always more influential on behavior than the latter two. But the high politics of power, war and peace, and economic factors, being perennially emphasized in scholarly treatments of Greek international life, need little highlighting by me for readers to appreciate their importance.

Yet I *have* argued that certain approaches, in particular to understanding why people comply with law, have indeed been overemphasized by others. Therefore, in Chapter 3, I argued for an understanding of law compliance different from the still-dominant deterrence views that are often based, wittingly or not, on a narrow form of rational-actor psychological theorizing. Despite the allure of simplifying theory, we must maintain a realistic picture of humans as psychologically complex, socially embedded creatures if we want to understand how and why people formulate, follow, break, and enforce rules at various levels of society. Although I did not, in this book, treat in detail Greek use of treaties or the laws of war, I would urge that to understand those international legal phenomena we should also take into account the social and psychological richness I have insisted on, including group identity.

This human complexity interacts with the complexity of many social groups at multiple scales in the Greek world, along with the norms and rules such groups always give rise to. Greek society had laws and law-like rules at all levels, from the household stratum of the *oikos,* through intra-city groupings such as *genos*, phratry, and deme, as well as private professional associations, to the centrally important *polis* and beyond to the *koinon*, alliance, kingdom, and empire. These social associations were interpenetrated by webs of *philia*, *xenia*, proxeny, trade relations, religious ties, and more. To pick out only one of these levels—the *polis*—as the exclusive domain of "genuine" law is, therefore, to misrepresent how Greeks themselves understood the rules they followed and applied to each other. Greeks understood at least some rules governing international activities to be laws just as much as domestic laws were, and they created, obeyed, and enforced them mostly for the same reasons: partly for "rational" reasons of maximizing gains and minimizing losses (especially financial); but largely from forces I have gathered under the label "legal socialization": ethics, religion, habit, group identity, personal relations.

It is not that variations in social scale have no meaning. There are both moral and psychological differences, for example, between family obligations, *polis* obligations, and the obligations of interstate treaties. But those differences can be hard to discern, dependent on context, and easily exaggerated. This is one reason a delicately refined conception of what constitutes "real law" has more importance for philosophers of law than for the psychology of ordinary people, for their law-abidingness or lack thereof. One consequence is that any "fuzziness" or continuity between levels of social scale need not cause conceptual problems concerning discernment of a *single* scale or level at which "law" existed for Greeks. We can treat a phenomenon as legal even if it is unclear whether it occurs on the domestic or international stage or somewhere between.

If taken very far in a certain direction, this line of argument can result in questioning the usefulness of the category "legal" at all for understanding human society or history. We need not be tempted so far. To consider an example from a different realm of inquiry, just because biology, geology, and chemistry must comply with and may be ultimately explicable in terms of physics (four fundamental forces, certain laws of thermodynamics and mathematics), few people deny the usefulness of studying certain phenomena as variously "chemical," "geological" or "biological."[3] Just because all human phenomena *may* be reducible to certain facts of individual human biology does not mean this is always the most interesting scale at which (or perspective from which) to view them. Legal phenomena are subject to a similar and common multiperspectivism. This is the cause of the strange disconnection some law students feel between most of society's ordinary understanding of law—one shaped largely by the dramatic interpretations of television, film, and books—and the version they learn in law school, based mostly on statutes and legal opinions. Learning to "think like a lawyer" traditionally means, in part, replacing one's understanding of "law as drama" with "law as practical science." In fact, however, being a successful lawyer means often exploiting both versions of law—performance and practical science—simultaneously. The historian of law can and ought to incorporate even more perspectives on law, depending on what kind of history he or she is writing. This is another reason that, while I have tried to reclaim the "legal" as a useful and interesting perspective from which to study Greek international life, I have avoided taking a narrow view of what "legal" means. I have brought to bear on Greek history more "behavioral" than "practical" jurisprudence.

Indeed, I have tried to present a broadly humanist version of Greek international law, one in which people act for many reasons and from diverse motives—reasons and motives familiar not only to economists and international relations theorists, not only to sociologists and psychologists, but to novelists, dramatists, and poets. I have also insisted it is always people acting: "states" do not do anything. And while the legal is humanist in my conception, there is no need to conceive of it as encompassing all human experience. We can admit the Greek international sphere was legal in important ways without insisting this implies a metaphysical change of status requiring rejection of prior approaches that ignored law as an element of Greek international life.

A central aspect of that life was economic, and much of the international law I have discussed in detail closely implicated economic activity. I have tried to enrich the now-dominant new institutionalist and law and economics approaches to understanding the Greek economy with a legal-sociological tack. Perhaps my most fundamental claim in this regard is that we have to look beyond the rules of institutions to the underlying factors that made those rules effective in practice. Alain Bresson, in his monumental study of the Greek economy, emphasizes both the fundamental contribution of international trade to Greek economic activity and the role of *syla* and *symbola* as international legal institutions supporting that trade.[4] It is our responsibility to take his results further, lest we risk assuming that the mere existence and theoretical availability of a legal institutional process means that all legal disputes will be resolved through that process in a fair and unbiased manner. This assumption would be false. I have argued that, like any legal process, *syla* and *symbola* were affected by social and psychological factors including group identities.

Josiah Ober, in his equally ambitious study of an apparent "ancient Greek efflorescence," similarly stresses the importance, for Greek economic growth, of international trade; of what he calls the "small-state, dispersed-authority" ecology of the Greek international world; and of political and legal institutions. But the institutions he focuses on are internal to individual Greek cities, not those that helped the Greek international system as a whole to function effectively. I suggest that my discussions of *syla* and *symbola* in particular help bridge Ober's gap by means of international law, namely by showing how Greeks institutionalized beyond the domestic level.[5]

I mentioned above certain self-imposed limitations to the scope of this book's subject matter. A further limitation has been both conceptual and historical: I have restricted myself to international law among Greeks. This constraint, aside from being a practical result of my own scholarly limits, derives from a premise I argued for in Chapter 4: that Greeks saw themselves as a social group with a coherence distinguishing them from all those who were not Greek. Yet, to fully understand how international law operated in the Greek world, we must understand that world properly, which means giving up the idea that there was a "Greek" world at all, strictly speaking. Rather there was just the world, of which Greek-speaking people were a part, and international law existed among the many overlapping social, political, economic, linguistic, and religious groups inhabiting the Mediterranean region in the first millennium BCE. A full history of Greek international law would therefore be a history of international law in the ancient Mediterranean and beyond. It would probably begin in the second millennium, perhaps with the "Amarna" archive of letters between the Babylonian, Hittite, Egyptian, Mittani, and Assyrian kingdoms, and continue deep into the Roman imperial period.[6]

Expanding our view of international law could help to confirm or refute the validity of my interpretation of Greek international law with contemporary theories of group identity and legal socialization. For example, if we found that international law was used and adhered to just as robustly *between* major Mediterranean ethnic, linguistic, religious, and social groups as *within* particular groups, that would be evidence that group identity did not play a major role in socializing people to international law.[7] On the other hand, as I hinted in Chapter 9 with regard to piracy, a larger "Greco-Roman" identity may have developed, one that partly defined itself in opposition to the "barbarian." The notion of a perceived common Greco-Roman culture—and hence identity—is (because of the nature of our sources) most familiar in "high" culture: literature, philosophy, art, and architecture. And even here it is important not only to consider the "Hellenizing" Romans (Plautus, Cicero, Vergil) but also the "Romanizing" Greeks (Dionysius of Halicarnassus, Diodorus, Strabo, Statius).[8] And in these contexts the importance of elite networks as avenues for the formation of identity and the shaping and transmission of norms seems obvious. At first blush, refined literary "classicizing" may appear far removed from the hurly-burly contexts in which international law is seen as most relevant, but the idealistic elements of identity can ramify in many aspects of human behavior. Hence a common Greco-Roman identity, even if initially fostered largely by networks of elite people studying literature and philosophy, could ultimately have both encouraged the observance of international legal norms among those who identified with the group and also fostered biases that pushed the out-group members (such as Cilicians and Illyrians, for example?) to violate those norms at higher rates.[9]

My argument about the role of identity in Greek international law connects to questions about the larger and more general history and operation of international law. It has long been argued that modern international law arose in the sixteenth and seventeenth centuries as a European phenomenon rooted in common ties of heritage, legal culture, Christianity, and history, a pattern that repeated itself in the nineteenth century. These origins have left their mark, arguably, in the ways western countries have used international law as a tool for establishing long-term imperial dominance over non-European countries, which I mentioned in Chapter 1. They have also left their mark on the most official definition of international law, which still includes "the general principles of law recognized by civilized nations," *civilized* being a not-so-subtle euphemism for European, western, Christian, and white. My identity-based approach to international law suggests that some amount of compliance with and use of modern international law is due to common group identities among citizens of different nations. We may contrast this with the institutionally rooted Kantian theory of a "democratic peace," the claim that modern democracies (what were called "republics" in Kant's day) do not go to war with each other. Kant explained this in terms of how democracies make decisions about going to war, an institutional explanation distinct from group identity. But it could overlap with an identity-based account if democratic government itself becomes a ground for group identity, as it likely has.[10]

If it is true that group identities can nourish the operation of international law, then strengthening contemporary international law means more than altering its rules and structures; it also means taking group identity into consideration. But we must always remember identity cuts two ways. In Chapter 3, I quoted Socrates's claim, in Plato's *Republic*, that Greeks are "naturally friends" and should not fight wars against each other. The other side of this coin, for Socrates, is that Greeks and non-Greeks are "naturally enemies," and the word for their hostility is, simply, "war" (*Resp.* 470c). Although the modern ideology of contemporary international law denies such a Manichean view and asserts the universal validity of that law, the social reality of group identity that grounds the Platonic view is alive and well. We must remember this in our efforts not only to understand the successes and failures of international law today but also to make it a more effective tool in the quest for peace and justice. I began this book by noting similarities between law and architecture. A phenomenon noted by historians of modern architecture is that many architects have struggled with the question of how much they should adopt from ancient Greek styles, how much to adapt, and how much to reject. Modern international lawyers may find similarly productive an engagement with ancient Greek international law.[11]

Abbreviations

References to the works of ancient authors are abbreviated generally in accordance with the *Oxford Classical Dictionary* (4th ed.), edited by S. Hornblower and A. Spawforth (Oxford, 2012). References to inscriptions generally follow the recommendations of "GrEpiAbbr, Version 03, Septembre 2024: List of Abbreviations of Editions and Works of Reference for Alphabetic Greek Epigraphy," available online, e.g. at https://aiegl.org/grepiabbr.html. For the following collections of inscriptions I use abbreviations other than those of GrEpiAbbr:

AIUK	*Attic Inscriptions in UK Collections.* Available at: atticinscriptions.com/papers/aiuk/
ML	Meiggs, R., and Lewis, D.M. 1988. *A Selection of Greek Historical Inscriptions to the End of the Fifth Century BC.* Revised ed. Oxford.
Nomima	van Effenterre, H., and Ruzé, F. 1994. *Nomima. Recueil d'inscriptions politiques et juridiques de l'archaïsme grec.* 2 vols. Rome.
OR	Osborne, R., and Rhodes, P.J. 2017. *Greek Historical Inscriptions 478–404 BC.* Oxford.
RC	Welles, C.B. 1934. *Royal Correspondence in the Hellenistic Period. A Study in Greek Epigraphy.* New Haven.
RO	Rhodes, P.J., and Osborne, R. 2003. *Greek Historical Inscriptions 404–323 BC.* Oxford.
SvA	Bengtson, H., Schmitt, H.H., and Errington, R.M. 1969–2020. *Die Staatsverträge des Altertums.* Vols. 2–4. Munich.
Tod	Tod, M.N. 1933–48. *A Selection of Greek Historical Inscriptions.* 2 vols. Oxford.

Abbreviations

Notes

Unless otherwise noted, all translations are my own.

Chapter 1

1. I am not aware of any general social history of Greek architecture such as DeLaine (2023) offers for Roman architecture. But Zuchtriegel's (2023) account of the origins of the Doric order focuses on social processes; Nevett (2023) discusses the social forces shaping Greek domestic architecture; Barringer (2021) offers a social history of the built environment of Olympia; and Paga (2021) offers a political and social history of Athenian architecture of the sixth and fifth centuries. An earlier, socially contextualized study of domestic and urban architecture is Hoepfner and Schwandner (1986). On the increasing scholarly focus on social aspects of Greek architecture, see Barletta (2011, 627, 630).
2. The primary sources for the thirty years' peace are provided at *SvA* 156, i.e., entry 156 in the multi-volume collection edited by Bengtson, Schmitt, and Errington (1962–2020), *Die Staatsverträge des Altertums*, which gathers the literary and epigraphic sources for all known treaties of the ancient Mediterranean world from 700 to 31 BCE, together with German translations and select bibliography. The Athenian alliance known as the Delian League is *SvA* 132.
3. Thuc. 1.67.4; cf. Ar. *Ach.* 532–34. On the disputed question of the so-called "Megarian decree" or decrees, see Zahrnt (2010, 611–24); Stadter (1989, 274–82) and (1984); Gauthier (1975); Ste. Croix (1972, 225–89, 381–97); and my discussion below.
4. Thuc. 1.68.3–4. Epidamnos was a colony of Corcyra, which in turn was a colony of Corinth. When fighting broke out between Epidamnians and Corcyreans, the Corinthians took the side of their "granddaughter" city Epidamnos while the Athenians sided with the Corcyreans. Immediately after a naval battle at Corcyra, the Corinthians had accused the Athenians of "acting unjustly by starting a war and violating the peace," ἀδικεῖτε, ὦ ἄνδρες Ἀθηναῖοι, πολέμου ἄρχοντες καὶ σπονδὰς λύοντες, 1.53.2. Thucydides narrates the Corcyra episode at 1.24–55. See my further discussion in Chapter 3.
5. Thuc. 1.126–27. On Pericles's eagerness for war, see Thuc. 1.141, 2.13.
6. The Athenians said they "were ready to resolve their disputes by adjudication, in accordance with the treaty," δίκῃ δὲ κατὰ τὰς ξυνθήκας ἑτοῖμοι εἶναι διαλύεσθαι περὶ τῶν ἐγκλημάτων, Thuc. 1.145; see also 1.78.4, 1.140.2, 1.144.2. Modern translators and scholars universally translate δίκη in this context as "arbitration," and δίκη is sometimes used in that sense, but it may be significant that Thucydides uses this ordinary word for referring to a lawsuit or trial in Athens rather than the more specialized word for arbitration, δίαιτα (or, less commonly, ἐπιτροπή). In any case, it is unclear what form the adjudication would have taken, and the exact terms of the clause, as of the entire thirty years' peace treaty, are unknown. According to Thucydides, the Athenians at Sparta described the clause as providing that the parties would "resolve their differences by adjudication," τὰ δὲ διάφορα δίκῃ λύεσθαι, 1.78.4 (as implied by Pericles at 1.140.2), whereas the Spartans in 414 understood the provision to have stated that neither side would take up arms so long as the other wanted adjudication, ὅπλα μὴ ἐπιφέρειν, ἢν δίκας ἐθέλωσι διδόναι, 7.18.2. Ste. Croix (1972, 259) argues the latter formulation is more authoritative and that not all disputes had to be adjudicated; see also Piccirilli (1973, 104–08).
7. Thuc. 1.118.3. On later Spartan regret, see Thuc. 7.18.2. It may be that the Spartans in 432 judged the Athenians to have breached the peace, including the adjudication clause, by having already acted unilaterally with regard to certain disputed questions rather than bringing them to adjudication.
8. Thuc. 1.44.1: "to consider the same people enemies and friends," τοὺς αὐτοὺς ἐχθροὺς καὶ φίλους νομίζειν. See *Ath. pol.* 23.5, where the oath of the Delian League is expressed as "the same party is to be enemy and friend," τὸν αὐτὸν ἐχθρὸν εἶναι καὶ φίλον. Yates (2005, 71) argues the Peloponnesian League became a full offensive and defensive alliance only in the mid-fifth

century. The statement in the *Ath. pol.* is evidence that "having the same friends and enemies" was a feature not only of bilateral alliances, *contra* Hornblower (2002, 14).

9. On the contested question of the nature and rules of the Peloponnesian League, see Yates (2005); Bolmarcich (2005); Baltrusch (1994, 19–30); Lendon (1994); Cawkwell (1993); Ste. Croix (1972, 101–24, summarized at 339–40). For the binding quality of a majority decision for war or peace, see Thuc. 5.30.1; cf. 1.125.1; Cawkwell (1993, 364–5). At least one Spartan ally in the fifth century, the mysterious Erxadieis, agreed simply to go "wherever the Spartans led," [hεπομ]ένος hόπυι κα Λα[κεδαιμόνιο]ι hαγίονται, *OR* 128, 4–5 (see their commentary for questions of dating this inscription, perhaps ca. 450, in which case it is our earliest evidence for such a clause). Bolmarcich (2005) argues that Sparta had both "equal" and "subject" allies, reflecting different terms of alliance. Lendon (1994, 164) argues, against the common view, that the Peloponnesian League had no standing rule requiring a majority vote and that the binding nature of a majority decision suggested by these passages was "probably not an abiding 'constitution' of the Peloponnesian League, but instead part of Sparta's agreement with her allies for the prosecution of the war against Athens." This explanation seems overcomplicated. What would have been the earlier procedure for agreeing to such a majority-vote provision? Would it have required a mere majority agreement, or unanimity? Thucydides (1.125.1) states that "the majority voted to make war," τὸ πλῆθος ἐψηφίσαντο πολεμεῖν, with no indication a special procedural rule was applied. It is simpler and preferable to assume that a majority vote on matters of war and peace was normal although not always mentioned by our sources. Even if Lendon is correct, the League still had a constitutional rule regarding making war and peace, but the rule would be that the allies had to follow wherever Sparta led unless there was a prior agreement providing otherwise.
10. See Thuc. 1.96. A second rule was that members were not permitted to leave the alliance (at least not unilaterally), a stricture first enforced against the Naxians, Thuc. 1.98.4. Allies who tried to leave generally came under more direct Athenian control, as illustrated not only by the Naxians (Thucydides, exaggerating, says they were "enslaved," ἐδουλώθη) but also, e.g., in the Athenian decree setting legal and political procedures for the Erythraeans, on the mainland of Asia Minor, after they (with Persian support) rebelled from Athens, *IG* I^3 14 (*OR* 121; *SvA* 134) (dating perhaps to the late 450s but maybe two or three decades later, see Papazarkadas [2009, 78]). Other apparently universal rules of the empire were promulgated in the so-called standards decree, *IG* I^3 1453 (*OR* 155). Thucydides has Athenians boast (self-servingly, of course) of the stringent legality in accordance with which the empire was governed, 1.77.1–4; for an example they may have had in mind, see *IG* I^3 10 (*OR* 120; *SvA* 149), regulating cases brought at Athens against individuals from Phaselis (see my discussion in Chapter 8). By the time of the "fully developed imperial system" (the phrase is Meiggs's), it appears that cases arising in any of the allied cities, and in which the penalty was exile, death, or loss of citizen rights, had to be brought in Athens (or could at least be appealed there), see Meiggs (1972, 224–26); Antiph. 5.47 ("and it is not permitted for a city, without the Athenians, to put anyone to death," οὐδὲ πόλει ἔξεστιν ἄνευ Ἀθηναίων οὐδένα θανάτῳ ζημιῶσαι). But ordinary bilateral *symbola* agreements continued to be in force for most judicial cases, as suggested by the Phaselis decree cited above and by Alcibiades's treaty with the Selymbrians in 407, *IG* I^3 118 (*OR* 185; *SvA* 207), ll. 25–26: "whatever dispu[tes] they have, [the trials] are to be in accordance with *symbola*," ὅ τι δ' ἂν ἀμφισβη[τõσι, δίκας] εἶναι ἀπὸ χσυμβολõν. Meiggs's (1972, 232–33) interpretation of the Athenian statement at Thuc. 1.77.1, which I prefer to Hornblower's (1991–2008, i.122), supports the conclusion that *symbola* agreements continued in force where they had not been otherwise preempted; see James (2023).
11. For a thorough discussion, and attempt to reconstruct the specific wording, of the treaty creating the Delian League, see Scheibelreiter (2013, 89–253). On the early Delian League and its meetings, see Thuc. 1.96.2–97.1; Scheibelreiter (2013, 228–31); Meiggs (1972, 44–9). As Hornblower notes (1991–2008, i.147): "we hear of no meeting [of Athenian allies] in the preliminaries to the Peloponnesian War." Calling the fifth-century Athenian hegemony an "empire," as I do here, is a scholarly convention. It has been noted that "empire" is misleading when applied to the Athenian case, see Shaw (2022, 508); Morris (2009, 99). On Athenian conceptualization of their empire as a "tyranny," see Hoekstra (2016).
12. On relations between colonies and mother cities, see Malkin (2016, 39–46); Graham (1983); Werner (1971). On Greek colonization generally, see Tsetskhladze (2006–08); Boardman (1999). On Epidamnos, Corcyra, and Corinth, see Sheets (1994, 64–70); cf. Malkin (2016,

43): "The call for international arbitration . . . implies that both sides had confidence in the mutual recognition of colonial *nomoi* by the entire Greek world."

13. On foundation decrees, see Graham (1983, 40–68), focusing on those of Cyrene (*ML* 5; *SEG* 9.3; *SvA* 103), Naupaktos (*ML* 20) (a re-colonization or reinforcement decree), and Brea (*IG* I³ 46; *OR* 142). A few illustrative examples of mother cities exerting control over colonies in specific realms include: sending later settlers: *ML* 20 (East Lokris into Naupaktos); preventing uprising: *OR* 176, ll. 7–8 (Thasian decree regarding plots "in the colonies," ἐν τῆις ἀποικίησιν, or concerning "any of the colonists," τινὰ τῶν ἀποίκων); imposing criminal laws (Teos and Abdera, early fifth century, see Adak and Thonemann (2022, 139–42), discussing their Document 3 [*OR* 102C]); regulating commerce: *OR* 103 ii, l. 3 (Thasian decree regulating commerce in wine and mentioning officials "in charge of the mainland," οἱ πρὸς τὴν ἤπειρον ἐπιτετραμμένοι); having a say in treaties: *OR* 126 (*I. Cret.* I 30.1; *SvA* 148) (Argos to have a vote in confirming new treaties by the Cretan cities Knossos and Tylissos, which seem to have been considered colonies of Argos, as argued by Vollgraff (1948, 91–102); requiring colonies to contribute to sacrifices in the mother city: *RO* 29, ll. 3–6 (Athenians require their colony Paros to send a cow and panoply to the Panathenaia and a cow and phallus to the Dionysia; cf. J.L. Shear (2021, 128–30); requiring colonies to contribute first fruits to a god at the mother city (see Jim [2014, 203–25], and inscriptions cited there, esp. *I.Delphinion* 141, l. 28, describing as a *nomos* the requirement that the Milesian colony Kios contribute first fruits to the god in Miletos). We learn from Thucydides (1.56.2) that in the 430s the Corinthians still kept their own officials in Potidaia. Thucydides calls them *epidemiourgoi*, but it is not clear if that was their actual name nor what their function or extent of authority in Potidaia was. The term may indicate authority over a certain region (so Vatin [1961, 253 n.4]), or a duty to supervise or inspect other officials (*eine Aufsichtsbehörde*, according to Classen and Steup [1882–1967, i.140]); in either case it seems that these Corinthian officials had real authority in Potidaia, since they were apparently there constantly or regularly and the Athenians thought they posed a significant danger to their own authority.

14. Bauslaugh (1991, 37–38 and n.1) distinguishes between the protections accorded to heralds (κήρυκες) and ambassadors (πρέσβεις): "The exemption [from violence] of the former was unquestioned, but not that of the latter." But the letter claiming to be from Philip II to the Athenians, transmitted with the works of Demosthenes, complains the Athenians have illegally detained and ransomed Philip's ambassador (πρεσβευτής) Amphilochos and declares that violation of both heralds and ambassadors was considered impermissible: "Treating a herald and ambassadors illegally is considered to be an impiety by all other people and especially by you," τὸ παρανομεῖν εἰς κήρυκα καὶ πρέσβεις τοῖς ἄλλοις τε πᾶσιν ἀσεβὲς εἶναι δοκεῖ καὶ μάλιστα ὑμῖν, [Dem.] 12.4; see Buis (2018, 161–66). On the other hand, even heralds perhaps sometimes officially lost their protection, as discussed below.

15. Plut. *Per.* 30.2–3. The letter from Philip mentioned in the previous note confirms the Athenians took retribution on the Megarians for the death of Anthemokritos, [Dem.] 12.4. The provision that hostility between Athenians and Megarians be "without truce," ἄσπονδος, and "with no communication by herald," ἀκήρυκτος, might reflect a practice by which parties would occasionally declare ahead of time that even the inviolability of heralds would not be observed in certain conflicts; for this meaning of πόλεμος ἀκήρυκτος, see Xen. *Anab.* 3.3.5; Pl. *Leg.* 626a (perhaps); Aeschin. 2.37, 80; Dem. 18.262; Myres (1943).

16. The Plutarch passage cited in the previous note suggests the decree of Charinos was close in time, if not identical, to the "exclusion" decree. Scholarly opinion on their relative dates varies widely. Some have argued they were indeed the same (e.g., Stadter 1984; Holzapfel 1879, 176–86), while others have argued they were unrelated and even occurred in different centuries (e.g., Connor 1962; 1970). Barring new relevant epigraphical finds, the chronological problems appear insoluble, but I find Stadter's argument for identity most convincing. Namely, that the decree was motivated by multiple norm violations by the Megarians, not only the murder of a herald but also the cultivation of sacred land and the harboring of runaway Athenian slaves. Yet, if Stadter is correct, the latter two infractions originally gave rise to a preliminary decree that made "a gentle and humane legal demand," εὐγνώμονος καὶ φιλανθρώπου δικαιολογίας ἐχόμενον, Plut. *Per.* 30.3. Only after the death of Anthemokritos did the Athenians pass the stronger measures (including exclusion?) in the decree of Charinos.

17. On the importance of oaths in Greek international relations, see generally Scharff (2016); Sommerstein and Bayliss (2012, 147–322); and my discussion in Chapter 10. On *pacta servanda sunt* as a foundational principle of Greek international law, see Low (2007, 98–99); on

this principle as foundational, see Dworkin (2013, 10). The ethical value of not betraying your allies, even under the most desperate circumstances, is exalted by Polybius, 2.61.9–11. Bayliss (2012b, 249–55) offers a detailed account of the start of the Peloponnesian War as motivated largely by fear of and punishment of oath breaking.

18. Thuc. 1.78.4: ἕως ἔτι αὐθαίρετος ἀμφοτέροις ἡ εὐβουλία, σπονδὰς μὴ λύειν μηδὲ παραβαίνειν τοὺς ὅρκους, τὰ δὲ διάφορα δίκῃ λύεσθαι κατὰ τὴν ξυνθήκην. εἰ δὲ μή, θεοὺς τοὺς ὁρκίους μάρτυρας ποιούμενοι πειρασόμεθα ἀμύνεσθαι πολέμου ἄρχοντας ταύτῃ ᾗ ἂν ὑφηγῆσθε.
19. Thuc. 1.71.5: δρῷμεν δ' ἂν ἄδικον οὐδὲν οὔτε πρὸς θεῶν τῶν ὁρκίων οὔτε πρὸς ἀνθρώπων τῶν αἰσθανομένων· λύουσι γὰρ σπονδὰς οὐχ οἱ δι' ἐρημίαν ἄλλοις προσιόντες, ἀλλ' οἱ μὴ βοηθοῦντες οἷς ἂν ξυνομόσωσιν.
20. Thuc. 1.123.2: "You will not be the party first breaking the oaths that the god, in ordering you to go to war, recognizes have been violated already; instead you will be strengthening oaths that have been broken. The oath breakers are not those acting in defense but those who attack first"; σπονδάς τε οὐ λύσετε πρότεροι, ἅς γε καὶ ὁ θεὸς κελεύων πολεμεῖν νομίζει παραβεβάσθαι, ἠδικημέναις δὲ μᾶλλον βοηθήσετε· λύουσι γὰρ οὐχ οἱ ἀμυνόμενοι, ἀλλ' οἱ πρότεροι ἐπιόντες.
21. E.g., in *IG* II^2 111 (*RO* 39; *SvA* 289), an agreement from 363/2 between the Athenians and the cities of the island of Keos, lines 57–81 contain the text of the oaths the Athenian generals swore in the name of Zeus, Athena, Poseidon, and Demeter. *IG* II^2 42 (*RO* 23; *SvA* 258), an agreement by which the Methymnians joined the Second Athenian League in 378/7, specifies that the embassy of the Methymnians is to swear "the same oath that the other allies swore," ll. 11–14.
22. Because war was foreseen as a possible legitimate response to at least some violations of international law, resort to war by Greeks should not be seen as a failure of that law, in the same way that forceful imprisonment of convicted criminals should not be seen as a failure of domestic law. Contrast Hathaway and Shapiro's (2017) argument that legalization of war was the original sin of international law. As I will discuss below, however, some theorists argue that international law does not need sanctions in order to qualify as law.
23. Eckstein (2017, 491). He is not clear about what he sees as the minimum requirements for what he would consider international law. At one point (2017, 493) he states that it "requires both formally acknowledged rules of interstate conduct and . . . guaranteed mechanisms of enforcement." But, I would argue, no human legal system has ever had "guaranteed mechanisms of enforcement." Tober (2018), who also denies the existence of international law in ancient Greece, offers a similarly narrow definition of it as requiring "a neutral and powerful authority that could prevent either side from transgressing the terms of their covenant."
24. Recent works emphasizing violent or unjust elements of Greek law include Ma (2024, chs. 18–19); J. Butler (2023); Vădan (2022); Glazebrook (2021); Kamen and Marshall (2021); Ismard (2019). Two prominent critiques of modern international law are Pitts (2018) and Anghie (2005). See also Mutua (2000); and, for a recent critique in graphic novel format, Corten, Klein, and Bedoret (2022). On the violence of law more generally, see Cover (1986).
25. Buis (2021, 441–49) makes a similar point; and more briefly, Buis (2018, 27–29).
26. Thucydides (1.23.5–6) asserts he will explain all the disputes that led to the war, many of which I mentioned above. He then famously insists the "truest cause" (ἀληθεστάτην πρόφασιν) of the war was Spartan fear of "the Athenians becoming greater" (τοὺς Ἀθηναίους . . . μεγάλους γιγνομένους). Here Thucydides himself is probably distinguishing two, mutually compatible, levels of explanation of the cause of the war, both correct in his eyes. See Lane Fox (2024, 17–20); Eckstein (2017, 505–06); Rhodes (1987). A few authoritative discussions of the historical (and cultural) circumstances that led to the outbreak of war include Lendon (2010); D. Lewis (1992, 370–80); Ste. Croix (1972); Busolt (1904, 758–853).
27. Van Rooij (2020); Ehrlich (1936 [1913], 2–25).
28. On the lack of a Greek practical legal science, and its implications, see Wolff (1975, 5–12; 1961, 253–55). On different ways of doing legal history, see Lesaffer (2024, 22–30); E.A. Meyer (2004, 3–4); Maffi (2001). The death of a distinct genre of ancient "legal" history was already announced six decades ago by Momigliano (1964), who attributed it in part to the influence of sociologists such as Max Weber. Some relatively recent examples of heavily socially inflected studies of Greek and Roman law include, for Roman law: Czajkowski and Eckhardt (2020); du Plessis, Ando, and Tuori (2016); Kelly (2011); McGinn (1998). For Greek law: Kapparis (2019); Lanni (2016); Hunter and Edmondson (2000); D. Cohen (1995).
29. J. Austin (1832, 1–9, 18–19, 208). Austin argues that laws come from superiors and defines superiority as "the power of affecting others with evil or pain, and of forcing them, through fear of that evil, to fashion their conduct to one's wishes" (19). In an Austinian mode, Eckstein (2017,

493) cites the lack of an "outside authority" as evidence for the nonexistence of international law in ancient Greece. A classic critical discussion of Austin's definition of law is Hart (1961, 1–76).

30. See, e.g., Llewellyn (1930); for a recent defense of the power of sanctions in law, see Schauer (2015).
31. Hathaway and Shapiro (2017) have rightly been criticized for overemphasizing and oversimplifying the effects of a simple change in international law on war-making behavior in the twentieth century; see Diggelmann (2018, 304–08); Geis (2018, 347–51); response by Hathaway and Shapiro (2018, 376–78).
32. See, e.g., Bernstein (2019); Richman (2017); Greif (1993). Cf. Ostrom (1990, 93–102) (emphasizing the role of sanctions and downplaying the importance of shared community norms; but see 206–07); Landa (1981, 355–57). Contrast the collection of essays edited by Gabrielsen and Paganini (2021) on private associations in ancient Greece, in which the socializing role of group identity features prominently in explaining the efficacy of private regulations.
33. On *syla* the most important work is Bravo (1980), with Lintott (2004) being a concise treatment in English. On *symbola* Gauthier (1972) is still authoritative; Cataldi (1983) provides in-depth commentaries on fifth-century *symbola* agreements, concerning which see now also Faraguna (2023).
34. See the works cited in Chapter 5, n. 1, below.
35. Ober (2015, 61–70); Eckstein (2006, 12–13). Ober's view is perhaps anticipated by Virginia Senator Robert Hunter's claim, before the US Civil War, that "it was the competition among the free States of ancient Greece which gave even to that ill-fated confederacy its surpassing excellency in arts of literature" (quoted by Richard 2009, 50).
36. Representative works by these scholars include Koskenniemi (2001) (mapping the rise of international law as a specialized field of juridical concern), L. Benton (2010) (discussing law as a tool of European conquest), and Anghie (2005) (arguing that the experience of colonialism was formative of the doctrines of modern international law). The largest current project in international legal history is the multi-volume and multi-author *Cambridge History of International Law* edited by Randall Lesaffer, the first volume of which was published in 2024. The "historical turn" in international law is now so well established that it has inspired a backlash. See Orford (2021).
37. See Lesaffer (2024); Koskenniemi (2016, 2017). Certain post-Westphalian events, especially of the nineteenth and twentieth centuries, have been seen as similarly epochal and inaugurating separate eras of "modern" international law. See Armitage and Pitts (2017, 18–20); Hathaway and Shapiro (2017).
38. Old: Ténékidès (1956); V. Martin (1940); Phillipson (1911); brief: Neff (2010); working with translations: Bederman (2001). On the neglect of the international law of the ancient Greek and Roman worlds in most histories of international law, see Buis (2021). Recent work on specific aspects of Greek international law includes: R.J.G. Evans (2019) (laws of war relating to noncombatants); Buis (2018) (laws of war); Magnetto (2018), (2016), (1997) (interstate arbitration); Scheibelreiter (2010) (treaty clauses); Lanni (2008) (laws of war); Chaniotis (2004) (international boundary disputes); Daverio Rocchi (1999) (a survey of international relations scholarship); Chaniotis (1996) (treaties among Cretan cities); Ager (1996) (interstate arbitration); Rigsby (1996) (territorial *asylia*); Baltrusch (1994) (treaties and truces); Ober (1994) (laws of war); Bravo (1980) (*syla*); Gauthier (1972) (*symbola*). Work on Greek international law as a whole includes: Barta (2010, 1:442–511); Giovannini (2007); Low (2007, ch. 3); Alonso Troncoso (2007); Sheets (1994). Saba (2009/10) surveys much of the recent work to the date of that writing. Eidem, Giltaij, and Tuori (2026), the volume of the *Cambridge History of International Law* focused on the ancient Mediterranean and Near East, is being published at the same time as this book but I have been unable to consult it. It promises to offer fundamental, broad ranging contributions to questions of Greek international law.
39. On this question, see Lonis (1969).
40. For two recent behavioral approaches to law, see Tyler (2021); van Rooij (2020). For applications to international law, see Wallace (2024); Cohen and Meyer (2021); Aaken and Broude (2019); Hirsch (2015).

Chapter 2

1. On the blurry border between domestic and international law in the Greek world, see Low (2007, 84–102).
2. Benton and Clulow (2015, 82), discussing a time much closer to the present (roughly 1400 to 1800 CE), prefer the term "interpolity law" to "international law." They presumably intend to emphasize distinctions of some sort between that time and the present; cf. 2024, 198). Lesaffer (2024, 40) defends using the term "international law" to describe a wide family of phenomena across the globe over several millennia. For other useful recent approaches to the main issues addressed in this chapter, see Low (2007, 77–128); Bederman (2001, 1–21, 31–41).
3. Lauterpacht (1970, i.9). Phrased differently, "the state and the international context in which it finds itself [are] mutually constitutive yet opposed spheres," Bartelson (2001, 12). Kestemont (1974, 6–7) speaks of "un ensemble d'États constituant une communauté internationale."
4. I say "typically" because there are exceptions. E.g., aboriginal states or tribes with limited sovereignty (the limitations being both practically and conceptually tangled) exist within the borders of a number of modern countries. *McGirt v. Oklahoma*, 140 S. Ct. 2452 (2020), is a recent major decision by the US Supreme Court determining some of the extent of that sovereignty under US law; *R. v. Sparrow*, 1 *S.C.R.* 1075 (1990), is a major case on a similar question under Canadian law. For an application of the "inside/outside" dichotomy to a federal structure, see Beck and Funke (2015b, 2); cf. Bartelson (2001, 12–13).
5. The term "international law" was coined by Jeremy Bentham (1789, 6, 335) in place of the older expression "law of nations"; see M.W. Janis (1984, 408–10). As Bentham himself suggests, he may even have coined the word "international": his usage here is the earliest cited by the *Oxford English Dictionary*. Although "state" has now largely replaced "nation" in scholarly parlance, "international law" is still a more common term than "interstate law." "Nation" is sometimes used like German *Volk* to refer specifically to an ethnically and culturally unified community that may or may not also be a "state"; see Kumar (2010, 121). In this way, "nation" reveals its etymology from Latin *natio*, which often refers to a racial or ethnic grouping. On "nation" as specially applicable to ancient Athens, see E.E. Cohen (2000, 3–4, 79–103).
6. See Stirk (2015). Steinberger (2004, 3) complains about the unpopularity and subsequent dearth of theorizing about the ontological and metaphysical status of the state. On the development of the modern notion of the state, see Skinner (1989); on this question with particular application to the "statehood" of ancient Rome, see Shaw (2023). On the vagueness of the term *res publica* in Rome, see Mebane (2024, 3–8).
7. M. Weber (1968, i.56). The quotation is from Cudworth and McGovern (2007, 3), who note strong disagreement among political theorists, some of whom recently have "come to question any certainties there might have been surrounding the concept of the state" (1–2). Recognizing that he was primarily describing a modern state, Max Weber (1968, i.56) attempted to frame his definition "in terms which abstract from the values of the present day." Finer (1997, i.2–3) offers an elaborate definition (which I do not quote here) explicitly designed to encompass ancient states of Europe and Asia. Tilly (2010, 269) also attempts to encompass entities existing as early as the fourth millennium BCE: "A state is a structure of power involving four distinctive elements: 1) major concentrated means of coercion, especially an army, 2) organization that is at least partly independent of kinship and religious relations, 3) a defined area of jurisdiction, and 4) priority in some regards over all other organizations operating within that area"; cf. Scheidel (2013, 5–9); Manning (2010, 56–7); and Crone (1989, 6–10) on defining ancient states. Shaw (2023) argues persuasively that the Roman empire was a state even within narrow modern definitions. Steinberger (2004, 21) claims, "[t]he state is nothing other than, and nothing less than, a systematic structure of ideas on the basis of which the individuals of a society seek jointly to control the physical objects that surround them . . . [and] implement its judgments." Wendt (1999, 202) defines the "essential state" by its possession of "five properties: (1) an institutional-legal order, (2) an organization claiming a monopoly on the legitimate use of organized violence, (3) an organization with sovereignty, (4) a society, and (5) territory." See his useful discussion at 201–14.
8. See Smith (2004, 12).
9. M. Weber (1947, 101–2): states, like other "social collectivities," "must be treated as *solely* the resultants and modes of organization of the particular acts of individual persons, since these alone can be treated as agents in a course of subjectively understood action." On the importance

of attending to the role of people in considering the statehood of the early *polis*, see Lundgreen (2020, 184–87).

10. This has been noted, e.g., by McCorquodale (2010, 280–84); J.L. Cohen (2010, 262); Lauterpacht (1970, i.9); Lawrence (1895, 55). Finnis (2011, 238) at one point performs the converse operation, "us[ing] the term 'state' as a short form of reference to any entity acting in the sphere of international law as a subject or potential subject thereof."
11. See Grzybowski and Koskenniemi (2015, 38); Craven (2010, 202). Vladimir Putin (2021) disputes the legitimacy of Ukrainian borders with Russia, and even of Ukrainian sovereignty.
12. Phillimore (1871, i.93–132). Nineteenth-century Germany is a good example. Renzsch (1989, 18) describes the *Deutscher Bund* of the early nineteenth century as "a confederation of thirty-eight sovereign German-speaking states and free cities" that, although "renounc[ing] the right to leave the confederation, . . . kept their sovereignty and independence in many respects." Lawrence (1895, 61–2) describes it as a *Staatenbund* as opposed to the more recent German *Bundesstaat*: in the former the individual states retain some sovereignty in foreign affairs; in the latter they delegate all foreign affairs sovereignty to the federal government; see Phillimore (1871, i.134–51). Craven (2010, 209–10) discusses the problems that non-Western state-like entities historically created for Western notions of international law. Fowler and Bunck (2002, 42) point out that "European governments (and trading companies acting, more or less, on their behalf) had long been willing to negotiate formal agreements with many different political entities . . . such as the Rajah of Assam and the Nizam of Hyderabad, and with tribes in Africa, the Americas, and the East Indies." On this view, European states (when it was convenient) took a functional approach to statehood: whatever entity can be party to a treaty is a state.
13. See Fofana and Hébié (forthcoming). They argue against the "classical account" of modern international law, under which the seventeenth century Peace of Westphalia established a system of sovereign states in Europe that became the "primary subject" of international law in European eyes and that spread through processes of European colonization and imperialism.
14. On the constituents of the British Empire, see Anand (2010); Marks (1995). It has been argued that the Brits were simply seeking greater representation for their own points of view and assumed that the "British" members would represent them; see Anand (2010, 7–8). But the individual memberships have also been seen as the result of demands made upon Britain by the dominions and India; see Marks (1995, 191). On the Soviet republics, see Motyl (1982, 70–74). Similarly to the case of Britain, it has been argued that these independent memberships were largely an attempt by Stalin to expand Soviet influence in the United Nations (he originally proposed that all sixteen Soviet republics be members).
15. Lesaffer (2024, 36–39) argues that international law has never been the exclusive preserve of the sovereign state as that term is used in a narrowly modern, Western sense; Wendt (1999, 202) suggests we "think of the state as a fuzzy set."
16. Aside from the matter of a defined territory, much of the concern regarding the definition of states is with their internal rather than external characteristics: Are there government officials rather than simply a traditional group of rulers? Is there a legal system? Is there a police force?
17. There are countless exceptions to my blanket distinction, and many subnational governmental units, including cities, do have foreign relations of sorts, in particular with the goal of expanding international economic relations. Hence, e.g., California has a Senate Office of International Relations whose function is "to assist [California State] Senators in furthering strong economic and diplomatic ties between California and the rest of the world," https://soir.senate.ca.gov/. But the activities of such bodies are subject to restriction, oversight, and regulation by central federal governments.
18. On diplomacy in ancient Greece, see Grainger (2017); Piccirilli (2002); C.P. Jones (1999, 17–65); Adcock and Mosley (1975).
19. Ma (2024) provides a long history of the *polis*, its transformations, and its unity.
20. Ehrenberg's work on the Greek state (1969) is divided into three sections: *polis*, federation, and kingdom. On *ethne*, see Beck and Funke (2015b, 17–18); Davies (2000); Corsten (1999, 18–19). Ian Morris (2013, 280), recognizing the spectrum of Greek state or state-like forms and the corresponding difficulty of hitting on a fixed set of criteria for defining a Greek state, prefers to speak of processes of "state formation," which he defines with a focus on internal processes. Cf. Morris (2009) on Athens.
21. For strong arguments for the "statehood" of the *polis*, see Ma (2024, 6–17); Hansen (2013, 268–72); Harris (2013, 21–59) on Athens. Dreher (2024) insists the *polis* "became" a state at a certain point in its history; cf. Lundgreen (2020). Billows (2023, 3–4) is agnostic. The statehood of the

polis is, however, simply denied by some who insist on a narrow definition of the state (i.e., mostly denying fuzzy edges). E.g., Zuiderhoek (2017, 151–59) summarizes the arguments of Berent (that the *polis* was not a state) and Hansen (2002) (that it was) and concludes it is not "analytically useful" to call *poleis* "states" (157); cf. G. Anderson (2009) (focused on the case of Athens). As I argue in this section, I disagree with Zuiderhoek, especially to the extent that the concept "state" is a constituent of the concept "international." See Terpstra (2019, 9–10), adopting a "flexible approach" in calling eighth-century Phoenician Tyre, Classical Athens, and the Roman empire "states." There has been a debate among numismatists and historians over the degree to which minting coins was an indicator either of a *polis*'s identity as a *polis* or of its sovereignty, especially after the mid-fourth century BCE. See Meadows (2001); T.R. Martin (1995, 170–82) and (1985).

22. On the frequent primacy of *polis* identity, see J.M. Hall (2013, 91); Hansen and Nielsen (2004, 12–14). Consider, e.g., the particular case of Socrates: he was a member of the deme of Alopeke, and could be described as Ionian, but in the *Crito* Plato represents Socrates as flatly rejecting the possibility of living surrounded by non-*Athenians*. Yet this example also suggests the limits to my claim of the centrality of *polis* identity, because Crito's proposal is that Socrates live in Thessaly, surrounded by Thessalians (*Crito* 45c, 53e–54a); he does not bother to identify a specific *polis* within Thessaly. And Herodotus (7.172.1) reports that "the Thessalians medized" (i.e., fought on the side of Persia in the Persian Wars) without distinguishing members of particular *poleis* within Thessaly (on *polis* vs. *koinon* in Thessaly in particular, see my discussion in Chapter 11). Hence we see that, especially for outsiders looking in, the primary identification of those who were members of "ethnic" *koina* could be with the *ethnos* rather than a particular *polis* (R. Osborne 1996, 286). It has been emphasized that *ethnos* and *polis* should be viewed as not necessarily competing forms of identity but rather as different "tiers" or "categories" (the former term is from C. Morgan [2003, 1], the latter from Hall [2015, 46]). Ismard (2010) stresses the social and political importance of sub-*polis* social structures (including demes, phratries, and *gene*) in Athens; similarly Ma (2024, 232–35), with a wider view.
23. Hansen and Nielsen (2004, 87–92). With their typology of fifteen kinds of dependent *polis*, Hansen and Nielsen appear to subscribe to a Tolstoyesque belief that all autonomous *poleis* were alike, but all dependent *poleis* were dependent in their own way. On dependent *poleis*, see also Hansen (2015), with response to critics (especially Fröhlich 2010). On the disappearance of the dependent *polis* as a phenomenon in the fourth and third centuries, see Ma (2017, 280–81).
24. On autonomy as a norm and ideal, see Ma (2024, 174–78); Dmitriev (2011, 3–66); Low (2007, 187–99); Ostwald (1982); Ténékidès (1954, 7–44); V. Martin (1940, 76–103).
25. On the Spartan *perioikoi*, see Ducat (2017) and (2008); Shipley (1997) and (1992); on Thessaly, see Bouchon and Helly (2015, 233–34); on Crete, see Perlman (1996) and Chaniotis (1996, 160–68). The process of synoikism also seems usually to have dissolved the state-like nature of multiple individual *poleis* into a single whole.
26. Rhodes (1995, 91): "It is not always easy to say at what point a political unit of any size has lost so much independence that it should no longer be regarded as a *polis*."
27. On the relation between federalism and ethnicity, see J.M. Hall (2015); Vlassopoulos (2015, 4–7).
28. Beck and Funke (2015) provide a thorough overview of the phenomenon; Mackil (2013) discusses in depth the Achaians, Aitolians, and Boiotians; Lasagni (2009) deals with the more general problem of defining the "federal state" in the Greek world. The most important earlier treatment of Greek federalism is Larsen (1968); see also Giovannini (1971).
29. Beck and Funke (2015b) use "federal state" as the blanket term for all the *koina* discussed in their volume, while stressing their diversity (11–13). Mackil (2013) generally restricts "state" to *koina* that meet a certain level of unity and describes with nuance multiple factors indicative of it (2013, 346–90), and Mackil (2013b) is a sensible discussion of the relevant issues, but Mackil (2014, 271) seems to apply "state" to all *koina* (she is there more worried about misuse of the term "federal" than of the term "state," cf. Mackil 2013, 4–6). Catherine Morgan's *Early Greek States Beyond the Polis* (2003), aside from using "state" in its title, occasionally calls early *koina* "states" (e.g., 6, 24, 84). As the title of Bruno Helly's *L'état thessalien* (1995) suggests, he views the Thessalian *koinon* as a state as early as the sixth century (but see my argument against this view in Chapter 11).
30. Busolt and Swoboda (1920–1926, 1310–15); Larsen (1968, xiv–xv); similarly Lasagni (2009, 264); Giovannini (1971, 9–10). With regard to dual citizenship, our evidence suggests that the actual granting of citizenship remained almost entirely in the hands of individual *poleis* (even in

the uncommon instances when the *koinon* decreed that it be granted), and that each person was usually a citizen of only one *polis* within a *koinon*. On dual citizenship and the *polis*'s prerogative to grant citizenship, see Mackil (2013, 387–88 and n.262); Beck (1997, 174–79); Rizakis (2015, 122) on the specific case of Achaia. I agree that a *koinon*'s exclusive regulation of citizenship status, if it ever happened, would be a strong marker of statehood (Endicott [2010, 252] defines the state as "that which issues passports," although he is not concerned there with how to think about a pre-passport world). But the control over citizenship that *poleis* continued to have even in the more unified *koina* suggests that a *koinon* never did exercise anything close to exclusive regulation of citizenship. Sizov (2021) and (2021b) shows that it is unclear if "federal" citizenship in the relatively highly developed Achaian and Aitolian leagues provided a right of property ownership (ἔγκτησις) within individual member *poleis*. Larsen's and Busolt's second criterion, the exercise by the *koinon* of direct legal jurisdiction on individuals, is only infrequently attested and seems limited to offenses performed by people acting in official or semiofficial roles and in situations where the safety or well-being of the *koinon* as a whole was at stake. See Busolt and Swoboda (1920–1926, 1317, 1405 n.6, 1407 n.7) (citing (a) the Arkadian *koinon*'s decision in 364/63 to charge the leaders of Mantinea with harming the *koinon*, after the Mantineans resolved not to use sacred funds to pay the elite *eparitoi* soldiers, Xen. *Hell.* 7.4.33; and (b) the Arkadians' vote, after the razing of Thebes by Alexander, to condemn to death those who had persuaded them to support the Thebans, Arr. *Anab.* 1.10.1); cf. Busolt and Swoboda (1920–1926, ii.1553 n.5). Exercising jurisdiction only in such cases is arguably not indicative of statehood because it is not an exercise of necessarily domestic law, as suggested by the Spartan "trial" and execution of Plataians in 427 (Thuc. 3.68).

31. Beck and Funke (2015b, 11). Consider, e.g., Knoepfler (2015, 169) on the Euboians: "by the beginning of the third century there was undoubtedly some form of confederation extant in Euboia, but at best it was no more than an association of sovereign *poleis* and certainly not a federal association in the technical sense of the word." Ténékidès (1956, 578–83) takes a very broad view of what sorts of inter-*polis* organizations could be considered examples of "federal communities," with the result that, like me, he sees a blurry boundary between synoikism, federalism, and treaty-based *symmachia*.
32. In fact, because of the political and ethnic diversity of these kingdoms, "empire" may be a better word to describe them. But this term comes with its own objections (see Shaw 2022, 508–11); for this reason, because their rulers all styled themselves as "king" (*basileus*), and to keep with scholarly tradition, I mostly refer to them as kingdoms.
33. This variation in status began under Alexander, see Bosworth (1988, 251). Paschidis (2008, 19–23) briefly surveys the large literature on relations between *poleis* and kingdoms; his monograph is a detailed study of the intermediaries of those relationships. Ma (2000, 150–214) provides an analysis focused on the relations between the *poleis* of western Asia Minor and the Seleukids, but with broader implications. Capdetrey (2007) surveys the whole geographic breadth of the Seleukid realm. Boehm (2018) concentrates on the synoikizing urbanization of the monarchs.
34. E.g., Bagnall (1976, 1) notes the "wide fluctuations" in the Ptolemaic possessions outside of Egypt; cf. Boehm (2018, 29) (noting "a loose aggregate of constantly shifting borders and alliances"); Ma (2000, 44–47, 55–61). Kosmin (2014, 3–5 and *passim*), however, argues that the Seleukids, at least, were more concerned with defining, delimiting, and defending a specific "Seleukid" territory than was understood by earlier scholars. In any case, fluctuating borders does not mean the kingdoms were not states (especially since they were recognized as such by other "stately" actors; but see M.M. Austin [1986, 455–56]), but it is evidence that some of the "modular" pieces of those kingdoms—many of which were Greek *poleis*—were themselves states, because they had enough of an independent existence to be seen and treated as (mostly) self-governing units that were best dealt with as such, incorporated, and subsequently treated as corporate wholes. Citizens of the city of Mylasa, e.g., did not become "Seleukidians" under Seleukid domination.
35. Conceptual ambiguity in this regard is reflected in the scholarly literature; e.g., Strootman (2014, 7–8) in a single paragraph describes the Antigonid, Seleukid, Ptolemaic, and Attalid kingdoms as "states," as "empires," and as "supranational state systems." His primary claim, in a useful discussion, is that those kingdoms do not fall neatly within "modern definitions of 'territorial state' or 'national state'" (11). Lesaffer (2024, 36–37) comments on the complexities involved in writing a history of international law in imperial contexts.

36. As Hammond puts it (1988, 182), "what emerged in those years were Macedonian kingships and in some sense... Macedonian kingdoms"; cf. (1988, 194–96). On the continuities between Persian and Greek rule, see Briant (2017, 429–58; 2006); 1985, 168) (Alexander's conquest involved "une reprise des structures administratives achéménides"). On the nature of the post-Alexander kingdoms generally, see Ma (2013). Lerouge-Cohen (2022) focuses on the smaller post-Alexander kingdoms in former Persian realms.
37. Arr. *Anab.* 1.18.2: "And everywhere he ordered them to dismantle oligarchies, establish democracies and give them each their own laws, to stop the payment of tribute they had formerly paid to the barbarians," καὶ τὰς μὲν ὀλιγαρχίας πανταχοῦ καταλύειν ἐκέλευσεν, δημοκρατίας δὲ [τε] ἐγκαθιστάναι καὶ τοὺς νόμους τοὺς σφῶν ἑκάστοις ἀποδοῦναι, καὶ τοὺς φόρους ἀνεῖναι, ὅσους τοῖς βαρβάροις ἀπέφερον. Cf. Diod. Sic. 17.24.1; Bosworth (1988, 252–3); and generally Heisserer (1980). On the succession of hegemonic regimes to which the Greek cities of Asia Minor were subject, see Lund (1992, 107–15).
38. Diod. Sic. 19.61–62. On the policies of the *diadochoi* (successor kings to Alexander) toward Greek freedom and autonomy, see Dmitriev (2011, 112–42); Bertrand (2001); Billows (1990, 194–204); Gruen (1984, i.133–42); Simpson (1959). Polyperchon in 319 seems to have been the first to have offered to free the Greek cities, through the *diagramma*, or declaration, of Philip III (Diod. Sic. 18.55.2; *SvA* 417 [=403, iii]), but see the qualifications of Billows (1990, 198); Will (1984, 42–43). On the *diagramma*, see Poddighe (2013). Ptolemy echoed Antigonos's Tyre declaration in 314, Diod. Sic. 19.62.1. On the origin of the notions of the "freedom of the Greeks of Asia" in particular, see Seager and Tuplin (1980). The slogan was active, e.g., in Ptolemy II's support of Athens and Sparta in the Chremonidean War (*Syll.*^{3} 434/35 (*SvA* 476), ll. 16–18), and in the so-called Nicouria decree from ca. 279, *IG* XII 7, 506, l. 14 (on the date, see Constantakopoulou 2017, 40 and n.40).
39. Diodorus (19.105.1) briefly reports the terms of the treaty (*SvA* 428), including "that the Greeks be *autonomos*," τοὺς Ἕλληνας αὐτονόμους εἶναι. Antigonos took credit for this clause in his letter to the citizens of Skepsis announcing the treaty, in which he explained that all Greeks were to swear to guard each other's freedom and autonomy and suggested that the men of Skepsis take this oath, *RC* 1, ll. 53–56, 65–66. Will (1984, 51–52) suggests that the oath provision may be an invention by Antigonos. But oaths were universal elements of Greek treaties and truces (as I discuss in Chapter 10), so this skepticism seems unwarranted.
40. E.g., Antigonos "freed" cities, including the Milesians, from Asandros in 313 (Diod. Sic. 19.75; *I.Delphinion* 123, ll. 1–3); in 310, Ptolemy claimed that Antigonos illegally garrisoned some cities in Cilicia; Ptolemy "subdued" them, ἐχειρώσατο; but Antigonos subsequently "recovered" them, ἀνεκτήσατο, Diod. Sic. 20.19.3–5; cf. 20.37.2 (Ptolemy freeing other cities to gain their citizens' goodwill); in 307 Demetrios, on instructions from his father Antigonos "to free all the cities of Greece," ἐλευθεροῦν πάσας μὲν τὰς κατὰ τὴν Ἑλλάδα πόλεις, "freed" the Athenians from Kassandros and permitted restoration of the democracy among them, Diod. Sic. 20.45; see Habicht (1997, 66–67); Lysimachus "left free" the Lampsakians and Parians when they willingly came to his side in 302 against Antigonos; Antiochos I or II in the 260s "restored" the autonomy the Erythraians had enjoyed under Antigonos and Demetrios (*RC* 15); Ptolemy I relieved the Milesians "of many harsh forms of tribute" (*RC* 14); later, Antiochos II helped free the Milesians from the rogue Ptolemaic officer Timarchos, who had begun ruling Miletos as a tyrant, App. *Syr.* 65; *I.Didyma* 471; see Bagnall (1976, 80–81). Will (1984, 48) calls the freedom of the Greeks "a propaganda theme which makes its appearance in [the 310s] and recurs year in year out until the intervention of the Romans, who use it in their turn." See also Dmitriev (2011, 112–42).
41. Exceptions are Syria and Phoenicia, where much of the territory was owned by the king and directly governed by royal officials, see Hölbl (2001, 61); Bagnall (1976, 238). Strootman (2019, 117–18) argues that the Ptolemaic empire or "polity" should be viewed less as a territorial state (Egypt) that held overseas possessions than as "an organization aiming at creating routine access to resources" and for which Egypt was only one "province of importance."
42. Bagnall (1976); for Byzantium, see 159 n.1; for Iasos, 89–90; for the Cretan cities, 117–23; for Samos, 82–83 (source of the quotation); for Cyprus, 38–79; for Cyrene, 25–37. See also: generally, Huß (2011, 140–77); Buraselis (1993) on the mutual dependencies, material and ideological, between the early Ptolemies and Greek cities; Buraselis (2000, 5) on the independence but friendliness of Kos; Kossmann (2015) on the variety of Ptolemaic relations with the cities of Crete; Kossmann (2011) (*non vidi*) on Ptolemaic relations with cities of Asia Minor. Strootman (2019, 120) describes the Ptolemaic empire as "basically a dynamic and varied patchwork

of friends, allied cities, friendly kings, fortified strongholds held by garrisons, and more." Marquaille (2008, 43–45) distinguishes between a "core" and "periphery" of the empire, a distinction already suggested by Bagnall (1976, 210).

43. On Cyrene's history and Cyrenean relations with Ptolemaic rulers, see Rosamilia (2018), who argues for 250 as the most likely date for the reannexation of Cyrene into Ptolemaic hegemony; cf. Bagnall (1976, 25–37). Two important documents for understanding Cyrene's relationship to Ptolemaic rule are *IG Cyrenaica* 010800 (*SEG* 9.1), the so-called "Constitution of Cyrene" from between 322 and 320, and *IG Cyrenaica* 011100 (*SEG* 9.5), a *prostagma*, or ordinance, of Ptolemy IX Soter II and Kleopatra Selene from 108. Yet, between these dates, in the first half of the third century, came at least two rebellions, the rule of Magas, and temporary alignment with the Antigonids.
44. On the shifting realms and borders in Asia Minor in the post-Alexander era, see generally E. Meyer (1925). On the rule of Antigonos Monophthalmos in Asia Minor, see Billows (1990, 189–285); on Lysimachos, see Lund (1992, 107–52), emphasizing the continuities between Alexander, Antigonos, Lysimachos, and Antiochos I. I omit discussion here of the great bulk of Seleukid territory to the east and southeast, extending across present-day Turkey and Syria through Iraq and Iran to Afghanistan and Pakistan. On the great variety of peoples ruled by the Seleukids, see Kosmin (2014, 3), whose book explores the "territoriality" of the kingdom as a whole, far beyond the Greeks of western Asia Minor. Capdetrey (2007) similarly explores Seleukid relations with all of the political subentities of the empire, while bemoaning that our lopsided evidence has often reduced discussions of royal-city relations in particular to its western aspects (191). But it is my concern with Greek international law, in particular, rather than the imbalance in our sources, that determines my focus here.
45. Even this process was not uniform, since the citizens of some cities yielded to Alexander only after resisting. Therefore, already under Alexander, as Bosworth puts it (1988, 251), "the conditions of conquest allowed for great variation in the treatment of individual cities," in particular with regard to the imposition of garrisons and tribute.
46. Ma (2000, ch. 3 and esp. 150–74); on Smyrna and Lampaskos: 164; on "integrated" versus "non-integrated" territory: 158–59. Capdetrey (2007, 192–94) similarly emphasizes the variety of city-king relations. Ma (2000, 159–65) endorses Elias Bickerman's insistence that the freedom of the "autonomous" cities in the empire was not full autonomy in the sense of an absence of legal connection to the king but was in fact a Seleukid juridical status and therefore conditional: the freedom was given by the king, was still subject to his wishes, and could be taken away by him. On the subordinate cities in particular, see Ma (2000, 158–59); Bickerman (1938, 140–41). Capdetrey (2007, 209) suggests six categories in place of Ma's four.
47. Adding to the variety was the presence, in the Seleukid empire or sphere of influence, of "dynasts," individual rulers of smaller areas who were supported or tolerated by the Seleukids and exercised varying degrees of independence. See Capdetrey (2007, 112–33); Ma (2000, 175–76); Bickerman (1938, 166–69).
48. See generally Hatzopoulos (1996); and Ma (2018) for an assessment of the results to date of the "New Macedonian History." On the distinct nature of Macedonian (versus Ptolemaic or Seleukid) kingship, see Mooren (1983).
49. On Macedonian expansion, see Hatzopoulos (1996, 208). On Cassandreia and Philippi, see Hatzopoulos (2021, 204).
50. At the end of the third century, Philip V spoke of Demetrias, Chalkis, and Corinth as the "fetters of Greece" (Polyb. 18.11.5; cf. 38.3.3; Livy 32.37.4); these cities were probably controlled by the Antigonids already by the end of the fourth century, see Shipley (2018, 51); F.W. Walbank (1988, 269–70). On the Hellenic League, see Plut. *Demetr.* 25; cf. Diod. Sic. 20.102. The League's charter is partly preserved: *IG* IV^2 1, 68 (*SvA* 446). Shipley (2018, 52): "the treaty left member cities autonomous and ungarrisoned under their 'ancestral' constitutions, as in the [League of Corinth of 337 (*SvA* 403)], but required them to contribute military manpower, have the same friends and foes as Antigonos and Demetrios, and uphold their kingship. Macedonian control may have been firm."
51. Habicht (1997, 66–193) provides a detailed narrative and analysis of these vacillations, which he characterizes with his chapter titles: "Between Freedom and Dependency," "The Independent City," "Renewed Subjugation," and "Freedom and Neutrality" (see also Habicht 2006, the revised and expanded French translation). For non-Athenian examples, see Reger's argument (1994, 66–68) that, in the second half of the third century, islands in the Cyclades exercised a significant amount of independence.

52. Low (2007, 88–92) discusses the ambiguity between domestic and "external" law with specific Greek examples; cf. Low (2007, 128–29). She also speaks of "the shaping and reshaping of the boundaries of the many, often intersecting, 'communities' which participate in the Greek interstate system" (2007, 174).
53. On the internal point of view in law, see Hart (1961, 54–58, 86–88); cf. Marmor (2011, 53–55, 130–35). I do not mean to suggest that this internal aspect is the only factor affecting international behavior. On the contrary, part of my project is to see how much we can disentangle that subjective feeling of obligation to act lawfully into distinct aspects such as morality, habit, legal socialization, and group identity.
54. On the "rights and privileges" of at least some cities under royal hegemony, see Dmitriev (2011, 135, 140–41). I will not try to reinterpret the Ptolemaic, Seleukid, or Antigonid empires as international legal institutions along the lines I hint at here. But, to offer one example, I suggest that an international law approach to the Seleukid empire can help us synthesize the opposed views of Heuss and Bickerman (as discussed by Ma 2000, 152–68) on the status of some cities that fell within that empire. We may posit that some Seleukid-city relations were governed by a form of international law. E.g., an inscription documents a treaty, in the form of a renewal of "friendship and alliance" (φιλίαν καὶ συμμαχίαν), between Antiochos II and the Cretan city of Lyttos in 250 (*SvA* 486). Perhaps we can accept Heuss's argument that some cities were sovereign in a sense while also accepting Bickerman's argument that they were still subject to "formal, legal structures" effectively imposed by the Seleukids (Ma 2000, 152). We can do this because, in a regime of international law, sovereignty is not mutually exclusive of subjection to legal structures.
55. On the meanings of *nomos*, see Buis (2018, 34–38); Low (2007, 83–102); Ostwald (1969, 20–55); Stier (1928); Hirzel (1907, 359–86). The basic noun, *nomos*, and the nominalized neuter plural of the adjective, *nomima*, have overlapping but not entirely coincident meanings. When a distinction is intended, *nomos* more commonly refers to written laws and *nomima* to unwritten, as is explicit, e.g., at Dem. 23.70, "the decree has been proposed contrary both to the written *nomoi* and to the unwritten *nomima*," παρά . . . καὶ τοὺς γεγραμμένους νόμους καὶ τὰ ἄγραφα νόμιμα τὸ ψήφισμα εἴρηται. Cf. Pl. *Leg.* 793a10–b1. But the sources I cite in the main text make clear that both *nomos* and *nomima* could refer to customary international law. On the difference between written and unwritten laws in a domestic context, see Harris (2006, 52–57). On the various early Greek terms for "law" in both domestic and international contexts, see Avilés (2010). *Nomos* also referred to a musical melody or genre of musical composition, a meaning important for understanding Plato's *Laws*, see Panno (2017); Folch (2015, 305–09). To include this musical aspect, perhaps the best general translation of *nomos* is "regulation" or even "canon."
56. Hdt. 7.136.2, συγχέαι τὰ πάντων ἀνθρώπων νόμιμα ἀποκτείναντας κήρυκας.
57. Nevertheless, Polybius also emphasizes the universal recognition of some rules. E.g., he states that the Mantineans violated "the common laws of humans," τοὺς κοινοὺς τῶν ἀνθρώπων νόμους, when they murdered the Achaian soldiers they had previously invited to garrison the city, 2.58.6. Cf. Polyb. 1.70.5 (Libyan mercenaries act "contrary to the common customs of humans," παρὰ τὰ κοινὰ τῶν ἀνθρώπων ἔθη); 2.8.12 (Teuta queen of the Illyrians ignores "the rules of justice determined among humans," τῶν παρ' ἀνθρώποις ὡρισμένων δικαίων); 4.6.11; 4.67.3–4.
58. "Laws of the gods," νόμιμα θεῶν, Eur. *Supp.* 19; cf. "the ancient law of divinities," νόμος παλαιὸς δαιμόνων, 563; "laws of all Greece," νόμιμα πάσης Ἑλλάδος, 311; cf. "the law of all Greeks," τὸν πανελλήνων νόμον, 526.
59. Isoc. *Panath.* 170–71: τὸν νόμον τὸν κοινὸν ἁπάντων τῶν Ἑλλήνων. See also Isoc. *Paneg.* 55, where, in describing the same situation, he calls it an "ancient custom and inherited law," παλαιὸν ἔθος καὶ πάτριον νόμον.
60. On the Delion campaign and the subsequent dispute between the Athenians and Thebans, see Thuc. 4.89–101. For invocation of "the laws of the Greeks," see Thuc. 4.97.2: τὰ νόμιμα τῶν Ἑλλήνων. Cf. Thuc. 3.59.1: the Plataians invoke "the common laws of the Greeks," τὰ κοινὰ τῶν Ἑλλήνων νόμιμα, in seeking mercy from the Spartans. On the dating of the *Suppliant Women*, see Collard (1975, i.8–14), also discussing the debate over a connection between events at Delion and Euripides's play; cf. Morwood (2007, 26–30). On Diodorus's views, see Diod. Sic. 19.63.5 (when the Orchomenians in 315 removed suppliants from the shrine of Artemis and murdered them, it was "contrary to the common laws of the Greeks," παρὰ τὰ κοινὰ τῶν Ἑλλήνων νόμιμα); cf. 13.23.4–5: "the practices of the Greeks . . . the common rules of all," τοὺς τῶν Ἑλλήνων ἐθισμοὺς . . . τὰ κοινὰ πάντων νόμιμα; 30.18.2 (although war is a transgression of law, it has "so to speak, laws of its own," τινὰς ἰδίους καθαπερεὶ νόμους). On the war-related

aspects of customary law, see Buis (2018, 109–228); Lanni (2008); Giovannini (2007, 185–218); Ober (1994); Kiechle (1958).

61. Lanni (2008, 472); Romilly (1971, 25–49) comes to a similar conclusion. On the treatment of asylum in the *Suppliants*, see Buis (2018, 189–99). In the *Nicomachean Ethics* (10, 1180a35–36), in apparent contrast to the *Politics*, Aristotle says "there seems to be little difference between written and unwritten laws" in the context of law's role in educating people and making them virtuous. I do not here offer an account of how Greek international customary law was or might have been generated. But Finnis (2011, 238–45) offers a philosophical explanation of "how an authoritative rule can emerge (i.e., begin to regulate a community) without being made by anyone with authority to make it, and even without the benefit of any authorized way of generating rules." And Partington, Kamtekar, and Nichols (2025) offer a social-psychological explanation of how iterative learning can lead to the development of injuctive norms such as laws without operation of a central authority. On the frequent Greek attribution to the gods of even domestic systems of laws, see Willey (2016).
62. The evidence is collected systematically in the multi-volume collection edited by Bengtson, Schmitt, and Errington (1962–2020), *Die Staatsverträge des Altertums* (*SvA*), which is not limited to treaties between Greeks. Chaniotis (1996) provides texts and commentary for dozens of inscribed Cretan treaties.
63. *I.Olympia Suppl.* 6 (*SEG* 22.336).
64. See, e.g., Thuc. 1.23.4, 1.67. Many inroads are available to the large literature on Greek treaties, e.g., Couvenhes (2016); Giovannini (2007, 224–342); Baltrusch (1994); Bickerman (1950); Busolt and Swoboda (1920–26, ii.1240–1575).
65. E.g., *IG* II^3 10 (*OR* 120; *SvA* 149) (memorializing such an agreement between Athenians and Phaselites in the mid-fifth century); *IG* II^2 1 (*OR* 191), l. 18 (Athenians and Samians, 405 = *SvA* 209). On *symbola*, see especially Gauthier (1972); more briefly Faraguna (2023), focusing on the fifth century.
66. *RO* 12 (*Syll.*^{3} 135; *SvA* 231; Hatzopoulos 1996, ii no. 1). See also, e.g., *I.Delphinion* 149 (*SvA* 638), the *sympoliteia* agreement between Miletos and Pidasa from ca. 189 in which it was agreed that the Milesians would build an ox-cart road for the Pidasans to transport their wine to the sea.
67. E.g., *RO* 14 (*IPArk* 9), under which all Helissonians became Mantineans in the early fourth century; on this agreement, see Ma (2024, 177–78).
68. See, e.g., the several surviving examples from Miletos, *I.Delphinion* 136 (*RO* 93; *SvA* 408), 137 (*SvA* 409), 141, 142 (*SvA* 453), 146 (*SvA* 539), 150 (*SvA* 638).
69. See Dmitriev (2011, 134–35, 140–41). Royal decrees of *asylia*, "inviolability," insofar as they were part of mutual recognition of agreed obligations between king and city, might also be included in this category. E.g., Antiochos III's grant of *asylia* (and of relief from taxes or tribute) to Teos (*SEG* 41.1003; Ma 2000, 308–11; Rigsby 1996, no. 132), which the Teans frame as promises to them (Ma 2000, 205), seems conditioned explicitly on Teans granting royal honors to Antiochos and implicitly on them remaining loyal to Antiochos. If Antiochos had unilaterally withdrawn the rights and privileges he had guaranteed the Teans, it is likely the Teans (along with the international community) would have seen themselves as justified in withdrawing their loyalty (and military support) from the king, no matter what the king claimed was "Seleukid" law on the matter (*pace* Bickerman 1938, 140–41). That the behavior was frequently characterized rhetorically as resulting (in both directions) from "goodwill" or "gratitude" rather than legal obligation does not in itself, I propose, remove it from the realm (or "jurisdiction") of international law.
70. But see Low (2007, 85–93) for some possible examples.
71. We can catalog this process of treaties acquiring their legal power among the "general principles of law" that would fall under the third category of sources of international law listed in Article 38 of the Statute of the International Court of Justice, quoted above. In the same way, modern treaty law is subordinate to the customary law *pacta servanda sunt*, "agreements must be maintained."
72. On the question of "international law as law," see Dworkin (2013); Hathaway and Shapiro (2011, 255–70); Goldsmith and Posner (2005, 3); Buchanan (2004); Damrosch et al. (2001, 16–40); Hart (1961, 209). For claims of the absence or ineffectiveness of international law in the Greek world, see Eckstein (2017; 2008, 11; 2006, 37–42). Phillipson (1911, i.43, 60) notes that such views about ancient international law were in currency over a century ago. For claims of the absence or ineffectiveness of international law in the modern world, see Goldsmith and Posner (2005, 200–203); Bolton (2000); Bork (1989/90). Such criticisms have perhaps decreased

as the reach and complexity of international law in the contemporary world have continuously expanded. See, e.g., Arbour and Parent (2012, 31–35); O'Connell (2008, 1–16, 57–91); Morgenthau and Thompson (1984, 295). I am unaware of any careful scholarly comparison of ancient Greek conceptions of domestic versus international law, which remains a desideratum with regard to intellectual and philosophical history. Because my study is a historical and sociological analysis of Greek international law that, as I argue, does not depend on it standing in any particular relationship to domestic law, I do not undertake such a comparison here.

73. As Besson and Tasioulas (2010, 8) put it, "if international law does not fit the criteria of the concept of law used at the domestic level, it may . . . be a problem . . . for those criteria themselves and hence for a given legal theory." Cf. Tamanaha (1997, 128); Arbour and Parent (2012, 33–4).
74. This is essentially the position of G.L. Williams (1945). Hart (1961, 210) calls this sort of response "too short."
75. This is the strategy of Hathaway and Shapiro (2011).
76. Kelsen (1967, 214–17, 336–39); see Engelking (2025, 14–25); Bernstorff (2010, 10) (describing Kelsen's view of "international law as a law above the state . . . [that] delegate[s] the respective state legal orders and delimit[s] them from one another"); similarly Dworkin (2013, 19). Hathaway and Shapiro (2011, 257) argue that the focus on domestic legal systems as "paradigm instances of law" is "completely understandable" but also "a grave mistake"; cf. Ehrlich (1936, 163). This is an especially strong objection to a skeptic such as John Bolton, whose highly normative argument restricts law to states with "democratic" constitutions similar to that of the United States (2000, 2–3). Despite the primacy of the *polis* in Greek political thought, perhaps most famously expressed in Aristotle's claim that the *polis* exists by nature and humans are by nature *political* creatures (*Pol.* 1.2, 1253a1–3), a case could perhaps be made that some Greeks saw international law as more foundational than *polis* law. E.g., in the belief that there were "laws of all Greeks" or of "all humans," and in the attitude that pirates were the enemies of all humanity and not just of organized states (I discuss piracy, and Greek attitudes toward it, in Chapter 9).
77. This is not to say that the potential significance of differences between domestic and international law should be downplayed or ignored. I highlight those differences at various points, and I make little use of studies examining phenomena that seem tied to features of domestic law that Greek international law lacked, such as legal officials.
78. On Greek international arbitration, see Magnetto (2016) and (1997); Ager (2013, 497–504) and (1996). The fifth-century author known as "Anonymous Iamblichi" implies that war is a form of international law enforcement when he states that war is what often results for "those who act lawlessly," ἀνομοῦσι, DK 89 fr. 7.6 (= Laks–Most *Anon. Iambl.* 7.6). Citing the absence of an international "treaty police" as an argument against the legality of international law goes beyond privileging domestic law and privileges domestic *criminal* law as the archetype of "true law." But international law is arguably more like civil law, such as tort and contract law, in which both the bringing and the enforcement of legal claims is almost entirely left up to an aggrieved party rather than an enforcement authority. In both ancient Greek and ancient Roman law generally, self-help (both bringing claims and enforcing awards and penalties) played a larger role in legal disputes than it does in the modern world. For further discussion on the role of self-help in Greek law, domestic as well as international, see Chapter 5, below.
79. Hathaway and Shapiro (2011, 348) express a similar objection, anticipated by Ehrlich (1936, 83). John Bolton (2000, 2–3) falls into the formalist tautology. For Bolton, law (1) "has to exist within a coherent structural framework—a constitution—that defines the government's authority, and by so doing, limits it, thus preventing arbitrary authority"; and (2) "rests on popular sovereignty or public accountability through reasonably democratic popular controls over the creation, interpretation, and enforcement of laws. . . . Any other definition of law is either incoherent or unacceptable to a free person." While territoriality (a common element in definitions of states) is not explicitly mentioned by Bolton here, and while one might be able to imagine a non-territorial legal system that meets Bolton's definition, territoriality seems assumed in it. Harris (2015b, 3), while not explicitly concerned with international law, similarly seems to define it away: "a law must be enacted and enforced by a political authority, i.e., the state" (distinguishing "laws" from "non-legal" sacred regulations). Maffi (2001, 285) requires "legislation," if not a state; Daverio Rocchi (2006, 138) claims that human and divine laws ended at the borders of the Greek *polis*. On medieval Iceland as a stateless society with, nevertheless, a highly developed legal system, see W.I. Miller (1990, 219–57). None of this is to deny that there may be

important differences between legal systems within a state (narrowly defined) and other legal systems; but rather to insist they are differences of degree; cf. Wolff (1954, 406–08).

80. Hathaway and Shapiro (2011, 256) paraphrase the functionalist skeptic view: "international law cannot be real law because real law must be capable of affecting behavior through the threat and exercise of physical coercion. Since international law lacks mechanisms of physically coercive enforcement, it cannot affect behavior in the right way and hence cannot be a real legal system." We can classify as a "hyper-functionalist" criticism of international law Eckstein's (2017, 493) insistence that there must be "guaranteed mechanisms of enforcement," which, he claims, Greek international law lacked. Bolton, in addition to his formalism, is also a functionalist in his claim that law must have "forces that can compel behavior and enforce compliance with rules" (2000, 2). Goldsmith and Posner (2005, 3) argue, along the other axis of functionalist criticism, that "international law emerges from states acting rationally to maximize their interests, given their perceptions of the interests of other states and the distribution of state power." I argue against this sort of "rational actor" view of state behavior in the next chapter.
81. Shapiro (2011, 202) claims that "all legal philosophers agree that legal systems exist only if they are generally efficacious, i.e., they are normally obeyed." A focus on enforcement as a criterion of law may be peculiarly Anglo-American; see Michaels and Jansen (2006, 852–53).
82. Ancient domestic legal systems are also sometimes simply assumed to have "ensured" enforcement of their laws; this assumption is expressed, e.g., by von Reden (2022, 612, 623).
83. See O'Connell (2008, 8), claiming that there is "no empirical basis" for the view that the sanctions of international law are weak.
84. Wallace (2024, 1–3).
85. See "Criminal Victimization, 2017," U.S. Department of Justice, Office of Justice Programs, Bureau of Justice Statistics, doc. no. NCJ 252472 (December 2018); available at https://www.bjs.gov/content/pub/pdf/cv17.pdf.
86. See O'Connell (2008, 8).
87. Lowery, Kelly and Rich (2018). That study was of fifty-five US cities. The FBI (optimistically) reports the nationwide murder "clearance" rate (percentage of reported murders resulting in an arrest or equivalent outcome) in recent years to be around 60 percent. The number dropped to 50 percent in 2020 (Li and Lartey 2022).
88. E.g., the U.S. Department of Justice estimates that in 2016 only 44 percent of all violent crimes were even reported to police, and that 46 percent of the reported cases were "cleared" (i.e., resulted in an arrest or similar outcome). For property crimes, it estimates that 35 percent were reported, with a clearance rate of only 18 percent of reported cases. Clearance does not mean conviction. For reporting rates, see *Criminal Victimization, 2016: Revised*, U.S. Department of Justice, Bureau of Justice Statistics, Document no. NCJ 252121 (Oct. 2018), available at https://www.bjs.gov/content/pub/pdf/cv16.pdf; for clearance rates, see https://ucr.fbi.gov/crime-in-the-u.s/2016/crime-in-the-u.s.-2016/topic-pages/clearances, where it explains the conditions for "clearance": "that at least one person has been: [1] Arrested. [2] Charged with the commission of the offense. [3] Turned over to the court for prosecution (whether following arrest, court summons, or police notice). [C]learance calculations . . . [count] the number of offenses that are cleared, not the number of persons arrested. The arrest of one person may clear several crimes, and the arrest of many persons may clear only one offense."
89. Kachalia and Mello (2011, 1564–65); cf. Mello and Brennan (2002, 1609).
90. Henkin (1979, 47). Hathaway and Shapiro (2011, 260, 308–39) argue that enforcement of international law, in the guise of what they call "externalization and outcasting," is "ubiquitous" in modern international law.
91. See O'Connell (2008, 62–66) (describing the views of Morgenthau); Goldsmith and Posner (2005, 3).
92. See Howse and Teitel (2010, 129). To take one example, Hull (2014) shows at length that international law was a central consideration in the commencement and conduct of World War I. An "expressive" interpretation of international law, in the vein of Constructivist International Relations thought, might argue that international law can in fact change attitudes about what is in the material interests of states; see McGinn (2015, 10–16) on expressive effects of law; the references in Chapter 6, n. 41, below; and my discussion of Constructivist IR in Chapter 3. Golove (2006) argues that Goldsmith and Posner's (2005) arguments about the ineffectiveness of international law are based on misreadings of the historical record; Sloss (2006) offers a similar, historically informed rebuttal of their claims.

93. Kelsen (1967, 320–24). On Kelsen's views (more complicated than I suggest in the main text), see also Engelking (2025, 17–18, 32–33); Bernstorff (2010, 78–103); O'Connell (2008, 61–68). Raz (1970, 186) argues that law is coercive, through the imposition of sanctions, but that "Bentham, Austin, and Kelsen misunderstood the function of coercion in the law. Its function is not as the standard motive for any act guided by the laws. It is much more complicated and indirect, though no less essential. Coercion is the ultimate foundation of the law, in the sense of being (part of) the standard reason for obedience to some [laws] that are presupposed in many enormously varied ways by all the other legal norms."
94. Kletzer (2018, 22–25). Those circumstances can include self-help: "The law declares the self-help of the person defending his possession against an attacker to be a lawful act. . . . The act of force is no longer merely a private act of force, but is now also the enforcement of law" (24). There may be a certain irony that, although placing force at the center of law, close to where John Austin had placed it, Kletzer nevertheless argues, contrary to Austin, that international law is just as "legal" as domestic law.
95. Hart (1961, 230). Primary rules are the rules governing life in the society (both rules imposing duties and rules conferring powers), and secondary rules state how one is to determine what the primary rules are, how one may change the primary rules, and how one is to decide when a primary rule has been broken (89–96). On theories of international law that downplay the importance of sanctions, see O'Connell (2008, 68–91); Sheets (1994, 60–61).
96. E.g., if I am hungry, I may have a first-order reason to steal a loaf of bread, but the law against theft may act as an overriding exclusionary second-order reason not to steal the bread. On exclusionary reasons, see Raz (1999, 39–48); on norms as exclusionary reasons, see Raz (1999, 74–76); on a legal system as a normative system, see Raz (1999, 149–54).
97. Raz (1999, 150). For Raz, a legal system is "comprehensive," "open," and "claims to be supreme" (1999, 150–54). International law, according to Raz, meets these conditions but lacks an institutionalized, authoritative way of settling disputes. Raz elsewhere (1970, 3) describes law as "normative, institutionalized, and coercive."
98. Shapiro (2011, 203). He allows customary law to be part of a "planned" legal system, acknowledging that "certain fundamental aspects of legal systems have arisen purely through custom" and proposing that a legal system that contains customary law still counts as law under his theory if at least some part of the system was designed as a group plan and the customary parts are seen as integral to that plan (2011, 207–08).
99. Citing the permissibility and necessity of self-help under international law, Kletzer (2018, 25 n.10) states: "That there is a true continuity between national and international law, and that not only is international law fully law in the national sense, but also national law is fully law in the international sense, is usually overlooked." Self-help, including forceful self-help, is also a significant aspect of domestic law systems. I discuss forceful self-help under Greek domestic and international law in Chapter 5.
100. Greek international law arguably: (1) was "comprehensive" in not having pre-set limits on the forms of behavior it could claim to regulate; (2) claimed supremacy by claiming "authority to regulate the setting up and application of other institutionalized systems by its subject-community" (Raz 1999, 151) (e.g., the Athenian management of its empire); (3) was "open" in giving binding force to norms outside its own system, such as domestic laws and private contracts (e.g., some *symbola* agreements seem to have stated that a *polis*'s domestic laws would apply to another city's citizens just as they applied to local citizens).
101. With regard to other features Shapiro (2011, 210–12) points out, Greek treaty law was also "institutional," in the sense that treaties were entered into by legally recognized officials, and "compulsory," in the sense of binding even people who did not personally consent to them. I note, in addition, that the argument of Hathaway and Shapiro (2011) suggests that Shapiro sees at least modern international law as "real" law.
102. See Dworkin (2013) (on international law specifically); (2011) (morality, politics, and law more generally); cf. Bustamante (2024) (arguing for the "monism" of Dworkin's theories of domestic and international law).
103. See Low (2007, 129–74); Giovannini (2007, 42–47, 149–58); Karavites (2003); Bederman (2001, 48–87) (focusing on religion); Kiechle (1958) (sense of a Greek community and ethics underpinned laws of war); cf. Buis (2018, 139–228) (discussing ethical elements of the Greek laws of war). Ténékidès (1956, 486–88) argues that, in Greek law generally, there was no fine line between law and morality.
104. Dworkin (2013, 11); 2011 (311–24).
105. Dworkin (2013, 19).

Chapter 3

1. Sheets (1994, 40–44); Malkin (2016, 43–46) has a similar interpretation.
2. Thucydides claims the Corcyreans helped the Epidamnian exiles because of sympathies nourished by genetic connections, that the exiles came to Corcyra "gesturing to the tombs and their common ancestry," τάφους τε ἀποδεικνύντες καὶ ξυγγένειαν, 1.26.3. The strength and longevity of ties between colony and mother city are shown perhaps most strikingly in a long, recently discovered decree from Teos, dating to the mid-2nd century BCE and revealing continuing close relations with the citizens of Abdera, which had been founded as a Tean colony four centuries earlier. See the text, translation, and discussion by Adak and Thonemann (2022).
3. Considering the city's general importance in the Greek world, we know remarkably little about Corinth's government. The extensive excavations undertaken for over a century at the site of ancient Corinth have uncovered a shockingly small number of inscriptions from the pre-Roman period (i.e., before 146 BCE). They may have frequently been inscribed on bronze, which was often melted down and reused; see Cassayre (2010, 160); Kent (1966, 1–2); Dow (1942, 89).
4. The ordinary Greek word for education, *paideia,* more literally means "child training," and the concept was much wider than "school learning." Hence, Greek discussions of *paideia* often incorporate significant elements of what is now called socialization (cf. the French *formation* and perhaps English "rearing"). See, e.g., Pl. *Leg.* 1.643a–44b; 2.653a–56b; 7.788a–817e; 9.862d (cf. Balot 2024, 180–87; Folch 2015, 80–97); Arist. *Eth. Nic.* 2.1–4, *Pol.* 7.17–8.7. See also Xen. *Cyr.* 1.2.2–3, claiming that Greek *paideia* in fact failed to socialize people, unlike Persian education, which did so from a young age. A recent collection of essays interpreting the ancient Greek and Roman world in light of the findings of modern social psychology is Huitink, Glaveanu, and Sluiter (2025).
5. Megiddo (2021, 2019). The topic is attracting greater interest: see now Wallace (2024) and the collection of essays edited by Sparks and Peters (2024); more briefly, Lesaffer (2024, 37–39). On the individual in Roman international law, see Cowan (2024).
6. See Gilpin (1986, 318): "The state does not really exist. . . . Only individuals exist . . . [and o]nly individuals *act*," and although scholars "write as if some particular social or political entity really does exist and acts . . . it is a matter of convenience and economy to do so." Cf. Jessop (1990, 366–7); M. Weber (1947, 102). Sometimes the legal authority of the actor is contestable, in which case it may be unclear whether "the state" acted through that person. For critical reviews of the "statist" tendency in international law and international relations scholarship, see Megiddo (2021, 230–47; 2019, 221–33). My approach to "individual vs. state" in international law has affinities with Duplouy's (2018, 250) approach to understanding citizenship in the ancient Greek city: the early city was not "a theoretical entity gradually granting 'membership' to its affiliates," but rather was "the empirical result of the 'participation' of individuals in a community in the making."
7. Wendt (1999, 197). Pettit (2002) argues for the theoretical possibility that groups of humans—what he calls "integrated collectivities"—can be intentional subjects to which desires, beliefs, and judgments, as well as intentions, can be ascribed. But he does not claim that any states in the real world actually meet the conditions of being an integrated collectivity in this sense. Philosophers of law debate whether intent can be attributed to a legislature; for a recent argument that it can, see Collins and Tan (2024); Ekins (2012, 14); *contra* Roversi and Sardo (2019); Shepsle (1992); Dworkin (1986, 313–54). Ludwig (2017) denies that modern corporations, sometimes offered as "paradigms" of group agents, have minds or agency of their own. On the history of political theorists anthropomorphizing the state, see Nutkiewicz (1983, 15): "the image of the state as a biological body permeated medieval and Renaissance political theory." Plato's *Republic* assumes that a state and a person have important similarities: that is the premise for theorizing the ideal state in the first place (*Resp.* 2.368c–369a); some Athenian art portrays the entire citizen body, the *demos*, as a single man; and Greeks easily attributed thoughts and emotions to an entire state, see Lendon (2010, 9–10). On the intellectual history of the anthropomorphizing metaphor of the "body politic" in Roman political thought, see Mebane (2024). Perhaps the most famous example of such anthropomorphism is by Hobbes, in the frontispiece and introduction to *Leviathan* (1996 [1651], 7), where he calls the Leviathan "but an artificial man." According to d'Aspremont (2015, 506), anthropomorphism of the state had become intellectual by the sixteenth or seventeenth century, when "Pufendorf . . . pushed the Hobbesian human analogy further and constructed an image of the state as endowed with an intellect that is distinct from that of the sovereign." Hegel (1988, 27–28) argued not only that states had conscious awareness but

that there was also an overarching "World Spirit" governing global history. For intellectual anthropomorphism of the state by more recent theorists, see, e.g., the neorealist Waltz (1979, 91, 118), who "assume[s] that *states* seek to ensure their survival"; his theory "is built up from the assumed motivations of *states*" (emphasis added). Schafer and Crichlow (2010, 34) point out that "many of the major schools of thought in the [foreign relations] field have disregarded or ignored individual-level psychology in most of their research." See also P.T. Jackson (2004, 255); Hollis and Smith (1990, 143–70); and, in a less theoretical but sensitive mode, Beaton (2020, 2).

8. See Mearsheimer (2006, 72): "For structural realists, human nature has little to do with why states want power. . . . Structural realists treat states as if they were black boxes: they are assumed to be alike, save for the fact that some states are more or less powerful than others." Cf. Eckstein (2006, 14–15); Waltz (1979, 91–92, 102). On the difference between realism and structural realism (a variant of neorealism), see Schonberg (2009, 815).
9. Influential statements of the constructivist position are Onuf (1989) and Wendt (1999); cf. Schonberg (2009, 817). A broadly constructivist theory heavily rooted in Greek historical examples and political thought is offered by Lebow (2008). Much international relations thought, including institutionalism, liberalism, and the so-called English and New Haven schools, is distinct from both realism and constructivism, and I offer here nothing approaching a survey of contemporary or historical international relations thinking. For the former, see Smith, Hadfield, and Dunne (2012, 35–109). For the latter, see Knutsen (2016); Low (2007, ch. 1); Dunne (1998). On realism vs. constructivism in particular, see Kessler and Steele (2018).
10. See Waltz (1979, 91). Even the simplification is arguably a façade, because it requires introducing (or at least assuming) an offsetting complication: explaining how the "state" decision then translates into the acts of physical human beings with their own individual minds. That is, if we accept that the "state" makes a decision, we must still explain how it happens that its individual human members decide to act in specific ways to carry out that decision. Without making yet more radical ontological claims (which even Wendt does not make, admitting that people must "accept the obligation to act jointly on behalf of collective beliefs, whether or not they subscribe to them personally" (1999, 218)), the simplifying assumption of the "state as person" at most explains state decision-making but not state action; see Wight (2004, 276–7). Levy (2013, 301–2) notes the "tension between the goals of constructing parsimonious and generalizable theoretical explanations of international behavior and of providing nuanced and descriptively accurate explanations of individual historical episodes. Many would agree that the inclusion of psychological variables seriously complicates the first task but is necessary for the second task." On the potential conflict of *simplicity* and *accuracy* in constructing a theory, see Richards (2002, 5), who lists Kuhn's (1977, 321–22) five "values" that guide theory choice: "accuracy, consistency, breadth, simplicity, and fruitfulness," accuracy being in the eyes of most scientists "the most nearly decisive of all the criteria," although "accuracy by itself is seldom or never a sufficient criterion for theory choice" (1977, 323). On the importance of using *both* reductive and complicating strategies, see Ober (2018, 8–9).
11. The belief that only individual humans have mental states is often called "methodological individualism." Searle (2005, 21) defines it as the claim that "all observer-independent mental reality must exist in the minds of individual human beings." On using methodological individualism to understand political activity in ancient Greece, see Simonton (2017, 61–64). R.A. Wilson (2005, 235) defends "talk[ing] of groups of people as having intentions, beliefs, goals, and memories" on the ground that it "add[s] intelligibility to the actions of those groups, and a greater sense of their place in the causal and normative nexus, through their assimilation to human agents." Sociological theories of "distributed" and "collective" cognition challenge the truth of methodological individualism; see an overview in Tindale et al. (2007); and exploration of collective cognition in Athens by Budelmann (2019). Tollefsen (2015) reviews philosophical theories of groups as cognitive and moral actors. The application of such ideas to the political realm may trace back at least to Rousseau's idea of the "general will" in the *Social Contract* (Book 2, chs. 1–3) or even to Ibn Rushd's theory of the single human intellect (*Long Commentary on the De Anima of Aristotle* 3.5; see Ogden 2022).
12. Goodman and Jinks (2013, 13); see also Wallace (2024). For a survey of recent research on psychological factors in international relations, see Kertzer and Tingley (2018). In fact, what is often called "behavioral IR" has moved beyond psychology in a narrow sense to incorporate the biology of genetics and neuroscience; see Davis and McDermott (2021). Megiddo (2019, 228) argues that Goodman and Jinks do not go far enough, "allocat[ing] little theoretical weight to individuals and to sub-state dynamics."

13. On the debate over the meaning of ἀληθεστάτην πρόφασιν, see Eckstein (2017, 504–08); Hornblower (1991–2008, i.64–66); Rhodes (1987).
14. On the common view of Thucydides as a realist, and the problems with such an interpretation, see Ober (2009); Welch (2003); Lebow (2001). Luckily for my purposes, Thucydides was much more a historian than a political theorist.
15. See Fiske and Taylor (2017, 7); Higgins (2012, 359). Fiske and Taylor (2017, 34–35) offer nine "varieties of automatic and controlled" cognitive processes, ranging from the "full automaticity" of unintentional and unconscious processes to the "full control" of "intentional responses with conscious awareness." On the heritability of "core predispositions" such as values and personality traits, and their effect on political orientation, see Hibbing, Smith, and Alford (2014); Funk et al. (2013); Higgins (2012, 24). On motives, see Caprara and Vecchione (2013, 33–4), defining them as "internal states or forces experienced as wishes and desires that lead to the achievement of specific goals." This is better than calling them *preferences* since the latter term always implies a comparison.
16. See, e.g., L.M. Friedman (2016, 5) (three "clusters of motives" are rewards and punishments; peer pressure; and conscience and morality); Etienne (2011, 306) (humans act from "material, emotional, and normative goals"); Lindenberg and Steg (2007, 119–21) (positing three "goal frames": hedonic, gain, and normative); May (2004, 41–42) (people and firms comply with rules "either because they fear detection of violations and subsequent punishment, feel a duty to comply, or feel social pressure to comply").
17. The most famous version of this view of human cognition is probably Freud's notion of the unconscious, but there are many non-Freudian versions. As Frith and Singer claim (2008, 3875), decision-making is not a "unitary cognitive process." Perhaps the most important contemporary class of theories seeking to explain this phenomenon is so-called "dual-process" theories, which propose that humans have two primary methods of thinking, one fast, automatic, intuitive, and mostly impervious to introspection, and the other slow, conscious, and reflective. On the variety of theories that fall within the dual-process "family," see J.St.B.T. Evans (2018); see also Fiske and Taylor (2017, 34–43); Stanovich (2011, 16–25); Thaler and Sunstein (2008, 19–21). Stanovich (2011, 17–18) notes that dual-process theories are now "ubiquitous" in psychology and related fields and lists twenty-seven variants in the scholarly literature.
18. On mis-explaining our actions, see Fiske and Taylor (2017, 173); Kahneman (2011, 415–18); Olson and Stone (2005, 228–54). E.g., we tend to believe our own motives are guided more by self-interest than is—apparently—really the case; see Ratner and Miller (2001, 6). On unconscious stereotypes and biases, see Devine and Monteith (1999), who explain that although use of stereotypes is often automatic and unconscious, there are ways to become aware of and consciously counteract them. On emotions, see the overview by Brader and Marcus (2013); cf. Frith and Singer (2008, 3879–80); McDermott (2004, 695–98). On heuristics and biases, see Fiske and Taylor (2017, 188–217); Chong (2013, 101–23); Redlawsk and Lau (2013); Kahneman (2011, 109–95).
19. On framing effects, see Etienne (2011, 311–16); Lindenberg and Steg (2007, 119–22); Thaler and Sunstein (2008, 36–7); Kahneman and Tversky (1979, 286–87). A similar concept is David Friedman's (1994, 6–7) presentation of so-called "Schelling points," which can similarly be manipulated by rhetoric. In their prospect theory, Kahneman and Tversky point to three "principles" that govern judgments concerning future losses and gains, which Kahneman (2011, 282) reports: (1) "Evaluation is relative to a neutral reference point. . . . Outcomes that are better than the reference points are gains. Below the reference point they are losses." (2) A principle of diminishing sensitivity applies to . . . the evaluation of changes of wealth... [so that, e.g.,] the subjective difference between $900 and $1,000 is much smaller than the difference between $100 and $200." (3) Loss aversion: "When directly compared or weighted against each other, losses loom larger than gains." For an example of Greek awareness of framing effects, see Arist. *Rh.* 1, 1356a4–20; 2, 1377b31–78a5; cf. Stucki and Sager (2018).
20. On voter studies, see Caprara and Vecchione (2013, 45–6). On transference, see Andersen et al. (2016, 2).
21. There is no single standard model, and it does not always go under the name "rational choice theory," so any description is at best a broad sketch. Helpful overviews are provided by Ermakoff (2017, 162–67); Kroneberg and Kalter (2012); Mintz and DeRouen (2010, ch. 4). Ober (2022, esp. 1–31) argues that a "folk" version of rational choice theory arose among Greeks in the fifth and fourth centuries BCE. The normative notion of rationality is found more widely than just among rational choice theorists; see Stanovich (2011, 3–8). Henry Adams (1907, 72) concisely

diagnoses the defect of the concept of "utility" in his description of the value of certain life experiences for one's education: "They were also what men pay most for; but one's ideas become hopelessly mixed in trying to reduce such forms of education to a standard of exchangeable value, and, as in political economy, one had best disregard altogether what cannot be stated in equivalents."

22. For criticisms of rational choice theory, see, e.g., Zafirovski (2018); Ermakoff (2017, 167–72); Chong (2013); Redlawsk and Lau (2013); Mintz and DeRouen (2010, ch. 5); DellaVigna (2009); Lehtinen and Kuorikoski (2007); Green and Shapiro (1994). Bourdieu and Wacquant (1992, 120–23) criticize it under the label "rational action theory." Some suggest the theory might be useful so long as people act "as if" they were reasoning according to the model of rational choice theory. Lehtinen and Kuorikoski (2007) discuss this and other defenses. One large-scale attempt to build an entire social theory on the foundation of rational choice is Coleman (1990); this ambitious effort has in turn been criticized largely for the flaws introduced by its rigid adherence to rational choice theory; see, e.g., Cherkaoui (2005); R.H. Frank (1992); Smelser (1990).
23. Among Greek political forms, democracy, and Athenian democracy in particular, has received the most extensive scholarly treatment. Two influential sustained engagements with Athenian democracy in recent decades have been those of Josiah Ober, especially his "trilogy": (2008, 1998, and 1989); and Mogens Hansen, e.g., (1999, 1983). On the dynamics of the Athenian assembly in particular, see Ober (2022, 250–94); Canevaro (2018, 123–36). For references to scholarship on the various Greek political forms, see Simonton (2017, 1–2 nn.3 and 4); Giovannini (2007, 86–89). Even within the main categories of political organization, every real-life instantiation will have been unique and will have changed over time, both structurally and in the people who constituted them. One relatively well-documented case is the changes to the constitution of the Athenians from its beginnings to the time of Aristotle, described in the *Athenaion Politeia* probably written by a member of Aristotle's school; see *Ath. pol.* 1–41 (with the commentaries of Rhodes 2017 and 1981) and Hansen (1999, 27–54). The Spartans appear to have been exceptional in the stability of their constitution (Thuc. 1.18.1); it is reasonable to assume that constitutional change was common for most Greeks. E.g., the essays collected in Beck and Funke (2015) provide, on the whole, much evidence for significant changes over time in the constitutions of Greek confederacies. Similar claims can be made regarding the post-Alexander monarchies, but note that Herman (1997, 207) follows F.W. Walbank (1984, 65) in claiming that "over time the three kingdoms gradually came to resemble each other more and more, adopting some remarkably similar structural features." Similarly, Ma (2017) describes the "Great Convergence" of *polis* forms that had swept across the Greek world by the first half of the third century BCE.
24. Political psychology is approached from a variety of perspectives including cognitive psychology, personality psychology, affective and attitudinal psychology, neuropsychology, social psychology, social identity theory, and other subfields. Recent surveys of the field of political psychology are Nesbitt-Larking et al. (2014) and Huddy, Sears, and Levy (2013). On political psychology in international relations scholarship since the 1960s, see Davis and McDermott (2021, 149–53).
25. See, most recently, Wallace (2024); Davis and McDermott (2021) survey many examples; cf. Hollis and Smith (1990, 143–70).
26. Schafer and Crichlow (2010, 19); Horowitz et al. (2019); Mintz and Wayne (2016); Levy (2013).
27. I.L. Janis (1982, 2–13); Schafer and Crichlow (2010, 50–51); Mintz and DeRouen (2010, 97–104).
28. Seddon, Miller, and Schwarz (2023) offer an interpretation of Russia's 2022 invasion of Ukraine and continuing war and occupation, suggesting groupthink has played a significant role in Russian decision-making.
29. I omit here discussion of the important role of Pericles—and hence his psychology—in the determination of Athenian foreign policy in the fifth century, merely noting that Plutarch (*Per.* 30–32) justifiably makes much of it as a factor in the Athenian move to war with Sparta. I also omit discussion of the important role of individual and group psychology in the Athenian decision to launch the Sicilian expedition, see Thuc. 6.8–26.
30. Thuc. 1.87.2: "hoping that he would push them more toward declaring war by revealing their preference openly," βουλόμενος αὐτοὺς φανερῶς ἀποδεικνυμένους τὴν γνώμην ἐς τὸ πολεμεῖν μᾶλλον ὁρμῆσαι.

31. Anyone familiar with Thucydides's account of the Athenian change of mind concerning Mytilene will have been struck by how my description of it distorts Thucydides's own presentation. This is because, of the eleven pages the episode occupies in the Oxford text of Thucydides, about ninety percent is taken up by the two speeches Thucydides reports, by Cleon and Diodotos, often called "The Mytilene Debate." The bulk of scholarly commentary on the passage is also devoted to the speeches, generally taking them as reflecting Thucydides's opinion of the actual views that some Athenians took of the nature of their empire. To the degree that the speeches represent broad reflections with relevance beyond the specific question of how to treat the Mytileneans, this scholarly emphasis is understandable. But, as Andrewes has noted, if we want to understand why the Athenians acted as they did in this instance, Thucydides's presentation may mislead us, since the speeches reported at such length do not appear to have altered people's already-changed opinion: "[F]or the real occasion [of the Athenian reversal] we must not minimize the effect of the simpler feelings described in 36.4" (1962, 72). Thucydides reveals that it was more the feeling of pity than consideration of the reasoned, policy-based arguments of Cleon and Diodotos that prevented even greater slaughter in Mytilene, *contra* Ober (2022, 233–40), whose interpretation of the episode as an example of political rationality does not mention Thucydides's observations about regret for savagery as playing the decisive role in the assembly's final decree. On the role of emotion in Greek society generally, see the collections of essays edited by Sanders and Johncock (2016), Chaniotis and Ducrey (2013), and Chaniotis (2012). Kalliontzis and Papazarkadas (2019, 310–11) argue that empathy was an important factor motivating many of the cities that contributed funds to the rebuilding of Thebes in the late fourth century, almost two decades after that city had been destroyed by Alexander the Great.
32. F.W. Walbank (1984, 69). See Strootman (2014, 118–59), esp. 119–21: "The *philoi* first of all created and maintained bonds between the dynasty and cities; furthermore, they were the advisors of the king in all his undertakings, the accountants of the royal finances; the functionaries and tax-collectors who administered the provinces, the king's representatives in cities and his ambassadors at foreign courts, and most of all the generals and admirals who commanded troops and ships. . . . The upper stratum of the *philoi* at court had a seat in the royal council, or *sunedrion*, granting them access to the person of the king on a regular basis, and hence influence on political matters." See also Savalli-Lestrade (1998, 355–94), emphasizing their role as royal counselors (356–58). On the operation of royal courts, see Strootman (2014); Ma (2011); Spawforth (2007b); Herman (1997); F.W. Walbank (1984). On ancient court society more generally, see the essays in Spawforth (2007).
33. "Speaking freely," *isegoria* or *parrhesia* in Greek, was most commonly viewed as a feature of democracies, Athens above all. See Raaflaub (2004); Balot (2004). In Plato's *Gorgias*, Socrates famously calls the alleged *parrhesia* in the Athenian assembly its opposite: pure flattery; see esp. *Gorg.* 502e–503d.
34. On the value of *parrhesia* in royal courts, see Strootman (2014, 172–74); cf. Polyb. 28.2 (a sign of Philip V's corruption was that his *philoi* stopped daring to speak their minds to him, οὐκέτι γὰρ οὐδεὶς ἐτόλμα τῶν φίλων ἔχειν παρρησίαν).
35. See Polyb. 7.12; Plut. *Arat.* 49–51. Polybius does at one point (5.12.5) describe Aratos and Demetrios of Pharos as among Philip's *philoi.*
36. F.W. Walbank (1957–1979, ii.59–60) suggests our account originates with Aratos himself although it cannot derive from Aratos's published memoirs, which Polybius knew well but which stopped at about 220 BCE (we know this because Polybius styles himself as Aratos's continuator, 4.1.9–4.2.1; cf. Nicholson 2023, 31–33). In any case, Polybius's reliance here on Aratos as a source is no reason to doubt his attribution of Philip's decision to ethical and emotional rather than strategic factors. Part of Polybius's stated purpose is to narrate Philip's decline from an admired and beloved king to a detested tyrant (7.11, 13). This incident could have illustrated that trend just as well if Philip had ignored Aratos's advice here or followed it only for strategic purposes. On this episode, see Nicholson (2023, 81–100), who emphasizes Polybius's additional rhetorical efforts to "defend and glorify" Aratos (99). Again, though, that goal does not explain the attribution of ethical over strategic factors.
37. On Beccaria's deterrence theory and its influence on Bentham, see Harcourt (2014); Nagin (2013, 205–07). The theory is of course much older. Aristotle partly subscribes to it when he claims that "most people naturally obey not shame but fear, abstaining from bad deeds not because of the dishonor but the penalties," οὐ γὰρ πεφύκασιν [sc. οἱ πολλοί] αἰδοῖ πειθαρχεῖν ἀλλὰ φόβῳ, οὐδ' ἀπέχεσθαι τῶν φαύλων διὰ τὸ αἰσχρὸν ἀλλὰ διὰ τὰς τιμωρίας, *Eth. Nic.*

10, 1179b11–12; cf. Dem. 21.37. Justinian's *Digest* (1.1.1.1) opens with a passage from the jurist Ulpian stating that jurists like himself seek to make men good "not only by the fear of penalties but also by the encouragement of rewards," *bonos non solum metu poenarum verum etiam praemiorum quoque exhortatione efficere*. Schauer (2015) offers a spirited restatement of deterrence theory (but see the reply of Tyler 2016). The traditional alternative to deterrence theory in criminological thought has been the "criminal disposition" theory: that some people have psychological features making them more predisposed to commit crime. See Nagin and Paternoster (1993, 467), who point out that the two theories are compatible (490–91).

38. On connections between deterrence theory and rational choice theory, see Trinkner and Tyler (2016, 425); Cardi, Penfield, and Yoon (2012, 592); Robinson and Darley (2004, 178–82); von Hirsch et al. (1999, 6); Cornish and Clarke (1987, 944–45); Hirschi (1986) and generally the other essays collected in Cornish and Clarke (1986).

39. E.g., there is evidence that sharply increasing the *likelihood* of punishment moderately decreases violations of the law; and that increasing the *severity* of punishment does so even less, a difference already predicted by Beccaria (1781, 76) (the passage is in ch. 20 of early Italian editions and ch. 27 of early English translations); for recent studies, see Hertogh (2023, 316–17); Loughran et al. (2015); Travis, Western, and Redburn (2014, 134–40); Cardi, Penfield, and Yoon (2012, 575–76); von Hirsch et al. (1999, 45–48); Nagin (1998, 13–15); Braithwaite and Makkai (1991). And for homicide, the most widely and reliably tracked crime worldwide, there is evidence that increasing the severity of punishment is actually correlated to *increases* in homicide rates; see Lappi-Seppälä and Lehti (2014, 190–203). Tonry (2014, 53) argues that "it is no longer reasonable even to hypothesize that crime patterns can be explained in terms of punishment policies or imprisonment rates, although many academics, especially economists, try to do so." There is extensive evidence that tort liability has little or no deterrent effect in most areas of law; see Rooij and Brownlee (2021, 319); Cardi, Penfield, and Yoon (2012).

40. On nondeterrence explanations of law-abiding behavior generally, see Lane, Nosenzo, and Sonderegger (2023); Trinkner and Tyler (2016, 420); von Hirsch et al. (1999, 3–4). For Aristotle's basic view on the importance of deterrence, see n. 37 above. But Aristotle was likely responding to the theory of law-abiding action propounded by Democritus, who acknowledged the role of deterrence but emphasized the importance of socialized and internalized standards of behavior; see Johnson (2020, 230–32); Procopé (1989, 320–25).

41. Basic definitions of socialization and helpful inroads into the enormous literature concerning the phenomenon include Brenton (2017); Frønes (2016, 1–8, 89–97); Maccoby (2015); Lutfey and Mortimer (2006); Corsaro and Fingerson (2003). For economic modeling of socialization processes, see Bisin and Verdier (2011, 392–406). For Greek awareness of socialization, see, e.g., Plato (*Resp.* 3.395b–d, 401d, 411a; *Leg.* 1.643a–44b; 2.653a–56b; 7.788a–817e) and Aristotle (*Eth. Nic.* 2.1–4, 10.9; *Pol.* 7.17–8.7), both stressing the importance of socialization in education. On the socialization of citizen behavior (which he calls "performance") in early Greek cities, see Duplouy (2018, 270).

42. George Mead's theory of "symbolic interactionism" is credited with first emphasizing the reciprocal nature of socialization; see Lutfey and Mortimer (2006, 185). On the role of institutions in socialization, see Alesina and Giuliano (2015, 921–28), summarizing many studies. On socialization through media, see Potts, Maadad, and Yu (2018, 22–24); Genner and Süss (2017, 1–3).

43. On socialization in childhood, see Habashi (2018); Tyler and Trinkner (2017); Brenton (2017); L.M. Friedman (2016, 153–87); Frønes (2016); Lerner, Overton, and Molenaar (2015, vol. 3); Corsaro and Fingerson (2003). On later socialization, see Brown and Rohlinger (2016); Arnett (2015); Lutfey and Mortimer (2006).

44. On the multiplicity of overlapping groups in the Greek world, see Loy (2023, 16); Taylor and Vlassopoulos (2015, 2–8). On the importance of sub-*polis* groups in ancient Athens, see Carugati and Weingast (2018, 166–68); Ismard (2010).

45. On theories of deviance, see Kaplan (2003, 457–60). One contemporary theory of the socialization of deviance is Akers's social learning theory, see Akers (1998); cf. Cochran et al. (2017, 40–45).

46. On professional groups, see Granovetter (2017, 33–34). On private associations in the ancient Greek world, see the essays in Cazemier and Skaltsa (2022) and Gabrielsen and Paganini (2021). On reference group theory, see Merton and Rossi (1957, 234, 250–60), providing an influential formulation that people often affiliate themselves with a more prestigious group by adopting its values.

47. On socialization as "internalization" of norms and values, see Frønes (2016, 2); on internalization vs. "rational" decision-making, see Fagan and Piquero (2007, 715–22). On socialization as both conscious and unconscious, see Hopf (2018); van den Berg (1998, 440–46).
48. Tapp and Levine (1974) use the term "legal socialization" in relation to "the institution of law specifically and all authoritative rule-systems generally." See Tapp (1976, 371–73); Trinkner and Tyler (2016, 424). Trinkner and Cohn (2014) emphasize the similarities between domains of "law" in the narrow sense and "rule bound institutions." Studies of legal socialization that look beyond the world of law narrowly conceived include Trinkner and Cohn (2014); Tyler (2011); Ellickson (1994); Cohn and White (1990); Folger and Konovsky (1989); Tapp and Levine (1974). The broad view seeing law as one among a number of formal social rule systems is in line with new institutional economic thinking that calls all of society's rule systems "institutions" and distinguishes between formal and informal. See Alesina and Giuliano (2015, 901–02); North (1990, 3–10).
49. See Trinkner and Cohn (2014, 602–3).
50. Lanni (2008, 472). Ellickson (1994) shows how what he calls "informal norms" can have more effect on "legal" behavior than formally enacted law.
51. Some studies of legal socialization focus explicitly on the role of law enforcement rather than law establishment authorities, e.g., Gao and Zhao (2018, 170).
52. Trinkner and Tyler (2016) provide an overview of research. See Nagin and Telep (2017, 6–7); Bradford et al. (2015, 172–78); Tyler (2006, 62–68, 270–80); Robinson and Darley (2004); von Hirsch et al. (1999, 3–7, 45–48); Braithwaite and Makkai (1991); Cohn and White (1990, 194–96).
53. Gao and Zhao (2018, 173) (finding, in a study of Chinese law compliance, that "morality was by far the strongest motivation for compliance" with four different sets of laws); Trinkner and Tyler (2016, 422); Alesina and Giuliano (2015, 921–28); DeBacker, Heim, and Tran (2015, 123–25).
54. Bradford et al. (2015, 175); Parsons, Sulaeman, and Titman (2018) find this effect to be highly local, e.g., varying from city to city within the United States.
55. On the role of legal judgment, see Trinkner and Tyler (2016, 422); Cohn et al. (2010, 295–97); Tapp and Levine (1974, 1–31). On the multiple factors affecting legal socialization, see Gao and Zhao (2018, 174); Bradford et al. (2015, 183–84); Tyler (2006, 25); Fagan and Tyler (2005, 219–20, 231–37).
56. See Gaertner et al. (1999, 177). My use of "group" is similar to Loy's (2023, 14) use of "community," which he intends as a "neutral" term "that presupposes nothing about a group's composition nor about its behaviours." For discussion of specific communal activities that may have helped form group identity in early Greek communities, see Steidl (2024).
57. On the need for group membership, see Baumeister and Leary (1995). On the connection between personal and group welfare, see Abrams and Hogg (2010, 188). On how group membership can contribute to welfare generally, see F. Stewart (2005). The fifth- or fourth-century BCE Athenian author known as "Anonymous Iamblichi" posits a similarly close connection between community, respect for its laws, trust between people, and mutual well-being, DK 89 fr. 7.1–4 (= Laks–Most *Anon. Iambl.* 7.1–4).
58. Lind and Tyler (1988, 232).
59. W.I. Miller (1990, 21). Two recent studies by Ben Bradford and colleagues show connections between group identity and law-abidingness. In a study in Australia, Bradford, Murphy, and Jackson (2014, 540) found that increasing identification as a member of the group "Australian citizens" "was strongly associated with a positive change in perceived duty to obey" law in Australia. And a study in Scotland found that "people who identified more strongly as 'Scottish citizens' tended to believe that it was more wrong to break traffic laws in Scotland than those who identified less strongly" (Bradford et al. 2015, 183).
60. D. Cohen (1995, 61–118). Gabrielsen and Paganini (2021b, 9–18) discuss the close relationship between group identity and the establishment and following of rules within ancient Greek private associations.
61. On social motivations, see Tyler (2011, 1–26). He contrasts social motivations with "external motivations" in the form of rewards or sanctions that are not so closely tied to internalized values and attitudes (2011, 4–5). The distinction is useful, but the categories are intertwined. E.g., it is partly my internalized values and attitudes that make me responsive to some external rewards and punishments but not others. See also Gaertner and Dovidio (2012, 444–45);

Foddy and Yamagishi (2009, 35–37). On the multiple scales on which groups may exist, see Loy (2023, 15–16).

62. See Hogg (2016, 5–6; 2006, 483); Tajfel and Turner (1979); Tajfel et al. (1971). According to Hogg (2006, 480), "[a] group exists psychologically when two or more people define and evaluate themselves in terms of the defining properties of a common self-inclusive category." Tajfel and Turner (1986, 15) define a group as "a collection of individuals who perceive themselves to be members of the same social category, share some emotional involvement in this common definition of themselves, and achieve some degree of social consensus about the evaluation of their group and of their membership in it." Wildschut, Gaertner, and Insko (2002, 976–77) postulate a "norm of group interest," namely, "that one should take into account the interests of one's own group before taking into account the interests of other groups," and they compare it to the common Greek ethic of "helping friends and harming enemies."
63. Hogg, Abrams, and Brewer (2017, 574); see Hogg (2006, 484–5). On the self-esteem motivation of group identity, see Martiny and Rubin (2016). One way humans understand the world is by categorizing its elements, which includes assigning ourselves and other people to categories. People then minimize differences between those whom they have categorized together and exaggerate differences between those whom they have placed in different categories. See Gaertner et al. (1999, 175–6). On biases against out-group members, see Gaertner et al. (1999, 177–78). For a survey of research in social identity theory, see Kalin and Sambanis (2018).
64. Gaertner and Dovidio (2012, 444–45) summarize the divergences: people allocate more rewards to members of their in-group than to members of the out-group; evaluate them more favorably; retain more detailed information about them; have better memory of their own similarities with in-group members, but of their differences from out-group members; are more likely to attribute positive outcomes from in-group members to stable characteristics; are more likely to assume that undesirable actions by out-group members reveal intention, but to view desirable actions as bare facts. "In terms of social relations and behavioral outcomes, people are more cooperative and trustful of ingroup than outgroup members . . . and they exercise more personal restraint when using endangered resources shared with ingroup members than with others. . . . Additionally, shared group membership decreases psychological distance from and facilitates arousal of promotive tension or empathy toward ingroup members. . . . Relatedly, prosocial behavior is offered more readily to ingroup than to outgroup members." On group coherence, see Effron and Knowles (2015, 235), who call it "entitativity": "Entitative groups are characterized by high similarity, proximity, and interdependence among members who share information and have strong interpersonal bonds. . . . [T]he pursuit of common goals—and thus the existence of collective interests—is a central characteristic of entitative-group members."
65. On Cleisthenes's reforms, see *Ath. pol.* 21; Hdt. 5.66, 69. Recent discussions include Paga (2021, 16–20, 244–45, and *passim*); Dmitriev (2018, 223–42); Ober (2008, 134–42). On identification with multiple groups, see Wiater (2011, 21) talking (in the context of Dionysius of Halicarnassus's professional life in Augustan Rome) about "the 'cultures' of different communicative networks of which an individual is a part" as the basis for someone's "understanding and experiencing of their social identity." On applying social identity theory in the ancient Greek context, see J.L. Shear (2021, 21–26).
66. An early and influential formulation of contact theory is Allport (1954, 262–82). Pettigrew and Tropp (2006) is a major meta-analysis of hundreds of studies confirming Allport's main hypotheses. Tropp, Mazziotta, and Wright (2017) review more recent literature; Blouin and Mukand (2022) and Clayton, Ferwerda, and Horiuchi (2021, 177) offer even more recent confirmations. On "multiple social categorization" and the effects of blurring boundaries and decategorization, see Crisp and Hewstone (2007, esp. 165–57, 179–227); Brown (1996, 171–81). On transferred "liking," see Pettigrew and Tropp (2006, 753); Harmon-Jones and Allen (2001, 889–90). In fact, just being aware that a member of one's in-group has friends in the out-group, or hearing stories about such friendships, can make one more positively and cooperatively oriented toward the out-group; see Tropp, Mazziotta, and Wright (2017, 465–66); Gómez et al. (2013, 420). On increased empathy, see Selvanathan et al. (2018, 893–95).
67. On superordinate group identity, see Gaertner et al. (1999, 179–92). On common threat perception, see Flade, Klar, and Imhoff (2019, 1); Maitner and Stewart-Ingersoll (2016, 322). On the UAE and Khaliji identity, see Maitner and Stewart-Ingersoll (2016, 317–23). Wenzel, Waldzus, and Steffens (2017, 65–70) review the literature on the in-group projection model. One Greek example that may reflect the power of perceived group prototypicality is the Boiotian *koinon*,

which was often dominated by the Thebans and experienced significant internal conflict over the decades. This conflict may have been driven in part by a Theban belief and assertion that they were the most prototypical Boiotians. On the Boiotian *koinon*, see Mackil (2013, *passim*); Beck and Ganter (2015).

68. Granovetter (1973); on the interplay of "weak" and "strong" ties in the transfer of complex information such as behaviors and norms, see Collar (2022). See Ober (2008, 135–42) for an application of Granovetter's framework to Athenian politics.
69. For overviews, see Hirsch (2015, 17–45, 128–56); Goodman and Jinks (2013, 53–86); Gilardi (2013). On convergence in environmental policies, see Frank, Hironaka, and Schofer (2000, 106); in education: Meyer, Ramirez, and Soysal (1992, 146); in constitutional design: Elkins (2010); in economic policies: Cao (2010); Simmons and Elkins (2004); in human rights: Greenhill (2010, 140–41).
70. Afonso and Negash (2021).
71. Hainmueller and Hangartner (2013, 160–61).
72. Bayram (2017, 54–55).
73. Thuc. 3.10.3: ξύμμαχοι μέντοι ἐγενόμεθα οὐκ ἐπὶ καταδουλώσει τῶν Ἑλλήνων Ἀθηναίοις, ἀλλ' ἐπ' ἐλευθερώσει ἀπὸ τοῦ Μήδου τοῖς Ἕλλησιν.
74. The literature on social network analysis is enormous. A short introduction is J. Scott (2012). Useful collections of articles are Scott and Carrington (2011) and Newman, Barabási, and Watts (2006), the latter not restricted to social networks.
75. J. Scott (2012, 1). Some analyses of Greek networks treat cities as nodes and people as the connections between them.
76. See Heatherly, Lu, and Lee (2017, 1276).
77. Newman, Barabási, and Watts (2006) collects several articles studying the network dynamics of epidemics.
78. Constantakopoulou (2017, 85): networks "may be 'everywhere', but at the same time, they are extremely difficult to document." Cf. Leidwanger et al. (2014); I. Rutherford (2013, 7); Pleket (1992, 149). A helpful entry point to the large literature on ancient Greek and Mediterranean networks is Malkin (2011). Early work that helped spur research into Greek networks were Ma (2003), Malkin (2003), Perlman (2000), and Shipley (1993). Further explorations of Greek (and related) networks since 2003 include Loy (2023); Collar (2022b); W. Mack (2022) and (2015); Arrington (2021, ch. 3); Beck (2020, chs. 1 and 5); Dana and Savalli-Lestrade (2019); Leidwanger and Knappett (2018); Constantakopoulou (2017 and 2007); Taylor and Vlassopoulos (2015); I. Rutherford (2013 and 2007); Tartaron (2013); Fenn and Römer-Strehl (2013); Knappett (2013); Fröhlich and Hamon (2013); McInerney (2011); Ismard (2010); and Malkin, Constantakopoulou, and Panagopoulou (2009).
79. Malkin (2011, 38). On limitations in the study of ancient networks, see Kowalzig (2018, 101); I. Rutherford (2007, 33). This is just one instance of the larger difficulty of trying to use spotty ancient data to test theories, rather than using already-tested theories to propose interpretations of spotty ancient data.
80. Sometimes the mapping is quite theoretically informed, as with W. Mack (2022). At other times, network analysis simply does not seem to provide special insight into data, as noted by Brughmans (2018, 212).
81. See Granovetter (2017, 15–17). M.O. Jackson (2019) and J. Scott (2012, ch. 4) provide accessible discussions of some common and interesting applications of network analysis.
82. M.O. Jackson (2019, 13–43), distinguishing in detail four kinds of centrality.
83. M.O. Jackson calls this the "friendship paradox" (2019, 13).
84. One of the most prominent contemporary social media influencers is Kim Kardashian, who in May 2023 had 377 million followers on Instagram and 75.1 million on X (previously called Twitter). In 2018 she stated, "You can really tell someone's influence when they wear a makeup look or clothes, and they start trends and inspire people. Since everything is so digital and on social media these days, many people can become amazing influencers." Available at https://cfda.com/news/kim-kardashian-west-on-influence-in-the-digital-age. On the network centrality of Robert Parker and his influence on the international wine market, see M.O. Jackson (2019, 175–77). Tuori (2025) discusses the role of "middlemen" in the spread of legal knowledge and "sociability" in the Roman empire.
85. Bourdieu (1986, 248–49). M.O. Jackson (2019, 139) defines social capital more briefly as "the favors, resources, and information that a person can access from their network of social connections or as a result of their reputation." Cf. Häuberer (2011, 35–151).

86. My picture of Greek elites heavily networked both among each other and within their larger societies is different from Georg Simmel's description of the European nobility as a highly distinct and self-sufficient *internationale Adelsrepublik*, a closed circle sealed off from the rest of society (1908, 732–46). While he rightly stresses international connections among a cosmopolitan European nobility, Simmel does not account for influence between the nobility and the rest of society. For a contrasting view of how networks could connect social strata in Greek cities, see Taylor (2015). On defining "elite" in the Greek context and identifying them in our sources, see Fouchard (2010); Duplouy (2006, 1–35). On specific forums and modes of communication and connection between elites and non-elites, see Duplouy (2006, 251–71); Ober (1989, 104–91).

Chapter 4

1. Greek religion was a highly permeable, syncretistic polytheism sharing many features, including gods, with other religious traditions, as Greeks themselves pointed out. Yet Greeks commonly distinguished between the familiar "Greek" gods (especially the Olympians, and local deities such as rivers and nymphs) and "new" or "foreign" gods, such as Isis (from Egypt), Bendis (from Thrace), Sabazios (from Phrygia), and Cybele (from Anatolia). Allan (2004, 120–21) argues that a key criterion in Greek conceptions of "old" "Greek" versus "new" "foreign" gods was whether they appeared in the Homeric and Hesiodic poems, those foundational works of common Greek culture (cf. Hdt. 2.53). On the Greek adoption of "foreign" gods, see Versnel (1990–93, i.102–23); Burkert (1985, 176–79). On the almost inverse phenomenon of the spread of "Greek" gods far beyond dominantly Greek cultural centers, see Parker (2017). On "foreign" gods in Greek visual art, see L.E. Roller (1994, 245–46).
2. On the regional and the local in Greek religion, see Constantakopoulou (2015, 273–75); on Greek religion as encouraging identities from the hyper-local to the panhellenic, see Parker (1998).
3. On panhellenic sanctuaries as key sites of interaction that enabled the spread of innovation and sociopolitical change in the Greek world, see Renfrew (1986, 16); on their role in the early spread of coinage among Greeks communities, see Mooring (2022). On Greek networks and community formation outside the narrow framework of the *polis*, see the essays in Taylor and Vlassopoulos (2015).
4. A recent volume of essays concerns precisely this *Multifunktionalität* of international sanctuaries: Freitag and Haake (2019). See also Loy (2023, 273–74); Marinatos (1993). On sanctuaries generally as sites for the transmission of knowledge, see Palamidis (2025). The poetry and song now most closely associated with panhellenic festivals is the epinician odes written to celebrate victories in the athletic contests, poetry whose best-known practitioners are Simonides, Pindar, and Bacchylides. It is unclear whether these poems—not themselves entered into competitions—were even performed at the festivals or always had their first performance at a later date, usually in the celebrated victor's hometown. See Eckerman (2012); Gelzer (1985). In Athens, the City Dionysia and Lenaia festivals were major occasions for competitions of dramatic poetry. Greek festivals turned Renfrew's (1986, 8) symbolic entrainment into something more like symbolic entertainment.
5. See I. Rutherford (2013, 54–57, 288–93). Nilsson (1906) contains probably still the most thorough collection and discussion of religious festivals throughout Greece, but he excludes the festivals of Attica and those that he judged to have "keine religiöse Bedeutung," including the crown festivals and those honoring mortals (1906, iv–v). For most smaller festivals, we have little or no evidence whether or to what extent Greeks from abroad joined in the celebrations, as *theoroi* or participants. Even the size of the great "crown" festivals may at times be exaggerated: M. Scott (2010, 242–43, 247) points out that the sanctuary at Isthmia received dedications mostly from mainland Greek cities, and thus questions how panhellenic it really was. But he does not argue that its religious rituals and athletic contests were not attended by visitors from beyond the mainland. On the Panathenaic festival in Athens, and in particular the ways that it constructed varieties of identity, see the comprehensive study by J.L. Shear (2021).

6. Chaniotis (2018, 350); also Chaniotis (1997, 250–51); Ma (2024, 272) speaks of a "religious renaissance" in the second century. This impression of an increase in the number of festivals may be partly an artifact of source bias, the evidence left by an increase in the "epigraphic habit" in much of Greece after the fifth century; see Nawotka (2021b, 12–23) and generally the studies in Nawotka (2021), especially the cumulative graph at p. 226 showing a third-century peak in surviving inscriptions in the pre-Roman Greek world. On festivals instituted after the mid-fourth century, see the essays collected in Newby (2023); Giovannini (2007, 52–53); Parker (2004), in particular the catalog in his "Chronological Overview" (18–22); Robert (1984). Many of the texts collected in Rigsby (1996) refer to *asylia*, or sacred protection, for sanctuaries whose governing cities advertised a festival internationally. Rigsby's long index entries for θεωρός, θεωροδόκος, and "Panhellenic games" give an idea of the number of such festivals; see also Rigsby (1996, 12 and n.41).
7. I. Rutherford (2013, 1); cf. 201–10, 237–49. On major festivals as "centres de l'hellénisme," see Giovannini (2007, 51–59). Parker (2004, 9) notes that when "thinking of regular, institutionalised mobility—and the interconnectedness of different regions that goes with it—then perhaps the very first mobility-promoting institution that we should consider is the festival." The University of Groningen multi-investigator research project "Connecting the Greeks: Multi-scalar festival networks in the Greek and Roman world" (connectingthegreeks.com) is exploring how festival culture fostered international connectivity in the Greek world.
8. Isoc. 4.43–45: Τῶν τοίνυν τὰς πανηγύρεις καταστησάντων δικαίως ἐπαινουμένων ὅτι τοιοῦτον ἔθος ἡμῖν παρέδοσαν ὥστε σπεισαμένους καὶ τὰς ἔχθρας τὰς ἐνεστηκυίας διαλυσαμένους συνελθεῖν εἰς ταὐτὸν, καὶ μετὰ ταῦτ' εὐχὰς καὶ θυσίας κοινὰς ποιησαμένους ἀναμνησθῆναι μὲν τῆς συγγενείας τῆς πρὸς ἀλλήλους ὑπαρχούσης, εὐμενεστέρως δ' εἰς τὸν λοιπὸν χρόνον διατεθῆναι πρὸς ἡμᾶς αὐτοὺς, καὶ τάς τε παλαιὰς ξενίας ἀνανεώσασθαι καὶ καινὰς ἑτέρας ποιήσασθαι. . . . Πρὸς δὲ τούτοις καὶ φιλίας εὑρεῖν πιστοτάτας καὶ συνουσίαις ἐντυχεῖν παντοδαπωτάταις μάλιστα παρ' ἡμῖν ἔστιν.
9. Lys. 33.2: "For he believed that gathering here would be a start of friendship for Greeks toward each other," ἡγήσατο γὰρ τὸν ἐνθάδε σύλλογον ἀρχὴν γενήσεσθαι τοῖς Ἕλλησι τῆς πρὸς ἀλλήλους φιλίας. Founding of the Olympic contests was attributed by Greeks variously to Heracles, Zeus, and Pelops; see Barringer (2021, 131–32).
10. This speech is described by Philostratos in his third century CE work *Lives of the Sophists* (1.9, Olearius p. 493): "For, seeing Greece in conflict, [Gorgias] became a counselor of unity, turning them against the barbarians and urging them to have armed contests not against each other's *poleis* but against the land of the barbarians." στασιάζουσαν γὰρ τὴν Ἑλλάδα ὁρῶν ὁμονοίας ξύμβουλος αὐτοῖς ἐγένετο τρέπων ἐπὶ τοὺς βαρβάρους καὶ πείθων ἆθλα ποιεῖσθαι τῶν ὅπλων μὴ τὰς ἀλλήλων πόλεις, ἀλλὰ τὴν τῶν βαρβάρων χώραν. Philostratos reports that Gorgias also delivered a celebrated speech at the Pythian festival but does not describe its content (p. 493). On the date of the Olympic speech, see Flower (2000, 92). Gorgias was honored by his great-nephew with a statue at Olympia, Paus. 6.17.7–9; the inscribed base survives: *I.Olympia* 293.
11. Diog. Laert. 6.1.2: προείλετο ἐν τῇ τῶν Ἰσθμίων πανηγύρει ψέξαι τε καὶ ἐπαινέσαι Ἀθηναίους, Θηβαίους, Λακεδαιμονίους· εἶτα μέντοι παραιτήσασθαι ἰδόντα πλείους ἐκ τῶν πόλεων ἀφιγμένους. Like Philostratos, who reported Gorgias's speech, Diogenes wrote in the third century CE. The episode he relates must have taken place in the early fourth century BCE.
12. On unifying messages at festivals, see Perlman (1995), arguing that a much smaller festival, of Zeus Diktaios, celebrated at his sanctuary in Palaikastro in eastern Crete, had as one of its ritual goals in the late fourth or third century the maintenance of a set of peaceful alliances between local communities. If correct, this indicates a "unifying" function for international festivals even on a local scale. On the practice of giving speeches at festivals, see Flower (2000, 92–95).
13. We do not know when it started, but a panegyric speech was part of the Greater Panathenaia at least by the first century CE; see *IG* XII 4, 939, l. 4: ἐ[γ]κωμίοις, which J.L. Shear (2021, 178) interprets as referring to speeches. On the role of the major sanctuaries in defining and expressing various notions of Greek identity, see M. Scott (2010, 265–72); on the role of Olympia in particular, see Papakonstantinou (2019, 73–78); Nielsen (2007).
14. I. Rutherford (2013) is the most comprehensive study of all the practices involved in announcing and attending Greek religious festivals. Important studies focusing on the announcement of festivals include Perlman (2000) and Boesch (1908). Dimitrova (2008) provides an in-depth study of the case of Samothrace. On logistics within sanctuaries generally, see the essays in Barringer, Ekroth, and Scahill (2025). Perlman (2000, 13) notes that the earliest surviving uses of the term *theoros* dates to the first half of the fourth century. Because part of their task was

announcing the truce (*spondai*), *theoroi* were sometimes called *spondophoroi*; see *IG* II^3 1, 1145 (Thessalian inscription from the late third century BCE in which the Athenians announcing the Panathenaic festival are called *spondophoroi*); cf. J.L. Shear (2021, 130–31). On *theorodokoi*, see Perlman (2000, 60). Nielsen (2007, 63) notes that it is "a reasonable assumption that an Eleian web of *theorodokoi* [*viz.*, those announcing the festival at Olympia] covered virtually all of Hellas in the Classical period." Our ignorance about the details of Greek religious festivals is deep, as Parker (2011, 175) notes: "we know . . . much less . . . about Greek festivals than about almost any other aspect of Greek religion."

15. On the size and makeup of delegations, see I. Rutherford (2013, 156–58); cf. Parker (2004, 10): "Prestigious festivals acted as a magnet . . . to anybody with the means and leisure to attend. Plato, for instance, can casually present the Eleatic philosophers Zeno and Parmenides coming to Athens for the Great Panathenaea (Parmenides, 127a–b)." On total visitor counts, see I. Rutherford (2013, 55). On Olympia as "the center in a Panhellenic network of communication," see Nielsen (2007, 61–71). Based on the calculated seating capacity of *stadia*, it has been estimated that Olympia, which apparently attracted the largest number of spectators for athletic events, drew around 25,000 in the late sixth century and around 45,000 in the fourth (Nielsen 2007, 56–57). The seating capacities at Nemea and Isthmia were smaller.
16. On the role of the ritual space in encouraging and maintaining international networks and identities, see C.G. Williamson (2023, esp. 278–80).
17. The main events of the Olympic and Pythian festivals lasted about three days in the early years, eventually expanding to five. See M. Scott (2014, 123–24); Parker (2011, 173 and n.7); Barringer (2005, 214).
18. On the overlapping categories and duties of *proxenoi* and *theorodokoi*, see Perlman (2000, 20–22). On the *proxenos* generally, see W. Mack (2015); Gschnitzer, *RE* Suppl. XIII (1973), cols. 629–730, *s.v. Proxenos*. On guesthouses at Olympia, see Barringer (2021, 58); *I.Olympia Suppl.* 4.
19. Plut. *Alc.* 12.1. Cf. [Andoc.] 4.30. On the frequency of tent camping at festivals, see Harter-Uibopuu (2002, 149 n.31). Specific references include: the fourth century BCE comic poet Heniokhos (*PCG* fr. 5.6–8) mentions a "theoric tent," σκηνὴ θεωρική, at Olympia, presumably a tent set up by a theoric delegation; cf. Diod. Sic. 14.109 (tent of Dionyios I of Syracuse); Ael. *VH* 4.9 (Plato camped in a tent at Olympia); see Barringer (2021, 58); *I.Ilion* 1, l. 28 (Ilium, late fourth century); *Syll.*^{3} 422, l. 11 (Thermopylae, early third century); *Syll.*^{3} 523, l. 9 (Delphi, late third century); *Syll.*^{3} 995, l. 2 (Epidauros, early second century); *Syll.*^{3} 1000, l. 1 (Cos, late second century); *IG* V 1, 1390, ll. 34–39 (the sacred law of the mystery cult of Andania, probably first century).
20. At Olympia, most archaeological evidence for cooking and dining activities has been found to the west and southeast of the central sacred area, the *altis*, where animals were actually sacrificed to the god, Barringer (2021, 52). This seems similar to what happened at the sanctuary of Demeter and Kore at Corinth: the ritual sacrificial area of the Middle Terrace had, by the sixth century, restricted access through a single narrow doorway, separated by walls and landscaping from the many dining rooms of the Lower Terrace, Bookidis and Stroud (1997, 426). Many of these dining rooms show evidence also of cooking, but not of sacrifice, Bookidis et al. (1999, 49–50), which tells us that actual ritual feasting happened not at the sacred center of the sanctuary but in these surrounding buildings; see generally Bookidis et al. (1999). It is also clear that nonsacrificed meat was eaten in sanctuaries, presumably during ritual times, see Scullion (2013, 247).
21. Athen. 1, 3e. He also mentions a certain Empedocles of Acragas (presumably not the philosopher), who did not sacrifice an animal since he was a Pythagorean, and hence a vegetarian, but instead created an enormous ox-shaped cake of myrrh, frankincense, and other expensive aromatics and shared it with all attendees (τοῖς εἰς τὴν πανήγυριν ἀπαντήσασιν).
22. J.L. Shear (2021, 148) emphasizes that, at the Greater Panathenaia festival in Athens, limitations on access to the sacrifices highlighted various restrictive group memberships—priests, Athenians, tribes, demes, Athenian allies and colonies, foreigners—and argues that the selective division of sacrificial meat "marked out the members of the sacrificial community from other less privileged participants and from mere spectators." But she does not discuss the actual feasts at which the meat was served. For evidence of joint sacrifices and sharing of meat at festivals, see I. Rutherford (2013, 201–05). On Greek practices of sacrifice and ritual feasting more generally, see Carbon and Ekroth (2024); Ekroth (2008).

23. On communal feasting as building society, see Clarke (2010); on communal dining as building community in early Cretan *poleis*, see Whitley (2018). On common sacrifices as community-building events at panhellenic festivals, see I. Rutherford (2013, 251): "'Joint sacrifice' between hosts and visiting *theōroi*, or between groups of visiting *theōroi*, implies a political bond, however briefly realised."
24. On puzzling group activities, see Parker (2011, 171–223). On festival markets, see Strabo (10.5.4), noting "the panegyric festival is a kind of market entity," ἥ τε πανήγυρις ἐμπορικόν τι πρᾶγμά ἐστι. Diogenes Laertius (8.8) reports a story about Pythagoras comparing life to a panegyric festival, to which some come as contestants, some for the market, and some—the best—as spectators, τὸν βίον ἐοικέναι πανηγύρει· ὡς οὖν εἰς ταύτην οἱ μὲν ἀγωνιούμενοι, οἱ δὲ κατ᾽ ἐμπορίαν, οἱ δέ γε βέλτιστοι ἔρχονται θεαταί. On ancient festival markets in general, see de Ligt and de Neeve (1988). For references to markets at specific festivals, see Parker (2011, 173 n.7); Giovannini (2007, 52 n.147).
25. Parker (1998, 10–11) emphasizes this point.
26. Parker (2011, 151). He adds: "The participants lead the animal to the altar in procession, form a circle, purify themselves with lustral water, and throw a handful of barley grains at the victim; these practices are consistently alluded to in a wide variety of texts, and their unifying function was so strongly felt that 'sharing lustral water' was a way of referring to membership of a group." Animal sacrifice was "the central ritual of Greek religion," Parker (2011, 124). On sacrifice and processions, see Bremmer (2007). On variations in Greek religious ritual, see R. Osborne (2015).
27. On the role of contact in reducing prejudice, see Pettigrew and Tropp (2006, 766), and my discussion in Chapter 3, n. 66 and accompanying text. See Kowalzig (2007, 36–41) on ritual as reinforcing a sense of community and social cohesion by enacting disintegration and reintegration of the community, but also sometimes being an attempt to create a unity that is in fact absent, or emergent. On panhellenic sanctuaries and festivals generally as sites of friendly, religiously-grounded contact, discourse, and exchange, see Daverio Rocchi (1999, 58–60).
28. E.g., in *IG* IV^2 1, 49, the Epidaurians appointed Hegesistratos of Kardia "to be *proxenos* of the *polis* of the Epidaurians and *thearodokos* of Asklepios," πρόξενον εἶμεν τᾶς πόλιος τᾶς Ἐπιδαυρίων καὶ θεαροδόκον τοῦ Ἀσκλαπιοῦ (ll. 5–8). See Perlman (2000, 28), and nos. E7–14 in her "Epigraphical Catalogue" (196–202).
29. On the role of oaths in the Peloponnesian War, see, e.g., Thuc. 1.71.5; 1.78.4, both discussed in Chapter 1. On oaths and their religious aspects, see my discussion in Chapter 10.
30. On displaying interstate agreements in sanctuaries, see Drauschke (2019), who catalogs the treaties displayed on the Athenian acropolis, at Olympia, at Delphi, and elsewhere (267–376). See also Drauschke (2019b); Alonso Troncoso (2012). We know from Pausanias (5.23.4), who saw it centuries later, that an inscribed version of the thirty years' peace (*SvA* 188) was posted at Olympia. Thucydides (5.18.10) reports that the Peace of Nicias, of 421, was posted at Olympia, Delphi, Isthmia, and Athens. One example of a treaty between unknown communities posted at Olympia is that between the Anaitioi and Metapioi, dated to the first half of the fifth century, *I.Olympia* 9 (*SvA* 110).
31. On festival truces generally, see Cogan (2014); I. Rutherford (2007, 187–89); Hornblower and Morgan (2007, 30–35); Lämmer (1982–83); Rougemont (1973). I. Rutherford (2007, 188) lists sources for truces in the fifth and fourth centuries. In the later period, truces are known for festivals at Kos, Magnesia on the Maiander, Kyzikos, and Ptoion. See Rigsby (1996, index *s.v.* ἐκεχειρία). The procedure for announcing a truce is indicated at Thuc. 5.49.2–3, when the Spartans argue that they did not technically violate the Olympic truce in 420: "The Spartans . . . argued that [the Eleans] had penalized them unjustly, explaining that the truce hadn't yet been announced in Sparta when they sent out their hoplites. But the Eleans said that the truce with them was already in effect, since they announce it among themselves first." Λακεδαιμόνιοι δὲ . . . ἀντέλεγον μὴ δικαίως σφῶν καταδεδικάσθαι, λέγοντες μὴ ἐπηγγέλθαι πω ἐς Λακεδαίμονα τὰς σπονδάς, ὅτ᾽ ἐσέπεμψαν τοὺς ὁπλίτας. Ἠλεῖοι δὲ τὴν παρ᾽ αὐτοῖς ἐκεχειρίαν ἤδη ἔφασαν εἶναι, πρώτοις γὰρ σφίσιν αὐτοῖς ἐπαγγέλλουσιν.
32. Rules about managing sanctuaries and cult activities are one category of what are called "sacred laws" or "ritual norms," a broad and contested category. See Carbon and Harris (2025); Parker (2018) and (2004c); Harris (2015b); Carbon and Pirenne-Delforge (2012); and the online database Collection of Greek Ritual Norms (*CGRN*, 2017–), available at cgrn.ulg.ac.be.

33. For the Eleusinia, see *IG* I^3 6 (*OR* 106; *I.Eleusis* 19); for Andania, see *IG* V 1, 1390. Both cover a variety of regulations, at least some of which explicitly apply to foreigners. A fourth-century inscription from the sanctuary of Hera at Arkesine on the island of Amorgos forbids foreigners from lodging in the sanctuary (*CGRN* 234; *IG* XII.7 2), but it is not clear if this related to celebration of a formal festival. On rules in Greek sport generally, see Papakonstantinou (2019, 67–69, 89–120); on Olympic rules, see Siewert (1992); also N.B. Crowther (1996, 38–42). The importance of establishing and enforcing rules for athletic contests was obvious to the Greeks. Consider the pseudojudicial dispute depicted in the *Iliad* at the funeral athletic contests for Patroclus (23.534–612), where Menelaus invokes a rule of chariot-racing that he claims Antilochos violated (23.584–85).
34. An example is provided by a late-sixth century fragment of a set of rules for wrestlers, and perhaps other athletes, inscribed on a bronze plaque with nail holes for posting. Its surviving text forbids finger-breaking by athletes and forbids officials from beating athletes on the head after a rule violation, *I.Olympia Suppl.* 2 (*SEG* 48.541); see commentary by Ebert and Siewert (1999); briefer discussion by Siewert (1992). On the general phenomenon of cheating in ancient athletic contests, and attempts to prevent and punish it, see Weiler (2014).
35. On the Zanes, see Paus. 5.21.1–18. None of the statues survives, but some of their bases do; see Barringer (2015, 19–20). On the punishment of flogging, see Crowther and Frass (1998). On the prominence of Zeus in the oath ritual as indicating that the god was the supreme authority of Olympic law, see Siewert (1992, 117).
36. Delphi is in fact a special case, because management of the sanctuary was divided, in ways not clear from our surviving evidence, between the Delphians and the members of the international Pylai-Delphi Amphictyony. There appears to have been a general division of responsibility: the Amphictyony mostly managed the festivals and the Delphians largely ran the oracle; see M. Scott (2010, 35–36); Lefèvre (1998, 42–51) (noting "une interpénétration constante des responsabilités" between the Amphictyony and Delphi, "malheureusement difficile à cerner," 42). The Delphians had more control over the sanctuary than members of any other Greek community, as emphasized by Sourvinou-Inwood (2000, 17–18), who however excessively downplays the importance of the Amphictyony as compared to the Delphians.
37. Sourvinou-Inwood (2000, 13); see also, especially, Sourvinou-Inwood (2000b). For critical reactions, see Kindt (2012, 12–35); Bremmer (2010).
38. Sourvinou-Inwood (2000, 17); Blok (2013, 163–65).
39. See Sourvinou-Inwood (2000, 16–17). Focusing on the case of Delphi, she in fact distinguishes four groups, in concentric circles: the Delphians innermost; next, citizens of members of the Amphictyony; next, all other Greeks; and, excluded entirely, non-Greeks. More generally, as Taylor (2015, 45) notes, "cult practice was just as likely to mark distinctiveness as it was to demonstrate similarity."
40. J.L. Shear (2021, 214); see more generally pp. 212–313. On the role of festivals in Athenian relations with allied cities in the fifth century, see Lazar (2024, 95–128).
41. Sixth-century Panathenaic prize amphorae have been found outside Athens, "presumably dedicated by [non-Athenian] victors," J.L. Shear (2021, 116 n.1). And Plato (*Parm.* 127a) tells us that Parmenides and Zeno, both from Elea on the southern Italian peninsula, attended the Greater Panathenaia in the mid-fifth century.
42. In the fifth and fourth centuries, the Athenians appear to have been able to coerce participation in the Greater Panathenaia by allies and colonies. See *IG* I^3 71, ll. 56–58 (*OR* 153); *IG* I^3 34, ll. 41–43 (*OR* 154); *RO* 29, ll. 2–6; J.L. Shear (2021, 128–30, 150–51). On cult fostering community, see Blok (2017, 57–63; 2013, 164).
43. See Loy (2023, 284–85); Vlassopoulos (2013, 40). Gribble (2012, 51) emphasizes the competitive political aspect of the Olympic festival in particular. Xenophon relates an occasion when it was the scene of actual military contestation. In 365, the Arkadians had invaded Elean lands and seized control of the Olympian territory (*Hell.* 7.4.14). As they still controlled it in the following (Olympic) year, 364, the Arkadians invited the Pisans to help conduct the festival. In the middle of the competitions, the Eleans marched on Olympia under arms and fighting erupted, with the Eleans eventually being driven out (7.4.28–32). The Arkadians and Eleans ultimately concluded a treaty that returned administration of the site to the Eleans (7.4.35).
44. On competitive sacrifice, see I. Rutherford (2013, 203–05). Plutarch describes the donations made to Alcibiades by the Ephesians, Chians, and Lesbians in 416 as being driven by a competitive spirit, φιλοτιμία, *Alc.* 12.1. On decorating sanctuaries with spoils of war, see, e.g., Pl. *Resp.* 469e–470a; Paus. 3.18.8; 5.26.1; 10.9.5; 10.10.4; 10.13.4. M. Scott's appendices (2010, 310–47)

listing every known dedication at Delphi note those believed to have commemorated a Greek victory over Greeks.

45. On spectator competition for honors, see I. Rutherford (2013, 207–08). On Nicias, see Plut. *Nic.* 3.4–6; I. Rutherford (2013, 339–41); V. Chankowski (2008, 93–94); Kowalzig (2007, 70–71). Plutarch does not reveal his source for this event, but Perrin (1902, 141) asserts that it "clearly comes from Philochoros, Kleidemos, or other *Atthis*-writers." On Alcibiades, see [Andoc.] 4.29.
46. Hornblower (2002, 212). On this episode, see Thuc. 5.47–49; Xen. *Hell.* 3.2.21; Paus. 3.8.3; Gribble (2012, 51–53); Hornblower (2000). Part of the Athenian copy of the treaty with the Eleans, inscribed in marble, was found near the Theater of Dionysus in Athens, *IG* I^3 83 (*OR* 165; *SvA* 193). The Spartans' argument shows that they agreed that a validly declared truce was binding.
47. On international festivals as fostering a "culture of policing" among Greeks and allowing them to "keep a close check on one another," see Kowalzig (2005, 54–55). Thucydides claims that all other Greeks, aside from the Spartans and the Lepreans (presumably prevented by the recent Spartan incursion that violated the Olympic truce, 5.49), attended the festival of 420. Not even Spartan allies boycotted in protest, suggesting that they accepted the Elean judgment against Sparta as legitimate. That boycott was at least sometimes seen as an option is shown by the Athenian boycott of the Pythia of 346, when that festival was led by Philip II of Macedon (Dem. 19.128); and of the Olympia of 332, when the Athenians were offended by a fine imposed on them by the Eleans because of attempted bribery by the Athenian pentathlete Kallipos (Paus. 5.21.5).
48. See Nielsen (2007, 12–21). In a famous incident related by Herodotus (5.22), Alexander I of Macedonia, ancestor of Alexander the Great, was permitted to compete in the Olympics in the early fifth century, over the objections of his opponents: they claimed that, as a Macedonian, he did not count as a Greek. The Elean officials disagreed. Cf. Hdt. 2.160; J.M. Hall (2002, 154–56).
49. Already by the end of the fourth century, according to M. Scott (2014, 138), Delphi was "groaning under the weight of dedications." See the comprehensive chronological list of monuments in M. Scott (2010, 310–47) and the detailed study by Jacquemin (1999). On the monuments and other dedications of Olympia, see Barringer (2021, 2015, and 2005); M. Scott (2010, 146–217); Nielsen (2007, 71–83).
50. On these maxims, see Plato *Prot.* 343a-b; Parke and Wormell (1956, i.386–87 and 392 n.24); Roscher (1900).
51. The inscriptions are *Choix Delphes* 57–58. The altar whose remains have been excavated, on which the inscriptions have been found, dates to the late fourth or third century, and must have been built to replace the original altar, as an almost exact replica, including the inscriptions (but with different letter forms). See U. Weber (2021, 84–89); Amandry (1986, 216–17); cf. M. Scott (2014, 173, 294).
52. The column is mentioned by Herodotus (9.81) and Thucydides (1.132). See generally Stephenson (2016). It was moved from Delphi (where a replica now stands) to Constantinople by the emperor Constantine, and its remaining portion still stands, open to public view, in the hippodrome near Hagia Sophia in Istanbul. For the inscription, see *Choix Delphes* 17 (*ML* 27).
53. Thucydides (1.132.2) quotes Pausanias's epigram: "When he had destroyed the Persian army, as leader of the Greeks, Pausanias erected this memorial to Apollo," Ἑλλήνων ἀρχηγὸς ἐπεὶ στρατὸν ὤλεσε Μήδων, / Παυσανίας Φοίβῳ μνῆμ' ἀνέθηκε τόδε. Liuzzo (2012, 38–41) argues that the replacement inscription with the cities' names was originally on the lip of the tripod cauldron, then re-inscribed lower down on the snake coils only in the fourth century. Thucydides (1.130–134) tells the whole gripping and gruesome story of Pausanias's downfall; his "injustice" is mentioned at 1.132.3.
54. Hdt. 9.81. Pausanias (5.23.1) describes the colossal bronze statue of Zeus dedicated at Olympia, whose base was inscribed with the names of the allied cities that defeated the Persians at the Battle of Plataia.
55. For the events depicted by the sculptures, see Paus. 5.10.6–8. For photos of the surviving sculptural fragments and an illustrated reconstruction of the pediments, see Barringer (2005, 213–18).
56. Pindar's first *Olympian* ode, ll. 93–96, may suggest that Pelops founded the Olympic competitions. Pausanias (5.10.8) informs us that the Lapith king Perithoos was a son of Zeus, and Theseus a great-grandson of Pelops.

57. Barringer (2005, 236). On a society's "memory" of paradigmatic models, see Hölscher (2018, 99). One potential objection to Barringer's interpretation is that, as has often been argued, viewers might have in mind a version of the Pelops story in which he won by subterfuge: namely, Oinomaos's charioteer Myrtilos was persuaded to replace one of his chariot's metal axle pins with a wax pin, which melted during the race, causing the wheel to fall off and Oinomaos to lose. One sub-version of this story reports that Pelops himself persuaded or bribed Myrtilos to use the wax pin. On this reading, cheating by competitors is potentially being praised rather than condemned in the east pediment sculptures. But this interpretation has two problems. First, Barringer (2005, 225) argues, it seems impossible that the Eleans who commissioned these sculptures would have depicted their local hero Pelops as a cheat. Second, the earliest surviving version in which Pelops is explicitly described as the cheater dates only to the first century BCE, in Diodorus Siculus (4.73), four centuries after the temple of Zeus was completed. Earlier reports of the broken chariot version of the story, the first of which is from the Athenian mythographer and historian Pherecydes, writing in the mid-fifth century, do not state that Pelops had any role in the sabotage scheme (Pherec., *FGrH* 3 fr. 37a; Eur. *Ores.* 988–1013; Apol. Rh. 1.752–58). And the scholiast on Apollonius of Rhodes who provides the Pherecydes fragment attributes no blame in the cheating scheme to Pelops: in this version, Hippodameia fell in love with Pelops; in the hope that he would win the race against her father and thus marry her, *she* persuaded Myrtilos to sabotage her father's chariot; see *FGrH* 3 fr. 37a.
58. As Zuchtriegel (2023, 197) argues with respect to the sculptural decoration on early Doric buildings, "the main purpose of the images was to evoke a Panhellenic, non-place-related framework of elite values and shared identity." 201: "The focus was not on locality, but on connectivity and shared values."
59. On this "Delphic monument war," see M. Scott (2014, 146); for a reconstruction of what the entrance looked like, crowded with competing monuments, M. Scott (2014, 129 fig. 6.2). For the Spartan and Arkadian inscriptions, see, respectively, *Choix Delphes* 25 and 33.
60. Paus. 5.10.4. He reports the entire inscription as:

    ναὸς μὲν φιάλαν χρυσέαν ἔχει, ἐκ δὲ Τανάγρας
    τοὶ Λακεδαιμόνιοι συμμαχία τ' ἀνέθεν
    δῶρον ἀπ' Ἀργείων καὶ Ἀθαναίων καὶ Ἰώνων,
    τὰν δεκάταν νίκας εἵνεκα τῶ πολέμω.

    Fragments of the inscription remain: *I.Olympia* 253; *SEG* 11.1207; see the discussion of Clairmont (1982). Thucydides (1.107–08) describes the battle of Tanagra. Spartans were on one side, facing Athenians, Argives, and other unnamed allies. Thessalian cavalry came to support the Athenians, but (according to Thucydides) switched sides during the battle. On the Thessalian role, see the inscriptions and commentary at *OR* 117. The Spartan monument was challenged, in turn, a few decades later by a soaring statue of Nike directly facing the front of the temple of Zeus bearing the Spartan shield. It was erected by the Messenians and Naupactians to commemorate a victory over the Spartans in the Peloponnesian War (*I.Olympia* 259; Paus. 5.26.1); see Chaniotis (2019, 137–38).
61. For a recent eloquent account, see Hölscher (2018, 134–42), who describes competing monuments as "efficient factors in a highly complex and polemical visual fight for public memory" (2018, 140). On "sanctuary competition" between Athenians and Boiotians, see van Wijk (2024, 279–381). See also Chaniotis (2019). On "art as competition" at sanctuaries, see Marinatos (1993, 231).
62. On community trust in and respect for *theoroi*, see I. Rutherford (2013, 161). On the international influence and prestige of athletes, see Scharff (2023).
63. Arist. *Eth. Eud.* 3.6, 1233b11–13: "They didn't think that the *theoria* he made to Olympia was appropriate for Themistocles, because of his former low status, but rather for Cimon," τὴν θεωρίαν οὐκ ᾤετο Θεμιστοκλεῖ πρέπειν, ἣν ἐποιήσατο Ὀλυμπίαζε, διὰ τὴν προϋπάρξασαν ταπεινότητα, ἀλλὰ Κίμωνι. See Plut. *Them.* 5. On Nicias leading a *theoria* to Delos, see V. Chankowski (2008, 93–94); Courby (1921, 185). On Alcibiades at Olympia, see Gribble (2012).
64. See Loy (2023, 273, 278); Mooring (2022, 87); I. Rutherford (2013, 161–62); Perlman (2000), who notes, e.g., that Neon son of Askondas, "one of the most prominent Thebans of his time," was appointed *theorodokos* by the Epidaurians in the late third century (2000, 269). The Nemeans appointed Nikokreon, king of Salamis in Cyprus, in the late fourth century (269); Hegesistratos of Kardia was son of the Kardian tyrant Hekataios and was appointed *theorodokos* by the Epidaurians in the late fourth century (261); Astynomos son of Lysiades, an Athenian

appointed by the Epidaurians in the late third century, "is the last known member of a prominent Athenian family from the deme Oion" (253). Plassart (1921, 41–43) finds several prominent individuals on a Delphic list of *theorodokoi* dating to the early second century. Cf. Hamon (2012, 199–200) on the elite status of "foreign judges."

65. On elites as "brokers" with network centrality, see Ch. 3, notes 81–86 and accompanying text, above. Papazarkadas (2019, 206–09) discusses the role of elites as officials in pan-Boiotian festivals of the second century as likely having "reinforced a sense of [Boiotian] regional identity."
66. Nielsen (2007, 62) describes Olympia as "the centre in a Panhellenic network of communication,"' therefore "every *polis* of the Hellenic world probably knew what happened there" (69). Sometimes, of course, contact could increase biases. If a *theoros* saw a particular delegation from another city behaving poorly, he would bring that negative view home with him. But modern research shows that increasing contact, overall and on average, reduces bias; see Ch. 3, note 66 and accompanying text, above.
67. On "professional" travel and mobility in Greece from the seventh through fourth centuries, see Stewart (2017, 33–64).
68. On amphictyonies generally (also spelled "amphictionies"), see Constantakopoulou (2015, 275–77); Forrest (2000); Tausend (1992). On the Pylai–Delphi amphictyony in particular, see Sánchez (2001); Lefèvre (1998).
69. Aeschin. 3.108–10. On the sacred wars concerning Delphi, see Sánchez (2001, index, *s.v. guerres sacrées*); Lefèvre (1998, 169–71). We will see another example of amphictyonic international law in Chapter 6, notes 109–114 and accompanying text, below.
70. Isoc. 19.6: πλάνης δὲ γενόμενος καὶ διαιτηθεὶς ἐν πολλαῖς πόλεσιν. On seers generally, see Flower (2008); on the sometimes overlapping categories of *mantis* and *chresmologos*, see Dillery (2005).
71. Eidinow (2011, 9). See Flower (2008, 29): seers "were 'migrant' because they traveled throughout the Greek world from South Italy to Asia Minor." Eidinow (2011) presents a view of Greek religious practice, including figures such as traveling seers, as networked across cities, and argues that this picture disrupts the *polis*-centered view of Greek religion advocated by Sourvinou-Inwood (2000 and 2000b).
72. MacDowell (1978, 234) argues that "Greek merchants in the fourth century were becoming a cosmopolitan community, in which the old distinctions of citizenship and nationality were unimportant. The new Athenian mercantile laws recognized this fact and were an important step towards the unity of the Greek world." On Athenian recognition of the importance of building goodwill with international merchants through the granting of honors and privileges, see Woolmer (2016, 72–74). On Athenian naval and trading networks as social as well as economic and military networks, see Gabrielsen (2015). On the formation of "moralized trading relationships of mutual goodwill" in modern Japan, see Dore (1983, 463). On Greek international trade networks, see chapters 9 to 16 in Harris, Lewis, and Woolmer (2016). On Greek international trade generally, see Bresson (2016, 286–438).
73. Isoc. 17.4: ἅμα κατ᾽ ἐμπορίαν καὶ κατὰ θεωρίαν (cf. 17.41). See also *Ath. pol.* 11.1, using the same formula to describe Solon; Pl. *Lg.* 12, 951a–c. Herodas (2.55–59) describes how much traveling a particular wheat merchant has done, going from city to city (yet he spends enough time in Kos to enroll as a metic there and have a *prostates*).
74. Examples of private associations whose members actively traveled include Dionysian *technitai* who traveled around performing at religious festivals, and associations of traders. On associations that were defined as consisting of foreigners, see Hasenohr (2022); Maillot (2015).
75. On colonization, see Malkin (2011, 53–64); and generally the essays collected in Tsetskhladze (2006–2008); Graham (1983). On close relations between Teos and its colony Abdera, see Adak and Thonemann (2022); Robin Osborne (2009, 11–13) discusses the close relations between Samos, Thera, and Cyrene, which seem to have been a product of *metropolis*–colony relations as well as trading connections. A "panhellenic" colony such as Thurii, founded by Athenian initiative but with no official *metropolis*, was exceptional, although many colonies had settlers of various origins; see, e.g., Diod. Sic. 12.9–11; Malkin (2011, 56–57).
76. Blok (2017, 152); W. Mack (2015, 15); see his work for a comprehensive discussion of the institution and history of proxeny; also Culasso Gastaldi (2004); Marek (1984); Gschnitzer, *RE* Suppl. XIII (1973), cols. 629–730, *s.v. Proxenos*; Gauthier (1972, 23–61).
77. Throughout this book, I use the term "metic" to refer to resident foreigners in Greek cities, a status that could go by various names depending on the time and place. "Metic" was the term

in Athens, the city for which we have the most evidence of this status. On metics in Athens, see E.A. Meyer (2023); Wijma (2014); Whitehead (1977). Akrigg (2015) argues that most Athenian metics were formerly enslaved. For an introductory attempt at understanding the institution of the metic outside of Athens, see Whitehead (1984). On the role of metics in Greek political theorizing, see Kasimis (2018). In a number of Greek cities, each metic had to have a local citizen representative or advocate called a *prostates*; these personal relationships were probably a significant source of international socialization. Gauthier (1972, 126–36) argues that the *prostates* was not someone appointed simply for the purpose of initial admission to the metic rolls but had continuous responsibilities, including going to court with the metic (although in Athens that requirement seems to have ended by 350). This repeated contact would have created network ties and contacts, hence socialization.

78. On the international mobility of professionals, especially visual artists and those in the building trades, see Linder (2020); Massar (2020, 71–75, 84–86); C. Feyel (2006, 341–68). On traveling poets, see Cinalli (2022). But see Larson (2013, 256), arguing that, at least in the case of sculptors, the frequency of highly itinerant artists has been overestimated by scholars. On the effects of international friendships between philosophers and similar intellectuals, see Sonnabend (1996). On Greek mercenaries as international transmitters of artifacts and ideas, see Luraghi (2006, 25–26).

79. On metics as a special class of foreigners in Athens, see Wijma (2014, 31–34). On distinction and alienation, see Vădan (2022), describing a "hierarchy" of violence in Greek cities, a hierarchy in which metics always held a lower rank than citizens. On slavery in Greece, a topic whose study has accelerated recently, see, e.g., Forsdyke (2021); Vlassopoulos (2021); Lenski and Cameron (2018); D.M. Lewis (2018b); Herrmann-Otto (2017); Ismard (2015).

80. Andoc. 1.145: πολλοῖς συγγενόμενος καὶ πλείστων πειραθείς, ἀφ᾽ ὧν ἐμοὶ ξενίαι καὶ φιλότητες πρὸς πολλοὺς καὶ βασιλέας καὶ πόλεις καὶ ἄλλους ἰδίᾳ ξένους γεγένηνται, ὧν ἐμὲ σῴσαντες μεθέξετε, καὶ ἔστιν ὑμῖν χρῆσθαι τούτοις, ὅπου ἂν ἐν καιρῷ τι ὑμῖν γίγνηται.

81. Hdt. 8.144.2; see also 5.49; 7.145; 8.3; cf. Ar. *Lys.* 1128–34; Isoc. (*Panath.*) 12.156–57, 163. On the origins of panhellenism and hellenic identity, see L.G. Mitchell (2015, 2007); Vlassopoulos (2013, 34–40); Malkin (2011, 53–64). J.M. Hall (1997, 47) emphasizes the centrality of the Persian War experience in providing an oppositional group against which "Greekness" was constructed. Malkin (2011, 63) emphasizes the common experience of colonization, which began earlier. Vlassopoulos (2013, 36–40) emphasizes shared language, literature, and religion going back perhaps even earlier. On Greek identity and its encouragement of international cooperation and law, see Giovannini (2007, 26–47); Daverio Rocchi (1999, 20–32); Ténékidès (1956, 567–73); V. Martin (1940, 103–18).

82. On the layers of Greek identity, see Malkin (2011, 17–18, 171); Lomas (2004, 2–9); J.M. Hall (2002, 35). On the salience of "Ionian" vs. "Dorian" identity, see L.G. Mitchell (1997, 25); Alty (1982). Many works discuss identities in particular Greek communities. A few recent examples include: on Athenian identity, J.L. Shear (2021); Volonaki (2021); on Erythraian identity, Liddel (2021). On the role of intra-*polis* civic subdivisions, see Cecchet (2017).

83. Thuc. 1.95.1: ἤδη δὲ βιαίου ὄντος αὐτοῦ οἵ τε ἄλλοι Ἕλληνες ἤχθοντο καὶ οὐχ ἥκιστα οἱ Ἴωνες καὶ ὅσοι ἀπὸ βασιλέως νεωστὶ ἠλευθέρωντο· φοιτῶντές τε πρὸς τοὺς Ἀθηναίους ἠξίουν αὐτοὺς ἡγεμόνας σφῶν γίγνεσθαι κατὰ τὸ ξυγγενὲς καὶ Παυσανίᾳ μὴ ἐπιτρέπειν, ἤν που βιάζηται.

84. On Athenians and Ionians as kindred, and Athens as the *metropolis* of the Ionian cities, see Hdt. 1.146–47; 5.97.2; 8.44.2; 9.106.3; Thuc. 1.12.4; 6.82.3–4; 7.57.4; Smarczyk (1990, 318–84); Barron (1964, 46–47); on kinship playing a role in formation of the Delian league, see Hornblower (2002, 13); Smarczyk (1990, 435–63); on Ionian kinship *and* Dorian hostility, see L.G. Mitchell (1997, 25); Alty (1982, 4 n.20). Tuplin (1999, 422) advises: "The emotional content of 478 in terms of liberation and ethnic identity is something we undervalue at our peril (it is arguably the *differentia* which made Athenian πόλις-imperialism both possible and inimitable)." On Thucydides's view of the *Athenian* motivation for taking on leadership of the alliance (*viz.*, that taking vengeance on the Persians was a mere pretext, self-aggrandizement the real goal), see Rawlings (1977).

85. Thuc. 3.104. See Meiggs (1972, 43), pointing out that "had military considerations alone been relevant Samos might have seemed the most appropriate headquarters as it had been in 479, but Delos had the strong advantage of its religious associations." On the Ionian and Athenian connections to Delos before 478, see V. Chankowski (2008, 9–32), who points out that Delos was also long associated with power in the Aegean (15) and concludes that Athenians used their long connections to Delos and their Ionian identity as justifying Athenian authority over the

islanders (28). Gomme (1945, 280) claims that basing the League on Delos even "emphasized overmuch the Ionian character of the League, which included many Dorian and Aeolian cities"; similarly Rhodes (1992, 36–7). Constantakopoulou (2007, 38–60), acknowledging the Ionian identity of Delos (49), argues it was not exclusively Ionian and that it had a stronger identity as an *island* community, making it part of a group that included Dorian islands; cf. Hdt. 4.35.3. She also argues that Athenians in the fifth century came to see Athens as metaphorically an island, strongly identified with Greeks who lived on islands, and that they even defined empire in Greece as an "island" phenomenon (90–175). On this view, we still have strong identification among members of the Delian League and the subsequent Athenian empire, only it is more of an "island" than an "Ionian" group identity.

86. On the date of the transfer, see Constantakopoulou (2007, 69 n.30). The 1/60th offerings were recorded in the so-called Athenian Tribute Lists, many of which survive (Meritt, Wade-Gery, and McGregor, 1939–53) and can be seen today in the Epigraphic Museum in Athens. Although the Athenians themselves, not the allies, made the 1/60th dedications (Tuplin 1999, 420), the lists of the size of the dedication deriving from each ally's contribution were still a way of giving the allies credit for the contribution and perhaps of connecting them more strongly to Athena; see J.L. Shear (2021, 128–30, 150–67, 286–92). A cow and panoply were demanded of all tributary allies by 425 (*OR* 153, l. 57; cf. *OR* 142, ll. 15–17). An inscription from the 450s indicates that some allies (here, Erythraeans) sent significant numbers of their own citizens to the Great Panathenaia, *OR* 121, ll. 3–4. It was not only the cult of Athena that likely had an internationally cohesive force: the Eleusinian Mysteries and the cult of Dionysus in Athens also had an international profile. On religion as a cohesive force in the Delian League and Athenian empire, see generally J.L. Shear (2021, 286–92); Parker (1996, 142–51); Smarczyk (1990); Barron (1964).

87. Thuc. 3.47.2–4; see also 3.82.1 (when cities were in *stasis*, leaders of the *demos* sought Athenian, and oligarchs sought Spartan, help). Phrynichos's later claim (in 412/11, Thuc. 8.48.5), that the allied cities would not wish to be slaves under either oligarchy or democracy more than being free under whatever government they happened to have, does not contradict Diodotos's claim. First, because Diodotos is talking about factions within *poleis*, whereas Phrynichos is referring to entire cities, ignoring the very identity distinctions Diodotos points to (see Gomme, Andrewes, and Dover 1981, 110). Second, because Phrynichos is not claiming that "oligarchic" and "democratic" identity did not exist or matter, but rather that the question of freedom trumped the question of which form of government that freedom existed under.

88. Ste. Croix (1954, 1); see (1954, 3–13) and (1972, 34–43); [Xen.] *Ath. pol.* 1.14 (survival of Athenian power relies on supporting the poor and oppressing the rich in the allied cities); Lys. 2.55–56 (Athens prevented "the few" from subjugating "the many" in the allied cities) (on this speech as genuinely by Lysias and dating to ca. 390, see Todd 2007, 157–63); Xen. *Hell.* 4.8.27 (when Athenians had changed the government of Byzantium from oligarchy to democracy, the *demos* was not upset at the Athenians); Isoc. 4.104–06 (in the allied cities the Athenians helped the many against the few and the powerful). Also, the emphasis on "the many," τὸ πλῆθος, of both Erythrai and Athens in the regulations established after the (likely Persian-supported) revolt of the Erythraians in the late 450s suggests an attempt to emphasize the common democratic nature of the two cities (as the commentary on *OR* 121, ll. 22–23 suggests). Ste. Croix (1972, 34 n.64) cites scholarship agreeing and disagreeing with his earlier-stated position. For a renewed defense of it, see Canevaro and Lewis (2024).

89. For a concise history of the league (sometimes called the Nesiotic League, τὸ κοινὸν τῶν νησιωτῶν), see Constantakopoulou (2017, 31–56); and more briefly Buraselis (2015, 358–66). On the dating dispute, see Constantakopoulou (2017, 33–35) and Buraselis (2015, 360–61), favoring a late fourth century Antigonid foundation; Meadows (2013) argues for a Ptolemaic foundation ca. 282. On the Nikouria decree (*IG* XII 7, 506; *Syll.*[3] 390), see Constantakopoulou (2017, 40), following the widely accepted date 280/79; Tully (2013) argues for 282.

90. On League activities, see Constantakopoulou (2017, 45–50); Buraselis (2015, 361–62). On sending delegates to meetings, see *IG* XII 7, 506, l. 1. Examples of proxeny decrees are collected by Rhodes (1997, 298). On Ptolemaic dominance, see Constantakopoulou (2017, 41–43); Bagnall (1976, 136–37).

91. Constantakopoulou (2017, 47–48) proposes that Delos, Kythnos, Naxos, Amorgos, Mykonos, Andros, Keos, Ios, and Thera were most likely members, and possibly also Samos, Paros, Astypalaia, and Siphnos.

92. Constantakopoulou (2017, 55). The League continued until at least the beginning of the second century, coming at some point under Rhodian hegemony; see Buraselis (2015, 363–65), who however interprets the survival of the League as being "perhaps the best proof of the suitability of the confederacy as a tool of control over the islands of the central Aegean in the framework of Antigonid and Ptolemaic policy" (363).
93. The prominence of *polis* identity may have played a role in the *polis*'s centrality in Greek political theorizing. Aristotle famously argues that "it is clear that the *polis* is among the things occurring naturally, and that the human is by nature a *polis*-creature," φανερὸν ὅτι τῶν φύσει ἡ πόλις ἐστί, καὶ ὅτι ὁ ἄνθρωπος φύσει πολιτικὸν ζῷον, *Pol.* 1.2, 1253a1–3. On what Aristotle means by these claims, see Reeve (2017, 215–21).
94. Isocrates decries this dissolution of the Greek alliance in the *Panathenaicus*, 12.158–59.
95. Consider also the much later case of Skepsis: although the Skepsians were compelled by Antigonos in the late fourth century to synoikize with the Kebreans (*RC* 1), constant conflict between Skepsis and Kebren led to dissolution of the union. According to Saba (2012, 276), "[t]his shows that rivalries did not die out with artificial new creations and the sense of identity of a community could not be put off by a forcefully promoted union."
96. Thuc. 3.82–83. Thucydides himself attributes the resulting conflicts to "desire for power arising from greed and ambition," ἀρχὴ ἡ διὰ πλεονεξίαν καὶ φιλοτιμίαν, 3.82.8 (on the text and translation of ἀρχή, see Hornblower 1991–2008, i.485), thus apparently leaving no role for identity. But he also claims that "kinship became more estranged than party affiliation," τὸ ξυγγενὲς τοῦ ἑταιρικοῦ ἀλλοτριώτερον ἐγένετο, 3.82.6, apparently recognizing the unifying role that kinship identity did usually play.
97. On the persistence of intergroup conflict, see Crisp and Hewstone (2007, 206–07). On acknowledging distinct contributions, see Hogg, Abrams, and Brewer (2017, 574–75).
98. On the rise of *koine* Greek, see Horrocks (2010, 79–123); on the "great convergence" of *polis* forms onto a specific set of democratic institutions, see Ma (2017); on the spread of the gymnasium, see Kah and Scholz (2004); Gauthier (1995) (describing it as "le conservatoire et le symbole de l'hellénisme," 10); on the formation of a Greek literary canon, see Netz (2020). On cultural homogenization spreading beyond the Greek world narrowly conceived and continuing long beyond the chronological boundaries of this book, see Chaniotis (2018, 6–7).
99. On the constant mixing of Greeks and non-Greeks, see Vlassopoulos (2013) and (2007); Demetriou (2012). On the complex dichotomy between "Greek" and "barbarian," see T. Harrison (2020).
100. On the ubiquity and ruthlessness of war in the fourth and third centuries, see Rostovtzeff (1941, i.192–201).

Chapter 5

1. On the neglect of private international law in histories of international law more generally, see Lesaffer (2024, 37–39). On the overemphasis of war in Greek history, see Garlan (1987, 18–20).
2. Horden and Purcell (2000, 178; cf. 205–06) call "redistribution" (their term for trade) "the most important strategy for coping with risks of all kind." I will not offer here an in-depth discussion of the ancient Greek economy, a dynamic research area in recent years, but rather highlight one salient feature. I describe below the long-dominant axes of scholarly debate. For recent detailed discussions of the Greek economy generally, see Bresson (2016); the essays collected in Harris, Lewis, and Woolmer (2016); Ober (2015); and Eich (2006); on Athens in particular, see O'Halloran (2019); on Greek trade, see Valente (2023); on the "ancient Mediterranean" economy, see Reden and Ruffing (2023); various chapters in Reden (2020–2022); Terpstra (2019) (focused on trade); Manning (2018); and Scheidel, Morris, and Saller (2007). An older, influential, but much-criticized account is Finley (1985), discussed below.
3. On the changing nature of interstate trade in Greece between 1300 and 700, see generally S.C. Murray (2017), in particular her summary in ch. 6. On trade from the eighth to fifth centuries, see Loy (2023, 31–144) (focused on the Aegean); van Wees (2022, 35–48); Broodbank (2013, 546–51); R. Osborne (1996, 42–43). On expansion through later centuries, see Bresson (2016, 346–47), describing a "vast international division of labor and the gains in productivity connected with it." Kron (2016, 357–62) presents evidence that per capita trade volumes in

fifth through second-century Greece were similar to those of early modern Europe. Over time, the center of this trade network shifted west, reflecting the rising dominance of the Romans both politically and economically (Kron 2016, 348). On Greek international trade generally, see Bresson (2016, 339–414). On Mediterranean trade more broadly, see Terpstra (2019); Manning (2018, 233–61).

4. [Xen.] *Ath. pol.* 2.3.1: οὐ γὰρ ἔστι πόλις οὐδεμία ἥτις οὐ δεῖται εἰσάγεσθαί τι ἢ ἐξάγεσθαι. Isoc. 4.42 (*Paneg.*): trade is necessary because "each [*polis*] possesses a territory that is not self-sufficient but is deficient in some thing and produces more than enough of others," τὴν χώραν οὐκ αὐτάρκη κεκτημένων ἑκάστων, ἀλλὰ τὰ μὲν ἐλλείπουσαν, τὰ δὲ πλείω τῶν ἱκανῶν φέρουσαν. Arist. *Pol.* 7, 1327a25–27: "It is among [a city's] necessities to import whatever doesn't exist there and to export its excess products," ὅσα τ' ἂν μὴ τυγχάνῃ παρ' αὐτοῖς ὄντα, δέξασθαι ταῦτα, καὶ τὰ πλεονάζοντα τῶν γιγνομένων ἐκπέμψασθαι τῶν ἀναγκαίων ἐστίν. He goes on to note that a city concerned with revenue (προσόδου χάριν) has particular reason to engage in trade (1327a29–30). For more examples and discussion of Greek views on the importance of international trade, see Bresson (2016, 339–47; 2000, 109–30) (available in English in Harris, Lewis, and Woolmer 2016, 41–65). For a list indicating the variety of items imported by Greeks, see van Alfen (2016, 280–83). Bresson argues (2016, 343–47) that although Greeks may not have theorized the ways in which international trade can result in an absolute increase in productivity, specialization based on absolute and comparative advantages and an international division of labor did take place and did increase wealth in the Greek world and the wider Mediterranean.
5. On the *agora* and *emporion*, see Bresson (2016, 234–50, 306–38). *Emporion* actually had two meanings, roughly equivalent to English "port" and "port city," respectively: the term could refer to a port and market area within a *polis* or to a settlement whose primary purpose was commercial and which typically brought together Greeks and non-Greeks. See Rouillard (2018, 20) and the discussions cited there; Demetriou (2012, 16–23); Hansen (2006).
6. In fact, in Attica there were multiple *agorai* in addition to the main market in Athens proper, including one at Piraeus near the great harbor as well as many small marketplaces in outlying demes; see Harris and Lewis (2016, 12–13). On the distinct culture of harbors, see Kosmin (2024, 12, 59–63).
7. Phenomena that illustrate the continuity between domestic and international trade are domestic wholesale trade (see Lytle 2007, 104–06, on wholesale fish selling in Attica) as well as regional shipping along the lines of "cabotage" or "tramping." On the importance of cabotage-like shipping in ancient Mediterranean trade generally, see Horden and Purcell (2000, 140; cf. 565), who argue that such small-scale transport was "probably responsible in aggregate for many more of the movements of goods and people around the sea than was *le grand trafic maritime*"; see also Arnaud (2012) (with cautions regarding terminology and over-simplification); Barnes (2006); D.M. Lewis (2022, 82) emphasizes frequent legal restrictions on international cabotage. On cabotage in early Ionia, see Greaves (2010, 84–85). Bresson (2016, 2–10, 351–58) emphasizes the complexity of trade networks in which raw materials might be imported from abroad and used to manufacture products that were in turn both sold in local markets and exported. Dana (2021, 364–71) emphasizes that surviving letters on lead reflect generally narrow geographic horizons for some commerce. On the high profits possible from international trade and its attendant high risk, see Bresson (2003, 148–51).
8. Legal disputes can arise from any sort of economic transaction, from the simplest to the most complex. It is not obvious that one sort is more prone than the other to give rise to legal action. Transactions with more parties involved may appear more likely to give rise to disputes. But parties often address more complex transactions with more complex contracts designed to explicitly address the additional questions that may arise and thereby to prevent misunderstandings that lead to legal quarrels.
9. The literature of both fields is enormous. Good starting points for law and economics are Parisi's three-volume collection (2017); Cooter and Ulen (2016); and Posner's classic casebook (9th ed., 2014). For new institutional economics, see Bresson (2016, 16–20); Richter (2015, 1–35); North, Wallis, and Weingast (2009); O.E. Williamson (2005); Ménard and Shirley (2005); and North (1990). For comparison of the two fields, see Richter (2015, 77–86); Posner (1993). The essays in Dari-Mattiacci and Kehoe (2020) apply elements of both approaches to the ancient Roman economy. Prominent practitioners of the "historical" school of new institutional economics are Douglass North, Avner Greif, and Joel Mokyr. Ronald Coase and Oliver Williamson are the most prominent theorists of a more general, less historical version.

10. As with international relations theory, the justification is that theorizing requires simplifying assumptions. See my discussion in Chapter 3, n. 10 and accompanying text, and, for examples of such justifications, see Posner (1993, 76–78); M. Friedman (1953, 41–43). On some shortcomings of this approach in economics in particular, see Bowles (2004, 1–19).
11. Bresson (2016, 19–21); North (2005, 13–19). Allen (2012, 2–43) focuses on problems of accurate measurement. On transaction costs in the context of the ancient economy, see Kehoe, Ratzan, and Yiftach (2015b).
12. North (2005, 57, 75, 158–59). There are varying definitions of institutions, one distinction being seeing them as rules versus seeing them as behavioral equilibria within a "system of social factors"; see Alesina and Giuliano (2015, 901–02). It appears to be taken as a truism by most economists that stronger and more well-defined property rights encourage economic growth. See, e.g., Karayiannis and Hatzis (2012, 623): "An efficient legal system reduces transaction costs by clearly delineating legal rights, avoiding their over- or under-protection by choosing the right mix of property and liability rules, allowing (in the case of the so-called 'inalienable' rights) and facilitating their transfer and finally reducing the cost of their legal protection." The data, however, are not so clear; see Vries (2013, 323–32).
13. Historians of the ancient Greek and Roman economies have taken to heart the teachings of new institutional economics. See, e.g., Zuiderhoek (2023); Reden and Kowalzig (2022); Blanton and Hollander (2019); Terpstra (2019, 9–32); O'Halloran (2019, 37–40); Manning (2018, 27–32); Bresson (2016, 16–21); Harris (2016); Ober (2015, 5, 14–18); the essays collected in Kehoe, Ratzan, and Yiftach (2015); and Frier and Kehoe (2007).
14. This broader approach is characterized by behavioral economics, prominently exemplified by the well-known work of Kahneman and Tversky mentioned in Chapter 3, n. 19 and accompanying text. Bowles (2004) provides an approach to microeconomics steeped in modern mainstream economic theory but trying to make it more accurate by incorporating advances from not only institutionalism but all the social sciences. See also the survey by Alesina and Giuliano (2015) of work at the intersection of culture, institutions, and economics. Joel Mokyr (2014, 2017) and Deirdre McCloskey (2006, 2010) are prominent examples of economic historians who incorporate a more holistic view of human social and psychological complexity into their research than that typically assumed in economic theories. D. Friedman (1994, 6–7) notes the importance of rhetoric and community, albeit in an account that posits humans as selfish utility-maximizers. See also Karayiannis and Hatzis (2012) for an application to ancient Greece. There have long been efforts to unify psychology and economics, or even all social sciences, into a larger science of human behavior; see Houkelon (2014, 5); Bowles (2004, 1–19).
15. Morley (2022, 88): "The widespread adoption of ideas from New Institutional Economics . . . can be seen . . . as a means of paying lip service to the importance of cultural practices and conceptions and noneconomic institutions but then recuperating them for conventional economics." See also Van Oyen (2024, 382–86). Stubborn reliance on the wealth-maximizing rational actor is compatible with asserting the importance of rules so long as one understands rules as having effects on human action only by virtue of the material benefits or losses (in the form of sanctions or punishments) that arise from following or breaking the rules. On this view, e.g., trust is merely a wealth-maximizing strategy that lowers transaction costs when effective, and the norms, or "rules," of honesty and fairness on which trust relies are purely the result of fear of reputational sanctions rather than socialized and internalized norms. For a strong assertion of this approach, see Allen (2012, 20–21); similarly Richman (2017, 37–85). The richer new institutionalist studies do not view the effects of law in such a simplistic manner. See my discussion of psycho-sociological understandings of legal compliance in Chapter 3.
16. North, Wallis, and Weingast (2009, 16): "Some organization must exist within which a set of officials enforce the rules in an impersonal manner. In other words, formal institutions control violence only in the presence of an organization capable of enforcing the rules impersonally." This is their analysis of what they call "contractual organizations" and "open access societies," which they contrast with "adherent" organizations, "characterized by self-enforcing, incentive-compatible agreements" and in which "cooperation . . . must be, at every point in time, incentive-compatible for all members" (North, Wallis, and Weingast 2009, 16). This rigid dichotomy ignores the importance of social motives and norms even in "modern open access societies," which I discussed in Chapter 3. For an early criticism of the approach, see Ehrlich (1936, 70–73). On the centrality of material punishment to institutionalist theories even of privately ordered legal systems, see Richman (2017, 40–62).

17. See, e.g., the criticisms by Manning (2018, 27–32); Manning and Oliver (2016); Bates (2014, 61–65); Vries (2013, 185–89). McCloskey (2016b, 63–68) (and more generally McCloskey 2016) argues that many new institutionalists in fact share the main neoclassical assumptions about humans as rational wealth-maximizers. D.M. Lewis (2018) proposes ways to keep both the baby and the bath water by applying new institutional economics, behavioral economics, and economic sociology to the study of the Greek economy. Taylor (2024) notes that new institutional studies have mostly been blind to the role of women in the Greek economy and proposes ways to incorporate women into new institutional analyses.
18. The debate has been described many times. See, e.g., O'Halloran (2019, 15–36); Bresson (2016, 2–15).
19. See the sources cited in n. 13 above. Zuiderhoek (2023, 53) notes the emergence of new institutional economics as a "common theoretical language" between the two schools. Van Berkel (2020) studies the complex and changing interaction of conceptions of friendship, reciprocity, money, and economic exchange in Athenian society of the fifth and fourth centuries BCE.
20. Compare the "silent barter" system that Herodotus (4.196) reports having been used between Carthaginians and inhabitants of the Atlantic coast of north Africa. He claims, notably, that ethical norms operated even here: "And they don't cheat each other; for [the Carthaginians] don't touch the gold until, in their opinion, it's equal in value to the cargo, nor do [the inhabitants] touch the cargo before the Carthaginians take the gold," ἀδικέειν δὲ οὐδετέρους· οὔτε γὰρ αὐτοὶ τοῦ χρυσοῦ ἅπτεσθαι πρὶν ἄν σφι ἀπισωθῇ τῇ ἀξίῃ τῶν φορτίων, οὔτ' ἐκείνους τῶν φορτίων ἅπτεσθαι πρότερον ἢ αὐτοὶ τὸ χρυσίον λάβωσι.
21. Decourt (2014, 45) notes "la grande sophistication" of Greek commercial practices already by the sixth century. On regulation of trade, see Arnaud (2012, 61–62). The financing of trade, in particular, was often elaborate. On maritime loan contracts generally, see Candy (2025). On the complexity of some commercial contracts as early as the beginning of the fifth century, see Bresson (2016, 232–34) and J.-P. Wilson (1997–98), both discussing, among other evidence, *IG France* 135 (*SEG* 38.1036), the so-called Pech-Maho lead, a lead tablet found at Sigean in southern France containing the terms of a fifth-century transaction among people of diverse citizenship that appears to include purchase of a half-share in a small commercial boat, partly on credit, perhaps for purposes of forming a partnership in a transport business. Cf. Bresson (2003, 142). In the fourth century, Chrysippos, the speaker of [Dem.] 34 (*Against Phormion*), states that "neither a ship nor a captain nor a merchant can put to sea if the lenders' share is taken away," οὔτε ναῦν οὔτε ναύκληρον οὔτ' ἐπιβάτην ἔστ' ἀναχθῆναι, τὸ τῶν δανειζόντων μέρος ἂν ἀφαιρεθῇ (34.51). But see also Bresson (2003, 142 n.9), citing several examples of merchants funding their own trading expeditions, e.g., the son of Sopaios of Bosporos, the speaker of Isoc. 17 (*Trapez.*) (see 17.4).
22. As David Lewis has suggested to me, despite its broad acceptance as genuine by generations of scholars, the text of the contract may have been inserted by a copyist sometime in the speech's long transmission, as it falls outside the speech's "stichometry" (see Canevaro 2020); nevertheless, many details are corroborated in the speech proper. The 3,000 drachmas were lent "on 3,000 jars of Mendaean wine," ἐπὶ οἴνου κεραμίοις Μενδαίοις τρισχιλίοις (35.10); the contract further stated: "and they pledge these in security, not owing anyone else any money with them as security, and they will not use them as security (for any other loan)," ὑποτιθέασι δὲ ταῦτα, οὐκ ὀφείλοντες ἐπὶ τούτοις ἄλλῳ οὐδενὶ οὐδὲν ἀργύριον, οὐδ' ἐπιδανείσονται (35.11). The Athenian lender, and speaker of this speech, was Androkles son of Xeinis of the deme Sphettos. For these details, see *IG* II³ 550, l. 20, and Lambert (2001, 57–58).
23. Indications that the speech took place in a maritime court are found at [Dem.] 35.1, 45–46, 49. The clearest contemporary description of the court is provided at Dem. 32.1 (*Against Zenothemis*): "The laws order . . . that the cases [*viz.*, in this court] be among ship-owners and traders, from liabilities [arising on voyages] to and from Athens, and concerning which there are written agreements," οἱ νόμοι κελεύουσιν . . . τὰς δίκας εἶναι τοῖς ναυκλήροις καὶ τοῖς ἐμπόροις τῶν Ἀθήναζε καὶ τῶν Ἀθήνηθεν συμβολαίων, καὶ περὶ ὧν ἂν ὦσι συγγραφαί. Harris (2015) argues persuasively (i) that συμβόλαιον means "actionable liability" rather than "contract," and (ii) against the dominant view that, to be litigated in this court, the dispute had to directly concern the written contract; but he goes too far in arguing there was no requirement of an underlying written contract; see Candy (2025, 83–84); Bresson (2016, 322–23). E.E. Cohen (1973) and Vélissaropoulos (1980, 235–67) are the most thorough treatments of the Athenian maritime court. There seems to have been a maritime court in Athens at least since the early fourth century, reformed sometime mid-century to be monthly, but the details are uncertain;

see E.E. Cohen (1973, 161–98); cf. MacDowell (1990, 393–94). On the possible connection of Athenian judicial officials called *nautodikai* to the maritime courts, see Erdas (2021, 50–52).

24. E.g., the "great code" of Gortyn (*I.Cret.* iv 72; Gagarin - Perlman, *Laws of Crete* G72) contains a provision (column 9, lines 43–54) for disputes concerning nonpayment of loans for "foreign ventures," πέραι. This may have granted legal access to foreign nonresident plaintiffs (but Gagarin and Perlman 2016, 409, state without argument that "[t]he plaintiff presumably resides in Gortyn"). For a concise overview of the varying legal statuses of foreigners in Greek domestic courts, see Harter-Uibopuu (2021).
25. The most in-depth treatment is Bravo (1980), which examines at length the Greek vocabulary concerning legal seizure. The most important early article is Dareste (1889). A concise recent treatment is Lintott (2004). See also Giovannini (2007, 303–08); Gauthier (1982) (a detailed review of Bravo 1980); Phillipson (1911, ii.353–57); Wilhelm (1911, 195–201); Lécrivain (1897).
26. Dareste (1889, 305–06); Bravo (1980, esp. 933–45). Bravo's disagreement was less with Dareste than with over-broad interpretations of the generalized statements in the opening pages of Dareste's article. Dareste (1889, 309 n.3) suggests that starting in the mid-fourth century, custom may have begun to require "declarations" of *syla* by a city in order to legitimize seizures against a fellow citizen of the wrongdoer. Bravo argues this was always the rule.
27. Bravo (1980, 944). Schlesinger (1933, 53–55) makes a similar argument.
28. Davies (1984, 287–88) makes similar observations.
29. On litigation rates after personal injury, see Engel (2016, 1–36); Kachalia and Mello (2011, 1564–65); Kritzer (2008, 876); Haltom and McCann (2004, 81–97); Burke (2002, 2–3); Saks (1992, 1169–1240). Engel offers a series of empathetic psychosocial explanations for the low rate of claims in cases of physical injury. On litigation rates generally, see Kritzer (2008, 876), citing studies from multiple countries. For references to socio-legal studies of how people respond to potential legal disputes, see Taylor Poppe (2019, 154 n.22).
30. In general, studies warn us not to accept popular perceptions of litigiousness as accurate. Just as Americans' perceptions of their own litigiousness are untethered from reality, we should give little credence to Athenian depictions of themselves as litigation lovers. The caution is doubly warranted since much of our evidence for this attitude is from Aristophanes, always playing the point for a laugh; see Ar. *Nub.* 206–08; *Av.* 40–41, 109–10; *Eccl.* 657; *Eq.* 1317; *Pax* 505; cf. Isoc. 7.51; Thuc. 1.77; and the discussions by Todd (1993, 147–54); Bonner and Smith (1930–38, ii.288–306).
31. Cooter and Ulen (2016, 385). I discuss the concept of administrative costs more in the next chapter.
32. One of the best-known demonstrations of this truth is Ellickson (1994), a study demonstrating how ranchers and property owners in California mostly used informal means to settle and avoid property disputes on terms that diverged from the rules of California law and without recourse to legal authorities. See also Taylor Poppe (2019, 154–57); Greenhouse, Yngvesson, and Engel (1994, 117–22); Merry and Silbey (1984, 172–76), 157: "disputes are cultural events, evolving within a framework of rules about what is worth fighting for, what is the normal or moral way to fight, what kinds of wrongs warrant action, and what kinds of remedies are acceptable."
33. On the tendency to self-blame, see Coates and Penrod (1980, 670–72). On economically "irrational" lawsuits, see Dunbar and Sabry (2007, 33–37). On Athenian litigation as feud, see D. Cohen (1995, 61–119); *contra* Cohen, and emphasizing civic duty, see Harris (2013, 60–98). On ethical and social considerations of litigation in the Roman republic, see Frier (1985, 30–32). On "conflicts of principles and values," see Merry and Silbey (1984, 154).
34. Such a *personal* sense of injustice could be at play in the "Letter of Berezan" discussed in Chapter 6, in which Achillodoros claims that he is being treated unjustly by Matasys. That is, his statement might not be evidence that seizing him was contrary to international law but simply that it was contrary to his own sense of right and wrong.
35. On the debate between Dareste and Bravo, see Maffi (1999, 12–14), also concluding that Dareste's rule is too broad for the evidence to bear.
36. On the use of the Homeric poems as evidence for Greek historical reality, see Chapter 6, n. 1. For a non-Greek example of a highly developed legal system that nevertheless relied on self-help rather than public enforcement of legal wrongs and judicial decisions, see W.I. Miller (1990) on saga-era Iceland.
37. For a theory of the development from self-help to judicial process in Greek law, see Wolff (1954, 405–11) with the comments of Maffi (2001, 281–83). The most common terms for legally justified seizure in a domestic context are: for seizure of goods, words or phrases based on ἐνέχυρον,

"pledge, security, collateral" (e.g., ἐνεχυράζειν and ἐνέχυρα λαμβάνεσθαι can both mean "to seize in restitution of a debt"); and, for seizure of people, ἄγειν. Seizure, and especially violent seizure, is not automatically implied by any of these terms, and its presence in any particular situation must be determined from the context. Perhaps the most general meaning of ἐνεχυράζειν is "to take something as security." This was often done peacefully and at the beginning of a transaction by a creditor receiving a surety or pledge. But it could also be done violently, after a debtor had defaulted; see Bravo (1980, 694–96). On ἐνεχυρασία, see Colorio (2014) (emphasizing the term's potential ambiguity); A.R.W. Harrison (1968–71, ii.244–47). On private seizure and imprisonment, especially in Gortyn and Athens, see Maffi (1999). On a state restricting self-help as a way to "squeeze out rival forms of social control," see Ellickson (1994, 276). On self-help in republican Roman law, see Lintott (1968, 22–34).

38. The monumentally inscribed version of this code, created in the mid-to-late fifth century, has been called the "Queen of Inscriptions" (Willetts 1967, vii) because of its grand scale and fine state of preservation.

39. *I.Cret.* iv 72 (Gagarin - Perlman, *Laws of Crete* G72), 1.2–7. I print the translation of Gagarin and Perlman. The Greek text is:

    ὅς κ' ἐλευθέροι ἒ δόλοι μέλλει ἀν-
    πιμολὲν, πρὸ δίκας μὲ ἄγεν. αἰ δ-
    έ κ' ἄγει, καταδικακσάτο τõ ἐλευθέρ-
    ο δέκα στατε̃ρανς, τõ δόλο πέντ-
    ε ὅτι ἄγει καὶ δικακσάτο λαγάσαι
    ἐν ταῖς τρισὶ ἀμέραις.

40. Gagarin and Perlman (2016, 340):

    "The decision to put this section first on the wall must mark its importance.... Although the opening sentence, strictly speaking, prohibits self-help by means of force only in cases of disputed ownership of persons, it may have been intended to apply implicitly to all disputes at Gortyn (with the exceptions noted in 1.56–2.2). A general prohibition of this sort would also be implicit in the act of writing such an extensive piece of legislation, which in itself would convey the message that members of the community were expected to submit their disputes to the judicial process that is elaborated in these laws rather than resorting to self-help." For a detailed discussion of the meaning of μὲ ἄγεν in this and other passages of the Gortyn code, see Maffi (1983, 3–114). On why Greeks inscribed laws, see Gagarin (2008, 67–109); R. Thomas (1995).

41. *I.Cret.* iv 72 (Gagarin - Perlman, *Laws of Crete* G72), 1.56–2.2: "There is to be immunity for one who seizes a person who has lost a case or has indentured himself," [τ]ọ̀ν δὲ νενικαμένοṿ κα[ὶ τὸν κα]τακείμενον ἄγοντι ἄπατον ἔμεν (Gagarin and Perlman trans.). κατακείμενον here acts as a passive of κατατίθημι meaning "pledge, mortgage." See *LSJ* (Supp.), *s.v.* κατάκειμαι; Gagarin and Perlman (2016, 345); Harris (2002, 419) (see this article on debt bondage generally, especially in Athens). Maffi (1983, 90–94) argues the term here may apply to someone who has guaranteed the debt of another, thereby subjecting himself to potential seizure. Kristensen (2004) argues that κατακείμενον refers to a person's (temporary) condition rather than (permanent) status.

42. *I.Cret.* iv 81 (Gagarin - Perlman, *Laws of Crete* G81; *Nomima* ii 47; Koerner, *Gesetzestexte* 155), ll. 16–22:

    κ' αἴ κ' ἐς στέγα-
    ς ἐνεκυράκσọντι, πονίον[τι μ]-
    [ὲ 'νϝ]οικε̃ν ὂ ἐνεκύρακσαν συν-
    εκσομόσαθθαι τõν ὀμό[ρον]
    [τõ]ṿ ἐννέα τρίινς, οἷς κα προ-
    ϝείπει, μὲ ἐνϝοικε̃ν ὂ ἐνεκύ̣[ρα]-
    [κσ]α[ν.]

    "And if they take something as security from a house, if the person from whom they received security asserts that he does not live in (the house), three of the nine neighbors whom he notified earlier are to swear with him that the one from whom they received security does not live in (the house)." (Gagarin and Perlman trans.)

    Apparently in Gortyn, it was legal to seize security for a debt but common to seize the wrong person's goods. To prevent this, they developed a procedural rule involving witnesses. Compare the similar situation in the "Letter of Apatorios" discussed in Chapter 6.

43. An earlier Cretan inscription, from north central Crete ca. 500, may supply evidence of a city in which seizure was still mostly permitted as an element of domestic law. It is an agreement

inscribed on a piece of bronze appointing an individual to the civic office of scribe, *poinikastas*. See Jeffery and Morpurgo-Davies (1970) (*SEG* 27.631) (*ed. pr.*); *Nomima* i 22; Gagarin and Perlman (2016, 181–96). The relevant sentence is: μήδ᾽ ἐπάγραν ἦμ[εν] μήδε ῥύτιον αἰλε̃ν τὸν ποινικαστὰν (B 6–7), which has been translated both as "There is to be neither seizure of the person nor of the property of the *poinikastas*" (Gagarin and Perlman) and as "There is to be no seizure, and the scribe is not to take any security" (Jeffery and Morpurgo-Davies). Whether the *poinikastas* is subject or object, the prohibition of seizure is narrowly tailored, suggesting that other forms of seizure were permitted.

44. Maffi (1983, 112) emphasizes the similarities between the Athenian and Gortynian rules. Demosthenes notes the importance of private initiative in enforcing the law in Athens in his speech *Against Meidias*, Dem. 21.39–40. On legal self-help in Athens, see Christ (1998). For a different perspective, emphasizing that public officials were chiefly or solely responsible for enforcing certain laws and regulations, see Harris (2013, 22–44).
45. The possibilities are listed at Dem. 23.53–60; see Harris (2010, 131–33). In addition, if a convicted murderer avoided death by going into exile, then subsequently returned to Attica, anyone could kill him, or arrest him and bring him to the archon to be publicly executed; see Dem. 23.28–32. Compare the similar provision in *OR* 123, a Milesian decree from the mid-fifth century permitting anyone to kill certain exiled men if they returned to Miletos, or to turn them over to magistrates to be executed.
46. See Harris (2013, 53–57). A private individual could also personally arrest an enslaver or a slave dealer, ἀνδραποδιστής, who was keeping a free person enslaved; *Ath. pol.* 52.1.
47. On seizure after a court judgment, see A.R.W. Harrison (1968–71, ii.188).
48. Dem. 21.11–12. The law quoted verbatim in the transmitted version of the speech is likely a forgery, see Harris (2013, 216–23). Later in the same speech (21.175–76), Demosthenes explains that a man from Boiotia had recently been found guilty of violating a similar Athenian law forbidding self-help seizures during the Eleusinian Mysteries. A certain Euandrus of Thespiae (who likely resided in Athens as a metic) had won a maritime suit against Menippus, from Caria in Asia Minor. Because Menippus did not promptly pay the court-ordered damages, Euandrus seized Menippus when Menippus returned to Athens to attend the Mysteries, a seizure that was illegal only because it occurred during the festival.
49. Dem. 47.33–38. An important detail here seems to be that the speaker did not force his way into a closed house—it was already open: ἔτυχεν γὰρ ἡ θύρα ἀνεῳγμένη, 47.38. Contrast the speaker's condemnation of his opponents' actions in having broken into his house when he was not present, 47.47–61. In Demosthenes 24.197 (*Against Timokrates*), seizure of a slave woman in response to debt to the *polis* is described as ἐνεχυράζειν.
50. Often, no actual seizure would have been required because the debtor already would have handed movable security over to the creditor, as with a pawn. This sort of security transaction is described, e.g., in [Dem.] 49.21, 51–53 (*Against Timotheos*), where the speaker's opponent has claimed a loan was secured by an amount of copper handed over to the lender. See A.R.W. Harrison (1968–71, i.254).
51. Dem. 41.7 cites "the law that expressly does not permit anyone who has pledged any amount of real security, nor his heirs, to bring suit over it," τὸν νόμον ὃς οὐκ ἐᾷ διαρρήδην, ὅσα τις ἀπετίμησεν, εἶναι δίκας, οὔτ᾽ αὐτοῖς οὔτε τοῖς κληρονόμοις; cf. 41.10 (describing it there as "the law that does not permit litigation against those possessing property pledged as security," τὸν νόμον ὃς οὐκ ἐᾷ τῶν ἀποτιμηθέντων ἔτι δίκην εἶναι πρὸς τοὺς ἔχοντας). I follow here Harris's interpretation and discussion (2006, 235–36). It is supported by Isaeus 10.24: "the man possessing a piece of disputed land must produce the mortgagor or seller, or have clearly won it in litigation," τῶν ἀμφισβητησίμων χωρίων δεῖ τὸν ἔχοντα ἢ θέτην ἢ πρατῆρα παρέχεσθαι ἢ καταδεδικασμένον φαίνεσθαι. Here, gaining possession directly from the mortgagor is distinguished from winning it in litigation, which suggests the former situation excluded the latter. Modern US law contains a similar provision. Under the Uniform Commercial Code, which has been mostly adopted by all fifty US states, self-help can be used to seize goods securing a defaulted loan, but only if done peacefully. See UCC 9-609, "Secured Party's Right to Take Possession after Default": "(a) . . . After default, a secured party: (1) may take possession of the security; and (2) without removal, may render equipment unusable and dispose of security on a debtor's premises under Section 9-610. (b) . . . A secured party may proceed under subsection (a): (1) pursuant to judicial process; or (2) without judicial process, if it proceeds without breach of the peace."

52. On the ejectment suit, δίκη ἐξούλης, see Harpokration, *s.v.* ἐξούλης; García Domingo (2017); Harris (2013, 57); A.R.W. Harrison (1968–71, i.217–21, 311–12). The risk in refusing to cede the property, thereby forcing the claimant to bring a δίκη ἐξούλης, was that if the defendant lost the case, he not only had to give up the property but also had to pay to the state a fine equal to the property's value.
53. On the social and economic use of debt bondage in Gortyn, see Kristensen (2004, 77–79). Harris (2002) persuasively argues that Solon's reforms abolished debt slavery but not debt bondage, and (at 420–25) presents the evidence for debt bondage in Athens. Debt bondage was crucially distinct from slavery in Athens, where there were legal remedies and heavy penalties for treating a free person as a slave; see Din. 1.23; Kapparis (2021, 34).
54. *Nub.* 240–41: ὑπὸ γὰρ τόκων χρήστων τε δυσκολωτάτων / ἄγομαι, φέρομαι, τὰ χρήματ' ἐνεχυράζομαι. Note the verb ἄγομαι in particular, "I'm being led off." This interpretation is the suggestion of Harris (2002, 423). Strepsiades hopes that speaking persuasively, whether in court or face to face with a creditor, will help him evade his debts.
55. E.g., in the surviving fragments of Menander's *Heros*, the character Gorgias appears to be in debt bondage to Laches, "working off the debt" (τὸ χρέος ἀπεργαζόμενος, 36) incurred by both his deceased father and himself. He is described not as having been seized but as having come, and brought along his sister: "he came to us, brought along his sister, and here he remains," πρὸς ἡμᾶς ἐνθάδε / ἐλθὼν ἀγαγών τε τὴν ἀδελφὴν ἐπιμένει, 34–35). A slave of Laches describes the sister as "sort of" a slave, "in a certain way" (ἡσυχῇ; τρόπον τινά, 20), a description that presumably applies to Gorgias as well. See the comments of Gomme and Sandbach (1973, 390–91).
56. On the procedures for seizure of a debtor's property in Ptolemaic Egypt, see Keenan, Manning, and Yiftach-Firanko (2014, 259–65); Llewelyn (1994, 200–12). *P. Enteux.* 14, from 223 BCE, mentions seizure of a mortgaged building by a creditor after a judgment (ἐπικαταβολὴν . . . [κα]τὰ τὸ διάγραμμα, 4). *P. Erasm.* 1, 1, a petition from 148/47 BCE, describes a creditor violently coming into the petitioner's house and seizing pledged property, εἰσβιάζεσθαι εἰς τὴν οἰκίαν μου καὶ τὸ ἐνεχυράζειν (ll. 36–37), apparently with the assistance of a police official, ἀρχιφυλακίτης (l. 19). Bauschatz (2013) argues that police and police-like officials were more common and played a larger role in law enforcement in Ptolemaic Egypt than elsewhere in the ancient Mediterranean, including Greece.
57. Polyb. 12.16. In the case he describes (of uncertain date), one man forcibly took away the other man's slave while he was away ("since the master wasn't home he forcibly led off the slave," μὴ παρόντος τοὺ δεσπότου μετὰ βίας εἰς οἶκον ἀπηχέναι τὸν δοῦλον), claiming the slave as his own property. The man now deprived of his slave went to the first man's house and took back the slave, bringing him directly to the magistrates (καὶ λαβόντ' ἀπάγειν ἐπὶ τὴν ἀρχήν) for them to decide who should have the slave while the question of ownership was being litigated. As Polybius tells the story, there was no claim either man had violated the law by making the seizure. Rather, the relevant legal questions were (i) to whom did the slave belong and (ii) who should possess him while that question was being litigated.
58. On Greek legal *Denkformen*, see Wolff (1975, 14–17); on the unity of Greek law, see Harris (2024) (there was substantive but not procedural unity); Gagarin (2005) (there was procedural but not substantive unity); Finley (1975, 134–46) (there was no meaningful unity at all); Mitteis (1891, 61–79) (Greek law presents a grand unity). Notably, both Harris (2024, 136–37) and Mitteis (1891, 72–76) ground their arguments partly in the unifying force of Greek international law.

Chapter 6

1. On the validity of treating the *Iliad* and *Odyssey* as reflecting aspects of Greek society of the eighth and early seventh centuries, when the poems were likely written down roughly in their extant forms, see Ma (2024, 53–58); Papakonstantinou (2008, 21 and n.10); Raaflaub (1997, 626–28). On the Homeric (and Hesiodic) poems as offering important evidence for early Greek law in particular, see Gagarin (1986, 19–50). On the immense cultural influence of Homer in the ancient Greek world, see Netz (2020, 15, 24, 45); Lamberton (1997); Schmid and Stählin (1929, I.i.175–86); on Homeric influence on visual art, literature, and philosophy, see the studies

by Blome (2008), Bierl (2008), and Flashar (2008), respectively. Homer's centrality to Greek education can be seen in the pains that Socrates takes, in Plato's *Republic*, to remove Homer from education (*Resp.* 2–3.376–98, 10.595–607). Socrates in the *Republic* can acknowledge the apparently popular claim about Homer that "this poet has educated Greece," τὴν Ἑλλάδα πεπαίδευκεν οὗτος ὁ ποιητής, 10.606e.

2. On Nestor as a skillful speaker, see Clay (2014); Roisman (2005). On rhetoric in Homer generally, see Pelliccia (forthcoming).
3. On the act as legal, see Pritchett (1991, 360). Hainsworth (1993, *ad* 704–05) sees here "a certain confusion (doubtless also in practice) between forcible restitution of debt and simple pillage: Neleus is entitled to his four horses or their value and takes it, the δῆμος then makes assignments in language appropriate to the distribution of booty." But the *demos* among whom the other items are divided has already been limited to those to whom a debt was owed, which distinguishes this from the distribution of booty. Of course, this is rough and ready compensation: the total amount seized could be more or less than what was owed. See the discussion of "error costs" below.
4. As in our later evidence, the Homeric world's permitting of legal seizure is in contrast to its condemnation of illegal seizure in the form of piracy, which I discuss in Chapter 9. Gagarin (1986, 19–50) does not include this episode from *Iliad* 11 in his consideration of Homeric law, probably because it involves international law and not judicial procedure. The world of the Homeric poems is recognizably international. It is also a world of regulated international athletic competition. Nestor's story makes apparent allusions to Olympic competition. The Pylians are fighting the Eleans, who controlled the Olympic sanctuary in historic times. Major action takes place by the banks of the Alpheios (11.726), famous as the river that flows through Olympia. Neleus was robbed of four "prizewinning" (ἀθλοφόροι) horses and their chariot, on their way to the "contests" (ἄεθλα) to compete for a tripod (11.699–701). Any Greek of the sixth century or later would assume these are the Olympic contests. And it is likely that Olympic athletic contests were already taking place when the *Iliad* was composed or written down in the eighth or seventh century. Hippias of Elis dated the first athletic contests at Olympia to 776; and tripods were being dedicated there in large numbers by the early eighth century, perhaps with a connection to athletics at this early time (Barringer 2021, 21; Christesen 2007, 478–79; C. Morgan 1990, 47–49) (large numbers of spectators may not have started attending the festival until the seventh century, Kyrieleis 2012, 64–65). In short, Nestor's story takes place in a recognizable Greek international world of rule-bound competition.
5. Strabo comments on Miletos's large number of colonies (14.1.6). Pliny the Elder counted ninety Milesian colonies (*NH* 5.112); Seneca, sixty-five (*Consol. ad Helv.* 7.2). D.W. Roller (2018, 788) notes that "over forty towns are known" to have been Milesian colonies; see Greaves (2002, 74–77); Gorman (2001, 59–71, 243–58); and the list in Hansen and Nielsen (2004, 1088).
6. On contacts between Greeks and non-Greeks around the Black Sea, see Donnellan (2021); Solovyov (2019).
7. Malkin (2011, 53–64). On the origins of Ionian identity, see Mac Sweeney (2013, 158–59). Both the *Iliad* (13.685) and the Homeric *Hymn to Apollo* (146–55) mention "Ionians," and a temple that may have been the site of early "panionion" cult to Poseidon seems to have been in use by the late seventh century, Mac Sweeney (2013, 181–83). Herodotus (1.170) reports both Bias of Priene and Thales of Miletos as having proposed that the Ionian cities come together under a single government in the early sixth century. Almost all the surviving letters on lead from the Black Sea are in Ionian dialect, see Dana (2021, nos. 19–54).
8. For the geography, see the detailed maps in Bravo (2021, Cartina I–III); Asheri, Lloyd, and Corcella (2007, 546–47, 590); or Dubois (1996, xvi–xvii). Eusebius tells us that Borysthenes was founded in the second year of the 33rd Olympiad, i.e., in 647/46 BCE (Euseb. *Chron.*, p. 95 Helm ed., p. 167 Fotheringham ed.). This date may be a quarter century too early, see Tsetskhladze (2018, 19–21). On the founding of Olbia, see Müller (2022, 334); Solovyov (2019, 177); Braund (2019, 222); and generally Vinogradov and Kryžickij (1995).
9. *Emporion* of Olbia: Hdt. 4.17; see Braund (2007, 45). For nearby Greek cities, see the table in Tsetskhladze (2018, 48–55). On Berezan and Olbia as a trade hub, see Braund (2007, 59–60). Berezan may have been founded as essentially a commercial and trade center. Excavations have revealed signs of at least a dozen foundries for working iron and copper, dating to the first half of the sixth century (Čistov 2012, 234), as well as remains of thousands of transport amphorae from throughout the century, almost all from Ionia and the northwest Aegean (Chistov 2021, 203). Salted fish was probably a main export from this region famed for its fisheries, see Lytle (2016, 11–18); Greaves (2002, 76). Parmenter (2020) documents and discusses the region's slave trade. On the link between the region's trade and "mercantile literacy," see Lamont (2023).

10. For this and the next letter, I follow the Greek text from the recent thorough edition of Dana (2021, nos. 25 and 26), which contains an up-to-date bibliography (but lacking Bravo 2021, 263–87; Parmenter 2020, 75–80). The Greek text is as follows:

[side A:]
Ἀχιλλοδώρο̄ τὸ μολί-
βδιον· παρὰ τὸμ παῖδα
κἀναξαγόρην.

[Side B:]
Ὦ Πρωταγόρη, ὁ πατήρ τοι ἐπιστέλλε̄. Ἀδικε̃ται
ὑπὸ Ματάσυος· δο̄λο̃ται γάρ μιγ καὶ το̃
φορτηγεσίο̄ ἀπεστέρεσεν. Ἐλθὼμ παρ᾽ Ἀναξαγό| (←)ρην
ἀπήγησαι· φησι γὰρ αὐτὸν Ἀναξαγόρεω
δο̃λον ε̃ναι μυθεόμενος· "Τα̃μ᾽ Ἀνα⟨ξα⟩γόρης ἔχε̄
καὶ δο̄́λο̄ς καὶ δο̄́λας κοἰκίας." ὁ δὲ ἀναβω̃ι τε
καὶ οὔ φησιν ε̃ναι οὐδὲν ἐωυτω̃ι τε καὶ Ματασ⟨υι⟩
καί φησιν ε̃ναι ἐλεόθερος καὶ οὐδὲν ε̃ναι ἐωυτ⟨ῶ⟩ι
καὶ Ματά{τα}συ⟨ι⟩· ε̄̓ δέ τι αὐτω̃ι τε κἀναξαγόρῃ, αὐτοὶ
οἴδασι κατά σφας αὐτο̄́ς. Ταῦτ᾽ Ἀναξαγόρῃ λέγε̄ν
καὶ τῇ γυναικί. Ἕτερα δέ τοι ἐπιστέλλε̄· τὴμ μητέρα
καὶ το̄̀ς ἀδε⟨λ⟩φε⟨ο̄́⟩ς, ⟨ο⟩ἵ ἐσσιν ἐν Αρβινατηισιν, ἄγε̄ν ἐς τὴμ πόλιν·
αὐτὸς δέ γ᾽ ọ νεο̄ρὸς ἐλθὼμ παρά ⟨μ⟩ιν ⟨ἰ⟩θύωρα καταβήσεται.

11. Dana (2021, 123, 348) claims this "epistolary third person" has parallels in literary evidence and indicates the perspective of the letter's recipient. Bravo (1980, 883) suggests that Achillodoros entrusted the letter to the boat captain, as though in secret. The question of delivery also arises for the similar fourth-century letter of Lesis found in the Athenian agora (Jordan 2000; *SEG* 50.276), in which Lesis, apparently a slave or apprentice, complains of treatment by his *despotes* and seeks help from the letter's addressees. Because that letter was found in a well, Jordan (2000, 95) surmises it was never delivered.
12. Here again I reproduce the text of Dana (2021, no. 26) and refer to her bibliography, with the addition of Lamont (2023, 3–4); Bravo (2021, 287–300); Parmenter (2020, 76–80):

[side A:]
Ἀπατο̄́ριος
Λεάνακτι

[side B:]
Λήνακτι Ἀπατο̄́ριος: τὰ χρήματα σισύλημαι: ὑπ᾽ Ἡρακ-
λείδεω το̃ Εὀθήριος: κατὰ δύναμιν τὴν σὴν: μὴ ἀπολέ-
σω τὰ χρήματα: τὰ γὰρ χρήματạ σạ̀ ἐφάμην ε̃ναι: καὶ Μένω-
ν: ἔφατό: σε ἐπịθε̃ναι ἐωυτω̃ι: καὶ τα̣̃⟨λ⟩λα ὅσα σὺ αὐτω̃ι ἐπέ-
θηκας: καὶ π[ρὸ]ς ἔφατο· {σ'} ἐ⟨μ⟩οὶ σạ̀ τὰ χρήματα ἐνη̃ν: ἰὰν ἐπιθε-
ίης διφθέρια πρ[ὸς] Ἡρακλείδην καὶ Θαθαίην ⋮ τὰ χρήματα σ-
εωυτο̃ ΠỌ[ca. 2–3 ἀποδ?]οσε̄· κε̃νοι γάρ φασιν: ὅ τι σὸν: ἔχο̄σιν ἀποδώ-
[σε̃ν] τὸ: συλη[θὲν? ὅλ?]ον ἑπτὰ καὶ εἴκοσ:ιν στατη̃ρες: *vac.*
[Τὶ? θε]λήσε̄ς; Περὶ τω̃ν οἰκιητέων: Θυμώλεω
[- - ca. 6-7 - - Εὀ?]θυμίωι: αὐτω̃ι μοι οὐκ οἶδα ἢν {ε} γένηται εο̃.

13. Or, taking the verb ἐπιτίθημι here as "deliver a message," this sentence could be translated: "And Menon said you sent him a message; and whatever other messages you sent him." This is the translation preferred by Dana (2021, 131–32) and Bravo (2011, 76–77). For my translation, see Santiago Álvarez and Gardeñes Santiago (2006, 59).
14. On the calm, legalistic nature of this matter, see Dana (2021, 391). Regarding the language of seizure, there is a lexical difference (but overlap) between seizure under domestic and under international law. While ἄγειν, an ordinary word in any case, was used to describe seizure of a person in both contexts, the specialized terminology differed. E.g., ἐνέχυρον and ἐνεχυράζειν were rarely used in the international context. Instead, the most common words for legal seizure performed as a form of self-help legal remedy were the nouns σῦλον or σύλη (both often found in the plural) and the verb συλα̃ν. But this was not the only family of words so used. The noun ῥύσια and its verb ῥυσιάζειν also referred to roughly the same phenomenon. These words also had meanings beyond the form of private, legitimized seizure that concerns me

here. Noteworthy among meanings I do not discuss is the common use of συλᾶν to refer to "the plundering of sanctuaries and sacred things of the gods" (Pritchett 1991, 117), which is part of public international law and outside the scope of this chapter (see generally Knäpper 2018; Rigsby 1996). For detailed discussion of the relevant vocabulary, see especially Bravo (1980); also Pritchett (1991, 73–132); Wilhelm (1911, 197–201).

15. On these letters as evidence for a law of seizure, see the commentaries of Dana (2021) as well as her further discussion at 388–92; Harris (2013b, 113–18); Bravo (2011, 81–82; 1980, 885); Santiago Álvarez and Gardeñes Santiago (2006, 67–69). On uncertainty regarding an international context, see Bravo (1980, 884); Wąsowicz (1975, 59–65).
16. Greek merchants certainly communicated by letter in the course of long-distance trade, but letters were also used for regional and even local commercial communications; see Dana (2021, 363–71); for evidence of long-distance commercial use of letters, see [Dem.] 56.7–10; cf. Gabrielsen (2013, 78–79).
17. If "and houses" is in fact the proper translation there for κοἰκίας in line 6, and if the dispute between Matasys and Anaxagoras concerns ownership of those houses, it makes the situation here murkier. Ownership of real property in Greek *poleis* was often restricted to citizens or people who had received special permission (Maffi 2014, 198; on connections between land ownership and *polis* citizenship generally, see Faraguna 2024). If two people could make legitimate legal claims to a house, they likely both also had a right to use the local courts, with a correspondingly narrower scope for the kind of self-help reflected in this letter. In other words, it is hard to see how a dispute over ownership of a house between two locals would lead to creation of this letter, except in a community in which self-help was still a central aspect of the legal system; Bravo's (1980, 884) suggestion that Matasys *used* to live in the same town as Anaxagoras does not appear to solve this problem. We can avoid the difficulty if we interpret κοἰκίας as something like "and moveable household effects" or, more speculatively, "female slaves of the household" or "prostitutes" (on Greek periphrases and euphemisms relating to prostitution, see Anastasiadis and Lewis 2024).
18. Parmenter (2020, 78) describes both letters as related to litigation processes, but no language in the letters, or other evidence, supports this conclusion. My argument that the legal context is international risks circularity, since if these letters did reflect purely domestic law disputes they would be evidence that, in Berezan and Olbia (or in whichever *polis* or *poleis* they took place), self-help could be used in place of judicial procedure. Different legal rules from what we see in our Athenian and Gortynian evidence could certainly have been in place: these letters were found far from Athens and Gortyn, and date half a century before the Gortyn code.
19. "Matasys" may be a Scythian name (Dana 2021, 119). But, as Vlassopoulos (2013, 117) points out specifically in the Olbia/Berezan context, "[w]e should not assume that everybody bearing a non-Greek name was non-Greek in origin, as non-Greek names could be assumed through marriage or guest-friendship"; cf. Vlassopoulos (2013, 133–35); Kryzhitskiy (2007, 21). One might guess that Matasys was one of the mysterious Kallipidai whom Herodotus calls "Greek Scythians," Ἕλληνες Σκύθαι, 4.17. Dana (2021, 133) argues that the name *Thathaie* in the second letter is Greek.
20. The presence of Matasys in the Berezan letter, however, may cause a problem from the other direction: maybe he is not Greek, and that letter indicates a customary law not restricted to Greeks but even more international, encompassing at least some non-Greek peoples. Such broader international law certainly existed, as I note in Chapter 1, but the extension of international law beyond Greek communities is outside the scope of this book.
21. Lamont (2023, 4, 18).
22. *I.Olympia* 11 (*Nomima* i 21; Koerner 1981, 201–06), ll. 5–7: αἰ δέ τις συλαίε, ϝέρρεν αὐτὸν ποτ τὸν Δία, αἰ μὲ δάμοι δοκέοι. I follow *LSJ*, *s.v.* ἔρρω (A)(2), in taking ϝέρρεν as the Lokrian form of Attic ἔρρειν. The Chaladriens were likely a local community, perhaps under broad Elean authority since they gave Deukalion a piece of land in Pisa. On the meaning of ϝράτρα here, see Avilés (2010, 33–34); and his pp. 76–78 on the text as a whole.
23. See Dreher (2003, 78–79). The language is ambiguous whether someone pondering *syla* against Deukalion must get pre-approval from the *demos* or if he can seek official approval of his seizure after the fact. But the approval must be formal and public (αἰ μὲ δάμοι δοκέοι).
24. Litigation is prominent in Hesiod, e.g., *Th.* 80–93, *Op.* 213–85; and visible in Homer, e.g., *Il.* 18.497–508. On early Greek litigation, see Cantarella (2021, 329–47); Papakonstantinou (2008, 24–46); Gagarin (1986, 19–50).

25. *IG* IX 1² 717 (*Nomima* i 53; *SvA* 146; Tod i 34; Oikonomides 1850 (*ed. pr.*)); see Zunino (2017); Avilés (2010, 66–75); Zelnick-Abramovitz (2004, 94–96); Lintott (2004, 343–44); Cataldi (1983, 53–86); Maffi (1983, 173–243); Bravo (1980, 890–911); Gauthier (1972, 222–25, 286–92); Lerat (1952, ii:31–34). Images of the bronze, which was found at Chaleion (not Oianthea as Tod reports) and measures 8 x 32 cm., are available at http://www.britishmuseum.org/collection/object/G_1896-1218-2. This treaty is perhaps the most significant surviving piece of evidence for these little-known *poleis*; see the entries in Hansen and Nielsen (2004, nos. 159 and 166).
26. Lines 1–4:

    ⁝ τὸν ξένον μὲ hάγεν ⁝ ἐ(τ) τᾶς Χαλεΐδος ⁝ τὸν Οἰανθέα μ-
    εδὲ τὸν Χαλειέα ⁝ ἐ(τ) τᾶς Οἰανθίδος ⁝ μεδὲ χρέματα. αἴ τι(ς) συ-
    λõι ⁝ τὸν δὲ συλõντα ἀνάτο(ς) συλε͂ν. τὰ ξενικὰ ἐ(θ) θαλάσας *hάγεν* ⁝
    ἄσυλον ⁝ πλὰν ἐ(λ) λιμένος ⁝ τõ κατὰ πόλιν ⁝

27. My focus here is on the implications of my reading rather than a word-by-word defense of it (the issues are aired in detail in the literature cited two notes above). I note here that a key ambiguity in the first sentence is: what are the subjects and what are the objects of the infinitive hάγεν (i.e., ἄγειν)? Another is whether hάγεν ἐ(τ) (i.e., ἄγειν ἐκ) is used as essentially a synonym for the legally justified act of συλᾶν (my preferred interpretation), i.e., an action that might constitute only part of a *syla* (seizure of a person, rather than goods); or to refer to an act of forcible seizure with no legal justification. A third is whether αἴ τι(ς) συλõι is the protasis of the first or the second sentence. As indicated, my preferred reading is to take it with the second sentence. Cataldi (1983, 56–57) and Zunino (2017, 127–28) take it with the first. But all six other instances of αἴ ("if") in this inscription occur at the beginning of a clause or sentence; we should read this one the same way.
28. Zunino (2005, 113 n.3).
29. Thuc. 1.5.2: τινὲς ἔτι καὶ νῦν, οἷς κόσμος καλῶς τοῦτο δρᾶν. I discuss this passage in Chapter 9, notes 41–45 and accompanying text. See Hornblower (1991–2008, *ad* 1.5.3); also Gabrielsen (2013b, 141); de Souza (1999, 29). Tod, in his note to the inscription (i 34), refers to "the piratical practices of the Ozolian Locrians and their Aetolian neighbours," but does not explain the precise connection he adduces between those alleged practices and this inscription; similarly Oikonomides (1850, 51). Against any connection between this inscription and piracy, see Zunino (2017, 132); Lerat (1952, ii.32–33).
30. In fact, the exception is not limited only to the open sea, since it appears to include harbors other than those "by the city."
31. Gauthier (1972, 224–25).
32. Greif (2005, 738) notes that the inability of a government judicial panel to verify the information relevant to a litigation may restrict the ability of a court to enforce contracts. If we assume that most people believe that a court, under such a lack of verifiable information, will tend to err on the side of dismissing claims for damages, this is evidence that commercial parties may prefer to pursue their claims privately under such circumstances. But it is not apparent to me that acknowledging the existence of such cases—which occur in any legal system—would cause a government to carve out a special exception such as we see in this treaty.
33. The passage, Dem. 58.55 (*Against Theokrines*), is about who is primarily responsible (αἴτιος) when things go wrong on the open sea versus in Athenian territory, by virtue of being in a better position to police activities in one place or the other. It is not about who has authority to enforce law against piracy as opposed to domestic law. See Maffi (1983, 185–86).
34. Maffi (1983, 184–89). His interpretation takes hάγεν (=ἄγειν) as having two entirely different valences in use just two lines apart: "seizure" in l. 1 vs. neutral "transport" in l. 3. It assumes a subject for the second ἄγειν that is not at all apparent from the context (namely, the foreign trader who owns τὰ ξενικά). But most problematically to my eyes, permitting seizure in the port (as Maffi argues the agreement does) seems even more counter to the general goal of the agreement than having an open sea exception. I agree with Maffi (1983, 202) that we must interpret every clause of the agreement in view of the parties' aim in the agreement as a whole. That aim is, I take it, to replace self-help with judicial resolution in the territories of the two cities (not, as Maffi takes it, to have self-help seizures take place under circumstances where the community can control them). The reason for mentioning harbors here is to make clear they are considered part of the cities' territories for purposes of this agreement. After creating an exception permitting seizures at sea, the agreement has to specify that the exception is limited to the "open sea," which it does by explaining that "sea" does not include a "harbor by the city."

35. Cooter and Ulen (2016, 385). One objection to adding administrative and error costs into one sum is that there is no obvious way to measure them with the same units. Administrative costs will be measured largely in person-hours, but error costs will take multiple largely immeasurable forms, such as degrees of injustice and undeserved punishments including imprisonment and death. And even administration costs would include the unmeasurable cost of "justice delayed."
36. See, e.g., the comparative analysis by Greif (2005, 732–39) of "private" and "organic" vs. "public" and "designed" contract-enforcement institutions. He claims (731 n.3) that "[o]rganic institutions often evolve to acquire designed components" (a proposed mixing of "evolution" and "design" that students of biological evolution might find distasteful).
37. On the path-dependence of institutional evolution, see Greif (2005, 776). The idea that law tends to "evolve toward efficiency" is encountered in new institutionalist and law and economics literature, despite a lack of evidence supporting it; see Niblett, Posner, and Schleifer (2010, 325–27); Fitzpatrick (2006, 996–97).
38. See North (1981, 33–34). Greif (2005, 729) argues that an "effective supply" of public designed contract-enforcement institutions (among which he would likely categorize *symbola* agreements) will tend to arise when the members of the commercial sector have a political voice by which they can persuade or compel a state's "coercive power" to supply such institutions. This is an example of his model of the "co-evolution" of markets and political institutions.
39. Cooter and Ulen (2016, 446) admit to deliberately omitting possible benefits of litigation, insisting without argument that "full trials are not worthwhile socially unless the stakes are substantial." One perhaps could charitably reframe Cooter and Ulen's formula as a pursuit of positives rather than an avoidance of negatives. E.g., one could describe the *avoidance* of administrative costs and error costs as instead the *pursuit* of efficiency benefits and accuracy benefits, respectively. But even seen from this perspective their formula omits important elements.
40. Arist. *Rhet.* 1.14, 1374b33: ἡ γὰρ δίκη καὶ κόλασις καὶ ἴασις (alternatively but less likely in the context, and because most manuscripts do not print the second καί, "the trial is both punishment and healing"). On the importance of voice for satisfaction with legal procedure, see Landsman (2012, 243); Zimmerman and Tyler (2010, 486–87); Hensler (1989, 98–100); Lind and Tyler (1988, 101–06); cf. Richman (2017, 96–97). On the "intangible benefits of trial" in the modern United States, see P. Butler (2004, 629–35).
41. On jury service as citizenship, see Arist. *Pol.* 3.1 (defining the citizen as one who participates in judging, κρίσις, and ruling, ἀρχή); Ar. *Vesp.* 548–627 (celebrating the juror's power in Athens). On trials as a form of norm reinforcement, see Lanni (2016, 119–70), discussing how trials in Athens were important in both shaping and enforcing norms not only through verdicts and sentences but as public venues for parties to discuss community rules and how they applied to the case at hand. Webber (2006, 180–81) discusses the benefits of litigation and similar "democratic" institutions: "They provide concrete and knowable mechanisms for popular participation; they allow citizens to speak in their own voice; and they do so on a basis of rough equality." On the expressive function of law, which has been robustly supported in recent studies, see Lane, Nosenzo, and Sonderegger (2023); Galbiati et al. (2021); McGinn (2015) (focusing on Roman law); Funk (2007); Sunstein (1996). On the communicative function of punishment, see Hadjimatheou (2016); Tadros (2011, 88–110); Duff (2001, 75–98).
42. On business reluctance to litigate, and even to appear prone to litigate, see Bernstein (1996, 1787–90). On the importance of reputation to Athenian businessmen, see Leese (2021, 136–77). On hesitancy to report sexual violence, seen across modern societies, see Lilley et al. (2023); Lowe (2022); Hohl and Stanko (2015).
43. A passage of Thucydides (3.101) suggests that Lokrian cities may have had a tendency to act in common, as when they all switched sides in the sixth year of the Peloponnesian War from the Athenians to the Spartans.
44. On the elements of Lokrian identity, and east–west differences, see Petrochilos (2019); Daverio Rocchi (2015, 179–85). On the Lokrian cult of Athena *Ilias*, see Lerat (1952, i.156–58), who located the (or *a*) sanctuary of that goddess in the vicinity of the modern town of Malandrino, 20 or 25 kilometers inland from Oianthea and Chaleion; Lerat (1951, 141–42); cf. Rousset (2006, 351–52). At least until the fifth century, Lokrians shared a distinctive practice of burying some deceased people in large clay jars, see Petrochilos (2019, 50–51). He also notes (2019, 56) that all Lokrians might have felt bound together by their joint duty of expiating Ajax's legendary sin of raping Cassandra at Troy. This expiation was performed by sending two "Lokrian maidens" each year to Troy, where they could be killed with impunity. This may have been practiced from

the seventh to fourth centuries, paused for several decades, then renewed; see generally Hughes (1991, 166–84).

45. *Contra* Petrochilos (2019, 54), who goes too far in concluding from this austere text that it forbids us from saying "that the two contracting parties had very close ties . . . or even that they shared consciousness of a common descent." This is to read the agreement as though it were an Athenian decree in which one expects a motivation clause, but even in Athens we do not see those until the very end of the fifth century.
46. Daverio Rocchi (2015, 193–94) emphasizes that the terms of this agreement underline the (continuing) independent *polis* status of Oianthea and Chaleion, especially compared to the federalization that had already taken hold in east Lokris and would eventually arise in the west. This view supports a liberal reading of the agreement as reifying the stateness of these two cities.
47. On the "open sea" in the Greek world, see Lytle (2016b, 107–11). The open sea is part of what Kosmin (2024, 3–4) calls the ungovernable "planetary": "a cosmos of vast, untamable, and heedless geological, climatic, and astronomical processes." The Oiantheans and Chaleians seem to have respected its ungovernable nature, in this way contrasting themselves to would-be *thalassocrats* such as Athenians, Rhodians, and especially Romans; see Chapter 9, below; and Kosmin (2024, 139–61).
48. *Against Nikomachos* (Lys. 30) was delivered in 399 or 398. On the likely procedure used to bring this case (*eisangelia*), see Todd (1996, 104–06).
49. Lys. 30.22: καὶ ταῦτα ὁρῶν αὐτὴν ἀποροῦσαν χρημάτων καὶ Λακεδαιμονίους μὲν ἀπειλοῦντας, ὅταν μὴ ἀποπέμψωμεν αὐτοῖς τὰ χρήματα, Βοιωτοὺς δὲ σύλας ποιουμένους, ὅτι οὐ δυνάμεθα δύο τάλαντα ἀποδοῦναι.
50. The sources are assembled by Migeotte (1984, 19–22).
51. Migeotte (1984, 22–23 and n.15).
52. The speech is Isocrates no. 3, *Nikokles*. On the date, see Münscher, *RE* 9,1 (1916), col. 2194, *s.v.* Isokrates. Salamis on Cyprus is not to be confused with the island Salamis just off the coast of Attica, although there are meaningful connections, which I discuss in Chapter 8, notes 56–65 and accompanying text.
53. Isoc. 3.33: ἀβάτου δὲ τῆς Ἑλλάδος ἡμῖν οὔσης διὰ τὸν πόλεμον τὸν γεγενημένον, καὶ πανταχῇ συλωμένων ἡμῶν, τὰ πλεῖστα τούτων διέλυσα, τοῖς μὲν ἅπαντ' ἀποτίνων, τοῖς δὲ μέρη, τῶν δ' ἀναβαλέσθαι δεόμενος, πρὸς δὲ τοὺς ὅπως ἠδυνάμην περὶ τῶν ἐγκλημάτων διαλλαττόμενος.
54. The depleted treasury is described at 3.31: "having inherited a royal treasury empty of money and completely spent," παραλαβὼν . . . τὰ μὲν βασίλεια χρημάτων κενὰ καὶ πάντα κατηναλωμένα. On the debt as public, see also Bravo (1980, 927); Gauthier (1972, 214), not noting the context, interprets the seizures as the result of private debts by individual Salaminians. On the significance of Nikokles's settlement of the claims, see Garlan (1965, 339).
55. This paragraph draws heavily from Iacovou (2008). On Cyprus especially in the sixth through fourth centuries, see also Körner (2016); Maier (1994, 297–317).
56. Iacovou (2008, 244). Phoenicians in Cyprus were by no means restricted to Kition. On the extent and variability of Phoenician identities in Cyprus, see Fourrier (2021).
57. On the history of the Cypriot Greek dialect, see Iacovou (2008, 235) and the essays collected in Karageorghis and Masson (1988). On the history of writing on Cyprus, see Steele (2019).
58. See Pestarino (2022, 55); Ulbrich (2020); Papantoniou (2013, 170–78); Maier (1994, 306); but note the cautions of Mehl (2013, 149) about the sparseness of our evidence. On use of alphabetic Greek, see Pestarino (2022, 16–17).
59. This is clear from, among other things, the many treaties between Greeks and non-Greeks for which we have evidence.
60. On the geography, see Kenrick (2013, 1); Laronde (1996). On Cyrene as a grain producer and exporter, see Bresson (2011, 69–70). On geography and agriculture both, see Schaus (2024, 11–14, 86–90); Horden and Purcell (2000, 65–74).
61. *IG Cyrenaica* 097100 and *GVCyr* 033 (Pugliese Carratelli 1961–62, 273–80, no. 103 (*ed. pr.*); Daux 1963; Bravo 1980, 918–28); see Laronde (1987, 149–61); Lintott (2004, 349–51); Laronde and Lefèvre (2009). Nowakowski (2013) adds a new fragment, which is included in the *IG Cyrenaica* edition; I follow his line numbers.
62. Line 7: σῦλ[α] διελύ⟨θ⟩η; cf. σῦλον διελύθ[η], l. 32; τό τε σῦλον ἐλύσαμες ὀκτὼ ταλάντων, l. 17.
63. "Harassed" here may be an understatement. Lines 15–20 describe what appears to have been multiple deaths caused by a certain Teisilaos, presumably during a seizure attempt by him upon Cyreneans. The Cyreneans did pay off that seizure, but Teisilaos was ultimately exiled and put to death for the killings.

64. On the founding of Cyrene, see Hdt. 4.150–67; Schaus (2024, 17–33); M. Austin (2008, 187–201); Chamoux (1953, 69–127). Neer and Kurke (2019, 163–65) emphasize the diversity of Greeks who inhabited Cyrene; but their common Greekness connected them, especially in a land that continued to be inhabited by native Libyans. And although marriage between Greek Cyreneans and Libyans may have been common, it seems only to have taken place between Greek men and Libyan women, see M. Austin (2008, 209).
65. On the political revolution, see Arist. fr. 611.17 (Rose); B.M. Mitchell (1966, 110–13); Chamoux (1953, 202–10). On the period from this time until Alexander the Great, see Laronde (1987, 27–39). On Cyrenean connections generally with other Greeks, see Laronde (1987, 137–68). **Architecture**: the early sixth century temple of Apollo shows close stylistic and technical affinities to the approximately contemporary temple of Hera at Olympia, see Sapirstein (2016, 587–93); **sculpture**: on "Ionicizing" *korai* and *kouroi* as a consciously "panhellenic" gesture, see Neer and Kurke (2019, 181–83); the influence of Athenian styles on local craftsmen has been noted, see Laronde (1987, 137–40); **theater**: Cyrene had one of the earliest theaters in the Greek world, far from Athens where both drama and its architectural setting were invented; the earliest phase of the theater in the sanctuary of Apollo at Cyrene has been dated to the first half of the fifth century, already at this time at least partly built in stone; see Ensoli (2012, 111–13); Csapo and Wilson (2020, 791–805); **trade**: Cyrene was famous for export of its silphium plant, which was in high demand in Greece (Ar. *Pl.* 925; Schaus 2024, 81–86); it was a major exporter of grain, see Bresson (2011, 69) and below; and a large number of ceramics attest to strong trade ties with mainland Greece (Schaus 2024, 90–91; Laronde 1996, 14–17); Laronde (1987, 140–42); **legend**: Herodotus (4.153) reports a story of Samians helping with the founding of Cyrene and a resulting long-term friendship between Cyreneans and Samians; **religion and festivals**: the Cyreneans had a treasury at Olympia (Paus. 6.19; Barringer 2021, 78–79), made personal dedications there (Paus. 6.13.7; Neer and Kurke 2019, 184), and attended activities there in significant numbers, as spectators (*I.Olympia Suppl.* 4, dated 500 BCE) and contestants (Laronde 1987, 146), and Cyrenean victories at the Pythian games in Delphi in 474 and 462 were celebrated by Pindar in three victory odes (*Pyth.* 4, 5, and 9, on which, see Neer and Kurke 2019, 159–217); they dedicated statues at Delphi in the fifth century (Paus. 10.13.5, 10.15.6; Neer and Kurke 2019, 185–89) and built a treasury there in the fourth (Laronde 1987, 147); over two dozen Panathenaic prize amphoras dating before 320 BCE are known from Cyrene (Laronde 1987, 143–45); and the cult of Apollo Karneios continuously connected Cyrene to Thera and Sparta in particular (Malkin 1994, 143–58); **quasi-military relations**: Cyreneans provided assistance to Athenian soldiers fleeing their catastrophic participation in the failed Egyptian revolt against the Persians in 454 (Thuc. 1.110) and guided a Peloponnesian naval force to Sicily in 413 (Thuc. 7.50).
66. Bresson (2011, 78; cf. 92–93). The inscription is *IG Cyrenaica* 010900 (*RO* 96; *SEG* 9.2). Bresson's important study argues persuasively, among other things, that the Cyreneans permitted larger grain exports than usual to the recipient cities, perhaps at a subsidized or controlled price, and did not give the grain outright as a gift (2011, 79).
67. Neer and Kurke (2019, 169–72). The inscription is *IG Cyrenaica* 011000 (*ML* 5; SEG 9.3) and usually dated ca. 370–60 but sometimes ca. 330–20; see Graham (1960, 100); *BE* 2008, no. 606.
68. Also, since the original settlement of Cyrene was believed to have been ordered by Apollo at Delphi (*IG Cyrenaica* 011000, ll. 24–25), the very existence of Cyrene may have been seen to depend on a certain divine ordering of the Greek international world.
69. [Dem.] 35.26: ἐν γὰρ τῇ πόλει τῇ ἡμετέρᾳ αὐτῶν, οὐδὲν ἀδικοῦντες οὐδὲ δίκην οὐδεμίαν ὠφληκότες τούτοις, σεσυλήμεθα τὰ ἡμέτερ' αὐτῶν ὑπὸ τούτων Φασηλιτῶν ὄντων, ὥσπερ δεδομένων συλῶν Φασηλίταις κατ' Ἀθηναίων. ἐπειδὰν γὰρ μὴ ἐθέλωσιν ἀποδοῦναι ἃ ἔλαβον, τί ἄν τις ἄλλο ὄνομα ἔχοι θέσθαι τοῖς τοιούτοις ἢ ὅτι ἀφαιροῦνται βίᾳ τὰ ἀλλότρια;
70. This is noted by Bravo (1980, 744) and Dareste (1889, 309 n.3).
71. [Dem.] 35.13: ἐὰν δὲ μὴ εἰσβάλωσι, μείναντες ἐπὶ κυνὶ ἡμέρας δέκα ἐν Ἑλλησπόντῳ, ἐξελόμενοι ὅπου ἂν μὴ σῦλαι ὦσιν Ἀθηναίοις. On the contract text's questionable provenance, see Chapter 5, n. 22 (that this clause is not mentioned in the text of the main speech may count for the contract's authenticity, however). The difficulty here is the translation of μὴ σῦλαι ὦσιν Ἀθηναίοις. In the previously quoted passage, the party in the dative is given the right to perform seizures, and κατά with the genitive means "against" (cf. *Anecd. Bekk.* i.303, 27–28, quoting the expression σῦλα δοῦναι κατὰ τῆς Χαλκηδονίων πόλεως, "to grant *syla* against the city of the Chalkedonians," from a fourth-century Attic work). But following that construction here would give an odd result by suggesting that cities other than Athens regularly granted Athenians a right of seizure. It is hard to imagine the circumstances under which that might ever happen, much less how it could be common. And in this case the right of seizure would presumably be granted

against some specific party. But if Ἀθηναίοις means "granted to Athenians," the contract here would not have specified whom the seizures could be against, which would be a major omission. Better to take Ἀθηναίοις as a dative of "disadvantage" and accept that the construction simply varies from Androkles's expression in his speech (we see a similar construal of the dative in Polybius's statement that Eleutherna declared *rhysia* against the Rhodians: ῥύσια κατήγγειλαν τοῖς Ῥοδίοις, 4.53.2, discussed below). Böckh (1851, i.194–95) in effect interprets ὅπου ἂν μὴ σῦλαι ὦσιν Ἀθηναίοις to mean "in whichever city the Athenians have not granted the right of seizure to Athenians." He suggests that the lenders were afraid that cities against whose citizens or residents Athens had permitted seizures would likely be home to people who thought they had suffered unjust seizures at the hands of Athenians and would therefore be likely to make counteracting seizures upon Athenian property that came to their city. But this seems to stretch the meaning of ὅπου too far: I am aware of no evidence that, in peacetime, cities granted rights of seizure against whoever was in a particular city, regardless of the victim's own citizenship. On the contrary, as in the passage above, it seems that seizures were granted against citizens of a particular city (κατ' Ἀθηναίων). Bravo (1980, 741) argues that the use of the dative means the Athenians could be the perpetrators or the victims of seizures. MacDowell (2004, 136) translates as I do.

72. E.g., *IG* XII 5, 24 (Sikinos), l. 11: ἐσσύλωι ἀσυλίαν; *IG* XII 5, 481 (Siphnos), l. 24: ἐν σύλοις ἀσυλίαν; cf. *IG* XII 5, 798, ll. 18–19; *IG* XII Supp. no. 177, ll. 6–7; *IG* XII 5, 9, ll. 9–13 (Ios).
73. See Bravo's (1980, 735–40) survey of the evidence.
74. The Egyptians were enemies either because the Athenians were still at war with the Persians in the Social War and Egypt was a Persian possession; or because the Social War had ended, the Athenians had reconciled with and were now friendly with the Persians, but the Egyptians were in revolt from them. The former view is implied by Hypothesis 1.1 to Dem. 24; the second is the more common scholarly view; see Harris (2018, 123 n.55); Harding (1976, 196).
75. On authorship of this speech, see Gorman and Gorman (2024, 88–90); Trevett (1992, 73); Blass (1893, iii.242–43).
76. πάντας ἀνθρώπους ἄγει καὶ φέρει, καὶ τὰς μὲν ὠφελίας ἰδίᾳ καρποῦται, τὰς δὲ δίκας τούτων ὁ τυχὼν δίδωσιν ὑμῶν, καὶ μόνοις ὑμῖν οὐδαμόσε ἔστιν ἄνευ κηρυκείου βαδίσαι διὰ τὰς ὑπὸ τούτων ἀνδροληψίας καὶ σύλας κατεσκευασμένας· . . . τὸν γὰρ ὑπὲρ τῆς πόλεως τριήραρχον οὐκ ἀπὸ τῶν κοινῶν προσδοκᾶν χρὴ πλουτήσειν, ἀλλ' ἀπὸ τῶν ἰδίων τὰ τῆς πόλεως ἐπανορθώσειν, εἴπερ ἔσται τι τῶν δεόντων ὑμῖν. τούτων δὲ τἀναντία ἕκαστος ἐγνωκὼς ἐκπλεῖ· καὶ γάρ τοι τὰ τῶν αὐτῶν τρόπων ἁμαρτήματα ταῖς ὑμετέραις βλάβαις ἐπανορθοῦνται.
77. Dem. 23.61: πάντες οἱ στράτευμ' ἔχοντες, ὧν ἂν οἴωνται κρείττους ἔσεσθαι, ἄγουσι καὶ φέρουσι χρήματ' αἰτοῦντες. It was permitted, and even expected, for Athenian trierarchs to collect booty from the defeated enemy; indeed, this was an important element of financing the navy in wartime; see, e.g., Xen. *Hell.* 6.2.36–37; Pritchard (2015, 57–58). But, as Pritchard notes, Athenian naval officers and their men were not allowed to enrich themselves with booty: it was only to be used to pay ordinary wages and expenses. Hence the Athenian system can be contrasted with how, for centuries, the British navy gave officers and their men a significant portion of any booty they won at sea, thereby creating large financial incentives for them to attack and defeat enemy vessels; see Allen (2012, 106–45).
78. The context of the speech is that Aristokrates has proposed a law forbidding anyone to kill Charidemos under any circumstances, even those normally permitted by law (23.16), and Demosthenes is showing what absurdities would result. 23.61: "And isn't it awful, O earth and gods, and obviously illegal, not only contrary to written law but also contrary to the common law of all people, for me not to be able to defend myself against the man who tries to seize me and carry off my goods by force as though I'm an enemy in war, or at any rate if one is not permitted to kill Charidemos under these circumstances but, on the contrary, if he attacks someone like a pirate and pillages his property, a man who kills him will be sent to prison, although the law provides that the man is innocent under such circumstances?" εἶτ' οὐ δεινόν, ὦ γῆ καὶ θεοί, καὶ φανερῶς παράνομον, οὐ μόνον παρὰ τὸν γεγραμμένον νόμον, ἀλλὰ καὶ παρὰ τὸν κοινὸν ἁπάντων ἀνθρώπων, τὸν ἄγοντ' ἢ φέροντα βίᾳ τἄμ' ἐν πολεμίου μοίρᾳ μὴ ἐξεῖναί μοι ἀμύνεσθαι, εἴ γε μηδὲ τοῦτον τὸν τρόπον ἐξέσται Χαρίδημον ἀποκτεῖναι, ἀλλά, ἐὰν ἀδικῶν ἄγῃ καὶ φέρῃ βίᾳ τά τινος ληζόμενος, ἀγώγιμος ὁ κτείνας ἔσται, τοῦ νόμου διδόντος, ἐὰν ἐπὶ τούτοις, ἀθῷον εἶναι; On the phrase ἐν πολεμίου μοίρᾳ as almost a periphrasis for ἐν πολεμίου, see *LSJ*, *s.v.* μοίρα (A)(V).
79. Van Groningen and Wartelle (1968, xiii) conclude that books 1 and 2 of the *Oeconomica* were written in the late fourth century by a member of the Lyceum. If correct, this would place the Chalkedonian action in the fourth century or earlier. On the economics and politics of shipping through the Bosporos, see Gabrielsen (2007).

80. Χαλκηδόνιοι δέ, ξένων ἐν τῇ πόλει συχνῶν παρ' αὐτοῖς γινομένων, ὀφείλοντες αὐτοῖς μισθὸν οὐκ ἠδύναντο διαλῦσαι. ἀνήγγειλαν οὖν, εἴ τις τῶν πολιτῶν ἢ μετοίκων σῦλον ἔχει κατὰ πόλεως ἢ ἰδιώτου καὶ βούλεται λαβεῖν, ἀπογράψασθαι. ἀπογραψαμένων δὲ συχνῶν, τὰ πλοῖα τὰ πλέοντα εἰς τὸν Πόντον ἐσύλων μετὰ προφάσεως εὐλόγου. ἔταξαν δὲ χρόνον ἐν ᾧ λόγον ὑπὲρ αὐτῶν ἔφασαν ποιήσασθαι. συλλεγέντων δὲ χρημάτων συχνῶν, τοὺς μὲν στρατιώτας ἀπήλλαξαν, ὑπὲρ δὲ τῶν σύλων διεδικάσαντο. τοῖς δὲ μὴ δικαίως συληθεῖσιν ἡ πόλις ἀπὸ τῶν προσόδων ἀπεδίδου.
81. I discussed, above, reference to a person being seized for the debts of his city, in Athens at the end of the Peloponnesian War, and we see it again in third-century inscriptions from Delphi (*Syll.*[3] 437) and Delos (*IG* XI 4, 1049), discussed below.
82. It is not clear how the *syla* claims were judged (ὑπὲρ δὲ τῶν σύλων διεδικάσαντο), but a board of Chalkedonian judges may have heard competing arguments from the person who "signed up" with a claim and the person whose goods were seized.
83. I consider my interpretation likely but not certain: the Chalkedonians may been little concerned about giving their seizures a legal pretext. This possibility is suggested by the expression quoted in n. 71 above, "to grant *syla* against the city of the Chalkedonians," σῦλα δοῦναι κατὰ τῆς Χαλκηδονίων πόλεως (*Anecd. Bekk.* i.303, 27–28). Transmitted to us only as a contextless phrase, the expression could refer to historical incidents of retaliatory *syla* declared by cities who believed their citizens had been treated unfairly by the Chalkedonians in this very situation described by the author of the *Oeconomica*. It is also possible that the seizures granted against the Chalkedonians were in response to other incidents in the 360s, specifically when Chalkedonians and Byzantines, due to grain shortages, were forcing grain ships to put into harbor and unload their cargoes, see [Dem.] 50.6, 17 (*Against Polykles*).
84. *IG* II[3] 1 367 (*RO* 95), esp. ll. 36–40.
85. The decree instructs the Athenian ambassador to tell Dionysius not to wrong anyone sailing to Athens in the future (τὸ λοιπὸν μηδέν' ἀδικεῖν τῶν Ἀθήναζε πλεόντων, ll. 40–41), but this does not mean Herakleides's Athenian destination made him the target of the Herakleian seizure.
86. *Proxenoi*: an Athenian *proxenos* in Herakleia is attested in the 420s (*IG* I[3] 74) and in the late fourth century (*IG* II[3] 1 483), and a Herakleian *proxenos* in Athens in the 370s ([Dem.] 52.5). The Athenian *xenoi* were friends of a Herakleian named Lykon, described in the speech *Against Callippus* ([Dem.] 52), attributed to Demosthenes but probably written by the plaintiff, Apollodorus son of the banker Pasion; see Gorman and Gorman (2024, 77); Trevett (1992, 51). The decree for Herakleian grain traders is *IG* II[3] 1 339.
87. Polyb. 4.53.2: τὸ μὲν πρῶτον ῥύσια κατήγγειλαν τοῖς Ῥοδίοις, μετὰ δὲ ταῦτα πόλεμον ἐξήνεγκαν.
88. See Zimny (2021, 134–35).
89. The use of one element of international law (*symbola* treaties) to restrict use of another element (the customary law of *syla*) is evidence that Greeks understood their international law as being one logically connected system.
90. On personal *asylia*, see Knäpper (2018, 38–41). On *asylia*'s range of meanings, see Chaniotis (1996b, 66): it spans "from the inviolability of every sanctuary and the personal inviolability of an individual guaranteed by a foreign city, to the prohibition of reprisals agreed upon by two communities, or the inviolability of certain sanctuaries recognized by kings, cities, and confederations." The term *asphaleia* was sometimes used instead of *asylia*; see, e.g., *IG* IX 1[2] 136, ll. 3–4 (Aitolia, late third century); *Syll.*[3] 721, l. 35 (Knossos, late second century). An example of pre-fourth century *asylia* is in a decree from Thetonion, in Thessaly, dating to the second half of the fifth century. It grants *asylia*, among other privileges, to Sotairos of Corinth, his family, his slaves, and his property: *IG* IX 2 257.
91. *IG* XII 9, 191 (*I.jur.gr.* no. 9; see commentary without text by Knoepfler 2001). No city ethnic is given for Chairephanes, but also no patronymic, and the agreement appears to provide for copies of the text to be placed in Megara and Andros. Chairephanes is likely a citizen of one of those cities (as noted in the commentary in *I.jur.gr.*).
92. *IG* XII 9, 191, ll. 37–38: "*asylia* to himself while he performs the work for the city, both on l[and and at sea and during war and during peace, both] for himself and for all of those working with Chairephanes," [α]ὐτῶι ἀσυλίαν ἐργαζομένωι τὰ πρὸς τὴν πόλιν καὶ κατὰ γ[ῆν καὶ κατὰ θάλασσαν καὶ πολέμου καὶ εἰρήνης καὶ] αὐτῶι καὶ τοῖς μετὰ Χαιρεφάνους ἐργαζομένοις ἅπα[σιν].
93. *I.Ilion* 24; *Syll.*[3] 355; ll. 9–10: εἶναι δὲ καὶ ἀσυλίαν αὐτοῖς καὶ ἐν πολέμωι καὶ εἰρήνηι.

94. This is because, first, *asylia* protection limits the options available to a potential plaintiff. Second, a citizen plaintiff wanting to make a seizure would normally have more friends and native sympathy on his side than would a foreign defendant. On the other hand, to make a useful seizure you have to find some valuable property of the defendant's or seize the defendant himself, tasks presenting their own difficulties.
95. *Syll.*[3] 437 (*Choix Delphes* 111; Migeotte, *Emprunt* 30). Lines 4 to 6 state that "the *polis* has been released from all the seizures that Philistion complained of having paid off on behalf of the *polis*, having been seized by people, as he said, on behalf of the *polis*": ἀπολελύσθαι δὲ τὰν πόλιν ἀπὸ τῶν ῥυσίων πάντων / ὧν ἐπεκάλει Φιλ[ι]ọ[τί]ων ὑπὲρ τὰν πόλιν ἀποτετείκεν, ὑφ' ὧν ἔφατο / ἐρρυσιάσται ὑπὲρ τὰν πόλιν. Note that the Delphians are effectively reamortizing their debt to the unknown people who seized Philistion, in the form of future foregone tax payments from Philistion.
96. *IG* XI 4, 1049 (Migeotte, *Emprunt* 117), ll. 6–9: "And in a time of grain shortage, when grain had twice been taken away (as security) by Delians to whom the city owed money, he interceded with the creditors and sent it back to the people," ἔν [τε] τῆι σπανισιτίαι σῖτογ καταχθέντα ὑπὸ Δηλίω[ν] δὶς οἷς ὤφειλεν ἡ πόλις, [πα]ραιτησάμενος τοὺς ἐν[ε]χυράσαντας, ἀπέσ[τει]λεν τῶι δήμωι.
97. τό τε κατὰ τᾶς πόλιος σῦλον ἄρα[ι]ς, *IG* XII 2, 527, l. 4 (*IG* XII Suppl. p. 33; Labarre 1996, no. 68). See Paschidis (2008, 403–06); Gauthier, *BE* 1992, no. 343.
98. *I.Cret.* I 19.1 (*SvA* 511; Chaniotis, *Verträge* 11), ll. 8–10: "And let it not be permitted either to seize a Lyttian in the land of the Mallaians or a Mallaian in the land of the Lyttians"; μὴ ἐξέστω δὲ συλὲν [μήτε] τὸν Λύττιον ἐν τᾶι τῶν Μαλλαίων μήτε τ[ὸν Μαλ]λαῖον ἐν τᾶι τῶν Λυττίων; see Maffi (1999, 16–17). The treaty lays out consequences for breaking this rule.
99. *I.Delphinion* 148 (*SvA* 645; *Syll.*[3] 588), ll. 47–50. The exclusion applies to τοῖς δὲ ἔχουσιν σῦλον (47), which probably means "those exercising a right of seizure." On the date of this inscription likely being 196 rather than the late 180s, see Wörrle (2004), *contra* Errington (1989).
100. *I.Priene B-M* 378; see Bravo (1980, 930–31). A second-century agreement between Troizen and Arsinoe (formerly Methana), neighbors on the Argolid peninsula, refers to compensations for seizures, which Lintott (2004, 348) takes to refer to private legal seizures. But use of the verb ῥυσιάζειν rather than συλᾶν, as well as references to the *polis* itself making the seizures, makes it more likely that these were communal acts performed in the name of the *polis* rather than vindications of private legal claims. The agreement is reflected in two different inscriptions, *IG* IV 752 and *IG* IV[2] 1, 76 + 77 (*SvA* 669). See the authoritative edition of both texts by Carusi (2005) and her discussion at pp. 115–16 supporting my interpretation here. Zimny (2021) argues that both public and private seizures are the subject of the agreement.
101. *IG* XII 5, 798, ll. 18–19: καὶ ἐμ πολέμωι εἰρήνην καὶ ἐν σύλωι ἀσυλίαν. See also *IG* XII 5, nos. 801, 802, and 820.
102. *IG* XII 5, 715. The right to have his cases heard first is expressed as δίκας προδίκους, l. 6. δίκη πρόδικος can also mean "arbitration in lieu of a public trial" (Rigsby 1996, 361, citing Ar. fr. 278, *PCG*), and ἀπρόδικος can mean "without preliminary arbitration" (Gauthier 1972, 329), but here and elsewhere "judged before other cases" seems to be the better translation, cf. *LSJ s.v.* πρόδικος. Chaniotis (1996, 139–40), discussing the noun πρόδικος, notes the scholarly controversy over its meaning and emphasizes that it had different meanings in different contexts. Similarly with the adjective.
103. *IG* XII 5, 481, ll. 22–24: ἐν σύλοις ἀσυλίαν. Klaffenbach's revised text, published in *IG* XII Supp., p.111 (1939), replaces the original *IG* publication and is still the most reliable edition. The date of this inscription has long been contested, the two options being ca. 274–270 and ca. 217, depending on whether the Arsinoe mentioned is the queen with Ptolemy Philadelphos or Ptolemy Philopator. Hiller von Gaertringen (*IG* XII Supp., p.111) argued for 217; Holleaux (1905, 320–21) for 274–70; Robert (1936, 185) and Bagnall (1976, 146) opt for the earlier date. Cf. *SEG* 59.928. Another inscription from Siphnos, recently published and dated by the editors to the mid-to-late third century, contains identical phrasing (except ἐς σύλοις instead of ἐν σύλοις); see Papazarkadas and Papadopoulou (2010–13), at ll. 12–13.
104. *IG* XII 4, 135, ll. 46–47: ἐν σύλοις ἀσυ[λία]ν κα[ὶ ἐμ πο]ḷέμωι εἰρήνην. This inscription is translated into English and commented on by C.V. Crowther (1999, 257–66). Bravo (1980, 735–40) discusses the cases mentioned in this paragraph, along with others.
105. *IG* IX 1[2] 169 (*Syll.*[3] 522), ll. 2–4: μηθένα ἄγειν Αἰτωλῶν μηδὲ τῶν ἐν Αἰτωλίαι πολιτευόντων τοὺς Κείους μηθαμόθεν ὁρμώμενον μήτε κατὰ γᾶν μήτε κατὰ θάλατταν μήτε ποτ' Ἀμφικτυονικὸν μήτε ποτ' ἄλλο ἔγκλημα μηθέν.

106. See Knäpper (2018, 136–46); Kvist (2003); Rigsby (1996, 280–325) provides a dossier of documents and discussion.
107. *I.Cret.* II 26.1 (Rigsby 1996, no. 141), ll. 19–26: εἰ δέ τινές κα τῶν ὁρμι⟨ο⟩μένων ἐξυβρί{σ}τας ἀδικήσωσίν τινα Τηΐων ἢ τῶν παροίκων ἢ κοινᾶι ἢ ἰδίαι παρὰ τὸ γραφὲν δόγμα περὶ τᾶς ἀσυλίας ὑπὸ τᾶς πόλεος τῶν Συβριτίων, ἐξέστω τῶι παραγενομένωι Τηΐων ἢ τῶν παροίκων τῶν ἐν Τέῳ ἐπιλαβέσθαι καὶ τῶν σωμάτων καὶ χρημάτων, εἴ τίς κα ἄγηι· οἱ δὲ κόσμοι οἱ τόκα ἀεὶ κοσμίοντες ἐπαναγκαζόντων ἀποδιδόμεν τοὺς ἔχοντας. See the similar decrees concerning Teos from, e.g., the Aitolians (*IG* IX 1^2 192; Rigsby 1996, no. 132); the Kydonians (*I. Cret* II 10 2; Rigsby 1996, no. 139); the Latonians (*I.Cret.* I 16 2; Rigsby 1996, no. 142).
108. See Rigsby (1996, 19). The most thorough treatments of territorial *asylia* are Knäpper (2018) and Rigsby (1996). See also Kató (2014).
109. On the *technitai*, see the overview by Aneziri (2020) and the comprehensive works of Aneziri (2003) and Le Guen (2001). We should not assume that all traveling musicians at this time were *technitai*. Nocita and Guizzi (2009, 136) state that the *aulos* player Perigenes of Alexandria, honored by Siphnos and mentioned above (*IG* XII 5, 481), was "certainly" a *technites*, but they do not explain their reasoning, and neither Aneziri nor Le Guen list him among their known *technitai*.
110. *CID* iv 12, which also exists in a copy at Athens, *IG* II^2 1132, ll. 65–94 (our versions of the decree date from its renewal in 130/29). The quoted words are from line 11. On the notion of *syla* in this decree, see Bravo (1980, 675–91, 806–07).
111. *Syll.*[3] 507, ll. 6–8: [ἀπο]δόμεν τοῖς τεχνίταις τάν [τε ἀσφάλεια]ν καὶ τὰν ἀσυλίαν τοῖς ἐπ' Ἰ[ωνίας καὶ Ἑλλησπό]ντου τοῖς ἐνγεγραμ(μ)ένοις, κα[θὼς καὶ τοῖ]ς εἰς Ἰθμὸν καὶ Νεμέαν συντ[ρευομένοις]. See Le Guen (2001, no. 38). Aitolian *asylia* for *technitai* is mentioned again in the Aitolian decree for Tean *asylia*, which was to be "just like what the law of the Aitolians regarding the Dionysian *technitai* commands," καθὼς καὶ τοῖς Διονυσιακοῖς τεχνίταις ὁ νόμος τῶν Αἰτωλῶν κελεύει, *IG* IX 1^2 192, ll. 15–16.
112. See *CID* iv 12, ll. 18–20: "unless the *technites* is indebted and in arrears to a city, or if he owes on a private liability," εἴ κα [μὴ χρέος ἔχων πόλει ἧι] ὑπόχρεως, καὶ ἐὰν ἰδίου ἧι συν[βολαίου ὑπόχρεος ὁ τεχν]ίτας. See Le Guen (2001, ii.70).
113. *IG* XII 9, 207; text, French translation, and commentary in Le Guen (2001, no. 1). It seems that music and theater performers were paid in advance, which was apparently uncommon for wage labor in the Greek world. See Slater (2010, 265–66), who quotes an inscription from Epidauros, dated ca. 100 CE (*IG* IV 1^2 99 III), stating that some *technitai* were found guilty of not performing *after* they were paid.
114. Our decree specifically mentions Thessalians, Aitolians, Boiotians, and Phokians as amphictyonic officials when the decree was enacted (*CID* IV 12, ll. 3–5); the Amphictyony also included, at this time, delegates from Delphi, from Aenis (west of Thermopylae), and from Dorian, Ionian (i.e., Athens and Euboia), and Lokrian cities. See the amphictyonic membership tables in Sánchez (2001, 524) and Lefèvre (1998, 284–85). It is unclear to what degree the Amphictyons saw themselves as creating a new legal protection for the *technitai* as opposed to attempting to codify a protection already recognized in customary law; the decree claims that this protection is recognized, or agreed, "by all the Greeks," ὑπὸ πάντων τῶν Ἑλλάνων (11); see commentary to *CID* IV 12, pp. 88–89.
115. See Knoepfler (2015, 167–70).
116. On the role of *technitai* in cult, see Aneziri (2003, 33–34, 65–66, 127–38); Le Guen (2001, ii.83–90). On monarchs' use of them, see Le Guen (2001, ii.133).
117. Arist. *Pol.* 3.9, 1280a14–16. On both the fear of violence and the desire for third-party judgment as encouraging people to pursue judicial resolution of disputes, see Ellickson (1994, 217 n.7, 253, 276).
118. On the transaction costs of litigation pushing people toward nonjudicial resolution of disputes, see Ellickson (1994, 280–83).
119. Protagoras, DK 80 B fr. 6b: τὸν ἥττω . . . λόγον κρείττω ποιεῖν, as quoted by Aristotle in the *Rhetoric* (1402a23), where he adds that people rightly abhorred Protagoras's claim to be able to do exactly this. Compare Gorgias's claim, as reported by Plato, that a skilled practitioner can use the persuasive power of rhetoric in the courtroom, council, or assembly to make the listeners effectively his slaves, Pl. *Gorg.* 452e. And in Aristophanes's *Clouds* Strepsiades goes to Socrates's "thinkery" to learn to win court cases whether he has the weaker argument or the stronger, the just or the unjust, Ar. *Nub.* 99, 112–18, 657. Many essays in a recent volume are concerned with "the abuse of law in the Athenian courts," Carey, Giannadaki, and Griffith-Williams (2018). The double edge of legal rhetoric is an enormous topic, which I plan to address in future work.

Chapter 7

1. Arist. *Pol.* 3, 1275a9–10; Harp. *s.v.* σύμβολα: τὰς συνθήκας, ἃς ἂν ἀλλήλαις αἱ πόλεις θέμεναι τάττωσιν τοῖς πολίταις ὥστε διδόναι καὶ λαμβάνειν τὰ δίκαια. The major work on *symbola* is Gauthier (1972), still authoritative (on that work and its influence, see Fröhlich 2023). Hitzig's paired studies (1907 and 1907b) continue to be helpful; cf. Lipsius (1905–15, iii.965–77) and Dindorf's condensed essay (1853, ii.428–30). Cataldi (1983) analyzes in detail the surviving fifth-century *symbola* agreements. Faraguna (2023) focuses on Athenian *symbola* of the fifth century, reevaluating and updating Gauthier's interpretation in particular. Gauthier (1972, 100, 201) seems to suggest that Athenian *symbola* in the fifth century were multilateral, with perhaps one agreement binding all the Athenian allies to Athens, in a sort of parallel agreement to the charter of the Delian League. But there is no particular evidence for this, as Faraguna (2023) points out. On the term *symbola* and its variations, see my discussion below. In keeping with scholarly convention, I generally use "*symbola*" (a neuter plural) to refer to all such agreements, even when a singular form might seem to make more sense grammatically.
2. On *symbola* as replacement for *syla*, see [Andoc.] 4.18, speaking specifically of Athens: "And in our *symbola* agreements with other *poleis* we agree that it's not permissible to lock up or tie up a free man," καὶ πρὸς μὲν τὰς ἄλλας πόλεις ἐν τοῖς συμβόλοις συντιθέμεθα μὴ ἐξεῖναι μήθ' εἶρξαι μήτε δῆσαι τὸν ἐλεύθερον. *Symbola* often did more than simply grant a private right to legal process. Some specified aspects of that process; some enumerated particular penalties; and some *symbola* covered situations in which a state could be a party. Examples are discussed below.
3. ὁ δὲ πολίτης οὐ τῷ οἰκεῖν που πολίτης ἐστίν, καὶ γὰρ μέτοικοι καὶ δοῦλοι κοινωνοῦσι τῆς οἰκήσεως, οὐδ' οἱ τῶν δικαίων μετέχοντες οὕτως ὥστε καὶ δίκην ὑπέχειν καὶ δικάζεσθαι, τοῦτο γὰρ ὑπάρχει καὶ τοῖς ἀπὸ συμβόλων κοινωνοῦσιν. πολλαχοῦ μὲν οὖν οὐδὲ τούτων τελέως οἱ μέτοικοι μετέχουσιν, ἀλλὰ νέμειν ἀνάγκη προστάτην, ὥστε ἀτελῶς πως μετέχουσι τῆς τοιαύτης κοινωνίας, ἀλλὰ καθάπερ καὶ παῖδας τοὺς μήπω δι' ἡλικίαν ἐγγεγραμμένους καὶ τοὺς γέροντας τοὺς ἀφειμένους φατέον εἶναι μέν πως πολίτας, οὐχ ἁπλῶς δὲ λίαν ἀλλὰ προστιθέντας τοὺς μὲν ἀτελεῖς τοὺς δὲ παρηκμακότας ἤ τι τοιοῦτον ἕτερον (οὐδὲν γὰρ διαφέρει· δῆλον γὰρ τὸ λεγόμενον).... πολίτης δ' ἁπλῶς οὐδενὶ τῶν ἄλλων ὁρίζεται μᾶλλον ἢ τῷ μετέχειν κρίσεως καὶ ἀρχῆς.
4. For close analysis and translation of the text, thorough bibliography, and a balanced approach, see Fröhlich (2016), with response by Sebillotte Cuchet (2017). Also Blok (2017, 13–21); Müller (2014); Schütrumpf (1991, 381–95); cf. Hansen (1999, 97–99). Filonik, Plastow, and Zelnick-Abramovitz (2023) offer a broad survey of current scholarship on citizenship in the Greek world; see also Brock (2015).
5. Blok (2005) did much to set the terms of this debate, which has been carried on by the works in the previous note. See also Faraguna (2024); Campa (2022).
6. Kamen (2013), adopting the terminology used by Moses Finley, refers to and thoroughly discusses a "spectrum" of statuses in Athens, from chattel slave at one end to full male citizen at the other. Kamen follows what we might call the "Aristotelian" lead in arguing that "even non-citizens and naturalized citizens were, to varying degrees, partial shareholders in the Athenian polis" (2013, 1). Müller (2014, 553–54) criticizes the Finley/Kamen notion of a "spectrum" of statuses, insisting that there were always three core, entirely distinct statuses in Greek cities: citizen, slave, and foreigner. But her objection seems focused against the idea of a *legal* continuum, and she agrees that "the situation was also more complex, for on top of these [legal] statuses were superposed privileges granted to foreigners," and claims that "the system of privileges, as invented by the Greeks, thus gave civic societies their social fluidity and allowed them to integrate the mobility of people without changing the hierarchy of legal statuses"; similarly D.M. Lewis (2025) and (2018b, 72–76), who insists there was no "fuzziness" in the juridical reality of slave vs. free status in particular, despite the complexity of Greek thinking about slavery and "slavishness." On the status of short-term visitors in Greek cities, see Roubineau (2012); on the variety of statuses in Rhodes, see Boyxen (2018, 25–95).
7. In fact, the statement here that metics needed a *prostates* to go to court is one of our pieces of evidence that *symbola* agreements typically provided a right to go to court on one's own behalf, without a *prostates*. On the disputed question of the role of the *prostates*, see W. Mack (2015, 74–75); Kamen (2013, 47–48).
8. Aristotle's discussion in the section immediately after the quotation above makes clear that he is talking here about the juror, δικαστής; see 1275a24–33. On the centrality to democratic

citizenship of participation in city governance by serving as a juror, both in Aristotle's thought and in Greek practice, see Walser (2012).

9. As we will see, after Aristotle's day it became more common, in some circumstances, to empanel jurors or judges from a third city to rule in cases brought under *symbola*.
10. See Arist. *Pol.* 1275a24–33. As we will see, some *symbola* seem to have included agreement on a certain set of substantive offenses and penalties that applied only between the two cities.
11. Gauthier (1972, 307) agrees with Aristotle's assessment: "L'affirmation est certainement vraie pour l'essentiel: les étrangers liés par *symbola* étaient, sur le plan judiciaire et sous certaines réserves, comparables à des concitoyens."
12. Forsdyke (2005, 210–22) argues that the fifth-century Athenian decree regarding the Chalkidians (*IG* I[3] 40) operated in a similar manner: "The Athenians, far from treating the Chalcidians as defeated rebels, were in fact extending to them certain privileges intimately tied to their own concept of citizenship" (221).
13. See Wolff (1954, 406–07).
14. *I.Delphinion* 136 (*RO* 93; *SvA* 408); text and discussion by Müller (2022), who argues for a date in the first half of the third century; see Saba (2020, 37–44), who is chary of calling it simply an *isopoliteia* agreement.
15. The distinctions between the three categories, in particular between categories (1) and (2), are not made entirely clear, but I believe my reading makes best sense of the text. See Müller's (2022, 336–39) similar but more detailed interpretation.
16. We see a temporary "foreigners' court," ξενικὸν δικαστήριον, set up at Tegea in 324/23 to adjudicate property claims of returning exiles, as part of Alexander the Great's wider "exiles decree," *IG* V 2, pp. vi–xxxvii (*RO* 101; *IPArk* 5), ll. 24, 27. Most commentators take the name to indicate that the judges were not Tegeans, presumably to ensure greater disinterest (see, e.g., the commentaries to *RO* 101 and to *IPArk* 5 [p. 65]). Alternatively, the court's name was politically motivated, since the litigants—exiled citizens—would not have been foreigners, *xenoi*, in the ordinary sense. Gauthier (1972, 359) suggests that *demotikon dikasterion* in the agreement between Miletos and Olbia indicates a citizen jury and implicitly contrasts a trial before the *demotikon dikasterion* with a hearing before a magistrate with no jury, which a foreigner without benefit of a *symbola* agreement might have typically received in both Olbia and Miletos. Müller (2022, 339) rightly calls this explanation excessively complicated.
17. Müller (2022, 344) notes that the inscribed text, which survives complete, begins abruptly without the prefatory language typical of city decrees, and she suggests that an official copy of the Milesian decree confirming the agreement with the Olbians was kept in the Miletos city archives.
18. See Hdt. 4.18.1; Strabo 7.3.17. Müller (2022, 350) proposes that the relationship between Milesians and Olbians reflected in this document was not continuous from the founding of Olbia but was reactivated at this time by means of a "memory" of the former relationship between the two cities. It is interesting, as noted by Saba (2020, 38) and by Rhodes and Osborne in their commentary (*RO* 93), that this agreement does not mention that Olbia was a Milesian colony or indicate this relationship played a role in the terms memorialized here.
19. Demosthenes's authorship of the speech was asserted by Callimachus but already perhaps doubted by Dionysius of Halicarnassus (Dilts 2002, v). Libanius, the fourth-century CE scholar whose prefaces to each speech are transmitted in the Demosthenic corpus, reports that others had proposed Hegesippus as the author ([Dem.] 7, *Hypothesis* 2). This judgment has largely been followed by modern scholars; see Harris (2018, 379); Schäfer (1886, ii.434–35).
20. [Dem.] 7.7–9. On the incident generally, see Griffith (1979, 511–13).
21. ἐπεὶ ὅτι γε συμβόλων οὐδὲν δέονται Μακεδόνες πρὸς Ἀθηναίους, ὁ παρεληλυθὼς ὑμῖν χρόνος τεκμήριον γενέσθω· οὔτε γὰρ Ἀμύντας ὁ πατὴρ ὁ Φιλίππου οὔθ' οἱ ἄλλοι βασιλεῖς οὐδεπώποτε σύμβολα ἐποιήσαντο πρὸς τὴν πόλιν τὴν ἡμετέραν. καίτοι γε πλείους γε ἦσαν αἱ ἐπιμειξίαι τότε πρὸς ἀλλήλους ἢ νῦν εἰσίν· ἐφ' ἡμῖν γὰρ ἦν ἡ Μακεδονία καὶ φόρους ἡμῖν ἔφερον, καὶ τοῖς ἐμπορίοις τότε μᾶλλον ἢ νῦν ἡμεῖς τε τοῖς ἐκεῖ κἀκεῖνοι τοῖς παρ' ἡμῖν ἐχρῶντο, καὶ ἐμπορικαὶ δίκαι οὐκ ἦσαν, ὥσπερ νῦν, ἀκριβεῖς, αἱ κατὰ μῆνα, ποιοῦσαι μηδὲν δεῖσθαι συμβόλων τοὺς τοσοῦτον ἀλλήλων ἀπέχοντας. ἀλλ' ὅμως οὐδενὸς τοιούτου ὄντος τότε, οὐκ ἐλυσιτέλει σύμβολα ποιησαμένους οὔτ' ἐκ Μακεδονίας πλεῖν Ἀθήναζε δίκας ληψομένοις, οὔθ' ἡμῖν εἰς Μακεδονίαν, ἀλλ' ἡμεῖς τε τοῖς ἐκεῖ νομίμοις ἐκεῖνοί τε τοῖς παρ' ἡμῖν τὰς δίκας ἐλάμβανον.
22. See A.R.W. Harrison (1960); cf. Gauthier (1972, 171); Ste. Croix (1961, 111).

23. Arist. *Rhet.* 1, 1360a12–17: ἔτι δὲ περὶ τροφῆς, πόση ἱκανὴ τῇ πόλει καὶ ποία ἡ αὐτοῦ τε γιγνομένη καὶ εἰσαγώγιμος, καὶ τίνων τ' ἐξαγωγῆς δέονται καὶ τίνων εἰσαγωγῆς, ἵνα πρὸς τούτους καὶ συνθῆκαι καὶ συμβολαὶ γίγνωνται· πρὸς δύο γὰρ διαφυλάττειν ἀναγκαῖον ἀνεγκλήτους τοὺς πολίτας, πρός τε τοὺς κρείττους καὶ πρὸς τοὺς εἰς ταῦτα χρησίμους. A number of editors (including Madvig and Kassel) print σύμβολα in this passage instead of συμβολαί, based on usage in other Aristotelian passages, although the latter is the only form attested in the manuscripts.
24. On the importance of property rights and contracts, see Leese (2021, 158); Harris (2016); Greif (2015, 71); Cooter and Schäfer (2012, 64–100); North (2005, 157–61). On the importance of court enforceability, see Cooter and Schäfer (2012, 90–96); Shirley (2005, 613–15); Greif (2000, 253–60). Xenophon, in his short work *Poroi* (3.3) discussing how Athenians could increase state revenues, suggests they should offer prizes to *emporion* officials for swift and fair dispute resolution, arguing that this would increase the number of merchants doing business in Athens. This represents a similar "law and economics" point of view.
25. On *symbola* as lowering transaction costs, see Woolmer (2016, 81–83). On economies of scale and government enforcement, see Cooter and Ulen (2016, 78); Greif (2005, 737); and in the Greek context, Ober (2015b, 58–68).
26. [Dem.] 7.5, 17, 45.
27. The reason Hegesippus claims to oppose a *symbola* agreement with Philip makes no sense, namely that it would amount to Athens putting a stamp of approval on Philip's aggression at Potidaia (7.10). We have no evidence—and Hegesippus himself offers none—that a *symbola* agreement would by its nature include such a clause, or that a draft agreement with such a clause had been proposed by Philip. The suggestion seems to be pure fearmongering; see Trevett (2011, 118 n.19).
28. In mid-fourth century Athens, *symbola* agreements were ratified by a jury, *dikasterion*, presided over by one of the *thesmothetai.* See *Ath. pol.* 59.6; [Dem.] 7.9 (*Hal.*); *IG* II^2 466, ll. 32–35; Gauthier (1972, 191 and n.46); Lipsius (1905–15, iii.968–9 and n.10).
29. When negotiations or ratification failed, however, the rhetoric of enmity that must have dominated in such circumstances likely decreased social identity formation. Hegesippus seems to have persuaded the Athenians not to enter into a *symbola* with the Macedonians, and active hostilities between them soon broke out again. On the expressive function of law, see Chapter 6, n. 41 and accompanying text.
30. On the connection between trust, contracts, and economic productivity in fifth- and fourth-century Athens, see Faraguna (2012); Anonymous Iamblichi, DK 89 fr. 7.1–4 (= Laks–Most *Anon. Iambl.* 7.1–4).
31. Lanni (2016, 120); see generally her chapters 4 and 5.
32. The Homeric epics contain examples of both forms of *xenia.* For the former, see *Od.* 14.56–58 (Eumaeus addressing Odysseus in disguise); for the latter, see *Il.* 6.119–236, esp. 215–21 (familial *xenia* between Diomedes and Glaukos, discussed below). On *xenia,* see Hiltbrunner (2005); Herman (1987); Gauthier (1972, 18–24). On the treatment of *xenia* in Homer and Herodotus, see Basile (2016); in Athenian tragedy, Verheij (2016); Roth (1993). My discussion here concerns the wider phenomenon of ξενία, the formal recognition of someone as a foreigner, not the narrower practice of providing ξένια, food and hospitality, to official delegates to a city, which is attested epigraphically starting in the fifth century. On the latter, see Cinalli (2015).
33. Herman (1987, 10–11). On the continuities between *xenia* and both kinship and friendship, see Herman (1987, 16–31).
34. See Beltrán Lloris et al. (2020).
35. Thuc. 2.13.1; Plut. *Per.* 33.3 (Thucydides may be Plutarch's source here, Stadter 1989, 306). On the potential conflict between duties to one's *xenos* and to one's community, see Herman (1987, 1–9).
36. Herman (1987, 10).
37. On naming practices, see Herman (1987, 19–21). One example is Alcibiades of Athens, son of Kleinias, named after Kleinias's *xenos* Alcibiades of Sparta, son of Endios. On *xenia* as an elite practice, see Basile (2016, 230–33); Herman (1987, 34). On *xenia* ritual, see Herman (1987, 59); cf. Basile (2016, 230, 238, 245).

38. On the role of competitive elites in the early *polis*, see Ma (2024, 128–39). On the connections between *xenia* and proxeny, see Gauthier (1972, 17–28); Müri (1931, 10–12). The earliest known epigraphical use of the term *proxenos*, perhaps from the seventh century, is on the cenotaph of Menekrates of Oianthea, *proxenos* to the Corcyreans; *IG* IX 1, 867 (*Nomima* i 34; *ML* 4) (Jeffery 1990, 234 proposes a late seventh-century date; *Nomima* suggests about 550). Mataranga (1994) argues unpersuasively that *proxenos* in this inscription is a term for a local official, and Menekrates merely born in Oianthea; see Zelnick-Abramovitz (2004, 96). A stone seat at Olympia bears an inscription, dated to the first half of the sixth century, honoring a Spartan *proxenos* named Gorgos: Γόργος / Λακεδαιμόνιο/ς πρόξενος / ϝαλείον, *I.Olympia Suppl.* 49. Another seat, dedicated to the Spartan Euwanios, is dated to the fifth century: Εὐϝανίου ⁝ Λακεδαιμονίου ⁝ προξένου, *I.Olympia Suppl.* 50.
39. W. Mack (2015, 24). The parallelism but distinction between *xenos* and *proxenos* was obvious to Greeks and is explained in the first- or second-century CE lexicon of synonyms attributed to a certain Ammonius (*Diff.*, *s.v.* πρόξενος): "*Proxenos* and *idioxenos* and *doruxenos* are different. A *proxenos* belongs to a *polis* and *ethnos*, as in Thucydides. A *xenos* is one person acting as *xenos* to one person. And *idioxenos* is the same thing"; πρόξενος καὶ ἰδιόξενος καὶ δορύξενος διαφέρει. πρόξενος πόλεως καὶ ἔθνους, ὡς παρὰ Θουκυδίδῃ. ξένος δ᾽ ὁ εἷς ἑνός· ὁ δ᾽ αὐτὸς καὶ ἰδιόξενος; for earlier passages implying such a parallelism, see Gschnitzer, *RE* Suppl. XIII (1973), col. 632. On the continuities between *xenia* and proxeny, see Herman (1987, 130–42); Gschnitzer, cols. 632, 644–46; Gauthier (1972, 24–25).
40. *Il.* 6.232–33: ὣς ἄρα φωνήσαντε καθ᾽ ἵππων ἀΐξαντε / χεῖράς τ᾽ ἀλλήλων λαβέτην καὶ πιστώσαντο.
41. W. Mack (2015, 35–36). On the affective aspects of *xenia*, see Herman (1987, 61).
42. On the main services provided by *proxenoi*, see W. Mack (2015, 65–76); Gschnitzer, *RE* Suppl. XIII (1973), cols. 721–29. On legal services, see W. Mack (2015, 74–75); Gschnitzer, cols. 726–27. We have little evidence for the concrete ways in which a *proxenos* might help a visitor with legal problems, but Mack argues that a central service would have been to formally attest to the visitor's identity.
43. For discussions of *symbolon* in a wider sense than "judicial treaty," see Finglass (2023); Struck (2004, 79–82); Gauthier (1972, 65–85); Müri (1931, 2–15).
44. See Faraguna (2023); Gauthier (1972, 62–65); Müri (1931, 12–17).
45. *Hymn. Hom. Merc.* 526–30: ἐκ δὲ τέλειον / σύμβολον ἀθάνατον ποιήσομαι ἠδ᾽ ἅμα πάντως / πιστὸν ἐμῷ θυμῷ καὶ τίμιον· αὐτὰρ ἔπειτα / ὄλβου καὶ πλούτου δώσω περικαλλέα ῥάβδον / χρυσείην τριπέτηλον. I follow the text of Vergados (2011), which differs from the transmitted text accepted by O. Thomas (2020) but not in a way to change the interpretation of *symbolon* here (contra O. Thomas 2020, 437). On the date of composition, see O. Thomas (2020, 1–23) (probably fifth century); Vergados (2011, 130) (probably sixth century).
46. Thgn. 1150: αἰσχρὰ κακοῖς ἔργοις σύμβολα θηκάμενοι.
47. For the *Hymn to Hermes*: O. Thomas (2020), "covenant"; Vergados (2011), "contract"; West (2003), "pact"; M. Feyel (1946), "convention, accord." In the Theognis passage, Hudson-Williams (1910, 241) takes *symbola* to mean "compacts"; Carrière (1975, 121) translates it as "*marché*" (i.e., "deal" or "contract") and also suggests (191) that these lines may date to the late fifth or early fourth century.
48. See *Hymn. Hom. Merc.* 475–77: "But since your heart is set on lyre-playing, sing and play and be festive, accepting it from me; and you, my friend, grant me glory," ἀλλ᾽ ἐπεὶ οὖν τοι θυμὸς ἐπιθύει κιθαρίζειν, / μέλπεο καὶ κιθάριζε καὶ ἀγλαΐας ἀλέγυνε / δέγμενος ἐξ ἐμέθεν· σὺ δέ μοι, φίλε, κῦδος ὄπαζε. Vergados (2011, *ad loc.*) notes that φίλε here "is the first indication of friendship between Hermes and Apollo." Struck (2004, 79) and Gauthier (1972, 69–70) make suggestions similar to mine. O. Thomas (2020, 437) considers the translation "token of agreement" but prefers "covenant."
49. Hdt. 6.86.α.5: σύ δή μοι καὶ τὰ χρήματα δέξαι καὶ τάδε τὰ σύμβολα σῷζε λαβών· ὃς δ᾽ ἂν ἔχων ταῦτα ἀπαιτέῃ, τούτωι ἀποδοῦναι.
50. The Milesian's sons did eventually come, showed the *symbola* to Glaukos, and asked for the money: ἀποδεικνύντες τὰ σύμβολα ἀπαίτεον τὰ χρήματα, 6.86.β.1. Herodotus was writing in the late fifth century, but his use here of the word *symbola* probably carries over from an earlier version of the story of Glaukos and the Milesian, reflecting a sixth-century use. On this passage, see also Finglass (2023, 26–27).
51. Eur. *Med.* 610--13: ἀλλ᾽, εἴ τι βούληι παισὶν ἢ σαυτῆι φυγῆς / προσωφέλημα χρημάτων ἐμῶν λαβεῖν, / λέγ᾽· ὡς ἕτοιμος ἀφθόνωι δοῦναι χερὶ / ξένοις τε πέμπειν σύμβολ᾽, οἳ δράσουσί σ᾽ εὖ.

52. Schwartz (1887–91, *ad Med.* 613): σύμβολα: οἱ ἐπιξενούμενοί τισιν ἀστράγαλον κατατέμνοντες θάτερον μὲν αὐτοὶ κατεῖχον μέρος, θάτερον δὲ κατελίμπανον τοῖς ὑποδεξαμένοις, ἵνα, εἰ δέοι πάλιν αὐτοὺς ἢ τοὺς ἐκείνων ἐπιξενοῦσθαι πρὸς ἀλλήλους, ἐπαγόμενοι τὸ ἡμιαστραγάλιον ἀνανεοῖντο τὴν ξενίαν. Εὔβουλος Ξούθῳ· τί ποτ' ἐστὶν ἅπαντα διαπεπρισμένα ἡμίσε' ἀκριβῶς ὡσπερεὶ τὰ σύμβολα; The Euboulos passage is fr. 70, Kassel–Austin, *PCG*. Finglass (2023, 27–31), discussed below, provides further evidence for *symbola* as "divided tokens."
53. For discussion of the literary and, especially, archaeological evidence, see Beltrán Lloris et al. (2020). One example, from Lilybaeum in western Sicily and dating to the second or first century, memorializes *xenia* between a Greek and a Carthaginian, as the Greek text states: "Imulch Inibalos Chloros, son of Imilchon, entered into *xenia* with Lyson son of Diognetos and their descendants," Ἰμύλχ Ἰμ(λ)χωνος / Ἰνίβαλος Χλωρὸς ξενίαν / ἐποήσατο πρὸς Λύσων / Διογνήτου καὶ τῶν ἐγγόνων, *IG* XIV 279; see Beltrán Lloris et al. (2020, 492).
54. *CIL* I[2] 3465: *Tessera hospitalis cum P. Turullio P. f. Mai(cia)*, dated to the late second or early first century.
55. Plaut. *Poen.* 1047–48: *tesseram conferre si vis hospitalem, eccam attuli.*
56. Plaut. *Bacch.* 261–68. See Finglass (2023, 37–38). On the Greek original of the *Poenulus*, see de Melo (2012, 3).
57. See Müri (1931, 13–14), comparing similar "abstracted concrete" plurals such as σπονδαί, ὅρκια, ὅρκοι, δεξιαί; Gauthier (1972, 65–66); cf. Gkikaki (2023b, 4–5).
58. Struck (2004, 79–80) cites further examples. The seal, *sphragis*, was another common means of guaranteeing the integrity of documents in particular. On the public use of seals in Athens, and comparison with the use of *symbola*, see Pébarthe (2006, 297–300).
59. *IG* II[2] 141 (*RO* 21; *AIUK* 11, 1), ll. 18–25: ποιησάσθω δὲ καὶ σύμβολα ἡ βολὴ πρὸς τὸν βασιλέα τὸν Σιδωνίων, ὅπως ἂν ὁ δῆμος ὁ Ἀθηναίων εἰδῆι ἐάν τι πέμπηι ὁ Σιδωνίων βασιλεὺς δεόμενος τῆς πόλεως, καὶ ὁ βασιλεὺς ὁ Σιδωνίων εἰδῆι ὅταμ πέμπηι τινὰ ὡς αὐτὸν ὁ δῆμος ὁ Ἀθηναίων. On the dating, see de Lisle (2020, 13–14). It has been suggested that use of physical *symbola* of this sort was largely defunct by the fourth century; de Lisle (2020, 17); Gauthier (1972, 85–86).
60. Ar. *Av.* 1214–15: οὐδὲ σύμβολον ἐπέβαλεν ὀρνίθαρχος οὐδείς σοι παρών;
61. Likely examples of Athenian military *symbola* tokens have been found; they are published (with images) and discussed by Kroll and Mitchel (1980). On *symbolon* as a password rather than a physical token, see Eur. *Rhes.* 573. "*Symbolon*" is used twice to refer to the signal fire in Aeschylus's *Agamemnon*, at ll. 8 and 316; this may be a metaphor meaning something like "military message"; see Struck (2004, 80–81 n.12). Other Athenian *symbola* tokens, with an apparently civilian use and dating to the fifth century, have been found in the Athenian *agora*. They are about three centimeters on a side, one edge cut into a saw-tooth pattern, with tribe and deme names painted on. They may have been used to determine by lot which demes would be charged with filling certain minor magistracies in a particular year. For recent full discussion (with images) and theories about their use, see Kierstead (2023). See also Finglass (2023, 29–35). As of 2023, a few examples were on long-term display in the Agora Museum in Athens. For recent discussions of our evidence of the use of many different kinds of physical tokens in Athens (and beyond), see the essays in Gkikaki (2023).
62. The *Symposium* is set in 416 but was likely composed sometime after 390.
63. Pl. *Symp.* 191d3–5: ἕκαστος οὖν ἡμῶν ἐστιν ἀνθρώπου σύμβολον, ἅτε τετμημένος ὥσπερ αἱ ψῆτται, ἐξ ἑνὸς δύο· ζητεῖ δὴ ἀεὶ τὸ αὑτοῦ ἕκαστος σύμβολον.
64. As Finglass (2023, 27–29) notes, Aristotle uses a similar metaphor for friendship in the *Eudemian Ethics*, 7, 1239b23–32; and elsewhere (*Gen. an.* 722b8–17) quotes Empedocles's comparison of the mother's and father's contributions to a child's nature as being each like a *symbolon*, because "the whole [child] comes from neither one" (ὅλον δ' ἀπ οὐδετέρου ἀπιέναι, Empedocles D171 Laks–Most); *viz.* reproduction requires putting together the contributions from both parents.
65. χαρακτῆρ', 572; τεκμήριον, 575; συμβόλοισι, 577. The *Electra* was produced probably between 427 and 417.
66. Eur. *Ion* 1385–86: "I'm fighting against the wish of the god who saved *symbola* of my mother for me," τοῦ θεοῦ προθυμίᾳ πολεμῶ, τὰ μητρὸς σύμβολ' ὅς σέσωκέ μοι. The use of *symbola* in Euboulos's play *Xouthos*, mentioned in the scholion to Euripides I quote above, may also refer to the character Ion, since Xouthos was Ion's father. The comic poet Euboulos may be parodying Euripides's *Ion*, which was produced probably between 412 and 406.

67. We have nothing aside from stylistic criteria for dating the *Oedipus Tyrannus* within Sophocles's long career. Using such criteria, Finglass (2018, 1–3) argues that sometime in the wide window from 440 to 420 is very likely.
68. Soph. *OT* 219–23:
    ἁγὼ ξένος μὲν τοῦ λόγου τοῦδ' ἐξερῶ,
    ξένος δὲ τοῦ πραχθέντος· οὐ γὰρ ἂν μακρὰν
    ἴχνευον αὐτός, μὴ οὐκ ἔχων τι σύμβολον.
    νῦν δ', ὕστερος γὰρ ἀστὸς εἰς ἀστοὺς τελῶ,
    ὑμῖν προφωνῶ πᾶσι Καδμείοις τάδε.
69. On σύμβολον as "connection," see Finglass (2018, 240–41). I agree with Finglass that "connection" is better than "clue," a common translation here. See his further discussion, Finglass (2023, 39–41).
70. Soph. *Phil.* 403–05: ἔχοντες, ὡς ἔοικε, σύμβολον σαφὲς λύπης πρὸς ἡμᾶς, ὦ ξένοι, πεπλεύκατε, καί μοι προσᾴδεθ'.
71. The emotional resonances seem to have survived for centuries. Diogenes Laertius, writing perhaps in the third century CE, calls the maxims of Pythagoras his *symbola* and describes them as entrées into the wise man's circle. Diog. Laert. 8.16: "If Pythagoras learned someone made use of his *symbola* he would immediately associate with him and make him a friend"; εἴ τινα πύθοιτο τῶν συμβόλων αὐτοῦ κεκοινωνηκότα, εὐθύς τε προσηταιρίζετο καὶ φίλον κατεσκεύαζεν; see Connor (2021, 27–33).
72. See Müri (1931, 17); Gauthier (1972, 201–05), summarizing his longer discussion at 173–201; cf. *BE* 1989, no. 380, reiterating this basic picture; Cataldi (1983, xx–xxiii).
73. *IG* I^3 6 (*I.Eleusis* 19), regulations concerning the Eleusinian Mysteries, ca. 470–60 (χσυ⟨μ⟩βολῶν); *IG* I^3 10 (*OR* 120), Athenians and Phaselites, 420s (ξυμβολῶν; ξυμβολὰς); *IG* I^3 66, Athenian decree concerning Mytilene, 427 or 412 (χσυ[μβο]λὰς); *IG* I^3 113, agreement between the Athenians and Evagoras of Cyprus, ca. 410 ([χ]σ̣υμβολα[. . .]); *IG* I^3 118 (*OR* 185), Athenian decree concerning Selymbria, 408/07 (χσυμβολõν); *IG* I^3 127, Athenian decrees concerning Samos, 405–03 (τὰς συμβολὰς).
74. Thuc. 1.77.1 uses an adjectivalized form with the expression ξυμβολαίαι δίκαι; Antiph. 5.78 has the gender-ambiguous ἀπὸ συμβολῶν; [Andoc.] 4.18 has the neuter τοῖς συμβόλοις, but it is unclear whether this speech was composed in the fifth or fourth century. The manuscripts of Aristotle's *Rhetoric* have συμβολαί in one passage (1.1360a15).
75. The Athenian decree for the Phaselites, *IG* I^3 10 (which I discuss in detail in the next chapter), is problematic for both theories. As Faraguna (2023) observes, its language suggests that the *symbola* between Athenians and Phaselites covered more than mercantile disputes, which does not fit with Gauthier's theory (similarly, as Faraguna notes, with the Selymbria decree, *IG* I^3 118). And several scholars have recently downdated it from the 450s to the 420s, which does not fit well with Cataldi's theory. On the redating, see James (2023, 133 and n. 1). As we will see, the evidence also does not support Gauthier's hypothesis that Athenian *symbola* shifted from a focus on distant cities to those nearer to Athens.
76. Faraguna (2023) reaches a similar conclusion.
77. The total number of inscribed treaties of any sort dated before 500 that survive today can be counted on one hand.
78. Hdt. 6.42.1: Ἀρταφέρνης ὁ Σαρδίων ὕπαρχος μεταπεμψάμενος ἀγγέλους ἐκ τῶν πολίων συνθήκας σφίσι αὐτοῖσι τοὺς Ἴωνας ἠνάγκασε ποιέεσθαι, ἵνα δωσίδικοι εἶεν καὶ μὴ ἀλλήλους φέροιέν τε καὶ ἄγοιεν. L. Scott (2005, 191–92 and Appendix 11, esp. 534–37) discusses this passage thoroughly, providing an analysis with which I largely agree.
79. See L. Scott (2005, 534); Bravo (1980, 802); Gauthier (1972, 212). On piracy, see my discussion in Chapter 9.
80. This is one of only two appearances of the adjective δωσίδικος in surviving sources. The other is Polyb. 4.4.3, also in the context of interstate seizures (ca. 222 the Messenians captured the Aitolian commander Dorimachos and refused to release him unless he handed over Aitolians accused of murder to be tried in court: ἐὰν μὴ . . . περὶ δὲ τῶν τεθνεώτων δωσιδίκους παράσχῃ τοὺς ἠδικηκότας.
81. See Ehrhardt (2017, 262); Cataldi (1983, 4–7 and nn.42–43); Piccirilli (1973, no. 11); Gauthier (1972, 379–80), all citing earlier literature; Tod (1913, 65–66). Briant (2002, 494–95) takes Artaphernes to have been mainly concerned with the resolution of border disputes between cities. But he offers no evidence of Ionian border disputes from this time.
82. *RO* 16 (*I.Nordkarien*, Myūs T23; *Milet* I.ii.9; *Syll.*^{3} 134); see also the text, German translation, and discussion by Ehrhardt (2017).

83. O. Murray (1988, 489). Both Thucydides (1.115) and Plutarch (*Per.* 25) tell us that the Samians and Milesians went to war in about 441 and that only after the Samians had won, or were close to doing so, the Athenians intervened on behalf of the Milesians. In response, the Athenians either took immediate military action against the Samians (Thuc. 1.115.3) or first told them to arbitrate the case before Athenians (Plut. *Per.* 25.1). Even on Plutarch's account the parties refused to arbitrate (οὐκ ἐπείθοντο), and the Athenians then moved against the Samians. Neither author suggests the Samians and Milesians violated an arbitration treaty. Thucydides does not mention arbitration, and the proposed arbitration that Plutarch describes does not resemble what later took place between the Milesians and Myusians: the latter was judged by perhaps fifty judges from other Ionian cities and only ratified by Persian authority. See Cataldi (1983, 4–7). As L. Scott notes (2005, 536), "the 390 dispute is a false friend." Nudell (2016) argues that the conflict was not "about" Priene but merely fought near Priene.
84. Piccirilli (1973, nos. 1–10) lists ten known likely interstate arbitrations between Greeks before 500.
85. Thuc. 1.78.4; 1.85.2; 1.140.2; 1.144.2; 7.18.2–3. On the arbitration (or "adjudication") clause of the thirty years' peace, see my discussion in Chapter 1. On what the actual terms of this clause might have been, see Ste. Croix (1972, 259). On later treaties with arbitration clauses, see Magnetto (2016, 1, 4–5); Ager (1996, 7–8).
86. On conflict as a formative element in Ionian identity, see Mac Sweeney (2013, 187) and below. On intra-Ionian peace at the turn of the fifth century, see L. Scott (2005, 534).
87. Artaphernes may have assumed that judicial resolution was more economically efficient overall than self-help. J.A.S. Evans (1976, 346–47) argues that Artaphernes's assessment of tribute was probably not based solely on quantity of land but also its productivity.
88. Mac Sweeney (2013, 157–97); Crielaard (2009); Kowalzig (2005, 46–56). On the "Ionian League" up to the time of Herodotus, see also Roebuck (1955), emphasizing (at p. 29) that the Ionian *koinon* was primarily a religious organization, used for military and political organization only under force of circumstances; cf. Tausend's (1992, 90–95) concurring analysis.
89. On the economic activity and wealth of Ionians in the sixth century, see Loy (2023, 267–68); Mac Sweeney (2013, 26–28); Greaves (2010, 69–94), emphasizing the importance of agriculture and local trade via cabotage; Georges (2000, 2–10), emphasizing the importance of coinage and Ionian mercenaries in Persian armies. On economic factors in Ionian relations, see Lateiner (1982, 135–37).
90. Mac Sweeney (2013, 187); cf. 196: "Being Ionian . . . meant squabbling with other Ionians" (but Tausend 1992, 91–92 interprets Vitruvius 4.1.4 (who calls Melie "Melite") as implying that the Panionion preexisted this conflict). Loy (2023, 268); cf. Crielaard (2009, 59): "The East Ionian cities found friends and foes first and foremost among their own kind."
91. Briant (2017, 43–73; 2002, 70–76).
92. *IG* IX 1^2 717; cf. Zunino's (2017) recent edition with extensive bibliography. The complete Greek text as it appears in *IG* is:

[side A:]
⁝ τὸν ξένον μὲ hάγεν ⁝ ἐ(τ) τᾶς Χαλεΐδος ⁝ τὸν Οἰανθέα μ-
εδὲ τὸν Χαλειέα ⁝ ἐ(τ) τᾶς Οἰανθίδος ⁝ μεδὲ χρέματα. αἴ τι(ς) συ-
λõι ⁝ τὸν δὲ συλõντα ἀνάτο(ς) συλε̃ν. τὰ ξενικὰ ἐ(θ) θαλάσας hάγεν ⁝
ἄσυλον ⁝ πλὰν ἐ(λ) λιμένος ⁝ τõ κατὰ πόλιν ⁝ αἴ κ' ἀδίκο(ς) συλõι ⁝ τέ-
τορες δραχμαί ⁝ αἰ δὲ πλέον δέκ' ἀμαρᾶν ἔχοι τὸ σῦλον, hε-
μιόλιον ὀφλέτο ⟨h⟩ότι συλάσαι ⁝ αἰ μεταϝοικέοι πλέον μενὸς ἒ
ὁ Χαλειεὺς ἐν Οἰανθέαι ἒ Οἰανθεὺς ἐν Χαλειõι, τᾶι ἐπιδαμίαι δίκαι χ-
ρέστο ⁝ τὸν πρόξενον : αἰ ψευδέα προξενέοι· διπλ-
είοι θοιέστο.

[side B:]
αἴ κ' ἀνδιχάζοντι ⁝ τοὶ ξενοδίκαι : ἐπομότας ⁝ hελέσ-
το ⁝ ὁ ξένος : ὀπάγον : τὰν δίκαν : ἐχθὸς προξένο
καὶ ϝιδίο ξένο : ἀριστίνδαν : ἐπὶ μὲν ταῖς μναια-
ίαις : καὶ πλέον : πέντε καὶ δέκ' ἄνδρας : ἐπὶ ταῖς
μειόνοις : ἐννέ' ἄνδρας : αἴ κ' ὁ ϝασστὸς ποὶ τὸν ϝ-
αστὸν δικάζεται κὰ(τ) τᾶς συνβολᾶς· δαμιοργὸς
hελέσται : τὸς hορκομότας ἀριστίνδαν τὰν πε-
ντορκίαν ὀμόσαντας : τὸς hορκομότας τὸν αὐτὸ-
ν hόρκον ὀμνύεν : πλεθὺν δὲ νικε̃ν.

93. To review the many debates, see the sources cited in Chapter 6, n. 25.
94. E.g., Zunino (2017, 134–35); Maffi (1983, 208) (the second part is a supplement); Gauthier (1972, 286–87); Klaffenbach (commentary to *IG* IX 1^2 717 [1968]); Hitzig (1907, 13); Dareste (1889, 308).
95. This is Gauthier's view (1972, 243). On identification of the find-spot—modern Galaxidi—as Chaleion, see Lerat (1952, i.198–209).
96. Hitzig (1907, 13) also sees the entire text as part of a treaty between the two cities. It is true that many of the provisions in Part 2 seem more appropriate to domestic regulations of a single city than to an international pact. But this is also true of lines 6 to 7, which everyone agrees are part of the joint agreement. In these lines, two cities are agreeing to mutual rules about how they will treat foreign residents from the other city, rules that were typically a purely domestic legal matter. If the two cities are already agreeing to jointly regulate the ground rules for citizens of each city to become resident metics in the other, it is no *more* surprising for them to jointly regulate specific details of legal procedures involving those metics. And nothing else here signals that the text is transitioning from international agreement to domestic regulation. The incompleteness of the surviving text was already proposed by Oikonomides (1850, 50), who thought it was part of a longer agreement or one in a series of related agreements between the Oiantheans and Chaleians. Maffi (1983, 208) suggests the regulations here simply presuppose well-known procedural rules. That may be so even if our text is also incomplete. The text of oaths is often inscribed with the regulations requiring them to be sworn, e.g., Koerner, *Gesetzestexte* 46 (Delphi), *ML* 32 (Halicarnassus), and often in treaties; the text of oaths to be sworn is also sometimes omitted, e.g., *IG* IX 1^2 718 (Opous), *IG* XII 8, 264 (Thasos).
97. The confusion arises in part because of the fines provided for in lines 4 to 6. They clearly apply only "if someone seizes illegally," αἴ κ' ἀδίκο(ς) συλõι. And the judicial procedures described later could, on a strict grammatical reading, apply only to determining whether someone had seized illegally and therefore now owed a fine for that illegal act. For an interpretation along these lines, see Gauthier (1972, 243).
98. See, e.g., Gauthier (1972, 242–43, 291).
99. On the uncertain meaning of ἐπιδαμίαι δίκαι, see Zelnick-Abramowitz (2004, 95 and n.9). On the *proxenos*'s likely role, see Zunino (2017, 135).
100. The notion of juror selection in light of likely bias is strikingly relevant to the modern US trial system, in which jury selection is considered a crucial aspect of trying a case and can be highly contested. Maffi (1983, 227) argues that the rule here as I interpret it would encourage excessive bias in the other direction, permitting the foreign litigant, in consultation with friends in the city that is the venue for the trial, to choose local jurors hostile to his opponent. His alternative interpretation is that the *epomotai* of line 10 are "oath-helpers" (*Eideshelfer*), by which he seems to mean, following Meister (1908, 560), people who vouch for the litigant's character, thereby making the litigant's own oath at trial carry more weight. But Maffi does not adequately explain why the foreign litigant is not permitted to select a *proxenos* or *idioxenos* for this role of oath-helper; and on his theory there could be the problem that, while there was likely a rich social network between the two cities (a point I insist on, in fact) some foreigners still might not be able to find enough reliable oath helpers in a city not his own.
101. That judges be selected from the best men, ἀριστίνδην, also seems to have been required by Draco's seventh-century homicide law in Athens, see *IG* I^3 104, l. 19.
102. This perhaps somewhat strained interpretation is nevertheless more satisfactory than the even more strained alternative, under which the agreement is providing for two citizens of the same city to be suing each other under a *symbola* agreement. Such suits would have been covered entirely by domestic law. Gauthier (1972, 290–91) and Dareste (1889, 308) argue, on the premise that this second part is a law of Chaleion, that the provision covers cases in which a Chaleian would bring suit against another Chaleian on behalf of an Oianthean who was unable, for some practical reason, to sue on his own behalf. This scenario strikes me as too uncommon to require special treatment, and unlikely to have been given special treatment in any case. Eduard Meyer (1892, 315) argues that this *symbola* agreement was an essentially commercial law agreement (*Recht der Handelsverträge*), granting simplified and expedited procedures that would have been superior even to the domestic procedures of either city, and therefore presumably similar to the maritime courts of fourth-century Athens. Therefore, people would want to use the *symbola* procedures even for domestic disputes that fell within the *symbola*'s commercial law purview. But that sort of domestic law provision

would be purely a matter of domestic law, not of a treaty. Since I see the entire document here as containing the text of a treaty, I disagree with Meyer.

103. The *damiourgia* (*demiourgia* in Attic dialect) seems at some times and places to have been a collegiate magistracy (see L.G.H. Hall 1982, 821), and the plural here could refer to a group of *damiourgoi* from only one city. *Damiourgos* may have been a common early office in the cities of western Lokris: it is referred to (also in the plural) in the so-called Pappadakis Bronze, a legal inscription of the late sixth century from an unknown *polis* in western Lokris, *IG* IX 1^2 609 (*Nomima* i 44; *ML* 13); and in an inscription from Lokrian Naupaktos (*ML* 13). It is also known from sixth-century Argos (*Nomima* i 87, 88, 101) and fifth-century Elis (*Nomima* i 23); and later from Molossia (*I.Molossie* 30, ca. 370 BCE [or later: see E.A. Meyer 2013, 47–48]).

Chapter 8

1. Ste. Croix (1954, 1). For a recent summary and reconsideration of the debate, see Canevaro and Lewis (2024); also Lazar (2024).
2. See, in this vein, Low (2013) and (2005); Meiggs (1972, 228–33); Ste. Croix (1961) and (1961b). Papazarkadas (2014, 234) emphasizes that Athenian imperialism was a "flexible phenomenon"; Forsdyke (2005, 206) describes how "the Athenians engaged in a policy of moderation as well as brute force in their relations with other Greeks." Kallet (2009) discusses more general patterns of modern scholarly evaluations of the Athenian empire, warning against simple categories such as "pro-" and "anti-" Athenian (2009, 53).
3. [Xen.] *Ath. pol.* 1.16: ὅτι τοὺς συμμάχους ἀναγκάζουσι πλεῖν ἐπὶ δίκας Ἀθήναζε. On the date of the *Athenaion Politeia* now attributed to the "Old Oligarch" but transmitted with Xenophon's works, see Marr and Rhodes (2008, 3–6).
4. Antiph. 5.47: ὃ οὐδὲ πόλει ἔξεστιν ἄνευ Ἀθηναίων οὐδένα θανάτῳ ζημιῶσαι.
5. The Erythrai decrees: *IG* I^3 14, 15a, 16 (*OR* 121), dating probably to the 450s or 430s (see Moroo 2014); the Chalkis decree: *IG* I^3 40 (*OR* 131), dating probably to the 440s or 420s (see Lambert 2017, 28–31; Papazarkadas 2009, 73–74); Kleinias's decree: *IG* I^3 34 (*OR* 154), dating probably to the 420s; the standards decree: *IG* I^3 1453 (*OR* 155), dating probably to the 420s or 410s (see Psoma 2024; Blok 2022, 126; Hatzopoulos 2013–14, 251–59; Kroll 2009, 201–02). Regarding evidence that there were multiple standards decrees, see Hatzopoulos (2013–14, 259–64). For discussion of many aspects of the standards decree (or decrees), see Psoma (2024); Figueira (2006) and (1998, 319–423).
6. See *IG* I^3 14 (*SvA* 134), ll. 29–35; *IG* I^3 15a, ll. 27–30; *IG* I^3 16, l. 17; and Forsdyke (2005, 209).
7. *IG* I^3 40 (*SvA* 155), ll. 70–76. Forsdyke (2005, 210–222) argues the Chalkis decree is less about punishing the Chalkidians, and more about reconciliation and projecting an image of just empire, than has typically been acknowledged by scholars.
8. *IG* I^3 1453, sections 2–3.
9. Most scholars believe the speech is not by Andocides. The debate is summarized by Gribble (1997, 367–73). Noting that the speech "excels in its knowledge of constitutional detail, and of persons" (382), he argues it was written by a member of Aristotle's school in the late fourth century. Raubitschek (1948, 207), in a sustained attack on the skeptics, argues that the speech "must be either authentic or else must have been written by an extremely careful and well-informed man." On either of these analyses the description of a provision of Athenian *symbola* agreements is fairly reliable.
10. [Andoc.] 4.17. The only source I am aware of that reports Agatharchos's citizenship is the 13th-cent. Byzantine lexicon-*cum*-onomasticon transmitted under the name of Zonaras (Tittmann, 1808), which states (*s.v.* Ἀγάθαρχος) that he was from Samos and a son of Eudemos. Since the speaker of our speech strongly implies that Agatharchos was a foreigner, I see no reason to suspect the lexicon's information.
11. [Andoc.] 4.18: καὶ πρὸς μὲν τὰς ἄλλας πόλεις ἐν τοῖς συμβόλοις συντιθέμεθα μὴ ἐξεῖναι μήθ' εἶρξαι μήτε δῆσαι τὸν ἐλεύθερον· ἐὰν δέ τις παραβῇ, μεγάλην ζημίαν ἐπὶ τούτοις ἔθεμεν· τούτου δὲ τοιαῦτα πράξαντος οὐδεμίαν οὐδεὶς οὔτ' ἰδίαν οὔτε δημοσίαν τιμωρίαν ποιεῖται.

12. *IG* I^{3} 6 (*I.Eleusis* 19; *AIUK* 4.2, no. 1 [with high-quality photos]; *OR* 106); housed in the British Museum.

13. [μιν . . . .]· πρᾶχσαι δ' ἔκπραχ⟨σι⟩[ν·]
[ἐὰν δὲ μὲ] ἐγδõι τὸν ὀφλόντα, μ-
[ὲ χρέσθο] τ̣õι hιερõι : ἐὰν ἀμφι-
[σβετõσι] μὲ κλεθε͂ναι ἐμ πό[λε]
[ι. . . .7. . .]εν ἐλθõσαν ἀδικ[. .]
[. . . .8. . . .] hύστερον hε̣ [β]ο̣[λ]ὲ α̣
[. . . .9. . . . .]ι : τõν Ἀθεναίον μὲ[λ]-
[αθ]ε͂ν̣[αι τ]ούτον τõν πόλεον μ[ε]-
δὲ *h*αμõ [ἀν]ιᾶσθαι ἐὰν μὲ δ[ί]κ[ε]-
ν̣ ὀφλόν[τα] ἐπιχορίαν ἒ ἐς πο[λ]-
εμίος λ[εφ]θ̣έ̣ντα· hέτις δ' ἂν τ-
[õ]μ πόλεον μὲ ἐθέλει, δ[ί]κας δ̣ι-
[δ]όναι καὶ δέχεσθαι Ἀθ̣εναίο-
[ι]σιν ἀπὸ χσυ⟨μ⟩βολõν.
vacat

I print the text as in *IG* I^{3} 6, except at ll. 36–40 I print Clinton's text and supplements as proposed in the commentary to *I.Eleusis* (= Clinton 2005–08) no. 19 and adopt his translation.

14. See Scafuro (2010, 31); Clinton (2005–08, ii.39); Sokolowski (1962, 17).

15. The text contains many obscurities. Among these is that, at first reading, the expression hέτις δ' ἂν τ[õ]μ πόλεον μὲ ἐθέλει (40–41) suggests that hέτις, i.e., a *polis* itself, is also the subject of δ[ί]κας δ̣ι[δ]όναι καὶ δέχεσθαι, and on this interpretation the passage appears to envisage public law disputes between cities (see Meritt 1946, 250). Because of the earlier focus on τὸν ὀφλόντα ("the debtor/accused"), however, there is also reason to understand here an implied subject such as τινα or τὸν ὀφλόντα. Lambert seems to agree, translating lines 40–43 as "any city that is not willing shall give and receive court cases with the Athenians according to the existing conventions" (translation in *AIUK* 4.2, no. 1). My interpretation is reinforced by the provisions on face B declaring that a sacred truce (σπονδάς, B 8) will be in force before, during, and after the celebration of the Mysteries. This truce, notably, does not apply (only) to the cities from which the foreign celebrants are coming, but directly to those celebrants themselves and their attendants, as well as to all Athenians (B 8–17).

16. For the theory that Ionian cities had *symbola* agreements at least as early as the 490s, see Chapter 7, notes 78–91 and accompanying text.

17. On the panhellenism of the Mysteries, see Clinton (2005–08, ii.39); also Clinton (1994). One of the early dedications at Eleusis was made around 500 by a certain Aristodamos of Metapontum, *IG* I^{3} 1006; as Clinton (2005–08, ii.31) notes, "this dedication offers material testimony to the respect the Eleusinian cult was receiving from foreigners toward the end of the sixth century." Parker (1996, 99–100) argues that Eleusinian myths were "overhaul[ed]" in the sixth century to emphasize that "the Mysteries attracted distinguished initiates from abroad: none other than Heracles . . . and the Dioscuri."

18. The most obvious examples of "imperial" use of religion by Athenians may be the requirements, at various times, that allies send a cow and panoply to the Panathenaia festival (e.g. *IG* I^{3} 34, ll. 41–43); that they offer a "first fruit," *aparche*, of 1/60 of their imperial tribute to Athena (*IG* I^{3} 259, l. 1); and that they offer first fruits to the Eleusinian goddesses (*IG* I^{3} 78, l. 14). On the cow and panoply requirement, see J.L. Shear (2021, 128); on the first fruits requirements, see Jim (2014, 203–21). Smarczyk (1990, 549–62) describes a change in the Panathenaia, in the second half of the fifth century, from a *Nationalfest* to a *Reichsfest*. See also Parker (1996, 142–51).

19. On Phaselis, see Grainger (2009, 15–21, 50–57, and *passim*); Blackman (1981); *TAM* II pp. 413–16; on Phaselis and Naukratis, see Hdt. 2.178; Möller (2000, 75–79). Phaselis's commercial significance in the sixth century is suggested by Hdt. 2.178; in the fifth by Thuc. 2.69.1; in the fourth by Dem. 35 (*Against Lacritus*). See Bresson (2016, 320) and (2000, 67–73); Malkin (2011, 72). But as Robert (1966, 40–44) suggests, Phaselis should not be seen as purely a trading state, since it appears to have had agricultural and in particular woodland resources; cf. Grainger (2009, 33–34).

20. *IG* I^{3} 10 (*OR* 120; *SvA* 149); see James (2023); Beretta Liverani (2013) (with photo); also Bresson (2016, 319–20); Pébarthe (2007); Cataldi (1983, 99–143); Fornara (1979); Gauthier (1972, 158–61, 177–80); Seager (1966); Ste. Croix (1961, 100–08); Hopper (1943, 39–45). As

Papazarkadas (2009, 70) notes: "Few, if any, would question the importance of this document for our understanding of Athens' treatment of her allies, judicial procedures etc." In the wake of resolution of the three-barred sigma debate, arguments for a date in the 420s have recently become predominant; see Blok (2022, 98–99); Beretta Liverani (2013, 138–48); Papazarkadas (2009, 70–71); M.J. Jameson (2000–03). For a date in the 450s, see the commentary to *OR* 120; Rhodes (1997, 504 and n.9).

21. Plut. *Cim.* 12.3–4.
22. See Grainger (2009, 50–53); on the other hand, Grainger's (2009, 50 n.23) doubt of the Chians brokering the surrender of the Phaselites, and his positing of a pure military victory by the Athenians instead, is too cynical.
23. . . . τοῖ]ς Φασηλίταις τὸ ψ[ήφ]ι-
[σμα ἀν]αγράψαι· ὅ τι ἂμ μὲ[ν] Ἀθ-
[ήνησι ξ]υ[μβ]όλαιον γένηται
[πρὸς Φ]ασηλιτ[ῶ]ν τινα Ἀθή[ν]η-
[σι, τὰς δ]ίκας γίγνεσθαι παρ-
[ὰ τῶι πο]λεμάρχωι, καθάπερ Χ-
[ίοις, καὶ] ἄλλοθι μηδὲ ἀμõ· τῶ-
[ν δὲ ἄλλω]ν̣ ἀπὸ ξυμβολῶν κατ-
[ὰ τὰς ὅσας] ξυμβολὰς πρὸς Φα-
[σηλίτας] τὰς δίκας ἐν[α]ι· τὰς
[. . .7. . .]το[ς] ἀφελε͂ν. ἐὰν δέ τ-
[ις ἄλλη τῶ]ν̣ ἀρχῶν δέξηται δ-
[ίκην κατὰ] Φασηλιτῶν τινος
[Ἀθήνησιν, ε]ἰ μὲν καταδικάσ-
[ει, ἡ καταδίκ]η ἄκυρος ἔστω. ἐ-
[ὰν δέ τις παραβ]α[ί]νηι τὰ ἐψη-
[φισμένα, ὀφ]ε[λέτ]ω μυρίας δ[ρ]-
[αχμὰς ἱερ]ὰς τῆι Ἀθηναίαι· . . .
24. See James (2023). Unlike all earlier editions, in lines 8–9 I place the comma after rather than before Ἀθή[ν]η[σι]; and in line 18 I print Wilhelm's restoration Ἀθήνησιν, creating a parallel with the newly punctuated line 9.
25. "Legal dispute" here translates [ξ]υ[μβ]όλαιον. There is a long and ongoing scholarly debate over the meaning of συμβόλαιον, generally divided between "contract," on one hand, and "actionable liability" or "legal dispute" on the other. The former view has recently been defended by Pébarthe (2007); the latter notably by Harris (2015) and Ste. Croix (1961); see also James (2026). Cataldi (1983, 105–19) argues that its core meaning related especially to creditor–debtor relations.
26. On close Athenian–Chian relations, see Thuc. 2.56.2; 4.51; 4.129; Eupol. fr. 246 Kassel–Austin; Meiggs (1972, 232). In the fourth century, only those foreigners in Athens with some sort of privileged status—metics, *proxenoi*, and *isoteleis* (foreigners with certain tax exemptions)—were entitled to have their lawsuits heard in the polemarch's court, *Ath. pol.* 58.2. A.R.W. Harrison (1968–71, i.193) suggests the polemarch's jurisdiction "arose out of . . . an executive function . . . of protecting the interests of this privileged group of foreigners." But no surviving source explains the actual concrete benefit of having a case in the polemarch's court. Speculation what that benefit might be includes: that in cases before the polemarch the Phaselites would not need to present an Athenian *prostates* (Wade-Gery 1958, 188); and that the polemarch's docket was less congested, and trial therefore quicker, than in other venues (Ste. Croix 1961, 101). On the polemarch's judicial role generally, see E.A. Meyer (2010, 32–35); Rhodes (1981, 652–57); A.R.W. Harrison (1968–71, i.192–96, ii.9–11); Ste. Croix (1961, 100–01); Busolt and Swoboda (1920–26, ii.1094–95).
27. On the fines, see James (2023, 135 n.9); Blok (2022, 117–27). On the significance of the Ionic alphabet in an Athenian decree, see Low (2005, 108), who argues that it exemplifies, on the part of the Athenians, a "more subtle, homogenizing approach to the construction of power, in which Athens is not so much the enforcer of an Athenian way of life as a facilitator of some wider, perhaps Panhellenic, relationship." For interpretations generally agreeing with mine, see Osborne and Rhodes (*OR* 120); Bresson (2016, 319–21); Beretta Liverani (2013, 136–37); Cataldi (1983, 129–30); Meiggs (1972, 231–32); Ste. Croix (1961, 100–08); Hopper (1943, 39–45). For the "imperial imposition" interpretation, see Fornara (1979); Seager (1966).

28. Gauthier (1972, 186–87) (approved by Cataldi 1983, 123). Use of the verb καταδικάζειν (l. 18) does not indicate that the official was actually deciding cases. Although καταδικάζειν can mean to determine that someone is guilty, i.e., to have the decision-making authority, it can also refer to the presiding magistrate's act of simply "announcing" a verdict of guilt, see Pl. *Leg.* 12.958b–c. Hence, its possible usages matched those of its base verb δικάζειν, which could mean either "preside over a trial and announce the verdict" or "act as decisionmaker and determine the verdict." For examples of the former, see *IG* I³ 104, ll. 11–13 (Draco's homicide law: the *ephetai* are to decide (διαγν[õ]ỵ[α]ị) the verdict, but the *archons basileias* are to "deliver" it ([δ]ικάζεν); on this inscription, see now Harris and Canevaro 2023); *Ath. pol.* 52.3 (with the note of Rhodes 1981, 586–87) and 57.4. For discussion with reference to this inscription, see Sealey (1964, 16–17); cf. Rhodes (1972, 204 n.1). Insistence on a narrow meaning for καταδικάζειν, as well as acceptance of a date probably forty years too early, led Wade-Gery (1958, 180–86) to misinterpret this decree as evidence that, in the 460s, shortly before Ephialtes's reforms, judicial magistrates in Athens still heard cases (valued at any amount) and rendered verdicts without juries. They may have done so, but this decree is not evidence of the fact. Gauthier (1972, 186–87) proposes that the new rules also permitted a Phaselite defendant to post bond and remain free until the trial, rather than be held in custody until trial as a foreigner and therefore a high flight risk.
29. The evidence is mostly from the fourth century, e.g., *Ath. pol.* 52.3 (the *apodektai* could decide suits up to ten drachmas); 53.2 (the "Forty," up to ten drachmas). Nikophon's law on silver coinage (*RO* 25; *SEG* 26.72), from 375/74, mentions several situations, including violations valued at up to ten drachmas, in which officials were permitted to judge and punish unilaterally (see ll. 16–26). For unilateral enforcement by officials, see also *IG* II² 380, ll. 25–28 (from 320/19: officials can make people clean up their garbage); *SEG* 30.61, ll. A31–33 (from between 380 and 350: supervisors of the Eleusinian Mysteries can fine disorderly initiates up to a certain amount—the specific amount is no longer readable on the stone—but must institute a jury trial for larger amounts); cf. Lipsius (1905–15, i.53–54). Aside from small fines, in the fourth century at least certain criminals who were caught in the act and confessed their guilt to one of the officials known as the "Eleven" could be summarily executed by him without a jury trial, see Aeschin. 1.91, *Ath. pol.* 52.1; cf. Dem. 24.113.
30. Mid-fifth-century Athenian judicial reforms reinstituted the thirty Peisistratid "deme justices," δικαστὰς κατὰ δήμους, who went round the demes hearing cases and had authority to decide disputes up to ten drachmas, *Ath. pol.* 16.5, 26.3, 53.1–3 (in the fourth century the number of deme justices was increased to forty). If such suits were permitted under the original *symbola* between the Athenians and Phaselites, this decree would have forbidden them.
31. See *Ath. pol.* 59.6. Ste. Croix (1961, 100) believes the *thesmothetai* were in charge of ordinary *symbola* suits already by the 460s but offers no evidence. If *thesmothetai* were the only officials who heard *symbola* suits when this decree was passed, it seems that the decree would have specified them by name as no longer authorized to hear suits against Phaselites. Another, highly fragmentary, Athenian inscription mentioning a *symbola* agreement, with Salamis on Cyprus, perhaps fifteen or twenty years after this decree, mentions a [. . .]ạρχος in close proximity to [χσ]υμβολα; Cataldi (1983, 288) reasonably reconstructs the word as πολέμαρχος, which would mean that the polemarch was to play some role in *symbola* cases between Athenians and Salaminians. I discuss this decree further below.
32. As subjects of Persia living in the eastern Mediterranean, Phaselites had probably focused their earlier maritime trade on points east of Athens. This is evidenced, e.g., by their co-founding of Naukratis and by a papyrus documenting customs fees paid by Phaselite ships in Egypt in the early fifth century, see Briant and Descat (1998, 63).
33. For Athenian prayers for Chians, see Ar. *Av.* 879 and the scholion to 880 (=*FGrH* 115, fr. 104, Theopompus of Chios). The *Birds* was produced in 414 but it is not clear when this practice originated in Athens.
34. On Chios as a "land of traders" (as it can still be described in modern times), see Arist. *Pol.* 4, 1291b24; cf. Hdt. 1.165. Herodotus reports that Phaselis was a Dorian *polis*, not Ionian like Chios, but their connection in co-founding Naukratis and its *Hellenion* may have fostered positive early relations between Phaselites and Chians. On the economic benefits of Athenian-Phaselite relations, see Lazar (2024, 187–90).
35. Phaselite dedications to Athena *Polias*: *SEG* 64.1408; *TAM* II, 1184; grave marker of Athenodotos: *IG* I³ 1360. Athena *Polias* was, admittedly, worshipped in many cities. In contrast, perusal of *LGPN* indicates that the name "Athenodotos/Athanodotos" was always uncommon (I count only eight attested instances in the sixth through fourth centuries), which makes its

appearance on a Phaselite gravestone even more marked. ("Athenodoros/Athanodoros" was more common—about fifty instances in the same time period—but as frequent in Attica as in all the rest of the Greek world combined.)

36. Antiphon's speech 5, *On the Murder of Herodes*, provides evidence that the Mytilenean revolt from Athens in 428 led to just such alienation, which was in turn used to bias Athenian judges against Mytileneans. The speaker's defense of his father's behavior during and after the revolt (sections 76–79) is framed as a response to the prosecution's attack on his character as an alleged participant.
37. Thuc. 2.69. On the identity of Phoinike, see Hornblower (1991–2008, i.355–56).
38. Οὐδὲν καινὸν διαπράττονται οἱ Φασηλῖται, ὦ ἄνδρες δικασταί, ἀλλ' ἅπερ εἰώθασιν. οὗτοι γὰρ δεινότατοι μέν εἰσιν δανείσασθαι χρήματα ἐν τῷ ἐμπορίῳ, ἐπειδὰν δὲ λάβωσιν καὶ συγγραφὴν συγγράψωνται ναυτικήν, εὐθὺς ἐπελάθοντο καὶ τῶν συγγραφῶν καὶ τῶν νόμων καὶ ὅτι δεῖ ἀποδοῦναι αὐτοὺς ἃ ἔλαβον, καὶ οἴονται, ἐὰν ἀποδῶσιν, ὥσπερ τῶν ἰδίων τι τῶν ἑαυτῶν ἀπολωλεκέναι, ἀλλ' ἀντὶ τοῦ ἀποδοῦναι σοφίσματα εὑρίσκουσιν καὶ παραγραφὰς καὶ προφάσεις, καὶ εἰσὶν πονηρότατοι ἀνθρώπων καὶ ἀδικώτατοι. τεκμήριον δὲ τούτου· πολλῶν γὰρ ἀφικνουμένων εἰς τὸ ὑμέτερον ἐμπόριον καὶ Ἑλλήνων καὶ βαρβάρων, πλείους δίκαι εἰσὶν ἑκάστοτε αὐτῶν τῶν Φασηλιτῶν ἢ τῶν ἄλλων ἁπάντων. οὗτοι μὲν οὖν τοιοῦτοί εἰσιν.
39. Harding (1987, 37) argues that ancient orators "were liars and cheats and their words cannot be trusted on any topic, unless supported by independent evidence." Cf. Gagarin (1989, 13); Dover (1974, 14). Aristotle classifies such attacks as part of the emotional form, *pathos*, of artificial proof; see *Rhet.* 2.4.32 (1382a16–19); 2.7.5–6 (1385a33–b10); 3.15.1–2 (1416a3–14). On the use of such devices in Greek oratory generally, see Carey (1994, 26–34).
40. [Dem.] 35.7: "I knew nothing, gentlemen of the jury, nor did Thrasymedes, of these men's bad character, but I believed that they were fair people, as they held themselves out to be and said they were, and I believed they would do everything they promised and Lakritos acknowledged." οὐδὲν εἰδώς, ὦ ἄνδρες δικασταί, οὐδ' ὁ Θρασυμήδης τὴν τούτων πονηρίαν, ἀλλ' οἰόμενος εἶναι ἐπιεικεῖς ἀνθρώπους καὶ οἱοίπερ προσεποιοῦντο καὶ ἔφασαν εἶναι, καὶ ἡγούμενος ποιήσειν αὐτοὺς πάντα ὅσαπερ ὑπισχνεῖτο καὶ ἀνεδέχετο Λάκριτος ουτοσί.
41. ἄλλους γ' ἂν οὖν οἰόμεθα τὰ ἡμέτερα λαβόντας δεῖξαι ἂν μάλιστα εἴ τι μετριάζομεν· ἡμῖν δὲ καὶ ἐκ τοῦ ἐπιεικοῦς ἀδοξία τὸ πλέον ἢ ἔπαινος οὐκ εἰκότως περιέστη. καὶ ἐλασσούμενοι γὰρ ἐν ταῖς ξυμβολαίαις πρὸς τοὺς ξυμμάχους δίκαις καὶ παρ' ἡμῖν αὐτοῖς ἐν τοῖς ὁμοίοις νόμοις ποιήσαντες τὰς κρίσεις φιλοδικεῖν δοκοῦμεν. καὶ οὐδεὶς σκοπεῖ αὐτῶν τοῖς καὶ ἄλλοθί που ἀρχὴν ἔχουσι καὶ ἧσσον ἡμῶν πρὸς τοὺς ὑπηκόους μετρίοις οὖσι διότι τοῦτο οὐκ ὀνειδίζεται.
42. Interpretation has focused on whether the sentence should be translated not along the lines I have followed, with the participles coordinate with each other (and both concessive), but rather with the first participle being causal of the second, which is then read with a strong aoristic aspect, as in Hornblower's translation (1991–2008, i.122): "for because we find ourselves at a disadvantage in law-suits against our allies, in cases controlled by inter-state agreements, and so have transferred such cases to Athens where the laws are equal for all, we are supposed to be too fond of dragging people into court." Parmeggiani (2021) offers a novel and interesting "third way"; but I find his reading of the Greek unpersuasive, and it loses the irony I find in the Athenians' comment. He takes the (admittedly odd) phrase ξυμβολαίαις δίκαις to refer not to private lawsuits brought in accordance with *symbola* agreements but to lawsuits brought by Athenian generals against allied communities, alleging public law violations of their treaty commitments; but he offers no parallels for this reading. Also, on Parmeggiani's interpretation, the Athenians claim it is because of "suffering loss," ἐλασσούμενοι, that they take allies to court both in cases abroad and at Athens. But suing after suffering loss is characterizable unironically as litigation-loving, φιλοδικεῖν, and the label would merit no special offense on the part of the Athenians such as they seem to take in this passage (as noted by Liberman 2017, 211, the opposition between the "suffering" and the "litigiousness" is key to the meaning). For yet a different recent interpretation, see Liberman (2017, 210–11). For interpretations that the Athenians here are talking about more than just cases brought under *symbola* agreements, see Forsdyke (2005, 228–29); Meiggs (1972, 232–33).
43. Ste. Croix (1961, 96–100). The contrary stance is taken by Hornblower (1991–2008, i.122–23), who also follows Fornara's (1979) interpretation of the Phaselis decree; Liberman (2017, 211) sees reference here only to lawsuits held in Athens. My interpretation is supported by Antiphon 5.78, an admittedly difficult and possibly corrupt passage, in which the speaker claims that some Mytileneans have become citizens of other *poleis* and sued Athenians under *symbola* agreements. The implication is that these lawsuits took place in those other cities, not

in Mytilene or Athens. This speech likely dates to the 410s, hence before the reconciliation between Athens and Mytilene discussed below.

44. Forsdyke (2005, 230) takes this passage as evidence of an Athenian imperial ideology "that the judicial measures were intended to allow legal procedures, not force, to govern their relations with their allies." The comment about *philodikein* may be intended by the Athenian speaker partly as a comic quip based on an Athenian reputation—even among themselves—for litigiousness. Consider the plot of Aristophanes's *Wasps* (produced 422), and see, e.g., Ar. *Nub.* 207–08 (produced 423); and *Pax* 505 (produced 421). But as Turner (1946) shows, the use of *philodikein* here refers to an Athenian propensity to sue rather than to an Athenian enjoyment of serving as jurors, although Aristophanes mocks both alleged Athenian characteristics.
45. *IG* I^3 66 (Cataldi 1983, no. 9; *SvA* 169; Tod i.63); see also the text and discussion of Saldutti (2016). This decree has traditionally been dated to within a few years after 428/27; Fornara (2010) argues for a date about 412; Saldutti (2016, 255–59) argues for between 422 (the Peace of Nicias) and 416 (when two Lesbian ships accompanied the Athenian invasion of Melos).
46. Lines 15–16: [δί]κας διδόν[τα]ς πρὸς Ἀθεν[αίος καὶ δεχομένος κα]τὰ τὰς χσυ[μβο]λὰς hαὶ ἔσαν [πρὸ τõ].
47. *IG* I^3 118 (*RO* 185; Cataldi 1983, no. 12; *SvA* 207).
48. See Plut. *Alc.* 30.2–4; Diod. Sic. 13.66.4; Xen. *Hell.* 1.3.10. Alcibiades is persuasively reconstructed as the proposer in line 31 of the decree: [Ἀλ]κιβ[ιάδες] εἶπε.
49. Lines 22–26: [ὅσα δὲ ἄ]λλα χσυμβόλαια πρὸ τõ ἒν τοῖς ἰ[διόταις πρ]ὸς τὸς ἰδιότας ἒ ἰδιώτει πρὸς τὸ κ[οινὸν ἒ κο]ινõι πρὸς ἰδιότεν v ἒ ἐάν τι ἄλλο γίγ[νεται, δια]λ̣ύεμ π[ρ]ὸς ἀλλέλος· ὅ τι δ' ἂν ἀμφισβη[τõσι, δίκας] ἔναι ἀπὸ χσυμβολõν.
50. As correctly noted by Cataldi (1983, 343 n.91) and Gauthier (1972, 163), *contra* Hopper (1943, 48), who takes the provision to concern disputes among Selymbrians. If we follow Cataldi and Gauthier, as I do, it is noteworthy there is no provision between "*koinon* and *koinon*," i.e., for the resolution of purely public disputes between the two communities.
51. As already noted by Lipsius (1905–15, ii.967 and n.5).
52. That this agreement does not refer to the *symbola* as "the *symbola* agreements that existed previously," as does the Mytilene decree discussed above, suggests either that the *symbola* agreement between the Athenians and Selymbrians was continuously in force, at least officially, even during the years of the Selymbrians' revolt from the empire; or that a *symbola* was entered into about the same time as this decree.
53. This is the dispute between Orchomenos and two men from Amphissa, Kalliontzis (2020, no. 33), discussed below. We have much evidence for cities taking out loans from private individuals, especially starting in the fourth century. On Greek civic loans in general, see the foundational work of Migeotte (1984). The story told by Philochoros (*FGrH* 328 fr. 121) that Pheidias—an Athenian artist—was put to death by the Eleans for fraud or embezzlement during his construction of the statue of Zeus in Olympia, indicates an awareness that interstate building contracts could easily give rise to legal disputes. I know of no evidence that the Athenians and Eleans had a *symbola* agreement in the fifth century under which Pheidias might have been prosecuted, but the possibility should not be dismissed out of hand. And it seems likely that Athenian craftsmen undertook many contracts in both allied and non-allied cities, especially before the outbreak of war in 431. One form of "insurance" for cities dealing with foreign contractors was to require them to provide (local) guarantors; see, e.g., *IG* II^2 1678, ll. 17–18, 20–21; *IG* VII 3073, ll. 24–29; Pitt (2016). A comparable modern practice is the use of letters of credit.
54. See Papazarkadas (2014, 227), comparing the "conciliatory nature" of this decree to those from the same period for Neapolitans, Halicarnassians, Klazomenians at Daphnous, and Sigeians: "Approbation instead of opprobrium and protection instead of maltreatment, these were the ingredients of Athens' new emollient approach towards her allies in the Ionian War." Cf. Hornblower (2002, 181); Cataldi (1983, 320–21).
55. Lines 44–45: [ἔναι δὲ καὶ] Ἀπολλοδόροι τὲμ προ[χσε]νίαν κα[θάπερ τõι] π̣ατρὶ αὐτõ. Proxeny relations between Athenians and Selymbrians reached back decades earlier. A prominent and strikingly minimalist, even modernist, grave monument in the Kerameikos cemetery in Athens, dated to the middle of the fifth century, marks the remains of a certain Pythagoras, a Selymbrian *proxenos* to the Athenians, who apparently died while in Athens. It is inscribed with two elegiac couplets praising the deceased in an Athenian voice (*IG* I^3 1154): "Because of proxeny and excellence, both his ancestors' and his own, the Athenians placed here, publicly, Pythagoras son of Dionysius, but grief for the deceased man reached horse-pasturing Selymbria, his homeland."

προξενίας ἀρετῆς τε χάριμ προ<γ>όνων τε καὶ αὐτõ
ἐνθάδ' Ἀθηναῖοι Πυθαγόρην ἔθεσαν
υἱὸν δημοσίαι Διονυσίο, ἱππόβοτον δὲ
πατρίδα Σαλυβρίαν ἵκετ' ἄχος φθιμένο.

On this monument, see the architectural study of Hoepfner (1973) (suggesting it was designed on proportions dear to the Pythagoreans because of the coincidence of the dead man's name with that of the famous philosopher and guru); on the epigraph, see Ferrario (2014, 47–49).

56. *IG* I^3 113 (Cataldi 1983, no. 10). Lines 8–9 appear to refer to a citizenship grant ([ἐ]σγράφσα[σθαι αὐτὸν . . . φυλ]εν hέντινα); lines 22–23 to lawsuits and a *symbola* agreement (τὰς δίκ[ας . . . χ]σ̣υμβολα). Isocrates (9.54) confirms that Evagoras was made an Athenian citizen by law, νόμῳ; cf. [Dem.] 12.10.
57. On Evagoras generally, see Maier (1994, 312–17). Evagoras seized the throne of Salamis from a Phoenician named Abdemon, possibly the successor of the Phoenician who usurped the crown from Evagoras's family in perhaps the 440s or 430s. Isoc. 9.19–32; Diod. Sic. 14.98; Theopompus, *FGrH* 115, fr. 103. On connections between Evagoras and Athenians, see Isoc. 9.54–56; Xen. *Hell.* 4.3.10–12; Diod. Sic. 14.39; Pestarino (2022, 31).
58. I suggest ratification as a possible function of this decree but note that in later years in Athens *symbola* were ratified not by the assembly but by a *dikasterion*; see n. 211, below.
59. Paus. 1.3.2 (describing Evagoras's assistance to Conon): "And he did this as an Athenian and, in origin, from Salamis [the island], since tracing his genealogy to his ancestors he arrived at Teucer and the daughter of Kinyras"; ἔπραξε δὲ ὡς Ἀθηναῖος καὶ τὸ ἀνέκαθεν ἐκ Σαλαμῖνος, ἐπεὶ καὶ γενεαλογῶν ἐς προγόνους ἀνέβαινε Τεῦκρον καὶ Κινύρου θυγατέρα. Aeschylus's *Persians* implies that Athens was the *metropolis* of Salamis the island ("and Salamis, whose mother city is the cause of all these lamentations," Σαλαμῖνά τε, τᾶς νῦν ματρόπολις τῶνδ' αἰτία στεναγμῶν, ll. 891–95). And in Euripides's *Helen* (146–50), Teucer foreshadows his founding of Cypriot Salamis in the following words to Helen: "Introduce me [to Theonoe] so that I might learn by prophecy in which direction I should dispatch my ship with fair-winded oar to Cyprus in the sea, where Apollo prophesied I would live, bearing the island name of Salamis in honor of my fatherland in that place":

    σὺ προξένησον, ὡς τύχω μαντευμάτων
    ὅπηι νεὼς στείλαιμ' ἂν οὔριον πτερὸν
    ἐς γῆν ἐναλίαν Κύπρον, οὗ μ' ἐθέσπισεν
    οἰκεῖν Ἀπόλλων, ὄνομα νησιωτικὸν
    Σαλαμῖνα θέμενον τῆς ἐκεῖ χάριν πάτρας.

    See Pestarino (2022, 33).
60. A section of Salamis's city wall dated to the eleventh century, and reinforced in the eighth, has been excavated (Petit 2019, 23–24). On connections between Salamis and mainland Greece (including Attica) visible in the archaeological record, see Matthäus (2009, 171); Guía (2005, 63, 67); Coldstream (1989); Pouilloux (1976, 452–57; 1975, 115–16).
61. On the myth and cult of Aglauros, see Sourvinou-Inwood (2011, chs. 2–3); Gourmelen (2004, 151–71); Dontas (1983) (= *SEG* 33.115; honorary decree for the priestess of Aglauros, ca. 246 BCE, found in situ on the east slope of the Acropolis). Their priesthood of Aglauros is attested by the famous decree of the Salaminioi, *RO* 37, ll. 12, 45 (363/62 BCE).
62. Porph. *Abst.* 2.54.3: ἐν δὲ τῇ νῦν Σαλαμῖνι, πρότερον δὲ Κορωνίδι ὀνομαζομένῃ, μηνὶ κατὰ Κυπρίους Ἀφροδισίῳ ἐθύετο ἄνθρωπος τῇ Ἀγραύλῳ τῇ Κέκροπος καὶ νύμφης Ἀγραυλίδος. καὶ διέμενε τὸ ἔθος ἄχρι τῶν Διομήδους χρόνων· εἶτα μετέβαλεν, ὥστε τῷ Διομήδει τὸν ἄνθρωπον θύεσθαι· ὑφ' ἕνα δὲ περίβολον ὅ τε τῆς Ἀθηνᾶς νεὼς καὶ ὁ τῆς Ἀγραύλου καὶ Διομήδους. ὁ δὲ σφαγιαζόμενος ὑπὸ τῶν ἐφήβων ἀγόμενος τρὶς περιέθει τὸν βωμόν· ἔπειτα ὁ ἱερεὺς αὐτὸν λόγχῃ ἔπαιε κατὰ τοῦ στομάχου, καὶ οὕτως αὐτὸν ἐπὶ τὴν νησθεῖσαν πυρὰν ὡλοκαύτιζεν. This passage is also quoted by Eusebius, *Praep. evang.* 4.16.2. On Porphyry's account, see Girgenti and Sodano (2005, 432–33). Unfortunately, the dating of the ritual that Porphyry describes is unclear and his chronological marker (ἄχρι τῶν Διομήδους χρόνων) mysterious.
63. The term "colony" in this context is Pouilloux's (1975, 117). Conon was in Salamis from 405 to 397, married a woman and raised a son there. A nephew of Conon's stayed in Salamis and managed the family property. Nicophemos settled and married there while retaining Athenian citizenship. And Andocides had many stays there and received a land grant from Evagoras; (Pouilloux 1975, 118). Cf. Lys. 19.36.
64. Furthermore, one of the Athenians' two official "dispatch galleys" was called the *Salaminia*. Casson (1971, 353) claims correctly that the name "recall[s] . . . the island which saw Athens'

great naval victory over Persia," but it also recalls Salamis on Cyprus, reachable only by ship across a vast expanse of sea. The overlapping fields of meaning of the name "Salamis" may have encouraged positive feelings toward the Cypriot *polis* among Athenians after 479.

65. In what may be a comment on both legal and social harmony between Athenians and Salaminians under Evagoras, the speaker of Lysias 19 claims that Conon and Nicophemus "believed that their property was equally safe there [in Salamis] as here [in Athens]," ἡγοῦντο δὲ καὶ τὰ ἐκεῖ ὁμοίως σφίσιν εἶναι σᾶ ὥσπερ καὶ τὰ ἐνθάδε, 19.36. The exact meaning of this phrase is uncertain, even in context, an uncertainty exacerbated by textual problems. Still, the passage indicates that Conon and Nicophemus had family and property in Salamis, from which we can presume strong local networks; cf. Lys. 19.44.
66. *IG* I^{3} 127 (*OR* 191; Cataldi 1983, no. 12; *SvA* 209) and *IG* II^{2} 1 (*RO* 2). See now Elsner (2015) for a unified and illustrated publication of the editions and translations in *OR* 191 and *RO* 2. There were three separate decrees: the first (*IG* I^{3} 127) passed in 405, on a *stele* likely destroyed during the oligarchic, pro-Spartan reign of the "Thirty" in Athens, and then reaffirmed by and reinscribed on the same stele as the two decrees of *IG* II^{2} 1, in 403/02 after the restoration of democracy in Athens.
67. Lines 17–18: καὶ περὶ τῶν ἐνκλημάτων ἃ ἄγ γίγνηται πρὸς ἀλλήλος διδόναι καὶ δέχεσθαι τὰς δίκας κατὰ τὰς συμβολὰς τὰς ὄσας. It is clear that ἀλλήλος here means "Athenians and Samians" because the previous sentence ends, "in accordance with the oaths and the agreements, just as they have been made between Athenians and Samians," κατὰ τὸς ὅρκος καὶ τὰς συνθήκας καθάπερ ξύνκειται Ἀθηναίοις καὶ Σαμίοις, 16–17.
68. As noted in the commentary to *OR* 191.
69. Lines 9–12: ὅτι ἐσὶν ἄνδρες ἀγαθοὶ καὶ πρόθυμοι ποιε͂ν ὅ τι δύνανται ἀγαθόν, καὶ τὰ πεπραγμένα αύτοῖς ὅτι δοκο͂σιν ὀρθῶς ποιῆσαι Ἀθηναίοις καὶ Σαμίοις· καὶ ἀντὶ ὧν εὖ πεποιήκασιν Ἀθηναίοις καὶ νῦν περὶ πολλο͂ ποιο͂νται καὶ ἐσηγο͂νται ἀγαθά.
70. Ma (2000, 215).
71. This explanation is offered by editors of all three versions of the collection *Greek Historical Inscriptions* (Tod; Meiggs and Lewis; Rhodes and Osborne); see Elsner (2015, 48–50, and n.23), who accepts the hypothesis.
72. On Spartan interference on Samos, see Xen. *Hell.* 2.3.6–7; Diod. Sic. 14.3.5. On this period of Samian history, see esp. Shipley (1987, 129–37); the second decree on our *stele* praises the Ephesians and Notians for taking in Samian refugees, *IG* II^{2} 1, ll. 48–49.
73. On the Samian statue of Lysander at Olympia, see Paus. 6.3.14–16. On the great Spartan dedication at Delphi, see the commentary to *OR* 192; Bommelaer (2015, 108–10); M. Scott (2010, 105–07); Jacquemin (1999, 191–92). For the verses by Ion of Samos, see *F.Delphes* III, 50–51 (*OR* 192, b and c). It is uncertain whether they were inscribed when the statues were erected or decades later.
74. We know from the third decree that Cephisophon was secretary not at the time of the first decree (when Alexias was archon, line 6), but in 403/02 when Euclides was archon.
75. See the cover image of this book. Elsner (2015) also contains excellent photos.
76. On who is represented by the non-Athena figure, see Blanshard (2007, 27–31). It is unlikely the figure on the left is human, since she is the same size as Athena. Examples of similar Attic *stelai* memorializing interstate agreements include: *IG* I^{3} 61 (Athens and Methone, 424/23); *IG* I^{3} 86 (*SvA* 196; Athens and Argos, 417/16); *IG* I^{3} 96 (Athens and Samos, 412/11 or 405); *IG* I^{3} 101 (*SvA* 204; Athens and Thracian Neapolis, 410/09); *IG* I^{3} 124 (Athens and Kios, 406/05); *IG* II^{2} 97 (*SvA* 263; Athens and Kerkyra, 375/74?); *IG* II^{2} 112 (*SvA* 290; Athens and Arkadia, Achaia, Elis, and Phleious, 362/61); *IG* II^{2} 128 (*SvA* 312; Athens and Thracian Neapolis, 356/55). See Lawton (1995, 36, and accompanying catalog and plates).
77. Arrington (2018, 20).
78. Elsner (2015, 56). Elsner's complication of the relation between relief and text here is generally anticipated by Blanshard (2007). For a more straightforward interpretation, see Lawton (1995, 30, 36). On *dexiosis* between humans in Athenian funerary sculpture, see Estrin (2023, 85–122); Arrington (2018).
79. Elsner (2015, 68): "Material culture . . . should provoke us to question our history as we write it and read it; to question the limitations of what we can know, based on a speculative and imaginative reconstruction from tiny and fragmentary parts of a totality now lost." Cf. Blanshard (2007, 20–21, 33–36).
80. Recall the "divine" *symbola* between Apollo and Hermes in the *Hymn to Hermes*, discussed in Chapter 7, notes 45–48 and accompanying text.
81. Gagarin (1989, 87).

82. Of course, the credibility of the claim in the eyes of a restored democratic Athenian assembly may itself reflect democratic bias against the oligarchs who took over in 411.
83. Hence the evidence does not support M.B. Walbank's (1986, 350) claim that, during the Athenian empire, *symbola* with Athens were "frequently biased in Athens' favor, thus reflecting her status as an imperial power."
84. Ste. Croix (1961, 94–95); see also Low (2013).
85. The three decrees are: *IG* I³ 68 (*OR* 152), "Kleonymos's decree," ca. 428–25; *IG* I³ 71 (*OR* 153), "Thoudippos's decrees," 425/24; and *IG* I³ 34 (*OR* 154), "Kleinias's decree," ca. 425–23. The two providing for trial in Athens are *IG* I³ 34, ll. 31–41; and *IG* I³ 68, ll. 43–52. In the third, *IG* I³ 71, all the penalties seem aimed at Athenians.
86. *IG* I³ 1453 (*OR* 155). Low (2013, 31) takes the decree as requiring "wholesale centralisation" of legal action in Athens for the cases contemplated; similarly, Ste. Croix (1961b, 269). But it is not clear that non-Athenians are to be brought before the court of the *thesmothetai*, or to Athens at all. As Osborne and Rhodes note in their commentary, "When our text starts it appears to be concerned . . . with sanctions against those not putting the decree into operation," i.e., with magistrates. There may be three categories of such magistrates contemplated: those of clause 2 ("if anyone," ἐὰν δέ τις [accepting *OR*'s restoration from the Hamaxitus fragment]); those of clause 3 ("if any other of the archons in the cities," ἐὰν δέ [τις ἄλλος τ]ῶν ἀρχόν[των ἐν τ]αῖσι πόλεσι); and those of clause 4 ("and if there are not archons of the Athenians," [καὶ εἰ μ]ή εἰσι ἄρχοντες Ἀθηναίων). The clause 4 phrase suggests that the first two groups are envisioned as Athenian magistrates and the last group as local non-Athenian magistrates. Clause 4 is too fragmentary to know what is to happen to this last class of magistrates, but the structure of the decree suggests it is different from the penalty for the first two groups. It may be that a local court was to hear claims against them, with loss of local citizenship the penalty. Clause 6 contemplates penalties against Athenian citizens (*contra OR* p. 337), clause 7 against Athenian generals. And clause 8 appears to require local magistrates to have the decree inscribed in each city, but with no penalty for disobeying. Overall, then, the decree as we have it appears more directly concerned with establishing punishments for the noncompliance of Athenians than of allies.
87. See, e.g., *IG* I³ 19; Meiggs (1949); Wilhelm (1939, 21–24).
88. Gauthier (1972, 203).
89. Athens and Troizen: *IG* II² 46 (*Agora* XVI 35; *SvA* 235); see Gauthier (1972, 166–67); D. Lewis (1959); Woodhead (1957, 225–29). Athens and Stymphalos: *IG* II² 144, but the most authoritative current edition and discussion is by M.B. Walbank (1986), whose text is reproduced at *Agora* XVI 47. *IG* II² 46 appears to refer to itself as *symbolai*: [συ]μβολὰς τάσδε, 38.
90. *IG* II² 46, l. 13: wounding (τρώση[ι]); l. 15: blinding (ἐκτυφλ[ῶσηι]); l. 20: crippling ([χ]ωλὸν ποι[ήσηι]); l. 34: intentional murder ([ἐὰν ἀποκτ]είνηι ἐκ [προνοίας]). *IG* II² 144, fr. k, ll. 4–5: killing ([ἀποκ]τείνηι, [ἀπο]κ̣τείνηι).
91. On the documents' similarity, see M.B. Walbank (1986, 338) (cf. 348 n.37), who suggests that the Troizen decree served as a deliberate model for the Stymphalos decree. The decrees' detailed rules can be seen, e.g., in their mention of: quantities of *drachmas* in several places, presumably as fines; officials (*xenodikai*, archons, *praktores*, *strategoi*, *proxenoi*, *presbeus*, *damiourgoi*); periods of time; and other court or lawsuit terms (δικαζ-; δίκης; δικαιότατα; [ὑπ]όδικος ὀφειλέτω; τὰς πράξεις; [ἔ]νδικον; μάρτυς; [μαρ]τύρησα).
92. Kirchner in *IG* II² (citing Wilhelm's opinion) and D. Lewis (1959) prefer an earlier date based on letter forms and layout. The irregularity of the checker pattern on this inscription is especially uncommon in Attica by the fourth century (Woodhead 1957). Woodhead connects *symbola* agreements to the Second Athenian naval confederacy in the early 370s: "commercial treaties . . . may have been a feature of the revival of Athenian influence in the Aegean area" and "perhaps marked the beginning of a new and vigorous phase in Athenian foreign policy" (1957, 227–28). But, as I noted, the language of these agreements indicates they are not commercial in a narrow sense.
93. Xen. *Hell.* 4.2.16, 6.2.3, 7.2.2.
94. For evidence of good relations, see *IG* II² 1425, ll. 227–32 (dating from 368/67, and mentioning crowns given by the Troizenians to the Athenian *boule* and *demos*). On the date of the *symbola* inscription, see the discussion in *Agora* XVI 35. Woodhead (1957, 224) argues that "Sparta's revived control of her League" in the 380s and 370s "appears to exclude the possibility" that a city in military alliance with Sparta could enter a *symbola* agreement with the Athenians (cf. Gauthier 1972, 166–67), but he does not argue the point further, and *IG* II² 1425, with the other evidence I discuss in this paragraph, indicates that the occasional hostilities between Troizenians and Athenians were confined to the surface of a deeper affinity.

95. On the terms of the King's Peace (*SvA* 242; also called the Peace of Antalcidas after the Spartan commander who was instrumental in its conclusion), see Xen. *Hell.* 5.1.31; Diod. Sic. 14.110.3. In 371, according to Xenophon (*Hell.* 6.3.7–8), the Athenian Autokles accused the Spartans of having violated their allies' autonomy by making them go to war against *poleis* toward which they were well disposed, τοὺς εὐμενεστάτους. This group of Spartan allies could very well have included Troizen.

96. Discussing what may be a similar situation, Funke (2009, 10) argues that the *sympoliteia* agreement between the Mantineans and Helissonians (*IPArk* 9), likely dating between 400 and 385, is evidence that "Mantinea was now no longer using treaties of alliance, but rather sympolities, [as] a clever trick to circumvent the corresponding clauses of [Mantinea's] thirty-years peace with Sparta." Both Funke and the inscription's first editor (te Riele, *SEG* 37.340) date the inscription before 385; the editors of *IPArk* date it to 350–40.

97. Plut. *Thes.* 3–6; Paus. 2.32.7–9 mentions sites in Troizen that the locals associated with Theseus. On Theseus as a connection between Athenians and Troizenians, see Nobili (2022, 13–17). The importance and long influence of the Theseus connection can be seen in both the iconography and written meaning of an Attic inscription dated to 140/39 (*IG* II^2 971; M.J. Osborne 1981, no. D102). The text indicates that Telesias of Troizen has taken advantage of the right to Athenian citizenship granted to his ancestors based both on their own good deeds for Athenians (ll. 16–17) and on the long-standing goodwill of Troizenians toward Athenians (ll. 13–15). The relief at the top of the stele portrays Theseus "lifting the rock which covered the *gnorismata* [or *symbola*??] by which he would prove his own Athenian citizenship, an event that took place in his youth in Troizen" (Lawton 1995, 157; photo on pl. 96). See M.J. Osborne's (1981, ii.189–91) commentary on the inscription. Pausanias (2.32.7) saw what the Troizenians believed to be the original rock in Troizen. He also (1.27.7–8) relates the story and tells us that a bronze statue of Theseus lifting this rock stood on the Athenian acropolis (a remarkable mixed-media sculpture, all in bronze except the rock itself). This late *stele* reveals long patterns of friendliness and mutually beneficial behavior between citizens of the two cities.

98. On the cult and sanctuary of Hippolytus at Troizen, see Paus. 2.32.1–4, calling it "extremely notable," ἐπιφανέστατος (2.32.1); cf. Rassia (2021) and the sources cited there. For evidence of Hippolytos cult in Athens, see *IG* I^3 255, l. 7 (late fifth century); *IG* I^3 369, l. 66 (second half of fifth century). Pausanias (3.12.9) mentions a hero shrine of "Hippolytos son of Theseus" in Sparta, but it has been suggested he may have erred here and that the object of cult in Sparta was one of at least two other Hippolytoses known from Greek legend; see Barrett (1964, 3 n.2).

99. In addition to his still-extant *Hippolytos*, sometimes known as the *Hippolytos Stephephoros* ("Crowned Hippolytos"), Euripides wrote a *Hippolytos Kalyptomenos* ("Veiled Hippolytos") that now exists only in fragments. Sophocles wrote a *Phaedra* that also is known only through fragments. The fragments of both plays are collected in an appendix by Roth (2015, 373–86).

100. See Barrett (1964, 5); cf. Roth (2015, 10–12). Lietzmann (*RE s.v. Hippolytos*, col. 1867) observes that the entire Athenian cult complex related to Hippolytos was probably adopted from Troizen.

101. Hdt. 8.41; Plut. *Them.* 10.3; Paus. 2.31.7. It is widely believed that the version of the "Decree of Themistocles" (relating to Athenian flight on the eve of Salamis) inscribed on a stone found in Troizen and first published in 1960 by M.H. Jameson (*ML* 23) is not genuine. See generally Knoepfler (2010); Johansson (2001). If that inscription is based on a late fourth-century literary version of Athenian preparations for the Persian invasion of Attica, as has been proposed, it is still evidence of the long afterlife enjoyed by Troizenian kindness toward Athenians in 480.

102. "And you, jurors, took them in after they were exiled, and made them citizens, and let them share in all your advantages, having remembered their good deed against the Barbarian across more than one hundred fifty years, and thinking it was only right that those who had helped you amidst dangers should, when suffering their own ill fortunes, be sheltered by you." καὶ ὑμεῖς μὲν ὦ ἄνδρ[ε]ς δικασταὶ ἐκπ[ε]σόντας αὐτοὺς ὑ̣πεδέ[ξ]ασ̣θε, καὶ πολίτας ἐποιήσασθε, καὶ τῶν ὑμετέρων ἀγαθῶν πάντ̣ω̣ν μετέδοτε, ἀπομνημονεύσαντες τὴν εὐεργεσίαν [τὴ]ν πρὸς τὸν βάρβαρον δι' ἐτῶν πλει̣[ό]νω̣ν̣ [ἢ π̣ε̣]ντήκοντα κ[αὶ] ἑκατόν, καὶ οἰόμ̣ε̣νοι [δεῖ̣ν̣] τοὺς ἐν τοῖς κινδύνοις ὑμῖν χ[ρ]ησίμους γενομένους, τούτο[υ]ς ἀτυχοῦντ̣[ας π̣]ε̣ρι[ποιηθῆναι] ὑφ' ὑμῶν, Hyp. *In Athenogenem* 31, col. 15.12–21 (Jensen ed.). The defendant in the speech is a former metic in Athens who subsequently became a citizen of Troizen (29, col. 14.1–6; 31, col. 15.5–8), hence this case may have been brought under the terms of the very *symbola* agreement documented in our inscription.

103. As M.B. Walbank (1986, 352 n.51) suggests, "Troizen . . . had claims of sentiment that may, in part, have promoted the establishment of its agreement with Athens." Two much-later inscriptions, from the first half of the second century (*IG* IV^2 1, 76 + 77 and *IG* IV 752; revised texts at *SEG* 55.425 and 55.418, respectively), recording the results of a Ptolemaic arbitral decision regarding a dispute between Troizen and nearby Arsinoe (the former Methana), indicate both the varied economic activity of the area (tuna fishing, salt production, stone quarrying, timber) and the fact that at this time the Athenians were seen as trusted third parties who had both sufficient good will and interest to assist the Ptolemaic arbitrators in resolving the dispute (see *IG* IV^{2}1, 76 + 77, ll. 51–56). Some of the economic, legal, and political facts revealed by these inscriptions may reflect long-standing economic and social patterns in the Saronic Gulf and the continuing interdependence of Athenians and Troizenians.
104. Nielsen (2015, 265; cf. 258–59); Xen. *Hell.* 7.4.6: τοῖς μέντοι Ἀρκάσι πέμπειν ἠναγκάζοντο τοῦς ἱππέας ἐπικούρους διὰ τὴν συμμαχίαν. On paleographic and historic grounds, M.B. Walbank (1986, 352) dates the *symbola* to 368, following Woodhead's (1957, 223–24) suggestion that "the period of rapprochement between Athens and Arkadia" matched well with the epigraphic considerations. The commentary to *IG* II^2 144 notes that Adolf Wilhelm found the omegas in this inscription to be identical to those in *IG* II^2 105 (*RO* 34), an Athenian treaty with Dionysius of Syracuse datable to 367, but Tracy (1995, 67–70) does not include 144 among the inscriptions carved by his "Cutter of *IG* II^2 105." One of the generals of the Arkadian confederacy in 367/66 was a certain Aineas of Stymphalos (Xen. *Hell.* 7.3.1; Ps.-Skylax 44), who may have been the Aineas "*Tacticus*" known as the author of a surviving work on siege warfare.
105. The date is uncertain because Iphikrates is reported to have invaded Arkadia twice, first in 392/91 (Xen. *Hell.* 4.4.16) and again in 370/69 (Xen. *Hell.* 6.5.49). Strabo (8.8.4) describes Iphikrates as having attempted to flood Stymphalos by blocking an underground stream with sponges, and Schaus (2015, 8 and n. 23) believes this tactic was more likely after the city center had been moved closer to Lake Stymphalos, which archaeological evidence suggests happened shortly after 392/91. See also Woodhead (1957, 224 n.4). Concerning the events in Arkadia that led to Athenian forces attacking Arkadia, see Nielsen (2015, 258–60).
106. That this treaty is between Athenians and Stymphalians rather than between Athenians and the Arkadian confederacy is of uncertain significance concerning the nature of that confederacy, since we cannot date the agreement precisely. If the agreement was concluded when the confederacy was a united organization, Stymphalos's independent entrance into an interstate pact would suggest the confederacy did not exercise full statehood by assuming all foreign relations powers (although the Athenian *symmachia* was with τοῖς Ἀρκάσι). Or, if we assume that the confederacy did assume all foreign relations powers, we must date the *symbola* agreement either before or (preferably) after the confederacy's existence. On confederacies, statehood, and international law, see my discussion of the Thessalians in Chapter 11.
107. E.g., most coins found in excavations at Stymphalos, especially those of the fourth century or earlier, have been from Sikyon; I have seen report of only a single Attic coin, dating to the late fourth century. See Weir (2014); Williams et al. (2002, 278).
108. Woodhead (1957, 225): "The goodwill generated by the[] negotiation and agreement [of *symbola* agreements] could have been regarded as a useful aim of Athenian diplomacy, and served as an additional support for the new league and the new military alliances on which the Athenians laid the foundation of their revived hegemony."
109. *Agora* XVI 56; *I.Eleusis* 138; Clinton (1980).
110. Mylonas (1961, 130–39); Clinton (1980, 275).
111. M.B. Walbank (1986, 352). See *IPArk* 18 (*SEG* 11.1107), lines 8 and 28: ἐν τῶι ἱερῶι τᾶς Ἀρτέμιτος τᾶς Βραυρωνίας.
112. Neither identification is by any means secure. On the acropolis sanctuary, see the thorough publication of Schaus (2015); on the lower sanctuary, see Seiler (1986, 120–29) with Morizot's cautions (1994, 204 n. 8). Another temple has been located east of the palaestra but with no indication of which divinity it was dedicated to (Williams et al. 2002, 180).
113. On Artemis and water sanctuaries, see Cole (2004, 192). Xenophon (*Anab.* 5.3.7–8) may have been reflecting a belief in the importance of water to Artemis in his dedication of an Artemis sanctuary alongside a river that he notes resembles the river near her temple in Ephesos. M.B. Walbank (1986, 352 n.51) concludes, "I should judge Stymphalos' agreement with Athens to partake more of sentiment or religious interest than of propinquity."

114. On the Athenian siege, see Diod. Sic. 15.34.3–35.2. For doubt whether Naxos was ever a member of the Confederacy, see Dreher (1995, 137); cf. Rutishauser (2012, 165). Naxos does not appear on the list of members in the Confederacy's "prospectus," *IG* II^2 43 (*RO* 22; *SvA* 257). An Athenian inventory inscription indicates that the Naxians gave a crown to the Athenians in 345/44: *IG* II^2 1443, col. 2, ll. 114–15.
115. *IG* II^2 179 (*SvA* 321). The rough dating is based on epigraphic features. See the survey by Rutishauser (2012, 165–67) of various proposed dates. On provisions for courts in Naxos and Athens: lines a9, a12; for *thesmothetai*: a10, a17; for court fees (τά τε πρυτανεῖα): a15; for cases with a right to appeal or transfer (τάς τε ἐφεσίμους δίκας): a16 (on the meaning of *ephesis* in an Athenian context, see Pelloso 2016). *Thesmothetai* were overwhelmingly associated with Athens and known as an Athenian legal magistracy, but non-Athenian *thesmothetai* are attested in a few inscriptions, in particular two from Amorgos, a neighbor of Naxos in the Cyclades (*IG* XII 7, 57, l. 12, ca. 300; *IG* XII 7, 515, l. 130, late second century); one from Larisa in Thessaly (*IG* IX 2, 634, undated).
116. Line C9, [το]ῖς Θηραίοις κύρια; l. c11, εἰς Θήραν ἀφικ[νουμένος]. See below for discussion of more certain cases.
117. Dreher (1995, 137–38) proposes that the reconciliation is internal to Naxos, a position that Berti (2012, 327–28) endorses. Reference to conflict between Athenians and Naxians is proposed by Gauthier (1972, 168) and Woodhead (1957, 225 n.7).
118. *Agora* XVI 51. Reference to Knossians in l. 12, καθάπτερ Κνωσ[ίοις]; likely references to a Knossos agreement also in ll. 8, 10, 16. The inventory inscription mentioned by Woodhead is *IG* II^2 1443, col. 2, ll. 114–15. It is impossible to say which *polis* is the Athenians' partner in the surviving *symbola* fragment, despite Dušanić's (1980–1981, 26) confidence that it must be Kydonia, also on Crete ("there is no other plausible restoration"). Dušanić follows Woodhead's (1957, 230) "very tenuous but plausible hypothesis" based on the appearance of [- - - κ]ρίναντες κυ[- - -] in l. 5. But even if κυ- is the beginning of a *polis* toponym or city-ethnic, Kydonia is not the only possible or plausible contender. Kytaion on Crete is another possibility; or Kyllandos or Kyrbissos in Karia; Kyrene in north Africa; or Kythnos in the Cyclades, just to name *poleis* that, for an Athenian, might be cognitively related to Knossos because of geographic proximity (compare how the fifth century Athens–Phaselis *symbola* discussed above [*IG* I^3 10; *OR* 120] referred to an Athenian agreement with Chios, not a close neighbor to Phaselis). In fact, if Dušanić is correct in his plausible (but by no means certain; see Woodhead 1957, 230 n.13) hypothesis that the -ωλλ- in l. 2 once held a form of the name Μαύσσωλλος, the satrap of Karia, that may increase the likelihood that the *polis* here was Karian; after all, both Kyllandos and Kyrbissos in Karia had been members of the Delian League and appear on fifth-century tribute lists and therefore had a history of relations with Athenians (on Mausolus's good relations with Knossos, see *RO* 55). But it may be that the κυ- in l. 5 does not hide a *polis* name at all. Following κρίναντες it may be a form of κύριος, as in the expression κύριος κρίνειν, "having power to pass legal judgment" (see, e.g., *Ath. pol.* 3.5; Arist. *Pol.* 2, 1273a11; 3, 1287b16; cf. Isoc. 18.68, κύριος ἀφεῖναι). A late second-century Cretan treaty between Lato and Olous (Chaniotis, *Verträge* 56A; *SvA* 706(III); coincidentally also involving Knossians) contains the phrase ἐγγράψαι δὲ ὥστε κυρίος ἦμεν κρίνοντας Κνωσίος ἐν μησὶν δέκα δύο, "and they are to publish that the Knossians have the power to make a decision within twelve months," ll. 9–10 (similarly Chaniotis, *Verträge* 55A [*SvA* 706(II)], ll. 16–18; Chaniotis, *Verträge* 54 [*SvA* 706(I)], ll. 11–13). Our inscription thus may have declared someone's authority to make a binding verdict.
119. *Contra* Dušanić (1980–1981, 27), who argues, "Athens' motive for approaching the two Cretan cities was imperialist rather than consular." Plato's *Laws* may also reflect close Athenian-Knossian connections at this time, see Morrow (1960, 25–27).
120. See his commentary to *Agora* XVI 35, p. 49. I also do not agree that there are good grounds for believing that *Agora* XVI 50 and 58 are *symbola* agreements. On *Agora* XVI 50 (relating to Athens and Siphnos), see now the edition by Matthaiou (2010), rejecting the restoration that would indicate that this is a *symbola* agreement, and dating it to between 409 and 385. *Agora* XVI 58 is simply too fragmentary to draw any conclusions.
121. See the "prospectus" of the confederacy, *IG* II^2 43 (*RO* 22; *SvA* 257), ll. 9–11, asserting its purpose as being "so that the Lacedaimonians will let the Greeks live in peace, free and autonomous," ὅπως ἂν Λακεδ[αιμό]νιοι ἐῶσι τὸς Ἕλληνας ἐλευθέ[ρ]ος [καὶ] αὐτονόμος ἡσυχίαν ἄγειν. Woodhead (1957, 227–28) suggests that these *symbola* agreements "perhaps marked the beginning of a new and vigorous phase in Athenian foreign policy, in which a threefold

approach, offering a choice of League membership, looser military symmachia, or purely commercial agreement, was adapted to the needs and wishes of the various cities."

122. The Greek text is reproduced with my earlier discussion of the passage, Chapter 7, notes 19–27 and accompanying text.
123. It is, however, possible that Hegesippus first came to believe that a *symbola* agreement would not have increased commerce with Macedonians and that this belief caused his opposition. But the general tenor of the speech as a whole suggests that his claim, even if sincere, was shaped by his hostility to Philip.
124. Since there never had been *symbola* between Athenians and Macedonians, he would have a poor basis for this claim unless he based it on observations of citizens of other distant states with which Athens did have *symbola* agreements. Again, any such claim would be highly impressionistic and biased and should be met with skepticism.
125. See his criticisms of pro-Macedonian Athenians at, e.g., 7.5, 17, 45.
126. See Trinkner and Tyler (2016, 421): "when people develop a healthy relationship with the law that is stable and based on mutual respect and shared values, they are more likely to support the legal system, comply with laws, and cooperate with legal authority. In these cases, people are motivated by . . . feelings of obligation and consent to legal regulation."
127. On Athenian epigraphic exceptionalism in the fifth century, see Lazar (2024b). On the waxing and waning of epigraphic habits across the Greek world over the centuries, see Nawotka (2021b) and Chapter 4, n. 6.
128. This is one way in which the use of *symbola* resembles that of international arbitration, submission to which powerful kings and the Romans consistently avoided; see Magnetto (2018, 86). The apparent exception that proves the rule that kings did not enter into *symbola* is Philip V, who did so—tellingly—only *after* his defeat to the Romans in 197. Polybius (23.1.1–13) reports that in 184/83 a large number of communities (including Thessalians, Perrhaibians, Athamanians, Epirotes, and Illyrians) sent envoys to Rome to complain that Philip was not complying with the dispute resolution procedures he was bound to "in accordance with the *symbolon*" (τοῦ γὰρ Φιλίππου συγκλεισθέντος εἰς τὴν κατὰ τὸ σύμβολον δικαιοδοσίαν, 23.1.2; cf. 23.1.12, οὐ φάσκοντες δύνασθαι τυχεῖν τοῦ δικαίου κατὰ τὸ σύμβολον). It is unclear if the *symbolon* between Philip and these communities was compelled by Rome or independently negotiated, but in any case it reflects Philip's loss of status in the international realm: he was now a peer of communities he used to rule. On Philip's self-acknowledged subservience to Rome, see Livy 39.26.11–12 (the Romans gave him certain cities and could take them away).
129. *IG* II^2 466. The *symbola* provision reads, "And in order that the *symbola* between Teneans and Athenians be in force, let the *thesmothetai* ratify the *symbola* when they first convene the *dikasteria*" (ὅπως δ' [ἂν κα]ὶ τὰ σύνβολα κύρια ἧι τὰ πρὸς Τηνίους κα[ὶ Ἀθην]αίους, τοὺς θεσμοθέτας ἐπικυρῶσαι τὰ [σύνβ]ολα, ὅταν πρῶτον δικασ[τήρι]α πλ[η]ρῶσιν, ll. 32–35). This inscription is noteworthy as the earliest certain occurrence of the neuter plural, τὰ σύνβολα, in an Athenian inscription. It also confirms the *Ath. pol.*'s statement (59.6) that by the second half of the fourth century in Athens a *dikasterion* headed by the *thesmothetai* had to ratify *symbola* agreements. But it shows that the *boule* could order the *thesmothetai* to do so, suggesting that, by this date at least, the *thesmothetai* were acting as a rubber stamp.
130. On the freeing of Athens by Demetrios Poliorketes, see Diod. Sic. 20.45–46. Reger (1992, 366–68) proposes the Teneans assisted him; cf. Buraselis (1982, 52–53 n.58).
131. This is the upper decree of *IG* II^3 1, 883 (ll. 1–8), which is confirmed in the later decree (dated to 281/80) that makes up most of the inscription. Étienne (1990, 176–78) has argued there were "profondes solidarités" between Athenians and Teneans. E.g., a speech composed by Demosthenes (*Against Polycles*) reveals that, in the 360s, Alexander of Pherai attacked Tenos and enslaved some of the citizens, and the Athenians took military action in response (Dem. 30.4–6).
132. The primary evidence is two inscribed letters from Antigonos to the Teans, *RC* 3–4 (*Syll.*[3] 344). For recent bibliography and a close analysis of the sections of *RC* 3 discussed here, see Egetenmeier (2016–2017).
133. The full provision (*RC* 3.24–30) is: "The lawsuits and actionable liabilities existing in each community among yourselves should be resolved or decided in accordance with each city's laws and in accordance with our declaration, within two years of when the declaration is publicly displayed. And regarding whatever lawsuits and actionable liabilities you have against the Lebedeans, or the Lebedeans against you, you should make an agreement, and it should

be written up, and if there is any opposition to the agreement it should be arbitrated by another city within six months. And the arbitral city is to be, by mutual agreement, Mytilene." I translate here the text of *RC* 3, altered in one immaterial respect by Wilhelm (1935, 283); cf. Klaffenbach (1948, 180). For discussion of the terms I translate as "lawsuits and actionable liabilities," τὰ δὲ ἐγκλήματα καὶ τὰ συμβόλαια, see Egetenmeier (2016–17, 172–78), who calls συμβόλαια a sort of procedural preliminary stage to ἐγκλήματα (177).

134. See Gauthier (1972, 315). The importance to Antigonos of having all existing lawsuits resolved within two years is apparent throughout this entire section, from lines 24 through 43. This overriding concern with timely resolution means we should be cautious in generalizing from the terms described here to what the terms of "ordinary" *symbola* of the period might have been.

135. Diod. Sic. 21.1.4–5; see Will (1984, 60). Pausanias (1.9.7; 7.3.5) reports that, in the first decade of the third century, Lysimachus forced the Lebedeans to settle in Ephesos and razed their city. This seems to indicate that the Lebedeans were still, or again by that time, politically distinct from the Teans. For discussion of the evidence whether the synoikism between Teans and Lebedeans was ever consummated, and if so for how long, see Ager (1998).

136. *I.Priene B-M* 8 (=*I.Priene* 28; *SvA* 782).

137. On these matters, see Polyb. 21.43–46; Livy 37.38–39; Ma (2000, 79–89, 162 and n.197); Will (1982, 228–29); Hiller von Gaertringen (1906, xvii).

138. See Ma (2000, 162 n. 197). Similarly noticeable is the lack of mention of Antigonos Gonatas in two documents arising out of a dispute in accordance with a *symbola* between the Athenians and the Boiotian *koinon* in 250, five years after Antigonos withdrew his garrison and declared the Athenians free (Euseb. *Chron.* 2, p. 120 [Schöne ed., 1866]: Ἀθηναίοις Ἀντίγονος τὴν ἐλευθερίαν ἀπέδωκεν). Habicht (1997, 152) notes that this grant of "freedom" by Antigonos meant "only that the king's exercise of his power had become less visible." The surviving *symbola*-related documents reflect this decreased visibility.

139. For one version of the now-dominant "vitalist" view of the *polis* after Alexander, see Gruen (1993). On *polis*—monarch interactions, focused on Antiochus III, see Ma (2000, 179–242). On *polis*—monarch and *polis*—Rome relations, see Rhodes (1997, 542–49).

140. *I.Priene B-M* 8, ll. i.8–9: "And those bringing charges against anyone after the da[te this *symbola* has become valid are to liti]gate thus: Milesians in Priene and Prieneans in Mi[letos]," τοὺς δὲ ἐγκαλοῦντας περί τινων ἀφ' οὗ χρό[νου ταῦτα τὰ σύμβολα ἐγένετο δικάζ]εσθαι Μιλησίους μὲν ἐμ Πριήνῃ, Πριηνεῖς δὲ ἐμ Μι[λήτωι·].

141. Lines i.10–11: "The Milesians in Priene before the gen[erals, and the Prieneans in Miletos before the em]porion overseers," Μιλήσιοι μὲν ἐμ Πριήνῃ τοῖς στρα[τηγοῖς, Πριηνεῖς δὲ ἐμ Μιλήτωι τοῖς τοῦ ἐμπ]ορίου ἐπιμεληταῖς. These lines show that at this time the office of *strategos*, "general," in Priene was concerned at least partially, if not wholly, with civil duties. Compare the similarly civil function of the *strategos* in Ptolemaic Egypt, and the entirely civil function of the Athenian polemarch (literally, "war archon") by the middle of the fifth century at the latest. For further examples of nonmilitary *strategoi*, see Hdt. 5.38; Polyb. 2.43.1.

142. The Prieneans seem to have been particularly prone to public boundary disputes with their neighbors, so much that Welles felt justified in speaking of their "penchant" for them, see commentary to *RC* 46 (p. 189). Ager (1996) collects inscriptional evidence of a number of arbitrated disputes between the Prieneans and their neighbors from the fourth through the first centuries: with the Milesians (Ager, *Arbitrations* 100 [=*I.Priene B-M* 141], 171 [=*I.Priene B-M* 67, 74, 75]); with the Magnesians (Ager, *Arbitrations* 25, 120); and with the Samians (Ager, *Arbitrations* 26, 74, 99).

143. See Gruen (1984, 96–131). He contrasts Roman responses to Greek appeals in legal matters with that toward appeals of political or military matters, to which the Senate was more responsive but still often minimally involved (1984, 117).

144. Polyb. 23.1.1–2.11. See further discussion in note 128, above.

145. The incident is described by Polybius, 32.7; cf. 30.20 for his account of and judgment on the Roman grant of Delos to the Athenians.

146. Polybius (32.7.5) reports the Roman response as that "the arrangements concerning the Delians made by the Achaians in accordance with the laws should be authoritative," κυρίας εἶναι τὰς κατὰ τοὺς νόμους γεγενημένας παρὰ τοῖς Ἀχαιοῖς οἰκονομίας περὶ τῶν Δηλίων. As F.W. Walbank correctly notes (1957–1979, iii.526), this seems to mean that, if the Achaians considered the Delians now to be Achaians and therefore covered by the *symbola*, the disputes should be resolved according to the *symbola*. See Habicht (1997, 248–49). Note that the

Athenians, in seeking to cut off Delian access to justice via both *symbola* and *syla*, were trying to make it impossible for the Delians to take any legal recourse at all.

147. On Greek federalism, see briefly Chapter 2, notes 27–31 and accompanying text. I discuss *koina* further in Chapter 11. On the apogee, see Ager (2015, 473).

148. Aitolians and Athenians (ca. 268–65): *IG* IX 1^{2} 176 (*SvA* 470); Aitolians (probably) and Delphians (late 3rd cent.): *F.Delphes* iii 1, 451; Boiotians and Athenians (ca. 250): *IG* II^{3} 997 and 998 (*SvA* 487); Achaians and Athenians (159): Polyb. 32.7; Thessalians and Philip V (190s): Polyb. 23.1.1–13; Perrhaibians and Thessalians (mid-second century): *SvA* 784. Scholars have connected two second-century inscriptions mentioning *symbola* to which the Perrhaibians were a party, both included under *SvA* 784. The first, published by Arvanitopoullos in 1910 and dated around 170, states that the other party was the Thessalians. In the other (*IG* IX 2 1106, dated around 130), "Thessalians" was restored by Stählin (1929, 212) and accepted as likely by Errington (*SvA* 784) and Gauthier (1972, 340 n.143), but is not certain (Ager 1996, App. 7 prefers "Magnesians"). Perrhaibia was a perioikic region of Thessaly, often politically part of the Thessalian *koinon*. The short-lived Perrhaibian *koinon* is generally ignored in accounts of Greek federalism and seems to be considered more an *ethnos* than a federal state proper. On evidence for it, and its second century reabsorption into the Thessalian *koinon, see* Kramolisch (1979).

149. The centralization was always qualified, however, and never complete. Hence the evidence for a *symbola* agreement between Athenians and Delphians is two decrees for Lamians, who sent individuals to judge a dispute covered by the agreement. Yet Lamia itself was at the time a member of the Aitolian *koinon*, while still being seen from the outside as independent enough to serve as *ekkletos polis* in such matters. See *Agora* XVI, p. 297; Habicht (1982, 25).

150. See Gauthier (1972, 308–38).

151. On international arbitration, see Magnetto (2018) and (1997); Ager (1996); Piccirilli (1973); Tod (1913). We know of about sixty international arbitrations before 338, and about three times that number between 338 and the early first century BCE. On "foreign judges," see the foundational article by Robert (1973); Scafuro (2014); and the many articles on the topic by C.V. Crowther, including (2008, 2006, 1999, 1993). On their increasing frequency after the fourth century, see Scafuro (2014, 365); C.V. Crowther (2006, 33). For an overview of both phenomena, see Magnetto (2016).

152. *IG* XII 7, 67B, ll. 36–90 (Migeotte, *Emprunt* 49; *Syll.*^{3} 955; *I.jur.gr.* i 15, pp. 312–41; Bagnall and Derow 72 (English trans.)); see Gabrielsen (2008, 128); Ager (1996, 514); Gauthier (1980, 197–205; 1972, 325–26); Tarn (1923, 108–12). An earlier example of an *ekkletos polis* may be found in the fragmentary *symbola* agreement between the Naxians and Athenians dated between 375 and 350, *IG* II^{2} 179, discussed above; see Cataldi (1979, 7); Gauthier (1972, 168). It is not certain that the Therans there played the role of *ekkletos polis*. But since that case also involved the Naxians, our evidence suggests the latter may have been early adopters of using foreign judges with *symbola*.

153. *IG* XII 7, 67B, ll. 63–64: καθάπερ δίκην ὠφληκότων ἐν τῆι ἐκκλήτωι κατὰ τὸ σύμβολον τὸ Ναξ[ίω]ν καὶ Ἀρκεσινέων. The word πόλις is implied (although not required) by the gender of τῆι ἐκκλήτωι.

154. "To exact payment": πράξεσθαι (l. 59), εἰσπράξεσθαι (l. 65); "to seize a deposit or amount owed": ἐνεχυράζεσθαι (l. 65). Another inscription from Amorgos (*IG* XII, 7, 69; Magnetto 1997, no. 18) reveals that, around this same time, the Arkesineans entered into a loan contract on similar terms with a certain Alexandros from an unknown city. Although fragmentary, this inscription appears to make no mention of a *symbola* agreement between Arkesine and Alexandros's home city, suggesting that no underlying *symbola* was seen as necessary for the Arkesineans to grant such broad self-help rights to major creditors of the city. But Magnetto (1997, 118) suggests, reasonably, that a relevant *symbola* may nevertheless have existed.

155. On cities borrowing from private lenders, see generally Migeotte (1984). The leverage such wealthy people held may be emblematic of the Greek civic culture of "euergetism" by rich private people that expanded about this time and continued, by some accounts, until perhaps the second century CE. For inroads into this large topic, see von Reden (2021); Quaß (1993); Gauthier (1985); Veyne (1976, section II).

156. *IG* II^{3} 997 and 998. See Gauthier (1999, 157–64; 1972, 172, 337–38); Roesch (1982, 401–03). The *symbola* agreement is mentioned at *IG* II^{3} 997, l. 11; *ekkletos polis* at 12–13; "decided justly" ([ἔκ]ριναν δικαίως) is stated at *IG* II^{3} 998, l. 5. The Lamians later judged more disputes

between Athenians and Boiotians, in the late third or early second century, presumably under the same agreement: *IG* II^3 1171.

157. A public law dispute between the city of Athens and the Boiotian *koinon* would likely have been handled through bespoke procedures in international arbitration. See Gauthier (1999, 158); Magnetto (1997, 206); Robert (1929, 163).
158. *I.Delphinion* 152 (with the supplementary material of *I.Milet* 1, pp. 189–91). The original editor, Albert Rehm, interpreted the disputes as public law disputes between the cities of Eresos and Methymna, but Robert (1925, 32–36) correctly recognized that they were between private citizens; cf. Gauthier (1972, 344). The three decrees on the stone, which was found in Miletos, refer to both a συνθήκα and an ἐπισυνθήκα (e.g., ll. 4–5, 20–21), which Robert (1925, 35–36) reasonably interprets as referring to a primary treaty (συνθήκα) between all four cities of Lesbos and a special rider (ἐπισυνθήκα) between only the Methymnians and Eresians. Robert (1925, 38–41) also first connected this inscription to another, from roughly the same time, containing the text of the "founding charter" of a Lesbian *koinon*, *IG* XII Suppl. 136 (*IG* XI 1064; Labarre 1996, no. 89). On the Lesbian *koinon*, see Labarre (1996, 70–74); cf. Buraselis (2013, 177–79).
159. Kalliontzis (2020, no. 33, pp. 201–17) (*SEG* 70.191).
160. Kalliontzis (2020, 211–12).
161. My translation and discussion are indebted to Kalliontzis's French translation and his rich commentary.
162. I translate this sentence following the text suggested by Rousset (*BE* 2021 no. 237). See the text and apparatus printed as an appendix to this chapter.
163. Kalliontzis (2020, 210–11) calculates that close to twenty years must have passed, even at a relatively high interest rate of between 15 and 20 percent. He also notes that the "seventy minas times two" must mean that the plaintiffs calculated the amount owed by starting from an original loan of seventy minas, which they doubled as an automatic penalty under the terms of the loan.
164. If Nion and Lioukos were designated as trial judges, they must have been so designated by a preliminary tribunal, by the judges described in lines 22–23 as having "decided": on this interpretation, these "preliminary" judges did not decide on a verdict but rather decided to appoint Nion and Lioukos as trial judges. My thanks to Flavio Santini for suggesting this possibility to me, and for helpful discussion of this inscription. For the process of appeal in the agreement between the Athenians and Naxians, see *IG* II^2 179, l. a16, where the fragmentary phrase survives, "to introduce the appealable lawsuits," [ἐ]νάγειν δὲ τάς τε ἐφεσίμους δίκας. On appeals in Athenian domestic procedure, see Pelloso (2016); MacDowell (1978, 30–33); A.R.W. Harrison (1968–71, ii.72–74); Lipsius (1905–15, iii.953–64); on the availability of appeal in some suits in Ptolemaic Egypt, see, e.g., *P.Lille* 1, 29 (*C.Ptol.Sklav.* 1), ll. 4–5. Another possibility is that the Orchomenians have received a favorable judgment that they are recording for posterity while awaiting a second, damages phase of the trial, to be presided over by Nion and Lioukos. But it is not obvious that damages would be available here, since Orchomenian victory would presumably mean dismissal of the suit. We do know, however, that in Athens penalties were sometimes available for "frivolous" lawsuits, as judged by the plaintiff failing to receive a certain minimal percentage of jurors' votes; see Andoc. 1.33; Dem. 21.47; A.R.W. Harrison (1968–74, ii.83). Such a rule seems unlikely in this situation.
165. The inscription was recently re-edited as *IG* XII 4, 4044 (Magnetto, *Arbitrati* 14; Ager, *Arbitrations* 21; *Tit. Calymnii* 79; *Syll.*^{3} 953). See also the recent discussion by Paschalidis (2023), who provides an English translation.
166. Demetrios's role is made clear by a Kalymnian decree honoring a Milesian citizen named Hekatomynos specifically for acting as advocate in this trial against the Koans, *IG* XII 4, 3952. It describes the proceeding as taking place "before the court appointed by the Knidians and in accordance with the command of King Demetrios," ἐπὶ [τὸ] δικαστήριον [τὸ ἀ]ποδειχθὲν [ἁ]μῖν ὑπὸ Κνιδίω[ν καὶ κα]τὰ τὸ βασιλέως π[ρόστ]αγμα Δαματρί[ου], ll. 10–12.
167. Comparison with our Boiotian case also emphasizes that the Kalymnian-Koan dispute regarded a matter of essentially private rather than public law. In both inscriptions describing the suit, the Kalymnians describe their lawsuit as being against apparently private individuals, "the children of Diagoras" (*IG* XII 4, 3952, l. 5; *IG* XII 4, 4044, ll. 134–35). Although one party was a city, the other party was neither one of its own citizens nor another city. So the case does not fit within the standard form of public law international arbitrations that are the main concern in the collections of Magnetto (1997) and Ager (1996). Nor does it fit the ordinary view of

public law as the state's regulation of relations with and between its own residents and citizens; see Paschalidis (2023, 2).

168. *IG* VII 3172 (Migeotte, *Emprunt* 13).
169. Kalliontzis (2020, 204–05) lists the officials named in both inscriptions: Kaphisodoros son of Damatrichos, Perilaos son of Anaxion, Euareis son of Euchoros, Philomeilos son of Philon, and Athanodoros son of Hippon.
170. The two men named as judges near the bottom of the surviving stone, Nion the Theban and Lioukos the Kalydonian, are known from other sources to have been federal officials in the Boiotian and Aitolian federations, respectively (Kalliontzis 2020, 205–07). But this does not illuminate which entities were parties to the *symbola*.
171. Since the Amphissans did not join the Aitolian *koinon* until sometime between about 272 and 262, the *symbola* agreement could even have predated that event. The Amphissans probably joined the *koinon* after an Aitolian decree dated to 272 granting Aitolian citizenship to a particular Amphissan (*IG* IX I^2 1, 12, l. 1), and before an inscription commemorating Aitolian proxeny grants, dated ca. 262, in which an Amphissan is named as guarantor (ἔνγυος) of several Rhodian *proxenoi* (*IG* IX 1^2 1, 17, l. 33–35). Another Amphissan is named as an Aitolian official in an inscription from ca. 250 (*SEG* 62.347, l. 2). See Scholten (2000, 29 n.1, 55 n.86, 61 n.8).
172. On Boiotian-Aitolian relations at this time, see Kalliontzis (2020, 115–17). Most notably, about a thousand Boiotian soldiers died in a major loss to Aitolians in a battle at Chaeroneia in 245, after which the Boiotians were forcibly allied to the Aitolians for perhaps a decade, until they were "freed" from the alliance by the Macedonian king Demetrios II.
173. An inscription from Thermon in Aitolia, dated to "ca. 246–236," grants Aitolian proxeny to Diogeiton son of Potammeis, Διογẹίτονι Ποτάμμẹιος Ὀρχομεγίω, *IG* IX 1^2 1, 25a, l. 34. Another inscription from Thermon, dated less specifically to "ca. 262-236," appears, in a badly damaged section, to name two men from Orchomenos as Aitolian *proxenoi*, *IG* IX 1^2 1, 17, ll. 102–105.
174. *F.Delphes* iii 1, 451. See Gauthier (1972, 97, 262); Roussel (1926, 128).
175. Although Delphi was under effective Aitolian control from the 270s, it does not appear to have been a member of the *koinon*. See Grainger (1999, 105, 121–22, 142–46); Roussel (1926, 133). Therefore it seems that, as the inscription suggests, these disputes fell under a true international *symbola* agreement rather than being required by the governing law of the Aitolian *koinon*. Because of the major role played by Aitolians in the Pylai–Delphi Amphictyony after 279, it seems that there was a large presence of Aitolians in Delphi for the next century or so; see Scholten (2000, 97–104); Grainger (1999, 184–85); Roussel (1926, 133).
176. *F.Delphes* iii 4, 169, l. 3. See Robert (1929, 162–64).
177. Béquignon (1935, 64–69 no. 3) (*ed. pr.*); see the edition by Gauthier (1999, 165–74) (text printed at *SEG* 49.621), with new restorations, photo, and French translation.
178. *IG* VII^2 2, 1 292; see Gauthier (1993, 592–98). The first editors (Roesch and Argoud 1993) attributed the decree to the Thebans, but Gauthier argues persuasively that the decree was issued by the *polis* whose name does not survive and that this *polis* was Eretria. I have not attempted here a comprehensive catalog of *symbola* providing for decisions by judges from a third *polis*. Probably to be included, e.g., is the second-century resolution by judges from Larisa of disputes between the Boiotian *polis* Akraiphia and its neighbors, although the surviving decree in their honor mentions not a *symbola* but simply a "writing," γραπτόν: *IG* VII 4130, l. 4; see Ager (1996, appendix 12); Roesch (1985, 130); Gauthier (1972, 343–44).
179. See Magnetto (2016, 31–32); Ager (1996, 11); Robert (1973, 75). Many decrees for foreign judges and arbitrators say they acted "fairly and justly," ἴσως καὶ δικαίως, but this is not the same as calling them neutral or unbiased.
180. See, e.g., Waldron (2008, 7–8); Summers (1993, 130–35); Raz (1979, 217).
181. This is Plutarch's point in the opening sentence of his brief treatise "On Love for One's Offspring," Περὶ τῆς εἰς τὰ ἔγγονα φιλοστοργίας, *Moralia* 493a–497e, where he compares resorting to foreign judges to the practice of international trade: "Arbitral decisions and the bringing of cases before foreign courts were first conceived among Greeks out of distrust of each other, out of a need for foreign justice just like that for any other necessity that does not grow among themselves"; ἔκκλητοι κρίσεις καὶ ξενικῶν δικαστηρίων ἀγωγαὶ τοῖς Ἕλλησι τὸ πρῶτον ἀπιστίᾳ τῇ πρὸς ἀλλήλους ἐπενοήθησαν, ἀλλοτρίας δικαιοσύνης ὥσπερ ἑτέρου τινὸς τῶν ἀναγκαίων μὴ φυομένου παρ' αὐτοῖς δεηθεῖσιν, 493a–b. Failure of neutrality was not the only reason to resort to foreign judges: some other sort of systemic political or

judicial crisis might drive a community to constitute a tribunal from outsiders. C.V. Crowther (1995, 122) argues that "the disruptive effects of warfare, compounded ... by natural disaster" motivated a series of appeals to foreign judges by Iasos in the third and second centuries; Robert (1929, 165) argues that in second-century Delphi "une anarchie judiciaire prolongée" had a similar result.

182. On a wholesale shift toward foreign judges, see Gauthier (1972, 345–46). But C.V. Crowther (1995, 123) is surely correct that such use did not become routine and that this is indicated by the fact that special honors were granted when foreign judges *were* called upon.

183. Such clauses are practically universal in these decrees. E.g., the Athenian decree of 109/08 for judges from Larisa notes the "friendship and goodwill" exhibited toward Athenians by the *demos* of Larisa, [τὴν π]ρὸς Ἀθηναίους φιλίαν καὶ εὔνοιαν, *SEG* 49.621, l. 16. The decree for judges from Oropos states that the Oropians wished to demonstrate their preexisting *syngeneia* with one or both of the disputing communities, θέλοντες ἀ[ποδεῖξαι ἡμῖν? ὅτι διατηροῦσι] τὴν ὑπάρχουσαν αὐτοῖς συγγένειάν τε κα[ὶ φιλίαν], *SEG* 43.210, ll. 4–6.

Chapter 9

1. Our earliest version of the story is from Cicero, *Rep.* 3, fr. 1 (Powell ed.): *Nam cum quaereretur ex eo, quo scelere inpulsus mare haberet infestum uno myoparone, 'Eodem,' inquit, 'quo tu orbem terrae.'* The quotation is reported differently by Augustine (*De civ. D.* 4.4) and by Nonius (125.12; 318.18 *s.v. habere*; 534.14 *s.v. myoparo*), the source of the fragment as it appears in modern editions of Cicero's *De republica.* Nonius, unlike Augustine, is presumably quoting Cicero verbatim. Cicero may have taken the story from Carneades (who lived ca. 214–129 BCE), see *Rep.* 3.7 (Powell ed.).
2. It is also Augustine's point in relating the story: human nations lacking justice are in fact no better than pirate regimes.
3. To be clear, the "marginality" I am talking about here is not socioeconomic marginality within a relatively small community such as a single city. Greeks with a reputation for piracy were not the poor or destitute, those "born on the wrong side of the tracks." Rather they were large sub-Hellenic ethnic groups that included within themselves rich and poor, socially high- and low-born.
4. On the economic logic of piracy and its suppression, see Gabrielsen (2013b; 2003, 399–403); Davies (1984, 290); A.H. Jackson (1973, 243–48). On elite participation, see D.M. Lewis (2019, 82, 101); Gabrielsen (2013b, 138); Brulé (1978, 180–83). On states as inherently antipiratic, see Kosmin (2024, 139–61); Garlan (1972, 22–23); on some states embracing piracy, see Gabrielsen (2013b, 138–39).
5. For the "naïve" view, consider the opening sentence of Ormerod (1924, 13): "Throughout its history the Mediterranean has witnessed a constant struggle between the civilised peoples dwelling on its coasts and the barbarians, between the peaceful trader using its highways and the pirate who infested the routes that he must follow." For "piracy in the eye of the beholder," see Gabrielsen (2001, 221); Jacoby, *FGrH* 3B Suppl. 2, p. 322; cf. de Souza (1999, 241). Kosmin (2024, 139–61) presents a view of pirate marginality similar to my own: socially constructed in part but no less real for all that; in fact, the geographic literalness of pirate marginality is central to Kosmin's account.
6. Versions of this account are offered by Gabrielsen (2013b, 2001); Giovannini (2007, 303–04); Rihll (1993); van Wees (1992). According to Gabrielsen (2013b, 142), the "raid mentality" was not eliminated from "respectable" Greek society; rather it was channeled into and legitimized by particular military situations. Avidov's (1997) approach is sympathetic to mine. Positing the unchanging antiquity of a certain marginal ethnic group risks bordering on a sort of romanticizing anthropology such as Fermor (2004, 31–33) engages in (self-consciously) when he suggests the twentieth-century transhumant Sarakatsans of northern Greece are the direct and unmixed descendants of the Dorian invaders of millennia earlier.
7. Helpful overviews are provided by Kosmin (2024); J.R. Hall (2024); D.M. Lewis (2019); Gabrielsen (2001); de Souza (1999); Ferone (1997); Davies (1984, 285–90); Garlan (1978); A.H. Jackson (1973); Ormerod (1924). On some of the earliest evidence for piracy by Greeks, see Luraghi (2006, 30–34).

8. On the ambiguous vocabulary of piracy, see Wiemer (2002, 112–16); de Souza (1999, 2–12); Ferone (1997, 43–67); Pritchett (1991, 315–18); Garlan (1978, 2–5); Ormerod (1924, 59–61); cf. Rigsby (1996, 17). See Pritchett's (1991, 324–48) catalog of occurrences of *leistes* and *peirates* and their cognates in works dating from the seventh to second centuries. A less common word of narrower meaning is καταποντιστής, literally "one who [throws] into the sea"; see de Souza (1999, 9–10).
9. On the distinction and continuing ambiguity between "pirate" and "privateer" in the early modern period, see E. Murphy (2020). On their common characteristics, see Gabrielsen (2001, 223–24); de Souza (1999, 19–26). On the importance of distinguishing between them, see Avidov (1997, 15).
10. On *leistes* as derogatory, see de Souza (1999, 6–7); Avidov (1997, 7–8); Pritchett (1991, 316–17); Wankel (1976, ii.788).
11. The Aitolians had a reputation for stretching this rule to, or even beyond, its limits, see Polyb. 18.4.8–5.4.
12. The first quotation is from Gabrielsen (2001, 221); the second is adapted from Jacoby, who attributes the attitude to Greek historians, *FGrH* 3B Suppl. 2, p. 322; cf. J.R. Hall (2024, 182).
13. See Cic. *Off.* 3.107: "For the pirate is not counted among the number of military opponents but is the common enemy of everyone," *nam pirata non est ex perduellium numero definitus, sed communis hostis omnium*; cf. Cic. *Verr.* 2.4.21: "You acted exactly in a manner typical of pirates, who are the common enemy of all," *fecisti item ut praedones solent, qui . . . hostes communes sint omnium.* The idea is not confined to Cicero. See, e.g., *Dig.* 49.15.24 (Ulpian): "Enemies are those against whom the Roman people have publicly declared war, or who have declared it against the Roman people; others are called highway robbers or pirates," *hostes sunt quibus bellum publice populus Romanus decrevit vel ipsi populo Romano: ceteri latrunculi vel praedones appellantur.* On the Roman legal treatment of the bandit (*latro*) as a non-person outside the law, see Shaw (2004, 342–43). Polybius (2.12.6) calls the Illyrians "the common enemies of all," πᾶσι κοινοὺς ἐχθρούς, and he likely has in mind their practice of "private" piracy (ἰδίᾳ, 2.8.8) whose restriction by the Romans he narrates at 2.2–12. On customary laws that our surviving sources *do* describe as "laws of the Greeks," see Chapter 2, notes 55–61 and accompanying text.
14. Hdt. 6.17: ὁρμώμενος δὲ ἐνθεῦτεν ληιστὴς κατεστήκεε Ἑλλήνων μὲν οὐδενός, Καρχηδονίων δὲ καὶ Τυρσηνῶν.
15. On Herodotus's description of Dionysios, see J.R. Hall (2024, 180).
16. On the date and other aspects of this inscription (last seen by scholars in the nineteenth century), see the new edition and commentary by Adak and Thonemann (2022, 97–116).
17. Adak and Thonemann (2022, Document 2) (*OR* 102B; *Nomima* i 104; *Syll.*[3] 37/38), ll. 18–27:

    . . . [ἢ κιξα]-
    λλεύοι : ἢ κιξάλλας : ὑπο-
    δέχοιτο : ἢ ληΐζοιτο : ἢ λ-
    ηιστὰς : ὑποδέχοιτο : εἰ-
    δὼς : ἐκ γῆς : τῆς Τηΐης : ἢ [θ]-
    αλάΤης : φέροντας : ἢ [τι κ]-
    ακὸν : βολεύοι : περὶ Τ[ηΐ]-
    ων : τῶ ξυνῶ : εἰδὼς : ἢ π[ρὸς]
    Ἕλληνας : ἢ πρὸς βαρβάρο-
    υς : ἀπόλλυσθαι.

18. An earlier provision (ll. 3–6) curses anyone participating in domestic revolution.
19. The potential breadth of concern in this final quoted portion of the inscription is already indicated in the previous clause, by the applicability of the curses to those who receive "pirates who are carrying things off from the Tean land *or the sea*": not only is "the sea" not qualified as Tean harbors or territorial waters; there is no limitation to Tean seaborne victims or Tean property. This clause, then, also reaches toward a condemnation of all piracy, not just that which targeted Teans and their property or even all Greeks. Contrast the interpretation of A.H. Jackson (1995, 98), who sees this inscription as evidence that piracy was perfectly respectable so long as it was practiced "from a base at a sufficiently discreet distance from home."
20. For text and discussion of the other set of curses, see Adak and Thonemann (2022, Document 3, 116–36), with their proposal (139–40) that the curses were displayed at both Teos and Abdera. On Tean settlement of Abdera, see Adak and Thonemann (2022), esp. 75–94. They explain (82–84) that Teans actually joined a preexisting settlement founded by Klazomenians.

21. Democr., DK 68 B fr. 260 (= Laks–Most *Atom.* D384) (Stob. 4.2.18): κιξάλλην καὶ ληστὴν πάντα κτείνων τις ἀθῷος ἂν εἴη καὶ αὐτοχειρίῃ καὶ κελεύων καὶ ψήφῳ. The similarity of his collocation of "highway robbers" and "pirates" to that in the Tean curses is likely not a coincidence, since the word in both texts for "highway robber," κιξάλλης, is attested nowhere else (Adak and Thonemann 2022, 112).
22. He adds, "Local shrines in each community, and truces, and oaths, forbid it." Democr., DK 68 B fr. 259 (= Laks–Most *Atom.* D383) (Stob. 4.2.17): ὅκωσπερ περὶ κιναδέων τε καὶ ἑρπετέων γεγράπται τῶν πολεμίων, οὕτω καὶ κατὰ ἀνθρώπων δοκεῖ μοι χρεὼν εἶναι ποιεῖν· κατὰ νόμους τοὺς πατρίους κτείνειν πολέμιον ἐν παντὶ κόσμῳ, ἐν ᾧ μὴ νόμος ἀπείργει· ἀπείργει δὲ ἱερὰ ἑκάστοισιν ἐπιχώρια καὶ σπονδαὶ καὶ ὅρκοι.
23. On these passages, see Adak and Thonemann (2022, 112–13); Procopé (1990, 26–27); Paneris (1983), who argues (p. 302) the first passage quoted is the text of a law drafted by Democritus for the Abderites. On Democritean ethics generally, see Johnson (2020).
24. Aesch. *Sept.* 602–04: ξυνεισβὰς πλοῖον εὐσεβὴς ἀνὴρ / ναύτῃσι θερμοῖς καὶ πανουργίᾳ τινὶ / ὄλωλεν ἀνδρῶν ξὺν θεοπτύστῳ γένει.
25. Nep. *Them.* 2.3; Plut. *Cim.* 8.3–4: ληϊζόμενοι δὲ τὴν θάλασσαν ἐκ παλαιοῦ. Thucydides (1.98.2) is less generous about the Athenian action, stating that the Athenians "enslaved" Skyros, ἠνδραπόδισαν, and settled it with Athenians. Plutarch's account suggests that what was normally private piracy practiced by the Dolopes had become sanctioned by the Dolopian state in one instance and that this was the instigation for Cimon's attack.
26. Canevaro and Lewis (2024, 196–98); Bresson (2016, 303); Woolmer (2016, 74–76); Ober (2015, 201); Gabrielsen (2013b, 140–44). But de Souza (1999, 27–29) finds little evidence that the Athenians and the Delian League actively suppressed piracy before the Peloponnesian War. Avidov (1997, 21–22) is more generally skeptical of supposed Athenian anti-piracy efforts, suggesting they may be seen as part of a larger exploitative and, itself, essentially "piratic" approach to foreign policy, with the main difference being the patina of state legitimacy on Athenian acts.
27. *IG* I^3 75 (*SvA* 184), ll. 8–10: "And [the Halieians shall] not harbor raiders nor commit raiding themselves nor wage war with the enemy against Athenians or the Athenians' allies," καὶ λ[ειστὰς μὲ hυποδέχεσθαι μεδ' α]ὐτọ̀ς [λε]ίζẹ[σ]θαι μεδὲ χσ[υστρατεύεσθαι μετὰ τõν πο]λ̣εμίον ἐπ̣' [Ἀθε]ναίος μεδ' ἐ[πὶ τὸς χσυμμάχος τὸς Ἀθεναί]ον. An even more fragmentary treaty with (perhaps) the Mytileneans, from around the same time, appears to contain a similar anti-raiding clause, *IG* I^3 67 (*SvA* 167), ll. 7–8.
28. We hear of the Spartans authorizing privateering at, e.g., Thuc. 5.115.2, "The Spartans . . . announced that anyone among them could make raids against the Athenians," Λακεδαιμόνιοι . . . ἐκήρυξαν δὲ εἴ τις βούλεται παρὰ σφῶν Ἀθηναίους λῄζεσθαι; Xen. *Hell.* 5.1.1, "And, with the ephors' approval, he permitted whoever wished to make plundering raids upon Attica [or, "upon shipping coming out of Attica"]," συνδόξαν καὶ τοῖς ἐφόροις ἐφίησι λῄζεσθαι τὸν βουλόμενον ἐκ τῆς Ἀττικῆς.
29. Pl. *Leg.* 7.823e: μηδ' αὖ ἄγρας ἀνθρώπων κατὰ θάλατταν ληστείας τε ἵμερος ἐπελθὼν ὑμῖν θηρευτὰς ὠμοὺς καὶ ἀνόμους ἀποτελοῖ· κλωπείας δ' ἐν χώρᾳ καὶ πόλει μηδὲ εἰς τὸν ἔσχατον ἐπέλθοι νοῦν ἅψασθαι.
30. [Dem.] 7.14: περὶ δὲ τῶν λῃστῶν δίκαιόν φησιν εἶναι κοινῇ φυλάττειν τοὺς ἐν τῇ θαλάττῃ κακουργοῦντας ὑμᾶς τε καὶ αὐτόν. Cf. 7.3: "For all pirates seize places that belong to others and make those places secure, and from there they harm others," ἅπαντες γὰρ οἱ λῃσταὶ τοὺς ἀλλοτρίους τόπους καταλαμβάνοντες καὶ τούτους ὀχυροὺς ποιούμενοι, ἐντεῦθεν τοὺς ἄλλους κακῶς ποιοῦσιν.
31. Arist. *Rhet.* 1.12, 1372a23–28: ἀδικοῦσι δὲ . . . οἱ συλῶντες τοὺς Καρχηδονίους.
32. *IG* XII 5, 653, ll. 10, 26, 30 (Bielman, *Retour à la liberté* 52); cf. *SEG* 59.931. See also Polyb. 13.8.2: he states that Nabis of Sparta "participated with the Cretans in piracy at sea," ἐκοινώνει μὲν γὰρ τοῖς Κρησὶ τῶν κατὰ θάλατταν ληστειῶν, and continues with the claim that Nabis gave refuge to temple robbers, highway robbers, and murderers in exchange for a share of their profits. For Polybius, the *leisteia* referred to here is apparently on the same level as banditry and temple robbery rather than war and privateering. Xenophon is able, when he wishes, to distinguish plundering undertaken for official military purposes from that done for personal enrichment, κατὰ τὰς ἰδίας λείας (*Hell.* 1.2.4–5) (although in this passage he does not explicitly condemn the latter).
33. Hegesippus, the speaker of *On Halonnesus*, does not trust Philip's motives. The quotation above continues ([Dem.] 7.14): "But he really has nothing in mind other than to be established at sea

by you, and for you to agree that without Philip you aren't strong enough to establish safety at sea," οὐδὲν ἀλλ' ἢ τοῦτ' ἀξιῶν, ὑφ' ὑμῶν εἰς τὴν θάλατταν κατασταθῆναι, καὶ ὁμολογῆσαι ὑμᾶς ὡς ἄνευ Φιλίππου οὐδὲ τὴν ἐν τῇ θαλάττῃ φυλακὴν δυνατοί ἐστε φυλάττειν.

34. [Dem.] 12.2: "When the Thasians received the Byzantine triremes and whichever pirates wanted to come, you paid no attention, although the agreements explicitly state that those who do such things are enemies." Θασίων ὑποδεχομένων τὰς Βυζαντίων τριήρεις καὶ τῶν λῃστῶν τοὺς βουλομένους οὐδὲν ἐφροντίζετε, τῶν συνθηκῶν διαρρήδην λεγουσῶν πολεμίους εἶναι τοὺς ταῦτα ποιοῦντας.

35. Dem. 18.145: Philip suffered terribly from pirates, τῶν λῃστῶν μυρία ἔπασχεν κακά (here the reference may in fact be to Theban or Thessalian privateers); 18.241: if Philip had allied with the Euboians, Demosthenes's political opponents would have complained that "the sea had become unnavigable because of pirates setting out from Euboia," ἄπλους δ' ἡ θάλαττα ὑπὸ τῶν ἐκ τῆς Εὐβοίας ὁρμωμένων λῃστῶν γέγονεν; Dem. 19.315: Philip's territory and harbor markets were overrun by raiders, διαφορουμένης αὐτοῦ τῆς χώρας ὑπὸ τῶν λῃστῶν καὶ κεκλειμένων τῶν ἐμπορίων (here the reference may be to brigands or pirates, or both).

36. On opposition to piracy, see Kosmin (2024, 151–53); J.R. Hall (2024, 183); de Souza (1999, 48–56, 78–96). On possible Parian anti-piracy efforts in the fourth century, see Liddel, Constantakopoulou, and Kourayos (2025, 57–58). Alexander's offensive against Cretan pirates is reported only by Curtius (4.8.15); Diodorus Siculus describes Eumelos's efforts against Black Sea pirates (25.2.2). On Ptolemaic attitudes, see Criscuolo (2013); de Souza (1999, 53–54); Pritchett (1991, 342–43). On Roman anti-piracy, see de Souza (1999, 92–224); Whitcomb (2025) on Augustus. I discuss the case of Rhodes further below. For inscriptions honoring anti-piratic activity, see Pritchett (1991, 340–47), briefly describing many of them. One example is *IG* XII 7, 386, a third-century decree by the people of Amorgos honoring two brothers who retrieved residents of Amorgos from the custody of pirates. A number of the inscriptions presented by Bielman (1994) relate to piracy.

37. Thucydides sometimes simply mentions raiding as an aspect of war, such as when the Athenian general Nicias in 427 established a base off Megara to prevent both triremes and *leistai* from sailing out (3.51.2); cf. 2.69.1: the Athenians sent a force to stop Peloponnesian raiders, τὸ λῃστικὸν τῶν Πελοποννησίων, from harming (βλάπτειν) the merchant ships sailing from Phaselis and Phoenicia; 4.45.2: Athenians raided, ἐλῄστευον, portions of the Argolid from Methana. Similarly, Xenophon in the *Hellenica* reports raiding parties as a normal part of warfare in the early fourth century, describing mutual raids between Athenians and Spartans as "making war": λῃστὰς διαπέμποντες ἐπολέμουν ἀλλήλοις (*Hell.* 4.8.35); cf. *Hell.* 5.1.1: the Spartans encouraged raiding, λῄζεσθαι, upon Attica; 5.4.42: Phoibidas sent raiders, λῃστήρια, against the Thebans to ravage the land; 3.4.19: in a passage praising Agesilaos, Xenophon describes how he paraded naked some "barbarians" seized "in raids," ὑπὸ τῶν λῃστῶν. Diodorus Siculus (20.82.4, 83.1, 97.5) reports, as an apparently ordinary fact, that *peiratai* made up part of Demetrios's fleet when he besieged Rhodes in 305–04.

38. *Hell.* 6.4.35: ἄδικος δὲ λῃστὴς καὶ κατὰ γῆν καὶ κατὰ θάλατταν. On his raiding tactics, see Diod. Sic. 15.95.1: Alexander used "raiding ships," λῃστρίδας ναῦς, against the Cyclades, "taking many captives," πολλῶν σωμάτων ἐκυρίευσεν.

39. Diod. Sic. 28.1–2. Diodorus's description is likely based on Polybius (18.54.6–11), who had already emphasized Dicaearchus's wickedness and the impiety of the task that Philip had sent him on, ἐπὶ πρόδηλον ἀσέβειαν ἐκπεμπόμενος (18.54.9). On Dicaearchus's activities for Philip, see Holleaux (1920). That Dicaearchus was Aitolian likely contributed to Polybius's (and hence Diodorus's) negative evaluation. See below on Polybius's anti-Aitolianism.

40. See, e.g., D.M. Lewis (2019, 82); Gabrielsen (2013b, 138–39); Shaw (2004, 344–46); A.H. Jackson (1995, 96–99); van Wees (1992, 213–17).

41. 1.5.2: οἱ παλαιοὶ τῶν ποιητῶν τὰς πύστεις τῶν καταπλεόντων πανταχοῦ ὁμοίως ἐρωτῶντες εἰ λῃσταί εἰσιν, ὡς οὔτε ὧν πυνθάνονται ἀπαξιούντων τὸ ἔργον, οἷς τε ἐπιμελὲς εἴη εἰδέναι οὐκ ὀνειδιζόντων.

42. *Od.* 3.72–74; 9.253–55; *Hymn. Hom. Ap.* 453–55.

43. *Od.* 3.72–74:

ἦ τι κατὰ πρῆξιν ἦ μαψιδίως ἀλάλησθε
οἷά τε ληϊστῆρες ὑπεὶρ ἅλα, τοί τ' ἀλόωνται
ψυχὰς παρθέμενοι, κακὸν ἀλλοδαποῖσι φέροντες;

The wording is exactly the same at *Od.* 9.253–55 and at *Hymn. Hom. Ap.* 453–55.

44. The forms found in the two poems are μάψ, μαψίδιος, and μαψιδίως. Passages illustrating their universally negative use in the *Odyssey* and *Iliad* are: *Od.* 2.58; 3.72; 3.138; 7.310; 9.253; 14.365; 16.11; 17.451; 17.537; *Il.* 2.120; 2.214; 5.374; 5.759; 13.627; 15.40; 20.298; 20.348; 21.510.
45. According to van Wees (1992, 214), "Those who ask this question merely want to know whether the new arrivals have a particular reason for visiting or are just drifting, as freebooters might. It is not an anxious or hostile question"; cf. A.H. Jackson (1995, 97). It may not be anxious or hostile, but that is because it is formulaic and because in none of the three instances cited is there an indication that the speaker actually fears the visitor. We may imagine that, like pirates and gangsters in the modern popular imagination, pirates in the world in which the Homeric poems were composed were proud of their transgressive activities, but even this attitude plays on a dominant social repudiation of piracy.
46. Van Wees (1992, 213–14).
47. *Od.* 17.424–25: ἀλλὰ Ζεὺς ἀλάπαξε... μ' ἅμα ληιστῆρσι πολυπλάγκτοισιν ἀνῆκεν.
48. The "Thucydidean" interpretation of the *Odyssey* is most thoroughly defended by van Wees (1992, 213–17); see also Luraghi (2006, 33); Crielaard (2002, 265); A.H. Jackson (1995, 96–99); Mele (1979, 59).
49. On Odysseus as learning from his mistakes, see R.B. Rutherford (2009, 165–71). An alternative interpretation of the attack on the Cicones, as David Lewis points out to me, is that the Cicones are non-Greeks and therefore fall outside of a Greek prohibition on piracy against Greeks. For another unequivocal criticism of piracy in the *Odyssey*, see Eumaeus's comments (*Od.* 15.449–84). For other articulations of the anti-piracy interpretation of the *Odyssey*, see Avidov (1997, 8–11); Bravo (1980, 975–77); and more briefly Bowie (2013, 178); Hornblower (1991–2008, i.24). And recall, again, the *Iliad* passage discussed at the beginning of Chapter 6 (*Il.* 11.670–707): Nestor makes clear the Pylians engaged in a justified retaliatory raid. Why would the poet put those words in his mouth if he were portraying a world in which unprovoked raiding held no dishonor or illegitimacy? Contrast the Homeric evidence of a blanket condemnation of piracy with Andersson's (1984, 497–98) description of medieval Icelandic attitudes regarding similar activity. Icelandic sagas distinguish between the heavily condemned thief, *ránsmaðr*, who secretly steals someone else's goods, and the more morally ambiguous robber or raider, *þjófr*, who openly seizes them with force; cf. W.I. Miller (1990, 77–78, 93–100). I am aware of no equivalent piracy-relevant distinction in the Homeric poems.
50. Solon fr. 117a (Schmitz) (fr. 76a, Leão and Rhodes 2016; *Digest* 47.22.4). The entire quoted law is difficult to translate because it is not grammatical as transmitted, but it runs roughly as follows: "If a *demos*, or *phratriai*, or members of religious associations, or sailors, or feasting companions, or those who share burial plots, or members of a religious group, or those who travel for plunder or to a trading port, whatever they agree with each other shall be authoritative unless it is forbidden by public written things," ἐὰν δὲ δῆμος ἢ φράτορες ἢ ἱερῶν ὀργιῶν ἢ ναῦται ἢ σύσσιτοι ἢ ὁμόταφοι ἢ θιασῶται ἢ ἐπὶ λείαν οἰχόμενοι ἢ εἰς ἐμπορίαν, ὅτι ἂν τούτων διαθῶνται πρὸς ἀλλήλους κύριον εἶναι, ἐὰν μὴ ἀπαγορεύσῃ δημόσια γράμματα. For an alternative text and translation, see N.F. Jones (1999, 34).
51. Van Wees (2013, 59–60); A.H. Jackson (1995, 98).
52. There are four obvious problems: (1) the phrase ἱερῶν ὀργιῶν ἢ ναῦται makes grammatical nonsense with the rest of the sentence; (2) there is no verb completing the clause opened by "if," ἐάν; (3) *demos* seems to be used in a post-Solonian (i.e., Cleisthenic) sense; and (4) "it has been generally accepted that the final clause, referring to *demosia grammata*, is most unlikely to give the wording of Solon's law," Leão and Rhodes (2016, 134). See also the discussions by Schmitz (2023, ii.727–33); Ismard (2010, 44–57); Arnaoutoglou (2003, 44–57) (suggesting this is a Hadrianic-era reformulation of early Athenian legislation); N.F. Jones (1999, 33–37, 311–20); Lambert (1993, 250); Ferguson (1944, 64–68); Wilamowitz (1881, 278–79).
53. Radin (1910, 48): they "were nothing more than men engaged in time of war in fitting out ships as privateers,—men equipped with letters of marque." Ma (2024, 133) interprets the expression as referring to privateering; similarly Arnaoutoglou (2003, 52–54); Bravo (1980, 857, 864) (either privateering or legally justified private *syla*). The expression ἐπὶ λείαν is used of militarily justified raiding at, e.g., Xen. *Hell.* 3.2.2; *Anab.* 5.1.8, 17; Aen. Tact. 24.4–5. At *Anabasis* 6.6.2, Xenophon describes how he, as commander of Greek mercenary forces working their way through hostile territory, established regulations governing the soldiers' plundering, which they engaged in to acquire provisions. If a soldier went out alone in search of plunder (ἐπὶ λείαν) while the army remained in camp, he got to keep his plunder as personal property; but if the army as a whole went out, all the plunder was public property to be divided among

them. We can see how the Solonic, Athenian law as quoted in the *Digest* would have fit easily with this (Athenian) commander's regulatory scheme: that if a small group of soldiers went out plundering, whatever division they agreed among themselves would likely be considered authoritative, unless counter to other regulations the commander had established.

54. IRS Publication 17 declares that bribes, stolen property, and income from illegal activities must all be declared as income, see https://www.irs.gov/publications/p17.
55. I am not arguing against claims that piracy was economically significant and that there was a sometimes close relation between piracy and legitimate commerce, as Mele argues (1979, 59–64). As Mele (1979, 59, cf. 71–74) himself notes, however, even in the *Odyssey* commerce is presented as an *alternative* to piracy.
56. *Sept.* 380–81: "Ravenous and longing for battle, he screams with midday hissing like a snake," μαργῶν καὶ μάχης λελιμμένος / μεσημβριναῖς κλαγγαῖσιν ὡς δράκων βοᾷ. 391–94: "Raving in this way with his shocking equipment, he roars by the riverbanks, wishing for battle, like a horse struggling powerfully against his bit who impatiently waits for the war trumpet's call," τοιαῦτ᾽ ἀλύων ταῖς ὑπερκόμποις σαγαῖς / βοᾷ παρ᾽ ὄχθαις ποταμίαις, μάχης ἐρῶν, / ἵππος χαλινῶν ὣς κατασθμαίνων μένει, / ὅστις βοὴν σάλπιγγος ὁρμαίνει κλύων. See Antonetti (1990, 47–68). Tydeus is not specified as Aitolian in the play, but his ethnicity was familiar from the *Iliad* (e.g., 4.399; 23.470–72).
57. Eur. *Phoen.* 134: Ἄρη δ᾽ Αἰτωλὸν ἐν στέρνοις ἔχει. 138: ὡς ἀλλόχρως ὅπλοισι, μειξοβάρβαρος.
58. Thuc. 1.5.3: ἐλῄζοντο δὲ καὶ κατ᾽ ἤπειρον ἀλλήλους. καὶ μέχρι τοῦδε πολλὰ τῆς Ἑλλάδος τῷ παλαιῷ τρόπῳ νέμεται περί τε Λοκροὺς τοὺς Ὀζόλας καὶ Αἰτωλοὺς καὶ Ἀκαρνᾶνας καὶ τὴν ταύτῃ ἤπειρον· τό τε σιδηροφορεῖσθαι τούτοις τοῖς ἠπειρώταις ἀπὸ τῆς παλαιᾶς λῃστείας ἐμμεμένηκεν.
59. On the Greek view that "raw meat is linked to those who are outside the bounds of civilized society," see Ekroth (2008, 101).
60. I discuss these truces in Chapter 4, notes 14 and 31 and accompanying text.
61. *RO* 35 (*Agora* XVI 48), ll. 13–14: παρὰ τοὺς νόμους τ[ο]ὺς κοι[ν]οὺς τῶν Ἑλλήνων. The inscription does not mention the Trichonians' justification for the arrest.
62. Commentators on the inscription have observed that decrees of presumably brief significance, such as this, were rarely inscribed on stone (*Agora* XVI, p. 77). The stone's location suggests this inscription may have been paid for by officials of the Eleusinian cult rather than from the Athenian *boule*'s funds. In any case, a special effort was made to commemorate the Aitolians' misbehavior.
63. The hymn's lyrics are reported to us in the work of Athenaeus, who quotes Douris, the Samian historian (and sometime ruler of Samos) who was probably writing in the early third century, *FGrH* 76 F13 (Ath. 6.63.253d–f): τὴν δ᾽ οὐχὶ Θηβῶν, ἀλλ᾽ ὅλης τῆς Ἑλλάδος / Σφίγγα περικρατοῦσαν, / Αἰτωλὸς ὅστις ἐπὶ πέτρας καθήμενος, / ὥσπερ ἡ παλαιά, / τὰ σώμαθ᾽ ἡμῶν πάντ᾽ ἀναρπάσας φέρει, / κοὐκ ἔχω μάχεσθαι· / Αἰτωλικὸν γὰρ ἁρπάσαι τὰ τῶν πέλας, / νῦν δὲ καὶ τὰ πόρρω.
64. Polyaenus *Strat.* 6.4.18. The ten pirates were under the command of a certain Melatas. Polyaenus also states that one of Antigonos's commanders at Cassandreia was a certain Ameinias whom he calls a "pirate leader," ἀρχιπειρατής.
65. *IG* XII 5, 36 (*Syll.*[3] 520; Bielman, *Retour à la liberté* 26), ll. 1–13: "It was decreed by the Aulonians: Since, when two hundred and eighty people had been seized from the *demos* by the Aitolians, Charopos son of Amphikleides, Xenodokos son of Aristoxenes, Demon son of Mares, Aristokles [son of . . .], Pheidias son of Gnosiades sailed out and ransomed them from the Aitolians"; ἔδοξεν Αὐλωνίοις· ἐπειδὴ ἁλόντων σωμάτων ἐκ τοῦ δήμου [ὑ]πὸ τῶν Αἰτωλῶν [δ]ι[α]κοσίων καὶ ὀγδοήκον[τα κ]αὶ κ[α]ταπλεύσαντες δημοσίως Χάροπος Ἀμ[φ]ικλείδου, Ξενόδοκο[ς Ἀ]ριστοξένου, Δήμω[ν][Μ]άρ[ιο]ς, Ἀριστοκλῆς [. . . .]κου, Φειδίας Γνωσ[ί.]ου ἐλυτρ[ώ]σαν[το π]αρὰ τῶν Αἰτωλῶν. See Grainger (1999, 20).
66. *IG* II[3] 1137 (*Syll.*[3] 535).
67. *IG* XI 4, 692 (*Syll.*[3] 500).
68. See Scholten (2000, 109); Grainger (1999, 20–22).
69. Diod. Sic. 28.1: τοὺς μὲν ἐμπόρους ἐλῄστευε, τὰς δὲ νήσους λεηλατῶν ἀργύριον εἰσεπράττετο.
70. On Polybian hostility to Aitolians, see Nicholson (2020, 47); Scholten (2000, 4–5); Champion (1996, 316 n.5 and 323 n.45); Sacks (1975, 92); on Polybian prejudices more generally, see Fine (1940).

71. Loy (2023, 264–65) (speaking only of the seventh and sixth centuries but calling Crete "different in so many ways to the rest of the Aegean"; the sea acted as a barrier and kept Crete in "relative isolation"); Erickson (2005, 636) (describing an "almost total absence" of ceramic imports to Crete in the middle and late fifth century, but arguing against the two centuries of isolation posited by some earlier scholars); Chaniotis (1999, 183); Perlman (1999, 138–39); van Effenterre (1948, 19); cf. Wilamowitz (1893, ii.25–26) (at some unspecified time Crete lost contact with "Greek" culture).
72. *Od.* 14.199–359. Earlier, also disguised and speaking to Penelope, Odysseus says, "I have learned of Ithaca even in broad Crete, far across the sea," πυνθανόμην Ἰθάκης γε καὶ ἐν Κρήτῃ εὐρείῃ, τηλοῦ ὑπὲρ πόντου, *Od.* 13.256-57.
73. *Pol.* 2, 1272b2: πόρρω γ' ἀποικοῦσιν ἐν νήσῳ τῶν διαφθερούντων. Cf. 1272b18–23.
74. Minos had prayed to Poseidon to send him a bull from the sea as a divine sign confirming his kingship in Crete. In return Minos promised to sacrifice the bull. But when Poseidon sent a magnificent animal, Minos sacrificed an ordinary bull instead. Angry, Poseidon inspired a sexual passion for the bull in Pasiphae, who persuaded the inventor and craftsman Daedalus to devise a way for her to have sex with it; Apollod. *Bibl.* 3.1.3–4. Minos's demand for the Athenian sacrifice began after the death of his son in Attica while participating in the Panathenaic festival, a death that Minos blamed on the Athenians; Apollod. *Bibl.* 3.15.7–8.
75. On the popularity of Theseus and the Minotaur in Greek visual art, especially Athenian vase painting, see Gantz (1993, 262–70); *LIMC* 6(1):574–81, *s.v.* "Minotauros"; *LIMC* 7(1): 940–43, *s.v.* "Theseus"; Servadei (2005, 84–134). On literary sources, see Obsomer (2003, 142–49). The story was mentioned already by Sappho in the late seventh or early sixth century (fr. 206 Lobel-Page) and seems to have been told in a fairly complete form already by the early fifth-century Athenian historian and mythographer Pherekydes (*FGrH* 3 F148). In the middle of the fifth century, Bacchylides told the story from Theseus's point of view, emphasizing Minos's violence and dark intentions (Bacchyl. 17.21–23, 40–41). Euripides's tragedy *Cretans* seems to have focused on the Minotaur's birth, Daedalus's construction of the labyrinth, and Minos's punishment of Pasiphae and Daedalus (for helping Pasiphae mate with the bull), see Collard and Cropp (2008, 530–31).
76. *FGrH* 457 fr. 2: Κρῆτες ἀεὶ ψεῦσται, κακὰ θηρία, γαστέρες ἀργαί. Ignorance of the original literary context risks distorting the statement's meaning; see Jacoby's commentary on the fragment, drawing particular attention to the parallel to Hes. *Th.* 26; cf. West (1966, 162).
77. Leonidas of Tarentum 16 (Gow–Page, *HE*) (*Anth. Pal.* 7.654):

    Αἰεὶ ληϊσταὶ καὶ ἁλιφθόροι, οὐδὲ δίκαιοι
    Κρῆτες· τίς Κρητῶν οἶδε δικαιοσύνην;
    ὡς καὶ ἐμὲ πλώοντα σὺν οὐκ εὐπίονι φόρτῳ
    Κρηταιεῖς ὦσαν Τιμόλυτον καθ' ἁλός,
    δείλαιον. κἠγὼ μὲν ἁλιζώοις λαρίδεσσι
    κέκλαυμαι, τύμβῳ δ' οὐχ ὕπο Τιμόλυτος.

78. D.M. Lewis (2023, 26–41) (for a mainstream view of the meaning of courage in hoplite formation, see the text of the Athenian ephebic oath I quote in Chapter 10, notes 22–23 and 34–37 and accompanying text). Lewis cites, as evidence of a Cretan "obsession with acquisition and plunder," a number of treaties between Cretan cities that carefully lay out the rules for dividing plunder from war (41 and n. 95); cf. Lewis (2023b, 248). It is important to note that these treaties are not evidence for Cretan piracy, since they are concerned with plunder from war enemies; see, e.g., Chaniotis, *Verträge* 11 (*SvA* 511), ll. 4–8; Chaniotis, *Verträge* 26 (*SvA* 603), ll. 7–8; Chaniotis, *Verträge* 46 (*SvA* 746), ll. 2–5. In this latter treaty, I take the reference to "privately seized items," τὰ δ' ἰδίαι ληφθέντα (ll. 4–5), to mean booty taken during a war in individual raids upon the enemy territory, τῶν δ' ἐκ τῆς πολεμίας ὠ[φ]ελιῶν (l. 2). This is because the ὅσα μέν ... τὰ δέ phrases that introduce the clauses distinguishing between "common" and "private" booty seem to be describing two ways that soldiers seized booty from wartime enemy territory, perhaps like what Xenophon describes at *Anab.* 6.6.2, which I discuss in n. 53, above. Contrast the interpretation of Chaniotis (1996, 303), who considers the reference to "private" booty to be to pirate-like activity; and of Errington (in his translation of *SvA* 746), who considers the reference to be to private raids independent of any joint military action. I do not see why such raiding would be regulated in a treaty otherwise concerned with joint war-making.
79. *IG* II^3 1, 358, ll. 15–16; see the edition and commentary of Bielman, *Retour à la liberté* 6, who discusses the scholarly debate over whether pirates took these captives.

80. *I.Delphinion* 140A–C (*SvA* 482 I–III); French translation and discussion by Giovannini (2007, 328–31). In fact each agreement claims to include, among the parties, other Cretan cities along with the main Cretan treaty partner, so that the three agreements together memorialize Milesian agreements with 28 Cretan cities. The central provision of the Milesian-Knossian treaty states (*I.Delphinion* 140A, ll. 18–23): "The Knossian shall not purchase the Milesian, nor the Milesian the Knossian, knowing that he is free. Whoever knowingly buys shall forfeit the purchase price and the person shall be free. And if he unknowingly buys, let him give back the person and regain the purchase price, however much he paid." μὴ ὠνείσθω ὁ Κνώσιος τὸμ Μιλήσιον μηδὲ ὁ Μιλήσιος τὸν Κνώσιον εἰδὼς ἐλεύθερον ὄντα. ὃς ἂν δὲ ἀγοράσηι εἰδώς, στερέσθω τῆς τιμῆς καὶ τὸ σῶμα ἐλεύθερον ἔστω. ἐὰν δὲ μὴ εἰδὼς ἀγοράσῃ, ἀποδοὺς τὸ σῶμα τὴν τιμὴν κομισάσθω, ὅσου ἠγόρακεγ. The other two treaties contain similar provisions; all three also provide for slaves to be returned to their rightful owners.
81. Brulé (1978, 6–12). The Milesian-Knossian treaty states it is merely a reaffirmation of an existing treaty, agreed to by the Knossians in response to an embassy from Miletos and designed in part to encourage other Cretan cities to enter similar agreements with the Milesians; *I.Delphinion* 140A, ll. 1–18. Gauthier (1972, 244–45) reads the treaty as concerned with legal seizures.
82. Similarly, the fragmentary inscription offered by Willets (1955, 244) as the earliest evidence of Cretan piracy, *IG* XII 3 328 (dated ca. 260) makes no mention of pirates. It describes efforts by Therans to retrieve captives and slaves held by the people of Allaria, a town on the northern coast of Crete near modern Rethymno; in fact, the document appears to describe an exchange of captives between the two cities.
83. Diod. Sic. 27.3: Κρῆτες ναυσὶν ἑπτὰ πειρατεύειν ἐπιβαλόμενοι τῶν πλεόντων ἐλῄστευον οὐκ ὀλίγους. διὸ καὶ τῶν ἐμπόρων ἀθυμούντων, Ῥόδιοι πρὸς αὑτοὺς τἀδικήματα νομίσαντες ἥξειν πρὸς τοὺς Κρῆτας πόλεμον ἐξήνεγκαν. This fragment's position in the Byzantine collection known as *Excerpta de Virtutibus et Vitiis* places the episode reliably at the end of the third century, see Walton (1957, viii–ix).
84. Perlman (1999) argues that the Rhodians may have been spurred to war more by Cretan trade competition than by Cretan piracy.
85. Polyb. 13.8.2: ἐκοινώνει μὲν γὰρ τοῖς Κρησὶ τῶν κατὰ θάλατταν λῃστειῶν.
86. On Polybius's anti-Cretan views, see Nicholson (2020, 47); Perlman (1999, 133 and n.5); F.W. Walbank (1957–1979, i.508).
87. On Cretan piracy generally, see D.M. Lewis (2023, 33); Perlman (1999); Brulé (1978); Willetts (1955, 241–45).
88. See Chaniotis (2005, 134–37; 1999, 183–85); Wiemer (2002, 112); Scholten (2000, 12, 21–23); Perlman (1999, 137). As David Lewis has pointed out to me, the Aitolian and Cretan reputation for piracy may have been related to their simultaneous reputation for using war as a (thin) pretext for plunder, as Polybius reports of the Aitolians (18.4.8–5.4) and as the Kalymnians perhaps implied when describing a naval attack by the Hierapytnians as "unjust," *IG* XII 4, 5, 4022 (*Syll.*[3] 567), ll. 4–5. Insincere attempts to legitimize plundering fit with my picture of Aitolians and Cretans as rejecting the spirit of the Greek prohibition of piracy even when following the letter of the law.
89. *Anth. Pal.* 7.45, l. 3. Euripides's cenotaph lay on the road between Piraeus and Athens. On the epitaph's authorship and date, see Plant (2015).
90. On the "canonization" of various aspects of Athenian culture already in the fifth and fourth centuries, see Netz (2020, 195–213, 230–37, 255–64): "the sheer exceptional character of classical Athens . . . was unprecedented and, in some ways, never repeated" (256). See also W. Mack (2022); Csapo, Paillard, and Wilson (2022, 21–24); and the essays in Canevaro and Gray (2017). On the donation of buildings in Athens, see Habicht (1997, 220–27, 331–37). On the centrality of Athens in at least some Roman conceptions of Greece, see Cic. *Brut.* 26; *Flac.* 62. Cf. Plin. *Ep.* 8.24 (writing later, and about the whole province of Achaea rather than just Athens, but picking out Athens and Sparta for special mention and evincing what may have been a long-standing attitude that here, especially as opposed to other parts of the eastern empire, was "the true and pure Greece, where humanity, literature, the very fruits of the earth are believed to have been first discovered," *vera et mera Graecia, in qua primum humanitas, litterae, etiam fruges inventae esse creduntur*).
91. On the "centrality" of Rhodes in these centuries, see Gabrielsen (1997, 16–24); also W. Mack (2022).
92. Polyb. 5.88–90. Gabrielsen (1997, 77). The earthquake probably occurred in 227.

93. Diod. Sic. 20.81.4; Gabrielsen (1997, 18). On Athens and Rhodes as cities where Greeks went for education, see Robert (1973, 778–79).
94. Isoc. 4.115; for the decree of Moirikles, see [Dem.] 58 (*Against Theocrines*): τῶν τοὺς ἐμπόρους ἀδικούντων (58.53); καθαρὰν εἶναι τὴν θάλατταν (58.54). See also *IG* II^3 370 (*RO* 100), an Athenian decree of 324 providing for creation of a naval base in the Adriatic, probably in part to suppress Tyrrhenian piracy.
95. On Rhodian anti-piracy, see Bresson (2007); Wiemer (2002, 111–42); Gabrielsen (2001, 228–33; 1997, 44–45, 59–60, 108–11); de Souza (1999, 48–53, 80–84); Holleaux (1920, 243).
96. Diod. Sic. 20.81.3: ἐπὶ τοσοῦτον γὰρ προεληλύθει δυνάμεως ὥσθ' ὑπὲρ μὲν τῶν Ἑλλήνων ἰδίᾳ τὸν πρὸς τοὺς πειρατὰς πόλεμον ἐπαναιρεῖσθαι καὶ καθαρὰν παρέχεσθαι τῶν κακούργων τὴν θάλατταν. Similar credit is given the Rhodians by Strabo (14.2.5: with its navy Rhodes "ruled the sea for a long time and eliminated piracy," ἐθαλαττοκράτησε πολὺν χρόνον καὶ τὰ ληστήρια καθεῖλε) and in a speech transmitted among the works of Aelius Aristides (*Or.* 25.4 [*Rhodikos*]: the Rhodians have "bronze-mouthed rams, . . . some from Tyrrhenian pirates," ἐμβόλους χαλκοστόμους, . . . τοὺς μὲν ἀπὸ τοῦ Τυρρηνῶν ληστικοῦ).
97. "In charge of what happened at sea," προεστάναι τῶν κατὰ θάλατταν, Polyb. 4.47.1. Gabrielsen (2007, 293) argues tolls were imposed on commercial traffic going both directions through the Bosporos. For the enforcement and resolution, see Polyb. 4.52.5. On this episode and the broader questions of the importance of the Bosporos straits to trade and the history of tolls through the Bosporos, see Gabrielsen (2007); cf. Wiemer (2002, 39–45). There is irony in the fact that the Rhodian "police" action described here was against the Byzantines, whom Polybius earlier in the same book describes as "common benefactors of all," κοινοί . . . εὐεργέται πάντων (4.38.10), in part because of their protection of Greek shipping from "barbarians," presumably raiders or simple pirates.
98. *Syll.*^{3} 1225, ll. 7–8, ἀγω[νιζόμενος] ποτὶ Τυρρανοὺς ἐτελεύτασε; ll. 10–11, ποτὶ τοὺς λαιστὰς ἀγωνιζό[μενος ἐτελε]ύτασε. On this inscription, see Bresson (2007, 148–49, 162–63); Wiemer (2002, 130–33); cf. Sekunda (2014).
99. *IG* XI 4, 596 (*Choix Délos* I 39), ll. 4–5: ἐπὶ τῆς φυλακῆς τ[ῶν νήσων καὶ] ἐπὶ σωτηρίαι τῶν Ἑλλήνων. Cf. l. 9, τὴν φυλακὴν τῶν Ἑλλήνων. On this inscription, see Wiemer (2002, 135–36).
100. Roussel (1907, 359 n.4). On the likely overall ineffectiveness of Rhodian anti-piracy efforts, see Wiemer (2002, 137–42); de Souza (1999, 91).
101. Contrast D.M. Lewis's (2023) more persuasive argument that Cretan techniques of war exhibit continuities from the seventh to second centuries. Here too, however, Lewis's discussion suggests that these techniques were probably not simply living fossils from the Cretan past but continued to be responsive to current needs, such as the nature of the Cretan landscape and a steady demand for mercenaries with "Cretan" skills.
102. On Latino gang membership, see Ventura Miller, Barnes, and Hartley (2011, 345–46). On broader ties between ethnic discrimination and rule-breaking, see, e.g., Jeries-Loulou and Khoury-Kassabri (2022, 197) (Arabic Palestinians in Israel); D.I. Scott (2020, 30–32) (Latinos in the United States); Stevens and Thijs (2018, 564) (Moroccans in the Netherlands); Cano et al. (2015, 37) (Latinos in the United States); Burt, Simons, and Gibbons (2012, 663) (Blacks in the United States); Caldwell et al. (2004, 99–100) (Blacks in the United States); Simons et al. (2003, 847–50) (Blacks in the United States).
103. On strain theory, see Agnew (2001, 1992). On ethnic discrimination as a strain, see Mégret (2021, 869); D.I. Scott (2020, 31–32); Agnew (2001, 346–47). On ethnic discrimination as one element of "multiple marginality," see Vigil (2002, 7–13).
104. Mégret (2021) makes the case that studies on domestic law criminality are helpful in understanding contemporary international criminal law.
105. Kinkor (2001) interprets the participation in Atlantic piracy of Black men and escaped slaves as a response to their marginalization by mainstream society; see also Rediker (2004, 38–59).
106. On Crete, see Erickson (2005); Chaniotis (1999, 183); Perlman (1999). On Aitolia, see Mackil (2013, 52–103); Scholten (2000, 1–25). For Aitolians, a larger presence on the Greek stage may be connected to formation of a state-like federal league perhaps in the early fourth century; see Funke (2015, 86–101).
107. On contact's varying effects, see Chapter 3, n. 66 and accompanying text.
108. Bayram (2017a, 54–55). On identity and rule following, see Gaertner and Dovidio (2012, 444–45); Foddy and Yamagishi (2009, 35–37); Lind and Tyler (1988, 230–34).

109. On perceptions of legal legitimacy, see K. Murphy (2017) and Trinkner and Tyler (2016) for recent overviews. On "social bandits," see Hobsbawm (1981, 17–29); for a critique, see briefly Slatta (2004), referring to many other studies; on subaltern resistance and its problematic use as a form of historical explanation, see Wagner (2021).
110. Particularly unfortunate in this regard is our lack of Aitolian and Cretan voices. As Rigsby (1996, 17) notes, "If Polybius had been an Aetolian, we might today be assessing the difficult question of the 'popularity of the Aetolian Empire.'"

Chapter 10

1. On the uses and functions of oaths in Greek society, see the publications of the so-called Nottingham Oaths Project, including Sommerstein and Torrance (2014); Sommerstein and Bayliss (2012); Sommerstein and Fletcher (2007). An earlier treatment of Greek oaths in general is Plescia (1970). On oaths in Greek law, see Thür (1996). As is often the case, the surviving *polis*-specific evidence relates largely to practice in Athens. But Bayliss (2012) discusses the domestic use of oaths in other Greek political communities including Sparta, Delphi, Miletos, Thasos, Halicarnassus, Cyrene, Epirus, Dreros, and Gortyn. For further non-Athenian evidence, see the indexes of van Effenterre and Ruzé (1994, *s.v. (h)orkos*) and of Vélissaropoulos-Karakostas (2011, *s.v.* ὅρκος). On the use of oaths in international relations, see Scharff (2016); Bayliss (2012b); Bolmarcich (2007); Giovannini (2007, 46–47, 232–35); Bederman (2001, 67–71, 174–78); Baltrusch (1994, 60–63, 111–17, 196–97); Plescia (1970, 58–74). Although no extant source explicitly states that oaths were sworn at the formation of truces to gather the dead, Bayliss (2012b, 291–301) argues persuasively that they very likely were.
2. Bayliss (2012, 9; 2012b, 325). Scharff (2016, 15–17); Bolmarcich (2007, 26); Burkert (1985, 250); Phillipson (1911, i.389) make similar claims. For some skepticism, see Gray (2016, 305–08).
3. For the text of the oath, see *RO* 88. The quoted section is from lines 6 to 8: οὐκ αἰσχυνῶ τὰ ἱερὰ ὅπλα οὐδὲ λείψω τὸν παραστάτην ὅπου ἄν στειχήσω. For a recent discussion with further references, see Bayliss (2012, 13–22). Xenophon in the *Memorabilia* (4.4.16) reports Socrates as attributing to oaths a similar effect. Socrates argues to Hippias that "agreement is considered to be the greatest good for cities," and that "everywhere in Greece a law is in force that the citizens must swear to agree, and everywhere they swear this oath": ὁμόνοιά γε μέγιστόν τε ἀγαθὸν δοκεῖ ταῖς πόλεσιν εἶναι . . . καὶ πανταχοῦ ἐν τῇ Ἑλλάδι νόμος κεῖται τοὺς πολίτας ὀμνύναι ὁμονοήσειν, καὶ πανταχοῦ ὀμνύουσι τὸν ὅρκον τοῦτον.
4. See Scharff (2016, 14, 31); Sommerstein (2012, 3–4); Plescia (1970, 3). On the curse element of oaths, see Konstantinidou (2014).
5. *IG* I³ 9 (*OR* 116; *SvA* 142), ll. 4–14: χσ[υνθέσθαι μὲν τὲν χ]συνμαχίαν [καθάπερ hοι ἐκ τε͂ς] Πυλαίας ἀπ[αγγέλλοσιν hάπασ]ι τοῖς Ἀμφι[κτίοσι hοῖσπερ μέ]τεσστιν τõ h[ιερõ, ἐμμενε͂ν τε ὀ]μόσαντας ἐν [τε͂ι χσυνμαχίαι νὲ τ]ὸν Ἀπόλλο [καὶ τὲν Λετὸ καὶ τὲν] Ἄρτεμιν ἐ[χσόλειάν τε καὶ hα]ụτοῖς ἐπαρ̣[ομένος ἐὰν παραβαί]νομεν. I provide the translation by Osborne and Rhodes.
6. On the archons' oath, see *Ath. pol.* 55.5; 7.1. On touching a statue, see *IG* I³ 254, l. 10, an Athenian deme decree from Ikarion that appears to indicate that those nominated to serve as *choregoi* of dramatic performances in the deme's celebration of the rural Dionysia festival could avoid the expense of that liturgy if, while touching a statue of Dionysos, they swore an oath (ἐξωμοσία) that they could not afford the cost (note ἀντίδοσιν in l. 7). On ἐξωμοσία, cf. Dem. 19.129 and *schol. ad* 19.262. As I discuss in Chapter 4, n. 35 and accompanying text, Olympic competitors stood next to a statue of Zeus Horkios when swearing to compete fairly, Paus. 5.24.9.
7. For oaths involving animal sacrifice, ὁρκωμόσια, see *OGIS* 229 (*I.Smyrna* 573; *I.Magnesia Sipylos* 1), l. 82 (Smyrna, ca. 245); *IG* XII.4.1, 152, l. 9 (Kos, late third century); Paus. 5.24.9; Bayliss (2012b, 151–54). On the Delian League oaths, see *Ath. pol.* 23.5; Plut. *Arist.* 25.1. Herodotus (1.165.3) describes the Phokaians performing a similar ritual in the sixth century.

8. In stressing the communicative aspect of oaths my approach is along the same lines as Scharff's (2016, 23) method of using an "akteurszentrierte Sprachanalyse" to understand Greek oath practice.
9. See J.L. Austin (1975, 22). See also Dworkin's (2011, 303–311) philosophical account of how promises create ethical obligations. Understanding an oath as a form of promise will be useful below when I apply recent research on promising to help understand the efficacy of Greek oaths.
10. As MacLachlan (2007, 92) notes, "Oaths were normally sworn in situations of mistrust. . . . Hesiod reasonably makes Horkos the son of Eris (*Op.* 803) because tension and conflict could be resolved through the imposition of an oath." See Kozak (2014); Soph. *Phil.* 811–13. Of course, even in a society of universal truth-tellers, oaths could play a role in self-commitment. It is a common human experience that I might now sincerely want to perform an act in the future but not actually perform it when the time comes. In such circumstances an oath can help ensure that I follow through.
11. See Schilke, Reimann, and Cook (2021, 10.4–9), who criticize a strict conceptual dichotomy between general and particular trust; Foddy and Yamagishi (2009, 18). Because general trust is, by definition, not affected by the particularities of a given situation such as the making of an oath, I do not explore it here.
12. *Leoc.* 79: τοὺς μὲν γὰρ ἀνθρώπους πολλοὶ ἤδη ἐξαπατήσαντες καὶ διαλαθόντες οὐ μόνον τῶν παρόντων κινδύνων ἀπελύθησαν, ἀλλὰ καὶ τὸν ἄλλον χρόνον ἀθῷοι τῶν ἀδικημάτων τούτων εἰσί· τοὺς δὲ θεοὺς οὔτ' ἂν ἐπιορκήσας τις λάθοι, οὔτ' ἂν ἐκφύγοι τὴν ἀπ' αὐτῶν τιμωρίαν.
13. Lycurg. *Leoc.* 79: "If not the oathbreaker himself, then his children and his entire line meet with great misfortunes," εἰ μὴ αὐτός, οἱ παῖδές γε καὶ τὸ γένος ἅπαν τὸ τοῦ ἐπιορκήσαντος μεγάλοις ἀτυχήμασι περιπίπτει. On the inescapability of divine punishment see also, e.g., Hes. *Th.* 231–32, *Op.* 282–85; Thgn. 1195–96; Hdt. 6.86γ; Xen. *Anab.* 2.5.7 (cf. 3.2.10) and, for discussion, Torrance (2014b). Parker (2004b, 140) calls this Greek belief a "pious cliché." For caution on the point, see Lanni (2008, 475–76). The belief in divine deterrence aligns closely with the justifications, dominant at least until the nineteenth century, of the Anglo-American legal requirement that judicial witnesses swear an oath and of the rule that someone who did not believe in divine punishment could not offer testimony as a witness; see, generally, Campbell (2019).
14. Burkert (1985, 252); Scharff (2016, 55, 214–62); Bayliss (2012b, 168); Rauh (1993, 152–66). Cf. Plescia (1970, 94): "God acted here not only as a witness of the debtor's or delinquent's promise, but, most important of all as a surety of it. . . . The creditor was relying, therefore, not on the *pistis* (faith) of the debtor, but on the magical power of the oath-formula, namely, the curse to assure the performance of the debtor." On the importance of the divine element, see also C.G. Williamson (2013, 123).
15. Paus. 5.24.9: πάντων ὁπόσα ἀγάλματα Διὸς μάλιστα ἐς ἔκπληξιν ἀδίκων ἀνδρῶν πεποίηται. Scharff (2016, 47) calls Zeus "der erste Schwurgott"; cf. Bayliss (2012b, 160–61); Burkert (1985, 251). Torrance (2014, 295): "The official divine guardians of oaths are variously represented as Horkos (Oath), the Erinyes (as oath-curses), Zeus Horkios (guardian of oaths), and also Themis."
16. On the Erinyes' connection to oaths, see Hes. *Op.* 803–04; Scharff (2016, 49–55); Konstantinidou (2014, 8–19). On their connection to the Areopagus, see Din. 1.47 (accusing Demosthenes of having "perjured himself on the Areopagus against the *semnai theai* and the other gods whom the law states one must swear by there," ἐπιωρκηκὼς μὲν τὰς σεμνὰς θεὰς ἐν Ἀρείῳ πάγῳ καὶ τοὺς ἄλλους θεοὺς οὓς ἐκεῖ διόμνυσθαι νόμιμόν ἐστι).
17. Hdt. 6.86γ. Herodotus of course incorporates this episode partly for its literary effect, but that alone is no reason to think he invented Leotychidas's use of the story in a very public setting; see Bayliss (2012b, 168).
18. Zeus, Apollo, and Demeter were a common trio of *theoi horkioi* invoked by Athenian oath-takers. See, e.g., *IG* I^3 14, l. 16; *IG* II^2 1183, ll. 11–12; Dem. 52.9. Torrance (2014b, 297) has a slightly different interpretation: "Perjurers, then, could expect to be pursued by a variety of hostile divine forces, including any or all of the specific divinities named as oath-witnesses in the perjured oath and any of the official guarantors of oaths, whether or not these had been named in the original oath." It seems particularly telling that even the Delphic oracle, according to Herodotus, claims perjurers are punished not by Apollo but by "son of oath." Of course, Apollo *could* punish humans, at least in literature, as the opening of the *Iliad* makes clear.
19. At the ceremony to swear the truce in book 3 of the *Iliad*, Agamemnon invokes Zeus on Ida as well as "Helios, who sees everything and hears everything, and rivers and earth," 276–78.

Bayliss (2012b, 161) explains that "Zeus is thus invoked . . . implicitly as a god who will witness events from his vantage point on Mount Ida. Helios is explicitly chosen because his place in the sky makes him all-seeing and all-hearing. Gaea stands for the earth on which the swearers stand, and the Rivers presumably not only represent the earth itself, but also ensure that transgressors will be found out not just on dry land but on water too."

20. Hence (*contra* Plescia 1970, 94) the speech act is performing a request rather than, by itself, bringing about a "magical" outcome, as seems to have been the object with, e.g., some curse tablets. In Faraone's (1991, 5) terms, it utilizes the "prayer formula" rather than the "direct binding formula" of binding curse tablets. Thucydides indicates the importance of human vengeance by quoting the Athenian invocation of the oaths that sealed the thirty years' peace: "With the gods of the oaths as our witnesses, once war starts we will strive to defend ourselves just as vigorously as you attack," θεοὺς τοὺς ὁρκίους μάρτυρας ποιούμενοι πειρασόμεθα ἀμύνεσθαι πολέμου ἄρχοντας ταύτῃ ᾗ ἂν ὑφηγῆσθε, 1.78.4.
21. Janko (1992, 194). Plescia (1970, 5) notes that "the gods had to be local (*enchorioi*) and officially recognized (*nomimoi*), i.e., enjoying the public worship." On the list of oath gods, see C.G. Williamson (2013, 134 and 150–51). Sometimes the list of gods invoked would be customized for obvious reasons. E.g., in the oath prescribed in the gymnasiarchic law of Beroia (*I.Beroia* 1, l. A32), the list is Zeus, Ge, Helios, Apollo, Heracles, and Hermes: the last two are included, undoubtedly, as gods of the gymnasium. When Ares and Athena Areia were invoked, it was likely due to their association with war, which was seen as a possible result of violating an interstate oath (cf. Bayliss 2012b, 161). But in the case of war the vengeful gods were (mostly) acting through human agents.
22. *RO* 88, ll. 39–46.
23. *I.Beroia* 1, ll. 32–34: εὐορκοῦντι μέν μοι εἴη πολλὰ καὶ ἀγαθά, ἐφιορκοῦντι δὲ τἀναντία.
24. *IG* I^3 254. Line 10 states, καὶ τὸ χορεγὸ ἐχσομο[σα], and line 12 mentions τõ ἀγάλματος hαπ[τ...]. Romano (1982, 407) suggests the remains of an early colossal statue uncovered at Ikarion are likely from the statue mentioned here. On this decree as early evidence for dramatic performances as part of the rural Dionysia, see Whitehead (1986, 215–16).
25. Since the *Ath. pol.* does not report which gods were invoked at either location, we are left to guess. A statue, apparently of a goddess, appears to have stood directly in front of the Stoa Basileios at least starting in the second half of the fourth century, Camp (2010, 79–80). Directly next to the Stoa Basileios was the stoa of Zeus Eleutherios with a statue of Zeus in front, Camp (2010, 74). Perhaps the archons taking their oath on the stone of the Stoa Basileios swore in the name of these two gods. I am unaware of any regulations in Athens for particular human witnesses to be present at the oath ceremonies of the various magistrates. Cf. Bayliss (2012, 38–40); Hansen (1999, 227). On the punishment, see Pl. *Phdr.* 235d–e; cf. Plut. *Sol.* 25.2; T.L. Shear (1994, 242–45).
26. For the sake of completeness, I should add that Greeks must often have complied with oaths because they had an underlying desire to perform whatever action they swore to perform, because they had already planned to tell the truth anyway, or because the oath was in some other way purely superfluous to fulfillment of whatever was sworn to. Some people at times likely swore oaths only because they already had such an underlying proclivity.
27. See, e.g., Dem. 34.52 (emphasizing economic benefits); Din. 3.16–17 (emphasizing public safety benefits).
28. On reputation cultivation as a rational strategy, see Origgi (2018, 29–40), who points out that there is also a more minimally rational explanation, namely that people simply want a good reputation per se, regardless of the material benefits that may flow from it.
29. On rational reputation maintenance, see Henrich and Henrich (2007, 123–24), finding that, among Chaldean Catholics in the United States, a good reputation is believed to improve one's marriage prospects, make it easier to get loans, and help build profitable business relations. See also Semmann, Krambeck, and Milinski (2005, 615). On the importance of reputation in Athens, see Leese (2021, 136–77); Adamidis (2017, 147–48); Engen (2010, 50–51); Hunter (1994, 96–118); Dover (1974, 226–29, 235–36). On oaths and reputation in the Roman world, see Terpstra (2013, 23–31). On the form of concern for reputation that the Greeks called *philotimia*, see Whitehead (1983). On altruistic compliance, see Bereczkei, Birkas, and Kerekes (2007, 283), reporting results of experiments indicating that "people see altruism as a sort of a tool that increases their reputation in their group. In this sense . . . altruism may constitute an investment that later pays off in others' generosity." On evidence against this sort of theory of "rational reputation maintenance," see Capraro, Jordan, and Tappin (2021, 7–9); Uzzi (1997, 54–55).

30. Ederer and Schneider (2020, 3–4); Vanberg (2008, 1475–77). Dworkin (2011, 304) describes promising as falling under the umbrella of the general duty "not to harm other people by first encouraging them to expect that we will act in a certain way and then not acting in that way." Ederer and Stremitzer (2017, 161–63) note that the two motivations may not be mutually exclusive.
31. In Dworkin's (2011, 310) terms, "the point of promising is to set the bar very high for successful excuses for disappointing deliberately encouraged expectations." Greek oath-takers might also have wanted not to disappoint the expectations of gods, whether or not they feared divine deterrence. This could have been a subconscious motivation for invoking gods not especially associated with vengeance.
32. The flip side of close attention to formality and precision is "artful dodging," avoiding perjury with a carefully worded oath; see Bayliss (2014). The effect of linguistic formality on promises is demonstrated by the experimental finding that language characterized by experimenters as language of "promising" is significantly more effective than "empty talk" at encouraging people to follow through with commitments; Ederer and Stremitzer (2017, 167–68, 171). Hence I agree with C.G. Williamson (2013, 121–23) about the importance of the formal, ritual aspect of swearing oaths, although I focus on different reasons for that importance: instilling ethical commitment in addition to being a "coordinating mechanism" encouraging joint action; cf. Teegarden (2012, 451).
33. See especially *EN* 3.1, 3.5. The expression "up to us," ἐφ' ἡμῖν, occurs, e.g., in 3.5, 1113b7.
34. Hansen (2015b) has argued that Greek civic oaths such as the Athenian ephebic oath were voluntary enough to create a sense of ethical obligation in the swearers, but I find his arguments unpersuasive, partly for the reasons elaborated by Klosko (2020).
35. Foddy and Yamagishi (2009, 18) discuss studies indicating that shared group membership is a key factor in determining trust. They propose (35–36) that the likely basis for this elevated trust is a higher expectation of altruistic reciprocal behavior from in-group members. Although rational, cost-benefit reasoning often affects trust, it is just one of many factors, and trust itself is primarily an affective, emotional state; see K. Jones (2024, 4–7).
36. See Pollux (8.55); A.R.W. Harrison (1968–71, ii.99–100). Many oaths likely have multiple effects. Consider, e.g., the "Hippocratic Oath" still sworn by most medical school graduates in the United States: it likely (a) reinforces their sense of the serious ethical obligations of being a doctor; (b) makes them feel part of the general community of doctors; and relatedly (c) acts as a rite of passage.
37. Ephebic oath, "together with everyone": *RO* 88, ll. 15–16; Xen. *Mem.* 4.4.16.
38. *IOSPE* I³ 3, 100 (*Syll.*³ 360), ll. 5–6, 13, 20–21. See Makarov (2014), arguing it is an "ordinary" civic oath regularly required of all citizens, rather than a one-time requirement imposed in response to an emergency (a view that had become a scholarly consensus); also C.G. Williamson (2013, 127–30). Cf. *OGIS* 229 (*I.Smyrna* 573; *I.Magnesia Sipylos* 1), ll. 64–65: καὶ πολιτεύσομαι μεθ' ὁμονοίας ἀστασιάστως (a *sympoliteia* oath, not an "ordinary" civic oath).
39. This is what Teegarden (2012, 451) calls "the generation of common knowledge of credible commitment." An inscription describing procedures for *sympoliteia* between Kos and Kalymna in the middle or late third century states that certain city officials—*prostatai* and *strategoi*—are to swear the oath first, followed by all other adult citizens, *Tit. Calymnii* xii, ll. 10–11. Although the Koans and Kalymnians are to swear separately from each other—each group in its own city—the provision for citizens of both cities to swear the same oath seems designed to have been reassuring to all that this was a joint, mutual decision to come together into a single political community.
40. But note the "compensatory" use of, e.g., the recitation of the Pledge of Allegiance in US public schools and the singing of the US national anthem before many sporting events.
41. On the importance of local deities for civic oaths, see C.G. Williamson (2013, 139–40) (discussing *OGIS* 229 (*I.Smyrna* 573; *I.Magnesia Sipylos* 1)). The quoted portions of the ephebic oath are at *RO* 88, ll. 16–20. Other associations that seem explicitly evoked by the entities named in the ephebic oath are youth (Herakles, Aglauros, Thallo) and war (Ares, Athena *Areia*, Enyo, Enyalios). See Bayliss (2012, 16). Contrast Plutarch's report (*Alc.* 15.4) that Alcibiades interpreted the invocation of common food crops as indicating that the Athenians were taught to consider the (entire) cultivated earth as rightfully theirs, οἰκείαν ποιεῖσθαι διδασκόμενοι τὴν ἥμερον καὶ καρποφόρον. As Louis Robert (1938, 306) notes, Alcibiades "déformait étrangement" the meaning of the oath. The ephebic oath of Dreros, known from an inscription from the first half of the third century (Chaniotis, *Verträge* 7), invokes similarly "generic"

gods and entities (καὶ ἥρωας καὶ ἡρωάσσας καὶ κράνας καὶ ποταμοὺς καὶ θεοὺς πάντας καὶ πάσας, 33–36), probably with the implication that they are the local divinities; see Chaniotis (1996, 197) and Cole (2004, 29) for similar interpretations. And compare the Chersonesos oath mentioned above, *IOSPE* I³ 3, 100 (*Syll.*³ 360), which is sworn, in part, in the name not of generic heroes but of "the heroes who possess the *polis* and country and walls of the Chersonesitai," ἥρωας ὅσοι πόλιν καὶ χώραν καὶ τείχη ἔχοντι τὰ Χερσονασιτᾶν, ll. 3–4. The same limitation is probably implied even when not expressed.

42. See McAuley (2018); A.S. Chankowski (2010, 438–40); Ma (2008, 196–98); Vidal-Naquet (1992, esp. 120 and 146). Perhaps Plutarch's Alcibiades should be seen as an Athenian "Black Hunter" gone awry.
43. *I.Olympia* 9 (*ML* 17; *Syll.*³ 9; *SvA* 110), ll. 3–7: αἰ δέ τι δέοι : αἴτε ϝέπος αἴτε ϝάργον : συνέαν κ' ἀλ(λ)άλοις : τά τ' ἄλ(λ)⟨α⟩ καὶ παρ πολέμο : αἰ δὲ μὰ συνέαν : τάλαντόν κ' ἀργύρο : ἀποτίνοιαν : τοῖ Δὶ Ὀλυνπίοι : τοὶ κα(δ)δαλέμενοι : λατρειόμενον. I print the Meiggs and Lewis translation.
44. *IOSPE* I³ 3, 100 (*Syll.*³ 360), ll. 4–5. We may also compare the very early treaty between the Sybarites and Serdaioi, *I.Olympia Suppl.* 6 (*ML* 10; *SvA* 120), in which the parties agree to "faithful and steadfast friendship forever," ἐπὶ φιλότατι πιστᾶι κ' ἀδόλοι ἀείδιον, ll. 3–5. The inscription does not indicate if these are words of an oath, but it cites "Zeus, Apollo, other gods and the *polis* of Poseidonia" as "proxenoi," which Siewert and Taeuber (in their commentary in *I.Olympia Suppl.*) take to mean "guarantors," so there likely was an oath ceremony involved.
45. However, Pausanias reports (6.20.3) that the Eleans swore "on the most important occasions" not in the name of Olympian Zeus, as here, but in the name of Sosipolis ("city savior"), who had a separate sanctuary; see Bayliss (2012b, 164).
46. On the role of sanctuaries as locations for identity building, see my discussion in Chapter 4. C. Morgan (2003, 75–76) cautions against seeing Olympia as the site of the first actual "administrative center" of Elis, although Roy (1997, 295–98) argues that the sanctuary seems to have played some (uncertain) role in relations between Elis and its perioikic communities. In any case, Olympia could have been a site for cross-community identity formation even (or especially) if it was not an actual Elean governmental center.
47. The divine element of oaths likely varied in its identity-building effects. At times the gods invoked were so universal that they seem unlikely to have evoked much group identity besides a common humanity. This is especially the case with Helios and Gaia ("Ge"), commonly invoked among Greeks and non-Greeks alike, see Scharff (2016, 31–33, 158–60); Bayliss (2012b, 161–62). And sometimes the parties to a treaty oath did not swear by the same gods but rather by their own, often unspecified, oath gods. This seems to have been the case, e.g., in the treaty of 420 between the Athenians, Argives, Mantineans, and Eleans. Thuc. 5.47.8 reports that the treaty provided that each party should swear "the greatest local oath," τὸν ἐπιχώριον ὅρκον ἕκαστοι τὸν μέγιστον; see Bayliss (2012b, 162–63).
48. Neither term, *synoikismos* nor *sympoliteia*, had a precisely fixed meaning (see Piñol-Villanueva 2017, 26–30), but *sympoliteia* seems generally to have had a broader meaning of communities joining together (and was used, e.g., in the formation of federal leagues, *koina*), whereas synoikism seems more regularly to have referred specifically to combining into a single *polis*. On synoikism and *sympoliteia*, see the foundational work of Moggi (1976); cf. Mackil (2013, 359–62); Giovannini (2007, 244–45); Eich (2004, 98–102); and the commentary to *RO* 14. Because they were entered into so that two communities could become one, *sympoliteia* treaties are not purely international but inhabit a transitional ground between international and domestic.
49. *IPArk* 9 (*RO* 14), ll. 3–6: τὸς [Ἐ]λ[ισ]ϝασίος Μαντινέας ἦναι ϝίσος καὶ ὑμοίος, κ[ο]ινάζοντα[ς πάν]των ὅσων καὶ οἱ Μαντινῆς, φέρ[ο]ντας τὰν χώραν καὶ τὰν π[όλιν] ἰμ Μαντιν[έ]αν ἰν τὸς νόμος τὸς Μαντινέων.
50. *OGIS* 229 (*I.Smyrna* 573; *I.Magnesia Sipylos* 1), ll. 65–68: καὶ πολιτεύσομαι μεθ' ὁμονοίας ἀστασιάστως κατὰ τοὺς Σμυρναίων νόμους καὶ τὰ ψηφίσματα τοῦ δ[ή]μου καὶ συνδιατηρήσω τήν τε αὐτονομίαν καὶ δημοκρατίαν καὶ τἆλλα τὰ ἐπικεχωρημένα Σμυρναίοις ὑπὸ τοῦ βασιλέως Σελεύκου μετὰ πάσης προθυμ[ία]ς ἐμ παντὶ καιρῶι, καὶ οὔτε αὐτὸς ἀδικήσω αὐτῶν οὐθένα οὔτε ἄλλωι ἐπ[ι]τρέψω οὐθενὶ κατὰ δύναμιν τὴν ἐμήν. . . . βοιηθήσω ἀγωνιζ[όμ]ενος μετὰ πάσης φιλοτιμίας, καὶ οὐκ ἐγκαταλείψω κατὰ δύναμιν τὴν ἐμαυτοῦ. See C.G. Williamson's text, translation, and discussion (2013, 136–40, 161–64).
51. *Tit. Calymnii* xii, ll. 18–23. Even with *sympoliteia* there was likely a range of identity-building effects from the oaths themselves. Another inscription from the fourth-century Peloponnese, a synoikism agreement between Euaimon and Arkadian Orchomenos, states it is on terms of

"equality and commonality," ἐπὶ τοῖς ϝίσϝοις καὶ τοῖς ὑμοίοις (*IPArk* 15, ll. 4–6), but the oaths themselves, which are preserved in this case, do little to obviously evoke a common identity. And *sympoliteiai* imposed from above by kings, such as Antigonos Monophthalmos imposed on Teos and Lebedos (*RC* 3, 4), and on Skepsis to participate in the synoikism that created Antigonea Troas (Strabo 13.1.52), might not have been embraced, by all involved, in the spirit of unity that some *sympoliteia* oaths tend to invoke.

52. *IG* II^2 116 (*RO* 44), ll. 16–17, βοηθήσω π[α]ντὶ σθένει κατὰ τὸ δυνατόν; cf. ll. 26–27. The key phrase is nearly identical again in the alliance between the Erythraeans and Hermias, the tyrant of Atarneus and Assos, from the 340s: the Erythraeans swore "I shall aid Hermias and his companions by land and sea with all my strength as much as possible, and I shall accomplish the other things according to what has been agreed," βοηθήσω Ἑρμί[αι καὶ τ]οῖς ἑταίροις καὶ κατὰ γῆν [καὶ κατ]ὰ θάλασσαν παντὶ σθένει κ[ατὰ τὸ δ]υνατόν, καὶ τὰ ἄλλα ἐπιτελ[έω κατὰ τ]ὰ ὡμολογημένα; *RO* 68 (*SvA* 322; *Syll.*^{3} 229), ll. 14–18.
53. *IG* II^3 1, 912, ll. 88–89, [ἐ]μ[μ]ενεῖν ἐν τεῖ συμμαχίαι τεῖ γεγ[ενημένηι]. I mention only briefly another subcategory: oaths in clearly unequal treaties, such as in the Peloponnesian and Delian Leagues. For reasons discussed in Chapter 3, notes 62–67 and accompanying text, the oaths of such uneven treaties seem more likely to have fostered feelings of hierarchy and subservience than of common identity (although those are not always mutually exclusive). On these oaths, see Scharff (2016, 102–18).
54. Blue et al. (2017, 201–04).
55. On who swore interstate oaths, see Bayliss (2012, 175–83); Giovannini (2007, 233–34). A well-known example of many high-status people swearing a treaty is the Peace of Nicias, where most of the Spartans and Athenians listed by Thucydides (5.19) are known figures, as detailed in Hornblower (1991–2008, ii.484–89); cf. Bayliss (2012, 180).
56. Studies show that both perceived control over outcome and perceived levels of expertise are positively correlated to trust in statements; see Blue et al. (2017, 191); Stevenson and Over (2001, 386–87); Evans and Twyman-Musgrove (1998, B15). Arrian, in his account of Alexander's campaigns (*Anab.* Praef. 2), states that he relies most on Ptolemy I's account because, "since he was a king, lying would have been more shameful for him than for another," βασιλεῖ ὄντι αἰσχρότερον ἤ τῳ ἄλλῳ ψεύσασθαι ἦν; cf. *Anab.* 7.5.2; Bosworth (1980–1995, i.43) cites "Hellenistic texts [that] emphasized the desirability of truthfulness in a monarch."
57. Procedure seems to have varied, even within a single *polis*. Sometimes an agreement was first approved by an assembly or council and then sworn, as with the Athenians' truce with the Spartans in 423 (Thuc. 4.118–19) and the Peace of Nicias in 421 (Thuc. 5.18–19). At other times it was negotiated and sworn and then approved, as with the Spartan-Athenian bilateral alliance that accompanied the Peace of Nicias (Thuc. 5.22.3).
58. Oaths in international affairs differed from those sworn in domestic *polis* ceremonies in that, while the latter bound only the individual who swore, the former bound an entire community, for years or even, theoretically, for ever. See Bolmarcich (2007, 26); Giovannini (2007, 233–35). For the most part this does not present problems, theoretical or practical, that are not already present in representative government generally. But in a domestic setting within communities, even in a context of communal or representative decision-making, the oath seems to have been seen as binding only on the individual person who swore it. An archon's oath bound only the archon, and my ephebic oath would impose no obligations on you, although the archon's official actions might affect the entire community and my vote in the assembly might impose a legal duty on you.

Chapter 11

1. As I noted in Chapter 2, I do not insist on a particular or narrow definition of what constitutes law. And as I noted in Chapter 3, legal socialization research is not limited by philosophical arguments concerning narrow definition of a "true legal system" but looks at various rule-bound social institutions.
2. As Larsen (1968, xviii) expresses it, the "great question" about Greek federal states "is whether they went so far beyond the symmachies as really to deserve the name. Did the cities actually co-operate much except in war?"

3. The traditional view is exemplified by Larsen's (1968, 12) description of Thessaly as "a strong feudal kingdom"; cf. Giovannini (1971, 63–67). Aston (2024, 60) now claims "the picture of the backward and isolated Thessaly has evaporated." On Thessaly as having an early *polis* culture, see Graninger (2011, 11) and my discussion below.
4. The best starting point for research into the history of Thessaly down to the third century is now Aston (2024). Major earlier works include Mili (2014); Helly (1995); Larsen (1968); Sordi (1958). On western Thessaly, see Rönnlund (2023). On the names of the tetrads, see Hellanikos of Lesbos, writing in the fifth century, *FGrH* 601a F1; cf. *IG* II^2 175, ll. 5–8 (first half of the fourth century); Aston (2024, 146–61, 227–29). On the *penestai*, see Ducat (1994); cf. Zingg (2023). Primary among the *perioikoi* (also called *hypekooi*) were the Phthiotic Achaians to the south, the Magnesians to the east, and the Perrhaibians to the north. They are mentioned by, e.g., Thucydides, 4.78.6, 8.3.1; and Xenophon, *Hell.* 6.1.9, 19. See Graninger (2011, 13–23); Sprawski (2008); Decourt, Nielsen, and Helly (2004, 680–82).
5. Sánchez (2001, 37–43, 518); see Aston (2024, 39–59); Mili (2014, 241–43).
6. Lefèvre (1998, 24) notes that there is no obvious evidence the two Thessalian representatives were appointed from different cities or regions on a rotating basis.
7. On the lack of Thessalian citizenship and regular federal political bodies, see Aston (2024, 225–87). On federal citizenship and political institutions as characteristic of federal states, see Beck and Funke (2015b, 14–19); Larsen (1968, xv). On political institutions in the Boiotian, Achaian, and Aitolian *koina*, see Mackil (2013, 335–46).
8. The lexicographer Harpokration (s.v. τετραρχία) records two mentions of these tetrads, one by the historian Hellanikos of Lesbos in the fifth century and one by Aristotle in the fourth. They are also mentioned in an Athenian inscription from the first half of the fourth century, *IG* II^2 175. On the significance of the tetrads, see Aston (2024, 9–10, 227–29); Helly (1995, 150–68); Sprawski (2012) advises extreme caution in interpreting Harpokration's text. The meager evidence does not suggest that the tetradic division formally played anything other than a military role, although Aston (2024, 227) emphasizes its possible pivotal role in Thessalian identity formation; see below.
9. On Aleuas and the Aleuads, see Arist. frr. 497–98 (Rose ed.); Sprawski (2012); Helly (1995, 112–18); Sordi (1958, 65–84); Morrison (1942, 60–62). On the Echekratidai, see Paus. 10.16.8. Morrison (1942, 61) argues the Echekratidai *were* Aleuads. On the Skopadai, see Plut. *Cimon* 10, reporting that Critias prayed for the "wealth of the Skopadai," πλοῦτον μὲν Σκοπάδων; cf. Plut. *Mor.* 527c (=*de Cup. Div.*). Herodotus (6.127.4) reports that one of the Skopadai, Diaktorides of Krannon, came to Sikyon in the tyranny of Kleisthenes (first half of the sixth century) as a suitor of the tyrant's daughter. On Skopas, see Helly (1995, 108–09); Sordi (1958, 62). He may have been the grandson of an elder Skopas, who likely flourished in the mid-sixth century, see Athen. 10, 438c; Quint. *Inst.* 11.2.15. On the family of Meno of Pharsalos, the title character in Plato's eponymous dialogue, see Morrison (1942, 59–64). On the social and political behavior of Thessalian elites in the sixth and fifth centuries, see Stamatopoulou (2007).
10. The Aleuads as "kings of Thessaly," Θεσσαλίης βασιλέες: Hdt. 7.6.2; Kineas as a "king," βασιλεύς: Hdt. 5.63.3; Echekratides as king, βασιλεύς, of Thessalians: Thuc. 1.111.
11. See Aston (2024, 232–34) (emphasizing the *polis*-centered nature of the authority of Thessalian "kings"); Helly (1995, 101–130). Contrast, e.g., T.R. Martin (1985, 74).
12. *Hell.* 6.1.8–9: "When Thessaly has a *tagos*, the cavalry number six thousand and the hoplites amount to more than ten thousand. . . . And all the peoples around are subjects, when a *tagos* is in power there," ὅταν ταγεύηται Θετταλία, εἰς ἑξακισχιλίους μὲν οἱ ἱππεύοντες γίγνονται, ὁπλῖται δὲ πλείους ἢ μύριοι καθίστανται. . . . πάντα τὰ κύκλῳ ἔθνη ὑπήκοα μέν ἐστιν, ὅταν ταγὸς ἐνθάδε καταστῇ. Jason became *tagos* "by common consent," ὁμολογουμένως: *Hell.* 6.1.18–19. In the first passage, Xenophon is reporting a speech by Polydamas of Pharsalos to the Spartans, in which Polydamas relates a conversation he had with Jason. The idea that the office of *tagos* was not always occupied seems confirmed by an inscription from Thetonion (*IG* IX 2, 257), probably from between 450 and 425 (see Jeffery 1990, 99 no. 10), recording a grant of honors by the Thetonians to Sotairos of Corinth κὲν ταγὰ κὲν ἀταγία (ll. 6–7). But there is debate whether this means "both when there is and is not a *tagos* in power" or "both in war and in peace." See Mili (2019, 280–81); Sordi (1996, 43 n.15); Helly (1995, 30); Hooker (1980, 272); Chadwick (1969, 231–34). To make the matter even less certain, because it is a *polis* decree this inscription could be referring to a local rather than Thessaly-wide office of *tagos*.
13. E. Meyer (1909, 249); Beloch (1926, 1.2:209–10). For the inscriptional evidence, see *SEG* 45.549, l. 8; *I.Atrax* 89 (*SEG* 27.183); *IG* IX 2, 257.

14. On the *tagos* as a military officer and not supreme leader, see Helly (1995, 13–38); on *archon*, *archos*, or *tetrarchos* as supreme leader, see Helly (1995, 39–68). The editors of *Choix Delphes* (p. 113), Sprawski (1999, 23), and Corsten (1999, 179) generally follow Helly's conclusions; Aston (2024, 274–75), Trevett (1999, 213), and Sordi (1996, 37 n.1; 1998, 418–19) are not persuaded. One sticking point is Helly's refusal to grant that Xenophon was privy to information we do not have about Thessalian institutions, especially when he states that Jason "was great because he became *tagos* in accordance with the law of the Thessalians," μέγας μὲν ἦν καὶ διὰ τὸ τῷ νόμῳ Θετταλῶν ταγὸς καθεστάναι, *Hell.* 6.4.28. This statement indicates Xenophon's understanding that Jason's position as *tagos* and the head of all Thessaly was in keeping with preexisting Thessalian law. On the role of the *tetrarchos*, Helly (1995, 42–44) cites an epigram attributed to Anacreon, *Anth. Pal.* 6.142, which calls Echekratidas a Θεσσαλίας ἀρχός, "ruler of Thessaly," seeing ἀρχός here as the technical term for leader of *all* Thessaly, although he admits that the closely related word ἄρχων "est vague et non significatif" (42). Sordi (1958, 64), on the other hand, takes the epigram as evidence that Echekratidas was *tagos*. Anacreon may simply mean that he was *one of the rulers* of Thessaly. Helly (1995, 45–46) also argues that two among the famous set of Daochos inscriptions from Delphi, erected in the second half of the fourth century after Thessaly was under Macedonian domination (*F.Delphes* iii 4 460; *Choix Delphes* 48), use the term τέτραρχος Θεσσαλῶν to mean a ruler of all four tetrads of Thessaly. But this leaves the question why the sole family member explicitly described as having been the ruler "of all Thessaly" is *not* called τέτραρχος: the inscription for Daochos (I) describes him as ἁπάσης Θεσσαλίας ἄρξας, "having ruled all Thessaly." Momigliano (1932, 50) suggests there was a college of four tetrarchs, each chosen by one tetrad; that together they administered all of Thessaly; and that this is why each could be called "tetrarch of the Thessalians."
15. Thessalian conflict with the Phokians: Hdt. 8.27–28; see Aston (2024, 60–72). Thessalians and Peisistratids: Hdt. 5.63. I pass over reported Thessalian participation in the shadowy Lelantine War, First Sacred War, and Battle of Keressos, but see Aston (2024, 43–48, 70–72); Helly (1995, 39–41); Tausend (1987, 510–11); Sordi (1958, 42–58, 85–91). As Aston (2024, 72) insists, "none of the[se] military actions . . . can be shown to have been a pan-Thessalian venture."
16. Aleuads invite Xerxes: Hdt. 7.6.2; Xerxes believes they represent all Thessalians: 7.130.3; Thessalians resist, then yield to, the Persians: 7.172–74. For arguments that resistance to the Aleuads' position may have originated in Pharsalos, see Morrison (1942, 61–2); Westlake (1936, 17). See also Hdt. 9.31.5 (Thessalians fight on the Persian side at the battle of Plataia); 9.1 and 9.58 (Aleuads help and advise Mardonios).
17. Pind. *Pyth.* 10.70–72, praising the brothers of Thorax of Larisa because they "raised high and increased the law of the Thessalians; and in the hands of good men resides the cherished inherited governance of cities," ὑψοῦ φέροντι νόμον Θεσσαλῶν / αὔξοντες· ἐν δ' ἀγαθοῖσι κεῖται / πατρώιαι κεδναὶ πολίων κυβερνάσιες. Stamatopoulou (2007, 313) takes the reference to *nomos* here to be to "custom" and "traditional law." On the brothers' identification and historicity, see Hdt. 9.58.
18. Xen. *Hell.* 6.4.28: τῷ νόμῳ Θετταλῶν ταγὸς καθεστάναι.
19. *F.Delphes* iii 4, 460(5) (*Choix Delphes* 48E; *Syll.*[3] 274): Δάοχος Ἀγία εἰμί, πατρὶς Φάρσαλος, ἁπάσης Θεσσαλίας ἄρξας, οὐ βίαι ἀλλὰ νόμωι, ἑπτὰ καὶ εἴκοσι ἔτη.
20. Aston reads *nomos* in both contexts as implying tradition or custom *rather* than law. Discussing the Xenophon passage, she describes the use of *nomos* as indicating merely "the accepted possibility . . . [of] the temporary command of an individual agreed by all. Nothing more elaborate, formal, or institutionalized is required" (2024, 242). Perhaps. But the verb used by Xenophon to indicate Jason's "appointment" as *tagos*, καθίστημι, is used frequently in constitutional and legal contexts to indicate both the appointment of officials in accordance with legal rules (e.g., Isoc. 12.132; Ar. *Pl.* 917; Dem. 3.10) and the very establishment of laws and constitutions (*Ath. pol.* 7.1; Lys. 12.42). Further, if Jason had become *tagos* through some informal and uninstitutionalized process (acclamation? passive acceptance?), one might expect Xenophon to explain how that could happen, since it would presumably appear mysterious to his non-Thessalian readers (compare Herodotus's more elaborate explanation of how Pisistratus became tyrant in Athens, Hdt. 1.59–61). Aston (2024, 285–86) reads *nomos* similarly in the Daochos inscription as "tradition" and not "law." But the inscription's expressed and implied contrast with "force," *bia*, counts strongly against that interpretation. If *nomos* meant "tradition" in this text, it would probably be contrasted not with "force" but with something by definition nontraditional, such as "novelty." Significantly, Diodorus describes Alexander of Pherai's later assumption of power in Thessaly as having been done "illegally and by force," παρανόμως καὶ βιαίως, Diod. Sic. 15.61.2. See

Mooren (1983, 221–22), who concludes Daochos is emphasizing that his grandfather "had acquired and fulfilled his function according to the 'constitution' or to the rules"; similarly Busolt and Swoboda (1926, ii.1482 n.1). A compromise position is to translate *nomos* in both passages as "customary law."

21. See Stamatopoulou (2013, 46); C. Morgan (2003, 87–88); Archibald (2000, 216); Helly (1995, 95). Rönnlund (2023, 19–46) argues that physical (as opposed to political) urbanization in Thessaly before the fourth century appears to have been confined to the east, although western Thessalians still lived together in "societies and communities forming complex political organisations" that took the form of "cities-across-villages," *poleis kata komas* (19–21), "probably forming small local federations or 'cantonal unions,' perhaps to be equated with *poleis*" (64).
22. The evidence includes the temple to Athena *Polias* on the acropolis of Gonnoi that has been dated to the late seventh century (although inscriptions naming the goddess are much later); and an inscription from Argoussa from the early-to-mid-fifth century mentioning Athena *Polias*, see *SEG* 45.549; Helly (1995, 95 n.62). On the cult of Athena *Polias* in Thessaly, see Mili (2014, 104–11). On the use of "*Polias*" as an epithet for Athena in many Greek cities, see Cole (1995, 301–04), explaining that "Πολιάς always referred first to the acropolis, and Athena with this name was the goddess on the acropolis."
23. "Hera of the *demos*," Ἕρας δαμόσιος. The inscribed stone is published by Doulgeri-Indzesiloglou (2000, 94–95, no. ΠΑ 1); reprinted by Helly (2018, 354); first published by Arvanitopoulos (1915, 159). The stone was found in Pagasai but is now apparently lost; see Mili (2014, 48 and n.163), who notes the reading has been doubted but should be taken seriously.
24. *FGrH* 1 frr. 133–36; Krannon, Photinaion, Olizon, and Eurumenai are each described as a πόλις Θεσσαλίας.
25. The inscription was originally published by Giannopoulos (1934/35, 140–45) (see *SEG* 45.549); revised text by Helly (2018, 355). It appears to be titled "A law for the *demos*," θεθνὸς τοῖ [δά]μοι, words highlighted on the first line. *Tagoi* are mentioned in line 8. Löbel (2014, 326) emphasizes its *polis*-based focus.
26. Rönnlund (2023, 36).
27. *IG* IX 2, 257 (*OR* 118; *Nomima* i 33; *Syll.*^{3} 55). "Forest warden": hυλορέων, l. 12. This inscription contains many difficulties of detail but its key elements are clear. As van Effenterre and Ruzé note in the commentary to *Nomima* i 33, the privileges are similar to those awarded in a proxeny decree but the term "proxeny" is not used. Aristotle mentions that in some cities the officials who manage the countryside around the city are called ὑλωρούς (*Pol.* 6, 1321b30).
28. Béquignon (1964, nos. 1 and 3) (*SEG* 23.415, 416).
29. W. Mack (2015, 3).
30. Enodia *Astike*: *IG* IX 2, 575 (but see the alternative interpretation of Nieto Izquierdo 2024). Athena *Agoraia*: *I.Atrax* 71 (*SEG* 27.184). Themis *Agoraia*: *I.Atrax* 89 (*SEG* 27.183).
31. Tziafalias et al. (2016, 177): "Thémis, comme plus haut Athéna, est ici une divinité non du marché, mais de la vie politique, déesse de la normalité, de la convenance et de la justice." See Mili (2014, 125–40) on Thessalian "cults in the agora" and (128–131) on Themis *Agoraia* and Athena *Agoraia*.
32. Arist. *Pol.* 3.2, 1275b26–30: "Thus Gorgias of Leontini, partly out of puzzlement and partly ironically, said that, just as mortars are the things made by mortar-makers, in the same way Larisaians are the people made by the *demiourgoi*. For there are some *larisapoioi*." Γοργίας μὲν οὖν ὁ Λεοντῖνος, τὰ μὲν ἴσως ἀπορῶν τὰ δ' εἰρωνευόμενος, ἔφη, καθάπερ ὅλμους εἶναι τοὺς ὑπὸ τῶν ὁλμοποιῶν πεποιημένους, οὕτω καὶ Λαρισαίους τοὺς ὑπὸ τῶν δημιουργῶν πεποιημένους· εἶναι γάρ τινας λαρισοποιούς. The joke works only in Greek and on the assumption that a *larisaios* was a name for a local type of vessel, as suggested by *Anth. Pal.* 6.305.3, τὼς Λαρισαίως κυτογάστορας ἑψητῆρας, "large-bellied Larisaian cauldrons." On *demiourgos* as a type of official, see Helly (1995, 28); Rougemont (1977, 65–66); Vatin (1961) (for examples from various cities, 236 n.2 and 237 nn.1–2). I follow the interpretation of Sprawski (1999, 46) and Sordi (1958, 122–23). It has been suggested that Gorgias's joke about Larisa was not made until the early fourth century, based on Pausanias's claim (6.17.9) that Jason of Pherai, active at that later time, admired him; see Sprawski (1999, 55–6). But in Plato's *Meno*, probably set in 404 (Morrison 1942, 76), Socrates refers to Gorgias as already popular in Thessaly.
33. On the first century of Thessalian coinage, see R. Mack (forthcoming) and (2021); a brief older treatment is T.R. Martin (1985, 34–59); see also Aston (2024, 235–36, 249–51); Liampi

(2015); Bouchon and Helly (2015, 238–39); Lorber (2008); Franke (1970). Minting coins is often recognized as a politically significant act by a Greek state, an assertion or at least reflection of civic identity and authority. See Bresson (2016, 268); Kurke (1999, 12–13); T.R. Martin (1995, 267).

34. On the dating and iconography of the earliest coins of Larisa and comparison with contemporary Macedonian coinage, see R. Mack (2021, 56–78); Kagan's (2004, 79–84) down-dating has also been accepted by Lorber (2008, 122).

35. The rodeo activity was a kind of bull-wrestling known as *taurokathapsia*, "tying down the bull." On these coins, and on *taurokathapsia* and its Thessalian associations, see R. Mack (2021, 79–112); also Aston (2024, 172–77); Liampi (2015). On the "Thessalians" coins, which are labeled ΦΕΤΑ or ΦΕΘΑ, see the thorough study by R. Mack (2021, 113–47); also Aston (2024, 177–80, 249–51); Rönnlund (2023, 35); Bouchon and Helly (2015, 238–39); T.R. Martin (1985, 36–37); Franke (1970).

36. R. Mack (forthcoming, Chapter 3) argues that the ΦΕΤΑ and ΦΕΘΑ coins may have been minted by the Pheraians.

37. See Aston (2024, 235–36); cf. R. Mack (2021, 112) (cities could "maintain individuality" within a cooperative coinage); Bouchon and Helly (2015, 238) (common coinage indicates some form of unity).

38. Pausanias 3.7.9: "And although he could have subdued all of Thessaly, since he was constantly winning the battles, he accepted a bribe from the Aleuads," καί οἱ καταστρέψασθαι Θεσσαλίαν πᾶσαν ἐξὸν ἅτε ἀεὶ νικῶντι ἐν ταῖς μάχαις, δῶρα ἔλαβε παρὰ τῶν Ἀλευαδῶν. Herodotus (6.72) describes the invasion and the bribe, although without stating the bribe's source.

39. Plut. *Mor.* 859d (=*de Mal. Herod.* 21): the Spartans "ended the *dynasteia* among Thessalians, deposing Aristomedes and Agelaos by the efforts of King Leotychidas," τὴν δ' ἐν Θετταλοῖς δυναστείαν ἔπαυσαν, Ἀριστομήδη καὶ Ἀγέλαον καταλύσαντες διὰ Λεωτυχίδου τοῦ βασιλέως.

40. Pausanias's specification that Leotychidas could have conquered "all of Thessaly," Θεσσαλίαν πᾶσαν, suggests that Leotychidas's original remit of attacking the Aleuads was only against part of Thessaly, *viz.*, the part ruled by the Aleuads.

41. I take the use of *dynasteia* by Plutarch, as also by Thucydides (4.78.3), to mean "rule by a narrow oligarchy" (following Hornblower 1991–2008, ii.259–60) but not to imply any form of lawlessness of the sort that the term "tyranny," *tyrannis,* could imply. Compare Xenophon's description of the *tagoi* of the Thessalian *koinon* after the death of Jason of Pherai, where they *are* likened to tyrants, *Hell.* 6.4.34–35.

42. Thuc. 2.22.3: ἡ δὲ βοήθεια αὕτη τῶν Θεσσαλῶν κατὰ τὸ παλαιὸν ξυμμαχικὸν ἐγένετο τοῖς Ἀθηναίοις, καὶ ἀφίκοντο παρ' αὐτοὺς Λαρισαῖοι, Φαρσάλιοι, [Παράσιοι], Κραννώνιοι, Πυράσιοι, Γυρτώνιοι, Φεραῖοι. ἡγοῦντο δὲ αὐτῶν ἐκ μὲν Λαρίσης Πολυμήδης καὶ Ἀριστόνους, ἀπὸ τῆς στάσεως ἑκάτερος, ἐκ δὲ Φαρσάλου Μένων· ἦσαν δὲ καὶ τῶν ἄλλων κατὰ πόλεις ἄρχοντες. "Aristonous" of Larisa has been believed to be the "Aristonos" awarded proxeny in an Athenian inscription dated to 431, *IG* I[3] 55; see M.B. Walbank (1978, 166). Hornblower (1991–2008, i.277–78) speculates that Menon may have been made *proxenos* at the same time. The meaning of ἀπὸ τῆς στάσεως ἑκάτερος is unclear. It is generally taken to mean "each from his own party" (see Bétant 1847 *s.v.*, defining στάσις here as "*factio, partes*"; see also citations at Rechenauer 1993, 239 n.3); Rechenauer (1993, 244) understands it as "each of the two as a result of the civil strife." Helly (1995, 234–35) more idiosyncratically takes στάσις here to be a technical term meaning a formation of troops, and Thucydides's expression to mean "qui relevaient respectivement de chacune des deux unités de mobilisation," and he concludes that this passage gives no support to theories of civil strife in Larisa. Aston (2024, 238) accepts Helly's interpretation, but Osborne and Rhodes reject it (in their commentary to *OR* 117).

43. See Mili (2019, 277–78).

44. Thuc. 3.93.2: οἵ τε Θεσσαλοὶ ἐν δυνάμει ὄντες τῶν ταύτῃ χωρίων.

45. E.g., in 422/21, Spartans attempted to traverse Thessaly again but the Thessalians "prevented" them, κωλυόντων δὲ τῶν Θεσσαλῶν, Thuc. 5.13.1. Thucydides does not say there was any fighting. And in 413/12 the Spartan king Agis demanded hostages and money from the Phthiotic Achaians, at the time subjects of the Thessalians. The latter registered their protests (μεμφομένων καὶ ἀκόντων τῶν Θεσσαλῶν) but apparently did not use violence to resist the Spartan action, 8.3.1.

46. The catalog of allies at the beginning of the war is at Thuc. 2.9. The allies in Sicily are listed at 7.57–58. On Thessalian neutrality, see Bauslaugh (1991, 121–24). In fact Thessaly could even be

described as being "at peace" during most of the war, as indicated in one inscription from the statues and bases in Delphi dedicated by Daochos (II) of Pharsalos and commonly dated to the mid-fourth century (*F.Delphes* iii 4, 460(5); *Choix Delphes* 48E; *Syll.*[3] 274). It claims that, in the reign of Daochos I, commonly dated to the final decades of the fifth century, "Thessaly teemed with much fruitful peace and with wealth," πολλῆι δὲ καὶ ἀγλαοκάρπωι εἰρήνηι πλούτωι τε ἔβρυε Θεσσαλία. On the dating of Daochos's reign, see *Choix Delphes* p. 115 and Sordi (1958, 117) (suggesting 440–413); Beloch (1926, i.2:208) (suggesting 432–405); E. Meyer (1909, 249) (suggesting 445–415). Geominy (1998, 374) argues unpersuasively for a reign in the mid-to-late fourth century.

47. Thuc. 4.78.3: εἰ μὴ δυναστείᾳ μᾶλλον ἢ ἰσονομίᾳ ἐχρῶντο τὸ ἐγχώριον οἱ Θεσσαλοί, οὐκ ἄν ποτε προῆλθεν. On the difference between δυναστεία and ἰσονομία, see Hornblower (1991–2008, ii.259–60); cf. Mili (2014, 69–71). I take τὸ ἐγχώριον here adverbially, as do most editors, but I propose that it means "locally" rather than "nationally" and modifies οἱ Θεσσαλοί, so that τὸ ἐγχώριον οἱ Θεσσαλοί means "the local Thessalians," "the Thessalians in that region." This makes more sense than the usual interpretation of τὸ ἐγχώριον as meaning "according to the traditions of the country," which Gomme (1956, 542–543) notes "is hard to parallel." Thucydides provides important information by specifying the local Thessalians, whereas on the traditional interpretation the adverbial expression could be omitted with little loss of meaning. And with my interpretation the usage of τὸ ἐγχώριον parallels Thucydides's adverbial use elsewhere of τὸ ἀρχαῖον meaning "originally" or "formerly," as Classen and Steup note (1882–1967, iv.158).
48. On Lycophron leading the Pheraians against other Thessalians, see Xen. *Hell.* 2.3.4. On Aristippus and Cyrus, see Xen. *Anab.* 1.1.10. Plato *Meno* 70b indicates that Aristippus was from Larisa and an Aleuad; Xenophon describes him only as "Thessalian." He was "hard-pressed by political opponents at home," πιεζόμενος ὑπὸ τῶν οἴκοι ἀντιστασιωτῶν, *Anab.* 1.1.10. On who Aristippus's opponents may have been, see Sprawski (1999, 40). Xenophon's use of ἀντιστασιώτης does not provide a definitive answer. It would seem to indicate an intra-*polis* opponent, but compounds of στάσις, unlike the uncompounded form, are not restricted in meaning to *civil* strife (e.g., ἀπόστασις, Thuc. 5.81.1).
49. In fact, except for the years of Jason of Pherai's hegemony, Pherai seems to have been politically distinct from Thessaly for most of the half century until Philip II finally defeated the "tyrants" Lykophron and Peitholaus in the late 350s, see Diod. Sic. 16.37.3.
50. The most complete edition and commentary is Albini (1968); see also text and discussion in E. Meyer (1909, 199–218, 259–83); discussion in Sprawski (1999, 34–38); Andrewes (1971, 218–21); Wade-Gery (1945); Morrison (1942, 68–74). Albini provides a balanced discussion of the authorship and dating questions, concluding reasonably that the work is likely from the time of Herodes Atticus even if not by Herodes (1968, 11–23); see also Sprawski (1999, 34–38); Russell (1983, 111) assigns the work to the second-century CE on stylistic grounds and is followed by Simonton (2017, 45 n.190). Funke (1980, 39–40 n.42) makes a case for the work's historical reliability.
51. Because there is no mention of Lykophron, some date it before Lykophron's attack in fall 404. See, e.g., Wade-Gery (1945, 22–23). E. Meyer (1909, 267–68) dates the speech to 399, arguing that before 399 Sparta was too busy consolidating more important affairs to even consider lending aid to a Thessalian *polis*. But as Adcock (1913, 250) notes, every possible date for an authentic speech presents problems.
52. In sections 9, 15, and 33 the author refers specifically to the "*polis*"; sections 7 and 30 also imply that the author is discussing a *polis* rather than a *koinon*. The leading candidate for the unnamed *polis* is Larisa (see, e.g., Andrewes 1971, 218; Albini 1968, 11; Wade-Gery 1945, 19; Morrison 1942, 69–70; E. Meyer 1909, 259), although the statement that the Phokians are their nearest neighbors (28) suggests Pharsalos (see Sprawski 1999, 36). Yet there is also a passage (14) that seems to identify the *polis* in question with all of Thessaly, stating, "we hold the most land among the Greeks, and the land capable of producing the most," χώραν γὰρ τῶν Ἑλλήνων ἔχοντες πλείστην καὶ πλεῖστα δυναμένην παρέχειν; see Albini (1968, 21). This apparent inconsistency is one reason I believe the speech to be late. Morrison (1942, 71) seems to take the speech to be primarily about Larisa, made by a Larisaian to the council of the Thessalians, but it seems unlikely such a speech would never name Larisa.
53. At least some writers of the first and second centuries CE (such as Plutarch, Arrian, and Lucian) had access to sources for Greek history that are lost to us. This speech could have been a "school

exercise" by an advanced student of rhetoric who had such access. On the other hand, works by historians other than Herodotus and Thucydides were not ordinary items on school syllabi at this time, so there is also a possibility that certain historical details were simply fabricated by the author; see Connolly (2001, 348–49); T. Morgan (1998, 94–100).

54. Ἀρχελάῳ δουλεύσομεν Ἕλληνες ὄντες βαρβάρῳ; The speech is called ὑπὲρ Λαρισαίων, DK 85 B fr. 2 (= Laks–Most *Thras.* D18) (Clem. Al. *Strom.* 6.16.6).
55. *Hell.* 4.3.3: Λαρισαῖοι μὲν οὖν καὶ Κραννώνιοι καὶ Σκοτουσσαῖοι καὶ Φαρσάλιοι, σύμμαχοι ὄντες Βοιωτοῖς, καὶ πάντες δὲ Θετταλοί, πλὴν ὅσοι αὐτῶν φυγάδες τότ' ἐτύγχανον, ἐκακούργουν αὐτὸν ἐπακολουθοῦντες.
56. On Medios, see Diod. Sic. 14.82.5–6. Sprawski (1999, 43) speculates that Lykophron of Pherai, likely a Spartan ally, may have been among the "exiled" Thessalians at this time. Perhaps φυγάδες here means "excluded [from the *koinon*]" rather than "exiled."
57. Plut. *Ages.* 16.3: "He was ravaging the land of the Thessalians who were allied to his enemies. But he sent Xenokles and Skythes into Larisa to make a pact. But when they were seized and guarded closely . . . he said that he wouldn't be willing to let one of those men die in exchange for taking all of Thessaly, and he got them back under a truce." τῶν δὲ Θετταλῶν τοῖς πολεμίοις συμμαχούντων ἐπόρθει τὴν χώραν. εἰς δὲ Λάρισσαν ἔπεμψε Ξενοκλέα καὶ Σκύθην περὶ φιλίας· συλληφθέντων δὲ τούτων καὶ παραφυλασσομένων . . . ὁ δὲ φήσας οὐκ ἂν ἐθελῆσαι Θεσσαλίαν ὅλην λαβεῖν ἀπολέσας τῶν ἀνδρῶν τὸν ἕτερον, ὑποσπόνδους αὐτοὺς ἀπέλαβε.
58. *Hell.* 4.3.8. On the other hand, in most of Xenophon's account he simply describes the actions of "the Thessalians," 4.3.4–8. As noted above, Medios of Larisa had seized Pharsalos the year before and driven out the Spartan garrison while enslaving the *katoikountes*, Diod. Sic. 14.82.5–6. These *katoikountes* seem not to have been Pharsalian citizens (since, e.g., Plutarch can discuss the Pharsalian cavalry in the following year) and may have been Spartan soldiers inhabiting Pharsalos. On *katoikountes* as military inhabitants, see G.M. Cohen (1991, 43), citing inscriptions from Asia Minor in which *katoikos* refers to Seleukid or Attalid military colonists; Gagliardi (2009/10, 312–20) cites inscriptions distinguishing *katoikountes* from *politai* and sometimes from other classes of non-citizen inhabitants (e.g., the careful distinction between πολῖται, πάροικοι, κάτοικοι, Ῥωμαῖοι, ξένοι, and δοῦλοι in *I.Priene B-M* 69, ll. 38–39).
59. Xen. *Hell.* 6.1.5, 18.
60. τῷ νόμῳ Θετταλῶν, *Hell.* 6.4.28. See Sprawski (1999, 100–101); contrast Diodorus's characterization (15.61.2) of how Alexander of Pherai came to power after Jason: "having acquired hegemony illegally and by force," παρανόμως καὶ βιαίως κτησάμενος τὴν δυναστείαν.
61. *Hell.* 6.1.8: ὅταν ταγεύηται Θετταλία, εἰς ἑξακισχιλίους μὲν οἱ ἱππεύοντες γίγνονται, ὁπλῖται δὲ πλείους ἢ μύριοι καθίστανται. On the *perioikic* tribute, see 6.1.19. There is no way to know the accuracy of Jason's claims about prior tribute, but it may be telling that Xenophon chose to put them in direct speech by Jason.
62. See Xen. *Hell.* 6.4.35; Diod. Sic. 15.61, 67, 71, 80; Tracy (2010, 28–9).
63. Diod. Sic. 15.80.6: ἠναγκάσθη καθ' ὁμολογίαν τοῖς μὲν Θετταλοῖς τὰς καταπεπολεμημένας πόλεις ἀποδοῦναι, Μάγνητας δὲ καὶ τοὺς Φθιώτας Ἀχαιοὺς παραδοῦναι Βοιωτοῖς, καὶ τὸ λοιπὸν Φερῶν μόνων ἄρχοντα σύμμαχον εἶναι Βοιωτοῖς.
64. *IG* II^2 116 (*RO* 44; *Syll.*^{3} 184; *SvA* 293). The treaty between the Athenians and the Thessalians is from 361/60 and specifically refers to a "war against Alexander" (l. 31). "The Thessalians" are mentioned throughout, and "the *koinon* of the Thessalians" at lines 17 and 25. The alliance between Alexander and the Athenians was struck about 368; see Diod. Sic. 15.71.3; Dem. 23.120; Tracy (2010, 28).
65. See, e.g., Diod. Sic. 3.64.7, 12.57.1; cf. Hdt. 8.3.1; Thuc. 3.82; Pl. *Resp.* 5.470B. At 15.61.1, Diodorus describes a *stasis* παρὰ Ῥωμαίοις of 369/68. On the core meaning of *stasis* being civil strife within a *polis*, see Lintott (1982, 34). *Stasis* could also break out among the soldiers or generals of an army; see, e.g., Diod. Sic. 14.40.4; 15.43.1; 16.78.3.
66. See Lintott (1982, 269): "The struggles in Thessaly cannot for the most part be strictly classified as *stasis*, since they were not conflicts inside cities, but conflicts between individual cities belonging to the league (*koinon*)." Gehrke, on the other hand, sees the early Thessalian *koinon* as a "politische Einheit" and includes intra-Thessalian conflicts in his survey of historical instances of *stasis*, although he admits "der Bund ein relativ loses Gebilde war" (1985, 184).
67. Parker (2011b, 112), discussing one of the very few decrees of "the Thessaloi" from the third century (Malay and Ricl 2009), notes "the existence of any form of centralized organisation during the period of Macedonian domination that ended only in 196 has been very uncertain."

68. As one of this book's anonymous readers rightly emphasized, "the collective ethnic ['Thessalians'] prevails over any other diplomatic formula" in Greek discussions of Thessalian foreign affairs.
69. Bouchon and Helly (2013, 223); see also Rönnlund (2023, 7).
70. For a brief account of the development of the story of Thessalos-descent in our surviving sources, see Mili (2014, 221–23).
71. Alcman fr. 16 Lobel-Page.
72. See n. 15, above.
73. See Lalonde (2019, 9–85), who concludes that "the cult of [Athena *Itonia*] probably originated [in Thessaly] in prehistoric time, that it eventually spread throughout Thessaly, and that its importance there was recognized by the wider Greek world" (84); see also Aston (2024, 167–68); Mili (2014, 225–34).
74. On the cult of Poseidon *Petraios* and the horse coins, see Aston (2024, 172–93); Mili (2014, 234–39). On the splitting of Tempe, see Hdt. 7.129. On the creation of the first horse, see schol. Pind. *Pyth.* 4.138.

Chapter 12

1. Kosmin (2024, 125) similarly describes a "Mediterranean world crisscrossed by treaties, oaths, and concords."
2. Menander Rhetor, writing perhaps in the reign of Diocletian in the late third century CE (Russell and Wilson 1981, xl), explains that it was no longer necessary to have a special term for relations between citizens and foreigners since everyone was now governed by "the common laws of the Romans," τοὺς κοινοὺς τῶν Ῥωμαίων νόμους (363.12, Russell–Wilson ed.). On the Greek world's gradual absorption into a Roman empire, see Ma (2024, chs. 11–12); Gruen (1984). On Greeks as *socii* of Rome, see Lavan (2013, 25–53). On early entanglements of Roman and Greek law, see Eberle (2016). On the legal implications of the mass citizenship grant of 212, see Mélèze Modrzejewski (2011, 475–96); Ando (2011, 19–36).
3. And there are many explicitly hybrid fields such as biophysics, biogeochemistry, etc.
4. On *syla* and *symbola*, see Bresson (2016, 318–23); on Greek international trade, see generally Bresson (2016, chs. 12–14). On the economic effects of domestic legal institutions, see Bresson (2016, ch. 9).
5. Ober (2015); see also Woolmer (2016). My approach also differs from Ober's strongly rationalistic vision of human behavior, in which social and psychological affect often seem absent. E.g., even when he suggests that ideology played a role in cooperative behavior among Greeks, Ober (2015, 67) depicts an ideology of fictive kinship as deliberately promoted by some cities, which seems to be positing rational, strategic behavior at the root even of group solidarity. See also Ober (2022, ch. 6), stressing at length the rationality of the Athenian legal order.
6. On the need to interpret Greek culture as part of and constantly mingling with the larger cultural world of the Mediterranean and Near East, see Morris (2000, 102–05). On the Amarna letters, see the editions by Rainey and Schneidewind (2015) and Moran (1992), and the essays in Cohen and Westbrook (2000). On international law (especially the laws of war and peace) in the ancient Near East, see Cox (2023); Altman (2012); on international commercial law in the Near East, see de Spens (1998). Von Scala (1898) is an early attempt to consider together (by way of collecting treaties) all Mediterranean and near-Mediterranean materials down to the fourth century BCE. Bederman (2001) considers the Near East, Greece, and Rome from the fifteenth to the second centuries BCE. See now also Eidem, Giltaij, and Tuori (2026), covering the ancient Mediterranean and Near East. On Roman international law, see Majer (2017); Ziegler (2008); Kaser (1993); Lombardi (1947).
7. Lonis (1969) makes the first steps on such a project, studying the use of laws of war between Greeks on one side and Persians and Carthaginians on the other, from the early fifth to mid-fourth century. He argues that the same general laws of war were followed as between Greeks alone, and that there is no sign of Greeks treating "barbarians" as an inferior race in this respect. But he does find evidence that treaties between Greeks and non-Greeks were less respected than those simply between Greeks (1969, 108–14).

8. On the former group, see, e.g., Feeney (2016); on the latter, see, e.g., Wiater (2011); Dueck (2000, 85–106). Bradley (2020, 256) claims that "Rome was a Hellenised society" already by the time of adoption of the Twelve Tables in the fifth century. On early Roman contacts with Greeks and Greek influence on Roman culture, see Bradley (2020, 47–55, 61–90, 204–209, 255–56, 350–53).
9. As Feeney (2016, 131–38) explains, Romans studied Greek language and literature as one means of belonging to a certain cultural elite. On Dionysius's circle of Greek and Roman intellectuals, see Wiater (2011, 22–27).
10. See Kant (2006, 75). On the theory of "democratic peace," see Ginsburg (2021, 31–59), citing extensive bibliography.
11. On modern use of Greek architecture, see, e.g., Temple, Piotrowski, and Heredia (2020); W.C. Miller (2016); Padovan (2013, 93–94, 146–50).

Bibliography

Aaken, A. van, and Broude, T. 2019. "The Psychology of International Law: An Introduction." *European Journal of International Law* 30:1225–36.

Abrams, D., and Hogg, M.A. 2010. "Social Identity and Self-Categorization." In *The SAGE Handbook of Prejudice, Stereotyping and Discrimination*, edited by J.F. Dovidio, M. Hewstone, P. Glick, and V. M. Esses. London: 179–193.

Adak, M., and Thonemann, P. 2022. *Teos and Abdera. Two Cities in Peace and War.* Oxford.

Adamidis, V. 2017. *Character Evidence in the Courts of Classical Athens. Rhetoric, Relevance and the Rule of Law.* Abingdon.

Adams, H. 1907. *The Education of Henry Adams.* Washington, D.C.

Adcock, F.E., and Knox, A.D. 1913. "Ἡρώδου περὶ πολιτείας." *Klio* 13:249–57.

Adcock, F.E., and Mosley, D.J. 1975. *Diplomacy in Ancient Greece.* London.

Afonso, A., and Negash, S. 2021. "Determinants of Selective Solidarity Across Borders." *SocArXiv.* April 7, 2021. doi:10.31235/osf.io/a75wx.

Ager, S.L. 1996. *Interstate Arbitrations in the Greek World, 337–90 BC.* Berkeley.

Ager, S.L. 1998. "Civic Identity in the Hellenistic World: The Case of Lebedos." *Greek, Roman, and Byzantine Studies* 39:5–21.

Ager, S.L. 2013. "Interstate Governance. Arbitration and Peacekeeping." In *A Companion to Ancient Greek Government*, edited by H. Beck. Chichester: 497–511.

Ager, S.L. 2015. "Peaceful Conflict Resolution in the World of the Federal States." In *Federalism in Greek Antiquity*, edited by H. Beck and P. Funke. Cambridge: 471–86.

Agnew, R. 1992. "Foundation for a General Strain Theory of Crime and Delinquency." *Criminology* 30:47–87.

Agnew, R. 2001. "Building on the Foundation of General Strain Theory: Specifying the Types of Strain Most Likely to Lead to Crime and Delinquency." *Journal of Research in Crime and Delinquency* 38:319–61.

Akers, R.L. 1998. *Social Learning and Social Structure. A General Theory of Crime and Deviance.* Boston.

Akrigg, B. 2015. "Metics in Athens." In *Communities and Networks in the Ancient Greek World*, edited by C. Taylor and K. Vlassopoulos. Oxford: 155–73.

Albini, U., ed. 1968. *Peri Politeias.* Florence.

Alesina, A., and Giuliano, P. 2015. "Culture and Institutions." *Journal of Economic Literature* 53:898–944.

Allan, W. 2004. "Religious Syncretism: The New Gods of Greek Tragedy." *Harvard Studies in Classical Philology* 102:113–55.

Allen, D.W. 2012. *The Institutional Revolution. Measurement and the Economic Emergence of the Modern World.* Chicago.

Allport, G.W. 1954. *The Nature of Prejudice.* Cambridge, Mass.

Alonso Troncoso, V. 2007. "War, Peace, and International Law in Ancient Greece." In *War and Peace in the Ancient World*, edited by K.A. Raaflaub. Malden, Mass.: 206–25.

Alonso Troncoso, V. 2012. "Olympie et la publication des traités internationaux." *Rivista Diritto Ellenico - Review of Hellenic Law* 2:1–25.

Altman, A. 2012. *Tracing the Earliest Recorded Concepts of International Law. The Ancient Near East (2500–330 BCE).* Leiden.

Alty, J. 1982. "Dorians and Ionians." *Journal of Hellenic Studies* 102:1–14.

Amandry, P. 1986. "Chios and Delphi." In *Chios. A Conference at the Homereion in Chios 1984*, edited by J. Boardman and C.E. Vaphopoulou-Richardson. Oxford: 205–32.

Anand, R.P. 2010. "The Formation of International Organizations and India: A Historical Study." *Leiden Journal of International Law* 23:5–21.

Anastasiadis, M., and Lewis, D. 2024. "The Inside Woman: A New Solution to the Riddle of the *Endothidia Dola* (*IC* IV 72 II 11–16)." *Zeitschrift für Papyrologie und Epigraphik* 232:129–41.

Andersen, S.M., Tuskeviciute, R., Przybylinski, E., Ahn, J.N., and Xu, J.H. 2016. "Contextual Variability in Personality from Significant-Other Knowledge and Relational Selves." *Frontiers in Psychology* 6:1–17.

Anderson, G. 2009. "The Personality of the Greek State." *Journal of Hellenic Studies* 129:1–22.

Andersson, T.M. 1984. "The Thief in *Beowulf*." *Speculum* 59:493–508.

Ando, C. 2011. *Law, Language, and Empire in the Roman Tradition. Empire and after.* Philadelphia.

Andrewes, A. 1962. "The Mytilene Debate: Thucydides 3.36–49." *Phoenix* 16:64–85.

Andrewes, A. 1971. "Two Notes on Lysander." *Phoenix* 25:206–226.

Aneziri, S. 2003. *Die Vereine der dionysischen Techniten im Kontext der hellenistischen Gesellschaft.* Stuttgart.

Aneziri, S. 2020. "Artists of Dionysus: The First Professional Associations in the Ancient Greek World." In *Skilled Labour and Professionalism in Ancient Greece and Rome*, edited by E. Stewart, E. Harris, and D. Lewis. Cambridge: 293–312.

Anghie, A. 2005. *Imperialism, Sovereignty, and the Making of International Law.* Cambridge.

Antonetti, C. 1990. *Les Étoliens. Image et religion.* Paris.

Arbour, J.-M., and Parent, G. 2012. *Droit international public.* 6th ed. Cowansville.

Archibald, Z.H. 2000. "Space, Hierarchy, and Community in Archaic and Classical Macedonia, Thessaly, and Thrace." In *Alternatives to Athens*, edited by R. Brock and S. Hodkinson. Oxford: 212–33.

Armitage, D., and Pitts, J. 2017. "*'This Modern Grotius': An Introduction to the Life and Thought of C. H. Alexandrowicz.*" In C.H. Alexandrowicz, *The Law of Nations in Global History*, edited by D. Armitage and J. Pitts. Oxford: 1–32.

Arnaoutoglou, I.N. 2003. *Thusias Heneka kai Sunousias. Private Religious Associations in Hellenistic Athens.* Athens.

Arnaud, P. 2012. "Ancient Sailing-Routes and Trade Patterns: The Impact of Human Factors." In *Maritime Archaeology and Ancient Trade in the Mediterranean*, edited by D. Robinson and A.I. Wilson. Oxford: 59–78.

Arnett, J.J. 2015. "Socialization in Emerging Adulthood. From the Family to the Wider World, from Socialization to Self-Socialization." In *Handbook of Socialization*, edited by J.E. Grusec and P.D. Hastings. New York: 85–108.

Arrington, N.T. 2018. "Touch and Remembrance in Greek Funerary Art." *Art Bulletin* 100:7–27.

Arrington, N.T. 2021. *Athens at the Margins. Pottery and People in the Early Mediterranean World.* Princeton.

Arvanitopoulos, A.S. 1915. "Ἀνασκαφαὶ καὶ ἔρευναι ἐν Θεσσαλίᾳ." Πρακτικὰ τῆς ἐν Ἀθήναις Ἀρχαιολογικῆς Ἑταιρείας (1915):131–200.

Asheri, D., Lloyd, A., and Corcella, A. 2007. *A Commentary on Herodotus Books I–IV*, edited by O. Murray and A. Moreno. Oxford.

Aston, E. 2024. *Blessed Thessaly. The Identities of a Place and Its People from the Archaic Period to the Hellenistic.* Liverpool.

Austin, J. 1832. *The Province of Jurisprudence Determined.* London.

Austin, J.L. 1975. *How to Do Things with Words.* 2nd ed. Oxford.

Austin, M.M. 1986. "Hellenistic Kings, War, and the Economy." *Classical Quarterly* 36:450–66.

Austin, M.M. 2008. "The Greeks in Libya." In *Greek Colonisation. An Account of Greek Colonies and Other Settlements Overseas*, Vol. 2, edited by G.R. Tsetskhladze. Leiden: 187–217.

Avidov, A. 1997. "Were the Cilicians a Nation of Pirates?" *Mediterranean Historical Review* 12:5–55.

Avilés, D. 2010. *Altgriechische Gesetze. Natur und Entwicklung eines Rechtsinstituts.* Diss. Freiburg.

Bagnall, R.S. 1976. *The Administration of the Ptolemaic Possessions outside Egypt.* Leiden.

Balot, R.K. 2004. "Free Speech, Courage, and Democratic Deliberation." In *Free Speech in Classical Antiquity*, edited by I. Sluiter and R.M. Rosen. Leiden: 233–59.

Balot, R.K. 2024. *Tragedy, Philosophy, and Political Education in Plato's Laws.* Oxford.

Baltrusch, E. 1994. *Symmachie und Spondai. Untersuchungen zum griechischen Völkerrecht der archaischen und klassischen Zeit (8. bis 5. Jahrhundert v. Chr.).* Berlin.

Barletta, B.A. 2011. "State of the Discipline. Greek Architecture." *American Journal of Archaeology* 115:611–40.

Barnes, C.L.H. 2006. "The Ferries of Tenedos." *Historia* 55:167–77.

Barrett, W.S. 1964. *Euripides Hippolytos.* Oxford.

Barringer, J.M. 2005. "The Temple of Zeus at Olympia, Heroes, and Athletes." *Hesperia* 74:211–41.

Barringer, J.M. 2015. "The Changing Image of Zeus in Olympia." *Archäologischer Anzeiger* (2015):19–37.

Barringer, J.M. 2021. *Olympia. A Cultural History.* Princeton.

Barringer, J.M., Ekroth, G., and Scahill, D., eds. 2025. *Logistics in Greek Sanctuaries. Exploring the Human Experience of Visiting the Gods.* Leiden.

Barron, J.P. 1964. "Religious Propaganda of the Delian League." *Journal of Hellenic Studies* 84:35–48.

Barta, H. 2010. *"Graeca Non Leguntur"? Zu den Ursprüngen des europäischen Rechts im antiken Griechenland.* 3 vols. Wiesbaden.

Bartelson, J. 2001. *The Critique of the State.* New York.

Basile, G.J. 2016. "*Xenía*: la amistad-ritualizada de Homero a Heródoto." *Emerita, Revista de Lingüística y Filología Clásica* 84:229–50.

Bates, R. 2014. "The New Institutionalism." In *Institutions, Property Rights, and Economic Growth*, edited by S. Galiani and I. Sened. Cambridge: 50–65.

Baumeister, R.F., and Leary, M.R. 1995. "The Need to Belong: Desire for Interpersonal Attachments as a Fundamental Human Motivation." *Psychological Bulletin* 117:497–529.

Bauschatz, J. 2013. *Law and Enforcement in Ptolemaic Egypt.* Cambridge.

Bauslaugh, R.A. 1991. *The Concept of Neutrality in Classical Greece.* Berkeley.

Bayliss, A.J. 2012. "2. Oaths and Citizenship; 3. Oaths of Office." In *Oath and State in Ancient Greece*, edited by A.H. Sommerstein and A.J. Bayliss. Berlin: 9–46.

Bayliss, A.J. 2012b. "Part Two: Oaths and Interstate Relations." In *Oath and State in Ancient Greece*, edited by A.H. Sommerstein and A.J. Bayliss. Berlin: 147–306.

Bayliss, A.J. 2014. "'Artful Dodging', or the Sidestepping of Oaths." In *Oaths and Swearing in Ancient Greece*, edited by A.H. Sommerstein and I.C. Torrance. Berlin: 240–80.

Bayram, A.B. 2017. "Good Europeans? How European Identity and Costs Interact to Explain Politician Attitudes towards Compliance with European Union Law." *Journal of European Public Policy* 24:42–60.

Beaton, R. 2020. *Greece. Biography of a Modern Nation.* London.

Beccaria, C. 1781. *Dei delitti e delle pene.* Edizione novissima di nuovo corretta, ed accresciuta coi commenti del Voltaire. Vol. 1. Venice.

Beck, H. 1997. *Polis und Koinon.* Stuttgart.

Beck, H. 2020. *Localism and the Ancient Greek City-State.* Chicago.

Beck, H., and Funke, P., eds. 2015. *Federalism in Greek Antiquity.* Cambridge.

Beck, H., and Funke, P. 2015b. "An Introduction to Federalism in Greek Antiquity." In *Federalism in Greek Antiquity*, edited by H. Beck and P. Funke. Cambridge: 1–29.

Beck, H., and Ganter, A. 2015. "Boiotia and the Boiotian Leagues." In *Federalism in Greek Antiquity*, edited by H. Beck and P. Funke. Cambridge: 132–57.

Bederman, D.J. 2001. *International Law in Antiquity.* Cambridge.

Beloch, K.J. 1926. *Griechische Geschichte.* 4 vols. in 8. Berlin.

Beltrán Lloris, F., Díaz Ariño, B., Jordán Cólera, C., Simón Cornago, I. 2020. "*Tesseram conferre.* Etruscan, Greek, Latin, and Celtiberian *tesserae hospitales.*" *Historia* 69:482–518.

Bentham, J. 1789 [1780]. *An Introduction to the Principles of Morals and Legislation. Printed in the Year 1780, and Now First Published.* London.

Benton, L. 2010. *A Search for Sovereignty. Law and Geography in European Empires, 1400–1900.* Cambridge.

Benton, L., and Clulow, A. 2015. "Legal Encounters and the Origins of Global Law." In *The Cambridge World History. Volume 6, The Construction of a Global World, 1400–1800 CE. Part 2, Patterns of Change,* edited by J.H. Bentley, S. Subrahmanyam, and M.E. Wiesner-Hanks. Cambridge: 80–100.

Benton, L., and Clulow, A. 2024. "Interpolity Law and Jurisdictional Politics." *Law and History Review* 42:197–209.

Béquignon, Y. 1935. "Études thessaliennes, VII (1)." *Bulletin de correspondance hellénique* 59:36–77.

Béquignon, Y. 1964. "Études thessaliennes, XI. Inscriptions." *Bulletin de correspondance hellénique* 88:395–412.

Bereczkei, T., Birkas, B., and Kerekes, Z. 2007. "Public Charity Offer as a Proximate Factor of Evolved Reputation-Building Strategy: An Experimental Analysis of a Real-Life Situation." *Evolution and Human Behavior* 28:277–84.

Beretta Liverani, M. 2013. "Il decreto ateniese per i Faseliti (*IG* i3 10) e le multe di 10.000 dracme nel V sec." *Historiká* 3:131–57.

Bernstein, L. 1996. "Merchant Law in a Merchant Court: Rethinking the Code's Search for Immanent Business Norms." *University of Pennsylvania Law Review* 144:1765–1821.

Bernstein, L. 2019. "Contract Governance in Small-World Networks: The Case of the Maghribi Traders." *Northwest University Law Review* 113:1009–70.

Bernstorff, J. von. 2010. *The Public International Law Theory of Hans Kelsen. Believing in Universal Law.* Cambridge.

Berti, M. 2012. "*Diallagai* e *diallaktai*: forme e strumenti della riconciliazione nelle testimonianze epigrafiche." In *Salvare le poleis,* edited by S. Cataldi, E. Bianco, and G. Cuniberti. Alessandria: 323–333.

Bertrand, J.-M. 2001. "La revendication de liberté, réflexions sur les modalités du discours politique dans les cités grecques." In *Images et représentations du pouvoir et de l'ordre social dans l'antiquité,* edited by M. Molin. Paris: 11–25.

Besson, S., and Tasioulas, J. 2010. "Introduction." In *The Philosophy of International Law,* edited by S. Besson and J. Tasioulas. Oxford: 1–27.

Bétant, E.-A. 1847. *Lexicon Thucydideum.* 2 vols. Geneva.

Bickerman, E.J. 1938. *Institutions des Séleucides.* Paris.

Bickerman, E.J. 1950. "Remarques sur le droit des gens dans la Grèce classique." *Revue internationale des droits de l'antiquité* 4:99–127.

Bielman, A. 1994. *Retour à la liberté. Libération et sauvetage des prisonniers en Grèce ancienne.* Athens.

Bierl, A. 2008. "Die Rezeption der Homerischen Dichtung in der griechischen Literatur." In *Homer. Der Mythos von Troia in Dichtung und Kunst,* edited by J. Latacz, T. Greub, P. Blome, and A. Wieczorek. Munich: 208–14.

Billows, R.A. 1990. *Antigonos the One-Eyed and the Creation of the Hellenistic State.* Berkeley.

Billows, R.A. 2023. *The Spear, the Scroll, and the Pebble. How the Greek City-State Developed as a Male Warrior-Citizen Collective.* London.

Bisin, A., and Verdier, T. 2011. "The Economics of Cultural Transmission and Socialization." In *Handbook of Social Economics, Volume 1A,* edited by J. Benhabib, A. Bisin, and M.O. Jackson. San Diego: 339–416.

Blackman, D.J. 1981. "Brief History of the City, Based on the Ancient Sources." In *Phaselis,* edited by J. Schäfer. Tübingen: 31–37.

Blanshard, A. 2007. "The Problems with Honouring Samos: An Athenian Document Relief and Its Interpretation." In *Art and Inscriptions in the Ancient World*, edited by Z. Newby and R. Leader-Newby. Cambridge: 19–37.

Blanton, T.R., and Hollander, D.B. 2019. "The Extramercantile Economy. An Assessment of the New Institutional Economics Paradigm in Relation to Recent Studies of Ancient Greece and Rome." In *The Extramercantile Economies of Greek and Roman Cities*, edited by D.B. Hollander, T.R. Blanton, and J.T. Fitzgerald. London: 8–28.

Blass, F. 1893. *Die attische Beredsamkeit*. 3 vols. in 4. Leipzig.

Blok, J. 2005. "Becoming Citizens. Some Notes on the Semantics of 'Citizen' in Archaic Greece and Classical Athens." *Klio* 87:7–40.

Blok, J. 2013. "Citizenship, the Citizen Body, and Its Assemblies." In *A Companion to Ancient Greek Government*, edited by H. Beck. Malden, Mass.: 161–75.

Blok, J. 2017. *Citizenship in Classical Athens*. Cambridge.

Blok, J. 2022. "Ten Thousand: Fines, Numbers and Institutional Change in Fifth-Century Athens." In *Numbers and Numeracy in the Greek Polis*, edited by R. Sing, T. van Berkel, and R. Osborne. Leiden: 96–130.

Blome, P. 2008. "Die Rezeption der Homerischen Dichtung in der griechischen Bildkunst." In *Homer. Der Mythos von Troia in Dichtung und Kunst*, edited by J. Latacz, T. Greub, P. Blome, and A. Wieczorek. Munich: 196–207.

Blouin, A., and Mukand, S. 2022. "Mistaking Noise for Bias. Victimhood and Hutu-Tutsi Reconciliation in East Africa." *Journal of Development Economics* 158: [unpaginated].

Blue, P.R., Hu, J., Peng, L., Yu, H., Liu, H., and Zhou, X. 2017. "Whose Promises Are Worth More? How Social Status Affects Trust in Promises." *European Journal of Social Psychology* 50:189–206.

Boardman, J. 1999. *The Greeks Overseas. Their Early Colonies and Trade*. 4th ed. London.

Böckh, A. 1851. *Die Staatshaushaltung der Athener*. 2nd ed. 4 vols. Berlin.

Boehm, R. 2018. *City and Empire in the Age of the Successors. Urbanization and Social Response in the Making of the Hellenistic Kingdoms*. Berkeley.

Boesch, P. 1908. *Theōros. Untersuchung zur Epangelie griechischer Feste*. Berlin.

Bolmarcich, S. 2005. "Thucydides 1.19.1 and the Peloponnesian League." *Greek, Roman, and Byzantine Studies* 45:5–34.

Bolmarcich, S. 2007. "Oaths in Greek International Relations." In *Horkos. The Oath in Greek Society*, edited by A.H. Sommerstein and J. Fletcher. Exeter: 26–38.

Bolton, J. 2000. "Is There Really 'Law' in International Affairs?" *Transnational Law & Contemporary Problems* 10:1–48.

Bommelaer, J.-F. 2015. *Guide de Delphes. Le site*. Athens.

Bonner, R.J., and Smith, G. 1930–38. *The Administration of Justice from Homer to Aristotle*. 2 vols. Chicago.

Bookidis, N., Hansen, J., Snyder, L., and Goldberg, P. 1999. "Dining in the Sanctuary of Demeter and Kore at Corinth." *Hesperia* 68:1–54.

Bookidis, N., and Stroud, R. 1997. *The Sanctuary of Demeter and Kore. Topography and Architecture*. Vol. 18, Part 3 of *Corinth. Results of Excavations*. Princeton.

Bork, R.H. 1989/90. "The Limits of 'International Law'." *The National Interest* 18:3–10.

Bosworth, A.B. 1980–1995. *A Historical Commentary on Arrian's History of Alexander*. 2 vols. Oxford.

Bosworth, A.B. 1988. *Conquest and Empire. The Reign of Alexander the Great*. Cambridge.

Bouchon, R., and Helly, B. 2013. "Construire et reconstruire l'état fédéral thessalien (époque classique, époque hellénistique et romaine)." In *Greek Federal States and Their Sanctuaries*, edited by P. Funke and M. Haake. Stuttgart: 205–26.

Bouchon, R., and Helly, B. 2015. "The Thessalian League." In *Federalism in Greek Antiquity*, edited by H. Beck and P. Funke. Cambridge: 231–49.

Bourdieu, P. 1986. "The Forms of Capital." In *Handbook of Theory and Research for the Sociology of Education*, edited by J.G. Richardson. New York: 241–258.

Bourdieu, P., and Wacquant, L.J.D. 1992. *An Invitation to Reflexive Sociology*. Chicago.
Bowie, A.M. 2013. *Homer,* Odyssey. *Books xiii and xiv*. Cambridge.
Bowles, S. 2004. *Microeconomics. Behavior, Institutions, and Evolution*. New York.
Boyxen, B. 2018. *Fremde in der hellenistischen Polis Rhodos. Zwischen Nähe und Distanz*. Berlin.
Brader, T., and Marcus, G.E. 2013. "Emotion and Political Psychology." In *The Oxford Handbook of Political Psychology*, 2nd ed., edited by L. Huddy, D.O. Sears, and J.S. Levy. Oxford: 165–204.
Bradford, B., Hohl, K., Jackson, J., and MacQueen, S. 2015. "Obeying the Rules of the Road: Procedural Justice, Social Identity, and Normative Compliance." *Journal of Contemporary Criminal Justice* 31:171–91.
Bradford, B., Murphy, K., and Jackson, J. 2014. "Officers as Mirrors. Policing, Procedural Justice and the (Re)Production of Social Identity." *British Journal of Criminology* 54:527–50.
Bradley, G. 2020. *Early Rome to 290 BC. The Beginnings of the City and the Rise of the Republic*. Edinburgh.
Braithwaite, J., and Makkai, T. 1991. "Testing an Expected Utility Model of Corporate Deterrence." *Law & Society Review* 25:7–40.
Braund, D. 2007. "Greater Olbia: Ethnic, Religious, Economic, and Political Interactions in the Region of Olbia, c. 600–100 BC." In *Classical Olbia and the Scythian World*, edited by D. Braund and S.D. Kryzhitskiy. Oxford: 38–78.
Braund, D. 2019. "Colonial Location: Olbia on the Hypanis." In *Greek Colonization in Local Contexts*, edited by J. Lucas, C.A. Murray, and S. Owen. Oxford: 215–30.
Bravo, B. 1980. "*Sulan*. Représailles et justice privée contre des étrangers dans les cités grecques (Étude du vocabulaire et des institutions)." *Annali della Scuola Normale Superiore di Pisa. Classe di Lettere e Filosofia* 10:675–987.
Bravo, B. 2011. "Tre lettere di mercanti del Mar Nero settentrionale rivisitate. Sui modi di organizzazione e gli attori del commercio e sulla 'giustizia privata' in poleis ed empória." *Palamedes* 6:37–91.
Bravo, B. 2021. *Pontica Varia.* Poleis *e città, culti e rappresentazioni religiose,* thiasoi *orfici, organizzazione del commercio, 'giustizia privata' nella periferia nord-orientale del mondo greco (secoli VII–IV A.C.)*. Athens.
Bremmer, J.N. 2007. "Greek Normative Animal Sacrifice." In *A Companion to Greek Religion*, edited by D. Ogden. Malden, Mass.: 132–44.
Bremmer, J.N. 2010. "Manteis, Magic, Mysteries and Mythography. Messy Margins of Polis Religion?" *Kernos* 23:13–35.
Brenton, J. 2017. "Socialization." In *The Cambridge Handbook of Sociology. Core Areas in Sociology and the Development of the Discipline*, edited by K.O. Korgen. Cambridge: 197–204.
Bresson, A. 2000. *La cité marchande*. Paris.
Bresson, A. 2003. "Merchants and Politics in Ancient Greece: Social and Economic Aspects." In *Mercante e politica nel mondo antico*, edited by C. Zaccagnini. Rome: 139–63.
Bresson, A. 2007. "Rhodes, Rome et les pirates tyrrhéniens." In *Scripta Anatolica. Mélanges Pierre Debord*, edited by P. Brun. Bordeaux: 145–64.
Bresson, A. 2011. "Grain from Cyrene." In *The Economies of Hellenistic Societies, Third to First Centuries BC*, edited by Z.H. Archibald, J.K. Davies, and V. Gabrielsen. Oxford: 66–95.
Bresson, A. 2016. *The Making of the Ancient Greek Economy: Institutions, Markets, and Growth in the City-States*. Princeton.
Briant, P. 1985. "Les Iraniens d'Asie Mineure après la chute de l'empire achéménide. À propos de l'inscription d'Amyzon." *Dialogues d'histoire ancienne* 11:166–95.
Briant, P. 2002. *From Cyrus to Alexander. A History of the Persian Empire*. Winona Lake, Indiana.
Briant, P. 2006. "L'Asie mineure en transition." In *La transition entre l'empire achéménide et les royaumes hellénistiques*, edited by P. Briant and F. Joannès. Paris: 309–51.
Briant, P. 2017. *Kings, Countries, Peoples. Selected Studies on the Achaemenid Empire*. Translated by A. Kuhrt. Stuttgart.

Briant, P., and Descat, R. 1998. "Un registre douanier de la satrapie d'Égypte à l'époque achéménide." In *Le commerce en Égypte ancienne*, edited by N. Grimal and B. Menu. Cairo: 59–104.

Brock, R. 2015. "Law and Citizenship in the Greek *Poleis*." In *The Oxford Handbook of Ancient Greek Law*, edited by E.M. Harris and M. Canevaro. Oxford. [https://doi.org/10.1093/oxfordhb/9780199599257.013.15]

Broodbank, C. 2013. *The Making of the Middle Sea. A History of the Mediterranean from the Beginning to the Emergence of the Classical World*. Oxford.

Brown, R. 1996. "Tajfel's Contribution to the Reduction of Intergroup Conflict." In *Social Groups and Identities*, edited by W.P. Robinson. Oxford: 169–89.

Brown, R.L., and Rohlinger, D.A. 2016. "The Effect of Political Generation on Identity and Social Change: Age Cohort Consequences." *Journal of Women and Aging* 28: 96–111.

Brughmans, T. 2018. "Lessons Learned from the Uninformative Use of Network Science Techniques." In *Maritime Networks in the Ancient Mediterranean World*, edited by J. Leidwanger and C. Knappett. Cambridge: 184–218.

Brulé, P. 1978. *La piraterie crétoise hellénistique*. Paris.

Buchanan, A.E. 2004. *Justice, Legitimacy, and Self-Determination. Moral Foundations for International Law*. New York.

Budelmann, F. 2019. "Group Minds in Classical Athens? Chorus and *Dēmos* as Case Studies of Collective Cognition." In *Distributed Cognition in Classical Antiquity*, edited by M. Anderson, D. Cairns, and M. Sprevak. Edinburgh: 190–208.

Buis, E.J. 2018. *Taming Ares. War, Interstate Law, and Humanitarian Discourse in Classical Greece*. Leiden.

Buis, E.J. 2021. "The Politics of Anti-Politics: Historiographies of International Law and the Paradox of Antiquity." In *Politics and the Histories of International Law*, edited by R. Schäfer and A. Peters. Leiden: 430–54.

Buraselis, K. 1982. *Das hellenistische Makedonien und die Ägäis*. Munich.

Buraselis, K. 1993. "Ambivalent Roles of Centre and Periphery. Remarks on the Relation of the Cities of Greece with the Ptolemies until the End of Philometor's Age." In *Centre and Periphery in the Hellenistic World*, edited by P. Bilde et al. Aarhus: 251–70.

Buraselis, K. 2000. *Kos between Hellenism and Rome*. Philadelphia.

Buraselis, K. 2013. "Confederacies, Royal Policies and Sanctuaries in the Hellenistic Aegean: The Cases of Nesiotai, Lesbioi and Kretaieis." In *Greek Federal States and Their Sanctuaries*, edited by P. Funke and M. Haake. Stuttgart: 173–83.

Buraselis, K. 2015. "Federalism and the Sea. The *Koina* of the Aegean Islands." In *Federalism in Greek Antiquity*, edited by H. Beck and P. Funke. Cambridge: 358–76.

Burke, T.F. 2002. *Lawyers, Lawsuits, and Legal Rights. The Battle over Litigation in American Society*. Berkeley.

Burkert, W. 1985. *Greek Religion*. Cambridge, Mass.

Burt, C.H., Simons, R.L., and Gibbons, F.X. 2012. "Racial Discrimination, Ethnic-Racial Socialization, and Crime: A Micro-sociological Model of Risk and Resilience." *American Sociological Review* 77:648–77.

Busolt, G. 1904. *Griechische Geschichte bis zur Schlacht bei Chaeroneia. Band III, Teil II: Der peloponnesische Krieg*. Gotha.

Busolt, G., and Swoboda, H. 1920–1926. *Griechische Staatskunde*. 3rd ed. 2 vols. Munich.

Bustamante, T. 2024. "Taking Dworkin's Legal Monism Seriously." *European Journal of International Law* 35:479–510.

Butler, J. 2023. "Fury and Justice in the Humanities." *Classical Antiquity* 23:1–18.

Butler, P. 2004. "The Case for Trials: Considering the Intangibles." *Journal of Empirical Legal Studies* 3:627–36.

Caldwell, C.H., Kohn-Wood, L.P., Schmeelk-Cone, K.H., Chavous, T.M., and Zimmerman, M.A. 2004. "Racial Discrimination and Racial Identity as Risk or Protective Factors for Violent Behaviors in African American Young Adults." *American Journal of Community Psychology* 33:91–105.

Camp, J.M. 2010. *The Athenian Agora. Site Guide.* 5th ed. Princeton.
Campa, N.T. 2022. "In Defence of Female Citizenship: Apollodorus, *Against Neaera* 113." *Classical Quarterly* 72:487–92.
Campbell, J. 2019. "Testimonial Exclusions and Religious Freedom in Early America." *Law and History Review* 37:431–92.
Candy, P. 2025. *Ancient Maritime Loan Contracts.* Ann Arbor.
Canevaro, M. 2018. "Majority Rule vs. Consensus: The Practice of Democratic Deliberation in the Greek *Poleis*." In *Ancient Greek History and Contemporary Social Science*, edited by M. Canevaro, A. Erskine, B. Gray, and J. Ober. Edinburgh: 101–56.
Canevaro, M. 2020. "The Documents in the Attic Orators. Early Antiquarians and Unintentional Forgers." In *Falsifications and Authority in Antiquity, the Middle Ages and the Renaissance*, edited by E. Gielen and J. Papy. Turnhout: 21–54.
Canevaro, M., and Gray, B., eds. 2017. *The Hellenistic Reception of Classical Athenian Democracy and Political Thought.* Oxford.
Canevaro, M., and Lewis, D.M. 2024. "Between 'The Character of the Athenian Empire' and *The Origins of the Peloponnesian War* (and beyond). The Popularity of the Athenian Empire Revisited." *Polis* 41:176–202.
Cano, M.A., *et al.* 2015. "Depressive Symptoms and Externalizing Behaviors among Hispanic Immigrant Adolescents: Examining Longitudinal Effects of Cultural Stress." *Journal of Adolescence* 42:31–39.
Cantarella, E. 2021. *Norma e sanzione in Omero. Contributo alla protostoria del diritto greco.* 2nd ed. Milan.
Cao, X. 2010. "Networks as Channels of Policy Diffusion: Explaining Worldwide Changes in Capital Taxation, 1998–2006." *International Studies Quarterly* 54:823–54.
Capdetrey, L. 2007. *Le pouvoir séleucide. Territoire, administration, finances d'un royaume hellénistique, 312–129 avant J.-C.* Rennes.
Caprara, G.V., and Vecchione, M. 2013. "Personality Approaches to Political Behavior." In *The Oxford Handbook of Political Psychology*, 2nd ed., edited by L. Huddy, D.O. Sears, and J.S. Levy. Oxford: 23–58.
Capraro, V., Jordan, J.J., and Tappin, B.M. 2021. "Does Observability Amplify Sensitivity to Moral Frames? Evaluating a Reputation-based Account of Moral Preferences." *Journal of Experimental Social Psychology* 94:1–10.
Carbon, J.-M., and Ekroth, G., eds. 2024. *From Snout to Tail. Exploring the Greek Sacrificial Animal from the Literary, Epigraphical, Iconographical, Archaeological, and Zooarchaeological Evidence.* Stockholm.
Carbon, J.-M., and Harris, E.M. 2025. "Policing Sanctuaries." In *The Logistics of Sanctuaries*, edited by J.M. Barringer, G. Ekroth, and D. Scahill. Leiden: 35–51.
Carbon, J.-M., and Pirenne-Delforge, V. 2012. "Beyond Greek 'Sacred Laws'." *Kernos* 25:163–82.
Cardi, W.J, Penfield, R.D., and Yoon, A.H. 2012. "Does Tort Law Deter Individuals? A Behavioral Science Study." *Journal of Empirical Legal Studies* 9:567–603.
Carey, C. 1994. "Rhetorical Means of Persuasion." In *Persuasion. Greek Rhetoric in Action*, edited by I. Worthington. London: 26–45.
Carey, C., Giannadaki, I., and Griffith-Williams, B., eds. 2018. *Use and Abuse of Law in the Athenian Courts.* Leiden.
Carrière, J. 1975. *Théognis. Poèmes élégiaques.* Paris.
Carugati, F., and Weingast, B.R. 2018. "Rethinking Mass and Elite: Decision-Making in the Athenian Law-Courts." In *Ancient Greek History and Contemporary Social Science*, edited by M. Canevaro, A. Erskine, B. Gray, and J. Ober. Edinburgh: 157–83.
Carusi, C. 2005. "Nuova edizione della homologia fra Trezene e Arsinoe (*IG* IV 752, *IG* IV^2 76 + 77)." *Studi Ellenistici* 16:79–139.
Casey, C. 2024. "Economic History and International Law. A Peculiar Absence." In *The Cambridge History of International Law*, Vol. 1, edited by R. Lesaffer. Cambridge: 162–83.

Cassayre, A. 2010. *La justice dans les cités grecques. De la formation des royaumes hellénistiques au legs d'Attale.* Rennes.

Casson, L. 1971. *Ships and Seamanship in the Ancient World.* Princeton.

Cataldi, S. 1979. "Atene 'Polis Ekkletos.' Ἐφέσιμοι ed ἔκκλητοι δίκαι." *Annali della Scuola Normale Superiore di Pisa. Classe di Lettere e Filosofia* 9:1–37.

Cataldi, S. 1983. *Symbolai e relazioni tra le città greche nel V secolo a.C.* Pisa.

Cawkwell, G.L. 1993. "Sparta and Her Allies in the Sixth Century." *Classical Quarterly* 43:364–76.

Cazemier, A., and Skaltsa, S., eds. 2022. *Associations and Religion in Context. The Hellenistic and Roman Eastern Mediterranean. Kernos* Supplement 39. Liège.

Cecchet, L. 2017. "Re-shaping and Re-founding Citizen Bodies: The Case of Athens, Cyrene and Camarina." In *Citizens in the Graeco-Roman World*, edited by L. Cecchet and A. Busetto. Leiden: 50–77.

Chadwick, J. 1969. "ταγά and ἀταγία." In *Studi linguistici in onore di Vittore Pisani.* Brescia: 231–34.

Chamoux, F. 1953. *Cyrène sous la monarchie des Battiades.* Paris.

Champion, C. 1996. "Polybius, Aetolia and the Gallic Attack on Delphi (279 BC)." *Historia* 45:315–28.

Chaniotis, A. 1996. *Die Verträge zwischen kretischen Poleis in der hellenistischen Zeit.* Stuttgart.

Chaniotis, A. 1996b. "Conflicting Authorities. Asylia between Secular and Divine Law in the Classical and Hellenistic Poleis." *Kernos* 9:65–86.

Chaniotis, A. 1997. "Theatricality beyond the Theater. Staging Public Life in the Hellenistic World." *Pallas* 47:219–59.

Chaniotis, A. 1999. "Milking the Mountains: Economic Activities on the Cretan Uplands in the Classical and Hellenistic Period." In *From Minoan Farmers to Roman Traders*, edited by A. Chaniotis. Stuttgart: 181–220.

Chaniotis, A. 2004. "Justifying Territorial Claims in Classical and Hellenistic Greece: The Beginnings of International Law." In *The Law and the Courts in Ancient Greece*, edited by E.M. Harris and L. Rubinstein. London: 185–228.

Chaniotis, A. 2005. *War in the Hellenistic World. A Social and Cultural History.* Malden, Mass.

Chaniotis, A. 2018. *Age of Conquests. The Greek World from Alexander to Hadrian, 336 BC – AD 138.* Cambridge, Mass.

Chaniotis, A. 2019. "Display and Arousal of Emotions in Panhellenic Sanctuaries in the Shadow of Rome." In *Griechische Heiligtümer als Handlungsorte*, edited by K. Freitag and M. Haake. Stuttgart: 137–54.

Chaniotis, A., ed. 2012. *Unveiling Emotions. Sources and Methods for the Study of Emotions in the Greek World.* Stuttgart.

Chaniotis, A., and Ducrey, P., eds. 2013. *Unveiling Emotions II. Emotions in Greece and Rome: Texts, Images, Material Culture.* Stuttgart.

Chankowski, A.S. 2010. *L'éphébie hellénistique. Étude d'une institution civique dans les cités grecques des îles de la mer Égée et de l'Asie Mineure.* Paris.

Chankowski, V. 2008. *Athènes et Délos à l'époque classique. Recherches sur l'administration du sanctuaire d'Apollon délien.* Athens.

Cherkaoui, M. 2005. "Micro-Macro Transitions: Limits of Rational Choice Theory in James Coleman's 'Foundations of Social Theory'." *Revue française de sociologie* 46 (Supp.):79–101.

Chistov, D. 2021. "Some Observations on the Dynamics of Trade in Transport Amphorae on the Berezan Settlement." In *The Greeks and Romans in the Black Sea and the Importance of the Pontic Region for the Graeco-Roman World (7th Century BC – 5th Century AD)*, edited by G.R. Tsetskhladze, A. Avram, and J. Hargrave. Oxford: 202–09.

Chong, D. 2013. "Degrees of Rationality in Politics." In *Oxford Handbook of Political Psychology*, edited by L. Huddy, D.O. Sears, and J.S. Levy. Oxford: 96–129.

Christ, M.R. 1998. "Legal Self-Help on Private Property in Classical Athens." *American Journal of Philology* 119:521–45.

Christesen. P. 2007. *Olympic Victor Lists and Ancient Greek History*. Cambridge.

Cinalli, A. 2015. *Τὰ ξένια. La cerimonia di ospitalità cittadina*. Rome.

Cinalli, A. 2022. *ΠΤΑΝΟΙΣ ΠΟΣΙΝ. Poeti vaganti, musici e conferenzieri di età ellenistica. Parte I – Delo e le Cicladi*. Rome.

Čistov, D.E. 2012. "La Borysthène archaïque (site de l'île de Bérézan). Première colonie grecque du nord de la mer Noire, d'après le matériel des fouilles récentes du Musée d'État de l'Ermitage menées dans la partie orientale de l'île." In *Études pontiques*, edited by P. Burgunder. Lausanne: 223–60.

Clairmont, C. 1982. "Sparta's 'Golden Phiale' at Olympia." *Zeitschrift für Papyrologie und Epigraphik* 48:79–85.

Clarke, M.J. 2010. "Akha Feasting. An Ethnoarchaeological Perspective." In *Feasts. Archaeological and Ethnographic Perspectives on Food, Politics, and Power*, edited by M. Dietler and B. Hayden. Tuscaloosa, Alabama: 144–67.

Classen, J., and Steup, J. 1882–1967. *Thukydides. Erklärt von Johannes Classen. Bearbeitet von Julius Steup*. Berlin.

Clay, J.S. 2014. "*Iliad* 1.282–284 and Nestor's Rhetoric of Compromise." *Mnemosyne* 67:987–93.

Clayton, K., Ferwerda, J., and Horiuchi, Y. 2021. "Exposure to Immigration and Admission Preferences: Evidence from France." *Political Behavior* 43:175–200.

Clinton, K. 1980. "A Law in the City Eleusinion Concerning the Mysteries." *Hesperia* 49:258–88.

Clinton, K. 1994. "The Eleusinian Mysteries and Panhellenism in Democratic Athens." In *The Archaeology of Athens and Attica under the Democracy*, edited by W.D.E. Coulson, O. Palagia, T.L. Shear Jr., H.A. Shapiro, and F.J. Frost. Oxford: 161–72.

Clinton, K. 2005–2008. *Eleusis, the Inscriptions on Stone. Documents of the Sanctuary of the Two Goddesses and Public Documents of the Deme*. 2 vols. Athens.

Coates, D., and Penrod, S. 1980. "Social Psychology and the Emergence of Disputes." *Law & Society Review* 15:655–80.

Cochran, J.K., Maskaly, J., Jones, S., and Sellers, C.S. 2017. "Using Structural Equations to Model Akers' Social Learning Theory with Data on Intimate Partner Violence." *Crime & Delinquency* 63:39–61.

Cogan, G. 2014. "De la reconnaissance des concours des cités grecques au IVe s. av. J.-C., ou la question d'un droit grecque international." In *Sport und Recht in der Antike*, edited by K. Harter-Uibopuu and T. Kruse. Vienna: 89–106.

Cohen, D. 1995. *Law, Violence, and Community in Classical Athens*. Cambridge.

Cohen, E.E. 1973. *Ancient Athenian Maritime Courts*. Princeton.

Cohen, E.E. 2000. *The Athenian Nation*. Princeton.

Cohen, G.M. 1991. "*Katoikiai, Katoikoi* and Macedonians in Asia Minor." *Ancient Society* 22:41–50.

Cohen, H.G., and Meyer, T. 2021. *International Law as Behavior*. Cambridge.

Cohen, J.L. 2010. "Sovereignty in the Context of Globalization: A Constitutional Pluralist Perspective." In *The Philosophy of International Law*, edited by S. Besson and J. Tasioulas. Oxford: 261–80.

Cohen, R., and Westbrook, R. 2000. *Amarna Diplomacy. The Beginnings of International Relations*. Baltimore.

Cohn, E.S., Bucolo, D.O., Rebellon, C.J., and Van Gundy, K. 2010. "An Integrated Model of Legal and Moral Reasoning and Rule-Violating Behavior: The Role of Legal Attitudes." *Law and Human Behavior* 34:295–309.

Cohn, E.S., and White, S.O. 1990. *Legal Socialization. A Study of Norms and Rules*. New York.

Coldstream, J.N. 1989. "Early Greek Visitors to Cyprus and the Eastern Mediterranean." In *Cyprus and the East Mediterranean in the Iron Age*, edited by V. Tatton-Brown. London: 90–96.

Cole, S.G. 1995. "Civic Cult and Civic Identity." In *Sources for the Ancient Greek City-State*, edited by M.H. Hansen. Copenhagen: 292–325.

Cole, S.G. 2004. *Landscapes, Gender, and Ritual Space. The Ancient Greek Experience*. Berkeley.

Coleman, J.S. 1990. *Foundations of Social Theory*. Cambridge, Mass.
Collar, A. 2022. "Strong Ties, Social Networks, and the Diffusion of New Ideas." In *Networks and the Spread of Ideas in the Past*, edited by A. Collar. London: 1–27.
Collar, A., ed. 2022b. *Networks and the Spread of Ideas in the Past. Strong Ties, Innovation and Knowledge Exchange*. London.
Collard, C. 1975. *Euripides. Supplices, Edited with Introduction and Commentary*. 2 vols. Groningen.
Collard, C., and Cropp, M. 2008. *Euripides. Fragments, Aegeus–Meleager*. Edited and translated by C. Collard and M. Cropp. Cambridge, Mass.
Collins, S., and Tan, D. 2024. "Legislative Intent and Agency: A Rational Unity Account." *Oxford Journal of Legal Studies* 44:231–56.
Colorio, A. 2014. "Note in tema de esecuzione forzata pignoratizia nella Grecia antica." *Rivista di diritto ellenico* 4:71–97.
Connolly, J. 2001. "Problems of the Past in Imperial Greek Education." In *Education in Greek and Roman Antiquity*, edited by Y.L. Too. Leiden: 339–72.
Connor, W.R. 1962. "Charinus' Megarean Decree." *American Journal of Philology* 83:225–46.
Connor, W.R. 1970. "Charinus' Megarean Decree Again." *Revue des études grecques* 83:305–08.
Connor, W.R. 2021. "Unmasking the Maxim: An Ancient Genre and Why It Matters." *Arion* 28:5–42.
Constantakopoulou, C. 2007. *The Dance of the Islands. Insularity, Networks, the Athenian Empire, and the Aegean World*. Oxford.
Constantakopoulou, C. 2015. "Regional Religious Groups, Amphictionies, and Other Leagues." In *The Oxford Handbook of Ancient Greek Religion*, edited by E. Eidinow and J. Kindt. Oxford: 273–89.
Constantakopoulou, C. 2017. *Aegean Interactions. Delos and Its Networks in the Third Century*. Oxford.
Cooter, R., and Ulen, T. 2016. *Law and Economics*. 6th ed. Boston.
Cooter, R.D., and Schäfer, H.-B. 2012. *Solomon's Knot. How Law Can End the Poverty of Nations*. Princeton.
Cornish, D.B., and Clark, R.V., eds. 1986. *The Reasoning Criminal. Rational Choice Perspectives on Offending*. New York.
Cornish, D.B., and Clark, R.V. 1987. "Understanding Crime Displacement: An Application of Rational Choice Theory." *Criminology* 25:944–45.
Corsaro, W.A., and Fingerson, L. 2003. "Development and Socialization in Childhood." In *Handbook of Social Psychology*, edited by J. Delamater. New York: 125–55.
Corsten, T. 1999. *Von Stamm zum Bund. Gründung und territoriale Organisation griechischer Bundesstaaten*. Munich.
Corten, O., Klein, P., and Bedoret, G. 2022. *De Salamanque à Guantanamo. Une histoire du droit international*. Paris.
Courby, F. 1921. "Le sanctuaire d'Apollon délien." *Bulletin de correspondance hellénique* 45:174–241.
Couvenhes, J-C., ed. 2016. *La symmachia comme pratique du droit international dans le monde grec: d'Homère à l'époque hellénistique*. Besançon.
Cover, R.M. 1986. "Violence and the Word." *Yale Law Journal* 95:1601–29.
Cowan, E. 2024. "The Individual and International Law in Antiquity." In *The Individual in International Law*, edited by T. Sparks and A. Peters. Oxford: 31–46.
Cox, R. 2023. *Origins of the Just War. Military Ethics and Culture in the Ancient Near East*. Princeton.
Craven, M. 2010. "Statehood, Self-Determination, and Recognition." In *International Law*, edited by M.D. Evans. 4th ed. Oxford: 201–47.
Crielaard, J.P. 2002. "Past or Present? Epic Poetry, Aristocratic Self-Representation and the Concept of Time in the Eighth and Seventh Centuries B.C." In *Omero tremila anni dopo*, edited by F. Montanari. Rome: 239–97.

Crielaard, J.P. 2009. "The Ionians in the Archaic Period. Shifting identities in a Changing World." In *Ethnic Constructs in Antiquity*, edited by T. Derks and N. Roymans. Amsterdam: 37–84.

Criscuolo, L. 2013. "Ptolemies and Piracy." In *The Ptolemies, the Sea and the Nile*, edited by K. Buraselis, M. Stefanou, and D.J. Thompson. Cambridge: 160–71.

Crisp, R.J., and Hewstone, M. 2007. "Multiple Social Categorization." *Advances in Experimental Social Psychology* 39:163–254.

Crone, P. 1989. *Pre-Industrial Societies. Anatomy of the Pre-Modern World*. New York.

Crowther, C.V. 1993. "Foreign Judges in Seleucid Cities (GIBM 421)." *Journal of Ancient Civilizations* 8:40–77.

Crowther, C.V. 1995. 'Iasos in the Second Century BC III: Foreign Judges from Priene." *Bulletin of the Institute of Classical Studies* 40:91–138.

Crowther, C.V. 1999. "Aus der Arbeit der *Inscriptiones Graecae* IV: Koan Decrees for Foreign Judges." *Chiron* 29:251–319.

Crowther, C.V. 2006. "Foreign Judges in Thessaly in the Hellenistic Period: A Second Century Phenomenon?" In *Inscriptions and History of Thessaly. New Evidence*, edited by G.A. Pikoulas. Athens: 31–48.

Crowther, C.V. 2008. "Foreign Judges and Regional Variations in Hellenistic Asia Minor." In *Regionalism in Hellenistic and Roman Asia Minor*, edited by H. Eltron and G. Reger. Pessac: 53–59.

Crowther, N.B. 1996. "Athlete and State: Qualifying for the Olympic Games in Ancient Greece." *Journal of Sport History* 23:34–43.

Crowther, N.B., and Frass, M. 1998. "Flogging as a Punishment in the Ancient Games." *Nikephoros* 11:51–82.

Csapo, E., Paillard, E., and Wilson, P. 2022. "Theatre and Autocracy: A Paradox for Theatre History." In *Theatre and Autocracy in the Ancient World*, edited by E. Csapo et al. Berlin: 1–14.

Csapo, E., and Wilson, P. 2020. *A Social and Economic History of the Theatre to 300 BC. Volume II. Theatre beyond Athens: Documents with Translation and Commentary*. Cambridge.

Cudworth, E., and McGovern, J. 2007. "Introduction." In *The Modern State*, edited by E. Cudworth, T. Hall, and J. McGovern. Edinburgh: 1–19.

Culasso Gastaldi, E. 2004. *Le prossenie ateniesi del IV secolo a.C. Gli onorati asiatici*. Alexandria.

Czajkowski, K., and Eckhardt, B., eds. 2020. *Law in the Roman Provinces*. Oxford.

Damrosch, L.F., Henkin, L., Pugh, R.C., Schachter, O., and Smit, H. 2001. *International Law. Cases and Materials*. 4th ed. St. Paul, Minn.

Dana, M. 2004. "Lettre sur plomb d'Apatorios à Léanax. Un document archaïque d'Olbia du Pont." *Zeitschrift für Papyrologie und Epigraphik* 148:1–14.

Dana, M. 2021. *La correspondance grecque privée sur plomb et sur tesson. Corpus épigraphique et commentaire historique*. Munich.

Dana, M., and Savalli-Lestrade, I., eds. 2019. *La cité interconnectée dans le monde gréco-romain (IVe siècle a.C.–IVe siècle p.C.)*. Bordeaux.

Dareste, R. 1889. "Du droit de représailles principalement chez les anciens Grecs." *Revue des études grecques* 2:305–321.

Dari-Mattiacci, G., and Kehoe, D.P., eds. 2020. *Roman Law and Economics*. 2 vols. Oxford.

d'Aspremont, J. 2015. "The Doctrine of Fundamental Rights of States and Anthropomorphic Thinking in International Law." *Cambridge Journal of International and Comparative Law* 4:501–20.

Daux, G. 1963. "Note sur une inscription de Cyrène." *Bulletin de correspondance hellénique* 87:388–90.

Daverio Rocchi, G. 1999. "Trent' anni di studi sulle relazioni interstatali della Grecia di V e IV secolo A.C." In *Storiografia ed Erudizione*, edited by D. Foraboschi. Milan: 19–66.

Daverio Rocchi, G. 2006. "Alle origini delle relazioni internazionali: frontiere e rapporti di amicizia in Magna Grecia dall'età arcaica all'età classica." In *Italo - Tusco - Romana*, edited by P. Amann, M. Pedrazzi, and H. Taeuber. Vienna: 135–42.

Daverio Rocchi, G. 2015. "The Lokrians and Their Federal Leagues." In *Federalism in Greek Antiquity*, edited by H. Beck and P. Funke. Cambridge: 179–98.

Davies, J.K. 1984. "Cultural, Social and Economic Features of the Hellenistic World." In *The Cambridge Ancient History. Second Edition. Vol. VII, Part 1. The Hellenistic World*, edited by F.W. Walbank, A.E. Astin, M.W. Frederiksen, and R.M. Ogilvie. Cambridge: 257–320.

Davies, J.K. 2000. "A Wholly Non-Aristotelian Universe: The Molossians as Ethnos, State, and Monarchy." In *Alternatives to Athens*, edited by R. Brock and S. Hodkinson. Oxford: 234–58.

Davis, J.W., and McDermott, R. 2021. "The Past, Present, and Future of Behavioral IR." *International Organization* 75:147–77.

DeBacker, J., Heim, B.T., and Tran, A. 2015. "Importing Corruption Culture from Overseas: Evidence from Corporate Tax Evasion in the United States." *Journal of Financial Economics* 117:122–138.

Decourt, J.-C. 2014. "Lettres privées grecques sur plomb et céramique." In *La lettre gréco-latine, un genre littéraire?*, edited by J. Schneider. Lyon: 25–79.

Decourt, J.-C., Nielsen, T.H., and Helly, B. 2004. "Thessalia and Adjacent Regions." In *An Inventory of Archaic and Classical Poleis*, edited by M.H. Hansen and T.H. Nielsen. New York: 676–731.

DeLaine, J. 2023. *Roman Architecture*. Oxford.

de Ligt, L., and de Neeve, P.W. 1988. "Ancient Periodic Markets: Festivals and Fairs." *Athenaeum* 66:391–416.

de Lisle, C. 2020. *Attic Inscriptions in UK Collections. Ashmolean Museum Oxford. AIUK* 11.

DellaVigna, S. 2009. "Psychology and Economics: Evidence from the Field." *Journal of Economic Literature* 47:315–72.

de Melo, W., ed. 2012. *Plautus:* The Little Carthaginian. Pseudolus. The Rope. Edited and translated by Wolfgang de Melo. Cambridge, Mass.

Demetriou, D. 2012. *Negotiating Identity in the Ancient Mediterranean. The Archaic and Classical Greek Multiethnic Emporia*. Cambridge.

de Souza, P. 1999. *Piracy in the Graeco-Roman World*. Cambridge.

de Spens, R. 1998. "Droit international et commerce au début de la XXIe dynastie. Analyse juridique du rapport d'Ounamon." In *Le commerce en Égypte ancienne*, edited by N. Grimal and B. Menu. Cairo: 105–26.

Devine, P.G., and Monteith, M.J. 1999. "Automaticity and Control in Stereotyping." In *Dual-Process Theories in Social Psychology*, edited by S. Chaiken and Y. Trope. New York: 339–60.

Diggelmann, O. 2018. "*The Internationalists* as Grand Narrative: Key Elements and Dilemmata." *Global Constitutionalism* 7:297–314.

Dillery, J. 2005. "Chresmologues and *Manteis*: Independent Diviners and the Problem of Authority." In *Mantikê*, edited by S.I. Johnston and P. Struck. Leiden: 167–231.

Dilts, M.R. 2002. *Demosthenis Orationes. Tomus I*. Oxford.

Dimitrova, N.M. 2008. *Theoroi and Initiates in Samothrace. The Epigraphical Evidence*. Princeton.

Dindorf, W. 1853. *Harpocrationis Lexicon in Decem Oratores Atticos*. 2 vols. Oxford.

Dmitriev, S. 2011. *The Greek Slogan of Freedom and Early Roman Politics in Greece*. Oxford.

Dmitriev, S. 2018. *The Birth of the Athenian Community. From Solon to Cleisthenes*. London.

Donnellan, L. 2021. "Understanding Greek-Native Interaction in Early Greek Black Sea Colonization. An Example from Istros/Histria." In *The Greeks and Romans in the Black Sea and the Importance of the Pontic Region for the Graeco-Roman World (7th Century BC–5th Century AD)*, edited by G.R. Tsetskhladze, A. Avram, and J. Hargrave. Oxford: 55–68.

Dontas, G.S. 1983. "The True Aglaurion." *Hesperia* 52:48–63.

Dore, R. 1983. "Goodwill and the Spirit of Market Capitalism." *British Journal of Sociology* 34:459–82.

Doulgeri-Indzesiloglou, A. 2000. *Θεσσαλικές επιγραφές σε τοπικό αλφάβητο*. Diss. Thessaloniki.

Dover, K.J. 1974. *Greek Popular Morality in the Time of Plato and Aristotle*. Berkeley.

Dow, S. 1942. "Corinthiaca." *Harvard Studies in Classical Philology* 53:89–119.

Drauschke, M.-K. 2019. *Die Aufstellung zwischenstaatlicher Vereinbarungen in griechischen Heiligtümern*. Hamburg.

Drauschke, M.-K. 2019b. "Die gemeinsame Aufstellung zwischenstaatlicher Vertragsurkunden (*koinē stēle*)." In *Griechische Heiligtümer als Handlungsorte*, edited by K. Freitag and M. Haake. Stuttgart: 121–36.

Dreher, M. 1995. *Hegemon und Symmachoi. Untersuchungen zum zweiten athenischen Seebund*. Berlin.

Dreher, M. 2003. "Hikesie und Asylie in den *Hiketiden* des Aischylos." In *Das antike Asyl*, edited by M. Dreher. Cologne: 59–84.

Dreher, M. 2024. "Der moderne Staatsbegriff und die Transformation der griechischen Polis zum Staat." *Dike* 27:9–64.

Dubois, L. 1996. *Inscriptions grecques dialectales d'Olbia du Pont*. Geneva.

Ducat, J. 1994. *Les Pénestes de Thessalie*. Besançon.

Ducat, J. 2008. "Le statut des périèques lacédémoniens." *Ktema* 33:1–86.

Ducat, J. 2017. "The Perioikoi." In *A Companion to Sparta*, edited by A. Powell. Hoboken, NJ: 596–614.

Dueck, D. 2000. *Strabo of Amasia. A Greek Man of Letters in Augustan Rome*. London.

Duff, R.A. 2001. *Punishment, Communication, and Community*. Oxford.

Dunbar, F.C., and Sabry, F. 2007. "The Propensity to Sue: Why Do People Seek Legal Actions?" *Business Economics* 42:31–42.

Dunne, T. 1998. *Inventing International Society. A History of the English School*. New York.

du Plessis, P.J., Ando, C., and Tuori, K., eds. 2016. *The Oxford Handbook of Roman Law and Society*. Oxford.

Duplouy, A. 2006. *Le prestige des élites. Recherches sur les modes de reconaissance sociale en Grèce entre les Xe et Ve siècles avant J.-C.* Paris.

Duplouy, A. 2018. "Citizenship as Performance." In *Defining Citizenship in Archaic Greece*, edited by A. Duplouy and R. Brock. Oxford: 249–74.

Dušanić, S. 1980–1981. "Athens, Crete and the Aegean after 366/5 BC." *Talanta* 12/13:7–29.

Dworkin, R. 1986. *Law's Empire*. Cambridge, Mass.

Dworkin, R. 2011. *Justice for Hedgehogs*. Cambridge, Mass.

Dworkin, R. 2013. "A New Philosophy for International Law." *Philosophy & Public Affairs* 41:2–30.

Eberle, L.P. 2016. "Law, Empire, and the Making of Roman Estates in the Provinces During the Late Republic." *Critical Analysis of Law* 3:50–69.

Ebert, J., and Siewert, P. 1999. "Eine archaische Bronzeurkunde aus Olympia mit Vorschriften für Ringkämpfer und Kampfrichter." *Bericht über die Ausgrabungen in Olympia* 11:391–412.

Eckerman, C.C. 2012. "Was Epinician Poetry Performed at Panhellenic Sanctuaries?" *Greek, Roman, and Byzantine Studies* 52:338–60.

Eckstein, A.M. 2006. *Mediterranean Anarchy, Interstate War, and the Rise of Rome*. Berkeley.

Eckstein, A.M. 2008. *Rome Enters the Greek East. From Anarchy to Hierarchy in the Hellenistic Mediterranean, 230–170 BC*. Oxford.

Eckstein, A.M. 2017. "Thucydides, International Law, and International Anarchy." In *The Oxford Handbook of Thucydides*, edited by S. Forsdyke, E. Foster, and R. Balot. Oxford: 491–514.

Ederer, F., and Schneider, F. 2020. "Trust and Promises over Time." *American Economic Journal: Microeconomics* 14:304–20.

Ederer, F., and Stremitzer, A. 2017. "Promises and Expectations." *Games and Economic Behavior* 106:161–78.

Effron, D.A., and Knowles, E.D. 2015. "Entitativity and Intergroup Bias: How Belonging to a Cohesive Group Allows People to Express Their Prejudices." *Journal of Personality and Social Psychology* 108:234–53.

Egetenmeier, P. 2016–2017. "Prozessrechtliche Überlegungen zum geplanten Synoikismos zwischen Teos und Lebedos (RC 3)." *Dike* 19/20:167–98.

Ehrenberg, V. 1969. *The Greek State*. 2nd ed. London.

Ehrhardt, N. 2017. "Der Schiedsspruch des Satrapen Struses: Prozedur und Politik." In *Von Magna Graecia nach Asia Minor*, edited by H. Beck, B. Eckhardt, C. Michels, and S. Richter. Wiesbaden: 255–65.

Ehrlich, E. 1936 [1913]. *Fundamental Principles of the Sociology of Law*. Cambridge, Mass.

Eich, A. 2004. "Probleme der staatlichen Einheit in der griechischen Antike." *Zeitschrift für Papyrologie und Epigraphik* 149:83–102.

Eich, A. 2006. *Die politische Ökonomie des Antiken Griechenland (6.–3. Jahrhundert v. Chr.)*. Cologne.

Eidem, J., Giltaij, J., and Tuori, K., eds. 2026. *The Cambridge History of International Law. Vol. IV. International Law in the Middle East and the Mediterranean during Antiquity*. Cambridge.

Eidinow, E. 2011. "Networks and Narratives: A Model for Ancient Greek Religion." *Kernos* 24:9–38.

Ekins, R. 2012. *The Nature of Legislative Intent*. Oxford.

Ekroth, G. 2008. "Burnt, Cooked, or Raw? Divine and Human Culinary Desires at Greek Animal Sacrifice." In *Transformations in Sacrificial Practices*, edited by E. Stavrianopoulou, A. Michaels, and C. Ambos. Berlin: 87–111.

Elkins, Z. 2010. "Diffusion and the Constitutionalization of Europe." *Comparative Political Studies* 43:969–99.

Ellickson, R.C. 1994. *Order without Law. How Neighbors Settle Disputes*. Cambridge, Mass.

Elsner, J. 2015. "Visual Culture and Ancient History: Issues of Empiricism and Ideology in the Samos Stele at Athens." *Classical Antiquity* 34:33–73.

Endicott, T. 2010. "The Logic of Freedom and Power." In *The Philosophy of International Law*, edited by S. Besson and J. Tasioulas. Oxford: 245–59.

Engel, D.M. 2016. *The Myth of the Litigious Society. Why We Don't Sue*. Chicago.

Engelking, W. 2025. "How Kantian Is Kelsen's Early Theory of International Law?" *Law and History Review* 43:1–34.

Engen, D.T. 2010. *Honor and Profit. Athenian Trade Policy and the Economy and Society of Greece, 415–307 B.C.E.* Ann Arbor.

Ensoli, S. 2012. "L'attività della Missione Archeologica Italiana a Cirene (MAIC) della seconda Università degli Studi di Napoli (SUN). Le ricerche svolte nel 2009 e 2010 in collaborazione con il Dipartimento alle Antichità (DoA) di Cirene: Strategie e prospettive future." In *For the Preservation of the Cultural Heritage in Libya*, edited by S. Ensoli. Pisa: 111–38.

Erdas, D. 2021. "I *nautodikai*. Note su una magistratura ateniese tra cause di *xenia* e giurisdizione sugli *emporoi*." *Dike* 24:33–62.

Erickson, B. 2005. "Archaeology of Empire: Athens and Crete in the Fifth Century B.C." *American Journal of Archaeology* 109:619–63.

Ermakoff, I. 2017. "On the Frontiers of Rational Choice." In *Social Theory Now*, edited by C.E. Benzecry, M. Krause, and I.A. Reed. Chicago: 162–200.

Errington, M. 1989. "The Peace Treaty between Miletus and Magnesia (I. Milet 148)." *Chiron* 19:279–88.

Estrin, S. 2023. *Grief Made Marble. Funerary Sculpture in Classical Athens*. New Haven.

Etienne, J. 2011. "Compliance Theory: A Goal Framing Approach." *Law & Policy* 33:305–33.

Étienne, R. 1990. *Ténos II. Ténos et les Cyclades du milieu du IVe siècle av. J.-C. au milieu du IIIe siècle ap. J.-C.* Paris.

Evans, J.A.S. 1976. "The Settlement of Artaphrenes." *Classical Philology* 71:344–48.

Evans, J.St.B.T. 2018. "Dual-Process Theories." In *The Routledge International Handbook of Thinking and Reasoning*, edited by L.J. Ball and V.A. Thompson. London: 151–66.

Evans, J.St.B.T., and Twyman-Musgrove, J. 1998. "Conditional Reasoning with Inducements and Advice." *Cognition* 69:B11–16.

Evans, R.J.G. 2019. "A Most Dangerous Place. Finding the Non-Combatant within the Greek Polis." Diss. Leicester.

Fagan, J., and Piquero, A.R. 2007. "Rational Choice and Developmental Influences on Recidivism among Adolescent Felony Offenders." *Journal of Empirical Legal Studies* 4:715–48.

Fagan, J., and Tyler, T.R. 2005. "Legal Socialization of Children and Adolescents." *Social Justice Research* 18:217–42.

Faraguna, M. 2012. "*Pistis* and *Apistia*: Aspects of the Development of Social and Economic Relations in Classical Greece." *Mediterraneo Antico* 15:355–74.

Faraguna, M. 2023. "Atene, gli alleati e l'impero: *symbolai* e *symbola* tra V e IV secolo." *Dike* 26: 127–62.

Faraguna, M. 2024. "Land and Citizenship in the Greek Polis: Real Property, Public Control, and Institutionalisation." *Dike* 27:121–74.

Faraone, C.A. 1991. "The Agonistic Context of Early Greek Binding Spells." In *Magika Hiera. Ancient Greek Magic and Religion*, edited by C.A. Faraone and D. Obbink. Oxford: 3–32.

Feeney, D.C. 2016. *Beyond Greek. The Beginnings of Latin Literature.* Cambridge, Mass.

Fenn, N, and Römer-Strehl, C., eds. 2013. *Networks in the Hellenistic World. According to the Pottery in the Eastern Mediterranean and Beyond.* BAR International Series 2539. Oxford.

Ferguson, W.S. 1944. "The Attic Orgeones." *Harvard Theological Review* 37:61–140.

Fermor, P.L. 2004 [1966]. *Roumeli. Travels in Northern Greece.* London.

Ferone, C. 1997. *Lesteia. Forme di predazione nell'Egeo in età classica.* Naples.

Ferrario, S.B. 2014. *Historical Agency and the "Great Man" in Classical Greece.* Cambridge.

Feyel, C. 2006. *Les artisans dans les sanctuaires grecs aux époques classiques et hellénistiques à travers la documentation financière en Grèce.* Athens.

Feyel, M. 1946. "Σμῆναι. Étude sur le v. 552 de l'*Hyme homérique à Hermès.*" *Revue archéologique* 25:5–22.

Figueira, T. 1998. *The Power of Money. Coinage and Politics in the Athenian Empire.* Philadelphia.

Figueira, T. 2006. "Reconsidering the Athenian Coinage Decree." *Annali dell'Istituto Italiano di Numismatica* 52:9–44.

Filonik, J., Plastow, C., and Zelnick-Abramovitz, R. 2023. *Citizenship in Antiquity. Civic Communities in the Ancient Mediterranean.* Abingdon.

Fine, J.V.A. 1940. "The Background of the Social War of 220–217 B.C." *American Journal of Philology* 61:129–65.

Finer, S.E. 1997. *The History of Government from the Earliest Times.* Oxford.

Finglass, P.J. 2018. *Sophocles. Oedipus the King.* Cambridge.

Finglass, P.J. 2023. "Tragic Tokens: Sophoclean *Symbola* in Context." In *Tokens in Classical Athens and Beyond*, edited by M.E. Gkikaki. Liverpool: 23–41.

Finley, M.I. 1975. *The Use and Abuse of History.* London.

Finley, M.I. 1985. *The Ancient Economy.* 2nd ed. London.

Finnis, J. 2011. *Natural Law and Natural Rights.* 2nd ed. Oxford.

Fiske, S.T., and Taylor, S.E. 2017. *Social Cognition. From Brains to Culture.* 3rd ed. Los Angeles.

Fitzpatrick, D. 2006. "Evolution and Chaos in Property Rights Systems: The Third World Tragedy of Contested Access." *Yale Law Journal* 115:996–1048.

Flade, F., Klar, Y., and Imhoff, R. 2019. "Unite against: A Common Threat Invokes Spontaneous Decategorization between Social Categories." *Journal of Experimental Social Psychology* 85:1–14.

Flashar, H. 2008. "Die Rezeption Homers durch die Philosophen." In *Homer. Der Mythos von Troia in Dichtung und Kunst*, edited by J. Latacz, T. Greub, P. Blome, and A. Wieczorek. Munich: 215–20.

Flower, M.A. 2000. "From Simonides to Isocrates: The Fifth-Century Origins of Fourth-Century Panhellenism." *Classical Antiquity* 19:65–101.

Flower, M.A. 2008. *The Seer in Ancient Greece.* Berkeley.

Foddy, M., and Yamagishi, T. 2009. "Group-Based Trust." In *Whom Can We Trust?*, edited by K.S. Cook, M. Levi, and R. Hardin. New York: 17–41.

Fofana, I.P-A., and Hébié, M. (forthcoming). "System of States in the Age of High Imperialism." *The Cambridge History of International Law*, Vol. 9 (general editor R. Lesaffer). Cambridge.

Folch, M. 2015. *The City and the Stage. Performance, Genre, and Gender in Plato's Laws.* Oxford.

Folger, R., and Konovsky, M.A. 1989. "Effects of Procedural and Distributive Justice on Reactions to Pay Raise Decisions." *Academy of Management Journal* 32:115–30.

Fornara, C.W. 1979. "The Phaselis Decree." *Classical Quarterly* 29:49–52.

Fornara, C.W. 2010. "The Aftermath of the Mytilenian Revolt." *Historia* 59:129–42.

Forrest, W.G. 2000. "The Pre-Polis Polis." In *Alternatives to Athens. Varieties of Political Organization and Community in Ancient Greece*, edited by R. Brock and S. Hodkinson. Oxford: 280–92.

Forsdyke, S. 2005. *Exile, Ostracism, and Democracy. The Politics of Expulsion in Ancient Greece.* Princeton.

Forsdyke, S. 2021. *Slaves and Slavery in Ancient Greece.* Cambridge.

Fotheringham, J.K., ed. 1923. *Eusebii Pamphili Chronici Canones.* London.

Fouchard, A. 2010. "Comment reconnaître les élites en Grèce ancienne?" In *La cité et ses élites*, edited by L. Capdetrey and Y. Lafond. Bordeaux: 359–78.

Fourrier, S. 2021. "Phoenician Identities in Cyprus in the Classical and Early Hellenistic Periods." In *Transformations and Crisis in the Mediterranean III*, edited by G. Garbati and T. Pedrazzi. Rome: 123–35.

Fowler, M.R., and Bunck, J.M. 2002. "The Nation Neglected: The Organization of International Life in the Classical State Sovereignty Period." In *International Law and the Rise of Nations*, edited by R.J. Beck and T. Ambrosio. New York: 38–60.

Franck, T. 2009. "Remarks." *American Society of International Law Proceedings* 103:161–63.

Frank, D.J., Hironaka, A., and Schofer, E. 2000. "The Nation-State and the Natural Environment over the Twentieth Century." *American Sociological Review* 65:96–116.

Frank, R.H. 1992. "Melding Sociology and Economics: James Coleman's *Foundations of Social Theory*." *Journal of Economic Literature* 30:147–70.

Franke, P.R. 1970. "ΦΕΘΑΛΟΙ - ΦΕΤΑΛΟΙ - ΠΕΤΘΑΛΟΙ - ΘΕΣΣΑΛΟΙ. Zur Geschichte Thessaliens im 5. Jh. v. Chr." *Archäologischer Anzeiger* (1970):85–93.

Freitag, K., and Haake, M., eds. 2019. *Griechische Heiligtümer als Handlungsorte.* Stuttgart.

Friedman, D. 1994. "A Positive Account of Property Rights." *Social Philosophy & Policy* 11:1–16.

Friedman, L.M. 2016. *Impact. How Law Affects Behavior.* Cambridge, Mass.

Friedman, M. 1953. *Essays in Positive Economics.* Chicago.

Frier, B.W. 1985. *The Rise of the Roman Jurists. Studies in Cicero's* pro Caecina. Princeton.

Frier, B.W., and Kehoe, D.P. 2007. "Law and Economic Institutions." In *The Cambridge Economic History of the Greco-Roman World*, edited by W. Scheidel, I. Morris, and R.P. Saller. Cambridge: 113–43.

Frith, C.D., and Singer, T. 2008. "The Role of Social Cognition in Decision Making." *Philosophical Transactions of the Royal Society. Biological Sciences*, 363 (1511):3875–86.

Fröhlich, P. 2010. "L'inventaire du monde des cités grecques. Une somme, une méthode et une conception de l'histoire." *Revue Historique* 312:637–77.

Fröhlich, P. 2016. "La citoyenneté grecque entre Aristote et les modernes." *Cahiers du Centre Gustave Glotz* 27:91–136.

Fröhlich, P. 2023. "1972–2022: conception, réception et portée des *Symbola* de Philippe Gauthier." *Dike* 26:9–43.

Fröhlich, P., and Hamon, P., eds. 2013. *Groupes et associations dans les cités grecques (IIIe siècle av. J.-C. – IIe siècle apr. J.-C.).* Geneva.

Frønes, I. 2016. *The Autonomous Child. Theorizing Socialization.* Cham.

Funk, C.L., Smith, K.B., Alford, J., Hibbing, M., Hatemi, P., Krueger, R.F., Eaves, L.J., and Hibbing, J. 2013. "Genetic and Environmental Transmission of Value Orientations." *Political Psychology* 34:805–19.

Funk, P. 2007. "Is There an Expressive Function of Law? An Empirical Analysis of Voting Laws with Symbolic Fines." *American Law and Economics Review* 9:135–59.

Funke, P. 1980. *Homónoia und Arché: Athen und die griechische Staatenwelt vom Ende des peloponnesischen Krieges bis zum Königsfrieden (404/3–387/6 v. Chr.)*. Wiesbaden.

Funke, P. 2009. "Between Mantinea and Leuctra. The Political World of the Peloponnese in a Time of Upheaval." In *The Politics of Ethnicity and the Crisis of the Peloponnesian League*, edited by P. Funke and N. Luraghi. Washington: 1–14.

Funke, P. 2015. "Aitolia and the Aitolian League." In *Federalism in Greek Antiquity*, edited by H. Beck and P. Funke. Cambridge: 86–117.

Gabrielsen, V. 1997. *The Naval Aristocracy of Hellenistic Rhodes*. Aarhus.

Gabrielsen, V. 2001. "Economic Activity, Maritime Trade and Piracy in the Hellenistic Aegean." *Revue des études anciennes* 103:219–40.

Gabrielsen, V. 2003. "Piracy and the Slave-Trade." In *A Companion to the Hellenistic World*, edited by A. Erskine. Oxford: 389–404.

Gabrielsen, V. 2007. "Trade and Tribute: Byzantion and the Black Sea Straits." In *The Black Sea in Antiquity*, edited by V. Gabrielsen and J. Lund. Aarhus: 287–324.

Gabrielsen, V. 2008. "The Public Banks of Hellenistic Cities." In *Pistoi dia tèn technèn. Bankers, Loans, and Archives in the Ancient World*, edited by K. Verboven, K. Vandorpe, and V. Chankowski. Leuven: 115–30.

Gabrielsen, V. 2013. "Rhodes and the Ptolemaic Kingdom: The Commercial Infrastructure." In *The Ptolemies, the Sea, and the Nile*, edited by K. Buraselis, M. Stefanou, and D.J. Thompson. Cambridge: 66–81.

Gabrielsen, V. 2013b. "Warfare, Statehood and Piracy in the Greek World." In *Seeraub im Mittelmeerraum*, edited by N. Jaspert and S. Kolditz. Paderborn: 133–53.

Gabrielsen, V. 2015. "Naval and Grain Networks and Associations in Fourth-century Athens." In *Communities and Networks in the Ancient Greek World*, edited by C. Taylor and K. Vlassopoulos. Oxford: 177–212.

Gabrielsen, V., and Paganini, M.C.D., eds. 2021. *Private Associations in the Ancient Greek World. Regulations and the Creation of Group Identity*. Cambridge.

Gabrielsen, V., and Paganini, M.C.D. 2021b. "Associations' Regulations from the Ancient Greek World and Beyond. An Introduction." In *Private Associations in the Ancient Greek World*, edited by V. Gabrielsen and M.C.D. Paganini. Cambridge: 1–23.

Gaertner, S.L., and Dovidio, J.F. 2012. "The Common Ingroup Identity Model." In *Handbook of Theories of Social Psychology*, Vol. 2, edited by P.A.M. Van Lange, A.W. Kruglanski, and E.T. Higgins. London: 439–57.

Gaertner, S.L., Dovidio, J.F., Nier, J.A., Ward, C.M., and Banker, B.S. 1999. "Across Cultural Divides: The Value of a Superordinate Identity." In *Cultural Divides*, edited by D.A. Prentice and D.T. Miller. New York: 173–212.

Gagarin, M. 1986. *Early Greek Law*. Berkeley.

Gagarin, M. 1989. *The Murder of Herodes. A Study of Antiphon 5*. Frankfurt.

Gagarin, M. 2005. "The Unity of Greek Law." In *The Cambridge Companion to Ancient Greek Law*, edited by M. Gagarin and D. Cohen. Cambridge: 29–40.

Gagarin, M. 2008. *Writing Greek Law*. Cambridge.

Gagarin, M., and Perlman, P. 2016. *The Laws of Ancient Crete, c.650–400 BCE*. Oxford.

Gagliardi, L. 2009/10. "I *paroikoi* delle città dell'Asia Minore in età ellenistica e nella prima età romana." *Dike* 12/13:303–22.

Galbiati, R., Henry, E., Jacquemet, N., and Lobeck, M. 2021. "How Laws Affect the Perception of Norms: Empirical Evidence from the Lockdown." *PLoS ONE* 16(9): e0256624.

Gantz, T. 1993. *Early Greek Myth. A Guide to Literary and Artistic Sources*. Vol. 1. Baltimore.

Gao, J., and Zhao, J. 2018. "Legitimacy versus Morality: Why Do the Chinese Obey the Law?" *Law and Human Behavior* 42:167–80.

García Domingo, E. 2017. "La δίκη ἐξούλης y la δίκη βιαίων." *Cuadernos de Filología Clásica (g): Estudios griegos e indoeuropeos* 27:117–32.

García-Villegas, M. 2018. *The Powers of Law. A Comparative Analysis of Sociopolitical Legal Studies.* Cambridge.

Garlan, Y. 1965. "Études d'histoire militaire et diplomatique." *Bulletin de correspondance hellénique* 89:332–48.

Garlan, Y. 1972. *La guerre dans l'antiquité.* Paris.

Garlan, Y. 1978. "Signification historique de la piraterie grecque." *Dialogues d'histoire ancienne* 4:1–16.

Garlan, Y. 1987. "War, Piracy and Slavery in the Greek World." In *Classical Slavery*, edited by M.I. Finley. London: 7–21.

Gauthier, P. 1972. *Symbola. Les étrangers et la justice dans les cités grecques.* Nancy.

Gauthier, P. 1975. "Les ports de l'empire et l'agora athénienne: A propos du 'décret mégarien.'" *Historia* 24:498–503.

Gauthier, P. 1980. "Études sur des inscriptions d'Amorgos." *Bulletin de correspondance hellénique* 104:197–220.

Gauthier, P. 1982. "Les saisies licites aux dépens des étrangers dans les cités grecques." *Revue historique de droit français et étranger* 60:553–76.

Gauthier, P. 1985. *Les cités grecques et leurs bienfaiteurs (IVe–Ier siècle avant J.-C.). Contribution à l'histoire des institutions.* Athens.

Gauthier, P. 1993. "Décrets d'Érétrie en l'honneur de juges étrangers." *Revue des études grecques* 106:589–98.

Gauthier, P. 1995. "Notes sur le rôle du gymnase dans les cités hellénistiques." In *Stadtbild und Bürgerbild im Hellenismus*, edited by M. Wörrle and P. Zanker. Munich: 1–11.

Gauthier, P. 1999. "*Symbola* athéniens et tribunaux étrangers à l'époque hellénistique." *Bulletin de correspondance hellénique* 123:157–74.

Gehrke, H.-J. 1985. *Stasis. Untersuchungen zu den inneren Kriegen in den griechischen Staaten des 5. und 4. Jahrhunderts v. Chr.* Munich.

Geis, A. 2018. "Outlawing War Is Not Enough to Promote International Peace: The Ambivalence of Liberal Interventionism." *Global Constitutionalism* 7:342–57.

Gelzer, T. 1985. "Μοῦσα αὐθιγενής. Bemerkungen zu einem Typ Pindarischer und Bacchylideischer Epinikien." *Museum Helveticum* 42:95–120.

Genner, S., and Süss, D. 2017. "Socialization as Media Effect." In *The International Encyclopedia of Media Effects*, edited by P. Rössler, C.A. Hoffner, and L. van Zoonen. Malden, Mass: [unpaginated].

Geominy, W. 1998. "Zum Daochos-Weihgeschenk." *Klio* 80:369–402.

Georges, P.B. 2000. "Persian Ionia under Darius: The Revolt Reconsidered." *Historia* 49:1–39.

Giannopoulos, N. 1934/35. "Επιγραφή εκ Θεσσαλίας." *Archaiologike Ephemeris* 1934/35:140–45.

Gilardi, F. 2013. "Transnational Diffusion: Norms, Ideas, and Policies." In *Handbook of International Relations*, 2nd ed., edited by W. Carlsnaes, T. Risse, and B.A. Simmons. Los Angeles: 453–77.

Gilpin, R.G. 1986. "The Richness of the Tradition of Political Realism." In *Neorealism and Its Critics*, edited by R.O. Keohane. New York: 301–21.

Ginsburg, T. 2021. *Democracies and International Law.* Cambridge.

Giovannini, A. 1971. *Untersuchungen über die Natur und die Anfänge der bundesstaatlichen Sympolitie in Griechenland.* Göttingen.

Giovannini, A. 2007. *Les relations entre états dans la Grèce antique. Du temps d'Homère à l'intervention romaine (ca. 700–200 av. J.-C.).* Stuttgart.

Girgenti, G., and Sodano, A.R. 2005. *Porfirio. Astinenza dagli animali.* Milan.

Gkikaki, M.E., ed. 2023. *Tokens in Classical Athens and Beyond.* Liverpool.

Gkikaki, M.E. 2023b. "Introduction." In *Tokens in Classical Athens and Beyond*, edited by M.E. Gkikaki. Liverpool: 1–20.

Glazebrook, A. 2021. *Sexual Labor in the Athenian Courts.* Austin.

Goldsmith, J.L., and Posner, E.A. 2005. *The Limits of International Law.* Oxford.

Golove, D.M. 2006. "Leaving Customary International Law Where It Is: Goldsmith and Posner's the Limits of International Law." *Georgia Journal of International and Comparative Law* 34:333–77.

Gómez, A., Dovidio, J.F., Gaertner, S.L., Fernández, S., and Vázquez, A. 2013. "Responses to Endorsement of Commonality by Ingroup and Outgroup Members: The Roles of Group Representation and Threat." *Personality and Social Psychology Bulletin* 39:419–31.

Gomme, A.W. 1945. *A Historical Commentary on Thucydides.* Vol. 1. Oxford.

Gomme, A.W. 1956. *A Historical Commentary on Thucydides.* Vol. 3. Oxford.

Gomme, A.W., Andrewes, A., and Dover, K.J. 1981. *A Historical Commentary on Thucydides. Vol. V. Book VIII.* Oxford.

Gomme, A.W., and Sandbach, F.H. 1973. *Menander. A Commentary.* Oxford.

Goodman, R., and Jinks, D. 2013. *Socializing States. Promoting Human Rights through International Law.* Oxford.

Gorman, V.B. 2001. *Miletos, the Ornament of Ionia. A History of the City to 400 B.C.E.* Ann Arbor.

Gorman, V.B., and Gorman, R.J. 2024. "A Morphosyntactic Authorship Attribution Study of the Speeches of Demosthenes and Apollodorus." *Journal of Hellenic Studies* 144:65–92.

Gourmelen, L. 2004. *Kékrops, le roi-serpent. Imaginaire athénien, représentations de l'humain et de l'animalité en Grèce ancienne.* Paris.

Graham, A.J. 1960. "The Authenticity of the ΟΡΚΙΟΝ ΤΩΝ ΟΙΚΙΣΤΗΡΩΝ of Cyrene." *Journal of Hellenic Studies* 80:94–111.

Graham, A.J. 1983. *Colony and Mother City in Ancient Greece.* 2nd ed. Chicago.

Grainger, J.D. 1999. *The League of the Aitolians.* Leiden.

Grainger, J.D. 2009. *The Cities of Pamphylia.* Oxford.

Grainger, J.D. 2017. *Great Power Diplomacy in the Hellenistic World.* London.

Graninger, D. 2011. *Cult and Koinon in Hellenistic Thessaly.* Leiden.

Granovetter, M. 1973. "The Strength of Weak Ties." *American Journal of Sociology* 78:1360–80.

Granovetter, M. 2017. *Society and Economy. Framework and Principles.* Cambridge, Mass.

Gray, B. 2016. Review of *Oath and State in Ancient Greece* by A.H. Sommerstein and A.J. Bayliss. *Klio* 98:302–09.

Greaves, A.M. 2002. *Miletos: A History.* New York.

Greaves, A.M. 2010. *The Land of Ionia. Society and Economy in the Archaic Period.* Malden, Mass.

Green, D.P., and Shapiro, I. 1994. *Pathologies of Rational Choice Theory. A Critique of Applications in Political Science.* New Haven.

Greenhill, B. 2010. "The Company You Keep: International Socialization and the Diffusion of Human Rights Norms." *International Studies Quarterly* 54:127–45.

Greenhouse, C.J., Yngvesson, B., and Engel, D.M. 1994. *Law and Community in Three American Towns.* Ithaca.

Greif, A. 1993. "Contract Enforceability and Economic Institutions in Early Trade: The Maghribi Traders' Coalition." *American Economic Review* 83:525–48.

Greif, A. 2000. "The Fundamental Problem of Exchange: A Research Agenda in Historical Institutional Analysis." *European Review of Economic History* 4:251–84.

Greif, A. 2005. "Commitment, Coercion, and Markets: The Nature and Dynamics of Institutions Supporting Exchange." In *Handbook of New Institutional Economics*, edited by C. Menard and M.M. Shirley. Berlin: 727–86.

Greif, A. 2015. "Coercion and Exchange. How Did Markets Evolve?" In *Institutions, Innovation, and Industrialization*, edited by A. Greif, L. Kiesling, and J.V.C. Nye. Princeton: 71–96.

Gribble, D. 1997. "Rhetoric and History in [Andocides] 4, *Against Alcibiades.*" *Classical Quarterly* 47:367–91.

Gribble, D. 2012. "Alcibiades at the Olympics: Performance, Politics and Civic Ideology." *Classical Quarterly* 62:45–71.
Griffith, G.T. 1979. "Part Two." In *A History of Macedonia. Volume II, 550–336 B.C.*, by N.G.L. Hammond and G.T. Griffith. Oxford: 203–646.
Gruen, E.S. 1984. *The Hellenistic World and the Coming of Rome.* 2 vols. Berkeley.
Gruen, E.S. 1993. "The Polis in the Hellenistic World." In *Nomodeiktes. Greek Studies in Honor of Martin Ostwald*, edited by R.M. Rosen and J. Farrell. Ann Arbor: 339–54.
Grzybowski, J., and Koskenniemi, M. 2015. "International Law and Statehood: A Performative View." In *The Concept of the State in International Relations*, edited by R. Schuett and P.M.R. Stirk. Edinburgh: 23–44.
Guía, M.V. 2005. "The Cult of Aglauros (and Aphrodite) in Athens and in Salamis of Cyprus: Reflections on the Origin of the *Genos* of the *Salaminioi*." *Ancient West & East* 4:57–76.
Habashi, J. 2018. *Political Socialization of Youth. A Palestinian Case Study.* New York.
Habicht, C. 1982. *Studien zur Geschichte Athens in hellenistischer Zeit.* Göttingen.
Habicht, C. 1997. *Athens from Alexander to Antony.* Cambridge, Mass.
Habicht, C. 2006. *Athènes hellénistique. Histoire de la cité d'Alexandre le Grand à Marc Antoine.* 2nd ed. Paris.
Hadjimatheou, K. 2016. "Criminal Labelling, Publicity, and Punishment." *Law and Philosophy* 35:567–93.
Hainmueller, J., and Hangartner, D. 2013. "Who Gets a Swiss Passport? A Natural Experiment in Immigrant Discrimination." *American Political Science Review* 107:159–87.
Hainsworth, B. 1993. *The Iliad: A Commentary. Volume III: books 9–12.* Cambridge.
Hall, J.M. 1997. *Ethnic Identity in Greek Antiquity.* Cambridge.
Hall, J.M. 2002. *Hellenicity. Between Ethnicity and Culture.* Chicago.
Hall, J.M. 2013. "The Rise of State Action in the Archaic Age." In *A Companion to Ancient Greek Government*, edited by H. Beck. Chichester: 9–21.
Hall, J.M. 2015. "Federalism and Ethnicity." In *Federalism in Greek Antiquity*, edited by H. Beck and P. Funke. Cambridge: 30–48.
Hall, J.R. 2024. "Piracy and the Western Greek Experience." In *The Greeks in Iberia and Their Mediterranean Context*, edited by J.A. Krasilnikoff and B. Lowe. London: 174–97.
Hall, L.G.H. 1982. Review of C. Veligianni-Terzi, *Damiurgen. Zur Entwicklung einer Magistratur* (Diss. Heidelberg 1977). *Gnomon* 54:821–23.
Haltom, W., and McCann, M. 2004. *Distorting the Law. Politics, Media, and the Litigation Crisis.* Chicago.
Hammond, N.G.L. 1988. Parts I and III in *A History of Macedonia. Volume III, 336–167 B.C.*, by N.G.L. Hammond and F.W. Walbank. Oxford.
Hamon, P. 2012. "Mander des juges dans la cité: notes sur l'organisation des missions judiciaires à l'époque hellénistique." *Cahiers du Centre Gustave Glotz* 23:195–222.
Hansen, M.H. 1983. *The Athenian* Ecclesia. *A Collection of Articles 1976–1983.* 2 vols. Copenhagen.
Hansen, M.H. 1999. *The Athenian Democracy in the Age of Demosthenes.* Revised ed. Norman, Okla.
Hansen, M.H. 2002. "Was the Polis a State or a Stateless Society?" In *Even More Studies in the Ancient Greek Polis*, edited by T.H. Nielsen. Stuttgart: 17–47.
Hansen, M.H. 2006. "*Emporion.* A Study of the Use and Meaning of the Term in the Archaic and Classical Periods." In *Greek Colonisation. An Account of Greek Colonies and Other Settlements Overseas*, Vol. 1, edited by G.R. Tsetskhladze. Leiden: 1–39.
Hansen, M.H. 2013. "Greek City-States." In *The Oxford Handbook of the State in the Ancient Near East and Mediterranean*, edited by P.F. Bang and W. Scheidel. Oxford: 259–75.
Hansen, M.H. 2015. "The Dependent *Polis*: Further Considerations, in Response to Pierre Fröhlich." *GRBS* 55:863–83.

Hansen, M.H. 2015b. *Political Obligation in Ancient Greece and in the Modern World.* Copenhagen.

Hansen, M.H., and Nielsen, T.H. 2004. *An Inventory of Archaic and Classical Poleis.* Oxford.

Harcourt, B.E. 2014. "Beccaria's *On Crimes and Punishments*: A Mirror on the History of the Foundations of Modern Criminal Law." In *Foundational Texts in Modern Criminal Law*, edited by M.D. Dubber. Oxford: 39–61.

Harding, P. 1976. "Androtion's Political Career." *Historia* 25:186–200.

Harding, P. 1987. "Rhetoric and Politics in Fourth-Century Athens." *Phoenix* 41:25–39.

Harmon-Jones, E., and Allen, J.J.B. 2001. "The Role of Affect in the Mere Exposure Effect: Evidence from Physiological and Individual Differences Approaches." *Personality and Social Psychology Bulletin* 27:889–98.

Harris, E.M. 2002. "Did Solon Abolish Debt-Bondage?" *Classical Quarterly* 52:415–30.

Harris, E.M. 2006. *Democracy and the Rule of Law in Classical Athens. Essays on Law, Society, and Politics.* Cambridge.

Harris, E.M. 2010. "Is Oedipus Guilty? Sophocles and Athenian Homicide Law." In *Law and Drama in Ancient Greece*, edited by E.M. Harris, D.F. Leão, and P.J. Rhodes. London: 122–46.

Harris, E.M. 2013. *The Rule of Law in Action in Democratic Athens.* Oxford.

Harris, E.M. 2013b. "Were There Business Agents in Classical Greece? The Evidence of Some Lead Letters." In *The Letter. Law, State, Society and the Epistolary Format in the Ancient World*, edited by U. Yiftach-Firanko. Wiesbaden: 105–24.

Harris, E.M. 2015. "The Meaning of the Legal Term *Symbolaion*, the Law about *Dikai Emporikai* and the Role of the *Paragraphe* Procedure." *Dike* 18:7–36.

Harris, E.M. 2015b. "Toward a Typology of Greek Regulations about Religious Matters." *Kernos* 28:53–83.

Harris, E.M. 2016. "The Legal Foundations of Economic Growth in Ancient Greece." In *The Ancient Greek Economy. Markets, Households and City-States*, edited by E.M. Harris, D. Lewis, and M. Woolmer. Cambridge: 116–46.

Harris, E.M., ed. 2018. *Demosthenes, Speeches 23–26. Translated with an Introduction and Notes by E.M. Harris.* Austin.

Harris, E.M. 2024. "Unity and Diversity in Ancient Greek Law." *Classica et Mediaevalia*, Vol. 73 Supplementum 1:129–57.

Harris, E.M., and Canevaro, M. 2023. "Towards a New Text of Draco's Law on Homicide." *Revue des études grecques* 136:1–52.

Harris, E.M., and Lewis, D.M. 2016. "Introduction. Markets in Classical and Hellenistic Greece." In *The Ancient Greek Economy*, edited by E.M. Harris, D.M. Lewis, and M. Woolmer. Cambridge: 1–37.

Harris, E.M., Lewis, D.M, and Woolmer, M., eds. 2016. *The Ancient Greek Economy. Markets, Households and City-States.* Cambridge.

Harrison, A.R.W. 1960. "[Demosthenes] *De Halonneso* 13." *Classical Quarterly* 10:248–52.

Harrison, A.R.W. 1968–71. *The Law of Athens.* 2 vols. Oxford.

Harrison, T. 2020. "Reinventing the Barbarian." *Classical Philology* 115:139–63.

Hart, H.L.A. 1961. *The Concept of Law.* Oxford.

Harter-Uibopuu, K. 2002. "Strafklauseln und Gerichtliche Kontrolle in der Mysterieninschrift von Andania." *Dike* 5:135–59.

Harter-Uibopuu, K. 2021. "Fremde vor Gerichten der griechischen Städte." In *Konfliktlösung in der Antike*, edited by N. Grotkamp and A. Seelentag. Berlin: 147–56.

Hasenohr, C. 2022. "The Italian Associations on Delos: Religion, Trade, Politics and Social Cohesion (2nd–1st c. BC)." In *Associations and Religion in Context*, edited by A. Cazemier and S. Skaltsa. *Kernos* Supplement 39. Liège: 79–91.

Hathaway, O.A, and Shapiro, S.J. 2011. "Outcasting: Enforcement in Domestic and International Law." *Yale Law Journal* 121:252–349.

Hathaway, O.A, and Shapiro, S.J. 2017. *The Internationalists. How a Radical Plan to Outlaw War Remade the World.* New York.

Hathaway, O.A, and Shapiro, S.J. 2018. "Response to Critics." *Global Constitutionalism* 7:374–82.
Hatzopoulos, M.B. 1996. *Macedonian Institutions under the Kings*. 2 vols. Paris.
Hatzopoulos, M.B. 2013–2014. "The Athenian Standards Decree: The Aphytis Fragments." *Tekmeria* 12:235–69.
Hatzopoulos, M.B. 2021. "Quatre nouveaux décrets d'asylie macédoniens: géographie historique et institutions." *Revue des études grecques* 134:199–213.
Häuberer, J. 2011. *Social Capital Theory. Towards a Methodological Foundation*. Wiesbaden.
Heatherly, K.A., Lu, Y., and Lee, J.K. 2017. "Filtering out the Other Side? Cross-Cutting and Like-Minded Discussions on Social Networking Sites." *New Media & Society* 19:1271–89.
Hegel, G.W.F. 1988. Introduction to *The Philosophy of History*. With Selections from *The Philosophy of Right*. Edited by L. Rauch. Indianapolis.
Heisserer, A.J. 1980. *Alexander the Great and the Greeks: The Epigraphic Evidence*. Norman, Okla.
Helly, B. 1995. *L'état thessalien. Aleuas le Roux, les tétrades et les tagoi*. Lyon.
Helly, B. 2018. "Some Materials for a Historical Grammar of the Thessalian Dialect." In *Studies in Ancient Greek Dialects*, edited by G. Giannakis, E. Crespo, and P. Filos. Berlin: 351–74.
Helm, R., ed. 1913. *Die Chronik des Hieronymus*. Vol. 7 of *Eusebius Werke*. Leipzig.
Henkin, L. 1979. *How Nations Behave. Law and Foreign Policy*. New York.
Henrich, J., and Henrich, N. 2007. *Why Humans Cooperate. A Cultural and Evolutionary Explanation*. Oxford.
Hensler, D.R. 1989. "Resolving Mass Toxic Torts: Myths and Realities." *University of Illinois Law Review* (1989):89–104.
Herman, G. 1987. *Ritualised Friendship and the Greek City*. Cambridge.
Herman, G. 1997. "The Court Society of the Hellenistic Age." In *Hellenistic Constructs*, edited by P. Cartledge, P. Garnsey, and E. Gruen. Berkeley: 199–224.
Herrmann-Otto, E. 2017. *Sklaverei und Freilassung in der griechisch-römischen Welt*. 2nd ed. Hildesheim.
Hertogh, M. 2023. "Traffic Justice." In *Combining the Legal and the Social in Sociology of Law*, edited by H. Hydén, R. Cotterrell, D. Nelken, and U. Schultz. Oxford: 307–18.
Hibbing, J.R., Smith, K.B., and Alford, J.R. 2014. *Predisposed: Liberals, Conservatives, and the Biology of Political Differences*. New York.
Higgins, E.T. 2012. *Beyond Pleasure and Pain. How Motivation Works*. Oxford.
Hiller von Gaertringen, F. 1906. *Inschriften von Priene*. Berlin.
Hiltbrunner, O. 2005. *Gastfreundschaft in der Antike und im frühen Christentum*. Darmstadt.
Hirsch, M. 2015. *Invitation to the Sociology of International Law*. Oxford.
Hirschi, T. 1986. "On the Compatibility of Rational Choice and Social Control Theories of Crime." In *The Reasoning Criminal*, edited by D.B. Cornish and R.V. Clark. New York: 105–18.
Hirzel, R. 1907. *Themis, Dike und Verwandtes. Ein Beitrag zur Geschichte der Rechtsidee bei den Griechen*. Leipzig.
Hitzig, H.G. 1907. *Altgriechische Staatsverträge über Rechtshilfe*. Zurich.
Hitzig, H.G. 1907b. "Der griechische Fremdenprozeß im Lichte der neueren Inschriftenfunde." *Zeitschrift der Savigny-Stiftung für Rechtsgeschichte, Romanistische Abteilung* 28:211–53.
Hobbes, T. 1996 [1651]. *Leviathan*. Edited by J.C.A. Gaskin. Oxford.
Hobsbawm, E.J. 1981. *Bandits*. Revised ed. New York.
Hoekstra, K. 2016. "Athenian Democracy and Popular Tyranny." In *Popular Sovereignty in Historical Perspective*, edited by R. Bourke and Q. Skinner. Cambridge: 15–51.
Hoepfner, W. 1973. "Das Grabmonument des Pythagoras aus Selymbria." *Mitteilungen des Deutschen Archäologischen Instituts. Athenische Abteilung* 88:145–63.
Hoepfner, W., and Schwandner, E.-L. 1986. *Haus und Stadt im Klassischen Griechenland*. Munich.

Hogg, M.A. 2006. "Intergroup Relations." In *Handbook of Social Psychology*, edited by J. Delamater. New York: 479–501.
Hogg, M.A. 2016. "Social Identity Theory." In *Understanding Peace and Conflict through Social Identity Theory*, edited by S. McKeown, R. Haji, and N. Ferguson. Cham: 3–17.
Hogg, M.A., Abrams, D., and Brewer, M.B. 2017. "Social Identity: The Role of Self in Group Processes and Intergroup Relations." *Group Processes & Intergroup Relations* 20:570–81.
Hohl, K., and Stanko, E.A. 2015. "Complaints of Rape and the Criminal Justice System: Fresh Evidence on the Attrition Problem in England and Wales." *European Journal of Criminology* 12:324-41.
Hölbl, G. 2001. *History of the Ptolemaic Empire*. New York.
Holleaux, M. 1905. "Sur un décret de Siphnos." *Bulletin de correspondance hellénique* 29:319–28.
Holleaux, M. 1920. "L'expédition de Dikaiarchos dans les Cyclades et sur l'Héllespont." *Revue des études grecques* 33:223–47.
Hollis, M., and Smith, S. 1990. *Explaining and Understanding International Relations*. Oxford.
Hölscher, T. 2018. *Visual Power in Ancient Greece and Rome. Between Art and Social Reality*. Oakland.
Holzapfel, L. 1879. *Untersuchungen über die Darstellung der griechischen Geschichte von 489 bis 413 vor Chr. bei Ephoros Theopomp u.a. Autoren*. Leipzig.
Hooker, J.T. 1980. "Thessalian ΤΑΓΑ." *Zeitschrift für Papyrologie und Epigraphik* 40:272.
Hopf, T. 2018. "Change in International Practice." *European Journal of International Relations* 24:687–711.
Hopper, R.J. 1943. "Interstate Juridical Agreements in the Athenian Empire." *Journal of Hellenic Studies* 63:35–51.
Horden, P., and Purcell, N. 2000. *The Corrupting Sea. A Study of Mediterranean History*. Oxford.
Hornblower, S. 1991–2008. *A Commentary on Thucydides*. 3 vols. Oxford.
Hornblower, S. 2000. "Thucydides, Xenophon, and Lichas: Were the Spartans Excluded from the Olympic Games from 420 to 400 B.C.?" *Phoenix* 54:212–25.
Hornblower, S. 2002. *The Greek World, 479–323 BC*. 3rd ed. New York.
Hornblower, S., and Morgan, C. 2007. "Introduction." In *Pindar's Poetry, Patrons, and Festivals*, edited by S. Hornblower and C. Morgan. Oxford: 1–43.
Horowitz, M., Stewart, B., Tingley, D., Bishop, M.,, Resnick Samotin, L., Roberts, M., Chang, W., Mellers, B., and Tetlock, P. 2019. "What Makes Foreign Policy Teams Tick: Explaining Variation in Group Performance at Geopolitical Forecasting." *Journal of Politics* 81:1388–1404.
Horrocks, G. 2010. *Greek. A History of the Language and Its Speakers*. 2nd ed. Chichester.
Houkelon, F. 2014. *Behavioral Economics. A History*. Cambridge.
Howse, R., and Teitel, R. 2010. "Beyond Compliance: Rethinking Why International Law Really Matters." *Global Policy* 1:127–36.
Huddy, L., Sears, D.O., and Levy, J.S., eds. 2013. *The Oxford Handbook of Political Psychology*. 2nd ed. Oxford.
Hudson-Williams, T. 1910. *The Elegies of Theognis. And Other Elegies Included in the Theognidean Sylloge*. London.
Hughes, D.D. 1991. *Human Sacrifice in Ancient Greece*. London.
Huitink, L., Glaveanu, V., and Sluiter, I. 2025. *Social Psychology and the Ancient World. Methods and Applications*. Leiden.
Hull, I.V. 2014. *A Scrap of Paper. Breaking and Making International Law During the Great War*. Ithaca.
Hunter, V.J. 1994. *Policing Athens. Social Control in the Attic Lawsuits, 420–320 B.C.* Princeton.
Hunter, V.J., and Edmondson, J.C. 2000. *Law and Social Status in Classical Athens*. Oxford.
Huß, W. 2011. *Die Verwaltung des Ptolemaiischen Reichs*. Munich.

Iacovou, M. 2008. "Cyprus: From Migration to Hellenisation." In *Greek Colonisation. An Account of Greek Colonies and Other Settlements Overseas*, Vol. 2, edited by G.R. Tsetskhladze. Leiden: 219–88.

Ismard, P. 2010. *La cité des réseaux: Athènes et ses associations, VIe–Ier siècle av. J.-C.* Paris.

Ismard, P. 2015. *La démocratie contre les experts. Les esclaves publics en Grèce ancienne.* Paris.

Ismard, P. 2019. *La cité et ses esclaves. Institution, fictions, expériences.* Paris.

Jackson, A.H. 1973. "Privateers in the Ancient Greek World." In *War and Society*, edited by M.R.D. Foot. London: 241–53.

Jackson, A.H. 1995. "An Oracle for Raiders?" *Zeitschrift für Papyrologie und Epigraphik* 108:95–99.

Jackson, M.O. 2019. *The Human Network. How Your Social Position Determines Your Power, Beliefs, and Behaviors.* New York.

Jackson, P.T. 2004. "Forum Introduction. Is the State a Person? Why Should We Care?" *Review of International Studies* 30:255–58.

Jacquemin, A. 1999. *Offrandes monumentales à Delphes.* Athens.

James, J. 2023. "Repunctuating Athenian Imperialism in the Phaselis Decree." *Zeitschrift für Papyrologie und Epigraphik* 225:133–41.

James, J. 2026. "Pragmata and the Unity of Greek Law in Hermias's Reconciliation at Airai." *Chiron* 56:[unpaginated].

Jameson, M.H. 1960. "A Decree of Themistokles from Troizen." *Hesperia* 29:198–223.

Jameson, M.J. 2000–2003. "Athens and Phaselis, *IG* I^3 10 (EM 6918)." *Horos* 14–16:23–29.

Janis, I.L. 1982. *Groupthink. Psychological Studies of Policy Decisions and Fiascoes.* Boston.

Janis, M.W. 1984. "Jeremy Bentham and the Fashioning of 'International Law'." *The American Journal of International Law* 78:405–18.

Janko, R. 1992. *The Iliad. A Commentary. Volume 4, Books 13–16.* Cambridge.

Jeffery, L.H. 1990. *The Local Scripts of Archaic Greece. A Study of the Origin of the Greek Alphabet and Its Development from the Eighth to the Fifth Centuries B.C.* Revised ed. Oxford.

Jeffery, L.H., and Morpurgo-Davies, A. 1970. "Ποινικαστάς and Ποινικάζεν: BM 1969.4–2.1, a New Archaic Inscription from Crete." *Kadmos* 9:118–54.

Jeries-Loulou, L. J., and Khoury-Kassabri, M. 2022. "Female Arab Teenagers' Involvement in Antisocial Behavior: Intersection of Perceived Ethnonational Discrimination, Sexual Victimization, and Affiliation with Delinquent Peers." *American Journal of Orthopsychiatry* 92:190–202.

Jessop, B. 1990. *State Theory. Putting the Capitalist State in Its Place.* Cambridge.

Jim, T.S.F. 2014. *Sharing with the Gods.* Aparchai *and* Dekatai *in Ancient Greece.* Oxford.

Johansson, M. 2001. "The Inscription from Troizen: A Decree of Themistocles?" *Zeitschrift für Papyrologie und Epigraphik* 137:69–92.

Johnson, M.R. 2020. "The Ethical Maxims of Democritus of Abdera." In *Early Greek Ethics*, edited by D.C. Wolfsdorf. Oxford: 211–42.

Jones, C.P. 1999. *Kinship Diplomacy in the Ancient World.* Cambridge, Mass.

Jones, K. 2024. "Wise Trust." *Proceedings of the Aristotelian Society* 124:95–113.

Jones, N.F. 1999. *The Associations of Classical Athens. The Response to Democracy.* Oxford.

Jordan, D.R. 2000. "A Personal Letter Found in the Athenian Agora." *Hesperia* 69:91–103.

Kachalia, A., and Mello, M.M. 2011. "New Directions in Medical Liability Reform." *New England Journal of Medicine* 364:1564–72.

Kagan, J. 2004. "The So-Called Persian Weight Coins of Larissa," in *'Οβολός 7: Το Νόμισμα στο Θεσσαλικό Χώρο.* Athens: 79–86.

Kah, D., and Scholz, P., eds. 2004. *Das hellenistische Gymnasion.* Berlin.

Kahneman, D. 2011. *Thinking, Fast and Slow.* New York.

Kahneman, D., and Tversky, A. 1979. "Prospect Theory: An Analysis of Decision under Risk." *Econometrica* 47:263–91.

Kalin, M., and Sambanis, N. 2018. "How to Think about Social Identity." *Annual Review of Political Science* 21:239–57.

Kallet, L. 2009. "Democracy, Empire and Epigraphy in the Twentieth Century." In *Interpreting the Athenian Empire*, edited by J. Ma, N. Papazarkadas, and R. Parker. London: 43–66.

Kallet, L. 2020. *Contribution à l'épigraphie et à l'histoire de la Béotie hellénistique. De la destruction de Thèbes à la bataille de Pydna*. Athens.

Kalliontzis, Y. 2020. *Contribution à l'épigraphie et à histoire de la Béotie hellénistique. De la destruction de Thèbes à la bataille de Pydna*. Athens.

Kalliontzis, Y., and Papazarkadas, N. 2019. "The Contributions to the Refoundation of Thebes: A New Epigraphic and Historical Analysis." *The Annual of the British School at Athens* 114:293–315.

Kamen, D. 2013. *Status in Classical Athens*. Princeton.

Kamen, D., and Marshall, C.W., eds. 2021. *Slavery and Sexuality in Classical Antiquity*. Madison, Wisc.

Kant, I. 2006. *Toward Perpetual Peace and Other Writings on Politics, Peace, and History*. Edited by P. Kleingeld, translated by D.L. Colclasure. New Haven.

Kaplan, H.B. 2003. "Social Psychological Perspectives on Deviance." In *Handbook of Social Psychology*, edited by J. Delamater. New York: 451–78.

Kapparis, K.A. 2019. *Athenian Law and Society*. London.

Kapparis, K.A. 2021. *Women in the Law Courts of Classical Athens*. Edinburgh.

Karageorghis, J., and Masson, O. 1988. *The History of the Greek Language in Cyprus*. Nicosia.

Karavites, P. 2003. "Morality and Expediency in Greek Inter-State Affairs." *Ancient World* 34:13–26.

Karayiannis, A.D., and Hatzis, A.N. 2012. "Morality, Social Norms and the Rule of Law as Transaction Cost-Saving Devices: The Case of Ancient Athens." *European Journal of Law and Economics* 33:621–43.

Kaser, M. 1993. *Ius Gentium*. Cologne.

Kasimis, D. 2018. *The Perpetual Immigrant and the Limits of Athenian Democracy*. Cambridge.

Kató, P. 2014. "Asylie-Variationen. Bemerkungen zu den Entstehungsgründen und Funktionen der hellenistischen Asylie." In *Stadtkultur im Hellenismus*, edited by A. Matthaei and M. Zimmermann. Heidelberg: 97–108.

Keenan, J.G., Manning, J.G., and Yiftach-Firanko, U. 2014. *Law and Legal Practice in Egypt from Alexander to the Arab Conquest*. Cambridge.

Kehoe, D., Ratzan, D.M., and Yiftach, U., eds. 2015. *Law and Transaction Costs in the Ancient Economy*. Ann Arbor.

Kehoe, D., Ratzan, D.M., and Yiftach, U. 2015b. "Introduction: Transaction Costs, Ancient History, and the Law." In *Law and Transaction Costs in the Ancient Economy*, edited by D. Kehoe, D.M. Ratzan, and U. Yiftach. Ann Arbor: 1–35.

Kelly, B. 2011. *Petitions, Litigation, and Social Control in Roman Egypt*. Oxford.

Kelsen, H. 1967. *Pure Theory of Law*. Translated from the 2nd German ed. by M. Knight. Berkeley.

Kenrick, P. 2013. *Libya Archaeological Guides. Cyrenaica*. London.

Kent, J.H. 1966. *Corinth. Results of Excavations Conducted by the American School of Classical Studies at Athens. Volume VIII, Part III: The Inscriptions 1926–1950*. Princeton.

Kertzer, J.D., and Tingley, D. 2018. "Political Psychology in International Relations: Beyond the Paradigms." *Annual Review of Political Science* 21:319–39.

Kessler, O., and Steele, B. 2018. "On Constructivism, Realism, and Contingency." In *Constructivism Reconsidered*, edited by M.E. Bertucci, J. Hayes, and P. James. Ann Arbor: 47–66.

Kestemont, G. 1974. *Diplomatique et droit international en Asie occidentale: 1600–1200 av. J.C.* Louvain-la-Neuve.

Kiechle, F. 1958. "Zur Humanität in der Kriegführung der griechischen Staaten." *Historia* 7:129–56.

Kierstead, J. 2023. "The Athenian Jigsaw Tokens." In *Tokens in Classical Athens and Beyond*, edited by M.E. Gkikaki. Liverpool: 43–61.

Kindt, J. 2012. *Rethinking Greek Religion.* Cambridge.
Kinkor, K.J. 2001. "Black Men under the Black Flag." In *Bandits at Sea. A Pirates Reader*, edited by C.R. Pennell. New York: 195–210.
Klaffenbach, G. 1948. "Zu König Antigonos' Schrieben an die Teïer." *Philologus* 97:179–80.
Kletzer, C. 2018. *The Idea of a Pure Theory of Law.* Oxford.
Klosko, G. 2020. "Oaths and Political Obligation in Ancient Greece." *History of Political Thought* 41:1–15.
Knäpper, K. 2018. *Hieros kai asylos. Territoriale Asylie im Hellenismus in ihrem historischen Kontext.* Stuttgart.
Knappett, C. 2013. *Network Analysis in Archaeology. New Approaches to Regional Interaction.* Oxford.
Knoepfler, D. 2001. "Le contrat d'Érétrie en Eubée pour le drainage de l'étang de Ptéchai." In *Irrigation et drainage dans l'antiquité*, edited by P. Briant. Paris: 41–79.
Knoepfler, D. 2010. "Les vieillards relégués à Salamine survivront-ils au jubilé de la publication du décret de Thémistocle trouvé à Trézène?" *Comptes rendus des séances de l'Académie des Inscriptions et Belles-Lettres* 154:1191–1233.
Knoepfler, D. 2015. "The Euboian League—an 'Irregular' *Koinon*?" In *Federalism in Greek Antiquity*, edited by H. Beck and P. Funke. Cambridge: 158–78.
Knutsen, T.L. 2016. *A History of International Relations Theory.* 3rd ed. Manchester.
Koerner, R. 1981. "Vier frühe Verträge zwischen Gemeinwesen und Privatleuten auf griechischen Inschriften." *Klio* 63:179–206.
Konstantinidou, K. 2014. "Oath and Curse." In *Oaths and Swearing in Ancient Greece*, edited by A.H. Sommerstein and I.C. Torrance. Berlin: 6–47.
Körner, C. 2016. "The Cypriot Kings under Assyrian and Persian Rule (Eighth to Fourth Century BC): Centre and Periphery in a Relationship of Suzerainty." *Electrum* 23:25–49.
Koskenniemi, M. 2001. *The Gentle Civilizer of Nations. The Rise and Fall of International Law, 1870–1960.* Cambridge.
Koskenniemi, M. 2016. "Expanding Histories of International Law." *American Journal of Legal History* 56:104–12.
Koskenniemi, M. 2017. "What Should International Legal History Become?" In *System, Order, and International Law*, edited by S. Kadelbach, T. Kleinlein, and D. Roth-Isigkeit. Oxford: 381–97.
Kosmin, P.J. 2014. *The Land of the Elephant Kings. Space, Territory, and Ideology in the Seleucid Empire.* Cambridge, Mass.
Kosmin, P.J. 2024. *The Ancient Shore.* Cambridge, Mass.
Kossmann, P. 2011. *Les Lagides et l'Asie Mineure.* Diss. École Pratique des Hautes Études. Paris.
Kossmann, P. 2015. "Les relations entre les Lagides et les cités crétoises," in *Afti inè i Kriti! Identités, altérités et figures crétoises*, edited by P. Louvier, P. Monbrun, and A. Pierrot. Bordeaux: 201–18.
Kowalzig, B. 2005. "Mapping out *Communitas*: Performances of *Theōria* in Their Sacred and Political Context." In *Pilgrimage in Graeco-Roman and Early Christian Antiquity*, edited by J. Elsner and I. Rutherford. Oxford: 41–72.
Kowalzig, B. 2007. *Singing for the Gods. Performances of Myth and Ritual in Archaic and Classical Greece.* Oxford.
Kowalzig, B. 2018. "Cults, Cabotage, and Connectivity." In *Maritime Networks in the Ancient Mediterranean World*, edited by J. Leidwanger and C. Knappett. Cambridge: 93–131.
Kozak, L.A. 2014. "Oaths between Warriors in Epic and Tragedy." In *Oaths and Swearing in Ancient Greece*, edited by A.H. Sommerstein and I.C. Torrance. Berlin: 60–66.
Kramolisch, H. 1979. "Das Ende des perrhäbischen Bundes." In *La Thessalie, actes de la table ronde, 21–24 juillet 1975, organisée par Bruno Helly.* Lyon: 201–19.
Kristensen, K.R. 2004. "Gortynian Debt Bondage. Some New Considerations on IC IV 41 IV–VII, 47 and 72 I.56–II.2, X.25–32." *Zeitschift für Papyrologie und Epigraphik* 149:73–79.

Kritzer, H.M. 2008. "To Lawyer or Not to Lawyer: *Is* That the Question?" *Journal of Empirical Legal Studies* 5:875–906.

Kroll, J.H. 2009. "What about Coinage?" In *Interpreting the Athenian Empire*, edited by J. Ma, N. Papazarkadas, and R. Parker. London: 195–209.

Kroll, J.H., and Mitchel, F.W. 1980. "Clay Tokens Stamped with the Names of Athenian Military Commanders." *Hesperia* 49:86–96.

Kron, G. 2016. "Classical Greek Trade in Comparative Perspective." In *The Ancient Greek Economy. Markets, Households and City-States*, edited by E.M. Harris, D. Lewis, and M. Woolmer. Cambridge: 356–80.

Kroneberg, C., and Kalter, F. 2012. "Rational Choice Theory and Empirical Research: Methodological and Theoretical Contributions in Europe." *Annual Review of Sociology* 38:73–92.

Kryzhitskiy, S.D. 2007. "Criteria for the Presence of Barbarians in the Population of Early Olbia." In *Classical Olbia and the Scythian World*, edited by D. Braund and S.D. Kryzhitskiy. Oxford: 17–22.

Kuhn, T.S. 1977. *The Essential Tension*. Chicago.

Kumar, K. 2010. "Nation-States as Empires, Empires as Nation-States: Two Principles, One Practice?" *Theory and Society* 39:119–43.

Kurke, L. 1999. *Coins, Bodies, Games, and Gold. The Politics of Meaning in Archaic Greece*. Princeton.

Kvist, K. 2003. "Cretan Grants of *Asylia* – Violence and Protection as Interstate Relations." *Classica et Mediaevalia* 54:185–222.

Kyrieleis, H. 2012. "Die frühe Geschichte Olympias: Mythos und archäologische Forschung." In *Mythos Olympia: Kult und Spiele*, edited by W.-D. Heilmeyer et al. Munich: 61–65.

Labarre, G. 1996. *Les cités de Lesbos, aux époques hellénistique et impériale*. Paris.

Lalonde, G.V. 2019. *Athena Itonia: Geography and Meaning of an Ancient Greek War Goddess*. Leiden.

Lambert, S.D. 1993. *The Phratries of Attica*. Ann Arbor.

Lambert, S.D. 2001. "Ten Notes on Attic Inscriptions." *Zeitschrift für Papyrologie und Epigraphik* 135:51–62.

Lambert, S.D. 2017. "Two Inscribed Documents of the Athenian Empire. The Chalkis Decree and the Tribute Reassessment Decree." *AIO Papers*, No. 8. Worcestershire. Available at: https://www.atticinscriptions.com/papers/aio-papers-8/]

Lamberton, R. 1997. "Homer in Antiquity." In *A New Companion to Homer*, edited by I. Morris and B. Powell. Leiden: 33–54.

Lämmer, M. 1982–83. "Der sogenannte olympische Friede in der griechischen Antike." *Stadion* 8–9:47–83.

Lamont, J.L. 2023. "Trade, Literacy and Documentary Histories of the Northern Black Sea." *Journal of Hellenic Studies* 143:1–23.

Landa, J.T. 1981. "A Theory of the Ethnically Homogeneous Middleman Group: An Institutional Alternative to Contract Law." *Journal of Legal Studies* 10:349–62.

Landsman, S. 2012. "Pro Se Litigation." *Annual Review of Law and Social Science* 8:231–53.

Lane, T., Nosenzo, D., and Sonderegger, S. 2023. "Law and Norms: Empirical Evidence." *American Economic Review* 113:1255–93.

Lane Fox, R. 2024. "OPW and de Ste. Croix: The Past and Present Views of a Pupil." *Polis* 41:9–50.

Lanni, A. 2008. "The Laws of War in Ancient Greece." *Law and History Review* 26:469–89.

Lanni, A. 2016. *Law and Order in Ancient Athens*. Cambridge.

Lappi-Seppälä, T., and Lehti, M. 2014. "Cross-Comparative Perspectives on Global Homicide Trends." *Crime and Justice: An Annual Review of Research* 43:135–230.

Laronde, A. 1987. *Cyrène et la Libye hellénistique. Libykai Historiai, de l'époque républicaine au principat d'Auguste*. Paris.

Laronde, A. 1996. "L'exploitation de la *chôra* cyrénéenne à l'époque classique et hellénistique." *Comptes rendus des séances de l'Académie des Inscriptions et Belles-Lettres* (1996):503–27.

Laronde, A., and Lefèvre, F. 2009. "Autour de la 'stèle des syla.'" *Comptes rendus de l'Académie des Inscriptions et Belles-Lettres* 153:807–40.

Larsen, J.A.O. 1968. *Greek Federal States. Their Institutions and History.* Oxford.

Larson, K.A. 2013. "A Network Approach to Hellenistic Sculptural Production." *Journal of Mediterranean Archaeology* 26:235–60.

Lasagni, C. 2009–2010. "La definizione di 'stato federale' nel mondo greco." *Dike* 12/13:219–70.

Lateiner, D. 1982. "The Failure of the Ionian Revolt." *Historia* 31:129–60.

Lauterpacht, H. 1970. *International Law. Being the Collected Papers of Hersch Lauterpacht.* 5 vols. Cambridge.

Lavan, M. 2013. *Slaves to Rome. Paradigms of Empire in Roman Culture.* Cambridge.

Lawrence, T.J. 1895. *The Principles of International Law.* Boston.

Lawton, C.L. 1995. *Attic Document Reliefs. Art and Politics in Ancient Athens.* Oxford.

Lazar, L. 2024. *Athenian Power in the Fifth Century BC.* Oxford.

Lazar, L. 2024b. "The Athenian Empire and Epigraphic Cultures." *Journal of Hellenic Studies* 144:144–63.

Leão, D.F., and Rhodes, P.J. 2016. *The Laws of Solon.* London.

Lebow, R.N. 2001. "Thucydides the Constructivist." *American Political Science Review* 95:547–60.

Lebow, R.N. 2008. *A Cultural Theory of International Relations.* Cambridge.

Lécrivain, M. 1897. "Le droit de se faire justice soi-même et les représailles dans les relations internationales de la Grèce." *Mémoires de l'académie des sciences de Toulouse*, 9 série 9:277–90.

Leese, M. 2021. *Making Money in Ancient Athens.* Ann Arbor.

Lefèvre, F. 1998. *L'amphictionie pyléo-delphique. Histoire et institutions.* Athens.

Le Guen, B. 2001. *Les associations de technites dionysiaques à l'époque hellénistique.* 2 vols. Nancy.

Lehtinen, A., and Kuorikoski, J. 2007. "Unrealistic Assumptions in Rational Choice Theory." *Philosophy of the Social Sciences* 37:115–38.

Leidwanger, J., et al. 2014. "A Manifesto for the Study of Ancient Mediterranean Maritime Networks." *Antiquity: A Review of World Archaeology* 88(342): [unpaginated]. Available at: https://www.antiquity.ac.uk/projgall/leidwanger342.

Leidwanger, J., and Knappett, C., eds. 2018. *Maritime Networks in the Ancient Mediterranean World.* Cambridge.

Lendon, J.E. 1994. "Thucydides and the 'Constitution' of the Peloponnesian League." *Greek, Roman and Byzantine Studies* 35:159–77.

Lendon, J.E. 2010. *Song of Wrath. The Peloponnesian War Begins.* New York.

Lenski, N., and Cameron, C.M., eds. 2018. *What Is a Slave Society? The Practice of Slavery in Global Perspective.* Cambridge.

Lerat, L. 1951. "Locride occidentale." *Bulletin de correspondance hellénique* 75:141–42.

Lerat, L. 1952. *Les Locriens de l'ouest.* 2 vols. Paris.

Lerner, R.M., Overton, W.F., and Molenaar, P.C.M., eds. 2015. *Handbook of Child Psychology and Developmental Science.* 4 vols. Hoboken.

Lerouge-Cohen, C. 2022 *Souvenirs du passé perse à l'époque hellénistique. Arménie; Cappadoce; Commagène; Perside; Pont; Royaume arsacide.* Brussels.

Lesaffer, R. 2024. "Scope, Scale and Humility in the History of International Law." In *The Cambridge History of International Law*, Vol. 1, edited by R. Lesaffer. Cambridge: 1–46.

Levy, J.S. 2013. "Psychology and Foreign Policy Decision-Making." In *The Oxford Handbook of Political Psychology.* 2nd ed., edited by L. Huddy, D.O. Sears, and J.S. Levy. Oxford: 301–33.

Lewis, D. 1959. "Athens and Troizen." *Hesperia* 28:248–50.

Lewis, D. 1992. "The Archidamian War." In *The Cambridge Ancient History. Second Edition. Vol. V. The Fifth Century B.C.*, edited by D. Lewis, J. Boardman, J.K. Davies, and M. Ostwald. Cambridge: 370–432.

Lewis, D.M. 2018. "Behavioural Economics and Economic Behaviour in Classical Athens." In *Ancient Greek History and Contemporary Social Science*, edited by M. Canevaro, A. Erskine, B. Gray, and J. Ober. Edinburgh: 15–46.

Lewis, D.M. 2018b. *Greek Slave Systems in Their Eastern Mediterranean Context, c.800–146 BC*. Oxford.

Lewis, D.M. 2019. "Piracy and Slave Trading in Action in Classical and Hellenistic Greece." *Mare Nostrum* 10:79–108.

Lewis, D.M. 2022. "Attic Deme Harbours, the Rural Economy, and State Oversight of Maritime Trade: The Incident at Φωρῶν Λιμήν ([Dem.] 35.28-29)." *Pnyx* 1:81–101.

Lewis, D.M. 2023. "The Cretan Way of War: Status, Violence and Values from the Classical Period to the Roman Conquest." *Journal of Hellenic Studies* 143:24–48.

Lewis, D.M. 2023b. "Did Serfdom Exist in Classical and Hellenistic Crete?" In *Symposion 2022*, edited by P. Scheibelreiter. Vienna: 225–51.

Lewis, D.M. 2025. "Greek Slavery and Honour: Institutional and Prototypical Approaches." In *Slavery and Honour in the Ancient Greek World*, edited by D.M. Lewis, M. Canevaro, and D.L. Cairns. Edinburgh: 38–59.

Li, W., and Lartey, J. 2022. "As Murders Spiked, Police Solved About Half in 2020." Analysis, The Marshall Project. Available at: https://www.themarshallproject.org/2022/01/12/as-murders-spiked-police-solved-about-half-in-2020.

Liampi, K. 2015. "A Hoard from Thessaly Containing Aeginetan Staters and Thessalian Issues of the 'Taurokathapsia' Type." In *Fides. Contributions to Numismatics in Honor of Richard B. Witshonke*, edited by P.G. Van Alfen, G. Bransbourg, and M. Amandry. New York: 1–19.

Liberman, G. 2017. *Les préliminaires de la guerre. Prolégomènes à la lecture du premier livre de Thucydide*. Bordeaux.

Liddel, P. 2021. "The Discourses of Identity in Hellenistic Erythrai: Institutions, Rhetoric, Honour and Reciprocity." *Polis* 38:74–107.

Liddel, P., Constantakopoulou, C., and Kourayos, Y. 2025. "An Inscribed Decree from the Paros Museum and the Parian Colonization of Pharos." *Journal of Hellenic Studies* 145:50–63.

Lilley, C., Willmott, D., Mojtahedi, D., Labhardt, D. 2023. "Intimate Partner Rape: A Review of Six Core Myths Surrounding Women's Conduct and the Consequences of Intimate Partner Rape." *Social Sciences* 12:34–53.

Lind, E.A., and Tyler, T.R. 1988. *The Social Psychology of Procedural Justice*. New York.

Lindenberg, S., and Steg, L. 2007. "Normative, Gain and Hedonic Goal Frames Guiding Environmental Behavior." *Journal of Social Issues* 63:117–37.

Linder, M. 2020. "Artists beyond Athens: The Freedoms and Restrictions of the Artistic Profession in Classical Greece." In *Skilled Labour and Professionalism in Ancient Greece and Rome*, edited by E. Stewart, E. Harris, and D.M. Lewis. Cambridge: 230–42.

Lintott, A.W. 1968. *Violence in Republican Rome*. Oxford.

Lintott, A.W. 1982. *Violence, Civil Strife, and Revolution in the Classical City, 750–330 B.C.* London.

Lintott, A.W. 2004. "*Sula*—Reprisal by Seizure in Greek Inter-Community Relations." *Classical Quarterly* 54:340–53.

Lipsius, J.H. 1905–1915. *Das attische Recht und Rechtsverfahren*. 3 vols. Leipzig.

Liuzzo, P.M. 2012. "Osservazioni sulle iscrizioni del trofeo di Platea e della colonna serpentina." *Epigraphica* 74:27–41.

Llewellyn, K.N. 1930. "A Realistic Jurisprudence – The Next Step." *Columbia Law Review* 30:431–65.

Llewelyn, S.R. 1994. *New Documents Illustrating Early Christianity. Volume 7: A Review of the Greek Inscriptions and Papyri Published in 1982–83*. Sydney.

Löbel, Y. 2014. *Die Poleis der bundesstaatlichen Gemeinwesen im antiken Griechenland. Untersuchungen zum Machtverhältnis zwischen Poleis und Zentralgewalten bis 167 v. Chr.* Alessandria.

Lomas, K. 2004. "Introduction." In *Greek Identity in the Western Mediterranean*, edited by K. Lomas. Leiden: 1–14.

Lombardi, G. 1947. *Sul concetto di "ius gentium."* Rome.

Lonis, R. 1969. *Les usages de la guerre entre grecs et barbares des guerres médiques au milieu du IVe s. avant J.-C.* Paris.

Lorber, C.C. 2008. "Thessalian Hoards and the Coinage of Larissa." *American Journal of Numismatics* 20:119–42.

Loughran, T.A., Brame, R., Fagan, J., Piquero, A.R., Mulvey, E.P., and Schubert, C.A. 2015. "Studying Deterrence among High-Risk Adolescents." *Juvenile Justice Bulletin*, August 2015. Available at: https://permanent.access.gpo.gov/gpo82827/248617.pdf.

Low, P. 2005. "Looking for the Language of Athenian Imperialism." *Journal of Hellenic Studies* 125:93–111.

Low, P. 2007. *Interstate Relations in Classical Greece. Morality and Power.* Cambridge.

Low, P. 2013. "Law, Authority and Legitimacy in the Athenian Empire." In *Law and Empire*, edited by J. Duindam, J. Harries, C. Humfress, and H. Nimrod. Leiden: 25–44.

Lowe, J. 2022. "Breaking the Silence: An Islamic Legal Approach to Facilitating Reporting and Testimony by Muslim Victims and Witnesses of Sexual Crimes." *Religions* 13:1017–31.

Lowery, W., Kelly, K., and Rich, S. 2018. "An Unequal Justice." *The Washington Post*, 29 July 2018, A1.

Loy, M. 2023. *Connecting Communities in Archaic Greece. Exploring Economic and Political Networks through Data Modelling.* Cambridge.

Ludwig, K. 2017. "Do Corporations Have Minds of Their Own?" *Philosophical Psychology* 30:269–301.

Lund, H.S. 1992. *Lysimachus. A Study in Early Hellenistic Kingship.* New York.

Lundgreen, C. 2020. "Schlüsselmonopole oder Governance-Funktionen? Alternative Annäherungen an Staatlichkeit in der griechischen Archaik." In *Konkurrenz und Institutionalisierung in der griechischen Archaik*, edited by J.B. Meister and G. Seelentag. Stuttgart: 157–92.

Luraghi, N. 2006. "Traders, Pirates, Warriors: The Proto-History of Greek Mercenary Soldiers in the Eastern Mediterranean." *Phoenix* 60:21–47.

Lutfey, K., and Mortimer, J.T. 2006. "Development and Socialization through the Adult Life Course." In *Handbook of Social Psychology*, edited by J. Delamater. New York: 183–202.

Lytle, E. 2007. "Fishless Mysteries or High Prices at Athens? Re-examining *IG* II2 1103." *Museum Helveticum* 64:100–11.

Lytle, E. 2016. "Chaerephilus & Sons: Vertical Integration, Classical Athens and the Black Sea Fish Trade." *Ancient Society* 46:1–26.

Lytle, E. 2016b. "Status beyond Law: Ownership, Access and the Ancient Mediterranean." In *The Inland Seas*, edited by T. Bekker-Nielsen and R. Gertwagen. Stuttgart: 107–35.

Ma, J. 2000. *Antiochos III and the Cities of Western Asia Minor.* Oxford.

Ma, J. 2003. "Peer Polity Interaction in the Hellenistic Age." *Past & Present* 180:9–39.

Ma, J. 2008. "The Return of the Black Hunter." *Cambridge Classical Journal* 54:188–208.

Ma, J. 2011. "Court, King, and Power in Antigonid Macedonia." In *Brill's Companion to Ancient Macedon*, edited by R.J. Lane Fox. Leiden: 521–44.

Ma, J. 2013. "Hellenistic Empires." In *The Oxford Handbook of the State in the Ancient Near East and Mediterranean*, edited by P.F. Bang and W. Scheidel. Oxford: 324–52.

Ma, J. 2017. "Whatever Happened to Athens? Thoughts on the Great Convergence and Beyond." In *The Hellenistic Reception of Classical Athenian Democracy and Political Thought*, edited by M. Canevaro and B. Gray. Oxford: 277–97.

Ma, J. 2018. "The *Polis* in a Cold Climate: Propositions, Consequences, Questions." In *Βορειοελλαδικά. Tales from the Lands of the* Ethne, edited by M. Kalaitzi, P. Paschidis, C. Antonetti, and A.-M. Guimier-Sorbets. Athens: 309–27.

Ma, J. 2024. *Polis. A New History of the Ancient Greek City-State from the Early Iron Age to the End of Antiquity*. Princeton.
Maccoby, E.E. 2015. "Historical Overview of Socialization Research and Theory." In *Handbook of Socialization*, edited by J.E. Grusec and P.D. Hastings. New York: 3–32.
MacDowell, D.M. 1978. *The Law in Classical Athens*. Ithaca.
MacDowell, D.M. 1990. *Demosthenes Against Meidias (Oration 21)*. Oxford.
MacDowell, D.M. 2004. *Demosthenes, Speeches 27–38*. Austin.
Mack, R. 2021. *The Role of the Horse on Thessalian Coinage, ca. 479-320 BC*. Diss. Reading.
Mack, R. (forthcoming). *Equine Currency. Thessalian Coinage and the Horse in the Classical and Hellenistic Periods*. Oxford.
Mack, W. 2015. *Proxeny and Polis. Institutional Networks in the Ancient Greek World*. Oxford.
Mack, W. 2022. "'Where Are the *Proxenoi*?' Social Network Analysis, Connectivity and the Greek *Poleis*." *Past and Present* 257:11–54.
Mackil, E. 2013. *Creating a Common Polity. Religion, Economy, and Politics in the Making of the Greek* Koinon. Berkeley.
Mackil, E. 2013b. "The Greek *Koinon*." In *The Oxford Handbook of the State in the Ancient Near East and Mediterranean*, edited by P.F. Bang and W. Scheidel. Oxford: 304–20.
Mackil, E. 2014. "Ethnos and Koinon." In *A Companion to Ethnicity in the Ancient Mediterranean*, edited by J. McInerney. Chichester: 270–84.
MacLachlan, B. 2007. "Epinician Swearing." In *Horkos. The Oath in Greek Society*, edited by A.H. Sommerstein and J. Fletcher. Exeter: 91–101.
Mac Sweeney, N. 2013. *Foundation Myths and Politics in Ancient Ionia*. Cambridge.
Maffi, A. 1983. *Studi di epigrafia giuridica greca*. Milan.
Maffi, A. 1999. "Emprisonnement pour dettes dans le monde grec." In *Carcer. Prison et privation de liberté dans l'antiquité classique*, edited by C. Bertrand-Dagenbach, A. Chauvot, M. Matter, and J.-M. Salamito. Paris: 7–17.
Maffi, A. 2001. "Hans Julius Wolff e gli studi di diritto greco a trent'anni dal I Symposion." *Dike* 4:269–91.
Maffi, A. 2014. "Identificare gli schiavi nei documenti greci." In *Identifiers and Identification Methods in the Ancient World*, edited by M. Depauw and S. Coussement. Leuven: 197–206.
Magnetto, A. 1997. *Gli arbitrati interstatali greci. Introduzione, testo critico, traduzione, commento e indici, Vol. 2, dal 337 al 196 a.C.* Pisa.
Magnetto, A. 2016. "Interstate Arbitration and Foreign Judges." In *The Oxford Handbook of Ancient Greek Law*, edited by E.M. Harris and M. Canevaro. Oxford: [unpaginated]. Available at: https://doi.org/10.1093/oxfordhb/9780199599257.013.20.
Magnetto, A. 2018. "Interstate Arbitration as a Feature of the Hellenistic Polis: Between Ideology, International Law and Civic Memory." In *The Polis in the Hellenistic World*, edited by H. Börm and N. Luraghi. Stuttgart: 85–107.
Maier, F.G. 1994. "Cyprus and Phoenicia." In *The Cambridge Ancient History. Second Edition. Vol. VI. The Fourth Century B.C.*, edited by D. Lewis, J. Boardman, S. Hornblower, and M. Ostwald. Cambridge: 297–336.
Maillot, S. 2015. "Foreigners' Associations and the Rhodian State." In *Private Associations and the Public Sphere*, edited by V. Gabrielsen and C.A. Thomsen. Copenhagen: 136–82.
Maitner, A.T., and Stewart-Ingersoll, R. 2016. "Social Identity and Peace in the Modern Middle East: Insights from the United Arab Emirates." In *Understanding Peace and Conflict through Social Identity Theory*, edited by S. McKeown, R. Haji, and N. Ferguson. Cham: 317–31.
Majer, C.F. 2017. *Das römische internationale Privatrecht*. Stuttgart.
Makarov, I.A. 2014. "Towards an Interpretation of the Civic Oath of the Chersonesites (*IOSPE* I2 401)." *Ancient Civilizations from Scythia to Siberia* 20:1–38.
Malay, H., and Ricl, M. 2009. "Two New Hellenistic Decrees from Agai in Aiolis." *Epigraphica Anatolica* 42:39–60.
Malkin, I. 1994. *Myth and Territory in the Spartan Mediterranean*. Cambridge.
Malkin, I. 2003. "Networks and the Emergence of Greek Identity." *Mediterranean Historical Review* 18:56–74.

Malkin, I. 2011. *A Small Greek World. Networks in the Ancient Mediterranean*. Oxford.
Malkin, I. 2016. "Greek Colonisation: The Right to Return." In *Conceptualising Early Colonisation*, edited by L. Donnellan, V. Nizzo, and G.-J. Burgers. Brussels: 27–49.
Malkin, I., Constantakopoulou, C., and Panagopoulou, K., eds. 2009. *Greek and Roman Networks in the Mediterranean*. London.
Manning, J.G. 2010. *The Last Pharaohs. Egypt under the Ptolemies, 305–30 BC*. Princeton.
Manning, J.G. 2018. *The Open Sea. The Economic Life of the Ancient Mediterranean World from the Iron Age to the Rise of Rome*. Princeton.
Manning, J.G., and Oliver, G.J. 2016. Review of J. Ober, *The Rise and Fall of Classical Greece* (Princeton 2015). *Journal of Economic History* 77:599–601.
Marek, C. 1984. *Die Proxenie*. New York.
Marinatos, N. 1993. "What Were Greek Sanctuaries? A Synthesis." In *Greek Sanctuaries. New Approaches*, edited by N. Marinatos and R. Hägg. London: 228–33.
Marks, S. 1995. "The Small States at Geneva." *World Affairs* 157:191–96.
Marmor, A. 2011. *Philosophy of Law*. Princeton.
Marquaille, C. 2008. "The Foreign Policy of Ptolemy II." In *Ptolemy II Philadelphus and His World*, edited by P. McKechnie and P. Guillaume. Leiden: 39–64.
Marr, J.L., and Rhodes, P.J. 2008. *The 'Old Oligarch.' The Constitution of the Athenians Attributed to Xenophon*. Oxford.
Martin, T.R. 1985. *Sovereignty and Coinage in Classical Greece*. Princeton.
Martin, T.R. 1995. "Coins, Mints, and the Polis." In *Sources for the Ancient Greek City-State*, edited by M.H. Hansen. Copenhagen: 257–91.
Martin, V. 1940. *La vie internationale dans la Grèce des cités (VIe–IVe s. av. J.-C.)*. Paris.
Martiny, S.E., and Rubin, M. 2016. "Towards a Clearer Understanding of Social Identity Theory's Self-Esteem Hypothesis." In *Understanding Peace and Conflict Through Social Identity Theory*, edited by S. McKeown, R. Haji, and N. Ferguson. Cham: 19–32.
Massar, N. 2020. "Skilled Workers in the Ancient Greek City: Public Employment, Selection Methods, and Evaluation." In *Skilled Labour and Professionalism in Ancient Greece and Rome*, edited by E. Stewart, E. Harris, and D.M. Lewis. Cambridge: 68–93.
Mataranga, K. 1994. "Un étrange «proxène» a Corcyre." *Revue archéologique*, n.s. 1:111–18.
Matthaiou, A.P. 2010. "A Treaty of Athens with Siphnos Revisited." In *Philathenaios*, edited by A. Tamis, C.J. Mackie, and S.G. Byrne. Athens: 45–54.
Matthäus, H. 2009. "Zeitenwenden im Mittelmeergebiet: Kunst und Kultur Zyperns zwischen 1100 und 750 v. Chr." In *Zypern — Insel im Schnittpunkt interkultureller Kontakte*, edited by R. Bol, K. Kleibl, and S. Rogge. Münster: 139–90.
May, P.J. 2004. "Compliance Motivations: Affirmative and Negative Bases." *Law & Society Review* 38:41–68.
McAuley, A. 2018. "From the Cradle: Reconstructing the *ephēbeia* in Hellenistic Megara." In *Megarian Moments*, edited by H. Beck and P.J. Smith. [*s.l.*]: 217–36.
McCloskey, D.N. 2006. *The Bourgeois Virtues: Ethics for an Age of Commerce*. Chicago.
McCloskey, D.N. 2010. *Bourgeois Dignity. Why Economics Can't Explain the Modern World*. Chicago.
McCloskey, D.N. 2016. "Max U *versus* Humanomics: A Critique of Neo-Institutionalism." *Journal of Institutional Economics* 12:1–27.
McCloskey, D.N. 2016b. "The Humanities Are Scientific: A Reply to the Defenses of Economic Neo-Institutionalism." *Journal of Institutional Economics* 12:63–78.
McCorquodale, R. 2010. "The Individual and the International Legal System." In *International Law*, edited by M.D. Evans. 4th ed. Oxford: 280–305.
McDermott, R. 2004. "The Feeling of Rationality: The Meaning of Neuroscientific Advances for Political Science." *Perspectives on Politics* 2:691–706.
McGinn, T.A.J. 1998. *Prostitution, Sexuality, and the Law in Ancient Rome*. Oxford.
McGinn, T.A.J. 2015. "The Expressive Function of Law and the *Lex Imperfecta*." *Roman Legal Tradition* 11:1–41.

McInerney, J. 2011. "Delphi and Phokis: A Network Theory Approach." *Pallas* 87:95–106.

Meadows, A.R. 2001. "Money, Freedom, and Empire in the Hellenistic World." In *Money and Its Uses in the Ancient Greek World*, edited by A.R. Meadows and K.M.W. Shipton. Oxford: 53–63.

Meadows, A.R. 2013. "The Ptolemaic League of the Islanders." In *The Ptolemies, the Sea and the Nile*, edited by K. Buraselis, M. Stefanou, and D.J. Thompson. Cambridge: 19–38.

Mearsheimer, J.J. 2006. "Structural Realism." In *International Relations Theories*, edited by T. Dunne, M. Kurki, and S. Smith. Oxford: 71–88.

Mebane, J. 2024. *The Body Politic in Roman Political Thought.* Cambridge.

Megiddo, T. 2019. "Methodological Individualism." *Harvard International Law Journal* 60:219–65.

Megiddo, T. 2021. "The Missing Persons of International Law Scholarship. A Roadmap for Future Research." In *International Law as Behavior*, edited by H.G. Cohen and T. Meyer. Cambridge: 230–64.

Mégret, F. 2021. "The Anti-deterrence Hypothesis. What if International Criminal Justice Encouraged Crime?" *Journal of International Criminal Justice* 19:859–76.

Mehl, A. 2013. "Zyperns Rolle im Überseehandel mit dem Ägäisraum (5.–4. Jh. v. Chr.)." In *Handels- und Finanzgebaren in der Ägäis im 5. Jh. v. Chr.*, edited by A. Slawisch. Istanbul: 135–53.

Meiggs, R. 1949. "A Note on Athenian Imperialism." *Classical Review* 63:9–12.

Meiggs, R. 1972. *The Athenian Empire.* Oxford.

Meister, R.M.E. 1908. "Eideshelfer im griechischen Rechte." *Rheinisches Museum für Philologie* 63:559–86.

Mele, A. 1979. *Il commercio greco arcaico prexis ed emporie.* Naples.

Mello, M.M., and Brennan, T.A. 2002. "Deterrence of Medical Errors: Theory and Evidence for Malpractice Reform." *Texas Law Review* 80:1595–1637.

Ménard, C., and Shirley, M.M., eds. 2005. *Handbook of New Institutional Economics.* Dordrecht.

Meritt, B.D. 1946. "Greek Inscriptions." *Hesperia* 15:169–253.

Meritt, B.D., Wade-Gery, H.T., and McGregor, M.F. 1939–53. *The Athenian Tribute Lists.* 4 vols. Cambridge, Mass.

Merry, S.E., and Silbey, S.S. 1984. "What Do Plaintiffs Want? Reexamining the Concept of Dispute." *The Justice System Journal* 9:151–78.

Merton, R.K., and Rossi, A.S. 1957. "Contributions to the Theory of Reference Group Behavior." In R.K. Merton, *Social Theory and Social Structure*, revised and enlarged ed. New York: 225–80.

Meyer, E. 1892. *Forschungen zur alten Geschichte. I. Zur älteren griechischen Geschichte.* Halle.

Meyer, E. 1909. *Theopomps Hellenika.* Hildesheim.

Meyer, E. 1925. *Die Grenzen der hellenistischen Staaten in Kleinasien.* Leipzig.

Meyer, E.A. 2004. *Legitimacy and Law in the Roman World.* Tabulae *in Roman Belief and Practice.* Cambridge.

Meyer, E.A. 2010. *Metics and the Athenian* Phialai-*Inscriptions. A Study in Athenian Epigraphy and Law.* Stuttgart.

Meyer, E.A. 2013. *The Inscriptions of Dodona and a New History of Molossia.* Stuttgart.

Meyer, E.A. 2023. "Metics and Freedmen: Conflicts of Social and Juridical Status in the Classical and Hellenistic Greek World." *American Journal of Legal History* 63:82–96.

Meyer, J.W., Ramirez, F.O., and Soysal, Y.N. 1992. "World Expansion of Mass Education, 1870–1980." *Sociology of Education* 65:128–49.

Michaels, R., and Jansen, N. 2006. "Private Law beyond the State? Europeanization, Globalization, Privatization." *American Journal of Comparative Law* 54:843–90.

Migeotte, L. 1984. *L'emprunt public dans les cités grecques. Recueil des documents et analyse critique.* Paris.

Mili, M. 2014. *Religion and Society in Ancient Thessaly.* Oxford.

Mili, M. 2019. "Ἄπιστα τὰ τῶν Θετταλῶν: The Dubious Thessalian State." In *Ethnos and Koinon*, edited by H. Beck, K. Buraselis, and A. McAuley. Stuttgart: 271–83.

Miller, W.C. 2016. *Nordic Modernism. Scandinavian Architecture, 1890–2015*. Ramsbury.

Miller, W.I. 1990. *Bloodtaking and Peacemaking. Feud, Law, and Society in Saga Iceland*. Chicago.

Mintz, A., and DeRouen, K. 2010. *Understanding Foreign Policy Decision Making*. Cambridge.

Mintz, A., and Wayne, C. 2016. "The Polythink Syndrome and Elite Group Decision-Making." *Political Psychology* 37(Supp.):3–21.

Mitchell, B.M. 1966. "Cyrene and Persia." *Journal of Hellenic Studies* 86:99–113.

Mitchell, L.G. 1997. *Greeks Bearing Gifts. The Public Use of Private Relationships in the Greek World, 435–323 BC*. Cambridge.

Mitchell, L.G. 2007. *Panhellenism and the Barbarian in Archaic and Classical Greece*. Swansea.

Mitchell, L.G. 2015. "The Community of the Hellenes." In *Federalism in Greek Antiquity*, edited by H. Beck and P. Funke. Cambridge: 49–65.

Mitteis, L. 1891. *Reichsrecht und Volksrecht in den östlichen Provinzen des römischen Kaiserreichs*. Leipzig.

Mélèze Modrzejewski, J. 2011. *Droit et justice dans le monde grec et hellénistique*. Warsaw.

Moggi, M. 1976. *I sinecismi interstatali greci. Volume 1: dalle origini al 338 a.C.* Pisa.

Mokyr, J. 2014. "Culture, Institutions, and Modern Growth." In *Institutions, Property Rights, and Economic Growth*, edited by S. Galiani and I. Sened. Cambridge: 151–91.

Mokyr, J. 2017. *A Culture of Growth. The Origins of the Modern Economy*. Princeton.

Möller, A. 2000. *Naukratis. Trade in Archaic Greece*. Oxford.

Momigliano, A. 1932. "Tagia e tetrarchia in Tessaglia." *Athenaeum* 10:47–53.

Momigliano, A. 1964. "Le conseguenze del rinnovamento della storia dei diritti antichi." *Rivista Storica Italiana* 76:133–49.

Mooren, L. 1983. "The Nature of the Hellenistic Monarchy." In *Egypt and the Hellenistic World*, edited by E. Van 't Dack, P. Van Dessel, and W. Van Gucht. Leuven: 205–40.

Mooring, J. 2022. "Weak and Strong Ties in the Diffusion of Coinage During the Archaic Period in Greece." In *Networks and the Spread of Ideas in the Past*, edited by A. Collar. London: 79–98.

Moran, W.L. 1992. *The Amarna Letters*. Baltimore.

Morgan, C. 1990. *Athletes and Oracles. The Transformation of Olympia and Delphi in the Eighth Century BC*. Cambridge.

Morgan, C. 2003. *Early Greek States beyond the Polis*. New York.

Morgan, T. 1998. *Literate Education in the Hellenistic and Roman Worlds*. Cambridge.

Morgenthau, H.J., and Thompson, K.W. 1984. *Politics among Nations. The Struggle for Power and Peace*. 6th ed. New York.

Morizot, Y. 1994. "Artémis, l'eau et la vie humaine." In *L'eau, la santé et la maladie dans le monde grec*, edited by R. Ginouvès, A.-M. Guimier-Sorbets, J. Jouanna, and L. Villard. BCH Supplément 28. Paris: 201–16.

Morley, N. 2022. "The Poetics and Politics of Exchange in Roman Agronomy." In *Debt in the Ancient Mediterranean and Near East*, edited by J. Weisweiler. Oxford: 84–101.

Moroo, A. 2014. "The Erythrai Decrees Reconsidered: *IG* I[3] 14, 15 & 16." In *ΑΘΗΝΑΙΩΝ ΕΠΙΣΚΟΠΟΣ. Studies in Honour of Harold B. Mattingly*, edited by A.P. Matthaiou and R.K. Pitt. Athens: 97–119.

Morris, I. 2000. *Archaeology as Cultural History. Words and Things in Iron Age Greece*. Malden, Mass.

Morris, I. 2009. "The Greater Athenian State." In *The Dynamics of Ancient Empires*, edited by I. Morris and W. Scheidel. Oxford: 99–177.

Morris, I. 2013. "Greek Multicity States." In *The Oxford Handbook of the State in the Ancient Near East and Mediterranean*, edited by P.F. Bang and W. Scheidel. Oxford: 279–300.

Morrison, J.S. (with H.T. Wade-Gery). 1942. "Meno of Pharsalus, Polycrates, and Ismenias." *Classical Quarterly* 36:57–78.

Morrow, G.R. 1960. *Plato's Cretan City. A Historical Interpretation of the* Laws. Princeton.

Morwood, J. 2007. *Euripides. Suppliant Women*. Oxford.

Motyl, A.J. 1982. "The Foreign Relations of the Ukrainian SSR." *Harvard Ukrainian Studies* 6:62–78.

Müller, C. 2014. "(De)constructing Politeia. Reflections on Citizenship and the Bestowal of Privileges upon Foreigners in Hellenistic Democracies." *Annales HSS* 69:533–54.

Müller, C. 2022. "Migration et mémoire: Milet et ses apoikiai à l'époque hellénistique." In *Ionians in the West and East*, edited by G.R. Tsetskhladze. Leuven: 333–60.

Müri, W. 1931. "ΣΥΜΒΟΛΟΝ. Wort- und sachgeschichtliche Studie." *Beilage zum Jahresbericht über das städtische Gymnasium im Bern* I–III:1–46.

Murphy, E. 2020. "Early Modern English Piracy and Privateering." In *The Routledge Companion to Marine and Maritime Worlds, 1400–1800*, edited by C. Jowitt, C. Lambert, and S. Mentz. London: 368–87.

Murphy, K. 2017. "Procedural Justice and Its Role in Promoting Voluntary Compliance." In *Regulatory Theory. Foundations and Applications*, edited by P. Drahos. Acton: 43–58.

Murray, O. 1988. "The Ionian Revolt." In *The Cambridge Ancient History. Second Edition. Vol. IV. Persia, Greece and the Western Mediterranean, c.525 to 479 BC*, edited by J. Boardman, N.G.L. Hammond, D. Lewis, and M. Ostwald. Cambridge: 461–90.

Murray, S.C. 2017. *The Collapse of the Mycenaean Economy. Imports, Trade, and Institutions, 1300–700 BCE*. Cambridge.

Mutua, M. 2000. "What Is TWAIL?" *American Society of International Law. Proceedings of the Annual Meeting* 94:31–38.

Mylonas, G.E. 1961. *Eleusis and the Eleusinian Mysteries*. Princeton.

Myres, J.L. 1943. "ΑΚΗΡΥΚΤΟΣ ΠΟΛΕΜΟΣ (Herodotus, v.81)." *Classical Review* 57:66–67.

Nagin, D.S. 1998. "Criminal Deterrence Research at the Outset of the Twenty-First Century." *Crime and Justice: An Annual Review of Research* 23:1–42.

Nagin, D.S. 2013. "Deterrence in the Twenty-First Century: A Review of the Evidence." *Crime and Justice: An Annual Review of Research* 42:199–263.

Nagin, D.S., and Paternoster, R. 1993. "Enduring Individual Differences and Rational Choice Theories of Crime." *Law & Society Review* 27:467–96.

Nagin, D.S., and Telep, C.W. 2017. "Procedural Justice and Legal Compliance." *Annual Review of Law and Social Science* 13:5–28.

Nawotka, K., ed. 2021. *Epigraphic Culture in the Eastern Mediterranean in Antiquity*. London.

Nawotka, K. 2021b. "Introduction. Epigraphic Habit, Epigraphic Culture, Epigraphic Curve: Statement of the Problem." In *Epigraphic Culture in the Eastern Mediterranean in Antiquity*, edited by K. Nawotka. London: 1–30.

Neer, R.T., and Kurke, L. 2019. *Pindar, Song, and Space. Towards a Lyric Archaeology*. Baltimore.

Neff, S.C. 2010. "A Short History of International Law." In *International Law*, edited by M.D. Evans. 4th ed. Oxford: 3–28.

Neff, S.C. 2014. *Justice among Nations. A History of International Law*. Cambridge, Mass.

Nesbitt-Larking, P., Kinnvall, C., Capelos, T., and Dekker, H. 2014. *The Palgrave Handbook of Global Political Psychology*. New York.

Netz, R. 2020. *Scale, Space and Canon in Ancient Literary Culture*. Cambridge.

Nevett, L. 2023. *Ancient Greek Housing*. Cambridge.

Newby, Z., ed. 2023. *The Material Dynamics of Festivals in the Graeco-Roman East*. Oxford.

Newman, M.E.J., Barabási, A.-L., and Watts, D.J., eds. 2006. *The Structure and Dynamics of Networks*. Princeton.

Niblett, A., Posner, R.A., and Shleifer, A. 2010. "The Evolution of a Legal Rule." *Journal of Legal Studies* 39:325–58.

Nicholson, E. 2020. "Hellenic Romans and Barbaric Macedonians: Polybius on Hellenism and Changing Hegemonic Powers." *Ancient History Bulletin* 34:38–73.

Nicholson, E. 2023. *Philip V of Macedon in Polybius' Histories. Politics, History, and Fiction*. Oxford.

Nielsen, T.H. 2007. *Olympia and the Classical Hellenic City-State Culture*. Copenhagen.

Nielsen, T.H. 2015. "The Arkadian Confederacy." In *Federalism in Greek Antiquity*, edited by H. Beck and P. Funke. Cambridge: 250–68.

Nieto Izquierdo, E. 2024. "Une Ennodia 'de la cité' a-t-elle existé en Thessalie? À propos de l'épithète ϝαστικα dans *IG* IX 2, No. 575." *Zeitschrift für Papyrologie und Epigraphik* 232:116–22.

Nilsson, M.P. 1906. *Griechische Feste von Religiöser Bedeutung*. Leipzig.

Nobili, C. 2022. "Teseo fra Trezene, Sparta e Atene." *Museum Helveticum* 79:9–24.

Nocita, M., and Guizzi, F. 2009. "At the Periphragma of Dionysos." In Πρακτικά Γ' Διεθνούς Σιφναϊκού Συμπόσιου. Σίφνος 29 Ιουνίου – 2 Ιουλίου 2006. Athens: 136–40.

North, D.C. 1981. *Structure and Change in Economic History*. New York.

North, D.C. 1990. *Institutions, Institutional Change, and Economic Performance*. Cambridge.

North, D.C. 2005. *Understanding the Process of Economic Change*. Princeton.

North, D.C., Wallis, J.J., and Weingast, B.R. 2009. *Violence and Social Orders. A Conceptual Framework for Interpreting Recorded Human History*. Cambridge.

Nowakowski, P. 2013. "A New Fragment of the 'Syla Inscription' from Cyrene." *Zeitschrift für Papyrologie und Epigraphik* 186:212–21.

Nudell, J.P. 2016. "The War between Miletus and Samos περὶ Πριήνης (Thuc. 1.115.2; Diod. Sic. 12.27.2; and Plut. *Per.* 25.1)." *Classical Quarterly* 66:772–74.

Nutkiewicz, M. 1983. "Samuel Pufendorf: Obligation as the Basis of the State." *Journal of the History of Philosophy* 21:15–29.

Ober, J. 1989. *Mass and Elite in Democratic Athens. Rhetoric, Ideology, and the Power of the People*. Princeton.

Ober, J. 1994. "Classical Greek Times." In *The Laws of War: Constraints on Warfare in the Western World*, edited by M. Howard, G.J. Andreopoulos, and M.R. Shulman. New Haven: 12–26.

Ober, J. 1998. *Political Dissent in Democratic Athens. Intellectual Critics of Popular Rule*. Princeton.

Ober, J. 2008. *Democracy and Knowledge. Innovation and Learning in Classical Athens*. Princeton.

Ober, J. 2009. "Thucydides *Theôrêtikos*/Thucydides *Histôr*: Realist Theory and the Challenge of History." In *Oxford Readings in Classical Studies. Thucydides*, edited by J.S. Rusten. Oxford: 434–78.

Ober, J. 2015. *The Rise and Fall of Classical Greece*. Princeton.

Ober, J. 2015b. "Access, Fairness, and Transaction Costs. Nikophon's Law on Silver Coinage (Athens, 375/4 B.C.E.)." In *Law and Transaction Costs in the Ancient Economy*, edited by D. Kehoe, D.M. Ratzan, and U. Yiftach. Ann Arbor: 51–79.

Ober, J. 2018. "Introduction." In *Ancient Greek History and Contemporary Social Science*, edited by M. Canevaro, A. Erskine, B. Gray, and J. Ober. Edinburgh: 1–12.

Ober, J. 2022. *The Greeks and the Rational. The Discovery of Practical Reason*. Oakland.

Obsomer, C. 2003. "Hérodote II 148 à l'origine du mot Labyrinthos? La Minotauromachie revisitée." In *Cretan Studies, Vol 9. Briciaka*, edited by Y. Duhoux. Amsterdam: 105–86.

O'Connell, M.E. 2008. *The Power and Purpose of International Law. Insights from the Theory and Practice of Enforcement*. Oxford.

Ogden, S.R. 2022. *Averroes on Intellect. From Aristotelian Origins to Aquinas's Critique*. Oxford.

O'Halloran, B. 2019. *The Political Economy of Classical Athens. A Naval Perspective*. Leiden.

Oikonomides, I.N. 1850. Λοκριῆς Ανεκδότου Επιγραφῆς Διαφώτισις. Kerkyrai.

Olson, J.M., and Stone, J. 2005. "The Influence of Behavior on Attitudes." In *The Handbook of Attitudes*, edited by D. Albarracin, B.T. Johnson, and M.P. Zanna. Mahwah, NJ: 222–72.

Onuf, N. 1989. *World of Our Making. Rules and Rule in Social Theory and International Relations*. Columbia, S.C.

Orford, A. 2021. *International Law and the Politics of History*. Cambridge.

Origgi, G. 2018. *Reputation. What It Is and Why It Matters*. Princeton.

Ormerod, H.A. 1924. *Piracy in the Ancient World. An Essay in Mediterranean History*. Liverpool.

Osborne, M.J. 1981. *Naturalization in Athens*. 2 vols. Brussels.
Osborne, R. 1996. "Pots, Trade and the Archaic Greek Economy." *Antiquity* 70:31–44.
Osborne, R. 2009. *Greece in the Making, 1200–479 BC*. 2nd ed. London.
Osborne, R. 2015. "Unity vs. Diversity." In *The Oxford Handbook of Ancient Greek Religion*, edited by E. Eidinow and J. Kindt. Oxford: 11–20.
Ostrom, E. 1990. *Governing the Commons. The Evolution of Institutions for Collective Action*. Cambridge.
Ostwald, M. 1969. *Nomos and the Beginnings of the Athenian Democracy*. Oxford.
Ostwald, M. 1982. *AUTONOMIA: Its Genesis and Early History*. Chico, CA.
Padovan, R. 2013. *Towards Universality. Le Corbusier, Mies and De Stijl*. Hoboken, NJ.
Paga, J. 2021. *Building Democracy in Late Archaic Athens*. Oxford.
Palamidis, A. 2025. "Les sanctuaires grecs antiques: des lieux de savoirs." *Revue de l'histoire des religions* 242:5–35.
Paneris, J.R. 1983. "Die eigenhändige Tötung des Räubers bei Demokrit und des nächtlichen Einbrechers bei Platon." *Philologus* 127:298–302.
Panno, G. 2017. "*Nomos* e *mousike*: uso politico delle emozioni in Platone (*Reppublica, Leggi*) e Aristotele (*Politica*)." *Rivista di Diritto Ellenico* 7:83–108.
Papakonstantinou, Z. 2008. *Lawmaking and Adjudication in Archaic Greece*. London.
Papakonstantinou, Z. 2019. *Sport and Identity in Ancient Greece*. London.
Papantoniou, G. 2013. "Cypriot Autonomous Polities at the Crossroads of Empire: The Imprint of a Transformed Islandscape in the Classical and Hellenistic Periods." *Bulletin of the American Schools of Oriental Research* 370:169–205.
Papazarkadas, N. 2009. "Epigraphy and the Athenian Empire: Reshuffling the Chronological Cards." In *Interpreting the Athenian Empire*, edited by J. Ma, N. Papazarkadas, and R. Parker. London: 67–88.
Papazarkadas, N. 2014. "Athens, Sigeion and the Politics of Approbation during the Ionian War." In *ΑΘΗΝΑΙΩΝ ΕΠΙΣΚΟΠΟΣ. Studies in Honour of Harold B. Mattingly*, edited by A.P. Matthaiou and R.K. Pitt. Athens: 215–40.
Papazarkadas, N. 2019. "Festival Networks in Late Hellenistic Boeotia: From Kinship to Political Rejuvenation." In *La cité interconnectée dans le monde gréco-romain*, edited by M. Dana and I. Savalli-Lestrade. Bordeaux: 205–21.
Papazarkadas, N., and Papadopoulou, Z.D. 2010–13. "Σιφναϊκὸ ψήφισμα ὑπὲρ Ἀμφιχάρους Σεριφίου." *Horos* 22–25:453–80.
Parisi, F., ed. 2017. *The Oxford Handbook of Law and Economics*. 3 vols. Oxford.
Parke, H.W., and Wormell, D.E.W. 1956. *The Delphic Oracle*. 2 vols. Oxford.
Parker, R. 1996. *Athenian Religion: A History*. Oxford.
Parker, R. 1998. *Cleomenes on the Acropolis. An Inaugural Lecture Delivered before the University of Oxford on 12 May 1997*. Oxford.
Parker, R. 2004. "New 'Panhellenic' Festivals in Hellenistic Greece." In *Mobility and Travel in the Mediterranean from Antiquity to the Middle Ages*, edited by R. Schlesier and U. Zellmann. Münster: 9–22.
Parker, R. 2004b. "One Man's Piety: The Religious Dimension of the *Anabasis*." In *The Long March. Xenophon and the Ten Thousand*, edited by R. Lane Fox. New Haven: 131–53.
Parker, R. 2004c. "What Are Greek Sacred Laws?" In *The Law and the Courts in Ancient Greece*, edited by E.M. Harris and L. Rubinstein. London: 57–70.
Parker, R. 2011. *On Greek Religion*. Ithaca.
Parker, R. 2011b. "The Thessalian Olympia." *Zeitschrift für Papyrologie und Epigraphik* 177:111–18.
Parker, R. 2017. *Greek Gods Abroad. Names, Natures, and Transformations*. Oakland.
Parker, R. 2018. "Regionality and Greek Ritual Norms." *Kernos* 31:73–81.
Parmeggiani, G. 2021. "Athens Struggling with Her Allies. A Note on Thucydides 1.77.1." *Ancient Society* 51:1–14.
Parmenter, C.S. 2020. "Journeys into Slavery along the Black Sea Coast, c. 550–450 BCE." *Classical Antiquity* 39:57–94.

Parsons, C.A., Sulaeman, J., and Titman, S. 2018. "The Geography of Financial Misconduct." *The Journal of Finance* 73:2087–137.
Partington, S., Kamtekar, R., and Nichols, S. 2025. "Norms Emerge through Iterated Learning." *Proceedings of the National Academy of Sciences* 122(29):1–10.
Paschalidis, P. 2023. "Note: The Heirs of Pausimachus v City of Kalymnos Arbitration." *Arbitration International* 39:[not yet paginated].
Paschidis, P. 2008. *Between City and King: Prosopographical Studies on the Intermediaries between the Cities of the Greek Mainland and the Aegean and the Royal Courts in the Hellenistic Period, 322–190 BC.* Paris.
Pébarthe, C. 2006. *Cité, démocratie et écriture. Histoire de l'alphabétisation d'Athènes à l'époque classique.* Brussels.
Pébarthe, C. 2007. "Contrats et justice dans l'empire athénien: les *symbolai* dans le décret d'Athènes relatif à Phasélis (*IG*, I^3, 10)." In *Scripta Anatolica*, edited by P. Brun. Bordeaux: 237–60.
Pelliccia, H. (forthcoming). "Homer as Model of Rhetorical Art." *The Cambridge History of Rhetoric*, edited by R. Copeland and P. Mack. Cambridge.
Pelloso, C. 2016. "*Ephesis eis to dikasterion*: Remarks and Speculations on the Legal Nature of the Solonian Reform." In *Symposion 2015*, edited by D.F. Leão and G. Thür. Vienna: 33–48.
Perlman, P. 1995. "*Invocatio* and *imprecatio*. The Hymn to the Greatest Kouros from Palaikastro and the Oath in Ancient Crete." *Journal of Hellenic Studies* 115:161–67.
Perlman, P. 1996. "Πόλις Ὑπήκοος: The Dependent Polis and Crete." In *Introduction to an Inventory of Poleis*, edited by M.H. Hansen. Copenhagen: 233–87.
Perlman, P. 1999. "KRETES AIEI LEISTAI? The Marginalization of Crete in Greek Thought and the Role of Piracy in the Outbreak of the First Cretan War." In *Hellenistic Rhodes: Politics, Culture and Society*, edited by V. Gabrielsen, P. Bilde, T. Engberg-Pedersen, L. Hannestad, and J. Zahle. Aarhus: 110–34.
Perlman, P. 2000. *City and Sanctuary in Ancient Greece: The Theorodokia in the Peloponnese.* Göttingen.
Perrin, B. 1902. "The Nikias of Pasiphon and Plutarch." *TAPA* 33:139–49.
Pestarino, B. 2022. Kypriōn Politeia, *the Political and Administrative Systems of the Classical Cypriot City-Kingdoms.* Leiden.
Petit, T. 2019. *La naissance des cités-royaumes cypriotes.* Oxford.
Petrochilos, N. 2019. "The Archaeological and Epigraphic Testimonies for the *ethnos* of the Western Lokrians." In *Ethnos and Koinon*, edited by H. Beck, K. Buraselis, and A. McAuley. Stuttgart: 45–64.
Pettigrew, T.F., and Tropp, L.R. 2006. "A Meta-Analytic Test of Intergroup Contact Theory." *Journal of Personality and Social Psychology* 90:751–83.
Pettit, P. 2002. "Collective Persons and Powers." *Legal Theory* 8:443–70.
Phillimore, R. 1871. *Commentaries upon International Law.* 4 vols. London.
Phillipson, C. 1911. *The International Law and Custom of Ancient Greece and Rome.* 2 vols. London.
Piccirilli, L. 1973. *Gli arbitrati interstatali greci, vol. 1: dalle origini al 338 a.C.* Pisa.
Piccirilli, L. 2002. *L'invenzione della diplomazia nella Grecia antica.* Rome.
Piñol-Villanueva, Adrià. 2017. "Halicarnassus – Salmakis. A Pre-Classical *Sympoliteia*?" *Klio* 99:26–50.
Pitt, R.K. 2016. "Inscribing Construction: The Financing and Administration of Public Building in Greek Sanctuaries." In *A Companion to Greek Architecture*, edited by M.M. Miles. Malden, Mass: 194–205.
Pitts, J. 2018. *Boundaries of the International. Law and Empire.* Cambridge, Mass.
Plant, I. 2015. "Thucydides, Timotheus and the Epitaph for Euripides." *Classical Journal* 110:385–96.
Plassart, A. 1921. "La liste des théorodoques." *Bulletin de correspondance hellénique* 45:1–85.
Pleket, H.W. 1992. "The Participants in the Ancient Olympic Games: Social Background and Mentality." In *Proceedings of an International Symposium on the Olympic Games, 5–9 September 1988*, edited by W. Coulson and H. Kyrieleis. Athens: 147–52.

Plescia, J. 1970. *The Oath and Perjury in Ancient Greece.* Tallahassee.
Poddighe, E. 2013. "Propaganda Strategies and Political Documents: Philip III's *Diagramma* and the Greeks in 319 BC." In *After Alexander. The Time of the Diadochi (323–281 BC)*, edited by V.A. Troncoso and E.M. Anson. Oxford: 225–40.
Posner, R.A. 1993. "The New Institutional Economics Meets Law and Economics." *Journal of Institutional and Theoretical Economics* 149:73–87.
Posner, R.A. 2014. *Economic Analysis of Law.* 9th ed. New York.
Potts, A., Maadad, N., and Yu, M. 2018. "Children and Television: Vicarious Socialisation Experiences." *Research on Education and Media* 10:20–29.
Pouilloux, J. 1975. "Athènes et Salamine de Chypre." *Report of the Department of Antiquities, Cyprus* (1975):111–22.
Pouilloux, J. 1976. "L'hellénisme à Salamine de Chypre." *Bulletin de correspondance hellénique* 100:449–60.
Pritchard, D.M. 2015. "Public Finance and War in Ancient Greece." *Greece & Rome* 62:48–59.
Pritchett, W.K. 1991. *The Greek State at War. Part V.* Berkeley.
Procopé, J.F. 1989. "Democritus on Politics and the Care of the Soul." *Classical Quarterly* 39:307–31.
Procopé, J.F. 1990. "Democritus on Politics and the Care of the Soul: Appendix." *Classical Quarterly* 40:21–45.
Psoma, S.E. 2024. "Deconstructing a Prussian Myth: The Athenian Standards Decree (*IG* I3 1453a–g)." *Tekmeria* 18:231–82.
Pugliese Carratelli, G. 1961–62. "Supplemento Epigrafico Cirenaico." *Annuario della Scuola Archeologica Italiana di Atene* 39–40:219–375.
Putin, V. 2021. "On the Historical Unity of Russians and Ukrainians." Available at: http://en.kremlin.ru/events/president/news/66181.
Quaß, F. 1993. *Die Honoratiorenschicht in den Städten des griechischen Ostens.* Stuttgart.
Raaflaub, K.A. 1997. "Homeric Society." In *A New Companion to Homer*, edited by I. Morris and B. Powell. Leiden: 624–48.
Raaflaub, K.A. 2004. *The Discovery of Freedom in Ancient Greece.* Chicago.
Radin, M. 1910. *The Legislation of the Greeks and Romans on Corporations.* New York.
Rainey, A.F., and Schneidewind, W.M. 2015. *The El-Amarna Correspondence. A New Edition of the Cuneiform Letters from the Site of El-Amarna Based on Collations of All Extant Tablets.* Leiden.
Rassia, A.-I. 2021. "The Hero-Cult of Hippolytus in Troezen." *Logeion* 11:108–27.
Ratner, R.K., and Miller, D.T. 2001. "The Norm of Self-Interest and Its Effects on Social Action." *Journal of Personality and Social Psychology* 81:5–16.
Raubitschek, A.E. 1948. "The Case against Alcibiades (Andocides IV)." *Transactions and Proceedings of the American Philological Association* 79:191–210.
Rauh, N.K. 1993. *The Sacred Bonds of Commerce. Religion, Economy, and Trade Society at Hellenistic Roman Delos, 166–87 B. C.* Amsterdam.
Rawlings, H.R. 1977. "Thucydides on the Purpose of the Delian League." *Phoenix* 31:1–8.
Raz, J. 1970. *The Concept of a Legal System. An Introduction to the Theory of a Legal System.* Oxford.
Raz, J. 1979. "The Rule of Law and Its Virtue." In *The Authority of Law.* Oxford: 210–29.
Raz, J. 1999. *Practical Reason and Norms.* Revised ed. Oxford.
Rechenauer, G. 1993. "Zu Thukydides II 22,3: . . . ἀπὸ τῆς στάσεως ἑκάτερος . . . " *Rheinisches Museum für Philologie* 136:238–44.
Reden, S. von, ed. 2020–2022. *Handbook of Ancient Afro-Eurasian Economies.* 2 vols. Berlin.
Reden, S. von. 2021. "The Politics of Endowments." In *Benefactors and the Polis*, edited by M. Domingo Gygax. Cambridge: 115–36.
Reden, S. von. 2022. "Economic Dynamics in the Hellenistic Empires." In *Handbook of Ancient Afro-Eurasian Economies*, Vol. 2, edited by S. von Reden. Berlin: 591–629.
Reden, S. von, and Kowalzig B. 2022. "New Institutional Economics, Economic Growth, and Institutional Change." In *The Cambridge Companion to the Ancient Greek Economy*, edited by S. von Reden. Cambridge: 347–59.

Reden, S. von, and Ruffing, K., eds. 2023. *Handbuch Antike Wirtschaft.* Berlin.

Rediker, M. 2004. *Villains of All Nations. Atlantic Pirates in the Golden Age.* Boston.

Redlawsk, D.P., and Lau, R.R. 2013. "Behavioral Decision-Making." In *The Oxford Handbook of Political Psychology.* 2nd ed., edited by L. Huddy, D.O. Sears, and J.S. Levy. Oxford: 130–64.

Reeve, C.D.C. 2017. *Aristotle Politics. A New Translation.* Indianapolis.

Reger, G. 1992. "Athens and Tenos in the Early Hellenistic Age." *Classical Quarterly* 42:365–83.

Reger, G. 1994. "The Political History of the Kyklades 260–200 B.C." *Historia* 43:32–69.

Renfrew, C. 1986. "Introduction: Peer Polity Interaction and Socio-Political Change." In *Peer Polity Interaction and Socio-Political Change,* edited by C. Renfrew and J.F. Cherry. Cambridge: 1–18.

Renzsch, W. 1989. "German Federalism in Historical Perspective: Federalism as a Substitute for a National State." *Publius* 19(4):17–33.

Rhodes, P.J. 1972. *The Athenian Boule.* Oxford.

Rhodes, P.J. 1981. *A Commentary on the Aristotelian* Athenaion Politeia. Oxford.

Rhodes, P.J. 1987. "Thucydides on the Causes of the Peloponnesian War." *Hermes* 115:154–65.

Rhodes, P.J. 1992. "The Delian League to 449 B.C." In *The Cambridge Ancient History. Second Edition. Volume V. The Fifth Century B.C.,* edited by D. Lewis, J. Boardman, J.K. Davies, and M. Ostwald. Cambridge: 34–61.

Rhodes, P.J. 1995. "Epigraphical Evidence: Laws and Decrees." In *Sources for the Ancient Greek City-State: Symposium August, 24-27 1994,* edited by M.H. Hansen. Copenhagen: 91–112.

Rhodes, P.J. 1997. *The Decrees of the Greek States.* With D. Lewis. Oxford.

Rhodes, P.J. 2017. *The Athenian Constitution Written in the School of Aristotle.* Liverpool.

Richard, C.J. 2009. *The Golden Age of the Classics in America. Greece, Rome, and the Antebellum United States.* Cambridge, Mass.

Richards, R. 2002. "Kuhnian Values and Cladistic Parsimony." *Perspectives on Science* 10:1–27.

Richman, B.D. 2017. *Stateless Commerce. The Diamond Network and the Persistence of Relational Exchange.* Cambridge, Mass.

Richter, R. 2015. *Essays on New Institutional Economics.* Cham.

Rigsby, K.J. 1996. *Asylia. Territorial Inviolability in the Hellenistic World.* Berkeley.

Rihll, T. 1993. "War, Slavery, and Settlement in Early Greece." In *War and Society in the Greek World,* edited by J. Rich and G. Shipley. London: 77–107.

Rizakis, A. 2015. "The Achaian League." In *Federalism in Greek Antiquity,* edited by H. Beck and P. Funke. Cambridge: 118–31.

Robert, L. 1925. "Lesbiaca, I: Décrets de Méthymna et d' Érésos en honneur de juges milésiens." *Revue des études grecques* 38:29–43.

Robert, L. 1929. "Notes d'épigraphie hellénistique." *Bulletin de correspondance hellénique* 53:151–65.

Robert, L. 1936. "Notes d'épigraphie hellénistique." *Bulletin de correspondance hellénique* 60:184–89.

Robert, L. 1938. *Études épigraphiques et philologiques.* Bibliothèque de l'École des Hautes Études fasc. 272. Paris.

Robert, L. 1966. *Documents de l'Asie Mineure méridionale. Inscriptions, monnaies et géographie* . Geneva.

Robert, L. 1973. "Les juges étrangers dans la cité grecque." In *XENION. Festschrift für Pan. J. Zepos. Anlässlich seines 65. Geburtstages am 1. Dezember 1973,* edited by E. von Caemmerer, J.H. Kaiser, G. Kegel, W. Müller-Freienfels, and H.J. Wolff. Athens: 765–82.

Robert, L. 1984. "Les concours grecs." In *Actes du VIIIe congrès international d'épigraphie grecque et latine.* Athens: 35–45.

Robinson, P.H., and Darley, J.M. 2004. "Does Criminal Law Deter? A Behavioral Science Investigation." *Oxford Journal of Legal Studies* 24:173–205.

Roebuck, C. 1955. "The Early Ionian League." *Classical Philology* 50:26–40.

Roesch, P. 1982. *Études béotiennes.* Paris.

Roesch, P. 1985. "La justice en Béotie à l'époque hellénistique." In *Actes du troisième congrès international sur la Béotie antique,* edited by J.M. Fossey and H. Giroux. Amsterdam: 127–34.

Roesch, P., and Argoud, G. 1993. "Décret de Thèbes pour des juges d'Oropos." *Zeitschrift für Papyrologie und Epigraphik* 95:141–46.

Roisman, H.M. 2005. "Nestor the Good Counselor." *Classical Quarterly* 55:17–38.

Roller, D.W. 2018. *A Historical and Topographical Guide to the Geography of Strabo.* Cambridge.

Roller, L.E. 1994. "Attis on Greek Votive Monuments. Greek God or Phrygian?" *Hesperia* 63:245–62.

Romano, I.B. 1982. "The Archaic Statue of Dionysos from Ikarion." *Hesperia* 51:398–409.

Romilly, J. de. 1971. *La loi dans la pensée grecque.* Paris.

Rönnlund, R. 2023. *The Cities of the Plain. Urbanism in Ancient Western Thessaly.* Oxford.

Rosamilia, E. 2018. "From Magas to Glaukon. The Long Life of Glaukon of Aithalidai and the Chronology of Ptolemaic Re-Annexation of Cyrene (ca. 250 BCE)." *Chiron* 48:263–300.

Roscher, W.H. 1900. "Die Bedeutung des E zu Delphi und die übrigen γράμματα Δελφικά." *Philologus* 59:21–41.

Rose, V., ed. 1886. *Aristotelis qui ferebantur librorum fragmenta.* Leipzig.

Rostovtzeff, M.I. 1941. *The Social and Economic History of the Hellenistic World.* 3 vols. Oxford.

Roth, P. 1993. "The Theme of Corrupted *Xenia* in Aeschylus' *Oresteia.*" *Mnemosyne* 46:1–17.

Roth, P. 2015. *Euripides Hippolytos. Herausgegeben, übersetzt und kommentiert.* Berlin.

Roubineau, J.-M. 2012. "La condition d'étranger de passage dans les cités grecques: statut de droit ou position *hors-la-cité.*" In *Mobilités grecques. Mouvements, réseaux, contacts en Méditerranée,* edited by L. Capdetrey and J. Zurbach. Bordeaux: 157–73.

Rougemont, G. 1973. "La hiéroménie des Pythia et les 'trêves sacrées' d'Éleusis, de Delphes et d'Olympie." *Bulletin de correspondance hellénique* 97:75–106.

Rougemont, G. 1977. *Corpus des inscriptions de Delphes.* Tome 1. Paris.

Rouillard, P. 2018. "The *Emporion*: Some Uses of the Term." In *The* Emporion *in the Ancient Mediterranean,* edited by É. Gailledrat, M. Dietler, and R. Plana-Mallart. Montpellier: 19–24.

Roussel, P. 1907. "Inscriptions anciennement découvertes à Délos." *Bulletin de correspondance hellénique* 31:335–77.

Roussel, P. 1926. "Les épimélètes aitoliens à Delphes." *Bulletin de correspondance hellénique* 50:124–34.

Rousset, D. 2006. "Affranchissements de Physkeis en Locride occidentale." *Bulletin de correspondance hellénique* 130:349–79.

Roversi, C., and Sardo, A. 2019. "Ekins on Groups and Procedures." *American Journal of Jurisprudence* 64:79–103.

Roy, J. 1997. "The *Perioikoi* of Elis." In *The Polis as an Urban Centre and as a Political Community,* edited by M.H. Hansen. Copenhagen: 282–320.

Russell, D.A. 1983. *Greek Declamation.* New York.

Russell, D.A., and Wilson, N.G., eds. 1981. *Menander Rhetor.* Edited with translation and commentary. Oxford.

Rutherford, I. 2007. "Network Theory and Theoric Networks." *Mediterranean Historical Review* 22:23–37.

Rutherford, I. 2013. *State Pilgrims and Sacred Observers in Ancient Greece. A Study of* Theōriā *and* Theōroi. Cambridge.

Rutherford, R.B. 2009. "The Philosophy of the Odyssey." In *Oxford Readings in Classical Studies. Homer's* Odyssey, edited by L.E. Doherty. Oxford: 155–88.

Rutishauser, B. 2012. *Athens and the Cyclades. Economic Strategies 540–314 BC.* Oxford.

Saba, S. 2009/10. "Hellenistic Institutions and Law: A Survey (2000–2010)." *Dike* 12/13:271–302.

Saba, S. 2012. "City Identity and Institutions." In *Identitätsbildung und Identitätsstiftung in griechischen Gesellschaften,* edited by M. Offenmüller. Graz: 273–84.

Saba, S. 2020. Isopoliteia *in Hellenistic Times.* Leiden.

Sacks, K.S. 1975. "Polybius' Other View of Aetolia." *Journal of Hellenic Studies* 95:92–106.

Saks, M.J. 1992. "Do We Really Know Anything about the Behavior of the Tort Litigation System—and Why Not?" *University of Pennsylvania Law Review* 140:1147–1292.

Saldutti, V. 2016. "Atene e Mitilene dopo il 427 A.C. Sulla datazione di *IG* I3 66." *Incidenza dell' antico* 14:247–62.
Sánchez, P. 2001. *L'amphictionie des Pyles et de Delphes. Recherches sur son rôle historique, des origines au IIe siècle de notre ère.* Stuttgart.
Sanders, E., and Johncock, M., eds. 2016. *Emotion and Persuasion in Classical Antiquity.* Stuttgart.
Santiago Álvarez, R.-A., and Gardeñes Santiago, M. 2006. "Algunas observaciones a la 'lettre d'Apatorios à Léanax'." *Zeitschrift für Papyrologie und Epigraphik* 157:57–69.
Sapirstein, P. 2016. "The Columns of the Heraion at Olympia: Dörpfeld and Early Doric Architecture." *American Journal of Archaeology* 120:565–601.
Savalli-Lestrade, I. 1998. *Les* philoi *royaux dans l'Asie hellénistique.* Geneva.
Scafuro, A.C. 2010. "Conservative Trends in Athenian Law: *IE* 138, a Law Concerning the Mysteries." In *Symposion 2009*, edited by G. Thür. Vienna: 23–46.
Scafuro, A.C. 2014. "Decrees for Foreign Judges: Judging Conventions--or Epigraphic Habits?" In *Symposion 2013*, edited by M. Gagarin and A. Lanni. Vienna: 265–95.
Schäfer, A. 1886. *Demosthenes und seine Zeit.* 4 vols. Leipzig.
Schafer, M., and Crichlow, S. 2010. *Groupthink versus High-Quality Decision Making in International Relations.* New York.
Scharff, S. 2016. *Eid und Aussenpolitik. Studien zur religiösen Fundierung der Akzeptanz zwischenstaatlicher Vereinbarungen im vorrömischen Griechenland.* Stuttgart.
Scharff, S. 2023. "Mediating, Arbitrating, Crossing Borders Constantly. Athletes as Envoys." *Erga - Logoi* 11:77–90.
Schauer, F. 2015. *The Force of Law.* Cambridge, Mass.
Schaus, G.P. 2024. "Cyrene." In *The Oxford History of the Archaic Greek World. Volume IV: Cyrene to Metapontion*, edited by P. Cartledge and P. Christesen. Oxford: 1–129.
Schaus, G.P., ed. 2015. *Stymphalos. The Acropolis Sanctuary.* Vol. 1. Toronto.
Scheibelreiter, P. 2010. "'*Die gleichen für Freunde und Feinde halten*': Rechtsvergleichende Untersuchungen zur Geschichte der Freund-Feindklausel." In *Staatsverträge, Völkerrecht und Diplomatie im alten Orient und in der griechisch-römischen Antike*, edited by M. Lang, H. Barta, and R. Rollinger. Wiesbaden: 51–70.
Scheibelreiter, P. 2013. *Untersuchungen zur vertragsrechtlichen Struktur des delisch-attischen Seebundes.* Vienna.
Scheidel, W. 2013. "Studying the State." In *The Oxford Handbook of the State in the Ancient Near East and Mediterranean*, edited by P.F. Bang and W. Scheidel. Oxford: 5–41.
Scheidel, W., Morris, I., and Saller, R.P., eds. 2007. *The Cambridge Economic History of the Greco-Roman World.* Cambridge.
Schilke, O., Reimann, M., and Cook, K.S. 2021. "Trust in Social Relations." *Annual Review of Sociology* 47:10.1–21.
Schlesinger, E. 1933. *Die griechische Asylie.* Göttingen.
Schmid, W., and Stählin, O. 1929. *Geschichte der griechischen Literatur. Erster Teil: Die klassische Periode der griechischen Literatur.* 2 vols. Munich.
Schmitz, W. 2023. Leges Draconis et Solonis (LegDrSol). *Eine neue Edition der Gesetze Drakons und Solons mit Übersetzung und historischer Einordnung.* Stuttgart.
Scholten, J.B. 2000. *The Politics of Plunder. Aitolians and Their Koinon in the Early Hellenistic Era, 279–217 B.C.* Berkeley.
Schonberg, K.K. 2009. "Robert E. Osgood and the Origins of Social International Relations Theory." *International Journal* 64:811–23.
Schütrumpf, E. 1991. *Aristoteles Politik Buch II/III.* Berlin.
Schwartz, E. 1887–91. *Scholia in Euripidem.* 2 vols. Berlin.
Scott, D.I. 2020. "The New Juan Crow?: Unpacking the Links between Discrimination and Crime for Latinxs." *Race and Justice* 10:20–42.
Scott, J. 2012. *What Is Social Network Analysis?* New York.
Scott, J., and Carrington, P.J., eds. 2011. *The SAGE Handbook of Social Network Analysis.* London.

Scott, L. 2005. *Historical Commentary on Herodotus Book 6*. Leiden.
Scott, M. 2010. *Delphi and Olympia. The Spatial Politics of Panhellenism in the Archaic and Classical Periods*. Cambridge.
Scott, M. 2014. *Delphi. A History of the Center of the Ancient World*. Princeton.
Scullion, S. 2013. "Bones in Greek Sanctuaries: Answers and Questions." In *Bones, Behaviour and Belief*, edited by G. Ekroth and J. Wallensten. Stockholm: 243–55.
Seager, R. 1966. "The Phaselis Decree: A Note." *Historia* 15:509–10.
Seager, R., and Tuplin, C. 1980. "The Freedom of the Greeks of Asia: On the Origins of a Concept and the Creation of a Slogan." *Journal of Hellenic Studies* 100:141–54.
Sealey, R. 1964. "Ephialtes." *Classical Philology* 59:11–22.
Searle, J.R. 2005. "What Is an Institution?" *Journal of Institutional Economics* 1:1–22.
Sebillotte Cuchet, V. 2017. "*Gender studies* et domination masculine. Les citoyennes de l'Athènes classique, un défi pour l'historien des institutions." *Cahiers du Centre Gustave Glotz* 28:7–30.
Seddon, M., Miller, C., and Schwarz, F. 2023. "How Putin Blundered into Ukraine - Then Doubled Down." *Financial Times*, Feb. 23, 2023. Available at: https://on.ft.com/3lUjcTn.
Seiler, F. 1986. *Die griechische Tholos: Untersuchungen zur Entwicklung, Typologie und Funktion kunstmässiger Rundbauten*. Mainz.
Sekunda, N. 2014. "A Note on the Rhodian Expedition against Aigila." *Grammateion* 3:13–14.
Selvanathan, H.P., Techakesari, P., Tropp, L.R., and Barlow, F.K. 2018. "Whites for Racial Justice: How Contact with Black Americans Predicts Support for Collective Action among White Americans." *Group Processes & Intergroup Relations* 21:893–912.
Semmann, D., Krambeck, H.-J., and Milinski, M. 2005. "Reputation is Valuable within and outside One's Own Social Group." *Behavioral Ecology and Sociobiology* 57:611–16.
Servadei, C. 2005. *La figura di Theseus nella ceramica attica. Iconografia e iconologia del mito nell'Atene arcaica e classica*. Bologna.
Shapiro, S.J. 2011. *Legality*. Cambridge, Mass.
Shaw, B.D. 2004. "Bandits in the Roman Empire." In *Studies in Ancient Greek and Roman Society*, edited by R. Osborne. Cambridge: 326–74. (Originally published in *Past and Present* 105 (1984): 3–52.)
Shaw, B.D. 2022. "Global Empires and the Roman Imperium." *American Journal of Philology* 143:505–34.
Shaw, B.D. 2023. "Was the Roman State a State?" *Medieval Worlds* 18:3–36.
Shear, J.L. 2021. *Serving Athena. The Festival of the Panathenaia and the Construction of Athenian Identities*. Cambridge.
Shear, T.L. 1994. "'Ισονόμους τ' Ἀθήνας ἐποιησάτην: The Agora and the Democracy." In *The Archaeology of Athens and Attica under the Democracy*, edited by W.D.W. Coulson et al. Oxford: 225–48.
Sheets, G.A. 1994. "Conceptualising International Law in Thucydides." *American Journal of Philology* 115:51–73.
Shepsle, K.A. 1992. "Congress Is a 'They,' Not an 'It': Legislative Intent as Oxymoron." *International Review of Law and Economics* 12:239–56.
Shipley, G. 1987. *A History of Samos, 800–188 B.C.* Oxford.
Shipley, G. 1992. "*Perioikos*: The Discovery of Classical Laconia." In *ΦΙΛΟΛΑΚΩΝ. Laconian Studies in Honour of Hector Catling*, edited by J.M. Sanders. London: 211–26.
Shipley, G. 1993. "Distance, Development, Decline? World-Systems Analysis and the 'Hellenistic' World." In *Centre and Periphery in the Hellenistic World*, edited by P. Bilde et al. Aarhus: 271–84.
Shipley, G. 1997. "'The Other Lakedaimonians': The Dependent Perioikic *Poleis* of Lakonia and Messenia." In *The Polis as an Urban Centre and as a Political Community*, edited by M.H. Hansen. Copenhagen: 189–281.
Shipley, G. 2018. *The Early Hellenistic Peloponnese. Politics, Economies, and Networks 338–197 BC*. Cambridge.

Shirley, M.M. 2005. "Institutions and Development." In *Handbook of New Institutional Economics*, edited by C. Menard and M.M. Shirley. Berlin: 611–38.

Siewert, P. 1992. "The Olympic Rules." In *Proceedings of an International Symposium on the Olympic Games*. Athens: 113–17.

Simmel, G. 1908. *Soziologie. Untersuchungen über die Formen der Vergesellschaftung*. Leipzig.

Simmons, B.A., and Elkins, Z. 2004. "The Globalization of Liberalization: Policy Diffusion in the International Political Economy." *American Political Science Review* 98:171–89.

Simons, R.L., Chen, Y.-F., Stewart, E.A., and Brody, G.H. 2003. "Incidents of Discrimination and Risk for Delinquency: A Longitudinal Test of Strain Theory with an African American Sample." *Justice Quarterly* 20:827–54.

Simonton, M. 2017. *Classical Greek Oligarchy. A Political History*. Princeton.

Simpson, R.H. 1959. "Antigonus the One-Eyed and the Greeks." *Historia* 8:385–409.

Sizov, S.K. 2021. "Federal Citizenship and the Right of ΕΓΚΤΗΣΙΣ in the Achaian *Koinon*." *Zeitschrift für Papyrologie und Epigraphik* 217:105–18.

Sizov, S.K. 2021b. "Federal Citizenship and the Right of ΕΓΚΤΗΣΙΣ in the Aitolian *Koinon*." *Zeitschrift für Papyrologie und Epigraphik* 217:119–27.

Skinner, Q. 1989. "The State." In *Political Innovation and Conceptual Change*, edited by T. Ball, J. Farr, and R.L. Hanson. Cambridge: 90–131.

Slater, W. 2010. "Paying the Pipers." In *L'argent dans les concours du monde grec*, edited by B. Le Guen. Vincennes: 249–81.

Slatta, R. 2004. "Eric Hobsbawm's Social Bandit: A Critique and Revision." *A Contracorriente* 1:22–30.

Sloss, D. 2006. "Do International Norms Influence State Behavior?" *George Washington International Law Review* 38:159–207.

Smarczyk, B. 1990. *Untersuchungen zur Religionspolitik und politischen Propaganda Athens im delisch-attischen Seebund*. Munich.

Smelser, N.J. 1990. "Can Individualism Yield a Sociology?" *Contemporary Sociology* 19:778–83.

Smith, J. 2004. *Federalism*. Vancouver.

Smith, S., Hadfield, A., and Dunne, T. 2012. *Foreign Policy. Theories Actors Cases*. 2nd ed. Oxford.

Sokolowski, F. 1962. *Lois sacrées des cités grecques. Supplément*. Paris.

Solovyov, S. 2019. "Borysthenes and Olbia: Reflections on the Character of Contacts between Greeks and Natives during the Initial Stage of Colonization." In *Greek Colonization in Local Contexts*, edited by J. Lucas, C.A. Murray, and S. Owen. Oxford: 159–82.

Sommerstein, A.H. 2012. "Part One: Oaths in the Polis. Introduction." In *Oath and State in Ancient Greece*, by A.H. Sommerstein and A.J. Bayliss. Berlin: 3–9.

Sommerstein, A.H., and Bayliss, A.J. 2012. *Oath and State in Ancient Greece*. With contributions by L.A. Kozak and I.C. Torrance. Berlin.

Sommerstein, A.H., and Fletcher, J., eds. 2007. *Horkos. The Oath in Greek Society*. Exeter.

Sommerstein, A.H., and Torrance, I.C. 2014. *Oaths and Swearing in Ancient Greece*. With contributions by A.J. Bayliss, J. Fletcher, K. Konstantinidou, and L.A. Kozak. Berlin.

Sonnabend, H. 1996. *Die Freundschaften der Gelehrten und die zwischenstaatliche Politik im klassischen und hellenistischen Griechenland*. Hildesheim.

Sordi, M. 1958. *La lega tessala fino ad Alessandro Magno*. Roma.

Sordi, M. 1996. "Larissa e la dinastia alevade." *Aevum* 70:37–45.

Sordi, M. 1998. Review of B. Helly, *L'état thessalien* (Lyon 1995). *Gnomon* 70:418–21.

Sourvinou-Inwood, C. 2000. "What Is Polis Religion?" In *Oxford Readings in Greek Religion*, edited by R. Buxton. Oxford: 13–37.

Sourvinou-Inwood, C. 2000b. "Further Aspects of Polis Religion" In *Oxford Readings in Greek Religion*, edited by R. Buxton. Oxford: 38–55.

Sourvinou-Inwood, C. 2011. *Athenian Myths and Festivals. Aglauros, Erechtheus, Plynteria, Panathenaia, Dionysia*, edited by R. Parker. Oxford.

Sparks, T., and Peters, A., eds. 2024. *The Individual in International Law. History and Theory*. Oxford.

Spawforth, A.J.S., ed. 2007. *The Court and Court Society in Ancient Monarchies*. Cambridge.

Spawforth, A.J.S. 2007b. "The Court of Alexander the Great between Europe and Asia." In *The Court and Court Society in Ancient Monarchies*, edited by A.J.S. Spawforth. Cambridge: 82–120.

Sprawski, S. 1999. *Jason of Pherae. A Study on History of Thessaly in Years 431–370 BC*. Krakow.

Sprawski, S. 2008. "Thessalians and Theirs [sic] Neighbours in the Classical Period." In *1ο Διεθνές Συνέδριο Ιστορίας & Πολιτισμού της Θεσσαλίας. Πρακτικά Συνεδρίου 9–11 Νοεμβρίου 2006*, Vol. 1, edited by L. Gklegkle. Thessaloniki: 131–37.

Sprawski, S. 2012. "Remarks on Aristotle's THETTALON POLITEIA." *Electrum* 19:137–47.

Stadter, P.A. 1984. "Plutarch, Charinus, and the Megarian Decree." *Greek, Roman and Byzantine Studies* 25:351–72.

Stadter, P.A. 1989. *A Commentary on Plutarch's* Pericles. Chapel Hill.

Stählin, F. 1929. "Zur Chronologie und Erklärung der Inschriften von Magnesia und Demetrias." *Mitteilungen des Deutschen Archäologischen Instituts. Athenische Abteilung* 54:201–26.

Stamatopoulou, M. 2007. "Thessalian Aristocracy and Society in the Age of Epinikian." In *Pindar's Poetry, Patrons, and Festivals from Archaic Greece to the Roman Empire*, edited by S. Hornblower and C. Morgan. Oxford: 309–41.

Stamatopoulou, M. 2013. "Thessaly (Prehistoric to Roman)." *Archaeological Reports* 59:35–55.

Stanovich, K.E. 2011. *Rationality and the Reflective Mind*. Oxford.

Ste. Croix, G.E.M. de. 1954. "The Character of the Athenian Empire." *Historia* 3:1–41.

Ste. Croix, G.E.M. de. 1961. "Notes on Jurisdiction in the Athenian Empire. I." *Classical Quarterly* 11:94–112.

Ste. Croix, G.E.M. de. 1961b. "Notes on Jurisdiction in the Athenian Empire. II." *Classical Quarterly* 11:268–80.

Ste. Croix, G.E.M. de. 1972. *The Origins of the Peloponnesian War*. London.

Steele, P.M. 2019. *Writing and Society in Ancient Cyprus*. Cambridge.

Steidl, C. 2024. "The Business of 'Becoming': Connectivity, Trade, and Community Formation in the Northwestern Mediterranean." In *Local Experiences of Connectivity and Mobility in the Ancient West-Central Mediterranean*, edited by L.R. Gosner and J. Hayne. Sheffield: 166–84.

Steinberger, P.J. 2004. *The Idea of the State*. Cambridge.

Stephenson, P. 2016. *The Serpent Column. A Cultural Biography*. Oxford.

Stevens, G.W., and Thijs, J. 2018. "Perceived Group Discrimination and Psychological Well-being in Ethnic Minority Adolescents." *Journal of Applied Social Psychology* 48:559–570.

Stevenson, R.J., and Over, D.E. 2001. "Reasoning from Uncertain Premises: Effects of Expertise and Conversational Context." *Thinking and Reasoning* 7:367–90.

Stewart, E. 2017. *Greek Tragedy on the Move. The Birth of a Panhellenic Art Form c. 500–300 BC*. Oxford.

Stewart, F. 2005. "Groups and Capabilities." *Journal of Human Development* 6:185–204.

Stier, H.E. 1928. "ΝΟΜΟΣ ΒΑΣΙΛΕΥΣ." *Philologus* 83:225–58.

Stirk, P.M.R. 2015. "The Concept of the State in International Relations." In *The Concept of the State in International Relations*, edited by R. Schuett and P.M.R. Stirk. Edinburgh: 1–15.

Strootman, R. 2014. *Courts and Elites in the Hellenistic Empires. The Near East after the Achaemenids*. Edinburgh.

Strootman, R. 2019. "The Ptolemaic Sea Empire." In *Empires of the Sea*, edited by R. Strootman, F. van den Eijnde, and R. van Wijk. Leiden: 113–52.

Struck, P.T. 2004. *Birth of the Symbol. Ancient Readers at the Limits of Their Texts*. Princeton.

Stucki, I., and Sager, F. 2018. "Aristotelian Framing: Logos, Ethos, Pathos and the Use of Evidence in Policy Frames." *Policy Sciences* 51:373–85.

Summers, R.S. 1993. "A Formal Theory of the Rule of Law." *Ratio Juris* 6:127–42.

Sunstein, C.R. 1996. "On the Expressive Function of Law." *University of Pennsylvania Law Review* 144:2021–53.

Tadros, V. 2011. *The Ends of Harm. The Moral Foundations of Criminal Law*. Oxford.
Tajfel, H., Billig, M.G., Bundy, R.P., and Flament, C. 1971. "Social Categorization and Intergroup Behaviour." *European Journal of Social Psychology* 1:149–78.
Tajfel, H., and Turner, J.C. 1979. "An Integrative Theory of Intergroup Conflict." In *The Social Psychology of Intergroup Relations*, edited by W. G. Austin and S. Worchel. Monterey, CA: 33–47.
Tajfel, H., and Turner, J.C. 1986. "The Social Identity Theory of Intergroup Behavior." In *Psychology of Intergroup Relations*, 2nd ed., edited by S. Worchel and W.G. Austin. Chicago: 7–24.
Tamanaha, B.Z. 1997. *Realistic Socio-Legal Theory. Pragmatism and a Social Theory of Law*. Oxford.
Tapp, J.L. 1976. "Psychology and the Law: An Overture." *Annual Review of Psychology* 27:359–404.
Tapp, J.L., and Levine, F.J. 1974. "Legal Socialization: Strategies for an Ethical Legality." *Stanford Law Review* 27:1–72.
Tarn, W.W. 1923. "The Social Question in the Third Century." In *The Hellenistic Age. Aspects of Hellenistic Civilization*. Cambridge: 108–40.
Tartaron, T.F. 2013. *Maritime Networks in the Mycenaean World*. Cambridge.
Tausend, K. 1987. "Der Lelantische Krieg – ein Mythos?" *Klio* 69:499–514.
Tausend, K. 1992. *Amphiktyonie und Symmachie. Formen zwischenstaatlicher Beziehungen im archaischen Griechenland*. Stuttgart.
Taylor, C. 2015. "Social Networks and Social Mobility in Fourth-Century Athens." In *Communities and Networks in the Ancient Greek World*, edited by C. Taylor and K. Vlassopoulos. Oxford: 35–53.
Taylor, C. 2024. "Women, Gender and the Ancient Economy: Towards a Feminist Economic History of the Ancient Greek World." *Journal of Hellenic Studies* 144:1–28.
Taylor, C., and Vlassopoulos, K., eds. 2015. *Communities and Networks in the Ancient Greek World*. Oxford.
Taylor Poppe, E.S. 2019. "Why Consumer Defendants Lump It." *Northwestern Journal of Law & Social Policy* 14:149–90.
Teegarden, D.A. 2012. "The Oath of Demophantos, Revolutionary Mobilization, and the Preservation of the Athenian Democracy." *Hesperia* 81:433–65.
Temple, N., Piotrowski, A., and Heredia, J.M., eds. 2020. *The Routledge Handbook on the Reception of Classical Architecture*. Abingdon.
Ténékidès, G. 1954. *La notion juridique d'indépendance et la tradition hellénique*. Athens.
Ténékidès, G. 1956. "Droit international et communautés fédérales dans la Grèce des cités (Vème–IIIème siècles avant J. C.)." *Académie de Droit International, Recueil des Cours* [1956 - II] 90:469–648.
Terpstra, T. 2013. *Trading Communities in the Roman World. A Micro-Economic and Institutional Perspective*. Leiden.
Terpstra, T. 2019. *Trade in the Ancient Mediterranean. Private Order and Public Institutions*. Princeton.
Thaler, R.H., and Sunstein, C.R. 2008. *Nudge. Improving Decisions about Health, Wealth, and Happiness*. New Haven.
Thomas, O. 2020. *The Homeric Hymn to Hermes*. Cambridge.
Thomas, R. 1995. "Written in Stone? Liberty, Equality, Orality and the Codification of Law." *Bulletin of the Institute of Classical Studies* 40:59–74.
Thür, G. 1996. "Oaths and Dispute Settlement in Ancient Greek Law." In *Greek Law in its Political Setting. Justification not Justice*, edited by L. Foxhall and A. Lewis. Oxford: 57–72.
Tilly, C. 2010. "Cities, States, and Trust Networks: Chapter 1 of Cities and States in World History." *Theory and Society* 39:265–80.
Tindale, R.S., Meisenhelder, H.M., Dykema-Engblade, A.A., and Hogg, M.A. 2007. "Shared Cognition in Small Groups." In *Blackwell Handbook of Social Psychology: Group Processes*, edited by M. Hogg. Oxford: 1–30.

Tittmann, J.A.H. 1808. *Iohannis Zonarae Lexicon ex Tribus Codicibus Manuscriptis.* 3 vols. Leipzig.

Tober, D. 2018. Review of J.D. Grainger, *Great Power Diplomacy in the Hellenistic World* (London 2017). *Bryn Mawr Classical Review.* Available at: bmcr.brynmawr.edu/2018/2018.06.05/.

Tod, M.N. 1913. *International Arbitration amongst the Greeks.* Oxford.

Todd, S.C. 1993. *The Shape of Athenian Law.* Oxford.

Todd, S.C. 1996. "Lysias against Nikomachos." In *Greek Law in Its Political Setting. Justifications not Justice,* edited by L. Foxhall and A.D.E. Lewis. Oxford: 101–31.

Todd, S.C. 2007. *A Commentary on Lysias, Speeches 1–11.* Oxford.

Tollefsen, D.P. 2015. *Groups as Agents.* Malden, Mass.

Tonry, M. 2014. "Why Crime Rates Are Falling throughout the Western World." *Crime and Justice: An Annual Review of Research* 43:1–63.

Torrance, I. 2014. "Ways to Give Oaths Extra Sanctity." In *Oaths and Swearing in Ancient Greece,* edited by A.H. Sommerstein and I.C. Torrance. Berlin: 132–55.

Torrance, I. 2014b. "Divine Responses." In *Oaths and Swearing in Ancient Greece,* edited by A.H. Sommerstein and I.C. Torrance. Berlin: 295–303.

Tracy, S.V. 1995. *Athenian Democracy in Transition. Attic Letter-Cutters of 340 to 290 B.C.* Berkeley.

Tracy, S.V. 2010. "The Thessalians and Athens from the Persian Wars to the Lamian War: The Literary and Epigraphical Evidence." In *Philathenaios,* edited by A. Tamis, C.J. Mackie, and S.G. Byrne. Athens: 23–32.

Travis, J., Western, B., and Redburn, F.S. 2014. *The Growth of Incarceration in the United States. Exploring Causes and Consequences.* Washington.

Trevett, J. 1992. *Apollodoros the Son of Pasion.* Oxford.

Trevett, J. 1999. Review of B. Helly, *L'état thessalien* (Lyon 1995). *Journal of Hellenic Studies* 119:213.

Trevett, J. 2011. *Demosthenes, Speeches 1–17.* Austin.

Trinkner, R., and Cohn, E.S. 2014. "Putting the 'Social' Back in Legal Socialization: Procedural Justice, Legitimacy, and Cynicism in Legal and Nonlegal Authorities." *Law and Human Behavior* 38:602–17.

Trinkner, R., and Tyler, T.R. 2016. "Legal Socialization: Coercion versus Consent in an Era of Mistrust." *Annual Review of Law and Social Science* 12:417–39.

Tropp, L.R., Mazziotta, A., and Wright, S.C. 2017. "Recent Developments in Intergroup Contact Research: Affective Processes, Group Status, and Contact Valence." In *The Cambridge Handbook of the Psychology of Prejudice,* edited by C.G. Sibley and F.K. Barlow. Cambridge: 463–80.

Tsetskhladze, G.R. 2018. "'Greek Penetration of the Black Sea': Twenty Years On." In *Essays on the Archaeology and Ancient History of the Black Sea Littoral,* edited by M. Manoledakis, G.R. Tsetskhladze, and I. Xydopoulos. Leuven: 1–64.

Tsetskhladze, G.R., ed. 2006–2008. *Greek Colonisation. An Account of Greek Colonies and Other Settlements Overseas.* 2 vols. Leiden.

Tully, J.A.N.Z. 2013. "Samos, Hegemony, and the Nicuria Decree." *Tyche* 28:177–82.

Tuori, K. 2025. "Middlemen. How Did Knowledge of Roman Law Spread Outside Rome?" *Historia* 74:101–28.

Tuplin, C. 1999. Review of B. Smarczyk, *Untersuchungen zur Religionspolitik und politischen Propaganda Athens im delisch-attischen Seebund* (Munich 1990). *Gnomon* 71:420–24.

Turner, E.G. 1946. "*ΦΙΛΟΔΙΚΕΙΝ ΔΟΚΟΥΜΕΝ* (Thuc. i.77)." *Classical Review* 60:5–7.

Tyler, T.R. 2006. *Why People Obey the Law.* 2nd ed. New Haven.

Tyler, T.R. 2011. *Why People Cooperate. The Role of Social Motivations.* Princeton.

Tyler, T.R. 2016. "Understanding the Force of Law." *Tulsa Law Review* 51:507–20.

Tyler, T.R. 2021. "Legal Socialization: Back to the Future." *Journal of Social Issues* 77:663–76.

Tyler, T.R., and Trinkner, R. 2017. *Why Children Follow Rules. Legal Socialization and the Development of Legitimacy.* Oxford.

Tziafalias, A., Bouchon, R., Darmezin, L., Decourt, J.-C., Helly, B., Lucas, G., and Pernin, I., eds. 2016. *Corpus des inscriptions d'Atrax en Pélasgiotide (Thessalie)*. Athens.

Ulbrich, A. 2020. "Adoption and Adaptation of Greek Iconography in Cypriot Votive Sculpture of the Late Archaic and Classical Periods." In *Classical Cyprus*, edited by M. Christidis, A. Hermary, G. Koiner, and A. Ulbrich. Vienna: 221–44.

Uzzi, B. 1997. "Social Structure and Competition in Interfirm Networks: The Paradox of Embeddedness." *Administrative Science Quarterly* 42:35–67.

Vădan, P. 2022. "Migration, Mobility, and the Hierarchy of Violence in the Classical and Early Hellenistic Polis." *TAPA* 152:381–425.

Valente, M. 2023. Emporia. *Elementi di razionalità economica nel commercio greco*. Pisa.

van Alfen, P. 2016. "Aegean-Levantine Trade, 600–300 BCE." In *The Ancient Greek Economy. Markets, Households and City-States*, edited by E.M. Harris, D.M. Lewis, and M. Woolmer. Cambridge: 277–98.

Vanberg, C. 2008. "Why Do People Keep Their Promises? An Experimental Test of Two Explanations." *Econometrica* 76:1467–80.

Van Berkel, T.A. 2020. *The Economics of Friendship. Conceptions of Reciprocity in Classical Greece*. Leiden.

Van den Berg, A. 1998. "Out of Habit. Notes toward a General Theory of Deliberate Action." *Amsterdams sociologisch tijdschrift* 25:429–63.

van Effenterre, H. 1948. *La Crète et le monde grec de Platon à Polybe*. Paris.

van Effenterre, H., and Ruzé, F. 1994. *Nomima. Recueil d'inscriptions politiques et juridiques de l'archaïsme grec*. 2 vols. Rome.

van Groningen, B.A., and Wartelle, A., eds. 1968. *Aristote: Économique*. Paris.

Van Oyen, A. 2024. "Why a Human Ancient Economy Should Be Posthuman." In *Models, Methods, and Morality*, edited by S.C. Murray and S. Bernard. Cham: 381–402.

Van Rooij, B. 2020. "Behavioral Jurisprudence: The Quest for Knowledge about the Ex-ante Function of Law and Behavior." *Jerusalem Review of Legal Studies* 22:57–77.

Van Rooij, B., and Brownlee, M. 2021. "Does Tort Deter? Inconclusive Empirical Evidence about the Effect of Liability in Preventing Harmful Behaviour." In *The Cambridge Handbook of Compliance*, edited by B. van Rooij and D.D. Sokol. Cambridge: 311–25.

van Wees, H. 1992. *Status Warriors. War, Violence and Society in Homer and History*. Amsterdam.

van Wees, H. 2013. *Ships and Silver, Taxes and Tribute. A Fiscal History of Archaic Athens*. London.

van Wees, H. 2022. "The Archaic Period." In *The Cambridge Companion to the Ancient Greek Economy*, edited by S. von Reden. Cambridge: 29–48.

van Wijk, R. 2024. *Athens and Boiotia. Interstate Relations in the Archaic and Classical Periods*. Cambridge.

Vatin, C. 1961. "Damiurges et épidamiurges à Delphes." *Bulletin de correspondance hellénique* 85:236–55.

Vélissaropoulos, J. 1980. *Les nauclères grecs. Recherches sur les institutions maritimes en Grèce et dans l'Orient hellénisé*. Geneva.

Vélissaropoulos-Karakostas, J. 2011. *Droit grec d'Alexandre à Auguste (323 av. J.-C. – 14 ap. J.-C.)*. 2 vols. Athens.

Ventura Miller, H., Barnes, J.C., and Hartley, R.D. 2011. "Reconsidering Hispanic Gang Membership and Acculturation in a Multivariate Context." *Crime & Delinquency* 57:331–55.

Vergados, A. 2011. *The Homeric Hymn to Hermes. Introduction, Text and Commentary*. Berlin.

Verheij, M.J.O. 2016. "Hospitality & Homicide. Violation of *Xenia* in Euripides' *Electra*." *Mnemosyne* 69:760–84.

Versnel, H.S. 1990–93. *Inconsistencies in Greek and Roman Religion*. 2 vols. Leiden.

Veyne, P. 1976. *Le pain et le cirque. Sociologie historique d'un pluralisme politique*. Paris.

Vidal-Naquet, P. 1992. "Le chasseur noir et l'origine de l'éphébie athénienne." In *La Grèce ancienne. 3. Rites de passage et transgressions*, edited by J-P. Vernant and P. Vidal-Naquet. Paris: 119–47.

Vigil, J.D. 2002. *A Rainbow of Gangs. Street Cultures in the Mega-City*. Austin, TX.

Vinogradov, J.G., and Kryžickij, S.D. 1995. *Olbia. Eine altgriechische Stadt im nordwestlichen Schwarzmeerraum*. Leiden.

Vlassopoulos, K. 2007. "Beyond and below the Polis: Networks, Associations, and the Writing of Greek History." *Mediterranean Historical Review* 22:11–22.

Vlassopoulos, K. 2013. *Greeks and Barbarians*. Cambridge.

Vlassopoulos, K. 2015. "Ethnicity and Greek History: Re-examining Our Assumptions." *Bulletin of the Institute of Classical Studies* 58(2):1–13.

Vlassopoulos, K. 2021. *Historicising Ancient Slavery*. Edinburgh.

Vollgraff, W. 1948. *Le décret d'Argos relatif à un pacte entre Knossos et Tylissos*. Amsterdam.

Volonaki, E. 2021. "Religious Identity in Athenian Forensic Oratory: Public Cases of *Eisangelia* Trials." *Polis* 38:47–73.

von Hirsch, A., Bottoms, A.E., Burney, E., and Wikström, P.-O. 1999. *Criminal Deterrence and Sentence Severity. An Analysis of Recent Research*. Oxford.

von Scala, R. 1898. *Die Staatsverträge des Altertums. Erster Teil*. Leipzig.

Vries, P.H.H. 2013. *Escaping Poverty. The Origins of Modern Economic Growth*. Vienna.

Wade-Gery, H.T. 1945. "Kritias and Herodes." *Classical Quarterly* 39:19–33.

Wade-Gery, H.T. 1958. *Essays in Greek History*. Oxford.

Wagner, K.A. 2021. "Resistance, Rebellion, and the Subaltern." In *The Oxford World History of Empire*, Vol. 1, edited by P.F. Bang, C.A. Bayly, and W. Scheidel. Oxford: 417–36.

Walbank, F.W. 1957–1979. *A Historical Commentary on Polybius*. 3 vols. Oxford.

Walbank, F.W. 1984. "Monarchies and Monarchic Ideas." In *The Cambridge Ancient History. Second Edition. Vol. VII, Part I. The Hellenistic World*, edited by F.W. Walbank, A.E. Astin, M.W. Frederiksen, and R.M. Ogilvie. Cambridge: 62–117.

Walbank, F.W. 1988. Part II in *A History of Macedonia. Volume III: 336–167 B.C.*, by N.G.L. Hammond and F.W. Walbank. Oxford.

Walbank, M.B. 1978. *Athenian Proxenies of the Fifth Century, B.C.* Sarasota.

Walbank, M.B. 1986. "Athens and Stymphalos: *IG* II2, 144+." *Hesperia* 55:319–54.

Waldron, J. 2008. "The Concept and the Rule of Law." *Georgia Law Review* 43:1–62.

Wallace, G.P.R. 2024. *International Law and the Public. How Ordinary People Shape the Global Legal Order*. Ithaca, NY.

Walser, A.V. 2012. "ΔΙΚΑΣΤΗΡΙΑ. Rechtsprechung und Demokratie in den hellenistischen Poleis." In *"Demokratie" im Hellenismus. Von der Herrschaft des Volkes zur Herrschaft der Honoratioren?*, edited by C. Mann and P. Scholz. Berlin: 74–108.

Walton, F.R. 1957. *Diodorus of Sicily. The Library of History Books XXI–XXXII*. Cambridge, Mass.

Waltz, K.N. 1979. *Theory of International Politics*. New York.

Wankel, H. 1976. *Demosthenes, Rede für Ktesiphon über den Kranz*. 2 vols. Heidelberg.

Wąsowicz, A. 1975. *Olbia pontique et son territoire. L'aménagement de l'espace*. Paris.

Webber, J. 2006. "Legal Pluralism and Human Agency." *Osgoode Hall Law Journal* 44:167–98.

Weber, M. 1947. *The Theory of Social and Economic Organization*. New York.

Weber, M. 1968. *Economy and Society*. 3 vols. Edited by G. Roth and C. Wittich. New York.

Weber, U. 2021. "The Role of Assembly Marks at Repairs and Restorations in Greek Architecture, Demonstrated with Case Studies from Delphi, Didyma and Samothrace." In *Ancient Architectural Restoration in the Greek World*, edited by J. Vanden Broeck-Parant and T. Ismaelli. Rome: 81–99.

Weiler, I. 2014. "Korruption und Kontrolle in der antiken Agonistik." In *Sport und Recht in der Antike*, edited by K. Harter-Uibopuu and T. Kruse. Vienna: 1–30.

Weir, R. 2014. "Coins." In *Stymphalos: The Acropolis Sanctuary*. Vol. 1, edited by G.P. Schaus. Toronto: 56–78.

Welch, D.A. 2003. "Why International Relations Theorists Should Stop Reading Thucydides." *Review of International Studies* 29:301–19.
Wendt, A. 1999. *Social Theory of International Politics*. Cambridge.
Wenzel, M., Waldzus, S., and Steffens, M.C. 2017. "Ingroup Projection as a Challenge of Diversity: Consensus about and Complexity of Superordinate Categories." In *The Cambridge Handbook of the Psychology of Prejudice*, edited by C.G. Sibley and F.K. Barlow. Cambridge: 65–89.
Werner, R. 1971. "Probleme der Rechtsbeziehung zwischen Metropolis und Apoikie." *Chiron* 1:19–73.
West, M.L. 1966. *Hesiod. Theogony. Edited with Prolegomena and Commentary*. Oxford.
West, M.L. 2003. *Homeric Hymns; Homeric Apocrypha; Lives of Homer*. Cambridge, Mass.
Westlake, H.D. 1936. "The Medism of Thessaly." *Journal of Hellenic Studies* 56:12–24.
Whitcomb, K. 2025. "Mare pacavi a praedonibus: Divus Augustus and the Pacification of the Seas." *Historia* 74:185–204.
Whitehead, D. 1977. *The Ideology of the Athenian Metic*. Cambridge.
Whitehead, D. 1983. "Competitive Outlay and Community Profit: Φιλοτιμία in Democratic Athens." *Classica et Mediaevalia* 34:55–74.
Whitehead, D. 1984. "Immigrant Communities in the Classical Polis: Some Principles for a Synoptic Treatment." *L'antiquité classique* 53:47–59.
Whitehead, D. 1986. *The Demes of Attica 508/7 – ca. 250 B.C. A Political and Social Study*. Princeton.
Whitley, J. 2018. "Citizenship and Commensality in Archaic Crete. Searching for the *Andreion*." In *Defining Citizenship in Archaic Greece*, edited by A. Duplouy and R. Brock. Oxford: 227–48.
Wiater, N. 2011. *The Ideology of Classicism. Language, History, and Identity in Dionysius of Halicarnassus*. Berlin.
Wiemer, H.-U. 2002. *Rhodische Traditionen in der hellenistischen Historiographie*. Frankfurt.
Wight, C. 2004. "State Agency: Social Action without Human Activity?" *Review of International Studies* 30:269–80.
Wijma, S.M. 2014. *Embracing the Immigrant. The Participation of Metics in Athenian Polis Religion (5th–4th Century BC)*. Stuttgart.
Wilamowitz-Moellendorff, U. von. 1881. *Antigonos von Karystos*. Berlin.
Wilamowitz-Moellendorff, U. von. 1893. *Aristoteles und Athen*. 2 vols. Berlin.
Wildschut, T., Gaertner, L., and Insko, C.A. 2002. "Intragroup Social Influence and Intergroup Competition." *Journal of Personality and Social Psychology* 82:975–92.
Wilhelm, A. 1911. "Die lokrische Mädcheninschrift." *Jahreshefte des Österreichischen Archäologischen Institutes in Wien* 14:163–256.
Wilhelm, A. 1935. "Zu König Antigonos' Schrieben an die Teïer." *Klio* 28:280–93.
Wilhelm, A. 1939. "Attische Urkunden. IV. Teil." *Sitzungsberichte der Akademie der Wissenschaften in Wien, philos.-historische Klasse* 217(5):5–97.
Will, É. 1982. *Histoire politique du monde hellénistique (323–30 av. J.-C.)*. Vol. 2. Nancy.
Will, É. 1984. "The Succession to Alexander." In *The Cambridge Ancient History. Second Edition. Vol. VII, Part I. The Hellenistic World*, edited by F.W. Walbank, A.E. Astin, M.W. Frederiksen, and R.M. Ogilvie. Cambridge: 23–61.
Willetts, R.F. 1955. *Aristocratic Society in Ancient Crete*. London.
Willetts, R.F. 1967. *The Law Code of Gortyn*. Berlin.
Willey, H. 2016. "Gods and Men in Ancient Greek Conceptions of Lawgiving." In *Theologies of Ancient Greek Religion*, edited by E. Eidinow, J. Kindt, and R. Osborne. Cambridge: 176–204.
Williams, G.L. 1945. "International Law and the Controversy Concerning the Word 'Law.'" *British Yearbook of International Law* 22:146–63.
Williams, H., Schaus, G., Gourley, B., Cronkite-Price, S.-M., Sherwood, K.D., and Lolos, Y. 2002. "Excavations at Stymphalos, 1999–2002." *Mouseion* 2:135–87.

Williamson, C.G. 2013. "As God Is My Witness. Civic Oaths in Ritual Space as a Means towards Rational Cooperation in the Hellenistic Polis." In *Cults, Creeds and Identities in the Greek City after the Classical Age*, edited by R. Alston, O.M. van Nijf, and C.G. Williamson. Leuven: 119–74.

Williamson, C.G. 2023. "Sacred Circles. Enclosed Sanctuaries and Their Festival Communities in the Hellenistic World." In *The Material Dynamics of Festivals in the Graeco-Roman East*, edited by Z. Newby. Oxford: 250–88.

Williamson, O.E. 2005. "Transaction Cost Economics." In *Handbook of New Institutional Economics*, edited by C. Ménard and M.M. Shirley. Dordrecht: 41–65.

Wilson, J.-P. 1997–98. "The 'Illiterate Trader'?" *Bulletin of the Institute of Classical Studies* 42:29–56.

Wilson, R.A. 2005. "Collective Memory, Group Minds, and the Extended Mind Thesis." *Cognitive Processing* 6:227–36.

Wolff, H.J. 1954. "Prozessrechtliches und materiellrechtliches Denken in rechtsgeschichtlicher Beleuchtung." In *L'Europa e il diritto romano*, Vol. 2. Milan: 405–23.

Wolff, H.J. 1961. "Rechtskunde und Rechtswissenschaft bei den Griechen." In *Beiträge zur Rechtsgeschichte Altgriechenlands und des hellenistisch-römischen Ägypten*. Weimar: 243–58.

Wolff, H.J. 1975. "Juristische Gräzistik. Aufgaben, Probleme, Möglichkeiten." In *Symposion 1971*, edited by H.J. Wolff. Köln: 1–22.

Woodhead, A.G. 1957. "Greek Inscriptions." *Hesperia* 26:221–36.

Woolmer, M. 2016. "Forging Links between Regions. Trade Policy in Classical Athens." In *The Ancient Greek Economy. Markets, Households and City-States*, edited by E.M. Harris, D.M. Lewis, and M. Woolmer. Cambridge: 66–89.

Wörrle, M. 2004. "Der Friede zwischen Milet und Magnesia. Methodische Probleme einer Communis opinio." *Chiron* 34:45–57.

Yates, D.C. 2005. "The Archaic Treaties between the Spartans and Their Allies." *Classical Quarterly* 55:65–76.

Zafirovski, M. 2018. "Rational Choice Theory or Pretense? The Claims, Equivalences, and Analogies of the 'Economic Approach to Human Behavior.'" *Sociological Spectrum* 38:194–222.

Zahrnt, M. 2010. "Das megarische Psephisma und der Ausbruch des peloponnesischen Krieges." *Historische Zeitschrift* 291:593–624.

Zelnick-Abramovitz, R. 2004. "The Proxenoi of Western Greece." *Zeitschrift für Papyrologie und Epigraphik* 147:93–106.

Ziegler, K.-H. 2008. "Ius Gentium als Völkerrecht in der Spätantike." In *Fata Iuris Gentium. Kleine Schriften zur Geschichte des europäischen Völkerrechts*. Baden-Baden: 81–92.

Zimmerman, N., and Tyler, T.R. 2010. "Between Access to Counsel and Access to Justice: A Psychological Perspective." *Fordham Urban Law Journal* 37:473–507.

Zimny, K. 2021. "*IG* IV 752 and Reprisals ΑΠΟ ΤΑΣ ΧΩΡΑΣ." *Zeitschrift für Papyrologie und Epigraphik* 220:127–36.

Zingg, E. 2023. "L'usage métaphorique du terme 'péneste' et la fin du pénestisme thessalien." *Revue des études grecques* 136:173–83.

Zuchtriegel, G. 2023. *The Making of the Doric Temple. Architecture, Religion, and Social Change in Archaic Greece*. Cambridge.

Zuiderhoek, A. 2017. *The Ancient City*. Cambridge.

Zuiderhoek, A. 2023. "Ancient Economic History and Scientific Theory." In *Handbuch Antike Wirtschaft*, edited by S. von Reden and K. Ruffing. Berlin: 41–64.

Zunino, M.L. 2005. "La συνβολά fra Oiantheia e Khaleion (*IG* IX I^2, 717): Il diritto di συλε̂ν." *Zeitschrift für Papyrologie und Epigraphik* 153:113–26.

Zunino, M.L. 2017. "Convenzione giudiziaria tra Eantea e Chaleion." *Axon* 1:125–44.

Index Locorum

For the benefit of digital users, indexed terms that span two pages (e.g., 52–53) may, on occasion, appear on only one of those pages.

Authors

Inscriptions

For the convenience of readers, some inscriptions are cited to multiple collections.

Papyri

General Index

For the benefit of digital users, indexed terms that span two pages (e.g., 52–53) may, on occasion, appear on only one of those pages.

Maps showing locations are indicated by *f.*